THE CONSTITUTION OF SOCIAL DEMOCRACY

This book is based upon the papers written by a group of leading international scholars on the 'constitution of social democracy', delivered at a conference to celebrate Professor Keith Ewing's scholarly legacy in labour law, constitutional law, human rights and the law of democracy. The chapters explore the development of social democracy and democratic socialism in theory and political practice from a variety of comparative, legal and disciplinary perspectives. These developments have occurred against a backdrop of fragmenting 'traditional' political parties, declining collective bargaining, concerns about 'juristocracy' and the displacement of popular sovereignty, the emergence of populist political movements, austerity, and fundamental questions about the future of the European project. With this context in mind, the chapters in this collection consider whether legal norms can and should contribute to the constitution of social democracy. This collection could not be more timely in addressing these fundamental constitutional questions at the intersection of law, democracy and political economy.

The Constitution of Social Democracy

Essays in Honour of Keith Ewing

Edited by
Alan Bogg
Jacob Rowbottom
and
Alison L Young

•HART•
OXFORD • LONDON • NEW YORK • NEW DELHI • SYDNEY

HART PUBLISHING

Bloomsbury Publishing Plc

Kemp House, Chawley Park, Cumnor Hill, Oxford, OX2 9PH, UK

1385 Broadway, New York, NY 10018, USA

HART PUBLISHING, the Hart/Stag logo, BLOOMSBURY and the Diana logo are trademarks of Bloomsbury Publishing Plc

First published in Great Britain 2020

A catalogue record for this book is available from the British Library.

Library of Congress Cataloging-in-Publication data

Names: Constitution of Social Democracy (Conference) (2018 : London, England) | Bogg, Alan, editor. | Rowbottom, Jacob, editor. | Young, Alison L, editor. | Ewing, K. D. (Keith D.), honouree.

Title: The constitution of social democracy : essays in honour of Keith Ewing / edited by Alan Bogg, Jacob Rowbottom and Alison L Young.

Description: Oxford ; New York : Hart, 2020. | Includes bibliographical references and index.

Identifiers: LCCN 2020004869 (print) | LCCN 2020004870 (ebook) | ISBN 9781509916573 (hardcover) | ISBN 9781509916580 (Epub)

Subjects: LCSH: Public law—Great Britain—Congresses. | LCGFT: Festschriften. | Conference papers and proceedings.

Classification: LCC KD3930.A75 C66 2020 (print) | LCC KD3930.A75 (ebook) | DDC 349.41—dc23

LC record available at https://lccn.loc.gov/2020004869

LC ebook record available at https://lccn.loc.gov/2020004870

ISBN: HB: 978-1-50991-657-3
ePDF: 978-1-50991-659-7
ePub: 978-1-50991-658-0

Typeset by Compuscript Ltd, Shannon

To find out more about our authors and books visit www.hartpublishing.co.uk. Here you will find extracts, author information, details of forthcoming events and the option to sign up for our newsletters.

PREFACE

It is a privilege to contribute a preface to this collection of chapters that enrich our understanding of social democracy, and in so doing to make my own tribute to my former student, colleague and co-author, Professor Keith Ewing.

The contents of this book will speak for themselves but in different ways they all relate to work that Keith Ewing has done, and is still undertaking, in a wide range of contexts, whether as sole or joint author. Leaving aside the editions of *Constitutional and Administrative Law*, of which he has been a joint author since 1993, I do not now list his extensive work on labour law and employment rights, nor his editing (with Tom Campbell and Adam Tomkins) of *Sceptical Essays on Human Rights* (2001) and *The Legal Protection of Human Rights: Sceptical Essays* (2011). His first book was on the Trade Union Act 1913, way back in 1982. This was followed by *The Funding of Political Parties in Britain* (1987), in which he gave prominence to a quotation from the Houghton report in 1976 that expressed a belief in democracy that has a special resonance in these Brexit years: 'Effective political parties are the crux of democratic government. Without them democracy withers and decays'.[1]

The importance of the political contest is stressed in *Freedom under Thatcher - Civil Liberties in Modern Britain* (1990), written jointly with Conor Gearty. The authors lamented the state of political life as it had become in the 1980s: 'In recent years, there has been a marked decline in the level of political freedom enjoyed in Britain. It is difficult if not impossible to point to a particular starting-point'.[2] This standpoint can be linked with their comment on the literature of public law: 'Textbooks catering for the upsurge in legal education in the 1950s and 1960s sought to capture in print the mysterious unwritten secrets of a constitution which had emerged into the democratic world without appearing to have changed at all'.[3]

This critique was developed by the same authors in *The Struggle for Civil Liberties – Political Freedom and the Rule of Law in Britain, 1914–1945* (2000):

> In writing this book it became painfully clear to us that the civil liberties dimension [of great events in the UK in the 20th century] has been either lost or neglected. As a result some scholars have unwittingly fed successive generations an account of civil liberties … which is at best complacent and at worst wholly out of touch with reality[4]

Ewing reverted to the subject of political funding in *The Cost of Democracy - Party Funding in Modern British Politics* (2007). Drawing into play the experiences of Canada, Germany and Sweden, he offered no simple solution to the funding of political parties, which 'is a

[1] KD Ewing, *The Funding of Political Parties in Britain* (Cambridge, CUP, 1987) 1.

[2] KD Ewing and C Gearty, *Freedom under Thatcher: Civil Liberties in Modern Britain* (Oxford, OUP, 1990) v.

[3] Ibid, 2.

[4] KD Ewing and C Gearty, *The Struggle for Civil Liberties: Political Freedom and the Rule of Law in Britain, 1914–1945* (Oxford, OUP, 2001) v.

problem in all parts of the world';[5] and, the author insisted, 'any package for reform must be based on a recognition of the central importance of political parties as constitutional players'.[6]

In 2010 came *Bonfire of the Liberties – New Labour, Human Rights and the Rule of Law*. In a disarming remark, the author comments that 'in most books only the introduction and conclusion are read' – so he gives us 'the edited highlights of the intervening six chapters', one of which is the 'blindingly obvious point … that the solution to the problem of liberty lies not with rights, lawyers, or judges, but with power, procedures and politicians'.[7] The content of the six chapters lives up to the challenge set by the book's stirring title.

This selective survey has left out a host of important articles and papers. All the evidence is that there is more to come. Published in 2019 has been the second edition of *Labour Law*, authored by Keith jointly with Hugh Collins and Aileen McColgan. And due to come in 2020 is *MI5, the Cold War and the Rule of Law*, written by Keith with Joan Mahoney and Andrew Moretta: this contribution to our knowledge of the secret side of the modern state in large part results from study of those MI5 files that have survived in the National Archives, and an article based on this research has already appeared in the *Modern Law Review*.

What has struck me in reading many chapters in this series of books (in particular, the two books on civil liberties plus *Bonfire of the Liberties)* is the sharply focussed research into innumerable struggles between individuals and the state in all its guises that it is vital to have on record and not lost from sight in press archives, journal comment, parliamentary reports and the like. Many of these events would all too easily be forgotten as the years roll on and other struggles occur: to mention just a few, the Zircon case, Spycatcher and the Ponting trial. And there is much to learn from more recent times – the police use of 'stop and account' and Forward Intelligence Teams; the Damian Green affair; *Chahal* and the Belmarsh case ('one of the most important public law decisions since *Entick v Carrington*' – p 237), with its complex sequels, and in *Bonfire* (at p 230) a startlingly apt quotation from Kafka's *The Trial*, which punctures the use of Special Advocates.

A striking feature of this treatment is the detail with which these clashes and contests are presented – detail that makes clear the issues in dispute, and how a particular case found its way through the courts. This is to treat readers with respect – we are not driven to accept every aspect of the author's conclusions and can form our own views about his criticisms of the judiciary, politicians and the other figures who exercise power. Taken together, these books provide a valuable record of our recent history. Running through them all is a deep concern for the social and economic rights of the many who are at risk of being ground down by current features of our governmental system.

I must add a few personal words. It was early in the 1970s that Keith moved a few miles from his home and school in Penicuik to begin studying law in Old College, Edinburgh. Four years later, his LL.B came with a First and this led him to apply to do research at Trinity Hall, Cambridge. The Cambridge Faculty had no difficulty in accepting him but, for reasons that still escape me, the college needed some extra persuasion that he had the

[5] KD Ewing, *The Cost of Democracy: Party Funding in Modern British Politics* (Oxford, Hart Publishing, 2007) 23.

[6] Ibid, vii.

[7] KD Ewing, *Bonfire of the Liberties: New Labour, Human Rights and the Rule of Law* (Oxford, OUP, 2010) 237.

calibre for a PhD before he was accepted. As a research student, he had the good fortune to be supervised by Patrick Elias, then a lecturer in the Faculty of Law. After two years came a problem – the Constitutional Law department at Edinburgh wished to offer him a lectureship, but Keith had still a year to go with his research, and Cambridge insisted that an Edinburgh supervisor be found for him in that year. Fortunately they agreed that I might fill the gap, a task that proved to be a sinecure. And the outcome? Keith completed and submitted his thesis punctually at the end of his third year's research – a period that doubled with his first year's lecturing.

It is well known that he soon moved back to Cambridge and then on to a chair at King's College, London. Not so many will know of his commitment to supporting Cambridge United, and his delight in making flying visits abroad to watch teams such as Real Madrid. The present volume will surely explain why I take much pleasure (with a touch of pride) that the work of an Edinburgh student whom I knew when he was young has stimulated such a rich and varied harvest of thinking and analysis on the constitution of social democracy today.

Anthony Bradley

EDITORS' PREFACE

In September 2018, a group of scholars met in the splendid surroundings of Somerset House for a workshop on 'The Constitution of Social Democracy'. We were a diverse band. There was a mix of experts in public law, labour law, civil liberties, political history and the law of democracy. We represented a range of jurisdictions. Nor were we all democratic socialists, though many of us might identify as such. What we shared was an admiration of the life and scholarly work of Professor Keith Ewing, and a desire to celebrate that legacy. The purpose of the workshop was to mark this in a fitting way – through an exploration of the ways in which different branches of the law might constitute or impede the realisation of democratic socialist objectives in the contemporary world. This of course reflects the vocation of Keith Ewing as scholar, teacher and activist. It is to this end that he has dedicated his professional life. The spirit of the workshop was conducted in the spirt of the man himself: a vigorous dialogue, based upon friendship, punctuated by much laughter, with papers developing imaginative and rigorous arguments on the legal underpinnings of the social democratic constitution.

Professor Ewing taught at the Universities of Edinburgh (1978–1983) and Cambridge (1983–1989) before becoming Professor of Public Law at KCL, where he has been since 1989. He has taught at several universities in Australia (Melbourne, Monash, Sydney, and Western Australia), Canada (Alberta and Osgoode Hall), and Japan (Fukuoka), and has presented papers in many countries. Professor Ewing is the author, co-author or editor of 40 books, including multiple editions of leading text books on *Constitutional and Administrative Law* (11th–17th editions, with A W Bradley and latterly C J S Knight), and Labour Law (1st–2nd editions, and two Cases and Materials books previously, with H Collins and A McColgan). His monographs and edited books cover a range of subjects, and include:

(i) Trade Unions, the Labour Party and the Law (Edinburgh University Press, 1982);
(ii) The Funding of Political Parties (Cambridge University Press, 1988);
(iii) Trade Union Democracy, Members' Rights and the Law (with P Elias, Mansell, 1988);
(iv) Freedom under Thatcher (with CA Gearty) (Oxford University Press, 1989);
(v) The Right to Strike (Oxford University Press, 1991);
(vi) Money, Politics, and Law (Oxford University Press, 1992);
(vii) Working Life: A New Perspective on Labour Law (ed, Lawrence and Wishart, 1995);
(viii) The Struggle for Civil Liberties – Political Freedom and the Rule of Law 1914–1945 (with CA Gearty, Oxford University Press, 2001);
(ix) The Cost of Democracy (Hart Publishing, 2007);
(x) The Bonfire of the Liberties (Oxford University Press, 2010).
(xi) MI5, The Cold War and the Rule of Law (with J Mahoney and A Moretta, Oxford University Press, 2020) is forthcoming).

He is also the author of many book chapters and journal articles and has published in leading journals around the world. Professor Ewing is President of the Institute of Employment

Rights (a trade union funded think tank) (IER), and President of the Campaign for Trade Union Freedom. He is also Vice President of the International Centre for Trade Union Rights and works closely with a number of trade unions in Britain and overseas.

In his work for the IER, Professor Ewing has campaigned since 1989 against Thatcher-led initiatives and to introduce more progressive labour laws. He has published many booklets, pamphlets and articles to this end, and given evidence to numerous parliamentary committees, and drafted private members' Bills on zero hours contracts and worker status. He advises the TUC on several matters, he is the Election Commissioner for Unite the Union (the UK's largest union), and he has been an advisor to the International Trade Union Congress and the European Trade Union Congress respectively. He has also worked as an adviser to the Labour Party and Labour Party affiliated trade unions on a number of constitutional and labour law questions for many years.

The latter works have involved drafting complaints to international agencies such as the ILO Committee of Experts and the ILO Freedom of Association Committee on behalf of the TUC and the Irish Congress of Trade Unions, and third party interventions to the ECtHR. He played a prominent role in defending the federal structure of the Labour Party from internal and external challenge. Most recently, with Lord Hendy QC he led the development of the IER *Manifesto for Labour Law*, coordinating the work of a number of leading scholars and activists. It was adopted by the Labour Party and many trade unions as a platform for a progressive Labour government.

Some brief comments are warranted on the structure of this volume. As editors, we resisted the temptation to stipulate a definition of democratic socialism to be circulated to the contributors. Most obviously, we did not do so because such an exercise is unlikely to be enlightening. There is no single account of democratic socialism. Rather, democratic socialism represents a discursive site where interlocutors explore its contrasts with free market capitalism; its constellation of values and the different ways in which those values can be configured in relation to each other; and the institutional mechanisms for implementing a democratic socialist vision. We also regarded it as artificial to treat this as a purely philosophical enterprise. Indeed, Ewing's intellectual development provides a living negation of that way of framing the enquiry. His understanding of democratic socialism has been dynamic rather than static. That approach is rooted in what is practically possibly within the existing political framework, rather than in pursuing an abstract ideal. The positions have shifted by praxis in light of his social activism.

In broad terms, three elements have provided the spine to Ewing's approach to democratic socialism: (i) popular sovereignty, embodied in a system of representative democracy and parliamentary sovereignty, is the basis of constitutional legitimacy; (ii) state power to be harnessed and directed at the promotion of the social, cultural and economic welfare of citizens; (iii) socio-economic objectives and the promotion of equality must be undertaken in accordance with civil and political liberties.[1] Within the compass of these broad principles, there is much scope for debate and contestation. Should civil and political liberties trump equality in every case of a conflict between them? Who should decide whether there has been a conflict in the first place, unelected judges or elected representatives? What about

[1] KD Ewing, 'Democratic Socialism and Labour Law' (1995) 24 *Industrial Law Journal* 103, 105.

the social, cultural and economic welfare of non-citizens? Should certain political liberties be curtailed through campaign finance laws in order to promote equality of democratic opportunity? The social democratic constitution must be both enabling and constraining. Over the last 50 years, some of the greatest advances of social and economic welfare have come through legislation and administrative action, which has depended upon an enabling constitution. During other periods, legislation and administrative action has also created a new 'precariat' that has been socially, economically and democratically disenfranchised. This has led some social democrats to forge alliances with liberal constitutionalists, identifying courts and the constitutionalisation of fundamental rights as a source of constitutional constraint.

We have also opted for a thematic division of chapters, rather than a disciplinary division between public law and civil liberties, labour law, and the law of democracy. The disciplinary division would have obscured a fundamental strength of Ewing's own work, which is to recognise the significance of an integrated and broad vision of the constitutional order. To paraphrase another great thinker of the Left, JAG Griffith, all of this material is constitutional. And all of it is political. While disciplinary boundaries are epistemologically useful in organising legal materials in a coherent way, the chapters in this volume make clear that the 'constitution of social democracy' depends upon an integrated vision of the different parts. Political representation is achieved not only in the formal electoral process, but also through collective action in the workplace. For example, the full and effective realisation of fundamental social rights, such as the right to collective bargaining, is as much a matter for public law and the law of democracy as it is for labour law. It invites questions about the possibilities for the will of the people to be translated into legislation through effective parliamentary democracy. Realising effective parliamentary democracy then necessitates measures to ensure that stark economic inequalities do not generate inequalities of political access and influence. In turn, this requires attention to the insulation of fundamental social rights from interference and disruption by the common law and an unelected judiciary. Finally, we must consider how the judicial protection of civil liberties might restrain the regressive programmes of right-wing governments dedicated to dismantling fundamental social rights, which is always a possibility where there are political freedoms and competing political parties. Ewing's position as one of the leading lights of English public law and labour law has enabled him to see these connections clearly, to escape the blinkers that come with excessive disciplinary specialisation.

The first part of the book is concerned with the role of judicial power in the social democratic constitution, focused on the protection of fundamental rights and civil liberties. As the diversity of contributions reveals, there is no single template. Indeed, the question of judicial power has always represented a site of intense disagreement within the tradition of democratic socialist thought. This is so in the field of labour law as in constitutional and administrative law. The various chapters in the first part demonstrate how it is mistaken to conflate a political culture of rights with a legal culture that is sanguine about the expansion of judicial power. It also exposes the troubling elisions that can sometimes occur in academic disagreements, where scepticism about the institutional position of judges is all too easily presented as a regressive hostility to citizens' fundamental rights. A constitution of fundamental rights may be realised through a variety of institutional mechanisms and regulatory techniques: Parliament, political parties, civil society, trade unions and collective bargaining. Furthermore, the resolution of these institutional dilemmas is unlikely to reflect timeless truths about human and political nature. They will reflect political choices, sensitive to the exigencies of particular times and places.

The second part considers the role of Parliament in the social democratic constitution. The principle of parliamentary sovereignty, as a vehicle for realising the will of the people, is the North Star of Ewing's constitutional vision. The chapters explore the different roles that might be undertaken by Parliament. Most obviously, it is a legislative institution. It is also a deliberative institution. And it is a political institution that holds the executive to account through its various committees. The chapters consider these different functions, and how they may need to be balanced differently and enhanced in order to realise a social democratic constitution.

The third part considers the ways in which constitutional norms mediate the tension between the distribution of resources in the economic and the political spheres. In the capitalist system, there are grave difficulties in minimising the spill-over of economic inequalities into the democratic system. At a time when economic and social inequalities appear to be widening and accelerating, the democratic socialist constitution must ensure that norms of political equality are protected from erosion. Indeed, this would appear to be the most pivotal element in the constitution of social democracy. Parliament's democratic legitimacy rests on the integrity of the electoral system. Where capital wields disproportionate influence in the political process, underpinned by constitutional rights of free speech and freedom of association, fundamental structural changes are unlikely to result from the legislative process.

The fourth part explores the different meanings of social justice in the social democratic constitution, and the ways in which the law and collective bargaining can realise social justice. Many of the chapters in this part reflect upon the role of labour law, given that the economic sphere and the organisation of production is one of the most crucial sites of social justice in the social democratic tradition. Among all of the contributions, there is an awareness that this is most likely to be achieved through strong and democratic trade unions, state supported collective bargaining conducted at the sectoral level, and a safety net or 'floor of rights' of basic labour standards for the most vulnerable workers. This provides an alternative social democratic narrative to the voluntaristic heritage of collective laissez-faire that has proved so captivating to the mythos of British labour law.

The final part considers the frontiers of the social democratic constitution. Some of the chapters examine the geographical idea of frontier, in various aspects such as the impact of Brexit or the position of migrants and non-citizens in the social democratic constitution based upon the nation-state. Other contributions identify new and emerging issues as the relevant frontier for the social democratic constitution, such as environmental crises or the use of state surveillance in relation to groups deemed threatening to the state.

The editors would like to record their gratitude to a number of individuals and institutions. Serena Crawshay-Williams has provided exemplary support to this project at every step along the way, from the planning and execution of the workshop to the finalisation of this volume. We would like to thank King's College, London and Professor Gillian Douglas for their moral and logistical support for the workshop. The Leverhulme Trust provided essential financial support for the workshop and the book project, through the Philip Leverhulme Prize. Professor Bogg records his gratitude to the Leverhulme for its ongoing support of his work. We would like to thank Hart Publishing for its support. The enthusiasm for the initial proposal, through to the logistical support in the preparation of the manuscript, has been absolutely exemplary. It continues to be a great pleasure to work with Hart. We record our gratitude to the contributors for producing marvellous chapters in a timely fashion. Finally, we take this opportunity to say thank you to Keith Ewing himself. To each of us, and to many others, he has been a loyal friend and supportive mentor. In the end, when the voluminous ink on the page eventually fades, the kindness will remain. That will be Keith's most important legacy.

TABLE OF CONTENTS

PART III
DEMOCRACY IN THE SOCIAL DEMOCRATIC CONSTITUTION

PART IV
SOCIAL JUSTICE IN THE SOCIAL DEMOCRATIC CONSTITUTION

PART V
FRONTIERS OF THE SOCIAL DEMOCRATIC CONSTITUTION

LIST OF CONTRIBUTORS

Alan Bogg is Professor of Labour Law at the University of Bristol, and Emeritus Fellow of Hertford College, Oxford.

Douglas Brodie is Professor of Employment Law, University of Strathclyde.

Anthony Bradley QC (Hon) is Emeritus Professor of Constitutional Law, University of Edinburgh and Research Fellow, Institute of European and Comparative Law, University of Oxford.

Nicola Countouris is Professor of Labour Law and European Law, University College, London, Faculty of Laws.

Ruth Dukes is Professor of Labour Law, University of Glasgow and PI on the European Research Council-funded project 'Work on Demand: Contracting for Work in a Changing Economy'.

Patrick Elias QC is Retired Judge, Court of Appeal.

Keith D Ewing is Professor of Public Law, King's College London.

Michael Ford QC is Professor of Law at the University of Bristol and a barrister at Old Square Chambers.

Mark Freedland QC (Hon), FBA is Emeritus Professor of Employment Law in the University of Oxford, and an Emeritus Research Fellow of St John's College Oxford.

Judy Fudge is LIUNA Enrico Henry Mancinelli Professor of Global Labour Issues School of Labour Studies, McMaster University.

Navraj Singh Ghaleigh is Senior Lecturer in Climate Law, University of Edinburgh.

Conor Gearty is Professor of Human Rights Law, LSE.

Michael Gordon is Professor of Constitutional Law, University of Liverpool.

James Grant is Senior Lecturer in Law, King's College London.

Lord Hendy QC is a barrister, Old Square Chambers, London, Honorary Professor, University College, London, Faculty of Laws, and life peer.

Ben Jackson is Associate Professor of Modern History at Oxford University and Co-Editor of *Political Quarterly*.

Timothy K Kuhner is Associate Professor, University of Auckland, Faculty of Law.

Virginia Mantouvalou is Professor of Human Rights and Labour Law, University College, London, Faculty of Laws.

Christopher McCorkindale is Senior Lecturer in Law, University of Strathclyde Law School.

Ewan McGaughey is Senior Lecturer, School of Law, King's College London and Research Associate, Centre for Business Research, University of Cambridge.

Alastair Mowbray is Professor of Public Law, University of Nottingham.

Cian C Murphy is Reader in Law, University of Bristol.

Tonia Novitz is Professor of Labour Law, University of Bristol.

Graeme Orr is Professor of Law, University of Queensland, Australia and Fellow of the Australian Academy of Law.

Marilyn J Pittard is Professor of Law and Associate Dean Academic Resourcing in the Faculty of Law, Monash University. She is President of the Australian Labour Law Association and deputy director of the Centre for Commercial Law and Regulatory Studies.

Jacob Rowbottom is Professor of Law at University of Oxford and Fellow of University College, Oxford.

Joo-Cheong Tham is Professor at Melbourne Law School and the Director of the Electoral Regulation Research Network.

PART I

Judicial Protection of Rights in the Social Democratic Constitution

1

Reflections on Judicial Power and Human Rights

PATRICK ELIAS

I. The Character of Judicial Review

The growth of judicial review has been one of the most striking features of the legal landscape in the last 50 years. It has led to a much greater holding to account of the executive by the judiciary. The basic techniques adopted by the courts for regulating the exercise of power are now firmly established. They were developed in part in the Victorian era but then virtually went into a cataleptic state for some 50 years or so until they were rediscovered, with some vigour, in the 1960s in such seminal cases as *Padfield,*[1] *Ridge v Baldwin,*[2] *Anisminic*[3] and, a little later, *Tameside.*[4] Lord Diplock identified the principles in the *GCHQ* case in 1984 as being illegality, irrationality and procedural impropriety[5] – a succinct if not entirely accurate summary. Save for the concept of irrationality, these principles are almost exclusively concerned with the manner of decision-making rather than the substance of the decision itself (although the division between the two is not rigid). In practice the test for irrationality was so high that it was almost fanciful to believe that it could ever justify invalidating a measure on merits grounds. Lord Diplock described it in these terms:

> By "irrationality" I mean what can by now be succinctly referred to as "Wednesbury unreasonableness". It applies to a decision which is so outrageous in its defiance of logic or of accepted moral standards that no sensible person who had applied his mind to the question to be decided could have arrived at it …[6]

In the last 20 years developments both at common law and stemming from the Human Rights Act have expanded judicial review of the merits, transforming the role of the courts and recalibrating the relationship between the courts, the executive and Parliament. The common law developments have in fact been strongly influenced by the Act. First, the common law concept of irrationality has been wholly recast. The courts first recognised that

[1] *Padfield v Minister of Agriculture, Fisheries and Food* [1968] AC 997 (HL).
[2] *Ridge v Baldwin* [1964] AC 40 (HL).
[3] *Anisminic v Foreign Compensation Commission* [1969] 2 AC 147 (HL).
[4] *Secretary of State for Education and Science v Tameside Metropolitan Borough Council* [1977] AC 1014 (HL).
[5] *Council of Civil Service Unions v Minister for the Civil Service* [1985] AC 374 (HL) 411.
[6] Ibid, 410 (Lord Diplock).

especially in cases where fundamental rights are involved, the decision needs to be subject to 'anxious consideration'.[7] In *Brind*,[8] a case involving free speech, Lord Bridge indicated what this might involve. He said that where fundamental human rights are at stake, the court should 'start from the premise that any restriction requires to be justified',[9] and that 'nothing less than an important competing public interest will be sufficient to justify it'.[10] As we shall see, this is essentially the principle of proportionality which lies at the heart of human rights' law. Another landmark case was *ex p Smith*.[11] The applicant was challenging the Ministry of Defence's policy of barring homosexuals from the armed services. The House of Lords accepted a formulation of the rationality principle in terms which stated that 'the more substantial the interference with human rights, the more the court would require by way of justification under the reasonableness test'.[12] This again is redolent of the proportionality analysis.

Subsequent cases in the Supreme Court have stressed the flexibility of the rationality test and whilst the courts have not in terms adopted the proportionality principle as part of the common law – in *Keyu*[13] Lord Neuberger expressed the view that it was a development of great constitutional significance which ought not to be taken by a five-judge court – the rationality test now employed by the courts is well capable of embracing it. In *Kennedy v Information Commissioner*,[14] Lord Mance reviewed the development of the rationality principle and observed that *Wednesbury* no longer rules; the test varies depending on the nature and gravity of the decision. *Kennedy* concerned the refusal by the Charity Commission to disclose certain information about the affairs of a particular charity. One of the arguments engaged article 10 on freedom of information. Lord Mance suggested that in that particular context, and given the way in which the common law had evolved, it was doubtful whether it mattered whether Convention or common law principles were applied. They would be likely to yield the same results. He expressed similar views in *Pham v Secretary of State for the Home Department*[15] when he said that whether the court is dealing with EU law, the Convention or the common law, the intensity of review will depend upon context and often the result will be the same whichever set of principles is adopted. Lord Sumption agreed, suggesting that the traditional rationality test at common law allowed for a more intensive review than was often thought to be the case, and that the Convention proportionality principle was not necessarily as intrusive as was often thought; it all depends on the context. Lord Reed observed that in a number of domestic cases the court had in substance applied a proportionality test, in the sense that there was a lack of proportionality between means and ends, without saying so in terms.[16] *Keyu* is therefore hardly a barrier

[7] Lord Bridge first adopted the concept in *Bugdaycay v Secretary of State for the Home Department* [1987] 1 AC 514. Lord Sumption has described it extra-judicially as no more than a slogan which fudged the question whether, and to what extent, the courts could review the merits of a decision: see the lecture, Lord Sumption, 'Anxious Scrutiny' (Administrative Law Bar Association, London, November 2014) www.supremecourt.uk/docs/speech-141104.pdf.

[8] *R v Secretary of State for the Home Department ex p Brind* [1991] 1 AC 696.

[9] Ibid, 748–749 (Lord Bridge).

[10] Ibid, 749 (Lord Bridge).

[11] *R v Ministry of Defence ex p Smith* [1996] QB 517.

[12] Ibid, 554 (Sir Thomas Bingham MR).

[13] *Keyu and ors v Secretary of State for Foreign & Commonwealth Affairs* [2015] UKSC 69, [2016] AC 1355.

[14] *Kennedy v Information Commissioner* [2014] UKSC 40, [2014] 2 WLR 808.

[15] *Pham v Secretary of State for the Home Department* [2015] UKSC 19, [2015] 1 WLR 1591.

[16] The judgments cited were *Hall & Co Ltd v Shoreham-by-Sea Urban District Council* [1964] 1 WLR 240 and *R v Barnsley Metropolitan Borough Council, ex p Hook* [1976] 1 WLR 1052.

to the application of the proportionality principle, albeit under another guise, even where Convention rights are not in play.

In a related development the courts have also recognised the significance of fundamental rights in the context of statutory interpretation. They have adopted what is termed the 'principle of legality'. In *R v Secretary of State for the Home Department ex p Simms*[17] the House of Lords accepted an argument that a blanket ban forbidding prisoners who protested their innocence from seeing journalists who might be able to assist them to establish their innocence was a breach of the common law right to freedom of expression. In so far as the prison rules appeared to be cast in sufficiently general terms to permit such a policy, they were read down so as to render the policy unlawful. Lord Hoffmann indicated that primary legislation could be similarly read down. He explained the principle thus:

> Parliamentary sovereignty means that Parliament can, if it chooses, legislate contrary to fundamental principles of human rights. The Human Rights Act 1998 will not detract from this power. The constraints upon its exercise by Parliament are ultimately political, not legal. But the principle of legality means that Parliament must squarely confront what it is doing and accept the political cost. Fundamental rights cannot be overridden by general or ambiguous words. This is because there is too great a risk that the full implications of their unqualified meaning may have passed unnoticed in the democratic process. In the absence of express language or necessary implication to the contrary, the courts therefore presume that even the most general words were intended to be subject to the basic rights of the individual. In this way the courts of the United Kingdom, though acknowledging the sovereignty of Parliament, apply principles of constitutionality little different from those which exist in countries where the power of the legislature is expressly limited by a constitutional document.[18]

Whether the courts would ever go further and refuse to apply legislation which infringed fundamental rights is a much disputed question,[19] although the traditional view, as famously enacted by Dicey, is that Parliament is sovereign and the function of the courts is to give effect to what Parliament has enacted. As Keith Ewing has recently argued,[20] the principle of Parliamentary sovereignty reflects a particular view of government: it is 'no more and no less than the legal principle underpinning the political principle that in a democracy there should be no legal limit to the wishes of the people'.[21]

II. The Impact of the Human Rights Act

All this has changed with the Human Rights Act 1998. Parliament has required the judges to test all public law decisions against the template of the European Convention on Human Rights (ECHR). More particularly, it has required the courts to interrogate for Convention compliance not only executive measures and subordinate legislation but even Acts of Parliament themselves. In so doing it has turned on its head the classic perception of

[17] *R v Secretary of State for the Home Department ex p Simms* [2000] 2 AC 115, [1999] 3 WLR 328.
[18] Ibid, 131 (Lord Hoffmann).
[19] Some judges believe that it could: see *R (Jackson) v Attorney General* [2006] 1 AC 262, [2005] 3 WLR 733.
[20] KD Ewing, 'The Resilience of the Political Constitution' (2013) 14 *German Law Journal* 2111.
[21] Ibid, 2118.

the judicial role. The courts do not give effect to the wishes of Parliament as expressed in the legislation; by section 3 of the Act they must where possible give a meaning which is Convention compliant, even where this involves a plain distortion of the natural and obvious meaning. This is akin to the doctrine of legality discussed above. And if they cannot adopt a Convention compliant construction, because the language of the Act will simply not permit it, they can issue a declaration of incompatibility under section 4. Parliament has chosen to limit its own powers and has conferred upon the courts the task of enforcing those limits.

It is true that constitutionally the Human Rights Act does not formally undermine the doctrine of Parliamentary sovereignty, for two reasons. First, the power conferred upon the judges is given by Parliament itself, and it can be taken back by Parliament. This is not a power grab by the judges but a devolution of power by Parliament. Second, the courts cannot formally strike down primary legislation (unlike secondary legislation) even where it concludes that the Act has infringed human rights. The courts can only make a declaration of incompatibility which, in theory at least, Parliament can choose to ignore, although the political pressure to give effect to it is very powerful. This is not least because if the government fails to put the matter right, it will be inviting challenges before the European Court of Human Rights from those whose rights are infringed and, save in the very exceptional case where the ECHR differs from the view of the domestic courts, the claims are certain to succeed.

For the most part, the Human Rights Act was given a good press both by lawyers and politicians. But some commentators did not welcome its enactment. Shortly after the Act was passed Keith Ewing, together with Tom Campbell and Adam Tomkins, edited a collection of essays entitled 'Sceptical Essays on Human Rights'.[22] They were not all sceptical about the existence of human rights, although some were and that is a perfectly tenable position. It was after all the utilitarian philosopher Jeremy Bentham who described the concept of natural rights as 'simple nonsense: .... rhetorical nonsense, – nonsense upon stilts'.[23] The principal concern of the sceptics was with the effect which the Act would have on the concept of a representative democracy. The mission statement which identified the intellectual starting point of the contributors to 'Sceptical Essays' included the following:

> All the participants endorse the importance of human rights within any democratic system of government but question whether the primary responsibility for the articulation of these rights ought to be taken away from the normal political processes of representative government.[24]

It may be questioned whether it is entirely accurate to say that the *primary* responsibility for the articulation and protection of human rights was being taken away from the normal political processes. After all, by section 19 of the Act the minister responsible for piloting a Bill through Parliament must make a statement in writing to the effect that in his or her view the Bill is in accordance with Convention rights, or must state in terms that this assurance cannot be given. This is not of course binding on the courts who can disagree with the Minister's views, and might even construe legislation as Convention

[22] T Campbell, KD Ewing, and A Tomkins (eds), *Sceptical Essays on Human Rights* (Oxford, OUP, 2001).

[23] J Bentham, 'Anarchical Fallacies' in J Waldron (ed), *Nonsense upon Stilts: Bentham, Burke and Marx on the Rights of Man* (London, Methuen & Coy Limited, 1987) 53.

[24] Campbell, Ewing and Tomkins (n 22) 2.

compliant where the Minister has been unable to give an assurance. In principle, therefore, Parliament still has both the primary responsibility, and the first opportunity, to ensure that legislation is not incompatible with human rights. In a very real sense it can be said that with respect to primary legislation the courts exercise a reviewing function which indirectly involves testing whether the Minister's statement of compatibility was correct. The more effective the Parliamentary procedures for assessing human rights' compliance, the fewer should be the cases where legislation is held to be incompatible. But however effectively Parliament polices its own laws, there will inevitably be cases where the judges simply take a different view from the politicians as to whether Convention rights have been unlawfully infringed or not. The critical question is: having been given this power, how should the judges exercise it?

The purpose of the Act was not consciously to give effect to a new philosophical perception of the nature of government; it had a more banal objective which was essentially to ensure that rights which were enforceable by the citizen before the European Court of Human Rights should now be enforceable in the domestic courts; hence the emphasis the government gave in the White Paper preceding the Act to the notion of 'bringing rights home', a pithy if somewhat jingoistic description of the process. But it does in fact mark an important shift in the nature of the constitution itself, and in particular the doctrine of the separation of powers, even if the doctrine of parliamentary sovereignty remains formally in place. Martin Loughlin in his chapter described it as a move from a liberal democratic model to a rights based conception of democracy. The former involves decisions taken after deliberation and discussion by representatives of the people, and the system envisages that traditions of liberty and tolerance will ensure that there are relatively few cases of legislation unacceptably infringing individual rights.[25] Rights-based constitutionalists see the role of government differently. The assumption is that citizens bear rights and do not intend to concede to their representatives the power to interfere with those rights save where there is a powerful collective interest justifying this. The HRA adopts the latter approach, though mitigated in favour of the former to the extent that as a matter of legal form it gives the last word to Parliament. An important element of a rights-based approach is that the rights in issue need to be identified with some clarity and that is precisely what the HRA seeks to do by adopting the provisions in the European Convention.

Contributors to Sceptical Essays were doubtful of the benefits of the Act for a number of reasons. Keith Ewing, for example, was concerned that giving special status to civil and political rights but not to social or economic rights distorted the constitution.[26] But the heart of the opposition was that the rights model – or at least the model ultimately adopted – involves giving judges the power to determine essentially political questions which in a representative democracy ought to be left with Parliament. A partisan objection was the fear that conservative judges will use human rights as a tool to frustrate radical policies. The more principled objection was that it is constitutionally inappropriate for unelected and unaccountable judges to curb the policies of the elected representatives, whatever the

[25] M Loughlin, 'Rights, Democracy and Law' in T Campbell, KD Ewing, and A Tomkins (eds), *Sceptical Essays on Human Rights* (Oxford, OUP, 2001).

[26] KD Ewing, 'The Unbalanced Constitution' in T Campbell, KD Ewing, and A Tomkins (eds), *Sceptical Essays on Human Rights* (Oxford, OUP, 2001).

political inclinations of the judges in question, and whether they are considering policies emanating from the political left or the political right. Rule by the judges should not replace the rule of Parliament.

There is no doubt that these commentators put a powerful and cogent case against re-balancing of the constitution in this way. But arguably it seems to me that the logic of the analysis is that the UK should not be bound by the Convention and subject to the jurisdiction of the ECHR either, otherwise there is a fundamental contradiction lying at the heart of this analysis. The HRA did not introduce the principle that judges could question measures, including legislation, for Convention compliance. That followed when the UK signed up to the Human Rights Convention and in particular when it acceded to the right of individual petition to the European Court of Human Rights. Moreover, the European Communities Act had already required the courts to strike down domestic laws which were inconsistent with EU principles, and many of the provisions in the EU Charter of Fundamental Rights explicitly drew upon Convention principles. So even before the HRA, judges – albeit not domestic judges – were reviewing both Acts of Parliament and acts of the executive on human rights grounds. If judicial review of parliamentary legislation based on human rights is unwarranted and undermines democracy, it is difficult to see why the UK should be a party to the Convention at all. It is true that by conferring power of review on the domestic courts the HRA has dramatically increased the number of decisions which will be subject to judicial scrutiny. But if it is in principle desirable to be a party to the Convention and to subject acts of government and Parliament to the template of the Convention, how can it be a bad thing to make the process easier for claimants by allowing them to pursue remedies in the domestic courts?

III. Why are Judges Thought to be Inappropriate?

James Allan in a chapter considering the New Zealand experience with their Human Rights Act,[27] crisply summarised the case against conferring the protection of human rights on the judges. He observed that we all put our hands up in favour of human rights, but when they have to be applied to particular situations where rights are typically in competition with each other or are to be balanced against some other public interest, 'any notion of consensus or even widespread agreement disappears'. He continued as follows:

> This point is crucially important. Once a constitutionalized Bill of Rights is in place, giving the judges power to strike down legislation and so, undeniably, enormous social policy making powers, the judges end up deciding controversial questions of social policy over which sincere, intelligent, well-meaning people disagree – questions about where to draw the line on abortion, privacy, police powers, free speech, religious practices, who can marry, how refugee claimants are to be treated, and much else besides .... There is no special moral goodness or acute ethical perspicacity inherent in judges which the rest of us lack.
>
> So what such a Bill of Rights does is to deliver from elected politicians to unelected judges power to decide highly contestable, debatable, social policy issues, under the guise of upholding and

[27] J Allan, 'The Effect of a Statutory Bill of Rights where Parliament is Sovereign: The Lessons of New Zealand' in T Campbell, KD Ewing, and A Tomkins (eds), *Sceptical Essays on Human Rights* (Oxford, OUP, 2001).

> protecting universally desired and uncontentious rights …. It is not the black and white, good versus evil, type issues, so often used to sell a Bill of Rights to the public, that the judges will be deciding. Rather it is the day to day but highly contentious political and social issues over which these unelected judges will have the first (and in all practical senses, the final) say.[28]

IV. The Judicial Approach to Balance; the Doctrine of Proportionality

James Allan accurately observes that the effect of the Act is that judges have made important decisions on all the areas he mentions and many more. They arbitrate between conflicting rights and the public interest. The starting point in cases where the relevant right is infringed is to identify the right. Some rights, such as the right to life, are absolute and no interference is justified. The court simply has to determine whether the right has been infringed. But many of the Convention rights are qualified, so that even where they are engaged, the interference with the right will not be unlawful if it can be justified. Article 8, which provides for the right to respect for family and private life, is a good illustration of the principles in action. It is frequently the relevant right involved because its ambit has been so broadly defined by the Strasbourg court. It is readily engaged and therefore the critical question is whether interfering with that right can be justified. Article 8 itself specifies, in broad terms, the legitimate reasons for interfering with the right. The interference must be 'such as is in accordance with the law and is necessary in a democratic society in the interests of national security, public safety or the economic well-being of the country, for the prevention of disorder or crime, for the protection of health or morals, or for the protection of the rights and freedoms of others.' In general terms, what is required is that a balance is struck between the constitutional right in issue and the wider public interest of the kind recognised in article 8(2); the interference must be proportionate.

The courts have adopted a concept of proportionality which is designed to provide a structured approach to the issue of justification. The essential features of the concept are now well established. Lord Reed set out the principles and made some observations about them in the *Bank Mellat* case.[29] The courts have to ask the following questions:

(1) whether the objective of the measure is sufficiently important to justify the limitation of a protected right;
(2) whether the measure is rationally connected to the objective;
(3) whether a less intrusive measure could have been used without unacceptably compromising the achievement of the objective, and
(4) whether, balancing the severity of the measure's effects on the rights of the persons to whom it applies against the importance of the objective, to the extent that the measure will contribute to its achievement, the former outweighs the latter.

As Lord Reed pointed out, however, the courts ought not to be too strict on the third requirement since it will almost always be possible to think of some alternative and less

[28] Ibid, 389.
[29] *Bank Mellat v HM Treasury* [2013] UKSC 39, [2014] AC 700 [74].

draconian means, particularly if the relevant practicalities and considerations of cost are ignored. Lord Reed concluded that the limitation should be one that is 'reasonable for the legislature to impose'.[30]

Interestingly the fourth criterion was not always seen as an element of the proportionality test; earlier authorities such as *de Freitas v Permanent Secretary of the Ministry of Agriculture*[31] simply identified the first three criteria. But since the judgment of Lord Bingham in the House of Lords in *Huang*[32] it has taken its place as one of the proportionality criteria – and often in practice the most important. This element is of profound importance. It means that even the least intrusive interference in pursuit of a legitimate objective may be unlawful; the objective may not be sufficiently important to warrant the interference with the Convention right at all. Where the court finds a decision, policy or law disproportionate on this ground, it is telling the executive or legislature that it must forego pursuing a legitimate public objective; the wider public benefit must be sacrificed to the individual Convention right affected.

The adoption of these criteria goes some way towards establishing a set of objective standards to guide the judges in the balancing exercise. They provide a degree of predictability to the process and a degree of consistency. The first two criteria in particular involve the exercise of a kind which judges habitually adopt in judicial review cases; they involve consideration of the purpose of the measure and whether the measure is rationally connected to the end in view in the sense that it is capable of achieving that objective. The requirement that there should be no less intrusive measure also has an element of objectivity, although it is more problematic. It is often closely linked to the fourth element; a measure which is more restrictive than it need be will be disproportionate, even if there are in principle legitimate public interest considerations to protect. But if the realistic observations of Lord Reed in *Bank Mellat* are followed, this ought not to involve the judges imposing unduly harsh standards on the decision maker so far as this element is concerned. Taking the first three factors identified by Lord Reed together, they go some way to countering Allan's objection that the courts are merely making a political decision under the guise of adjudication. They are in many cases exercising powers in a manner which is consonant with traditional common law concepts of judicial review.

The controversial area is the fourth requirement, the balance between the individual right and the countervailing public interest, and cases frequently turn on this assessment. This is not a simple comparison because one is not comparing like with like; there are no obvious objective criteria for making the assessment. In truth there is little which can properly be called judicial in this exercise, and the fact that Parliament has chosen to give these powers to the judges does not alter that fact. The courts are being given a power that is often essentially political in nature. That is particularly so where the courts are evaluating general policy measures. Moreover, the fact that Parliament has chosen to give special status to Convention rights means that the exercise is not even the classic balancing of competing interests involved in the political process. One of the factors, namely the human right interfered with, has been given particular weight in advance, and there must good and cogent reasons for interfering with it.

[30] Ibid.
[31] *de Freitas v Permanent Secretary of the Ministry of Agriculture* [1999] 1 A C 69.
[32] *Huang v Secretary of State for the Home Department* [2007] 2 AC 167, [2007] 2 WLR 581.

There is in my view a very powerful argument for saying that once the first three elements have been satisfied, the courts ought to apply a classic reviewing function to the fourth requirement by simply asking whether the balance is rational. One might have thought that once the decision maker had shown that there was a legitimate objective, that the means were directed to it, and that it was no more stringent than was necessary, the decision should stand unless the balance is manifestly out of kilter. The question would be whether the balance was in principle justifiable rather than whether the court thought it was justified. That would respect the policy choice of the decision maker whilst allowing the court to restrain clearly unjustified interference with human rights. But that is not the position. It has been firmly established by Lord Bingham in *Huang*[33] that the judges are not asking whether the decision maker could legitimately have struck the balance in the way it did; rather they are striking the balance for themselves.

On the face of it, this lends strong support to James Allan's contention that the unelected judges are simply usurping the decisions of the elected representatives as to where the appropriate balance lies. In fact, however, the position is more nuanced than this simple statement of principle might suggest. This is because the judges do not apply the same balancing technique in all cases. They have recognised that notwithstanding the broad power conferred upon them, they should exercise it with appropriate restraint. This is consistent with the jurisprudence of the European Court of Justice itself which has recognised that in areas of social and economic policy, for example, considerable leeway should be given to the decision maker and the courts should intervene only where the decision is manifestly without reasonable foundation[34] – a concept which sets a high hurdle for intervention. Lord Reed described the position as follows in the *Nicklinson* case;

> … the Human Rights Act introduces a new element into our constitutional law, and entails some adjustment of the respective constitutional roles of the courts, the executive and the legislature. It does not however eliminate the differences between them: differences, for example, in relation to their composition, their expertise, their procedures, their accountability and their legitimacy. Accordingly, it does not alter the fact that certain issues are by their nature more suitable for determination by Government or Parliament than by the courts. In so far as issues of that character are relevant to an assessment of the compatibility of executive action or legislation with Convention rights, that is something which the courts can and do properly take into account. They do so by giving weight to the determination of those issues by the primary decision-maker. There is nothing new about this point. It has often been articulated in the past by referring to a discretionary area of judgment.[35]

As a statement of principle, this would no doubt secure general approval from the judiciary. Even though Parliament has delegated the determination of human rights' issues to the courts, judges recognise that for institutional, constitutional or other reasons they may not be best placed to make the decision in issue and particular respect will be shown to the views of the decision maker. Parliament can give the power of review to the courts, but it cannot alter the fact that frequently the decision maker, whether the executive or Parliament, is better placed to make the right decision and the courts recognise that. Those

[33] Ibid [11].
[34] *Stec v United Kingdom* (2006) 43 EHRR 47.
[35] *R (Nicklinson) v Ministry of Justice* [2014] UKSC 38, [2015] AC 657 [296].

sceptical about the HRA will no doubt applaud the display of judicial humility. The problem, however, is that individual judges have very different views about when and how much respect should be shown to the assessment of the primary decision maker. Some judges are far more interventionist than others as the cases demonstrate.

A striking example of the fundamentally different perspectives which judges may hold is provided by the decision of the Supreme Court in *Lord Carlile of Berriew v Secretary of State for the Home Department*.[36] A group of cross bench MPs and peers wanted to invite a Ms Rajavi, a well-known Iranian dissident, to speak to them in Parliament. She had been banned from the UK since 1997 on the grounds that her entry was not conducive to the public good because she had formerly supported terrorism in Iran. The Home Secretary was asked to lift that order but after consulting the Foreign Office, she refused. In fact she considered the matter on three occasions but maintained her position, giving extensive reasons why. The MP claimants asserted that this was an unjustified interference with their right of free speech under article 10 and indeed, with Ms Rajavi's right also.

The Home Secretary concluded that if Ms Rajavi were allowed in it would be received very badly by the government in Iran, being perceived by the Iranians as a deliberately hostile act. It would as a result damage diplomatic relations, it could put at risk the safety of UK citizens in Iran, including staff in the embassy, and it could even provoke terrorist acts outside Iran against UK citizens. These were very serious concerns indeed, and the judges accepted that they could not gainsay the Home Secretary's assessment of the risks however dubious they may be about it. As Lord Sumption pointed out, the judges were not in a position to make their own assessment, and there was no basis for saying that the Home Secretary had erred in principle in taking the view she did.

The first three elements of the proportionality test were met, as all the judges accepted. There was a legitimate aim, namely to prevent Ms Rajayi being allowed into the UK in order to avoid the risks identified: the ban was rationally related to the aim (because it kept her out); and nothing less than a ban would have met the concerns (because the assessment was that the risks might materialise unless she was kept out.) So everything turned on the fourth element: was the interference justified? The context, security and foreign relations, was one where considerable leeway should be afforded to the decision maker, as the Supreme Court had unsurprisingly accepted in *Bank Mellat v HM Treasury*. Applying that test, and given the potentially grave consequences which might result from allowing Ms Rajavi entry, it is hardly surprising that the majority of the court concluded that the interference was justified.

However, Lord Kerr took a different view and felt no such inhibitions. His position was summarised in the following two paragraphs of his judgment:

> Ultimately, therefore, it is not a question of whether the Secretary of State has been shown to be guilty of an error of principle. We do not ask whether the Secretary of State's view is tenable; we ask whether it is right. Right, that is, by the standards that have been set for us by the Human Rights Act. Taking account, albeit with a suitably critical appraisal, of the Secretary of State's view as to the consequences of lifting the exclusion on Mrs Rajavi, the question is whether the interference with the appellant's right, notwithstanding those consequences, is justified.
>
> What it comes to is this. By enacting the Human Rights Act, the government has chosen to subject decisions which any public authority, including the executive or an individual minister, takes,

[36] *Lord Carlile of Berriew v Secretary of State for the Home Department* [2014] UKSC 60, [2015] AC 945.

> involving interference with citizens Convention rights, to the courts' independent review. In submitting to that review, the government is entitled to say to the courts, "respect our reasons for deciding why such interference is required". It is not entitled to say, however, "you must accept our view as to the importance of the right that has been interfered with."[37]

Lord Kerr did not consider that the balance had been properly struck in this case. In arriving at this conclusion he was influenced by two considerations which the rest of the court did not consider persuasive: first, that the reaction of the Iranian Government was unpredictable; and second, that if it did display the hostility which the Home Secretary feared it might, that would be an irrational and undemocratic reaction. So the Home Secretary's concerns should be afforded lesser weight on that count. The other judges – surely correctly – said that the Home Secretary was entitled to consider what in fact might happen; if in fact Iran might act so as to put UK citizens in jeopardy, that justified the Home Secretary's ban. It was hardly relevant to say that it would not be cricket for the Iranians to act in that way.

Lord Kerr assumes that the judges are better able than government to understand the importance of human rights. Even assuming that judges do have that particular expertise, it does not follow that the courts should therefore carry out the proportionality assessment. But the premise is far from self-evident: the fact that Parliament has given these rights a special protected status suggests that they are fully alive to their significance. Moreover, the politicians might argue that judges tend not to give sufficient weight to the wider public interests in play and are not as carefully attuned to the public mood as they are.

Lord Sumption gave an excoriating assessment of Lord Reed's analysis with which it is difficult to disagree:

> "We do not ask whether the Secretary of State's view is tenable", he says (para 158), "but whether it is right." Notwithstanding the respect which in earlier parts of his judgment Lord Kerr has acknowledged is due to the executive's assessment of questions of national security, this is in fact nothing less than a transfer to the courts of the constitutional function of the Home Secretary, in circumstances where the court is wholly incapable of performing it.[38]

Another area where the courts have recognised the need to afford particular respect for the views of government is in the field of social and economic policy. The current prevailing view, laid down by the majority in the very recent case of *R (on the application of DA) v Secretary of State for Work and Pensions*[39] is that when applying the proportionality test to such policies, the court must ask whether the measure in question was manifestly without reasonable foundation (MWRF). Prior to this clarification there was considerable uncertainty whether this was the test. There were a number of cases where judges in the Supreme Court had expressed the view that although the MWRF test would apply to the first three aspects of the proportionality test, it was not appropriate to apply it to the fourth. I confess that I found this a surprising analysis. One might have thought that particularly in aspects of government policy it is particularly in the application of the broad balancing exercise required by the fourth element that deference should be afforded to the decision maker. If anything a more intrusive approach could be adopted with respect to the other, more objective, elements. In *DA* both Lord Wilson (with whose judgment Lord Hodge agreed) and

[37] Ibid [158]–[159] (Lord Kerr).
[38] Ibid [49] (Lord Sumption).
[39] *R (on the application of DA) v Secretary of State for Work and Pensions* [2019] UKSC 21, [2019] 1WLR 3289.

Lord Carnwath (with whose judgment Lords Reed and Hughes agreed) analysed the relevant case law in some detail. They sought to lay down a clear test for the future. Lord Wilson accepted that he had been in error in previously having adopted what he now accepted was a misguided view of the law. Lord Kerr disagreed with the majority; he accepted that MWRF was the appropriate test for the first element, namely whether there was an legitimate purpose, but not for the fourth element; he in turn accepted that he had been in error in the earlier case of SG, where he had accepted that MWRF was the appropriate test in such cases! Lady Hale was content to say that this was a 'difficult question' which the court would no doubt have to revisit in the future (notwithstanding that Lord Carnwath had stated that it was surely settled for the future).[40]

The adoption of the MWRF test is an important recognition that the courts should not readily strike down important measures of government policy save in a very clear case indeed. In *DA* the case concerned the imposition of the benefit cap which set a cap on benefits made available to those in need. An exception was made for lone parents working for more than 16 hours a week. In separate actions lone parents with children under the age of two and lone parents with children under school age contended that they ought not, like other parents, to have been subject to this rule principally because it was more difficult for them, for a range of reasons, to obtain work. They should be exempted automatically. The young children were also joined as claimants. The claims were made under article 8 read with article 14. It was said to have been unlawful discrimination to impose the same rule on them as everyone else when they were in a markedly different situation (a so-called *Thlimmenos* claim).[41] A particular issue in the case was whether the policy as applied to these children had properly taken into account the best interests of the children as required by article 3 of the UN Convention on the Rights of the Child. The majority held that they had. The government relied upon evidence which showed that there were long term benefits for children who lived in households where a parent was at work. The majority held that it was not manifestly without reasonable foundation for the government to conclude that this was capable of overriding the undoubted shorter term hardships which the policy created, although it was, particularly in Lord Wilson's view, a very marginal case even applying the MWRF test. Lady Hale and Lord Kerr both dissented and held that there was a breach of article 3 and that the failure to make an exception for these groups was not justified.

One of the consequences of the Human Rights Act is that particularly in major human rights cases which raise socio-economic issues, there will often be a number of interveners providing written and sometimes oral argument. They are there to assist the court and they often do, but an observer might be forgiven for thinking that many of these groups perceive their role as special interest groups seeking to influence the proportionality analysis. Lord Carnwath in his judgment pointed out some of the very real practical difficulties which courts will face if they adopt too intrusive a test of proportionality in cases of this nature; it may require them to evaluate conflicting evidence which they are not necessarily in the best position to evaluate:

> We have been faced with detailed submissions based on conflicting factual and statistical evidence, much of it produced for the first time in this court. Some of this evidence has come in support of

[40] Ibid [152] (Lady Hale).

[41] Named after the case where the argument was first (successfully) advanced in the European Court of Human Rights: *Thlimmenos v Greece* (2004) 31 EHRR 15 (GC).

> submissions from interveners. Their experience of the practical implications of the legal issues can be of great value, but the court must be careful to ensure that such interventions do not lead to the introduction of new evidence which has not been fully tested, and which cannot be properly tested within the limitations of this court's proper function. At times it has seemed as though the court were being invited to take on the task of a Parliamentary Select Committee, undertaking a review of the policy and factual basis of the legislation. That is not our role.[42]

A case where the application of the MWRF test would probably have resulted in a different decision is the *Aquilar Quila* case.[43] This involved a change to an immigration rule designed to protect those forced into marriage. The new rule, approved by Parliament, provided that if a UK citizen married a non-UK citizen, the latter could only have a right to join his or her spouse if both were over the age of 21. Until the amendment, both had to be over 18. The claimants alleged that this was a disproportionate interference with their family lives contrary to article 8. The leading judgment in the Supreme Court was given by Lord Wilson. There was conflicting evidence whether the change would in fact deter forced marriage or not, although an EU Directive had allowed states to make this change specifically for that purpose and several European countries had done so. Notwithstanding this, Lord Wilson held that the rule was a disproportionate interference. In this case it was on the grounds that there was no clear evidence that the policy would deter forced marriage and therefore no legitimate objective. It is difficult to see how that conclusion could possibly be reached had he adopted the MWRF test.

Furthermore, the Secretary of State had not assessed the relative proportions of those aged 18–21 in a forced marriage as against those who were not, and would be prejudiced by the rule. Lady Hale gave a judgment essentially in agreement, and Lords Clarke and Phillips agreed with both judgments. Lord Browne, in a strong dissent, pointed out that for obvious reasons it is difficult to get reliable evidence as to whether the rule change would be likely to deter forced marriage given the secrecy surrounding such practices. He commented upon the strong policy implications of the majority's analysis:

> The extent to which the rule will help combat forced marriage and the countervailing extent to which it will disrupt the lives of innocent couples adversely affected by it is largely a matter of judgment. Unless demonstrably wrong, this judgment should be rather for government than for the courts. Still more obviously, the comparison between the enormity of suffering within forced marriages on the one hand and the disruption to innocent couples within the 18-21 age group whose desire to live together in this country is temporarily thwarted by the rule change, is essentially one for elected politicians, not for judges. Lady Hale suggests (at para 66 of her judgment) that: "The right to marry is just as important as the right not to marry." But she cannot possibly mean by this that the postponement by up to three years of a couple's wish to live together as man and wife in this country involves just as great a violation of human rights as a forced marriage. What value, then, is to be attached to preventing a single forced marriage? What cost should each disappointed couple be regarded as paying? Really these questions are questions of policy and should be for government rather than us. Of course, the ultimate decision on article 8(2) proportionality must be for the courts but in this particular context the courts should to my mind accord government a very substantial area of discretionary judgment.[44]

[42] Ibid [123] (Lord Carnwath).
[43] *R (Aquilar Quila) v Secretary of State for the Home Department* [2011] UKSC 45, [2012] 1 AC 621.
[44] Ibid [91] (Lord Browne).

He later observed:

> In a sensitive context such as that of forced marriages it would seem to me not merely impermissible but positively unwise for the courts yet again to frustrate government policy except in the clearest of cases. To my mind this cannot possibly be regarded as such a case.[45]

The possible implications of this decision are concerning. There will be circumstances particularly in the economic field where the government acts on a belief that a particular measure is likely to have a certain effect but there is no direct evidence one way or the other; it a judgment or prediction. It surely cannot be right simply to discount the minister's best assessment in such circumstances on the grounds that the belief is not sufficiently rooted in evidence. This case engaged a very important aspect of social policy, namely the deterrence of forced marriage. Nobody could say that the new rule might not assist in that objective, yet the decision of the court is that even if it does, it did not justify the interference. The balance to be struck between the realistic, if uncertain, prospect of deterring forced marriage as against deferring unforced marriage is not an easy one to strike, but what special qualities do judges have which warrants them carrying out the task? Lord Wilson thought that in adopting the stance he did, Lord Brown was effectively negating his duty to apply the proportionality test. He cited a passage from the judgment of Lord Bingham in *R (SB) v Governors of Denbigh High School* when Lord Bingham had said that 'Proportionality must be judged objectively, but by the court'.[46] Perhaps it is now more fully appreciated that it is not a failure to discharge a duty to give appropriate – which might sometimes be very considerable – weight to the views of the decision maker.

Another area where perceptions of the judicial role have a marked effect on the decision is where controversial ethical issues are in issue. In *Nicklinson*,[47] Mr Nicklinson was paralysed from the neck down following a stroke. He could communicate only by blinking to spell out words. For seven years his life was, in his own words, 'dull, miserable, demeaning, undignified and intolerable.'[48] He was unable to take his own life and wished to be helped to die by professional doctors. But assisting a suicide is a criminal offence: see section 2 of the Suicide Act 1961. He contended that he was being prevented from choosing the time of his death and thereby avoiding an undignified end. The Strasbourg Court had already accepted that this engaged article 8, although it had also held, in the *Pretty*[49] case which was a reference from the UK decided before the *Nicklinson* case, that states have a wide margin of appreciation in this area. Nevertheless, the Supreme Court held that it had jurisdiction to decide whether in its view article 8 had been infringed or not.

The case turned on utilitarian arguments. Surprisingly it was not argued – although in principle it could have been – that the sanctity of life was itself a moral principle capable of justifying the law. The Secretary of State submitted that if assisted suicide were made legal, other vulnerable parties would be pressured, or at least might well feel themselves pressured to end their lives, perhaps because they felt they were a burden on their families. There was no reliable evidence as to whether, or to what extent, this would be likely to be the case, and

[45] Ibid [97] (Lord Browne).
[46] *R (SB) v Governors of Denbigh High School* [2007] 1 AC 100, [2006] 2 WLR 719 [30] (Lord Bingham).
[47] *Nicklinson* (n 35).
[48] Ibid [13] (Lord Toulson).
[49] *Pretty v United Kingdom* (2002) 35 EHRR 1.

it would for obvious reasons be difficult to obtain such evidence. But it was the belief of many who worked with elderly patients. Lord Kerr held that nonetheless in these circumstances the Secretary of State had not even established that he was pursuing a legitimate objective to protect the lives of others. Perhaps not surprisingly, he was the only judge to take that view. Lady Hale conceded that this was a legitimate objective but was satisfied that it would be possible to adopt a less stringent interference by providing a procedure whereby someone in Mr Nicklinson's position could come before a judge and satisfy the judge that he had a properly settled wish to die. Both these judges would have granted a declaration of incompatibility. Lords Neuberger, Mance and Wilson did not go this far. They were not satisfied that the evidence before them demonstrated that the interference was disproportionate, but further evidence might establish that it was. This was not a no-go area as far as the courts were concerned. Although Parliament's view was entitled to great weight, it was not determinative.

Lord Sumption with, whose judgment Lords Hughes, Reed and Clarke were in agreement, took the view that Parliament's view should be determinative. This was plainly not an appropriate decision for the court; it was a complex issue and Parliament had relatively recently confirmed that it wished the law to remain in place. Also Parliament had access to a range of expert views not available to the court. This was classically a matter which should be determined by Parliament. He said this:

> The question whether relaxing or qualifying the current absolute prohibition on assisted suicide would involve unacceptable risks to vulnerable people is in my view a classic example of the kind of issue which should be decided by Parliament … … the issue involves a choice between two fundamental but mutually inconsistent moral values, upon which there is at present no consensus in our society. Such choices are inherently legislative in nature. The decision cannot fail to be strongly influenced by the decision-makers' personal opinions about the moral case for assisted suicide. This is entirely appropriate if the decision-makers are those who represent the community at large. It is not appropriate for professional judges. The imposition of their personal opinions on matters of this kind would lack all constitutional legitimacy.[50]

There was a similar difference of opinion in the recent case of *Human Rights Commission of Northern Ireland.*[51] The case concerned the ban on abortion in Northern Ireland, save where the life of the woman is at risk. There were a number of issues before the court. One was whether it infringed a woman's article 8 rights to refuse her an abortion where she had conceived as a result of rape or incest. The court held by a majority that the claimants had no standing to bring the action but the issues were discussed in detail nevertheless. Four judges thought that article 8 rights were infringed in these circumstances and three did not. The arguments were complex but again the minority were essentially influenced by the fact that the issue was properly a decision for Parliament. Lord Reed, with whom in respect of these issues Lord Lloyd-Jones and Lady Black agreed, made the following observation:

> It is difficult to envisage a more controversial issue than the proper limits of the law governing abortion. Diametrically opposed views, and every shade of opinion in between, are held with equal sincerity and conviction. Each side of the debate appeals to moral or religious values which

[50] Ibid [230] (Lord Sumption).
[51] *Northern Ireland Human Rights Commission's Application for Judicial Review* [2018] UKSC 27, [2019] 1 All ER 173.

> are held with passionate intensity. In a democracy on the British model, the natural place for that debate to be resolved is in the legislature.[52]

V. Conclusions

The HRA has conferred significant powers upon the courts. It requires them to review cases some of which are of a highly-charged political nature. A critical question in many, if not most, human rights' cases is whether the interference with the right in issue is justified. The courts are charged with answering that question and the controlling mechanism they employ is the concept of proportionality. There is general judicial agreement about what the concept entails and there is also broad agreement that institutional or constitutional considerations will sometimes require the courts to adopt a light touch – and sometimes a very light touch – review. The problem is that different judges have strikingly different conceptions about how these considerations should play out in particular practical situations. The fact that the Supreme Court itself is often divided in human rights' cases is not infrequently because underlying the disagreement are different perceptions of how intrusive judges are entitled to be. As the Lord Chief Justice has observed:

> All judges called upon to decide cases that occupy the intersection between judicial power and that of Parliament and the executive must work out for themselves where in the spectrum of judicial activism they lie. That such a spectrum exists cannot seriously be doubted. One need look no further than the nine judge decision in Nicklinson … to see its manifestation.[53]

So the perspectives of the judges hearing a particular case will have a substantial influence on the result. An obvious concern is how far a particular judge will be inclined to be more or less active depending upon his or her assessment of the merits of the measure under consideration. Lord Sumption thought that in some cases it was inevitable that the judge's personal views would influence any assessment of merits.[54] In the absence of objective criteria for carrying out the balancing exercise, which is necessarily the position where the fourth proportionality element is in play, that must surely be right.

If judges are perceived to be frustrating the decisions of politicians by what the latter see as inappropriate judicial activism, there will inevitably be pressure for the politicians to have some say over judicial appointments. This is not a fanciful possibility. Originally the Constitutional Reform Bill proposed that the Judicial Appointments Committee should put three names to the Lord Chancellor when filling a judicial post but the government changed this to one nominee only. The possibility of the final decision residing with the Lord Chancellor raises a whole host of issues which cannot be pursued here. Although I personally would be strongly opposed to any such change, one can well understand why it might be said to be the logical consequence of the direction which the constitution has taken with the advent of the HRA.

[52] Ibid [336] (Lord Reed).

[53] R Ekins, *Judicial Power and the Balance of Our Constitution* (London, Policy Exchange, 2018) 8.

[54] In the 2019 Reith lectures Lord Sumption has again expressed concerns that the Human Rights Act is requiring the judiciary to determine essentially political questions: see in particular, Lord Sumption, 'Human Rights and Wrongs' (Reith Lectures, BBC, June 2019) www.bbc.co.uk/programmes/m0005msd.

The move to a rights-based constitution has been largely the consequence of the HRA. But as I have pointed out, the common law was already providing greater protection for fundamental rights. In a number of recent cases the Supreme Court has emphasised the need to focus on the common law and not to assume that rights are only protected, or even primarily protected, under the Act.[55] Lord Toulson described the 'baleful tendency' to overlook the common law.[56] The court is keen to demonstrate that the common law is sufficiently vibrant to ensure that rights are often fully protected without the need for recourse to the HRA. This presupposes that the judicial protection of fundamental rights in a manner akin to that provided by the HRA is an inherently desirable objective for the common law. The combination of respect for fundamental rights coupled with the adoption of a common law doctrine of proportionality would in principle enable the courts to render much, if not all, of the HRA unnecessary. These developments would be of profound importance if at any time in the future the HRA were to be repealed. It would be difficult to turn back the clock for two related reasons. First, any legislative attempts to curb expanded common law powers of review would in all likelihood be very narrowly construed in accordance with the doctrine of legality; it would be difficult to draft them in a judge-proof way. Second, it would be politically difficult for any government to pass legislation which would be perceived as precluding judges from protecting human rights, whatever the merits of such legislation may be. So the HRA may have wrought a permanent and irreversible shift in the nature of our constitution, and to a permanently enhanced role for the judiciary.

[55] There have been observations to this effect in a number of cases including *Osborn v Parole Board* [2013] UKSC 61, [2014] AC 1115 and *Kennedy v The Charity Commission* [2014] UKSC 20, [2015] AC 455.

[56] In *Kennedy* (n 55) [133] Lord Toulson developed the point in a speech: 'Fundamental Rights and the Common Law' (Fundamental Rights Conference: A Public Law Perspective, London, October 2015) www.supremecourt.uk/docs/speech-151010.pdf.

2

Courting Trouble. The Role of the Courts in Contemporary Democracy

CONOR GEARTY

I. The Spectre of Juristocracy

Was Keith Ewing the first scholar to come up with this devastating term, 'Juristocracy', to describe the way democratic societies can be crushed by unelected judges under cover of ostensible principles like 'the rule of law' and 'the protection of human rights'?[1] Certainly Ran Hirschl uses it in the title for his well-known work, but this was published ten years later.[2] Now it turns up regularly. The sub-editors of a Rod Liddle article deployed it for a piece he wrote for the *Spectator* in July 2012, using Hirschl as a route in to critiquing judges but from the perspective of the populist right.[3] Jon Holbrook has the term in his attack on a recent Supreme Court case on abortion which, he says, 'should worry democrats'.[4] There are pages and pages on it in Google, much of it Hirschl-related or Hirschl-inspired – but no Keith Ewing. Adam Tomkins, who was Ewing's colleague at the time the chapter that seems to have coined the term appeared, acknowledges Ewing's parentage in his *Our Republican Constitution*[5] but Hirschl himself fails to do so, despite citing the chapter where it appears – even going so far as to truncate the title of that chapter in his footnote so as to excise the reference to juristocracy that appears there.[6] To paraphrase a man whom I know Ewing greatly admired, EP Thompson, it is time 'to rescue' the origins of this powerful word from the 'enormous [silence] of posterity'.[7]

[1] KD Ewing, 'The Bill of Rights Debate: Democracy or Juristocracy in Britain?' in KD Ewing, CA Gearty and BA Hepple (eds), *Human Rights and Labour Law. Essays for Paul O'Higgins* (London, Mansell, 1994) 147–187.

[2] R Hirschl, *Towards Juristocracy. The Origins and Consequences of the New Constitutionalism* (Cambridge, Mass., Harvard University Press, 2004).

[3] R Liddle, 'Rise of the juristocracy. Why have we handed unelected judges so much power?' *Spectator* (London, 7 July 2012).

[4] J Holbrook, 'Another step towards juristocracy' (*Spiked*, 11 June 2018) www.spiked-online.com/newsite/article/another-step-towards-juristocracy/21487#.W3uxY9VKjIU.

[5] A Tomkins, *Our Republican Constitution* (Oxford, Hart Publishing, 2005) 7 (fn 25).

[6] Hirschl (n 2) 256 (fn 41).

[7] EP Thompson, *The Making of the English Working Class* (London, Victor Gollancz, 1963) preface.

The chapter where as I say so far as I know it first appeared was part of a collection for Paul O'Higgins which Ewing, the late Professor Bob Hepple and I co-edited in 1994.[8] In it, Ewing laid out the 'central dilemma' he wanted to address in the form of a question: 'how can we reconcile with the first principles of democratic self-government the transfer of sovereign power from an elected legislature to an unelected judiciary?'[9] In Ewing's view, three fundamental points must underpin any answer to this question. First there is 'the principle of equal participation; that is to say, the right of us all to participate as equals in the policy-making institutions of government'.[10] Since it is obvious that 'the sheer size of contemporary society' makes it impossible 'for us all to participate in the making of decisions'[11] (more on this later), we are forced 'as a practical necessity' to embrace representative government, and so the second core principle 'is simply that in [such] a system … the representatives must be selected by the community they claim to represent'.[12] And thirdly, flowing also from the first two propositions, 'those who hold representative positions must in some sense be accountable to the people they represent for the decisions they purport to take on their behalf'.[13] The rest of Ewing's chapter is a magnificent exposure of quite the extent to which judges fail the democratic test on all these scores and should as a result most certainly not be empowered to exercise sovereign power either in general or (in particular) through enactment of any kind of entrenched Bill of Rights. Writing at a time when 'New Labour' was slowly emerging, and after the Party's leader John Smith had made an important speech on constitutional change in March 1993,[14] Ewing concludes that any change of this sort in the UK;

> would represent a monumental historic retreat, a step backwards from democracy to the creation of what could only be regarded as a juristocracy, a system of government predominantly by lawyers and judges, from participation in which the great bulk of the people would be permanently and irrevocably excluded.[15]

How does Ewing's essay read today? His 'central dilemma' rests on an assumption about the transfer of '*sovereign* power … to an unelected judiciary'[16] from which all else flows. Of course as we all know the Human Rights Act 1998 enacted by Parliament in the first term of Tony Blair's Labour Government did not transfer power in this way, in fact (not least because of the powerful case against made at the time by Keith Ewing) explicitly preserved parliamentary sovereignty.[17] The lively British debate ever since has been about the breadth of the legislation's interpretive mandate[18] and the extent to which the non-obligatory declarations

[8] Ewing, 'The Bill of Rights Debate' (n 1).
[9] Ibid, 147–148.
[10] Ibid, 149.
[11] Ibid, 149.
[12] Ibid, 150.
[13] Ibid.
[14] For the background see D Erdos, 'Charter 88 and the Constitutional Reform Movement: A Retrospective' (2009) 62 *Parliamentary Affairs* 537–551.
[15] Ewing 'The Bill of Rights Debate' (n 1) 182.
[16] Ibid, 147–148. (Emphasis added). The problem of course remains a highly topical one. Cf R Bellamy, *Political Constitutionalism. A Republican Defence of the Constitutionality of Democracy* (Cambridge, Cambridge University Press, 2007); and (more recently but very much in the Ewing spirit) G Webber et al, *Legislated Rights. Securing Human Rights Through Legislation* (Cambridge, Cambridge University Press, 2018). The issues have also been given a re-airing in Lord Sumption's Reith lectures for 2019: www.bbc.co.uk/programmes/m0005f05.
[17] HRA 1998, ss 3(2)(b), 6(2).
[18] HRA 1998, s 3(1).

of incompatibility in section 4 are or are not mandatory as a matter of political reality.[19] Of course it is putting it mildly to say that Ewing is no fan of this rights instrument: his *Bonfire of the Liberties. New Labour, Human Rights and the Rule of Law*, published in 2010, does not hold back, being particularly critical of how the interpretive power in the Act can be used to wreak policy havoc by escaping legislative intention in specific cases.[20] In his 1994 essay, however, Ewing was a little less sceptical about such an approach, at least in (what of course was then) theory:

> The problems, admittedly, would be much less acute if the Bill of Rights (or an incorporated European Convention) were to be limited in its scope by operating simply as a guide to the interpretation of statutes and as a means of regulating executive discretion, but not also as a device for limiting the sovereign power of Parliament.[21]

One's perspective here probably depends on the line one takes about the character of the declarations, and how much one is willing as well to see the hand of a de facto sovereign legislature in the judges' statutory mandate to do what is 'possible' to ensure that primary legislation is 'read and given effect in a way which is compatible with Convention rights' by giving (for example) the test of proportionality a far greater reach than the old pre-rights criteria for judicial review would have achieved.[22]

One line that was unequivocal in Ewing's chapter is his castigation of judicial review as an exercise in sovereign power under cover of supposedly seeking to maintain a society's fundamental values. Here the target is Alexander Bickel whose early book *The Least Dangerous Branch: The Supreme Court at the Bar of Politics*[23] was very influential in promoting acceptance in the US of the exercise of wide-ranging substantive power by the Warren and Burger supreme courts from the mid-1950s through to the 1970s. The exposure to criticism of the judges here is as to the certainty of their having to choose which values and principles to prioritise or (as in the US, if there is already a document to hand) how to interpret its 'inevitably open-textured' nature.[24] Because values are themselves political, giving the judges a definitive say on their content is indeed plausibly to set them up as juristocrats gazing down on rather than being part of the democratic struggle below. Ewing is very persuasive on the impact such reasoning has had on the US and Canadian frameworks of democratic decision-making.[25] An academic perspective from the US, published a decade or so after Bickel, the 'noble attempt to reconcile the practice of judicial review with the principles of democratic government' that 'is to be found in the work of John Hart Ely', was also the subject of

[19] HRA 1998, s 4: see *R (Nicklinson) v Ministry of Justice; R (AM and AP) v Director of Public Prosecutions* [2014] UKSC 38, [2015] AC 657.

[20] KD Ewing, *Bonfire of the Liberties. New Labour, Human Rights and the Rule of Law* (Oxford, Oxford University Press, 2010). CA Gearty, *On Fantasy Island. Britain, Strasbourg and Human Rights* (Oxford, Oxford University Press, 2016) offers a different perspective.

[21] Ewing 'The Bill of Rights Debate' (n 1) 181–182.

[22] HRA 1998, s 3(1). See A Young, *Parliamentary Sovereignty and the Human Rights Act* (Oxford, Hart Publishing, 2008); and also the same author's *Democratic Dialogue and the Constitution* (Oxford, Oxford University Press, 2017).

[23] A Bickel, *The Least Dangerous Branch: The Supreme Court at the Bar of Politics* (New York, Bobbs-Merrill, 1962).

[24] Ewing 'The Bill of Rights Debate' (n 1) 160.

[25] Ibid, 159–163.

withering critique from Ewing in his 1994 essay.[26] Eschewing Bickel's overtly value-laden approach, Ely argued in favour of 'a participation-oriented, representation-reinforcing approach to judicial review'[27] which would permit strike-downs of legislation 'only where the democratic process itself is malfunctioning'.[28] But as with Bickel, this 'representation-reinforcing function' inevitably 'requires the courts to confront hard questions about the very system of democracy itself'.[29] Which voting system is the 'right' one? Does campaign election expenditure legitimately amplify certain voices or disproportionately favour the already economically powerful?[30] Once again, there is no escaping important value judgments by recasting them as (merely) procedural.[31] So for Ewing, Ely falls at the same fence as Bickel, just in a way that is less easy for the passing reader to detect.

In 1994, it seemed unthinkable that the courts could ever assert an approach of any of these sorts in Britain, without even a Bill of Rights scaffold on which to hang it. True there had been drifts in the direction of constitutional rights of a sort, sometimes rooted in the common law,[32] sometimes drawing inspiration from the European Convention on Human Rights[33] and mainstream judicial review was certainly developing an increased robustness,[34] but all of this felt as though it fell well short of the sort of judicial engagement at which Ewing was taking aim. Then, a little more than ten years after Ewing's chapter appeared, against all expectations, the UK House of Lords threw a Bickel-shaped cat among the democratic pigeons, in *R (Jackson) v Attorney General*.[35] In that well-known case, a challenge to the use of the Parliament Acts to achieve a ban on hunting foxes with dogs, Lord Steyn asserted that parliamentary sovereignty was a common law construct, and that what the judges gave the judges could take away:

> it is not unthinkable that circumstances could arise where the courts may have to qualify a principle established on a different hypothesis of constitutionalism. In exceptional circumstances involving an attempt to abolish judicial review or the ordinary role of the courts, the Appellate Committee of the House of Lords or a new Supreme Court may have to consider whether this is a constitutional fundamental which even a sovereign Parliament acting at the behest of a complaisant House of Commons cannot abolish.[36]

Lord Hope agreed that 'the courts have a part to play in defining the limits of Parliament's legislative sovereignty'.[37] Baroness Hale considered that 'the courts will treat with particular suspicion (and might even reject) any attempt to subvert the rule of law by removing governmental action affecting the rights of the individual from all judicial scrutiny'.[38]

[26] Ibid, 163, with JH Ely's *Democracy and Distrust: A Theory of Judicial Review* (Cambridge, Mass., Harvard University Press, 1980) mainly in mind.

[27] Cited by Ewing, Ely (n 26) 87.

[28] Ewing 'The Bill of Rights Debate' (n 1) 163.

[29] Ibid, 164.

[30] J Rowbottom, *Democracy Distorted. Wealth, Influence and Democratic Politics* (Cambridge, Cambridge University Press, 2010).

[31] Ewing, 'The Bill of Rights Debate' (n 1) 163–167.

[32] *Derbyshire County Council v Times Newspapers Ltd* [1993] UKHL 18, [1993] AC 534.

[33] A line of cases that had begun as early as the 1970s: see, eg, *R (Bhajan Singh) v Secretary of State for the Home Department* [1976] QB 198.

[34] *R (Fire Brigades Union) v Secretary of State for the Home Department* [1995] UKHL 3, [1995] 2 AC 513.

[35] *R (Jackson) v Attorney General* [2005] UKHL 56, [2006] 1 AC 262.

[36] Ibid [102].

[37] Ibid [107].

[38] Ibid [159].

Rather more dramatically, albeit with greater circumspection, Lord Carswell wondered about the legitimacy of a law proposing 'a fundamental disturbance of the building blocks of the constitution'.[39]

Now all of this is pretty strong stuff for democrats, outrageous even to those who give credit to Ewing's fundamental democratic principles and how far such interventions would undermine them (yet to materialise in the UK post-*Jackson*, it has to be said[40]). The case was warmly applauded by judicial activists[41] but certainly much criticised at the time as well, particularly by those who take a 'Ewing' line on the restriction of judicial power.[42] Looking back on *Jackson* from the vantage point of the present, does the depth of the outrage expressed then depend on the relative health of the democratic process being put under (to coin a phrase) 'anxious scrutiny'[43] in this way? Reflect again on Lord Steyn's Ely-esque assumption that judges' would intervene to protect principle only in situations where the impugned executive excess had been made possible by the inaction of a 'complaisant' Commons. This is to turn the judicial oversight away from substance (Lady Hale's 'rights of the individual'; Lord Carswell's 'building blocks') and towards process: how active/complaisant have the elected representatives been? If the former there is no role for the courts; if the latter, there is.

But active/complaisant with regard to what? It must be in relation to the holding of elected representatives to account, the third of Ewing's three fundamental principles, applied now not to the accountability of all MPs to their constituents but rather to that subset of MPs who (with colleagues from the House of Lords) make up the executive branch of government, and are answerable not to the electors as such so much as to their colleague MPs (those not in government) in the lower House. Now without doubt in (by the standards we have grown accustomed to) normal constitutional times judgments about how proper parliamentary action/inaction has been is very much in the eye of the beholder: passive acquiescence to a savagely wrong intervention in the minds of some is necessary and responsible, supportive decision-making to others.[44] Thus while we may well have thought that times in which *Jackson* appeared to have been abnormal – there was the post 11 September 2001 attacks indefinite detention power in the Anti-Terrorism Crime and Security Act 2001 that had just been declared a breach of rights by the House of Lords,[45] and various proposals for the empowering of the executive and the restriction of judicial

[39] Ibid [178]. A theory that allows liberal democracy to fight back against its own destruction has Continental admirers: see A Sajó, *Militant Democracy* (Utrecht, Eleven International Publishing, 2004).

[40] But see *R (Privacy International) v Investigatory Powers Tribunal and others* [2019] UKSC 22, [2019] 2 WLR 1219.

[41] See the Symposium on 'The Changing Landscape of British Constitutionalism' (2011) 9 *International Journal of Constitutional Law* 79–273, esp T Allan, 'Questions of Legality and Legitimacy: Form and Substance in British Constitutionalism' Ibid 155–162.

[42] Including by myself: CA Gearty, 'Are Judges Now Out of Their Depth?' (The JUSTICE Tom Sargant Memorial Annual Lecture 2007) [2007] *Justice Journal* 8: https://2bquk8cdew6192tsu41lay8t-wpengine.netdna-ssl.com/wp-content/uploads/2015/02/JUSTICE-Journal-2007-vol4-no2.pdf.

[43] *Bugdaycay v Secretary of State for the Home Department* [1987] AC 514.

[44] Michael Heseltine's removal of the Mace from its place in the Commons Chamber on 27 May 1976, and his advancing towards the government benches with it menacingly in his hands, will be remembered by some. The *casus belli* was the reneging of a pairing agreement made by the government on a crucial matter related to the then controversial Aircraft and Shipbuilding Bill, but so far as I know no one thought for a moment that the relevant clause in the law subsequently enacted could be challenged in court.

[45] *R (A) v Secretary of State for the Home Department* [2004] UKHL 56, [2005] 2 AC 68.

review in the immigration context were swirling in the political ether[46] – they look from the perspective of today's Brexit-induced constitutional chaos to have been a model of calm. This fluidity in our perception of the import of any given moment surely tends to confirm the Ewing-esque scruples we might already have about the judges getting stuck in too quickly and too much. The Labour administration of the day may have had views about various matters that were controversial, extending beyond hunting with dogs into more sensitive matters related to national security and judicial review in specific arenas for sure, but (with hindsight, admittedly) it would be hard to see any of what was then proposed/defeated/enacted as beyond the pale of entirely proper vigorous democratic debate. The 'building blocks' of the constitution were hardly being challenged; rather parliamentary battles were being fought to achieve change on the margins.

How deep should such judicial self-denial go? Can anything at all push the courts into legitimate, protective action? So far in this chapter I (and Ewing in 1994) have been assuming a system that is operating with reasonably effective accountability to the legislature for the executive branch, and with a rule of law independent enough to prevent not executive activism (something well outside the judges' constitutional job description) but rather – to put it crudely – administrative unlawfulness, criminal actions by the executive even. Now of course I appreciate that hypotheticals have long been the bane of democrats: suppose this, suppose that and then, off the back of a never-to-materialise catastrophe, the proponents of judicial sovereign power secure what they want (a reordering of the basis of democratic decision-making away from elected representatives and towards courts), a normative reshaping which can then be deployed into the future in multiple sub-catastrophic situations. This is why the Ewings of this world are rightly sceptical of conceding anything on the basis of a doomsday they know will never come. Judicial sceptics are essentially upbeat about the corrective capacity of the democratic process, its ability to stop that doomsday before it happens rather than rely on courts to undo it afterwards. Is this optimism still warranted?

II. The Constitution of Social Democracy

The British Constitution was very well adapted to the growth of social democracy in Europe in the decades after World War Two. The electorate had already delivered a large majority for a radical Labour Government to reshape relations between the individual and the state, through the securing of a 'welfare' (as opposed to 'warfare') state.[47] The accountability of executive power to the voters via the legislative branch had been stunningly displayed by the removal by the electorate of a war-time Prime Minister at the very height of his powers. The team led by Clement Attlee that replaced Winston Churchill did not revolutionise the society that elected it. Rather it set about smoothing out the hard edges of the capitalism

[46] Clause 14 of the Asylum and Immigration Bill 2004 had proposed the ouster of court oversight of asylum and immigration claims but it was modified by the government after sharp criticism: see J Rozenberg, 'Labour U-Turn on Asylum Bill' *The Telegraph* (London, 16 March 2004).

[47] The term appears to have been coined by Archbishop William Temple, during the Second World War: see CA Gearty, *Liberty and Security* (Cambridge, Polity, 2013) 22.

that had so divided society in the 1930s[48] and so preventing (or so it was assumed and hoped) the plunge into Communism that was a far more credible threat after the war than it had been when the Special Branch had been harassing the likes of the aged Thomas Mann for his visits to Moscow a decade or so before.[49] The UK was an early social democratic space in a Western Europe that increasingly took on this character as the decades went by. Equality was the goal but modified capitalism was to be the means. The resurrected polities of NATO-protected Western Europe sought (whatever their governing parties called themselves) to deliver social gain via democratic systems that were specifically designed to prevent moves to the Right or (far more to the point) Left.

It was never thought necessary in victorious, Butskellite[50] Britain to deploy courts of any sort as the guardians of this social democratic consensus. The only Bill of Rights thought to be worth having was that through which Parliament had asserted its power against the Crown in 1688,[51] and the newly established judicial mechanism for the enforcement of human rights to be found in the European Convention on Human Rights likewise passed the UK by – it was not until 1966 that individuals could take the UK to the Convention's Strasbourg-based Court and even after this, no ruling of that body could possibly impugn the authority of any Act of the sovereign legislature.[52] The European Social Charter in 1961, policed by Strasbourg's Committee of Social Rights, marked the embracing of regional oversight of democratic choices in the field of social rights as well as the civil and political rights of the Convention,[53] but the UK chose not to engage in its collective complaints procedure when it became available.[54] And the same was, of course, the case with the Common Market which had as early as the late 1960s already embraced a strong judicial invigilation of state practice in the name of fundamental rights.[55] Even when the country joined what by then had become the European Economic Community, in 1973, it did so concerned about the possible intrusion into its sovereignty that this entailed, and in the decades that followed the more this Europeanisation took the shape of rights-assertion, the more the British authorities didn't like it, opting out if they could and downplaying and resisting if they could not.[56]

From the start the less secure democracies on the Continent had taken a different tack, initially insulating their political space from rupture by means of oversight by both national constitutional courts and the European authorities (Commission and Court) set up under the European Convention and then driving forward with exactly those various mechanisms of European oversight with which the British would have no truck. Michael Mandel's fine

[48] See generally KD Ewing and CA Gearty, *The Struggle for Civil Liberties* (Oxford, Oxford University Press, 2000) chs 5 and 6.

[49] Ibid, 254.

[50] The short-hand term given to the convergence of the names of two leading Labour (Hugh Gaitskell, Labour leader, 1955–1963) and Conservative ('Rab' Butler, holder of many important Cabinet positions under successive Conservative prime ministers from the 1940s through to 1964) whose views broadly converged on the need for social protection and the public interest in growing equality.

[51] Usefully set out at www.legislation.gov.uk/aep/WillandMarSess2/1/2/introduction.

[52] *James v United Kingdom* (1986) 8 EHRR 123.

[53] See www.coe.int/en/web/conventions/full-list/-/conventions/treaty/035.

[54] KD Ewing and S Weir, 'The European Social Charter Turns 50 Today, but Britain doesn't belong at the Party' (*Open DemocracyUK*, 18 October 2011) www.opendemocracy.net/ourkingdom/stuart-weir-keith-ewing/european-social-charter-turns-50-today-but-britain-doesnt-belong-.

[55] A O'Neill, *EU Law for UK Lawyers*, 2nd edn (Oxford, Hart Publishing, 2011) ch 6.

[56] D Gowland, *Britain and the European Union* (Abingdon, Routledge, 2017) is a good generalist account.

extended essay in the *Israel Law Review* in 1998, detailing the impact of the embracing of constitutional rights in Europe at this time, showed clearly how as he put it in the long title 'we changed everything so that everything would remain the same'.[57] The Strasbourg Court also did its part in this erection of a European democratic fortress. Communists found themselves starved of political space, and fascists too did not have everything their own way.[58] This European story was always different from the one that in books and articles Keith Ewing told about the UK. His confidence in the essential health of the democratic process made sense of his strictures against the Europeanisation of our judicial involvement in politics. While the right of individual application to Strasbourg under the European Convention was just about acceptable, it was neither necessary nor desirable to translate this into the domestic arena, especially given the historically poor performance of the British judges as guardians of civil liberties.[59]

The high point of this critique was the juristocracy chapter in 1994, though even then it was undeniable that – whatever the occasional winds of change in the case-law[60] – the reality of political change in Britain had been beginning to have its effect, eventually (I would tentatively suggest) calling into question certain assumptions about the democratic process that underpinned that critique. I am not thinking here so much of 'the constitution is broken' movement that emerged at the end of the Thatcher period and which manifested itself in the shape of Charter 88 and other similar organisations calling for radical change in the structure of government. The prescription offered by these groups struck Ewing as often worse than the disease, or at best like 'treating a heart attack with a used Band-aid'.[61] The underlying problem, of which Thatcherite excess in the field of civil liberties was an offshoot, lay in the deployment of executive power via the legislature to destroy the Butskellite consensus, replacing it with various policies that went under many names (monetarism; privatisation; trickle-down; etc) but which had a singular effect: the removal of guarantees of social protection and the growth of inequality. Started under the cautious leadership of Mrs Thatcher, this became the dominant theme of her successor John Major's five years in office, and was eventually embraced as well by a 'New' Labour opposition that had come close to despair at the prospect of never returning to office. When it eventually did win power, in 1997, it initially did nothing (quite explicitly) to challenge the policies of the preceding decades while however embarking on a noisy round of constitutionalisation to fill a space in governance that would otherwise have been empty, the Human Rights Act included among the initiatives taken at that time. Mrs Thatcher and Mr Major, and afterwards Mr Blair, all enjoyed strong legislative support for their policies, and they exercised power only because of the victories their respective Parties had achieved at successive general elections. If we recall Ewing's three basic principles of democratic self-government each was clearly being met: pretty well everybody could vote, the resulting government

[57] M Mandel, 'A Brief History of the New Constitutionalism, or "How We Changed Everything so that Everything Would Remain the Same"' (1998) 32 *Israel Law Review* 250. It was, perhaps unsurprisingly, Keith Ewing who first drew my attention to this article.

[58] *Communist Party of Germany v Germany* app 250/57. Cf *Vogt v Germany* (1996) 21 EHRR 205. On right-wing controls see *Kosiek v Germany* app no 9704/82 (28 August 1986).

[59] KD Ewing and CA Gearty, *Democracy or a Bill of Rights* (London, Society of Labour Lawyers, 1991).

[60] See text at nn 32–35 above.

[61] KD Ewing and CA Gearty *Freedom under Thatcher: Civil Liberties in Modern Britain* (Oxford, Oxford University Press, 1990) 275.

was (broadly) representative, and the MPs who kept these governmental shows on the road were always accountable to those who elected them, with the threat of defeat in the next election never far from many of their minds. To recall my earlier allusion to a potential fourth principle, not explicitly present in Ewing's 1994 formulation, the executive was also in constitutional terms answerable to the people's representatives in the Commons, though of course there were lively discussions about how realistic this was, with the Party system then operating very strongly to ensure disciplined support in the Commons for the government of the day.[62]

At exactly the same time, however, and far from disappearing with the passing of time, Europe's anxiety about the fragility of democratic governance was becoming if anything more pronounced than it had been in the immediate post-war decades. The issue has increasingly taken centre-stage in the years since 1994. Turkey's semi-engagement with Europe has led to its submission to the oversight of the Strasbourg Court and this has in turn produced a series of dramatic interventions by that tribunal in huge national debates about the legitimacy of certain kinds of democratic political activity. The main left wing Parties had won major victories in Strasbourg against government efforts to exclude them from the electoral process in 1998,[63] but in the *Refah Partisi* case three years later the European Court of Human Rights found that an Islamic-inspired Party then in government in Turkey and with a 22 per cent share of the vote could nevertheless be dissolved compatibly with human rights principles.[64] The Court came to this conclusion because it judged that an outright win for the Party at the next election (a real possibility) would have brought about a breach of fundamental democratic principle, and that democracy could not be allowed to eat itself in this way, even in situations where it appeared the electors' choice to do so.[65] The *Refah Partisi* decision was of course hugely controversial, but it set the Court's parameters for engagement with the governments of many of its new members in the years that followed. At the same time the attacks of 11 September 2001 in New York and Washington have generated in their wake a new atmosphere of tolerance for executive crackdown on dissent, while also bringing to the surface of public discourse a move back to national partisanship – wholly unexpected in the heady days of post-1989 globalisation – that had been slowly growing in the 1990s and to which the events of that day have given a large boost.

In that first decade of the 2000s, political leaders began to emerge who were happy to mine the democratic systems they had inherited for opportunities to grow much stronger individual powers out of them, with the invariable route to success being both a strong emphasis on threats posed to the very existence of the state by external enemies of various sorts and also at the same time a similar focus on enemies within, immigrants, terrorists and so on but also, in time, 'elites' whose behind-the-scenes manipulation of democracy ruined the life chances of the 'ordinary people'. The economic crises of the mid 2000s led to a dramatic reduction in life-chances for many, thus playing into this emerging feeling of anger. Democracy continued but often as a camouflage for real

[62] See Ewing and Gearty, *Struggle for Civil Liberties* (n 48) ch 1 for a discussion of this aspect of accountability.

[63] *United Communist Party of Turkey v Turkey* (1998) 26 EHRR 121; *Socialist Party of Turkey v Turkey* (1998) 27 EHRR 51.

[64] (2003) 35 EHRR 3. Cf *Herri Batasuna and Batasuna v Spain* app nos 25803/04 and 25817/04, 30 June 2009; *Vona v Hungary* app no 35943/10 9 July 2013.

[65] See Sajó (n 39).

power rather than a constraint upon its exercise.[66] This was not by any means a European phenomenon exclusively – one of its first and most effective exponents was Israeli Prime Minister Benjamin Netanyahu[67] – but it found a ready home in post-Soviet societies whose economic decline created a political nostalgia for a people's strongman. In recent years, therefore, it has not been surprising to see the Strasbourg Court drawn into ever-deeper appraisals of the democratic health of its Member States.[68] More recently but to potentially great effect the European Court of Justice has found itself being asked fundamental questions about the democratic health of EU states, 'fundamental' because if the score-card marks a failure then the continued membership of the Union can be put in severe doubt,[69] a power of escalation that is not so directly accessible in the Strasbourg system.

Today it is credible to say of the political developments just described that they are examples of 'populism' in action.[70] The European courts are being drawn into disputes because their founding documents assume a thicker version of democracy than that which regards as enough the election of accountable representatives on a universal suffrage. Putting it like this makes clear that the European vision of democracy goes beyond Ewing's three principles to include principles of the rule of law, separation of powers, respect for diversity and human rights etc. The result of this is that impeccably elected, accountable parliamentarians producing a government which can then do whatever it wants (including destroy the system under which it secured power) is not guaranteed to be seen as democratic by these unelected guardians of European democracy. We are back in the territory of Ely and the *Jackson* case, and (so far as Strasbourg is concerned) a jurisdiction greatly expanded from the days when it covered only Communists and fascists. When one surveys the organised shift to presidential styles of government in certain European states, deliberately using a power – sanctioned it is true by the people – to destroy inhibitors on the deployment of executive power (legal and political) and so as a result to centralise power more and more in the hands of a small group (or even in some cases a single individual and his or her family), then it is surely hard to say of the Strasbourg Court's attempts to stop or delay this that these are the actions of a juristocracy? True perhaps, but remembering that Ewing's 1994 piece had Britain mainly in mind it is a valid question certainly to ask what, if anything, this has to do with us?

III. Brexit

The answer to the question with which we ended the last section flows from closer scrutiny of what 'populism' means. Of course, this is not the same as 'popular': much of what

[66] Gearty, *Liberty and Security* (n 47).

[67] A Pfeffer, *Bibi: The Turbulent Life and Times of Benjamin Netanyahu* (London, C Hurst & Co, 2018) reviewed by A Shatz, 'The Sea is the Same Sea' (2018) 40 *London Review of Books* 24.

[68] See generally I Motoc and I Ziemele (eds), *The Impact of the ECHR on Democratic Change in Central and Eastern Europe: Judicial Perspectives* (Cambridge, Cambridge University Press, 2016).

[69] A Sikora, 'The CJEU and the rule of law in Poland: Note on the Polish Supreme Court Preliminary Ruling Request of 2 August 2018' (*EU Law Analysis*, 4 August 2018) http://eulawanalysis.blogspot.com/2018/08/the-cjeu-and-rule-of-law-in-poland-note.html.

[70] M Anselmi, *Populism. An Introduction* (London, Routledge, 2018); C Mudde and R Kaltwasser, *Populism. A Very Short Introduction* (Oxford, Oxford University Press, 2017).

Mrs Thatcher did, and after her that other charismatic politician Tony Blair, was popular (council house sales; anti-social control orders; terrorism laws; etc). There is an important distinction here between process and substance. 'Popular' politics use the procedures available to achieve the substantive desired outcomes, those pushing this or that specific goal believing that it will be well-liked and make them, or continue to make them, the sort of person people will (continue to) vote for. Described like this, all democratic politics is 'popular'. Rather than focusing on specific substantive outcomes, 'populist' politics, in contrast, attacks the pre-existing procedures of representative government. There is a vagueness on vision but a highly refined understanding of what makes that vision (vague though it is) impossible to realise: it is the democratic process itself (and perhaps other societal phenomena as well) that act as impediments to the realisation of the people's will. Old fashioned democratic government as such rather than its embodiment in this or that policy is the enemy of the people:

> In addition to being anti-elitist, populists are always antipluralist; populists claim that they, *and only they*, represent the people. Other political competitors are just part of the immoral, corrupt elite, or so populists say, while not having power themselves; when in government, they will not recognise anything like a legitimate opposition.[71]

The people are those who agree with them; the rest – judges; civil servants; politicians; voters not on their side – are 'enemies of the people' in their pursuit of a 'singular common good' that 'the people can discern and will' and that 'a politician or a party (or, less plausibly, a movement) can [then] unambiguously implement. as policy.'[72]

To use a sporting analogy, populism is going for the player rather than the ball. Of course, there has always been something like this in British (as in all democratic) politics but it has been kept very much to the margins. Tony Blair occasionally spiced up his pursuit of popularity with recognisably populist ingredients, inveighing against the public sector ('I bear the scars on my back after two years in government and heaven knows what it will be like after a bit longer'[73]) and the Human Rights Act (as on one occasion when (or so Blair claimed) probation staff had 'been so "distracted" by the prisoner's human-rights claims that they [had] lost sight of their duty to protect the public'[74]). The Conservative Party has of course also flirted with such policies in the past, one good example being its tendency to inveigh against the bureaucratic constraints on British enterprise, vowing to liberate the people from the 'Nanny State'.[75] The dislike of prisoner voting was driven much more by hostility to the body that wanted it, in this case the European Court of Human Rights,[76] than by any particular engagement with the issue itself, an example of a populist talent for reverse-engineering a policy out of a culture of animosity towards a particular institution. The attack on the Strasbourg Court which was mounted off the back of the prisoner votes

[71] J Müller, *What is Populism?* (London, Penguin, 2017) 20 (emphasis in the original; footnote omitted).

[72] Ibid, 25, footnote omitted.

[73] J Hyland, 'Blair denounces public sector workers to an audience of venture capitalists' (*World Socialist Website*, 12 July 1999) www.wsws.org/en/articles/1999/07/blai-j12.html.

[74] N Temko and J Doward, 'Revealed: Blair Attack on Human Rights Law' *The Observer* (London, 14 May 2006).

[75] David Cameron called bureaucratic necessities 'the enemies of enterprise' in a speech to a Party conference shortly after becoming Prime Minister: M Kite, 'David Cameron launches new war on red tape' *The Telegraph* (London, 6 March 2011).

[76] *Hirst v United Kingdom (No. 2)* (2005) 42 EHRR 849.

controversy was an early taste of the dislike of that other Europe, the European Union, that was to become the signature tune of British populists towards the end of the 2000s, eventually producing the referendum of 2016 under which the people 'took back control' of their destiny by voting for Brexit.[77]

A referendum is the perfect vehicle for populists, especially when it combines a proposed change that is very vague with an apparent opportunity to give 'elites' a kicking by voting for it (albeit without really knowing what 'it' is). It calls into question Ewing's assumption that we have to have representative government because of the 'sheer size of contemporary society:'[78] the people can speak directly now and indeed technology does allow us (if we are so inclined) to consult them far more frequently, turning Parliament from a law-making assembly into an executive body, charged with doing the people's will: there has been much talk along those lines by enthusiasts for the Brexit referendum result. The invariable challenge for successful populists is how to govern; on the one hand they are driven to accumulate power by destroying the 'elite' buffers that lie between themselves and total control; on the other, they are not at all sure how to exercise the power they are thereby accumulating. Brexit is a perfect case in point. The enemy is everywhere but the means of realising the fact of 'taking back control' are proving harder to pin down than had seemed to be the case in the excitement of the campaign. The vision remains vague while the elites etc who stand in its way are clearly visible to all. The inevitable result is the accumulation of power so as to be able to do whatever is necessary to achieve the vision, but without being at all sure what that necessity actually entails.

The result in the context of Brexit is the extraordinary European Union Withdrawal Act 2018 with its vast empowerment of the executive to make regulations to deal with 'deficiencies arising from withdrawal' from the EU[79] and – in advance of departure and assuming an orderly one rooted in agreement – to do whatever 'the Minister considers appropriate for the purposes of implementing the withdrawal agreement if the Minister considers that such provision should be in force on or before exit day'.[80] Both provisions expressly allow ministers to 'make any provision that could be made by an Act of Parliament'[81] with, however, the important caveat that certain areas are specifically declared to be outwith this legislative power.[82] Does this huge empowerment of the executive – the Minister doing what he or she thinks *appropriate* – take us close to the *Jackson* threshold in terms of potential judicial oversight? Close I would say, but not over the bar. For this we have Parliament to thank. As introduced, clause 9(2) envisaged the regulatory power under that section being used to amend the EU (Withdrawal) Act itself: 'Regulations under this section may make any provision that could be made by an Act of Parliament' as has been enacted and then the vital addition: '(including modifying this Act)'. So the no-go areas in the Act, the arrangements on devolved matters, the parliamentary oversight and so on, could have been changed by the Minister if he or she thought this 'appropriate' for

[77] My speech to the Canadian Institute for Advanced Legal Studies in Cambridge on 1 July 2019 covers the same ground from a UK perspective: 'She's Dead of Course! Brexit, the British Constitution and Human Rights' (copy of talk with the author).

[78] Ewing 'The Bill of Rights Debate' (n 1) 149.

[79] European Union Withdrawal Act 2018, s 8. This chapter was completed before enactment of the European Union (Withdrawal Agreement) Act 2020 which carries with it many implications for the balance of power between the executive and the legislature, eg ss 41(2) and 41(3).

[80] Ibid, s 9(1), now repealed by the European Union (Withdrawal Agreement) Act 2020 s 36(a).

[81] Ibid, s 8(5); s 9(2).

[82] Ibid, s 8(7); s 9(3).

the purposes of the withdrawal agreement. Could such a power survive the expunging of the parenthetic clarifier? Probably not: section 20 (2)-(5) sets out various provisions where it is desired by regulation to change one part of the main body of the Act, that related to specifying exactly when 'exit day' is. By allowing it in this specific instance, but only through the provision of direct statutory authority, it is surely strongly arguable that parliament has made clear its disinclination to allow such executive amending for any other parts of this parent Act. So far as the exercise of these Henry VIII clauses affects other pieces of primary legislation, schedule 7 now contains a framework for parliamentary scrutiny vastly more intensive and complicated than had appeared in the original Bill. We can agree with an expert legal commentary that 'given the scale of the delegated legislative exercise likely to be necessary to make retained EU law work, judicial review may have an important role.'[83] In the circumstances Parliament may be thought to have done a fair job of holding the executive to account, even though – of course – vast power has been gathered to the centre. (Indeed, as Tom Poole has perceptively argued, the effect of many contemporary arguments against judicial power along Ewing's lines from 1994 has been to facilitate the extension of executive rather than legislative power.[84])

IV. Conclusion

Parliament did its work with the EU Withdrawal Act 2018, just as it has done with other controversial legislation in the past when large-scale executive powers were sought to deal with this or that emergency.[85] But it was a fairly close-run thing – might clause 9 (2) as introduced have attracted the attention of today's judicial disciples of Lord Steyn had it been the focus of litigation, particularly if the proceedings involved some dramatic reworking of the 2018 Act via a regulation that (because of the precise wording of clause 9(2)) could not be credibly described as *ultra vires*? We shall never know. But the populist impulse remains strong across Europe and, as the Brexit phenomenon shows us, Britain is not immune. What will be next? Repeal of the Human Rights Act? A Westminster-led forced realignment of devolved powers, in the name of some kind of English-inspired populist animosity towards the Scots? The abolition of judicial review to avoid 'elite judges' calling into question execution of the people's will? The final shredding of the welfare state in the name of 'international competitiveness'? Political leaders capable of leading the UK out of the EU to foster their own careers are capable of anything. And the Trump presidency acts as an inspiration to this sort of politician, as one of their number (at the time of writing about to be Prime Minister) has frankly admitted.[86] If the Westminster system of parliamentary

[83] See J Segan, 'The European Union (Withdrawal) Act 2018: Ten Key Implications for UK Law and Lawyers' (*Blackstone Chambers*, 19 July 2018) www.blackstonechambers.com/news/european-union-withdrawal-act-2018-ten-key-implications-uk-law-and-lawyers/.

[84] T Poole, 'The Executive Power Project' (*LRB Blog*, 2 April 2019) www.lrb.co.uk/blog/author/thomas-poole.

[85] The Anti-terrorism, Crime and Security Act 2001 was sown with the seeds of its own collapse (so far as indefinite detention was concerned) during its passage through Parliament: see ss 122 and 123. Likewise the control order regime that followed the ending of that detention was greatly modified in Parliament: Prevention of Terrorism Act 2005.

[86] See Y Salam, 'Boris Johnson defends "Admiring" Donald Trump' (*Politico*, 26 June 2018) www.politico.eu/article/boris-johnson-defends-admiring-donald-trump-leaked-comments/.

sovereignty were used to transfer power indefinitely to the executive, under cover perhaps of an ongoing post-Brexit emergency (or some sort of terrorist atrocity), what then? To adapt Ewing's own 'central dilemma' in his 1994 chapter, 'how can we reconcile with the first principles of democratic self-government the transfer of sovereign power from an elected legislature to a [indirectly elected/presidential] executive'? Does the passivity of the courts extend to giving safe passage to this sort of move to what might reasonably quickly end up at least as an authoritarian and perhaps also a fascist state? A hypothetical question certainly, but not as hypothetical as it once was.

3

Conflicts of Rights and Constitutional Balance

JAMES GRANT*

'One of the great virtues of the British constitution', Keith Ewing wrote at the dawn of the twenty-first century, 'has been its relative neutrality.'[1] He meant that it contained no hierarchy of rights, other than the hierarchy of the sources from which legal rights are derived: the priority of statutes over the common law. The Human Rights Act 1998 changed that, Ewing argued, by introducing a new hierarchy: the priority of civil and political rights (such as rights to free speech, free association, privacy, and political participation) over social and economic rights (such as rights to minimum income, housing, education, and health care).[2] According to Ewing, this new priority rendered the constitution 'unbalanced'. He suggested that the constitution should be rebalanced by giving social and economic rights the same level of protection as civil and political rights.

For Ewing to make this claim is, as he acknowledges, 'counter-intuitive and paradoxical'.[3] He has long been one of our greatest critics of expanding judicial power, forcefully arguing that judges are ineffective and illegitimate enforcers of human rights. His chronicling of the judiciary's often dismal record on human rights has been a significant and stimulating contribution to legal scholarship, deeply enriching our understanding. What, then, explains his claim that there should be judicial enforcement of social and economic rights? Well, mainly 'defensive reasons', as he puts it.[4] Given how unlikely it is that countries will discard their judicially enforceable constitutional rights, he thinks that the only way to protect social and economic rights is to constitutionalise them.

We can think of the constitutional protection of social and economic rights as a solution to two perceived problems that are said to arise from constitutional imbalance. The first relates to conflicts of rights and gives rise to Ewing's defensive argument. The Human Rights Act, the argument goes, protects 'liberty *at the expense of* equality; or … civil and political rights *at the expense of* social and economic rights'.[5] Ewing gave examples from

* Thanks to Alan Bogg, Jeff King, Virginia Mantouvalou, and Alison Young for helpful comments.

[1] KD Ewing, 'The Unbalanced Constitution' in T Campbell, KD Ewing, and A Tomkins (eds), *Sceptical Essays on Human Rights* (Oxford, OUP, 2001) 104.

[2] On this distinction, see TH Marshall, *Citizenship and Social Class* (Cambridge, CUP, 1950).

[3] KD Ewing, 'The Case for Social Rights' in T Campbell, J Goldsworthy, and A Stone (eds), *Protecting Human Rights: Instruments and Institutions* (Oxford, OUP 2003) 323.

[4] KD Ewing, 'The Politics of the British Constitution' [2000] *PL* 405, 434.

[5] Ewing, 'The Unbalanced Constitution' (n 1) 111 (emphasis added).

other jurisdictions in which the former have been held to trump the latter, including the use of the right to free expression to curb trade union rights and to shield tobacco companies from laws restricting the advertisement of their products to children and other vulnerable groups.[6] His worry, at the birth of the Human Rights Act, was that similar examples would be found in the UK, a worry reinforced by the history of the common law.[7]

The second alleged problem stems from the belief that, even without any conflicts of rights, there ought to be constitutional protection for social and economic rights, guaranteeing a minimal standard of social provision. The social and economic rights guaranteed in the European Social Charter – the Council of Europe's counterpart to its more well-known Convention on Human Rights – have no equivalent to the duties contained in the Human Rights Act, which incorporates much of the Convention into domestic law. It is sometimes argued that the reasons for incorporating the Social Charter are just as compelling as those for incorporating the Convention.[8] And this is not only a domestic problem: the Council of Europe's enforcement mechanisms for the Social Charter are weaker than those for the Convention.

In this chapter, my focus is on the first problem: the alleged conflicts of rights and the defensive argument for balancing the constitution. Although Ewing suggests that, quite apart from any defensive need to protect social rights, there is a case for using the Human Rights Act as a template to promote them,[9] his concern for the most part is with the defensive argument. He is mainly concerned about the priority allocated to civil and political rights and the effect that has on social rights. I am unpersuaded that these concerns are justified. It seems to me that our unbalanced constitutional structure does not impede the protection of social and economic rights. My aim in this chapter is not to deny that it might be a good thing to balance the constitution and constitutionalise social rights, all things considered. However, I do want to explain why one argument for constitutionalising social rights is unpersuasive.

I. Conflicts of Rights

Can rights conflict with one another? The possibility that they can is far from straightforward. It needs to be emphasised that we are here concerned with the possibility of conflicts between moral rights. Laws such as the Human Rights Act are best understood as attempts to give legal effect to the subset of moral rights that we call human rights. In human rights adjudication, judges must try their best to form a correct moral judgment about the definition (or specification) of human rights. Does the right to vote extend to prisoners? Does the right to free expression protect hateful speech? Does the right to respect for private

[6] See KD Ewing, 'Constitutional Reform and Human Rights: Unfinished Business?' (2001) 5 *Edinburgh Law Review* 297, 303–6.

[7] See, eg, *Hornby v Close* (1867) LR 2 QB 153; *Boddington v Lawton* [1994] ICR 478.

[8] Those arguing for a greater role for the European Social Charter in the UK do not necessarily claim that it must have a status that is equal to the European Convention on Human Rights: see, eg, C O'Cinneide, 'The European Social Charter and the UK: Why it Matters' (2018) 29 *King's Law Journal* 275, 288.

[9] See, eg, Ewing, 'The Politics of the British Constitution' (n 4) 435–36. See also K Ewing, '*Just Words* and Social Justice' (1999) 5 *Review of Constitutional Studies* 53.

and family life protect illegal immigrants from deportation? That kind of thing. Of course, judges are as fallible as everyone else: sometimes they get it wrong. And they disagree. A right as defined by a judge might conflict with another right as defined by the same judge or it might conflict with the same right as defined by another judge. In that sense, then, legal rights can clearly conflict. But our concern is with the question whether moral rights, properly defined, can conflict.

The claim that rights conflict is sometimes given as one reason *against* constitutionalising social and economic rights. The thought here is that conflicts of rights only occur, or are more likely to occur, when social and economic rights enter the fray. Civil and political rights, the argument goes, are negative rights in the sense that they ground a duty of non-interference, and so do not conflict with one another; whereas social and economic rights are positive rights in the sense that they ground duties to provide assistance and resources, which are scarce goods and so conflict with one another.[10] The argument is flawed. If social and economic rights can conflict, there is no good reason to deny that civil and political rights can as well. It is not difficult to imagine, for example, how one's speaking freely might conflict with someone else's privacy. And civil and political rights can also give rise to positive duties and therefore conflicts based on scarcity.

But can rights conflict at all? Let's assume that the interest theory of rights is correct.[11] One has a right to privacy when one's interest in privacy is important enough to justify holding someone else to be under a duty. The question is: when is one's interest in privacy important enough to justify imposing a duty on someone else? Do we look only at the interest of the purported right holder, ignoring the interests of others? If so, rights can conflict: one's interest in privacy justifies one set of duties, but these duties might conflict with another set of duties arising out of someone else's interests – say, their interest in free speech. Or, to work out whether an interest justifies a right, do we have to look at all the circumstances, including the interests of others? If so, rights cannot conflict, because if one's interest in privacy conflicts with and is outweighed by someone else's interests, it will not be important enough to justify a right to privacy in the first place.

To put it another way, do rights conflict or is it only the underlying interests that conflict? Jeremy Waldron argued that rights can conflict: he argued that the interest theory entails that 'conflicts of rights, though not logically necessary, are in the circumstances of the real world more or less inevitable.'[12] For Waldron, this follows because he thinks that, to determine whether a person has a right to something, we should look only at the interests of the person claiming the right, and we should ignore the interests of others. He insists that this approach is necessary in order to capture the special importance of rights. It is what he thinks distinguishes the idea of rights from utilitarianism: we derive duties from rights by looking at the importance of the interest to the individual; and that, he insists, is different

[10] See, eg, C Fried, *Right and Wrong* (Cambridge Mass., Harvard University Press, 1978) 110. According to Robert Nozick, all rights are essentially negative 'side constraints', and so never conflict: see R Nozick, *Anarchy, State and Utopia* (Oxford, Basil Blackwell, 1974) 28–29.

[11] See J Raz, *The Morality of Freedom* (Oxford, Clarendon Press, 1986) 166: 'X has a right if and only if X can have rights, and, other things being equal, an aspect of X's well-being (his interest) is a sufficient reason to hold some other person(s) to be under a duty.'

[12] See, eg, J Waldron, 'Rights in Conflict' (1989) 99 *Ethics* 503, 505. cf FM Kamm, 'Conflicts of Rights' (2001) 7 *Legal Theory* 239.

from how we derive duties from a utilitarian calculus, which is by weighing the interest of the individual against every other interest that may be affected by the imposition of a duty.[13]

Waldron's argument as I have just summarised it is unsound for the following reason. As Cécile Fabre put it:

> It is perfectly plausible to aver that one has to take into account what would happen to Y if X were assigned a right, and that if it is thought that some interest of Y would be seriously harmed, then X's interest, although important in itself, is not important *enough* to justify holding someone else under some duty, disability, etc. In other words, one must adjudicate between competing interests *before* one assigns rights to them.[14]

Thus, Fabre says, rights do not conflict; only interests conflict. She uses this point to dismiss one argument against constitutionalising social rights, namely the claim that social rights give rise to conflicts of rights. Fabre is right that we should look at all the circumstances, including any competing interests of others, to work out whether one's interest is important enough to justify holding someone else to be under a duty. The proper definition of civil and political rights requires us to reach a moral judgment about the importance of – or, if you prefer, to weigh and balance – the competing interests, including interests in social and economic equality. Any property rights we have, for example, are rights to what we are left with after taxation as determined by standards of social justice.[15] Or, as Neil MacCormick put it in the context of liberty,

> we each have a right to as much liberty as everyone can equally enjoy; where, but only where, liberty competes with fairness in access to economic goods, the right is qualified to the extent necessary to satisfy our conception of economic fairness.[16]

Lawyers and judges may need to re-orientate their language away from speaking about justifiable infringements of human rights and towards speaking about defining or specifying the proper scope of the right. That is, instead of saying that we have a right to free speech, but it can be justifiably infringed in some circumstances, we should say that we do not have a right to free speech in those circumstances.[17]

But I doubt that there will never be conflicts of rights. Even if Fabre is right about how rights are determined, conflicts of rights might occur in the following way: the competing

[13] This is an over-simplification. Indirect forms of utilitarianism, often associated with David Hume, John Stuart Mill, Henry Sidgwick, and, more recently, RM Hare, make the apparently paradoxical claim that fundamental rights can be derived from, and place constraints on, the utilitarian calculus. See J Gray, 'Indirect Utility and Fundamental Rights' (1984) 1 *Social Philosophy and Policy* 73. cf HLA Hart, 'Between Utility and Rights' in his *Essays in Jurisprudence and Philosophy* (Oxford, OUP, 1983).

[14] C Fabre, 'Constitutionalising Social Rights' (1998) 6 *Journal of Political Philosophy* 263, 278 (emphasis in original).

[15] L Murphy and T Nagal, *The Myth of Ownership: Taxes and Justice* (Oxford, OUP, 2002). See also J Waldron, *The Rule of Law and the Measure of Property* (Cambridge, CUP, 2012) 70: 'property rights are not defined in isolation from the rest of the law. What my property rights amount to is partly a matter of how things stand in other areas of law.' Waldron is talking here about legal rights, but the same logic applies to moral rights. See also his *The Right to Private Property* (Oxford, Clarendon Press, 1988); *Liberal Rights: Collected Papers 1981–1991* (Cambridge, CUP, 1993); 'Socioeconomic Rights and Theories of Justice' (2011) 48 *San Diego Law Review* 773.

[16] N MacCormick, *Legal Right and Social Democracy: Essays in Legal and Political Philosophy* (Oxford, Clarendon Press, 1982) 43.

[17] See further, eg, TM Scanlon, 'Adjusting Rights and Balancing Values' (2004) 72 *Fordham Law Review* 1477; J Oberdiek, 'Specifying Rights Out of Necessity' (2008) 28 *OJLS* 127; G Webber, *The Negotiable Constitution: On the Limitation of Rights* (Cambridge, CUP, 2009).

interests might be roughly equal or incommensurable. That is, one's interests might be neither more nor less important than another's competing interests.[18] One might be tempted to say that this merely entails that neither interest is important enough to ground a right; that, for example, if your interest in free speech is incommensurable with the public's interest in curbing your speech in some contexts, then in those contexts you have no right to free speech and it is reasonable for the government to curb your speech. But another plausible conclusion is that both interests are important enough to ground conflicting rights.[19]

Waldron, then, might have been on to something when he argued that rights can conflict. He did not put it this way, but perhaps the example he uses to illustrate conflicts of rights is best understood as a conflict between rights grounded in roughly equal or incommensurable interests. In his example, we are to imagine that two people are drowning. Each has an interest in not drowning that is sufficiently important to justify holding some third person to be under a duty to rescue them. Now, suppose there are only enough resources available to rescue one of them. The conclusion to draw is not that neither of them has a right to be rescued, but that both of them do, and that their rights conflict. As Waldron observes, 'the tragedy of the conflict consists in the fact that we could rescue either of them, but not both.'[20] I think Waldron was right to conclude that there are rights that conflict in these circumstances, but wrong in how he reasoned towards that conclusion. The conflict arises because the competing interests are equal or incommensurable.

It is worth noting that there is another version of the argument that rights do not conflict, which also makes use of the incommensurability thesis. This version can be found in John Finnis's 1985 Maccabaean lecture on the proposals for a British Bill of Rights.[21] As well as making essentially the point I have already made – that moral rights are not defeasible premises, but are conclusions to moral reasoning, reached after all the competing interests have been evaluated – Finnis also claims that the specification of rights will often be underdetermined by reason, because the competing interests are incommensurable. In those circumstances, legislators and judges have to choose between different reasonable specifications of a right, none of which is uniquely correct. The problem with this argument is it entails that, whenever the interests are incommensurable, there is really no moral right, only what the legislature or judge has chosen as its preferred specification.[22] But as I said there is another possibility: that conflicts between incommensurable interests can lead to conflicts between incommensurable rights.

Anyway, what follows from all this? Only this: if and when two rights conflict, there are undefeated reasons for protecting each right, but no conclusive reason for choosing to protect one right rather than the other. This is what is tragic about the example of the two people drowning: each has a right to be rescued, but only one can be rescued and there is no conclusive reason to choose one over the other. But that, I suspect, is not the sort of conflicts Ewing has in mind.

[18] On incommensurability, see Raz (n 11) ch 13. For different perspectives, see R Chang (ed), *Incommensurability, Incomparability, and Practical Reason* (Cambridge Mass., Harvard University Press, 1997).

[19] cf L Zucca, *Constitutional Dilemmas: Conflicts of Fundamental Legal Rights in Europe and the USA* (Oxford, OUP, 2007).

[20] Waldron, 'Rights in Conflict' (n 12) 506.

[21] J Finnis, 'A Bill of Rights for Britain? The Moral of Contemporary Jurisprudence' (1985) 71 *Proceedings of the British Academy* 303. See also the book by one of Finnis's former doctoral students, Webber, *The Negotiable Constitution* (n 17).

[22] See T Hickman, 'Negotiable Rights, What Rights?' (2012) 75 *MLR* 437.

I am therefore going to focus on cases in which the competing interests are commensurable. Perhaps you think those are the only cases, but the existence or non-existence of incommensurability is not my concern in this chapter.[23] Remember, the worry that Ewing's 'unbalanced constitution' thesis presents is that, in some cases, civil and political rights might conflict with, and impede, social and economic rights. It is not that, in some cases, civil and political rights might be incommensurable with social and economic rights. In those cases (if they exist) it is reasonable to settle the conflict either way. Our worry is that some interests might be unjustifiably infringed when only civil and political rights are constitutionally protected. Our worry assumes that the underlying interests are commensurable. And what matters for our purposes is that in those cases, when the rights are properly defined, there are no conflicts of rights.

Of course, the proper definition of rights is complex and controversial. The question Ewing proposes can therefore be rephrased: does the constitutional ordering or structure help or hinder the correct definition of rights? Does the legal protection of civil and political rights create an imbalance that impedes the unprotected social and economic rights? Let's consider this question by first examining how rights are dealt with in the UK's relatively neutral constitution before the Human Rights Act, before examining the treatment of rights in the unbalanced constitution since the Human Rights Act, and in a possible rebalanced constitution in which social and economic rights receive the same legal protection.

II. The Neutral Constitution

Neutrality entails not taking sides. As Ewing suggests, the paradigm of a neutral constitution (which should not be confused with state neutrality) is one in which there are no substantive constitutional limits on lawmaking powers.[24] It seems an impossible ideal. Even in the UK's unwritten constitution, there seem to be substantive constitutional limits: simply put, although Parliament can pass any statute, it cannot fully determine the meaning of the law it makes, because the courts are the authoritative interpreters of statutes; and although judges have the power to make law, they cannot make any law, because the common law is subordinate to statute law.[25] And yet, if we take the legislative, interpretative, and adjudicative process as a whole, there are no substantive constitutional limits on what law we can end up with at the end of the process.

That is different from, for example, the US, where the Constitution does specify substantive limits on lawmaking power, and the Supreme Court has the power to enforce them. There, talk of neutrality can arguably be more pernicious. The most infamous use of the term 'neutrality' in constitutional scholarship is Herbert Wechsler's 1959 Holmes lecture at Harvard Law School. Wechsler used his lecture to criticise, among other things, the

[23] For what it is worth, I think value incommensurability exists but is a far less pervasive feature of moral reasoning than some people believe. For an argument along these lines, see B Williams, 'Conflicts of Values' in his *Moral Luck: Philosophical Papers 1973–1980* (Cambridge, CUP, 1980).

[24] Ewing, 'The Unbalanced Constitution' (n 1) 104. See also KD Ewing, 'Social Rights and Constitutional Law' [1999] *PL* 104, 112, describing the British constitution as 'the closest we come to' a constitution that is 'neutral on substantive issues'.

[25] See further J Grant, 'Unconstitutional Interpretation' (2018) 134 *LQR* 627.

US Supreme Court's decision in *Brown v Board of Education*, which declared racial segregation in schools unconstitutional.[26] As he saw it, the case boiled down to a clash between two groups wishing to associate freely – segregation denied blacks the freedom to associate with whites; integration denied whites the freedom to associate with only whites – and the Court had not provided any basis 'in neutral principles' for holding that the claims of those preferring desegregation should prevail.[27] Wechsler hoped that such a basis in neutral principles could be found, but he confessed he was unable to provide it.

The most infamous example in US constitutional law of what Cass Sunstein called 'status quo neutrality' is, of course, *Lochner v New York*.[28] The Supreme Court's invalidation of a state law setting minimum working hours for bakers in that case has become synonymous with economic libertarianism. But the *Lochner*-era Court presented its decisions as neutral. As far as it was concerned, the existing distribution of wealth and entitlements, under the common law's protection of property rights and contractual autonomy, provided a natural and impartial baseline for measuring the constitutionality of state action; any legislative attempts to redress inequalities of bargaining power were therefore impermissible.[29] But the status quo was not neutral. *Lochner*, the 'whipping boy' of American and indeed comparative constitutional scholarship, was a bad decision not so much because of judicial activism (as is often argued), but because of bad arguments.[30]

Nothing in the US Constitution compelled the decision in *Lochner*; nothing in the constitutional architecture inhibited the Court from relying on good arguments to make good decisions, decisions that would be more sympathetic to a reordering of social and economic relationships.[31] The text of the US Constitution is neutral to that extent – that is, its Fourteenth Amendment, on which that case turned, did not compel a decision one way or the other. But there are no neutral principles for interpreting the Bill of Rights. There is only one's best moral judgment of what the rights mean.

In the UK's legal systems, the way in which the courts have interpreted and developed the law has never been neutral either. Like the US Supreme Court in the *Lochner* era, our courts have earned a reputation for favouring economic liberty over other interests, including political liberty and social and political equality. Lord Atkinson's reactionary outburst in *Roberts v Hopwood*,[32] or Lord Diplock's in *Duport Steels v Sirs*,[33] are only two of the most prominent among many examples.[34] No doubt the myth of neutrality was partly responsible for the attachment to the status quo in cases of this kind.[35] Parliament may have been

[26] *Brown v Board of Education* 347 US 483 (1954).

[27] H Wechsler, 'Toward Neutral Principles of Constitutional Law' (1959) 73 *Harvard Law Review* 1, 34.

[28] *Lochner v New York* 198 US 45 (1905). See CR Sunstein, *The Partial Constitution* (Cambridge Mass., Harvard University Press, 1993) ch 3.

[29] See CR Sunstein, '*Lochner*'s Legacy' (1987) 87 *Columbia Law Review* 873.

[30] R Dworkin, *Freedom's Law: The Moral Reading of the American Constitution* (Cambridge Mass., Harvard University Press, 1996) 82.

[31] See, eg, *West Coast Hotel Co v Parish* 300 US 379 (1937).

[32] *Roberts v Hopwood* [1925] AC 578, 594 (Lord Atkinson): 'The council would, in my view, fail in their duty if … they … allowed themselves to be guided in preference by some eccentric principles of socialistic philanthropy, or by a feminist ambition to secure the equality of the sexes in the matter of wages in the world of labour.'

[33] *Duport Steels Ltd v Sirs* [1980] ICR 161, 177 (Lord Diplock), describing legislation on trade union action that provided immunity from tort as 'intrinsically repugnant to anyone who has spent his life in the practice of the law or the administration of justice.'

[34] Ewing, 'The Politics of the British Constitution' (n 4).

[35] TRS Allan, 'The Politics of the British Constitution: A Response to Professor Ewing's Paper' [2000] *PL* 374.

sovereign, but when interpreting statutes the courts would apply common law presumptions in favour of property rights and contractual autonomy.[36] Only towards the end of the twentieth century did judges show a greater willingness to extend these presumptions to political liberty.[37] The important point for our purposes is that the judicial hostility to social reform was caused by the political biases of the judges and the social conditions from which those biases derived. It was not the result of the constitutional structure in which they operated. And like the *Lochner*-era Court, they could have developed the law in a different direction.

When Ewing praised the 'relative neutrality' of the British constitution, he hastened to add: 'There is of course no such thing as a truly neutral constitution: all constitutions reflect certain economic structures, and are designed to ensure the political influence of dominant economic interests.'[38] He masterfully describes the change from the property-based Victorian constitution to liberal democracy, and then the change to a partial social democracy followed by the retreat from that social dimension.[39] A danger with this way of thinking about constitutional fluidity, familiar from Ivor Jennings, is that it can often further blur the (admittedly vague) line between the ebb and flow of ordinary political changes and changes that really deserve to be called constitutional. When Jennings wrote that '[t]he balance of the constitution has shifted', it was because the functions of the state had shifted: 'British political institutions are no longer concerned only with external relations, the maintenance of order, and the administration of justice; they closely regulate private enterprise and provide vast services directly to citizens'.[40] Of course, there have been great constitutional changes since the start of the twentieth century, the biggest being democracy. But all along the constitution was neutral to the extent that it allowed the state to pursue any ends it wanted.[41]

Still, there is nothing neutral about the preference for a neutral constitution. Many people believe that a good constitution is one that does take sides, by providing checks and balances that limit the power of an executive with a Commons majority. There is a distinction between two perspectives, broadly speaking, on what a constitution is for: those who see the constitution as the means by which the state is empowered to pursue any ends it wants (so that everything, every aspect of life, is vulnerable to state intervention); and those who see the constitution as the means to 'put the state in its place' (protecting spheres of private autonomy).[42] The distinction is crude, and constitutions do a bit of both, but there is

[36] See further JAG Griffith, *The Politics of the Judiciary*, 5th edn (London, Fontana Press, 1997) 104.

[37] See, eg, *R v Secretary of State for the Home Department, ex parte Simms* [2000] 2 AC 115.

[38] Ewing, 'The Unbalanced Constitution' (n 1) 104.

[39] See Ewing, 'The Politics of the British Constitution' (n 4).

[40] WI Jennings, *The Law and the Constitution*, 5th edn (London, University of London Press, 1959) 33. See KD Ewing, '*The Law and the Constitution*: Manifesto of the Progressive Party' (2004) 67 *MLR* 734.

[41] See further T Daintith and M Sah, 'Privatisation and the Economic Neutrality of the Constitution' [1993] *PL* 465; D Nicol, *The Constitutional Protection of Capitalism* (Oxford, Hart Publishing, 2010) 31–34.

[42] This is essentially the distinction Michael Oakeshott draws between an 'enterprise association' (or *universitas*) and a 'civil association' (or *societas*), the latter being 'a formal relationship in terms of rules, not a substantive relationship in terms of common action': M Oakeshott, 'On the Character of a Modern European State' in his *On Human Conduct* (Oxford, Clarendon Press, 1975) 201. In 1992, Ferdinand Mount argued that 'one of the great political changes of the past century has been the gradual transition from a civil-association to an enterprise-association view of government'; to get back to what he saw as the old ways, he favoured, among other things, modern bills of rights, because they 'support written constitutions in *putting government in its place* and thus help to restore the understanding of society as a civil association': F Mount, *The British Constitution Now: Recovery or Decline?* (London, William Heinemann, 1992) 75, 78 (emphasis in original).

a genuine disagreement or tension between these competing views. Even with an ostensibly neutral constitution such as ours, there is ultimately no neutral foundation.

The courts have taken sides in accepting the sovereignty of Parliament. That acceptance makes their biases in developing the common law less of a threat than they might otherwise be, because ultimately Parliament could enact legislation that displaces the common law. If the courts had rejected parliamentary sovereignty, social democrats would be reliant on the courts changing the direction of the common law. Trevor Allan, a defender of common law (or liberal) constitutionalism, strikes an optimistic note, suggesting that the common law constitution could be developed to protect social and economic rights.[43] Maybe. But the common law has not done a very good job so far, as Ewing has expertly shown us.[44] Pessimism about the common law's social-democratic potential is compounded, for Ewing, by a belief that Parliament, in enacting the Human Rights Act, has reinforced the biases of the common law. It leads Ewing to advocate constitutionalising social and economic rights. But will that make a difference?

III. The Unbalanced Constitution

When faced with two claims of rights, only one of which is explicitly guaranteed in the law of the constitution, can judges still reach the correct moral judgment in the definition of moral rights? Or are they bound to enforce the rights that are guaranteed in the law of the constitution at the expense of those that are not? That way of framing the issue fairly reflects Ewing's worry. He worries that constitutionalising one set of rights but not another introduces a hierarchy of rights, which is to the detriment of social and economic rights. 'Civil and political rights have a new priority over all others,' he warns.[45] Yet what I want to show is that the constitutional structure makes no difference. The problem, if there is a problem, is that judges have been reaching the wrong conclusions when they make their moral judgments about what the rights require.

Admittedly, the constitutional structure has changed. Although the Human Rights Act was designed to ensure that Parliament remains sovereign and so the Act does not enable the courts to strike down legislation, it does confer significant power on the courts. Yes, section 4 of the Act merely provides that courts may issue a 'declaration of incompatibility', which has no legal effect; however, the political effect of such a declaration should not be underestimated. And there is arguably great power in section 3 of the Act, extending the common law presumptions by requiring the courts to interpret primary legislation in a way that is compatible with Convention rights 'so far as it is possible to do so'. It was not much of an exaggeration for Joseph Raz to write in *The Morality of Freedom*: 'Interpretive presumptions, such as a presumption that parliament does not intend to derogate from

[43] TRS Allan, 'In Defence of the Common Law Constitution: Unwritten Rights as Fundamental Law' (2009) 22 *Canadian Journal of Law and Justice* 187, 201. cf Alan Brudner, *Constitutional Goods* (Oxford, OUP, 2004).

[44] But for a contrasting view, in the context of labour law, see A Bogg, 'Common Law and Statute in the Law of Employment' (2016) 69 *Current Legal Problems* 67.

[45] Ewing, 'The Unbalanced Constitution' (n 1) 108.

people's civil rights, are as powerful a tool in the hand of a judiciary keen on fulfilling a role in the protection of human rights as an entrenched bill of rights.'[46]

But any structural changes, transferring power to the judiciary, do not necessarily pose a danger to unprotected social and economic rights. It all depends on how the protected rights are interpreted. Now, Ewing acknowledges this point. He writes:

> But of course it is not only constitutional texts which matter: equally important are the values of those charged with the responsibility of determining what the texts mean. A liberal constitution could be made to serve social democratic ends if social democratic values were dominant and pervasive. Equally, a social democratic constitution could be rendered useless by the narrow reading by those educated and trained in a different tradition.[47]

Quite so. But rather than being 'equally important', as Ewing puts it, there are good reasons for thinking that this point about interpretation is much more important than the constitutional structure. When he writes that 'the Human Rights Act has created a constitutional imbalance', we should take this to mean that the Act has reinforced the judicial bias in favour of liberty and against equality, which leads them to incorrect definitions of rights. His argument for reform must therefore be that ensuring constitutional balance, putting social and economic rights on the same constitutional plane, will influence the values of the judiciary and re-orientate them towards social democratic values.

The suggestion that there is no difference between the common law and the Convention rights incorporated into domestic law by the Human Rights Act troubled Ewing. 'The obvious problem which this creates,' he wrote, 'is that it reinforces the liberal values of the common law, at the expense of other political values and constitutional principles'.[48] Convention rights have built-in limits, which require judges to consider whether something is 'necessary in a democratic society'. What this entails, properly understood, is the definition of the right: it requires, as I explained earlier, a judgment about whether an interest is important enough to justify holding another person or persons to be under a duty. That judgment is of course controversial, and as Ewing believed 'there is so far no recognition in the jurisprudence that social equality is a fundamental principle of democracy'.[49]

The judicial approach has indeed been a problem. But Ewing sees a further problem: 'the onus is on the person imposing the limit on liberty, not on those who wish to maintain limits on equality', and this 'reinforces the priority of liberal principles'.[50] I am less convinced that this is really a problem. Restrictions on liberty would still give rise to the same claims, and would still need to be justified, even if social and economic rights were constitutionally protected. And persuading the courts that restrictions on liberty are justified would not be a problem if the interests of social equality were adequately recognised by judges. The real problem, in other words, is the inadequacy of judicial recognition of social rights claims, not the constitutional structure or the burden of justification.

Things are not all doom and gloom for social and economic rights in the 'unbalanced constitution' under the Human Rights Act. There have been instances of individuals using

[46] Raz (n 11) 258.
[47] Ewing, 'The Unbalanced Constitution' (n 1) 112.
[48] Ibid, 108.
[49] Ibid, 111.
[50] Ibid.

the Human Rights Act to get access to welfare services, with varying degrees of success.[51] Of course, civil and political rights can only go so far. As Ewing puts it, 'by trying to use civil and political rights imaginatively as a vessel for social and economic rights, lawyers are trying to pour quarts into pint pots'.[52] But there have been some successes.

A high point came in November 2008, when the European Court of Human Rights announced its landmark decision in *Demir and Baykara v Turkey*.[53] Ewing, in an article written with John Hendy QC, went so far as to describe *Demir and Baykara* as 'a decision in which social and economic rights have been fused permanently with civil and political rights, in a process that is potentially nothing less than a socialization of civil and political rights'.[54] The Court held that the right to collective bargaining was an essential element of what Article 11 of the Convention calls 'the right to form and to join trade unions for the protection of [one's] interests'. It adopted what has been called an 'integrated approach' to the interpretation of the Convention,[55] knitting social rights into the fabric of the Convention.

Since then, the European Court of Human Rights has appeared to row back. In the *RMT* case of 2014, although extending the reasoning in *Demir and Baykara* to recognise a right to strike (something that English judges had refused to accept),[56] the Strasbourg Court held that under Article 11(2) a total ban on 'secondary' strike action was justified.[57] What we find in cases such as these is the kind of disagreement you would expect when it comes to the definition of rights. From the social democratic perspective, it looks like Strasbourg gets the judgment correct some of the time but not all of the time and maybe not even most of the time.

But when judges get it wrong, it is not because of the constitutional structure. The same is true of British judges. The question then is: how do we ensure judges properly recognise the values of social equality? One way that Ewing mentions is to fully realise the potential of section 2 of the Human Rights Act, which requires domestic courts to take into account Strasbourg jurisprudence. Strasbourg jurisprudence, in turn, has emphasised the need to have regard to other international treaties, including the European Social Charter and other treaties dealing with social rights. Those treaties, and the decisions of the institutions charged with interpreting them, might indeed enlighten our judges in their interpretation of Convention rights.[58] But Ewing struck a sceptical note: 'it would be a triumph of faith over experience to believe that this is likely to happen'.[59]

[51] See E Palmer, *Judicial Review, Socio-Economic Rights and the Human Rights Act* (Oxford, Hart Publishing, 2007).

[52] K Ewing, 'Book Review' (2009) 7 *I-CON* 155, 167.

[53] *Demir and Baycara v Turkey* (2009) 48 EHRR 54.

[54] KD Ewing and J Hendy, 'The Dramatic Implications of Demir and Baykara' (2010) 39 *Industrial Law Journal* 2, 47.

[55] V Mantouvalou, 'Labour Rights in the European Convention on Human Rights: An Intellectual Justification for an Integrated Approach to Interpretation' (2013) 13 *Human Rights Law Review* 529.

[56] See, eg, *Metrobus Ltd v Unite the Union* [2009] EWCA Civ 829, [2009] 7 WLUK 854 (Lloyd LJ): 'English law does not of course recognise a right to strike'. But compare *London Underground Ltd v RMT* [1995] IRLR 636, 641 (Millett LJ).

[57] *National Union of Rail, Maritime and Transport Workers (RMT) v United Kingdom* (2015) 60 EHRR 10. See A Bogg and KD Ewing, 'The Implications of the *RMT* Case' (2014) 43 *Industrial Law Journal* 221.

[58] On the use of unincorporated treaties in interpretation, see *R (SG) v Secretary of State for Work and Pensions* [2015] UKSC 16, [2015] 4 All ER 939.

[59] Ewing, 'The Unbalanced Constitution' (n 1) 113.

He has a point. The idea that British judges should follow Strasbourg jurisprudence faces hostility not only from some politicians and some sections of the press and the public, but also from some judges. For example, Sir John Laws, in his 2013 Hamlyn lectures, argued that law made in Europe is one of 'two contemporary threats to the constitutional balance'.[60] By 'the constitutional balance', he meant what he considered to be the proper relationship between Parliament and the courts:

> The sovereignty of Parliament itself only has life by means of the common law's methods. The judicial ascertainment of an Act's meaning, and the judicial elaboration of substantive principle, are indissolubly interwoven. This meeting of Parliament and judges is the constitutional balance.[61]

According to Laws, the influence (or at least perceived influence) of European law on domestic law may be considered an assault on the constitutional balance and 'may undermine virtues of the common law: its catholicity and its restraint'.[62] Noting the public's perception that 'the law of human rights has got too big', he argues that British courts should 'keep control of the proper place of human rights, and so protect the common law's restraint'.[63] Leaving their development to the slow creep of the common law, on this account, will ensure that human rights do not get too big, and will also protect the common law's 'presumption of liberty', which 'moderates the temper of the people'.[64] It's not surprising many people believe that social and economic rights need to be constitutionalised to be protected against judges. But it's less than clear that such a reform would make a real difference to the judgments of our courts.

IV. Balancing the Constitution

True, there would be significant consequences if the rights in the European Social Charter were protected in the same way as Convention rights are protected under the Human Rights Act. There would be an equivalent of sections 3 and 4 of that Act, imposing a duty on the courts to interpret legislation, so far as it is possible to do so, in a way that is compatible with European Social Charter rights and, where that is not possible, to make a declaration of incompatibility. There would be a new ground of judicial review of administrative action: an equivalent section 6 would require public authorities to act in a way that is incompatible with Charter rights. And the courts, being themselves public authorities, would also have to act compatibly with Charter rights, including in their development of the common law. These would undoubtedly be important changes. But we must not exaggerate them.

As evidence of the difference that an interpretative obligation (along the lines of the Human Rights Act's section 3) would make for protecting social rights, Ewing cites *Banks v Chief Adjudication Officer*.[65] In that case, the House of Lords held by a majority that,

[60] J Laws, *The Common Law Constitution* (Cambridge, CUP, 2014) 4.
[61] Ibid, 18.
[62] Ibid, 4.
[63] Ibid, 71, 72.
[64] Ibid, 85.
[65] *Banks v Chief Adjudication Officer* [2001] UKHL 33; [2001] ICR 877. See Ewing, 'The Case for Social Rights' (n 3) 335–36.

under the relevant legislation, a special needs assistant at a school was not entitled to income support for the school holidays, even though he was unpaid during that time. But the *Banks* case can also support the claim that incorporating the European Social Charter is unnecessary. The Law Lords were split three to two, and the decision very nearly went the other way (Lord Millett had the swing vote and changed his judgment at the last minute, having read a draft of Lord Hope's speech).[66] The two in the minority, Lord Scott and Lord Cooke, thought that the legislation could be interpreted so as to enable Mr Banks to get income support. Although the majority thought that such an interpretation was not possible, Lord Scott's conclusion – that the majority's interpretation created a 'poverty trap' and that 'the sooner the Secretary of State remedies the situation by making appropriate new Regulations the better' – was as strong as any declaration of incompatibility.[67] What the minority speeches in this case suggests, albeit not conclusively, is that enacting an equivalent Human Rights Act for social rights is not a necessary condition for their protection. It should go without saying that such an enactment would not be sufficient, either.

Ewing is of course acutely aware that constitutionalising social rights is insufficient to protect them. He points out that 'the courts in the common law tradition are likely to read down social rights and to dilute their effect, even before any question of balancing social rights against property arises whenever they clash'.[68] He claims that this problem could be addressed by using the template of section 2 of the Human Rights Act and requiring the courts to take into account the decisions of the European Committee of Social Rights.[69] But that, too, would have limits. There is always a danger with constitutionalising social rights: that the courts will set back the cause of social rights by defining them narrowly.[70]

This brings us to that other legal Europe, the European Union, and the highly controversial *Viking* and *Laval* cases of 2007.[71] These cases concerned two companies that operated in Nordic states but wanted to use workers from Baltic states, in order to take advantage of lower labour and regulatory costs. In each case, the relevant trade unions wanted to take industrial action to stop this. The European Court of Justice found in favour of the employers. It is common to criticise the Court's decisions in *Viking* and *Laval* for prioritising the employers' economic right to free movement over the trade unions' social right to collective action. According to Ewing, 'these cases reveal very clearly the dangers of unbalanced constitutional arrangements and the very real threat to democratic achievements that continues to be presented by unaccountable judges in the context of unprotected social rights'.[72] But was the problem really due to unbalanced constitutional protection of social and economic rights? The Court certainly talked the talk when it came to balance:

> Since the Community has thus not only an economic but also a social purpose, the rights under the provisions of the Treaty on the free movement of goods, persons, services and capital must

[66] See A Paterson, *Final Judgment: The Last Law Lords and the Supreme Court* (Oxford, Hart Publishing, 2013) 182.

[67] *Banks* (n 65) 902 (Lord Scott).

[68] Ewing, 'The Case for Social Rights' (n 3) 334, citing the example of *Council of Civil Service Unions v Minister for Civil Service* [1985] AC 274 (HL).

[69] Ewing, 'The Case for Social Rights' (n 3) 334–35.

[70] See M Tushnet, *Weak Courts, Strong Rights: Judicial Review and Social Welfare Rights in Comparative Constitutional Law* (Princeton NJ, Princeton University Press 2008).

[71] See Case C–438/05 *International Transport Workers Federation and Finish Seamen's Union v Viking Line* [2007] ECR I–10779; Case C–341/05 *Laval v Svenska Byggnadsarbetareförbundet* [2007] ECR I–11767.

[72] Ewing, 'Book Review' (n 52) 169.

> be balanced against the objectives pursued by social policy, which include … inter alia, improved living and working conditions … proper social protection and dialogue between management and labour.[73]

The Court recognised that the right to take collective action could be an overriding reason of public interest that could justify a restriction on free movement.[74] The problem, it seemed to many commentators, was that the Court did not walk the walk in balancing the interests, because it viewed collective action as a restriction on free movement and therefore a prima facie breach of Community law. 'This is balance in name, not substance,' Catherine Barnard wrote.[75]

The perceived problem, in other words, stems from the structure of the Court's analysis. Its 'restrictions' analysis, according to Barnard, 'gives primacy to the economic freedoms' and 'creates a presumption that the national rule is unlawful.'[76] This analysis, as Jeff King puts it, 'encourages and justifies' the belief that social rights have a lower status, 'being treated as a mere legitimate aim to be implemented by proportionate means, rather than as a competing right – a contest among equals.'[77] But is the problem really that social rights have an unequal status? After all, as King goes on to say, the *Viking* and *Laval* cases made clear that the protection of social rights 'provided a legitimate ground for limiting the commercial freedoms in EU law, and that balancing between the freedoms and social rights provisions was necessary.'[78]

The real problem is that the European Court of Justice in *Viking* and *Laval* reached the wrong moral judgment in defining the respective rights, which is to say, the moral judgment about the importance of the respective economic and social interests. The Court's error was not due to any unequal legal protection of the rights,[79] nor was it due to the structure of the proportionality analysis, in which the right to collective action, being a restriction on free movement, is placed in a defensive position. The error was in the Court's moral judgment – the consequence, perhaps, of an ideological preference for economic freedom over social equality.[80] We run the risk of absolving judges of responsibility if we place the blame on the structure of the constitution or the structure of the courts' proportionality analysis. You may think that judges should not be responsible for the highly controversial task of balancing the competing values in the first place. But for so long as the rights fall to be judicially interpreted, the balancing is unavoidable.

[73] *Viking* (n 71) [79], *Laval* (n 71) [105].

[74] Ibid [103].

[75] C Barnard, 'Social Dumping or Dumping Socialism?' (2008) 67 *CLJ* 262, 264.

[76] C Barnard, 'Restricting Restrictions: Lessons for the EU from the US?' (2009) 68 *CLJ* 575, 576. See also A Davies, 'One Step Forward, Two Steps Back? The *Viking* and *Laval* Cases in the ECJ' (2008) 37 *Industrial Law Journal* 126; S Garben, 'The Constitutional (Im)balance between "the Market" and "the Social" in the European Union' (2017) 13 *European Constitutional Law Review* 23; M Freedland and J Prassl (eds), *Viking, Laval and Beyond* (Oxford, Hart Publishing, 2016).

[77] J King, *Judging Social Rights* (Cambridge, CUP, 2012) 53.

[78] Ibid 55.

[79] It might be thought that the entry into force of the Lisbon Treaty in 2009 changes things, because it gives the EU Charter of Fundamental Rights an equal status to the Treaties, and the Charter includes the right to collective action. But the Court could have said – and in *Viking* and *Laval* did say – that the right to collective action is a fundamental right; and the rights still have to be interpreted, which involves the same moral judgment regardless of what formal legal status the rights have.

[80] See, eg, D Nicol, 'Europe's *Lochner* Moment' [2011] *PL* 308, 325: 'no substantive provision of the TFEU compels the ECJ to accord precedence to employers' interests over those of trade unions. Rather, an interpretative adventure by the ECJ secured this result.'

The EU proclaims itself a 'social market economy', but cases such as *Viking* and *Laval* suggest a preference for the values of the market over social values. And when the Court undermines social values, its decisions become very difficult to change. The EU's political power to intervene and pursue socially motivated regulation is meagre in comparison with the judicial power to intervene in pursuit of market deregulation.[81] The problem in the EU is wider. The supposed 'constitutional balance' between economic policy at the European level and social policy at the Member State level – which it was thought 'serves to ensure the relative neutrality of the Union's policies' and therefore to make integration acceptable – was always going to be difficult, if not impossible, to sustain.[82] The story of the rise and fall of 'social Europe' is well told by Ewing.[83] But although proposals to rebalance the EU towards social protection might be attractive,[84] they depend for their success on the support of political elites.[85] If the constitution is unbalanced, whether at the European or the domestic level, what matters is persuading the elites, including the judges, to take social values seriously.

The conflicts between market and social values will not disappear by balancing, or rebalancing, the constitution. 'Constitutions,' as John Griffith said in his seminal Chorley lecture in 1978, 'are often presented as descriptions of equilibrium', with the opposing forces of left and right, or of the social and the market, being understood to provide weights and measures that, somehow, 'hold even the scales of civilised constitutionalism'.[86] Instead, he pointed out, 'a society is endemically in a state of conflict between warring interest groups'.[87] In other words, it is conflict, not balance, that rules. As I have tried to explain in this essay, the most important conflicts are not conflicts between rights, but between the interests that must be assessed in defining rights. Griffith also thought that there are no conflicts of rights, but for a different reason: he thought that 'there are no over-riding human rights' at all, only 'political claims'.[88] I think he was wrong to put it like that. The fact that claims about human rights are politically controversial is no reason for denying that there are human rights. However, his general point – that the definition of rights is a matter of political controversy – is a valid one. And of course, that is why Griffith and others, including Ewing, opposed a Bill of Rights. They thought that these conflicts should be resolved by politicians who are politically accountable rather than judges who are not.[89]

In the context of the debate about social rights, the worry about judicialising political issues is often part of an argument against constitutionalising social rights.[90] But Pandora

[81] F Scharpf, 'The Asymmetry of European Integration, Or Why the EU Cannot Be a Social Market Economy' (2010) 8 *Socio-Economic Review* 211.

[82] M Dawson and F de Witte, 'Constitutional Balance in the EU after the Euro-Crisis' (2013) 76 *MLR* 817. See also S Giubboni, *Social Rights and Market Freedom in the European Constitution: A Labour Law Perspective* (Cambridge, CUP, 2006).

[83] KD Ewing, 'The Death of Social Europe' (2015) 26 *King's Law Journal* 76.

[84] C Barnard, 'EU Employment Law and the European Social Model: The Past, the Present, and the Future' (2014) 67 *CLP* 199; N Countouris and M Freedland (eds), *Resocialising Europe in a Time of Crisis* (Cambridge, CUP, 2013).

[85] For scepticism of the prospects of rebalancing EU towards social protection, see S Weatherill, *Law and Values in the European Union* (Oxford, Clarendon Press, 2016) 414.

[86] JAG Griffith, 'The Political Constitution' (1979) 42 *MLR* 1, 1.

[87] Ibid, 19.

[88] Ibid, 17.

[89] Ibid, 18–19.

[90] See, eg, Joint Committee on Human Rights, *A Bill of Rights for the UK?* (2007–8, HL 165-I, HC 150-I) para 167: 'including fully justiciable and legally enforceable economic and social rights in any Bill of Rights carries too great a risk that the courts will interfere with legislative judgments about priority setting.'

has already opened her box (actually a jar). According to Ewing, power has already shifted from an elected legislature to an unelected judiciary, a shift from democracy to what he called 'juristocracy'.[91] Ideally, there would be no juristocracy, but now we have one, he thinks, it must be ordered to ensure that social rights are equally protected.[92]

We can protect social rights without constitutionalising them.[93] As long as judges reach the correct moral judgments in defining constitutional rights, the judicial enforcement of constitutionally protected civil and political rights poses no threat to constitutionally unprotected social and economic rights. Ewing would no doubt respond that, as history shows, we cannot trust judges to reach the correct moral judgments themselves. We need to 'nudge' or enlighten judges to ensure they have due regard to social values.[94] One way of doing that, the argument goes, is to include social and economic rights in the constitution (or a Human Rights Act equivalent). Constitutionalising social rights, Ewing says, involves 'nothing less than the *socialization of the common law*, by displacing liberty as the only principle and introducing accompanying principles of substantive equality and solidarity'.[95]

I am sceptical about the ability of the constitutional protection of social rights to enlighten judges. There is still the risk that judges will reach the wrong moral judgments in defining social rights, with all the damage to the cause of social rights that ill-conceived judicial decisions entail. In any case, even if putting social rights in a Bill of Rights does have the effect of enlightening judges, the value of doing so – rather than seeking to enlighten judges in other ways – has to be considered against all the other objections to constitutionalising social rights and tasking the judiciary with their enforcement, which have not been my concern in this essay.[96]

In this chapter, I have raised a note of scepticism merely about the defensive case for constitutionalising social rights, namely the claims that rights conflict and that there is a constitutional imbalance that favours rights to economic liberty at the expense of social equality. If I am right, these two issues – conflicts of rights and constitutional balance – are red herrings. If the constitution were an obstacle to protecting and promoting the public good, it could indeed be described as unbalanced, unhinged, deranged. But it is not constitutional disorder that is to blame for the inadequacy of social rights protection. The problem stems from the decisions of judges and other political power-holders. That said, even if the defensive case fails, it might still be a good idea to constitutionalise social rights, all things

[91] KD Ewing, 'The Bill of Rights Debate: Democracy or Juristocracy in Britain?' in KD Ewing, CA Gearty, and BA Hepple (eds), *Human Rights and Labour Law: Essays for Paul O'Higgins* (London, Mansell, 1994). See also R Hirschl, *Towards Juristocracy: The Origins and Consequences of the New Constitutionalism* (Cambridge Mass., Harvard University Press, 2004).

[92] See further KD Ewing, 'The Resilience of the Political Constitution' (2013) 14 *German Law Journal* 2111.

[93] See G Webber et al, *Legislated Rights: Securing Human Rights through Legislation* (Cambridge, CUP, 2018).

[94] cf KD Ewing (2016) 132 *LQR* 683, 685 (emphasis added): 'In the real world of litigation competing economic freedoms and social rights cannot prevail simultaneously, and a court must allocate priority to one over the other. And in the real world of procedural law where this conflict is fought, *a nudge would be unlikely to affect the outcome* in cases such as *Viking* … the nudge is a fudge.'

[95] Ewing, 'The Unbalanced Constitution' (n 1) 116 (emphasis in original). See also J King, 'Social Rights in Comparative Constitutional Theory' in G Jacobsohn and M Schor (eds), *Comparative Constitutional Theory* (Cheltenham, Edward Elgar, 2018).

[96] See, eg, T Macklem, 'Entrenching Bills of Rights' (2006) 26 *OJLS* 107; C Gearty, 'Against Judicial Enforcement' in C Gearty and V Mantouvalou, *Debating Social Rights* (Oxford, Hart Publishing, 2011). cf V Mantouvalou, 'In Support of Legalisation' in *Debating Social Rights*, ibid; King (n 77).

considered. My intention has not been to oppose a non-defensive case for constitutionalising social rights. And, of course, it might be a good idea to go beyond a focus on social rights to more egalitarian redistributive projects.[97]

What a constitutional text says is often less important than what its interpreters do. For those who share Ewing's concerns about the effects of an unbalanced constitution, the important task is to fight the political fight, to engage in the moral debates about the proper definitions of civil and political rights, and to explain when liberal interests, on which claims of civil and political rights are based, are outweighed by the interests of social equality. Ewing's important body of scholarship has both demonstrated the need for a better understanding of social rights and helped to explain what that better understanding might be.

[97] See S Moyn, *Not Enough: Human Rights in an Unequal World* (Cambridge Mass., Belknap Press 2018).

4

The Human Rights Act and Labour Law at 20

VIRGINIA MANTOUVALOU*

In a typically inspiring and thought-provoking piece written in 1998, Keith Ewing presented the then newly enacted Human Rights Act 1998 (HRA) to an audience of labour lawyers through the pages of the Industrial Law Journal.[1] Ewing argued that 'it is far from clear that the HRA will have a decisive impact on the structure of labour law'.[2] He explained that the HRA/European Convention on Human Rights (ECHR) includes limited social and labour rights, as it primarily protects civil and political rights. He also explained that many of the provisions that can be relevant to the employment relation (such as articles 8–11 ECHR)[3] do not contain an absolute protection, but are qualified in the sense that they can be limited if there is a legitimate aim and the restriction is proportionate to the aim pursued, and that the Strasbourg Court has been reluctant to afford wide protection to workers in this context. Finally, Ewing was particularly concerned that article 11, which protects freedom of assembly and association, including the right to form and join trade unions, could have, not just a limited, but a negative effect on collective labour rights because of the jurisprudence of Strasbourg in the 'closed shop' cases.[4] An issue underlying Ewing's scepticism was the power that judges were conferred by the HRA, which he feared might even be used against workers' interests.

Was Ewing right to be sceptical about the effects of the HRA on labour law? This chapter revisits the question 20 years on. While we have not witnessed a profound reorientation of UK labour law to reflect human rights values, the HRA has not become 'a shield for the bearers of private power' against social regulation either.[5] In fact the ECHR/HRA has had a broader impact than Ewing originally predicted. There have been certain significant worker-protective developments in legal principles governing areas, such as the contract of employment and human rights, workers' access to justice, the protection from severe

* I am grateful to Alan Bogg, Hugh Collins and Alison Young for comments on a draft, as well as all conference organisers and participants at KCL in September 2018.

[1] K Ewing, 'The Human Rights Act and Labour Law' (1998) 27 *Industrial Law Journal* 275.

[2] Ibid, 276.

[3] Article 8 protects the right to private and family life, art 9 protects freedom of thought, conscience and religion, art 10 protects freedom of expression, and art 11 protects freedom of assembly and association, including the right to form and join trade unions.

[4] See among others, *Young, James and Webster v UK* (1983) 5 EHRR CD519.

[5] K Ewing, 'The Unbalanced Constitution' in T Campbell, K Ewing and A Tomkins (eds), *Sceptical Essays on Human Rights* (Oxford, OUP, 2001) 103 at 111.

labour exploitation, as well as in collective labour law issues. Ewing was concerned that the ECHR/HRA is 'unbalanced'[6] because it does not explicitly protect social rights. However, it is fair to say that it can still serve as a bulwark against arbitrary exercises of employers' power. For a human rights document to have the ability to affect more deeply the inequality of power of the employment relation, though, the incorporation of social rights would be essential, as Ewing rightly pointed.[7]

I. ECHR/HRA

The Human Rights Act was enacted in 1998, following what was described as 'an aggressive campaign for the incorporation into domestic law of the European Convention on Human Rights, a campaign in which the judges joined forces with other activists'.[8] The Convention itself was drafted in the aftermath of the Second World War in order to respond to the atrocities of the War, and came into force in 1953 under the auspices of the Council of Europe. This was also the period of the Cold War, which explains why the Convention contained primarily civil and political rights, with social and labour rights being protected in the 1961 European Social Charter (ESC). As an implication of this separation for a few decades it was taken for granted that there is a sharp dividing line between civil and social rights in case law that involved labour rights.[9] This is not the case anymore, as we will see later on.

The UK was the first country to sign the ECHR in 1950, and the British MP and lawyer David Maxwell-Fyfe was one of the main drafters. In 1966, the UK accepted the jurisdiction of the European Court of Human Rights (ECtHR) to hear individual complaints. Everyone within the UK's jurisdiction could lodge a petition to Strasbourg, having exhausted domestic remedies. Yet when the HRA was enacted that incorporated Convention rights into English law, Ewing said that it marked an 'unprecedented transfer of political power from the executive and legislature to the judiciary'.[10] How did this transfer of power occur? The key sections of the Act are section 3 that provides that '(1) So far as it is possible to do so, primary legislation and subordinate legislation must be read and given effect in a way which is compatible with the Convention rights', and section 4 that permits courts to issue a declaration of incompatibility when primary or subordinate legislation cannot be interpreted in a way that is compatible with Convention rights. Section 6 provides:

> (1) It is unlawful for a public authority to act in a way which is incompatible with a Convention right … (3) In this section "public authority" includes – (a) a court or tribunal, and (b) any person certain of whose functions are functions of a public nature … (5) In relation to a particular act, a person is not a public authority by virtue only of subsection (3)(b) if the nature of the act is private.

[6] Ibid.

[7] Ibid, 116.

[8] K Ewing, 'The Human Rights Act and Parliamentary Democracy' (1999) 62 *MLR* 79. On further issues of principle that explain Ewing's approach to the role of judges in human rights adjudication, see K Ewing, 'The Bill of Rights Debate: Democracy or Juristocracy in Britain?' in K Ewing, C Gearty and B Hepple (eds), *Human Rights and Labour Law* (London, Mansell, 1994) 147.

[9] See V Mantouvalou, 'Labour Rights in the European Convention on Human Rights: An Intellectual Justification for an Integrated Approach to Interpretation' (2013) 13 *Human Rights Law Review* 529, 532.

[10] Ewing, 'The Human Rights Act and Parliamentary Democracy' (n 8) 79. Cf A Kavanagh, *Constitutional Review Under the UK Human Rights Act* (Cambridge, CUP, 2005).

At the time that Ewing was writing in 1998, it was unclear whether the HRA would apply equally to public and private sector employers, namely whether it would have full horizontal effect. It was clear that the Act would not provide a direct cause of action against private employers, but the extent to which it would have indirect horizontal effect on the basis of section 3 was open to question. Ewing's concern was that the civil and political rights that we find in the ECHR/HRA are primarily addressed to state authorities, while social rights in the employment context are mostly about regulating the conduct of private employers.

However, it was established from early on that Convention rights apply in the private employment relation. The most significant decision on this is *X v Y*,[11] which involved the dismissal of a charity employee because his name was included in the sex offenders register for the reason that he was caught having consensual sexual intercourse with another man in a public space. The lawfulness of his dismissal had to be assessed under section 98 of the Employment Rights Act 1998 (ERA). Yet the further argument that was raised on the basis of section 3 of the HRA was that the test of fairness in dismissal should be interpreted in light of the HRA. The Court accepted that the ERA had to be interpreted in light of the HRA, according to section 3. In addition, considering whether the dismissal raised issues under article 8 of the ECHR (right to private life) in the private employment relationship, Mummery LJ said:

> In many cases it would be difficult to draw, let alone justify, a distinction between public authority and private employers. In the case of such a basic employment right there would normally be no sensible grounds for treating public and private employees differently in respect of unfair dismissal, especially in these times of widespread contracting out by public authorities to private contractors.[12]

The approach of the English courts to the issue of horizontality is in line with principles that we find in ECHR jurisprudence, which imposes a range of positive obligations on state authorities to protect individuals from violations of their rights by other private entities, including employers.[13] Even though the ECHR was drafted against the backdrop of atrocities committed by state authorities, the Court has developed positive obligations to legislate and enforce the law, which aim to protect human rights in the private sphere.[14] In this context, landmark labour law cases on positive obligations in the employment relation include *Wilson and Palmer v UK*,[15] to which I'll return, and *IB v Greece*[16] that involved the dismissal of an employee who was HIV-positive from his job in the private sector.

[11] *X v Y* [2004] EWCA Civ 662, [2004] ICR 1634 (CA).

[12] *X v Y* [57(4)]. See further V Mantouvalou, 'Human Rights and Unfair Dismissal: Private Acts in Public Spaces' (2008) 71 *MLR* 912.

[13] The HRA can also be used to interpret and develop common law principles. See, for instance, J Atkinson, 'Implied Terms and Human Rights in the Contract of Employment' (2019) *Industrial Law Journal*, available on advance access https://doi.org/10.1093/indlaw/dwz001.

[14] See D Spielmann, 'The European Convention on Human Rights – The European Court of Human Rights', in D Oliver and J Fedtke (eds), *Human Rights and the Private Sphere* (Abingdon, Routledge, 2007) 427; A Mowbray, *The Development of Positive Obligations Under the European Convention on Human Rights by the European Court of Human Rights* (Oxford, Hart Publishing, 2004). On this, see also the landmark *Marckx v Belgium* (1979) 2 EHRR 330.

[15] *Wilson, National Union of Journalists and Others v United Kingdom* (2002) 35 EHRR 523.

[16] *IB v Greece*, App No 552/10, Judgment of 3 October 2013.

II. Integrated Approach to the Interpretation of Civil and Political Rights

The rights of the HRA/ECHR are indirectly applicable in the private employment context, as has been clearly established. Are they relevant to the substantive regulation of the employment relation? One of the reasons that triggered Ewing's scepticism about the effect of the HRA on labour law was the fact that Convention rights are traditional civil and political rights, such as freedom of expression and the right to private life, with social rights, such as the right to work and the right to fair and just working conditions, being protected in the ESC, which is not incorporated in English law. UK governments have persistently resisted the legal protection of social rights through human rights law.[17]

Civil and political rights may of course be relevant to the employment relation. Like everyone else, employees have a right to privacy and a right to free speech, and these rights can be restricted both by the state and by the employer or other private entities. However, many wrongs that employees suffer in the workplace involve exploitation by the employer. It is primarily through social rights, such as the right to fair and just working conditions, that workers can be protected from these wrongs, but social rights are not explicitly included in the Convention.

The sharp divide between civil and social rights was indeed uncritically endorsed by the Court and the Commission in past case law. For about three decades, the ECtHR was reluctant to examine questions that raised social rights issues when these were brought under Convention provisions. If social rights materials, such as materials of the ILO or the ESC, were brought to their attention in support of a claim under the Convention, the Court and Commission viewed their inclusion in a separate document as a reason to reject the application. When applicants alleged that article 11 (the right to form and join a trade union), for instance, encompasses a right to strike, the claim was rejected.[18] Similarly, the right to consultation and the right of a union to be recognised for the purposes of collective bargaining were not regarded as essential components of article 11.[19] The Commission and Court created what has been called a 'ceiling effect';[20] the ceiling being, in this context, the ESC and the ILO. Claims that referred to the ESC were 'being used ingeniously as a source of restraint' as Ewing rightly observed,[21] rather than a source of inspiration as to the interpretation of Convention provisions.

However, the case law took an unpredictable turn in Strasbourg with *Wilson and Palmer* in 2002, when the Court adopted what has become known as an 'integrated approach to interpretation'.[22] It was described as an *integrated* approach, because it integrates certain socio-economic rights into a civil and political rights document. This integrated approach

[17] See K Ewing, 'Social Rights and Human Rights: Britain and the Social Charter – The Conservative Legacy' (2000) *European Human Rights Law Review* 91. See also the UK approach to the EU Charter of Fundamental Rights, which contains a long list of social and labour rights.

[18] *Schmidt and Dahlstrom v Sweden* A 21; 1 EHRR 637.

[19] *National Union of Belgian Police v Belgium* A 19; 1 EHRR 578.

[20] C Scott, 'Reaching Beyond (Without Abandoning) the Category of "Economic, Social and Cultural Rights"' (1999) 21 *Human Rights Quarterly* 633, 638–639.

[21] K Ewing, 'The Implications of Wilson and Palmer' (2003) 32 *Industrial Law Journal* 1, 3.

[22] See the discussion in Mantouvalou, above n 9.

characterises the work of the ILO more generally and has also been described as a 'holistic approach'.[23] Applied to the ECHR, it means that certain social and labour rights are essential elements of the Convention, and should therefore be protected as such. Instead of rejecting claims that could be viewed as grounded on social rights, the Court started to integrate them in the scope of the Convention, in order to make ECHR rights 'practical and effective' rather than 'theoretical and illusory'.[24]

In the area of labour rights, the adoption of the integrated approach is mainly found in the following fields: first, we have a line of cases that look at collective labour rights under article 11; second, case law that involves access to work and decent working conditions under articles 8 (the right to private life); and third, cases of particularly severe labour exploitation under article 4 (prohibition of slavery, servitude, forced and compulsory labour). In a series of cases, the Court took cognisance of social and labour rights materials of other international bodies that expanded the scope of the Convention. In *Sidabras and Dziautas v Lithuania*,[25] the Court read a social right, the right to work, in article 8 of the ECHR that protects the right to private life. *Siliadin v France*[26] held that lack of criminalisation of extremely harsh working conditions, such as those faced by the applicant migrant domestic worker, amounted to a breach of article 4. In making these findings, the Court relied on materials of the European Committee of Social Rights and the ILO in order to clarify the material scope of the Convention provisions. The adoption of this interpretive technique showed that the Court was open to labour rights. In a significant break with its past stance, the integrated approach brought social and labour rights a step closer.

The integrated approach to interpretation was best analysed by the Court itself in the landmark Grand Chamber case under article 11, *Demir and Baykara v Turkey*.[27] I am calling it landmark in this context because of its extensive analysis of the integrated approach, namely the interaction between the ECHR, on the one hand, and the ILO and other relevant international legal materials, on the other. The facts were as follows: Tum Bel Sen, a civil servants' trade union, had been recognised for the purposes of collective bargaining and had also concluded collective agreements. Following litigation, Turkish courts found that these agreements should be annulled. This was because civil servants' unions should not have been recognised a right to conclude them in the first place. In examining the complaint, the Court made mention of several ILO and other relevant documents, at which point Turkey raised an objection: how can it be legitimate for the Court to use ILO Conventions, even though Turkey had not signed and ratified some of them? How could the ECtHR impose on it international obligations that Turkey had never agreed to undertake?

[23] V Leary, 'The Paradox of Workers' Rights as Human Rights' in LA Compa and SF Diamond (eds), *Human Rights, Labor Rights and International Trade* (Pennsylvania, University of Pennsylvania Press, 1996) 22 at 40.

[24] On the principle that rights have to be practical and effective, see *Airey v Ireland* (1979–80) 2 EHRR 305.

[25] *Sidabras and Dziautas v Lithuania* 42 EHRR (2004) 104. For analysis of the case and discussion of the integrated approach, see V Mantouvalou, 'Work and Private Life: *Sidabras and Dziautas v Lithuania*' (2005) 30 *European Law Review* 573.

[26] *Siliadin v France* 43 EHRR (2006) 287. See V Mantouvalou, 'Servitude and Forced Labour in the 21st Century: The Human Rights of Domestic Workers' (2006) 35 *Industrial Law Journal* 395; H Cullen, '*Siliadin v France*: Positive Obligations Under Article 4 of the European Convention on Human Rights' (2006) 6 *Human Rights Law Review* 585.

[27] *Demir and Baykara v Turkey* 48 EHRR (2009) 54.

The Grand Chamber was clear: 'the Court has never considered the provisions of the Convention as the sole framework of reference'[28] for its interpretation. According to the rules of interpretation found in the Vienna Convention on the Law of Treaties, a treaty ought to be interpreted according to its object and purpose. The object and purpose of a document that protects human rights is to make these rights practical and effective, not theoretical and illusory.[29] The interpretation of the Convention must also take account of other rules of international law,[30] and to read it as a 'living' document in light of 'present-day conditions'.[31] Several materials can serve to elucidate the content of the Convention, both from other international organisations and from the Council of Europe itself. When taking note of the relevant materials, in addition, the Court stressed, it never distinguishes between documents that the respondent state has signed and ratified, and those that it has not.[32] Not only that, but at times it has paid attention to materials that are not, in any case, legally binding, such as the EU Charter of Fundamental Rights.[33]

The *Demir and Baykara* case was celebrated in scholarship by Ewing and Hendy. They described it as 'epoch-making' for being a 'decision in which social and economic rights have been fused permanently with civil and political rights, in a process that is potentially nothing less than a socialization of civil and political rights'.[34] They also said that in this decision 'human rights have established their superiority over economic irrationalism and "competitiveness" in the battle for the soul of labour law, and in which public law has triumphed over private law and public lawyers over private lawyers'.[35]

However, it turned out that *Demir and Baykara* did not mark a permanent reorientation for the Court. Materials of the ESC and the ILO were frequently invoked in subsequent case law, and sometimes endorsed by the Court, as it sought to establish a European or international consensus on difficult social and political questions. But it soon became evident that civil and social rights were not permanently fused. In *RMT v UK*,[36] the applicants invoked a wealth of international and regional materials in support of their claim that English law violated article 11 of the ECHR because of its blanket ban of secondary industrial action.[37] The Court said that these might indeed be relevant, but could not be viewed as decisive because the nature of review in Strasbourg is different to the supervision by the ILO and the ECSR:[38]

> … the Court considers that the negative assessments made by the relevant monitoring bodies of the ILO and European Social Charter are not of such persuasive weight for determining whether the operation of the statutory ban on secondary strikes in circumstances such as those complained of in the present case remained within the range of permissible options open to the national authorities under Article 11 of the Convention.

[28] Ibid at para 65.
[29] Ibid at para 66.
[30] Ibid at para 67.
[31] Ibid at para 68.
[32] Ibid at para 78.
[33] Ibid at para 80. For analysis against the background of Strasbourg's methods of interpretation more generally, see G Letsas, 'Strasbourg's Interpretive Ethic: Lessons for the International Lawyer' (2010) 21 *European Journal of International Law* 509, 521–523.
[34] K Ewing and J Hendy, 'The Dramatic Implications of Demir and Baykara' (2010) 39 *Industrial Law Journal* 2, 47.
[35] Ibid, 47–48.
[36] *RMT v UK* (2015) 60 EHRR 10.
[37] Ibid at para 57.
[38] Ibid at para 98.

The case *Unite The Union v UK*[39] was described as 'another disappointment in Strasbourg'[40] for not merging ESC rights with the Convention, but other recent case law on the right to strike was open to the use of ILO materials in order to find a violation of the Convention.[41] At domestic level, the judiciary was still reluctant to rely on materials of the ILO, as it became particularly evident in a case on injunctions for strike action, where these were invoked, described as interesting but then dismissed.[42]

To conclude, while the evolution of the case law is by no means linear, there is a noticeable change in the pattern when looking at pre-2002 and post-2002 case law. The ECtHR no longer views non-Convention materials as outright outside the scope of the Convention. It takes note of them and discusses them when they are invoked by applicants, and this has led to an opening up of the scope of the ECHR in the area of economic and social rights. This has not made the ECHR a balanced document in its protection of economic liberty, on the one hand, and political and social equality, on the other (to use Ewing's terminology).[43] However, it has put into question the traditional sharp separation of the two categories of rights that has been strongly supported by consecutive UK governments, and which partly underlies Ewing's scepticism on the HRA.

III. Structure of Convention Rights

The scepticism on the effect of the HRA on labour law that we find in Ewing's 1998 piece was not only limited to the exclusion of social rights from the scope of the Act. It was also due to the fact that many Convention rights are qualified, rather than absolute, which means that they may be restricted by the employer if there is a legitimate aim. The ECtHR applies a test of proportionality when it implements these rights, examining whether the limitation of a right is proportionate to the aim pursued. Despite the fact that many ECHR rights are not absolute, articles 8–11 of the ECHR, have had a significant impact on the employment relationship, either thanks to Strasbourg case law, or, perhaps more rarely, domestic jurisprudence.[44] The same observation can be made in relation to article 6, the right to a fair trial, which has a different structure to the aforementioned provisions, but is at times construed as a qualified right by the ECtHR when it examines the 'essence of the right' and applies a 'sui generis proportionality test'.[45] I will illustrate the effect of these provisions on the employment relation through a line of leading cases.

[39] *Unite the Union v UK* (2016) 63 EHRR SE7.

[40] K Arabadjieva, 'Another Disappointment in Strasbourg: Unite the Union v United Kingdom' (2017) 46 *Industrial Law Journal* 289.

[41] See *Ognevenko v Russia* (2019) 69 EHRR 9 and *Association of Academics v Iceland* (2018) 67 EHRR SE4. See the discussion in T Novitz, 'Protecting the Right to Strike in the ILO and the European Court of Human Rights: The Significance of Appn No 44873/09 Ognevenko v Russia' (*UK Labour Law Blog*, 8 April 2019) https://wordpress.com/view/uklabourlawblog.com.

[42] *Metrobus Ltd v UNITE the Union* [2009] EWCA Civ 829, [2009] 7 WLUK 854.

[43] Ewing, 'The Unbalanced Constitution' (n 5).

[44] See generally H Collins and V Mantouvalou, 'The Employment Contract and Human Rights' in M Freedland (ed) *The Contract of Employment* (Oxford, OUP, 2016).

[45] See D Vitkauskas and G Dikov, *Protecting the Right to a Fair Trial under the European Convention on Human Rights* (Strasbourg, Council of Europe, 2012) 9.

A. Qualified Rights

In the past, when assessing contractual terms that in effect waive fundamental rights, some decisions in connection with interference with the right to manifest a religion in the workplace under the Convention acknowledged that if an employee could resign and obtain another job, there was no violation of the ECHR since no-one was preventing the employee from manifesting a religion.[46] This approach suggested a fundamental misunderstanding of the employment relation, which is a relationship of submission and subordination, where the employer offers the terms on a take it or leave it basis and can unilaterally change them, against a background of scarcity of jobs. It is misleading to think that people can easily leave their job and take another job that matches their needs and interests, even if their current employer restricts their human rights. In 2013, however, the Court changed its approach to this matter. In *Eweida v UK*,[47] a majority in ECtHR held that:

> [g]iven the importance in a democratic society of freedom of religion, the Court considers that, where an individual complains of a restriction on freedom of religion in the workplace, rather than holding that the possibility of changing job would negate any interference with the right, the better approach would be to weigh that possibility in the overall balance when considering whether or not the restriction was proportionate.

The underlying rationale of this change in the Court's case law was probably that any decision to consent to limitations of rights in the workplace is unlikely to be voluntary, because for reasons of economic necessity the possibility of resignation is rarely a viable alternative.[48]

The reluctance of the Court to accept waivers of Convention rights through the employment contract because of the legal subordination of the employee was reaffirmed and further clarified in *Barbulescu v Romania*.[49] The case involved the question of whether the applicant, a sales engineer, who was dismissed from his job for using his work Yahoo Messenger account for private communications with his partner and brother on his health and sex life, suffered a violation of article 8 rights. Mr Barbulescu had signed internal regulations that prohibited using computers for personal purposes. When his employer found out that he had used his work Messenger account for communications that involved intimate aspects of his private life, he was dismissed. In examining the question of the reasonable expectation of privacy in light of the fact that the applicant had signed up to the internal regulations, the ECtHR said:

> an employer's instructions cannot reduce private social life in the workplace to zero. Respect for private life and for the privacy of correspondence continues to exist, even if these may be restricted in so far as necessary.[50]

This remarkable passage suggests that the Court sets limits on the extent to which the employee can agree to a waiver of human rights through the employment contract.

[46] *Stedman v UK* (1997) 23 EHRR CD168. See also G Morris, 'Fundamental Rights: Exclusion by Agreement?' (2001) 30 *Industrial Law Journal* 49.

[47] *Eweida and Others v UK* (2013) 57 EHRR 8.

[48] R McCrea, 'Religion in the Workplace: *Eweida and Others v UK*' (2014) 77 *MLR* 277.

[49] *Barbulescu v Romania*, App No 61496/08, Grand Chamber judgment of 5 September 2017, para 117. Noted by J Atkinson, 'Workplace Monitoring and the Right to Private Life at Work' (2018) 81 *MLR* 688.

[50] *Barbulescu* (n 49) para 80.

The Court has examined dismissals that engage Convention rights many times in recent years, and has often exhibited an appreciation of the particularities of the employment context.[51] Perhaps the most elaborate case on dismissal that violates Convention rights was the Grand Chamber judgment in *Denisov v Ukraine*.[52] This examined the question in detail under article 8 of the ECHR, and analysed the reasons that can give rise to a violation of the provision because of a dismissal. The Court said that it may be violated both when someone is dismissed because of his or her private activities, and when the dismissal has a significant impact on the employee's reputation. Cases such as *Eweida*, *Barbulescu* and *Denisov* indicate that the Court is willing to take seriously the character of human rights as inalienable rights, which cannot be taken away unless there is a legitimate reason, and in a manner that is proportionate to the aim pursued.

Against the background of these Strasbourg developments, it may be time to revisit the test of fairness in dismissal in English law.[53] In a famous passage from *Turner v East Midland Trains Ltd*, having gone through ECHR case law, Elias LJ said that 'Strasbourg therefore adopts a light touch when reviewing human rights in the context of the employment relationship', and went on to suggest that '[i]t may even be that the domestic band of reasonable responses test protects human rights more effectively'.[54] Given recent developments, particularly cases such as *Denisov*, it is questionable whether the test is compatible with ECHR standards. Strasbourg applies a stricter test than the test of reasonableness under section 98 of the Employment Rights Act 1996, which recognises great discretion to managerial prerogative. The Strasbourg Court's approach to workers' rights brings the law closer to the inalienability of moral human rights, namely the fact that human rights cannot be easily taken away through employers' power, without strict scrutiny of the lawfulness of the employer's decision.[55]

In addition to the above cases that reflect the character of human rights as inalienable rights in the workplace, there is also case law that supports the universality of human rights at work, expanding the personal scope of protection of labour legislation. This can be illustrated by the case *Redfearn v United Kingdom*.[56] In this case the ECtHR held that dismissal for membership of a political party is an interference with the right to freedom of association in article 11 of the ECHR. Such a dismissal should therefore be unlawful unless in the circumstances of the particular case the dismissal was a proportionate measure taken in pursuit of a legitimate aim pursued by an employer. Mr Redfearn's dismissal had resulted from his active membership of the British National Party (BNP), an extreme right-wing political party, which is notorious for its anti-immigration and anti-EU positions.[57] The reason why the claim was brought to Strasbourg was because the

[51] *Obst v Germany*, App No 425/03; *Schuth v Germany* (2011) 52 EHRR 32. Judgments of 23 September 2010; *IB v Greece* (n 16); Cf *Pay v UK* (2009) 48 EHRR SE2. Cf *Palomo Sanchez v Spain* (2012) 54 EHRR 24. But see also the strong and persuasive dissenting opinion of Tulkens et al.

[52] *Denisov v Ukraine*, App No 76639/11, Grand Chamber judgment of 25 September 2018.

[53] See generally, H Collins, *Justice in Dismissal* (Oxford, OUP, 1992). H Collins, 'The Protection of Civil Liberties in the Workplace' (2006) 69 *MLR* 619; V Mantouvalou, 'Human Rights and Unfair Dismissal' (n 12).

[54] *Turner v East Midland Trains ltd* [2012] EWCA Civ 1470, [2013] ICR 505 [56].

[55] H Collins and V Mantouvalou, 'Human Rights and the Contract of Employment' in M Freedland (ed) *The Contract of Employment* (Oxford, OUP, 2016) 188.

[56] *Redfearn v United Kingdom* (2013) 57 EHRR 2.

[57] British National Party, *Democracy, Culture, Freedom and Identity: General Election Manifesto* (April 2010) 5; http://communications.bnp.org.uk/ge2010manifesto.pdf.

dismissal occurred during the qualifying period, when employees have extremely limited protection. The Strasbourg Court ruled that dismissal for political activity during the qualifying period may violate the Convention, and that there should be a test examining the legality of such dismissals.[58]

At domestic level, the HRA has also given rise to cases that challenge arbitrary exclusions from the personal scope of Convention rights. A significant decision on this issue is *Vining*,[59] a case that involved the exclusion of parks police from unfair dismissal protection and collective redundancy consultation. The argument was made that these exclusions contravened, first, the right to private life (alone and together with the prohibition of discrimination) and second, the right to freedom of association under article 11 (alone and together with the prohibition of discrimination). The Court of Appeal went through Strasbourg case law on unfair dismissal, including *Sidabras*, *IB* and *Martinez v Spain*,[60] and concluded that not all dismissals engage article 8 of the ECHR. Even though it recognised that economic redundancies may give rise to article 8 issues, it ruled that this did not occur in the instant case. As to the second claim regarding the exclusion from redundancy consultation, the Court said that consultation for collective redundancy should be viewed as an essential component of article 11 of the ECHR. It concluded that the legislation that excludes the police force should be interpreted in a manner that is compatible with article 11 so as not to apply to parks police. In this way, it expanded the personal scope of the protection to cover a category of workers that was excluded. It remains to be seen whether this line of thinking will be used to challenge exclusions in the context of the gig economy, where workers are sometimes classified as self-employed, with the implication that they are excluded from the enjoyment of certain Convention rights.[61]

The right to a fair trial, to which Ewing referred in his 1998 article,[62] has also played a significant role in the employment context. Even though it does not usually apply in internal disciplinary procedures of the employers,[63] it applies when workers claim legal rights. In *Benkharbouche*,[64] the applicants who were working in foreign embassies in London brought claims of breaches of the law on dismissal, minimum wage and working time, as well as discrimination and harassment. These were barred because of the State Immunity Act 1978. Section 4 of the Act says that there is no immunity for contracts of employment with an individual in the UK, where the work performed by that individual will be 'wholly or partly' in the UK. However, section 16(1)(a) provides that 'section 4 does not apply to proceedings concerning the employment of members of a mission', namely embassy staff.

[58] H Collins and V Mantouvalou, 'Redfearn v UK: Political Association and Dismissal' (2013) 76 *MLR* 909.

[59] *Vining & Ors v London Borough of Wandsworth & Anor* [2017] EWCA Civ 1092, [2018] ICR 499.

[60] *Fernandez Martinez v Spain* (2015) 60 EHRR 3.

[61] *R (The IWGB) v Central Arbitration Committee* [2018] EWHC 3342 (Admin), [2018] 12 WLUK 17. Cf *Pastoral Cel Bun v Romania* (2014) 58 EHRR 10, which found that an 'employment relationship' is necessary for the right to form and join trade unions. For critical analyses, see J Atkinson and H Dhorajiwala, '*IWGB v RooFoods*: Status, Rights and Substitution' (2019) 48 *Industrial Law Journal* 278; A Bogg, 'Taken for a Ride: Workers in the Gig Economy' (2019) *LQR* 219.

[62] Ewing, 'The Human Rights Act and Labour Law' (n 1) 278–279.

[63] See A Sanders, 'Does Article 6 of the European Convention on Human Rights Apply to Disciplinary Procedures in the Workplace?' (2013) 33 *OJLS* 791.

[64] *Benkharbouche (Respondent) v Secretary of State for Foreign and Commonwealth Affairs (Appellant) and Secretary of State for Foreign and Commonwealth Affairs and Libya (Appellants) v Janah (Respondent)* [2017] UKSC 62, [2017] 3 WLR 957.

The UK Supreme Court (UKSC) had to decide whether this complies with article 6 of the ECHR on the right to a fair trial, as well as article 47 of the EU Charter of Fundamental Rights on the right to an effective remedy and a right to a fair trial, given that the case had an EU law element.[65] It ruled that the provisions of the State Immunity Act 1978 were incompatible with article 6 of the Convention (and article 47 of the EU Charter). This case could potentially help other situations in which legislation prevents access to the courts to protect labour law rights.

Finally, before concluding this section, mention should be made of *UNISON*,[66] a case of great significance in the employment field that ruled that the fees for bringing claims to employment tribunals were unlawful as a matter of common law and EU law. Even though the UKSC did not decide the case on the basis of article 6 of the ECHR, the provision had a supporting role to common law principles and article 47 of the EU Charter of Fundamental Rights.[67] Such was the importance of the case that Michael Ford described it as an 'important triumph of a revitalised rule of law',[68] and 'a powerful normative lens through which to scrutinise the practical realisation of employment and other social rights'.[69] These cases on access to justice underline the central or supporting value of Convention civil and political rights for the vindication of workers' economic and social rights.[70]

B. Absolute Rights

Another development that needs to be mentioned in this overview has been the case law under one of the absolute (rather than qualified) rights, article 4 of the ECHR that prohibits slavery, servitude, forced and compulsory labour. In his 1998 article, Ewing did not consider the effect of article 4 of the Convention on labour law. This is understandable, as at the time that the ECHR was incorporated in English law, the case law under article 4 was very limited, and the ECtHR and Commission had never found a breach of the provision. However, in 2005, in *Siliadin v France*, the Court ruled that the ill-treatment of a migrant domestic worker should be classified as servitude, and that the ECHR imposes a positive obligation to criminalise severe labour exploitation. This was the first case in which Strasbourg ruled that there was a breach of article 4 of the ECHR, and has been followed by cases involving sex trafficking, and other instances of severe labour exploitation.[71] This line of cases led to the

[65] The Working Time Regulations implement the EU Working Time Directive. For further analysis for the implications of the case in relation to the Charter, see A Young, 'Benkharbouche and the Future of Disapplication' (*UK Constitutional Law Blog*, 24 October 2017) https://ukconstitutionallaw.org/2017/10/24/alison-young-benkharbouche-and-the-future-of-disapplication/.

[66] *R (on the application of UNISON) (Appellant) v Lord Chancellor (Respondent)* [2017] UKSC 51, [2017] 3 WLR 409, noted by A Bogg, 'The Common Law Constitution at Work: *R (on the application of UNISON)* v *Lord Chancellor*' (2018) 81 *MLR* 509. See also M Ford, 'Employment Tribunal Fees and the Rule of Law: *R (Unison) v Lord Chancellor* in the Supreme Court' (2018) 47 *Industrial Law Journal* 1.

[67] *UNISON* (n 66) [108]–[117].

[68] Ford (n 66) 44.

[69] Ibid.

[70] The ECtHR recognised the links between civil and social rights in the context of article 6 early on in its case law. See *Airey v Ireland* (n 24).

[71] *Rantsev v Cyprus and Russia* (2010) 51 EHRR 1; *CN v UK* (2013) 56 EHRR 24; *Chowdury and Others v Greece*, App No 21885/15, Judgment of 30 March 2017.

adoption of new legislation in the UK. We first saw the introduction of section 71 of the UK Coroners and Justice Act 2009, entitled 'slavery, servitude, and forced or compulsory labour', and later on the Modern Slavery Act 2015 (MSA), which codified criminal legislation on slavery, servitude, forced and compulsory labour, and human trafficking.[72] The MSA brings English law in line with the substantive requirement under the ECHR to criminalise, but it is questionable whether it also brings it in line with the procedural obligation to enforce effectively the legislation. At the same time it raises questions on how genuine the government's commitment to protect workers from severe labour exploitation is, for the reason that it has not taken further steps to remove structural factors that create vulnerability to exploitation, as the example of the treatment of migrant domestic workers shows.[73]

IV. Collective Labour Law

The third key concern in Ewing's 1998 piece involved collective labour law. As was said earlier, in a line of cases that were decided in the 1970s, 1980s and 1990s, the ECtHR repeatedly ruled that when a right can be classified as social and protected in the ESC or in instruments of the ILO, it ought to be excluded from the ECHR. When applicants alleged that article 11 encompasses a right to strike, for instance, the claim was rejected.[74] Similarly, the right to consultation and the right of a union to be recognised for the purposes of collective bargaining were not regarded as essential components of article 11.[75] At the same time as the Court was reluctant to protect trade union rights, it was willing to protect individuals who did not want to be trade union members in the 'closed shop' cases.[76] The approach of the Court in these cases led Tonia Novitz to argue that the Court shows 'a greater interest on the defence of individual autonomy than collective solidarity',[77] and Lord Wedderburn described the case law as 'individual and formalistic'.[78] Ewing said that 'the contribution of article 11 to date has been disappointing, failing to deliver any meaningful protection for trade union activities, while being used as an instrument for undermining trade union security',[79] and that 'from a trade union point of view, Article 11 was showing a debit balance'.[80]

However, *Wilson and Palmer* introduced a new way of thinking about labour law and human rights in the area of the right to form and join a trade union. The case involved the discriminatory treatment of workers who chose to continue having their working

[72] Sexual Offences Act 2003, ss 57–59; Asylum and Immigration (Treatment of Claimants) Act 2004, s 4, as amended by Protection of Freedoms Act 2012, ss 109 and 110, and Coroners and Justice Act 2009, s 71.

[73] I analyse the Act and develop the criticisms in V Mantouvalou, 'The UK Modern Slavery Act 2015 Three Years On' (2018) 81 *MLR* 1017.

[74] *Schmidt and Dahlstrom v Sweden* A 21; 1 EHRR 637.

[75] *National Union of Belgian Police v Belgium* A 19; 1 EHRR 578.

[76] *Young, James and Webster* (n 4).

[77] T Novitz, *International and European Protection of the Right to Strike* (Oxford, Oxford University Press, 2003) 238.

[78] Lord Wedderburn, 'Freedom of Association or Right to Organise? The Common Law and International Sources' in Lord Wedderburn (ed) *Employment Rights in Britain and Europe* (London, Lawrence and Wishart 1991) 138 at 144.

[79] Ewing, 'The Human Rights Act and Labour Law' (n 1) 279.

[80] Ewing, 'The Implications of Wilson and Palmer' (n 21) 4.

conditions governed by a collective agreement, rather than a personal contract negotiated between the employer and the workers. The fact that UK law permitted employers to treat less favourably these workers who were not prepared to renounce 'a freedom that was an essential feature of union membership'[81] was found to be in breach of article 11, in a case that Ewing described as representing 'a significant break with the past', where the ECtHR went 'a long way to restore confidence in Article 11 of the Convention'.[82] *Wilson and Palmer* was 'the most important labour law decision for at least a generation, and is all the more important for the unusual fact that the trade unions won a considerable victory'.[83] Yet Ewing also expressed a word of caution in light of other case law: he said that 'it may be premature to pop the champagne corks to celebrate judicial defection in the class war'.[84]

After *Wilson*, the most important development was *Demir and Baykara*, which was discussed earlier. Here the Court ruled that the invalidation of a collective agreement that had been concluded between the union and the employer constituted a violation of article 11. As was said above, this case was not only significant for its substantive ruling, but also because of the reasoning by which the ruling was reached, and it was celebrated in labour law scholarship, and particularly by Ewing and Hendy.

However, the stance of Ewing and other labour law scholars changed following *RMT v United Kingdom*.[85] Here the Court addressed the issue of secondary industrial action, which is banned in English law. The applicant union of transport workers suggested that the ban violated their rights under article 11 of the Convention. The applicants were all members of the RMT union. They were initially employed by a company called Jarvis, and were then transferred to a smaller company, Hydrex. Their terms and conditions were at first kept as they were, according to a legal requirement, but deteriorated later on. Industrial action by Hydrex employees only would not be effective, so RMT sought to organise industrial action at the bigger company, Jarvis, but as English law does not protect secondary action, it was not possible to do this. The Court accepted that secondary action falls within the scope of article 11. It affirmed on the one hand that the right to strike is 'clearly protected' under article 11. On this basis, Bogg and Ewing stated that '[t]here is now a right to strike, albeit forged in jurisprudence rather than created by statute, and albeit emerging improbably from the Human Rights Act rather than purposefully from a dedicated statute drafted for this purpose'.[86] However, the Court ruled on the other hand that the ban on secondary industrial action in English law was justified under article 11(2) of the ECHR, as the state enjoys a wide margin of appreciation. *RMT* was therefore heavily criticised by Bogg and Ewing, who suggested that the Court was 'weak, bullied and timid'.[87]

The *RMT* judgment has been followed by further article 11 cases, which have disappointed labour law scholars, to the extent that Ewing and Hendy argued in a recent piece that there is an article 11(3) in the ECHR, which is 'created by and visible only to the judges of the European Court of Human Rights. This provides as follows: "(3) The foregoing provisions

[81] *Wilson and Palmer* (n 15) para 47.
[82] Ewing, 'The Implications of Wilson and Palmer' (n 21) 5.
[83] Ibid, 20.
[84] Ewing, 'The Implications of Wilson and Palmer' (n 21) 21.
[85] *RMT v United Kingdom* (n 36). See A Bogg and K Ewing 'The Implications of the *RMT* Case' (2014) 43 *Industrial Law Journal* 221.
[86] A Bogg and K Ewing (n 85) 222.
[87] Ibid, 251.

of this Article shall not apply to the United Kingdom".[88] In this piece, the authors placed special attention to the politics of the ECHR, and criticised the Court for 'subordinating justice to politics' in its decisions on UK compliance.[89]

V. Human Rights Instrumentalism

The above overview of the case law of Strasbourg and domestic courts shows that the Convention has brought about significant improvements in the scope of workers' rights at Council of Europe level, and at times in English law. Certain arbitrary exclusions have been challenged, and some changes have been introduced in the legislative framework that would not have occurred had we not had this human rights document. These changes are significant but also relatively limited. This reality may be explained to a certain degree by the character of the judiciary in the UK that is often criticised for being conservative, the composition of the legislature, and the sensitive task of the Strasbourg Court as a supranational court.[90]

It was noted earlier that as the case law evolved, so did Ewing's approach towards human rights in his academic scholarship. From deep scepticism in the early days, his position changed into increasing enthusiasm with cases such as *Wilson and Palmer* and *Demir and Baykara*, and then deep disappointment following *RMT*. The changes in Ewing's stance towards human rights, in his sole-authored and co-authored work, can be explained. Labour law scholars usually approach these rights instrumentally. When courts are willing to protect workers' rights, scholars endorse them in academic work and support the use of human rights in litigation. When litigation fails, their disenchantment leads to a rejection of this way of framing workers' claims and to scepticism about human rights altogether.

The instrumental approach to the protection of labour rights as human rights is evident in much labour law literature.[91] Its roots lie in the Marxist tradition that approaches the legal system with pragmatism, as Collins explains.[92] Certain legal rights, such as the right to join political associations, are useful for the promotion of the interests of the working class in this context, and these are endorsed by Marxian thinkers.[93] Bogg also suggested that this approach towards human rights is grounded on a 'radically empiricist ethos': 'the best test of a theory was not its elegance or its cleverness, but whether it worked: did it improve the lives of real people? That was also the metric for evaluating fundamental rights'.[94] On this analysis,

[88] K Ewing and J Hendy, 'Article 11(3) of the European Convention on Human Rights (2017) *European Human Rights Law Review* 356.

[89] Ibid, 375.

[90] On this latter point, see, for instance, D Spielmann, 'Whither the Margin of Appreciation?' (2014) 67 *Current Legal Problems* 49.

[91] I develop this in V Mantouvalou, 'Are Labour Rights Human Rights?' (2012) 3 *European Labour Law Journal* 151, 156.

[92] On the Marxist approach towards legal rights, see the discussion in H Collins, *Marxism and the Law* (Oxford, OUP, 1982) 142 ff.

[93] Ibid.

[94] A Bogg, 'The Hero's Journey: Lord Wedderburn and the "Political Constitution" of Labour Law' (2015) 44 *Industrial Law Journal* 299, 316.

> [t]he imperative to present [workers'] claims as human rights comes from the desire to utilise the potentially powerful legal methods of securing advantage to pursue their claims, and also from the perceived need to respond to employers' willingness to use these arguments and tools themselves.[95]

This strategic use of human rights law can be powerful and important, but it also carries some dangers. For instance, if a case is lost in courts, it is then harder to question the outcome than if we only had a political decision, which could be challenged through activism. A judicial decision may legitimise the employer's conduct, making it harder to then challenge it through politics.

That many labour law scholars' approach towards human rights is instrumental should by no means be viewed as suggesting that it is not grounded on moral principles. One of Ewing's key concerns, as we know from his work, is the lack of balance in the ECHR/HRA between liberty, on the one hand, and equality, on the other. Liberty in the British Constitution is analysed as economic liberty and encapsulated in civil and political rights primarily, and equality, analysed as political and social equality, in social rights. The incorporation of the HRA in English law reasserted this economic liberty and gave it 'a new legal priority'.[96] On this basis, no deep transformation of the inequality of economic power could ever be brought about without the incorporation of social rights into domestic law and without a change in the UK's stance towards the ESC and the findings of the European Committee of Social Rights. On this matter and looking at the bigger picture, Ewing was right. Without the incorporation of social rights in English law, there will be limitations to the arguments that can be brought and to the decisions that can be reached in order to address workers' submission and subordination.

Yet it is also important to appreciate that human rights are not just legal standards that are implemented by courts. Parliamentary committees, such as the UK Joint Committee on Human Rights, also consider domestic human rights issues that are not only limited in the ECHR/HRA.[97] Even more importantly perhaps, human rights are normative standards that exist outside the law and irrespective of whether litigation and other mechanisms are a successful strategy.[98] They are grounded on values such as dignity, equality and freedom, and have great moral force. Human rights theory itself can offer an important critical focus, a list of moral standards against which legislation, including human rights law, can be assessed, on the basis of which it can be criticised, and towards which it should develop. When the approach of courts disappoints, there should be calls for change, both at domestic level and at European level, so that the case law of courts and the legislation reflect these moral standards. This is an important task for labour law scholarship, and I hope that this is one with which labour lawyers will continue to engage.

[95] C Fenwick and T Novitz, 'Conclusion: Regulating to Protect Workers' Human Rights' in C Fenwick and T Novitz (eds), *Human Rights at Work: Perspectives on Law and Regulation* (Oxford, Hart Publishing, 2010) 587–588.

[96] Ewing, 'The Unbalanced Constitution' (n 5) 116.

[97] See A Kavanagh, 'The Joint Committee on Human Rights: A Hybrid Breed of Constitutional Watchdog', in M Hunt, HJ Hooper and P Yowell (eds) *Parliaments and Human Rights – Redressing the Democratic Deficit* (Oxford, Hart Publishing, 2015) 115.

[98] On three different approaches to labour rights as human rights, see Mantouvalou (n 91). On human rights as normative foundations of labour law, see J Atkinson, 'Human Rights as Foundations for Labour Law' in H Collins, G Lester and V Mantouvalou (eds) *Philosophical Foundations of Labour Law* (Oxford, OUP, 2018).

PART II

Parliament in the Social Democratic Constitution

5

Parliamentary Sovereignty and Constitutional Futures

MICHAEL GORDON*

Parliamentary sovereignty offers the potential to deliver democratic political change. The doctrine ascribes to the UK Parliament a legislative power which is legally unlimited, and can in principle be used to remake any aspect of our social, economic, legal and political order. This possibility provides a basis for the justification of the doctrine of parliamentary sovereignty as the UK's fundamental constitutional principle, and is strongly evident in the work of Keith Ewing.[1] At the same time, however, the idea of parliamentary sovereignty can be seen as an ostensibly archaic basis for a modern constitution, and its implications are increasingly misunderstood or misrepresented. The doctrine appears to have survived a period of doubt, among judicial actors and others,[2] and remains almost unshakably central in the UK's contemporary constitutional system. Yet if the endurance of the doctrine as the fundamental principle of the UK Constitution appears to have been reemphasised by the decision to exit the European Union, at the same time, scepticism about the potential of parliamentary sovereignty has been very much renewed.[3]

This scepticism about the potential of parliamentary sovereignty has a number of dimensions. The potential for change which parliamentary sovereignty symbolises and supports might seem increasingly beyond reach in a time of political and administrative turmoil induced by Brexit, with the UK stuck in a period of constitutional overload which may continue for an unknowable period of time.[4] In this context, the idea that parliamentary

* With thanks to Alison Young for valuable comments on my draft text, and to Keith Ewing for all of his generous support.

[1] See, eg, KD Ewing, 'The Resilience of the Political Constitution' (2013) 14 *German Law Journal* 2111; KD Ewing, *The Bonfire of the Liberties: New Labour, Human Rights and the Rule of Law* (Oxford, OUP, 2010) ch 8.

[2] In the courts, see especially the doubts in *R (Jackson) v Attorney General* [2005] UKHL 56, [2006] 1 AC 262. In the academic literature, see especially TRS Allan, *The Sovereignty of Law* (Oxford, OUP, 2013); V Bogdanor, *The New British Constitution* (Oxford, Hart Publishing, 2009) and 'Imprisoned by a Doctrine: The Modern Defence of Parliamentary Sovereignty' (2012) 32 *OJLS* 179.

[3] See, eg, S Douglas-Scott, 'Brexit, Article 50 and the Contested British Constitution' (2016) 79 *MLR* 1019; V Bogdanor, *Brexit and Our Unprotected Constitution* (London, The Constitution Society, 2018).

[4] M Gordon, 'Constitutional Overload in a Constitutional Democracy: The UK and the Brexit Process' in S Garben, I Govaere and P Nemitz (eds), *Critical Reflections on Constitutional Democracy in the European Union* (Oxford, Hart Publishing, 2019).

sovereignty can be an instrument through which to pursue positive democratic change – as opposed to the reactive, erratic and hasty reordering of our legal and political system – can appear as if an unattainable holy grail. Parliamentary sovereignty might instead seem synonymous with the empowerment of Westminster elites, to the detriment of the other nations of the UK, the other regions of England, and the citizens in whose name democratic authority ought to be exercised. In this discordant climate, we can see fundamental constitutional disagreements of different kinds at different levels. This includes disagreement between these different groups and actors about where democratic authority should be vested, how it should be exercised, and the substantive ends of political power. These deep rooted questions necessarily prompt debate about the constitutional framework in which democratic authority exists – in this context, among other things, there may be disputes about what kind of change can be delivered through the ordinary democratic process, whether the outcomes of that process should be substantively constrained, and whether there are certain categories of decision that require additional layers of democratic engagement. Against such a complex backdrop, the sovereignty of the UK Parliament might, understandably, seem an anaemic basis on which to structure the operation of the state.

Such multi-dimensional scepticism has potentially far reaching implications, for it can call into question both aspects of the doctrine of parliamentary sovereignty: the location and the scope of the law-making power which is established in accordance with this doctrine become open to challenge. For we can see reasons for scepticism about, first, the appropriateness of locating power in the UK Parliament in particular, and second, the propriety of allowing democratic power to be unconstrained by law, and left hostage to the ebbs and flows of party political fortune. As a result, parliamentary sovereignty might persist in the UK as a matter of constitutional law, but the constitutional legitimacy of both the 'parliamentary' and the 'sovereign' character of this doctrine might simultaneously be in question.

Yet there is also a more fundamental problem for a democratic account of parliamentary sovereignty. Parliamentary sovereignty may offer the potential to deliver a range of different constitutional futures, and this may be contested, both in terms of the substance of the constitutional futures themselves, and the suitability of parliamentary sovereignty as the vehicle for their pursuit. But in such circumstances, if the potential of parliamentary sovereignty is to be tangible, there must be some degree of clarity about the possible destinations. And it is for this reason that doubts about the potential of parliamentary sovereignty to deliver democratic political change may intensify – while constitutional reform has remained on the political agenda in the past two decades as perhaps never before,[5] we have a remarkably narrow conception of what the UK's constitutional future might look like. The appeal of radical constitutional alternatives is inevitably diminished if constitutional radicalism is simply an abstract idea, with little purchase in the real world. If this is the case, the potential of parliamentary sovereignty to deliver democratic political change becomes a theoretical nicety rather than a plausible prospect. And this may also diminish the appeal of

[5] See generally R Brazier, *Constitutional Reform: Reshaping the British Political System*, 3rd edn (Oxford, OUP, 2008), D Oliver, *Constitutional Reform in the UK* (Oxford, OUP, 2006).

parliamentary sovereignty as a constitutional fundamental, if – in practice – the doctrine is deprived of one of its core virtues.

Consequently, if we are to defend a constitutional vision founded on the idea that it is desirable to sustain the potential for democratic political change, we need to map out much more clearly what that potential might offer. Otherwise, it is entirely possible for that potential to continue to go unrecognised, unfulfilled, or over time to be diluted. For although the retention of parliamentary sovereignty itself provides a crucial starting point for facilitating significant political change, it is simply a starting point, and does not inherently guarantee that this potential will be exploited. Indeed, while parliamentary sovereignty is a key component of the UK's political constitution, it does not provide a singular constitutional model. Instead, the doctrine is compatible with different kinds of political constitutions, and it may be seen to perform different functions, and be exploited in different ways, depending on the principles (and the politics) which underpin the broader constitutional framework in which it operates.[6]

The constitutional ideas developed in this chapter are not, therefore, ones which inherently flow from an acceptance of parliamentary sovereignty, nor do they offer a direction of travel which all those who recognise the constitutional force of this doctrine must endorse. Perhaps it is the openness of parliamentary sovereignty to a range of constitutional futures which has made us reluctant to explore the specific possibilities in greater depth. Nevertheless, the aim of this chapter is to argue that if parliamentary sovereignty is to be sustained and justified as the centrepiece of the UK's Constitution, the more radical possibilities for the kind of constitutional future it could deliver need to be exposed and examined.

In developing this argument, the chapter will be divided into two sections. The first section will consider the idea of parliamentary sovereignty as an instrument for democratic political change, and the limitations on the potential offered by this constitutional norm. In particular, the chapter will discuss, first, the lack of a defined constitutional future for the UK, and second, our complacency about the possibilities for reforming the Constitution. The second section will then begin to explore what a radical constitutional future might look like in the UK. Or perhaps more accurately, it will try to sketch how a radical approach to UK constitutionalism might take shape, given the aim is not to delineate some particular ideal set of arrangements, but instead to open up discussion of the possibilities that could be considered. Indeed, these are possibilities that arguably ought to be considered, if we are to make the potential of parliamentary sovereignty more than just an attractive idea, and show how it might actually be utilised in the real world constitution. In starting to sketch these possibilities, the second section will explore the potential for substantive constitutional reform in the UK, but also the more complex question of the possibility of radicalism in terms of the form of the Constitution itself.

In large parts, this chapter is therefore obviously normative, contestable, and might seem removed from the practicalities of the day-to-day Constitution. Yet this normativity is not

[6] As Graham Gee argues, 'we may be witnessing the bifurcation of political constitutionalism into two less coherent and less unified traditions: a new conservative tradition associated with the right and a new radical variant associated with the left'; G Gee, 'The Political Constitution and the Political Right' (2019) 30 *King's Law Journal* 148, 171.

intended to be an exercise in indulgent hypothesising, or constitutional wish-fulfilment. Instead, it serves a broader purpose: when the constitutional appeal of parliamentary sovereignty is based on its potential for change, we must understand the possibilities for the UK's constitutional future if that potential is to be meaningful, let alone if it is ever to be realised.

I. Parliamentary Sovereignty as an Instrument for Democratic Political Change

Parliamentary sovereignty is the fundamental rule of the UK Constitution. In accordance with this doctrine, the UK Parliament has a legislative power which is legally unlimited. Parliament may 'make or unmake any law whatever', and no court or other body can override the legislation which is enacted by the House of Commons, House of Lords, and receives the royal assent.[7] This is, therefore, an incredibly broad foundational principle for a political system, which appears to prioritise institutional authority over constitutional values. However, to draw such a contrast between institutional authority and constitutional values is misplaced: parliamentary sovereignty must be situated in a wider context, in which the allocation of institutional authority is made on the basis of an assessment of constitutional values. In particular, the allocation of sovereign institutional authority to the UK Parliament can be justified by reference to democratic and political constitutional values.[8] At least in the modern UK, Parliament (and in particular the House of Commons, the primary chamber within it by law and convention) is the most democratic institution of central government.[9] And it is a legitimate constitutional choice to allocate to that democratic institution a legislative power which is free from substantive constraints established in law, on the basis that political rather than legal actors ought to be the ultimate decision-makers concerning matters of social importance.[10]

This basic justification for parliamentary sovereignty might also, however, seem quite thin. A core preference for decision-making through democratic politics rather than legal rationalising might tell us a lot about how other institutions should refrain from interfering with Parliament's legislation, but might not tell us a great deal about how Parliament should endeavour to exercise its legislative power. In part, this is inevitable, for the essential justification for parliamentary sovereignty is that social priorities should be established through the political process, rather than preordained by reference to absolute ideal (legal) principles. Yet at the same time, there remains considerable scope to think about the different ways in which legislative power can be utilised. Understood as part of a broader scheme of democratic constitutional values, parliamentary sovereignty can be seen as an instrument which readily facilitates (although does not demand) political change.

[7] AV Dicey, *Introduction to the Study of the Law of the Constitution*, 8th edn (London, Macmillan, 1915) 37–38.

[8] See M Gordon, *Parliamentary Sovereignty in the UK Constitution: Process, Politics and Democracy* (Oxford, Hart Publishing, 2015) chs 1 and 7.

[9] Parliament Acts 1911 and 1949; 'Conventions on the relationship between the Commons and the Lords', *House of Commons Library*, Briefing Paper 5996 (7 January 2016).

[10] See, eg, J Waldron, *Law and Disagreement* (Oxford, OUP, 1999); M Tushnet, *Taking the Constitution Away from the Courts* (Princeton NJ, Princeton, 1999).

A. Two Varieties of Democratic Political Change

The scope of this power to deliver political change can be seen more clearly if we start to analyse the different possibilities. We can draw a distinction between two varieties of democratic political change: first, ordinary political change, and second, transformative political change. Ordinary political change is part of the routine fabric of democracy. Political parties construct manifestos indicating how they would use legal, administrative and economic tools to alter the functioning of society. They stand for election, a victor emerges (sometimes definitively, sometimes less so), and sets about implementing that agenda to the best of its ability, within institutional constraints, and in light of changing circumstances. The party reaches the end of its mandate or the limits of its authority, a new electoral cycle begins, and the process repeats, with the social order constructed, reconstructed, and sometimes deconstructed, according to changing political beliefs and preferences.

In contrast, the aim of transformative political change is to reconfigure this cycle, shifting the underlying conditions on which the democratic system is based. This might involve reorganising the political process in some fundamental way, re-making core components of the state, or dramatically altering its functions. Such change might, for example, be to the central institutions of government, the voting system used in elections, the location of power at different levels within a nation, or the relationship with other regional, supranational or international legal or political systems. The potential for such transformative political change to be delivered by the doctrine of parliamentary sovereignty has long been clear. This idea underpins Ivor Jennings' stark claim that '[t]he Supremacy of Parliament is the Constitution',[11] because any aspect of the legal or political system could be transformed by an Act of Parliament. This has been drawn out in further detail in the work of Keith Ewing, who notes the 'latent transformative potential' of a political constitution in which the doctrine of parliamentary sovereignty is the 'core legal principle'.[12] The fundamental democratic basis of the state, and the opportunities for the people to engage with constitutional authority, could therefore be transformed via the exercise of existing constitutional authority, and in accordance with the established democratic process.

The purpose of drawing this distinction between ordinary and transformative democratic political change is not to suggest there is some clear cut distinction between the two varieties – what appears to be ordinary change may actually have transformative effects, over time or cumulatively.[13] What is intended to be transformative may fizzle into insignificance.[14] Political actors may design a programme of change which, intentionally or otherwise, cuts across these lines. Nor is the purpose of this distinction to demean ordinary political change, making it sound mundane or insignificant. It is a crucial part of

[11] WI Jennings, *The Law and the Constitution*, 5th edn (London, University of London Press, 1959) 314.

[12] Ewing, 'The Resilience of the Political Constitution' (n 1) 2117, 2118.

[13] For a recent example, see, eg, the Fixed-term Parliaments Act 2011, the effects of which on the dismissal and formation of governments were very uncertain, in particular as a result of establishing a 14-day period following a vote of no confidence in which the conduct required of key actors was wide open to debate.

[14] For a recent example, see, eg, the Constitutional Reform and Governance Act 2010, which Gordon Brown hoped to be a momentous recalibration of executive power, yet ultimately made few changes of substantive and enduring significance, and has had little impact overall.

the regular operation of a democratic system, exhibiting and sustaining many important constitutional values.[15]

Instead, these categories are intended to show the potential of parliamentary sovereignty. To draw this distinction establishes the possibility of transformative political change as a distinct option for constitutional reform in a system based on parliamentary sovereignty. Ordinary political change within the boundaries of the democratic cycle is both facilitated and valuable in a constitutional order based on legally unlimited parliamentary legislative authority. But it is not all that is possible. And this stands in contrast with the standard position in many constitutional systems where transformative political change is not readily available, in principle, because of deliberately constructed barriers, whether procedural or substantive, requiring a slower pace of reform. Indeed, that transformative change occurs through special procedures – rather than according to the same process by which ordinary political change occurs – is the norm across many democratic constitutional systems.[16]

The availability in principle of transformative political change, delivered through the very same democratic process as ordinary political change, shows the broad potential of parliamentary sovereignty as a constitutional norm. And the existence of this potential has a constitutional virtue, which adds to the core democratic justification for the doctrine of parliamentary sovereignty.

B. The Constitutional Virtue of Potential and its Limitations

A constitutional commitment to parliamentary sovereignty facilitates two distinct kinds of democratic political change: a continual flow of possible change associated with the ordinary democratic political cycle, and the possibility of dramatic reformulation of this cycle via transformative political change. Clarifying these different possibilities reveals the potential of parliamentary sovereignty. And this potential has a constitutional virtue. At the most, that virtue stems from the fact that a constitutional system based on parliamentary sovereignty makes a wide spectrum of change possible, and that where necessary, reform can be designed and delivered as appropriate. At the least, for those who may not feel radical change is desirable in our political system, the potential of parliamentary sovereignty is simply focused on opening up options. It does not generate any inherent commitment to any particular programme or volume of political change, rather the potential of parliamentary sovereignty creates space in principle for the uninhibited consideration of how the constitutional system can be enhanced.

There are, however, limitations to this potential, given it exists as a matter of constitutional theory. These limitations can serve to diminish the potential of parliamentary sovereignty. The first limitation is the lack of a clearly defined end to which to aspire. Many different constitutions are both possible to imagine and compatible with parliamentary sovereignty,

[15] See especially R Bellamy, *Political Constitutionalism: A Republican Defence of the Constitutionality of Democracy* (Cambridge, CUP, 2007).

[16] See generally R Albert, X Contiades and A Fotiadou (eds), *The Foundations and Traditions of Constitutional Amendment* (Oxford, Hart Publishing, 2017).

as is evident from the UK identity crisis fuelled by Brexit.[17] We might see parliamentary sovereignty as underpinning a deeply traditional conception of the Constitution, according to which national institutions should be left in splendid isolation, unfettered by any legal constraints flowing from supranational coordination.[18] Yet equally we can see this doctrine as compatible with the voluntary and contingent acceptance of qualifications on legislative authority, in furtherance of greater cooperation between nation states, and so generating a potential expansion of power.[19] Beyond this simple illustration, we can see many other conceptions of the Constitution which are framed around, or accommodate, the idea of parliamentary sovereignty. Increasingly influential, for example, is the kind of constitutional pluralism set out by Alison Young, according to which the Constitution is revealed by the cooperative and conflicting interactions between a range of institutions, yet legislative supremacy is not displaced, and remains a key part of the framework in which these activities occur.[20] Further differences in constitutional emphasis might derive from distinctions between conservativism and modernism,[21] liberalism and republicanism,[22] left and right political philosophies,[23] and legal and political constitutionalism.[24] Of course, such openness to all possibilities is a crucial element of the constitutional virtue of the potential of parliamentary sovereignty. Yet it is important to be aware that this level of openness could also be a weakness, if too much choice becomes debilitating, and therefore theoretical potential becomes a barrier to real world change.

The second limitation is complacency about constitutional possibilities. It is not the case that, in recent years, we have seen a lack of constitutional reform in the UK. Indeed, far from being averse to constitutional change, the main political parties have been open to this prospect almost as never before.[25] However, despite this level of activity, an extremely narrow conception of constitutional reform still dominates UK debates. From a purely functional perspective, we have not seen an overt hostility to parliamentary sovereignty. Indeed, the use of parliamentary sovereignty as a tool for delivering constitutional change was very much evident in the New Labour era of proactive constitutional reform.[26] Yet if we look past this instrumental embrace of parliamentary sovereignty, in so far as New Labour's rationalising project had any further overarching objective, the focus of these reforms was arguably

[17] See further M Gordon, 'Parliamentary Sovereignty and the Political Constitution(s): from Griffith to Brexit' (2019) 30 *King's Law Journal* 125.

[18] See, eg, Department for Exiting the EU, *The United Kingdom's exit from and new partnership with the European Union* (Cm 9417, February 2017), 13: 'Whilst Parliament has remained sovereign throughout our membership of the EU, it has not always felt like that.'

[19] See, eg, *R* v *Secretary of State for Transport, ex p Factortame (No 2)* [1991] 1 AC 603.

[20] AL Young, *Democratic Dialogue and the Constitution* (Oxford, OUP, 2018).

[21] See, eg, G Gee and G Webber, 'A Conservative Disposition and Constitutional Change' (2019) 39 *OJLS* 526; M Loughlin, 'Modernism in British Public Law, 1919–79' [2014] *PL* 56.

[22] See, eg, TRS Allan, *Law, Liberty and Justice: The Legal Foundations of British Constitutionalism* (Oxford, OUP, 1993); A Tomkins, *Our Republican Constitution* (Oxford, Hart Publishing, 2005).

[23] See, eg, JAG Griffith, 'The Political Constitution' (1979) 42 *MLR* 1; Gee (n 6).

[24] See, eg, A Kavanagh, 'Recasting the Political Constitution: From Rivals to Relationships' (2019) 30 *King's Law Journal* 43; M Goldoni and C McCorkindale, 'Three Waves of Political Constitutionalism' (2019) 30 *King's Law Journal* 74; T Hickman, 'In Defence of the Legal Constitution' (2005) 55 *University of Toronto Law Journal* 981.

[25] See, eg, M Gordon, 'Constitutional Reform under the Coalition Government' (*UKCLA Blog*, 18 December 2013) https://ukconstitutionallaw.org/2013/12/18/mike-gordon-constitutional-reform-under-the-coalition-government/.

[26] See, eg, R Hazell, K Donnelly and N Smith, *Delivering Constitutional Reform* (London, The Constitution Unit, 1996) 16–17.

on the constraint of central legislative authority: the Human Rights Act 1998 created new powers for the judiciary to review the substantive content of legislation,[27] primary legislative power was devolved to new institutions in Scotland, Northern Ireland and Wales,[28] a new Supreme Court was established for the UK, enhancing the authority and self-confidence of the senior judges.[29]

This presents a paradox. By explicit design, these reforms were not incompatible with parliamentary sovereignty,[30] and, indeed, in the case of devolution, serve the significant purpose of expanding, rather than contracting, the opportunities for democratic policy-making in the UK.[31] Yet the changes made in this period can also be framed as part of an (imperfect) pattern of constitutionalising, establishing a narrative that reforming energy should in future be directed towards completing this process, and subjecting public power to constitutional constraints.[32] This approach now dominates, and has gained considerable momentum – practically all suggestions for structural constitutional reform which are now openly discussed in UK public debates are premised on the assumption that codification would be the centrepiece of any dramatic reformation of the political system. This has been further complicated by Brexit, with many 'Leave' advocates misidentifying parliamentary sovereignty as a constitutional fundamental which can only be defended through reversion to a nostalgic conception of the state, based on unlimited national authority but a limited role for government intervention.[33] Between the purported modernity of calls for codification, and the regressive attempts to regain political sovereignty as a means of neutering public power, we have become constitutionally complacent. Any more radical thinking about the future of the UK Constitution, beyond these two crude alternatives, has been absent from public debates at an important moment in our political history.

We need to confront these two limitations if the constitutional virtue of parliamentary sovereignty is to be fully understood, let alone realised. We must start to move from abstract constitutional potential to tangible constitutional futures, and sketch out more precisely what might be pursued. This will respond to the first limitation by providing greater definition of the possible ends to which the transformative legislative authority of the UK Parliament might be directed. And it will respond to the second limitation by challenging the current complacency about constitutional reform with alternative options. To do this, the next section of this chapter will explore ideas of constitutional radicalism, examining in outline the broader spectrum of democratic political change made available in a

[27] Human Rights Act 1998, ss 3–4.

[28] Scotland Acts 1998, 2012 and 2016; Government of Wales Acts 1998, 2006 and the Wales Act 2017; Northern Ireland Act 1998 and many others since, including the Northern Ireland Act 2009.

[29] Constitutional Reform Act 2005.

[30] See the explicit statutory preservation of parliamentary sovereignty in the devolution legislation: Scotland Act 1998, s 28(7); Northern Ireland Act 1998, s 5(6); Government of Wales Act 2006, s 107(5). See also the inability of a declaration of incompatibility to undermine the validity of primary legislation in the Human Rights Act 1998, s 4(6)(a).

[31] See, eg, A Cheung, A Paun and L Valsamidis, *Devolution at 20* (London, Institute for Government, 2019) 5.

[32] See, eg, V Bogdanor, 'Our New Constitution' (2004) 120 *LQR* 242, 259.

[33] See, eg, C Hope and H Yorke, 'Boris Johnson plans Singapore-style tax-free zones around UK to power post-Brexit economy' *The Telegraph* (London, 2 July 2019) www.telegraph.co.uk/politics/2019/07/02/boris-johnson-plans-six-singapore-style-tax-free-zones-around/.

constitutional system founded on parliamentary sovereignty. In considering what a radical constitution for the UK might look like, the aim of this section is to establish a richer framework for thinking about the UK's constitutional future, and the place of parliamentary sovereignty within it.

II. What is a Radical Constitution for the UK?

To explore the possibilities for a radically reconceived constitution for the UK, this section will distinguish between issues of constitutional substance and those of constitutional form. While inevitably these categories will blur into one another, this distinction can nevertheless help to structure our thinking about the different ways in which the UK Constitution might be reformed. Questions as to the substantive constitutional reforms which might be attempted which remain compatible with parliamentary sovereignty are more familiar. They include discussion of the possibility of altering the institutions and processes operating within the UK Constitution, and here radical ideas for change might be more easily imagined given the historical nature of much of the UK's core constitutional architecture. Questions as to radical reform of the form of the UK Constitution are less familiar. From this perspective, we must consider the character and structure of the Constitution, including the legal and political dimensions of its norms and mechanisms. In doing so, we will encounter tensions between different conceptions of constitutional law, yet in thinking about these challenges, the way in which parliamentary sovereignty could generate more radical ideas for the UK's constitutional future will start to emerge.

In considering the potential for constitutional change which is established by the doctrine of parliamentary sovereignty, there may be some objections to adopting the terminology of constitutional radicalism. Is this language simply being appropriated to sustain an archaic legal principle which underpins the UK's constitutional status quo? To some extent, such an objection is well founded – indeed, it might be argued that the idea of radical constitutionalism is a contradiction in terms, especially if it is rooted in a desire to establish a more democratic political system. For as Martin Loughlin has argued, the relationship between democracy and law is complex, and based on a potentially fundamental tension: 'democracy fixes on the present and is orientated to the future', reflecting 'a principle of openness'. While law also addresses 'the concerns of the present', it is, in contrast, 'orientated to the past'. Law 'seeks to control, regulate and divide' the 'expansive force' of democracy, and aims to secure 'the closure of that which democracy tries to keep open'.[34] If the authority and content of law is rooted in the past, a constitution of any kind might inevitably establish and privilege (even if not necessarily entrench) a historical set of power arrangements. At the same time, however, we must recognise the extent to which constitutional law can be empowering and a tool for change. As Loughlin notes, we should view 'public law as a power-generating phenomenon', not simply as an instrument of limitation, and 'constitutional structures are the means by which political power itself is generated'.[35]

[34] M Loughlin, *The Idea of Public Law* (Oxford, OUP, 2003) 100.
[35] M Loughlin, *Foundations of Public Law* (Oxford, OUP, 2010) 11, 12.

The essential tensions between constitutional law and democracy cannot be circumvented, but must be accommodated in any attempts to explore the radical potential of constitutionalism. Law inevitably constrains possibilities by identifying certain arrangements as authoritative rather than others, yet it also institutionalises the possibility of democratic change, creating the conditions in which the law itself may be remade. We can only decide how to address this tension between law as a source of continuity with the past, and law as a lever for future change, in the context of specific constitutional systems. In that sense, the idea of radical constitutionalism employed in this chapter should be seen as providing one answer to the question of how to reconcile the inevitable tensions between law and democracy, and how to balance the past and future orientations of constitutional law.[36] Recognising the inevitable and significant extent to which constitutional law will be captured by and reinforcing of the social and political status quo, we must think about ways in which real world constitutional arrangements can be designed which unlock the capacity of law to channel democratic inputs and support rather than suppress transformative reform.

Consequently, the purpose of using the terminology of radicalism is to try to inspire fresh thinking about what a constitution might try to achieve, and how it might be organised. This is not to endorse a cult of the novel, but to mark a need for divergence from a constitutional status quo which in many respects we have a tendency to romanticise. It is all too easy to slip between thinking of the exceptionalism of the UK Constitution as being the result of its difference from prevailing constitutional norms, to being based on its brilliance as compared to the approach taken in the majority of other nation states.[37] This is a serious mistake, yet it is also wrong to believe, in contrast, that the only constitutional futures available in the UK are either to seek to defend or restore a set of traditional arrangements, or to follow the path to codification, whether slowly or quickly, inspired by liberal ideas of limited government. Of course, some may worry that, even if a radically different constitutional future is possible for the UK, adherence to a doctrine of parliamentary sovereignty could have no place in those future arrangements. It is the aim of this chapter, however, to demonstrate that this is not the case, and, rather, that the development of a radical constitution can run in parallel with the development of parliamentary sovereignty. To do this, we need to gain a more direct sense of the possible substantive and formal aspects of a radical constitution.

A. Issues of Substance: The Dominance of Constitutional Liberalism, the Impossibility of Laissez Faire

The substantive components of the Constitution are a familiar target when considering potential constitutional reform. In particular, when we think of the substance of the

[36] For an alternative approach to the idea of 'radical constitutionalism', rooted in the work of Rousseau and making the important point that 'constitutional analysis ought not be limited to the formal and legalistic dimension, but it should enquiry into the undergirding socio-economic and psychological dynamics', see M Goldoni, 'Rousseau's Radical Constitutionalism and Its Legacy' in MW Dowdle and MA Wilkinson (eds) *Constitutionalism Beyond Liberalism* (Cambridge, CUP, 2017) 41.

[37] See, eg, the quotations from Burke and Hallam, cited in Dicey (n 7) 2.

Constitution, we might focus on the institutions and processes which are most prominent within it. In institutional terms, this will most obviously include the UK Government, Parliament, Crown and courts, the executives and legislatures of the devolved administrations, the machinery of local and regional government, and the relationships between all these actors and supranational or international authorities (whether European or otherwise). In relation to constitutional process, again we can draw this category in broad terms, including the legal procedures according to which primary and secondary legislation is made, and potentially also open to judicial review in the courts, but also the formal processes within government by which policies are established and decisions are taken, the processes through which government accountability is sought in the functioning of Parliament and elsewhere, rules relating to the consent of the devolved administrations to central government decision-making, as well as those rules concerning the various democratic events which determine the composition of our constitutional institutions, or (attempt to) resolve directly major questions of national policy.

This is a wide spectrum of constitutional actors and activities, and all of it is open to reform through the legislative action of the UK Parliament. Indeed, many aspects of the UK Constitution's institutions and processes have been the subject of reform in the last 25 years, an era of proactive constitutional change started by the New Labour Government of Tony Blair in 1997,[38] but continued by the Conservative-Liberal Democrat coalition between 2010 and 2015.[39] This new constitutional consciousness – according to which the Constitution becomes an object to be deliberately altered and moulded – has also seeped into the approach of the subsequent Conservative governments of David Cameron and Theresa May, with their decisions to hold and deliver on the outcome of the referendum on withdrawal from the European Union set to prompt vast changes in the UK's legal and political system.[40] There are, of course, different levels of enthusiasm evident among the different political parties, and enthusiasm for different types of reform: the key Conservative proposal remains (eventually, after Brexit) to repeal the Human Rights Act 1998 and replace it with a 'British Bill of Rights',[41] whereas the Liberal Democrats have long been committed to a far-reaching programme of constitutional formalisation.[42] Yet despite these important differences in attitude, constitutional reform has become a core political issue in the UK.

However, while constitutional reform may now be mainstream among the UK's leading political parties, there is a distinct lack of radicalism in the substance of what has happened, and in what continues to be proposed. As Flinders argues, we might conclude that 'New Labour has largely failed to transform the British constitution in a radical way, preferring to accommodate reforms within a Westminster model that preserves

[38] See, eg, R Blackburn and R Plant (eds), *Constitutional Reform: The Labour Government's Constitutional Reform Agenda* (London, Longman, 1999).

[39] See, eg, R Hazell and B Yong, *The Politics of Coalition: How the Conservative-Liberal Democrat Government Works* (Oxford, Hart publishing, 2012) esp ch 9.

[40] See, eg, AL Young, 'The Constitutional Implications of Brexit' (2017) 23 *European Public Law* 757; M Gordon, 'Brexit: a challenge *for* the UK constitution, *of* the UK constitution?' (2016) 12 *EuConst* 409.

[41] The Conservative and Unionist Party, *Forward, Together* (2017) 37.

[42] The Liberal Democrats, *Change Britain's Future* (2017) 91.

executive dominance'.[43] Even the election manifesto of the Labour Party led by Jeremy Corbyn in 2017, which was explicitly framed around the need for 'real change',[44] was remarkably timid in its constitutional vision. The centrepiece of the proposals for 'Extending Democracy' was to offer to establish a Constitutional Convention, which in one sense could be a welcome methodological innovation if it engaged a wider body of citizens with questions of reform.[45] Yet the framing of both the purpose and the composition of this Convention was incredibly vague, with the broad intention 'to examine and advise on reforming of the way Britain works at a fundamental level', and no proposals as to the membership or terms of reference, which were to be the subject of a consultation.[46] This suggests the proposed Convention simply amounted to an attempt to displace substance with process, papering over a failure to offer any new proposals for extending democracy in the UK, beyond reiterating the traditional Labour commitment to reform the House of Lords.

Crucially, this absence of radicalism is arguably due to the fact that debates about reform are still largely conducted within the confines of constitutional liberalism. Assessing the proposals for political reform in Labour's 2017 manifesto, Keith Ewing argues that this is 'an agenda that owes more to Blair's liberalism than Corbyn's socialism'.[47] For Ewing, more attention needs to be given to reforms which take the Constitution 'as an institution that empowers rather than restrains', while also viewing 'parliamentary institutions as only one source of constitutional legitimacy'.[48] From this perspective, it might be argued that constitutional reform is actually a distraction, inevitably diluting the uninhibited potential of parliamentary sovereignty to deliver far-reaching economic and social change. In the social democratic pursuit of equality, Ewing suggests that we require an approach to the Constitution focused on 'embracing the state, concentrating on power rather than accountability', while reshaping the relationship between the political and the social or economic spheres.[49] This would occur in both directions, through expanding the scope of political decision-making to incorporate social actors, prime among them representative trade unions, and expanding the reach of democratic political values to restructure decision-making in social and economic arenas, most notably the workplace.[50] Yet in aiming to channel the power of the state to collapse boundaries between the political, social and economic arenas, there is a risk that we end up taking an approach to the Constitution shaped by collective laissez-faire: reform is viewed as desirable only to the extent that it supports the achievement of specified political objectives, and the Constitution should otherwise simply ensure it is not a barrier to change. This is particularly evident in Ewing's attitude to House of Lords reform, in relation to which he argues 'there is no virtue in a

[43] M Flinders, 'New Labour and the Constitution' in S Ludlam and MJ Smith (eds), *Governing as New Labour: Party and Politics Under Blair* (London, Palgrave Macmillan, 2004) 126. See also P Dorey, *The Labour Party and Constitutional Reform: A History of Constitutional Conservativism* (London, Palgrave Macmillan, 2008).

[44] The Labour Party, *For the Many Not the Few* (2017) 4.

[45] See, eg, G Smith, *Democratic Innovations: Designing Institutions for Citizen Participation* (Cambridge, CUP, 2009) esp ch 3.

[46] Labour Party (n 42) 102.

[47] K Ewing, 'Jeremy Corbyn and the Law of Democracy' (2017) 28 *King's Law Journal* 343, 346–47.

[48] Ibid, 361.

[49] Ibid, 344.

[50] Ibid, 344.

directly elected second chamber' due to 'the time it would take to enact the necessary legislation' and 'the obstacles' such a chamber 'would create for the enactment of a progressive manifesto'.[51]

We must certainly be aware of the historic liberal underpinnings of the idea of parliamentary sovereignty, and recognise the Whiggish individualism which may be reflected in our constitutional structures.[52] Indeed, as Jennings argued, so accepted is the Whig theory of democracy it might almost be considered 'a permanent part of the Constitution'.[53] However, while acknowledging these historic foundations, we need not be constrained by them. It must be possible in principle to move beyond an approach to constitutional reform which is designed to promote the values of constitutional liberalism, while also still seeking a radicalism which is defined by more than the outcomes of the political system. This becomes especially apparent when we appreciate that substantive political principles – whether Whig, liberal, conservative or socialist – can become deeply embedded in the seams of our constitutional order. In seeking to move beyond a classic constitutional liberalism, Ewing is surely right to emphasise the importance of focusing on public power when framing our ambitions for constitutional reform. Yet we do not need to conceptualise power as being in competition with accountability. Instead, we can understand the constitutional relationship between power and accountability to be mutually reinforcing: those who exercise power must be accountable in authentic ways to those who are subject to their decisions, and this in turn should contribute to a state of affairs where that power is used in ways which reflect the preferences of a majority. Substantive constitutional reform of institutions and processes within the legal and political system can be aimed at satisfying both of these connected aspirations, rather than adopting the liberal preference for constraint, or a purely instrumental approach to delivering change through the Constitution.

This is not to dismiss instrumental considerations when imagining the possibilities for reform, since the fundamental constitutional purpose is to facilitate collective decision-making in the public interest. Yet in addition to generating outcomes which advance our chosen principled commitments through that process, it is also important to reflect those substantive principles in our political arrangements. To take one example, the pursuit of equality certainly requires a constitution which contains the institutions and processes which can deliver social and political equality in substance, but these institutions and processes must also be organised so as to exhibit the spirit of equality in their operation. Beyond this point of principle, there is also a more pragmatic reason that an instrumental approach to the Constitution can no longer provide an adequate basis for constitutional radicalism. In an era of enhanced constitutional consciousness, a laissez-faire attitude leaves inevitable gaps which other actors can fill, deploying explicitly constitutional arguments to extend their powers. This risk is especially evident in the actions of the courts in high profile cases including *Miller*,[54] where expansive but superficial assertions about the scale of constitutional change flowing from Brexit were offered as a justification for judicial intervention to

[51] Ibid, 351.
[52] See, eg, Jennings (n 11) 314–16.
[53] Ibid, 316.
[54] *R (Miller) v Secretary of State for Exiting the European Union* [2017] UKSC 5, [2018] AC 61.

shape the domestic process of withdrawal from the EU.[55] To retreat from this debate about the nature of the Constitution, reducing it to a minimalist construct which must only get out of the way of radical social or economic change, is to potentially cede the Constitution to other groups. And the result may be the assertion of constitutional liberalism by other means, if the judges are effective in establishing a thicker framework of common law principle which increasingly restrains political action.[56]

Therefore, a radical approach to constitutionalism requires us to reimagine the Constitution, and in particular its institutions and processes, rather than keep it out of the way. There are obviously infinite ways in which our institutions might be realigned, or our processes might be reinvented. We can nevertheless outline some initial priorities which might provide an indication of a programme of reform, but do not (and could not) dictate a monolithic approach.

In terms of institutions, we should first consider the replacement of existing institutions, whether those which it has long been agreed are anachronistic, like the House of Lords, or those, like the monarchy, which are curiously immune from mainstream public scrutiny despite their incompatibility with basic democratic principles concerning the selection and removability of those in powerful positions. There are a range of proposals that might be considered as alternatives to the House of Lords – from a smaller, elected upper chamber representing regional interests,[57] to a legislative revising chamber composed of citizens chosen for a fixed period of time through random selection.[58] The same is true of proposals to establish a new Head of State – from passing relevant powers and responsibilities to the Speaker of the House of Commons,[59] while placing other royal prerogative powers on the statute book,[60] to an elected but largely ceremonial office modelled on the Presidency of the Republic of Ireland.[61] How these institutions should be reformed will be a matter for widespread debate, depending on the purposes they would be intended to fulfil, but a starting point for developing a radical constitution would be shedding the relics of a pre-democratic politics.

Yet updating the core constitutional architecture of the legislature and executive would not alone be sufficient. For pluralism among better institutions will not necessarily equate to popular or political pluralism – if those institutions all represent similar interests, it is simply a reshuffling of power, rather than an alteration of it.[62] Novel institutional alignments which fracture the traditional tripartite separation of powers would need to be explored,

[55] Ibid, esp [81]–[83].

[56] This theme is prominent in extra-judicial lectures by our senior judges, eg Lady Hale, 'UK Constitutionalism on the March?' (Keynote Address to the Constitutional and Administrative Law Bar Association, London, 12 July 2014) www.supremecourt.uk/docs/speech-140712.pdf; Lord Neuberger, '"Judge not, that ye be not judged": judging judicial decision-making' (FA Mann Lecture, London, 29 January 2015) www.supremecourt.uk/docs/speech-150129.pdf.

[57] See, eg, the Labour proposal under the leadership of Ed Miliband to replace the Lords with 'an elected Senate of the Nations and Regions'; The Labour Party, *Britain Can Be Better* (2015) 84.

[58] See, eg, R Askwith, *People Power: Remaking Parliament for the Populist Age* (London, Biteback, 2018).

[59] See the discussion in R Brazier, 'A British Republic' (2002) 61 *CLJ* 351, 369.

[60] See, eg, Tomkins (n 20) ch 4.

[61] Constitution of Ireland, arts 12–14.

[62] I therefore very much agree with Alison Young that we must 're-imagine' the Constitution to respond to changing patterns of democracy, yet enhancing political pluralism also requires us to look beyond attempts to rebalance the existing relationship between the legislature and the courts; see AL Young, 'Populism and the UK Constitution' (2018) 71 *Current Legal Problems* 17.

facilitating or capturing other inputs into political decision-making. This might involve, first, bolstering existing institutions by guaranteeing a greater input into the existing operations of the UK's central legislature, executive and judiciary. That could entail formalising consent rights for the devolved institutions in Scotland, Wales and Northern Ireland in relation to central intervention in devolved policy areas,[63] or regularising the rules which govern when referendums are held, to provide citizens with standing mechanisms of legislative initiative or override.[64]

Second, we should consider creating new institutions, rather than simply refreshing or reorganising the status quo. This is not a call for novelty for novelty's sake, but should be based on a functional approach: what do we need to do better? How could a more diverse set of interests be represented in our constitutional decision-making? By what means could we enhance the accountability of those in power to those subject to their power? An example of a significant proposal which merits serious attention comes from John McCormick, who argues for the creation of a 'People's Tribune', established for a fixed period of time composed of randomly selected citizens exercising a combination of legislative initiative, veto and accountability functions.[65] This is not to transfer political decision-making authority away from democratically elected actors, but instead to institutionalise the direct engagement of citizens with constitutional elites, bringing a wider range of expertise, concerns, and life experience to the centre of the Constitution. Rather than simply constituting singular citizens' assembles to make recommendations regarding specific issues before lapsing, a permanent institution with an evolving membership and a broad portfolio of oversight functions could establish some continuity in better connecting elected officials with the wider public. This could also be an opportunity to enhance our inadequate constitutional diversity, by guaranteeing the inclusion of underrepresented groups, whether judged by reference to gender, race, class, age, or other key characteristics.[66]

In addition to considering substantive reform of our institutions, we should also explore the possibilities for altering our constitutional processes. The relationship between reform of institutions and reform of the processes in which those institutions are crucially involved will be fluid, but although inevitably linked, it is important to consider both the 'who' and the 'how' of constitutional decision-making. Again, we can consider a number of examples. One crucial area of concern is the conduct of elections to select those in positions of constitutional authority. The starting point would be to replace the First-Past-the-Post system for

[63] See, eg, M Gordon, 'The Permanence of Devolution: Parliamentary Sovereignty and Referendum Requirements' (*Scottish Constitutional Futures Forum*, 30 September 2015) www.scottishconstitutionalfutures.org/OpinionandAnalysis/ViewBlogPost/tabid/1767/articleType/ArticleView/articleId/6113/Mike-Gordon-The-Permanence-of-Devolution-Parliamentary-Sovereignty-and-Referendum-Requirements.aspx.

[64] See, eg, JG Matsusaka, *For the Many or the Few: The Initiative, Public Policy, and American Democracy* (Chicago, University of Chicago Press, 2004).

[65] J McCormick, *Machiavellian Democracy* (Cambridge, CUP, 2011).

[66] See especially the debates about the institutionalisation of minority voice protection for indigenous peoples in Australia and Canada; see, eg, F Davis, 'The Problem of Authority and the Proposal for an Indigenous Advisory Body' (2015) 8 *Indigenous Law Bulletin* 23; S Morris, '"The Torment of Our Powerlessness": Addressing Indigenous Constitutional Vulnerability through the Uluru Statement's Call for a First Nations Voice in Their Affairs' (2018) 41 *University of New South Wales Law Journal* 629; H King and S Pasternak, 'Canada's Emerging Indigenous Rights Framework: A Critical Analysis' (*Yellowhead Institute*, 5 June 2018) https://yellowheadinstitute.org/wp-content/uploads/2018/06/yi-rights-report-june-2018-final-5.4.pdf.

selecting members of the House of Commons, which in a pluralistic age produces neither proportionate nor decisive election results.[67] There are a set of related issues concerning our primary democratic elections, including the possibility of compulsory or incentivised voting, lowering the voting age, automatic as opposed to individual voter registration, the funding of parties, and the regulation of political advertising (especially in light of shifts away from mainstream to social media as a primary source of information).[68]

In addition, we could also rethink our decision-making processes for the exercise of public power. There is increasing evidence of the effectiveness of citizens' assemblies in evaluating choices on the policy agenda.[69] The greater constitutional challenge may be to work out how these ad hoc decision-making tools could be incorporated into the legislative process, considering whether small groups of randomly selected citizens can ever do more than make recommendations for wider democratic consideration. A similar challenge exists in relation to referendums, which have become intensely controversial after the Brexit vote.[70] Yet their use is still supported by a strong democratic case,[71] especially if we can develop better regulatory systems, and perhaps even try to formalise the circumstances in which their use is appropriate.[72] A radical approach would also require us to think about the ways in which technology can be used to extend opportunities for popular participation and voting – while this undoubtedly raises challenges (not least concerns relating to the digital exclusion of older people or marginalised groups), there is scope to involve the electorate in decision-making far more regularly, and no reason to assume that periodic general and regional elections and occasional referendums provide the ideal level of political input. At a collective level, a debate about the decision-making powers of different groups within the UK will be required – this could extend to cover issues including the processes for obtaining the consent of devolved governments in relation to central legislation affecting devolved subject-matters, to whether we even have adequate representation of sub-national interests across the regions of England.

There would clearly be a range of other options for radical constitutional reform – this is simply an indicative attempt to map potential priorities, which could be significantly refined and augmented. However, a more significant final issue is whether constitutional radicalism in relation to the composition and design of our institutions and processes would mean the end of parliamentary sovereignty as a central organising principle of the Constitution. Even if Parliament itself is reformed and reinforced, would it be displaced from its centrality

[67] See, eg, J Garland and C Terry, 'The 2017 General Election: Volatile Voting, Random Results' (*Electoral Reform Society*, 2017) www.electoral-reform.org.uk/wp-content/uploads/2017/08/2017-UK-General-Election-Report.pdf.

[68] See, eg, P Dunleavy, A Park and R Taylor (eds), *The UK's Changing Democracy: The 2018 Democratic Audit* (London, LSE Press, 2018) esp pts 2 and 3.

[69] See, eg, ME Warren and H Pearse (eds), *Designing Deliberative Democracy: The British Columbia Citizens' Assembly* (Cambridge, CUP, 2008); D Farrell, J Suiter and C Harris, '"Systematizing" Constitutional Deliberation: the 2016–18 Citizens' Assembly in Ireland' (2019) 34 *Irish Political Studies* 113.

[70] See, eg, S Tierney, 'Was the Brexit Referendum Democratic?' (*UKCLA Blog*, 25 July 2016) https://ukconstitutionallaw.org/2016/07/25/stephen-tierney-was-the-brexit-referendum-democratic/.

[71] See esp, S Tierney, *Constitutional Referendums: A Theory and Practice of Republican Deliberation* (Oxford, OUP, 2013).

[72] See generally the 'Report of the Independent Commission on Referendums' (*The Constitution Unit*, 2018): www.ucl.ac.uk/constitution-unit/sites/constitution-unit/files/ICR_Final_Report.pdf.

as other actors are empowered, and authority is diversified? For Flinders, reflecting on the timidity of New Labour, a radical re-thinking of the Constitution would necessarily see parliamentary sovereignty diminished:

> It is these constitutional fuels, falling electoral turnout and weakening public trust that may force a future New Labour government to adopt a more radical approach to the constitution. At the heart of such a reappraisal would have to be a formal acknowledgement that parliamentary sovereignty has become a relative rather than an absolute concept.[73]

Yet on the contrary, radical constitutional change of the kind outlined above is change which could be delivered through the doctrine of parliamentary sovereignty, and with which parliamentary sovereignty would remain compatible. Indeed, we can also readily imagine change to parliamentary sovereignty, in the form of an institutional relocation of legally unlimited law-making power from the Queen, Lords and Commons, to some reformed alignment based on the basic removal of some of the existing component elements, to their replacement with new participants.[74] From this perspective, we can see the interactive and fluid nature of power in the contemporary Constitution: the idea of parliamentary sovereignty is simply a legal starting point for framing and understanding how a complex multiplicity of constitutional actors compete and engage across institutions, nations and political parties, rather than establishing the singular omnipotence of the legislature. The constitutional primacy of the UK Parliament, the key democratic institution of central government, is just one element of our democratic political system, and the unlimited character of legislative sovereignty is a tool to deliver, rather than a barrier obstructing, radical change to the substance of our constitutional framework.

B. Issues of Form: The Codification Consensus and a Federal UK

How we might reform the form of the Constitution is a more complex question than what changes we might make to the substance of our legal and political system. For we can imagine an infinite range of new institutional formations or procedural arrangements, with the previous section providing just an overview of some possibilities. Yet while the form of the Constitution presents a further and distinct set of issues, most engagement with them is premised on a binary approach. A constitution is either codified, in the sense of being contained in a singular written text or instrument, or uncodified, and dispersed across a range of sources and documents. Substantive institutional or procedural reform can occur within either framework, but beyond this basic formal distinction, deeper questions concerning the structure and character of the Constitution which will contain any modified arrangements are rarely addressed. In a constitutional reform context, this means that there is a significant amount of complacency about the possibilities for change to the form of the Constitution. We therefore need to open up discussion of the radical options for changing the structure and the character of the UK Constitution.

[73] Flinders, 'New Labour and the Constitution' (n 41) 143.
[74] Gordon (n 8) 339–347.

When debating change to the form of the UK Constitution, a codification consensus dominates the terrain. This is evident in practice, when constitutional actors consider formal reform to the UK's arrangements. A prime example of this was the 'New Magna Carta' project conducted by the Political and Constitutional Reform Committee of the House of Commons between 2010 and 2015, when it developed three different models for constitutional reform – a non-legal Code, a Consolidating Constitution Act, and a Written Constitution – all of which represented an attempt at codification by alternative means.[75] Similarly, when the Scottish Government outlined its plans for an interim Scottish Constitution in the event of a vote for Scottish independence at the 2014 referendum, a codified constitution was the proposed solution.[76]

This consensus is also evident in, and supported by, a significant body of academic work. Brexit has presented an obvious opportunity to consider restructuring the constitution, but perhaps more surprising is that suggestions that the end result should be a codified constitution have united the long committed, such as Vernon Bogdanor,[77] with some previous sceptics, such as Martin Loughlin.[78] This proposal has been prominent in mainstream public debate. Codification of the Constitution is positioned as the radical option: '[t]he writing of a constitution will itself be an exercise in radical optimism'.[79] It is presented as the solution to democratic discontent: 'the case for radical surgery' is now 'beyond argument'.[80] It would provide more 'grownup' arrangements than the current 'arbitrary, hyper-centralised empire-state', establishing the basis for a 'federal UK'.[81] There are of course some dissenting voices,[82] but the idea that codification is the key constitutional reform required to save the UK from break-up, and from itself, is shaping the terms of public discourse.

Does this mean there is no potential for alternative radicalism as a matter of constitutional form? If we seek to reform the Constitution, is the path one which inevitably leads to codification? Even in more innovative attempts to map a path to a reformed 'written constitution', a codified, entrenched, legal text is still the baseline. Jeff King, for example, argues that we may want to mitigate the potential for a written constitution to embed the values of one generation against the wishes of future generations by including an automatic sunset

[75] House of Commons Political and Constitutional Reform Committee, *A New Magna Carta?* (HC 463, 10 July 2014).

[76] The Scottish Government, *The Scottish Independence Bill: A Consultation on an Interim Constitution for Scotland* (2014).

[77] See, eg, V Bogdanor, 'Post-Brexit Britain may need a constitution – or face disintegration' *The Guardian* (London, 18 January 2019) www.theguardian.com/commentisfree/2019/jan/18/brexit-britain-constitution-disintegration-eu-uk-devolution-good-friday-agreement; V Bogdanor, 'Beyond Brexit: Towards a British Constitution' (*The Constitution Unit*, 22 February 2019) https://constitution-unit.com/2019/02/22/beyond-brexit-towards-a-british-constitution/.

[78] M Loughlin, 'The End of Avoidance' (2016) 38 *London Review of Books* 12.

[79] M D'Ancona, 'Time for a written constitution' (*Opinion: The Tortoise Take*, May 2019) https://members.tortoisemedia.com/2019/05/08/the-take-a-written-constitution/content.html?sig=3I_4D96VsK6vRKMQwotlLZ7qtw88b7AcOZpuHaMiUrs&utm_source=Twitter&utm_medium=Social&utm_campaign=8May2019&utm_content=Time_for_a_written_constitution_take.

[80] T Clark, 'Could a new constitution fix Britain's democracy?' (*Prospect*, 2 April 2019) www.prospectmagazine.co.uk/magazine/brexit-constitution-democracy-government-politics-tom-clark.

[81] A Barnett, 'Why Britain needs a written constitution' *The Guardian* (London, 30 November 2016) www.theguardian.com/commentisfree/2016/nov/30/why-britain-needs-written-constitution.

[82] J Rentoul, 'A written constitution can't save us from Brexit now – it could even make things worse' (*The Independent*, 9 February 2019) www.independent.co.uk/voices/brexit-latest-written-constitution-electoral-reform-vernon-bogdanor-a8771296.html.

clause in the terms of the constitution, requiring a new constituent assembly to complete a generational renewal of the text.[83] Yet even this democratically sensitive case for a written constitution provides a different means of reaching the same destination: a fundamental category of legal constitutional norms, an empowered judiciary to interpret and enforce them, fixed procedural and temporal barriers to political reform, and a less responsive politics. The process of establishing a constitution is certainly important, but the democratic gains of popular constitutional authorship, through a constituent assembly, a representative legislature and referendums, can be achieved without elevating a definitive 'Constitution', the text of which would be ripe for ossification.

It is from this perspective that the distinction between reform of the substance and the form of the constitution becomes especially important. Codification is not simply one option at the far end of a spectrum based on the intensity of reform – it does not simply provide a neutral vehicle through which a large volume of institutional and procedural reform can be implemented. Instead, it is a structural choice, which is based on a particular conception of the character of constitutional law. In thinking about these two related issues of structure and character, we can start to see the initial parameters for a radical approach to constitutional form.

First, in structural terms, codification functions to create a hierarchy between those norms and principles recognised as 'constitutional' and those which are not. The significance of constitutional norms, as those which frame the ordinary operation of the legal and political system, can be seen to create an imperative to entrench them in recognition of that importance. Yet a constitution does not need to be based on this structural hierarchy between the constitutional and the non-constitutional – if our aim is to clarify, systematise and publicise, we can identify constitutional norms and institutions without assuming they require any special protection against alteration. We can formalise a distinction between constitutional and non-constitutional norms without feeling a need to embrace and entrench a hierarchy, constraining the more fluid development of constitutional arrangements.

Second, we can rethink our approach to the character of constitutional law. Almost inevitably, codification will prompt a shift to greater legalism and the limitation of politics, assuming (as is the dominant paradigm) that it is effected through an enforceable legal text. This has the potential to sanctify and sanitise the constitution: certain categories of disagreement are pushed from the political to the legal realm, to be determined by reference to principles which are aspirational but still demand elaboration by judicial actors to establish their meaning and application. In that sense, adopting a codified text as a matter of constitutional form can be seen to derive from a particular conception of constitutional law, one which creates a (further) constitutional hierarchy between law and politics, replacing and simplifying what can otherwise be a more complex interactive relationship. However, we need not embrace this hierarchy – changing the form of the constitution does not inherently entail that we accept (constitutional) law as having a character which is categorically superior to (ordinary) politics. Constitutional reform does not require constitutional legalisation; instead we can try explicitly to craft a place for constitutional politics in the authoritative structures of our society. This means departing from a rationalistic approach

[83] J King, 'A Democratic Case for a Written Constitution' (2019) *Current Legal Problems* 33–4.

to decision-making focused on the judicial interpretation of constitutional norms and principles in courts, and instead cultivating the constitutional role of politics. In terms of constitutional form, this might include recognising an equivalence in status between legal and political norms, and establishing clear space for political (as well as legal) mechanisms of accountability and processes for resolving disputes.

These are abstract ideas, producing a constitutional preference to formalise rather than entrench, and politicise rather than legalise. How can we put these premises into action in the real world? To explore this, we can take an attempt to establish a federal relationship between the four constituent nations of the UK as an example. To federalise the Constitution is often one of the primary motivations behind a programme of codification, especially as Brexit has strained the precarious distribution of power between England, Scotland, Wales, Northern Ireland and the UK. Yet could we move towards federalisation of these relationships without adopting a codified constitutional form? It would be possible to formalise the relationship between devolved and central government in a new organising Act of Union[84] – there is no inherent need to give any such rules bolstering the relationship between these different levels of government any special legal status or entrenched protection. Similarly, it would be possible to develop political mechanisms to enhance inter-institutional cooperation and for the resolution of disputes[85] – a reinforced federalist architecture (inevitably also including provision for national government in England) would not need to be constructed primarily around maintaining formal legal divisions of competence.

There are some obvious objections to such an approach. The explicit cultivation of constitutional politics might be seen as too weak and erratic to serve as the means to structure such delicate relationships. The limitations of unenforceable declarations of principle might be observed in the *Miller* case, when the Supreme Court held that constitutional conventions did not provide a basis on which the rights of the devolved institutions could be guaranteed.[86] For King, this exposes 'the secrecy and unreliability of constitutional conventions'.[87] Yet to focus on the enforceability of conventions is the kind of approach we need to question when considering alternatives in terms of constitutional form. There would necessarily be a role for law in constructing a new federalist constitutional system, but we need not assume that the significance of every rule depends on its status in the courts, especially when the outcome of *Miller* may simply demonstrate a clear and unsurprising judicial commitment to the central state.[88] Instead, law can be a tool of institutionalisation as much as enforcement. A more federal constitution could therefore disperse authority within

[84] See, eg, the proposal for an Act of Union Bill, including an option for an English Parliament, promoted by the Constitution Reform Group (www.constitutionreformgroup.co.uk/). This was introduced in the House of Lords by Lord Lisvane on 9 October 2018 as a Private Members' Bill (HL Bill 132), which is unlikely to progress to a second reading.

[85] See, eg, proposals for a UK Council of Ministers by the Welsh Government, *Brexit and Devolution* (15 June 2017) 17.

[86] For criticism of this aspect of the decision in *Miller*, see KD Ewing, 'Brexit and Parliamentary Sovereignty' (2017) 80 *MLR* 711.

[87] King (n 79) 35.

[88] See also the repeated emphasis (perhaps even unnecessarily in the context of the case) on the sovereignty of the UK Parliament in the Supreme Court decision in *The UK Withdrawal from the European Union (Legal Continuity) (Scotland) Bill – A Reference by the Attorney General and the Advocate General for Scotland (Scotland)* [2018] UKSC 64, [2019] 2 WLR 1 at [12], [41], [43], [53], [61], [63], [64].

the state by institutionalising processes and principles which reflect a changed culture of political power. The success of such a scheme would depend on the quality of the politics, of course, but the aspiration could be to create space for productive political engagement between those in office at different national levels, rather than generate a series of technical legal boundary disputes.

Would such a flirtation with constitutional federalism ultimately pose questions about the doctrine of parliamentary sovereignty as a vehicle for reform? It might be thought that any shift to formalise a diversification of authority among the constituent nations of the UK would fracture that unitary vision of sovereignty. However, it is actually this approach to constitutional form, which departs from the codification consensus, which demonstrates the full potential of the doctrine of parliamentary sovereignty for delivering radical reform of the Constitution. Parliamentary sovereignty already attributes power to a composite institution, composed of Queen, Lords, and Commons. The institutional complexity of Parliament complicates the idea of legislative sovereignty as the authority of a unitary actor. In theory, then, the disaggregation of Parliament from its law-making sovereignty is possible: we could relocate sovereignty to a different alignment of institutions without necessarily abandoning the idea that legally unlimited legislative power should, on democratic principle, be vested somewhere in the Constitution.[89] This would be to make a conscious choice about the structure of a reformed UK Constitution, on the basis of a particular understanding of the character of constitutional law. In other words, it demonstrates that variation is possible in constitutional form, and the principled ideas underpinning the doctrine of parliamentary sovereignty could be relocated and even expanded, rather than dispensed with, if we think radically about reform of the UK Constitution.

Much would depend on the detail of such an approach to the Constitution, and in practice, removing parliamentary sovereignty as a constitutional ornament would risk creating circumstances in which constitutional judicial review of legislation would seem an inexorable next step. Nevertheless, there are possibilities here for constitutional design which deserve exploration, rather than sleepwalking into codification as the only alternative. In mapping ideas for a radical constitution, questions of form have freestanding importance. But what also emerges is the need to think about substantive constitutional reform in light of a clear sense of the implications for the form of the Constitution. For the substantive institutions and processes we establish would be key to delivering a functioning constitutional form which aimed to sustain and enhance the political dimensions of the UK's system of government. In that sense, an understanding of the different components of the Constitution's form is essential in providing the context to identify the priorities for substantive constitutional reform.

III. Conclusion: Parliamentary Sovereignty in a Radical Constitution

The purpose of this chapter has been to explore a series of possibilities for radical reform of the UK Constitution. Crucial to this task is rethinking our understanding of constitutional

[89] See further Gordon (n 8) ch 8.

reform – parliamentary sovereignty should not be viewed as a creaking obstacle to constitutional change, but a doctrine which facilitates change to the substance and the form of the UK Constitution. Rather than assume parliamentary sovereignty is a barrier to radical change, we need to more clearly explore the potential of parliamentary sovereignty to deliver a radically different Constitution. In so doing, we start to open up the full potential of parliamentary sovereignty, as well as create space to challenge timid assumptions about what a radically reformed constitution might look like.

This approach to constitutional change is underpinned by a democratic desire to prompt broad and fresh debate about how our political system could be changed: to establish a bigger space in which political contestation can occur, between a more equal and inclusive body of people, aimed at enhancing the use of public power, and more effective accountability for those in authority. Rather than offer definitive solutions or identify a singular constitutional future, my aim has been to map out the potential for a transformed constitution that could be developed in different directions depending on the objectives to be achieved. Inevitably this raises more questions than answers, but in thinking about constitutional substance and constitutional form – the institutions and processes, the structure and character of the Constitution – a framework for constructing a transformative programme of constitutional reform can start to be developed.

Parliamentary sovereignty can be a crucial part of a radical approach to the Constitution. While much writing about this fundamental constitutional doctrine is defensive, we fail to appreciate its democratic function and value unless we also explore its full potential in practice, rather than just acknowledge it in theory. A reformed Parliament could sit at the centre of a pluralistic, non-elitist Constitution, or we could take inspiration from the ideas underpinning parliamentary sovereignty, and seek to attach legally unlimited legislative authority to a better democratic political input, if we can make one. For some, this will go far beyond idealism into unreality, based on the present imperfections of our political order. Yet the central argument of this chapter is that until we think seriously about the unlimited potential of parliamentary sovereignty for radical constitutional transformation, and start to examine exactly how this might be exploited to shape the UK's Constitution, the virtue of that potential will ultimately be squandered, and a better constitutional future will elude us.

6

Parliament, Sovereignty and the Paradox of the Political Constitution

CHRIS McCORKINDALE

I. Introduction

Keith Ewing has made an outstanding – indeed, an inspiring – contribution to the way in which we perceive and understand the United Kingdom's (still)[1] political Constitution, both in theory[2] and in practice.[3] In this chapter, however, I will take as my point of departure what in my view is a tension between two claims that he has made about that tradition. The first is made in defence of Parliamentary sovereignty, which for Ewing is the 'core legal principle of the political constitution,' and this, he says, for two reasons. First, because it defines the power of the legislature itself, having evolved to become 'no more and no less than the legal principle underpinning the political principle that there should be no legal limit to the wishes of the people.'[4] Second, because Parliament, in the exercise of its legislative function, delineates the proper scope of lawful executive action. Seen in this light, Ewing defends judicial review on traditional *ultra vires* grounds as being 'not so much a usurpation of the sovereignty of Parliament as its vindication, to the extent that the courts do not permit Ministers or others to stray beyond their Parliamentary mandate.'[5] For Ewing, the *problem* of judicial review (against which so much of modern political constitutionalism has been defined)[6] emerges where judicial activism has gone further than this in order to wash through (and by implication to constrain) progressive social and economic legislation and government action with conservative common law values.[7] For these reasons, Ewing found it frustrating that JAG Griffith, in his seminal 1978 Chorley Lecture, *The Political Constitution*,[8] paid such little attention to the principle of

[1] KD Ewing, 'The Resilience of the Political Constitution' (2013) 14 *German Law Journal* 2111.
[2] Ibid.
[3] See, eg, Ewing's prescriptions for the constitution of social democracy in 'Jeremy Corbyn and the Law of Democracy' (2017) 28 *King's Law Journal* 343.
[4] Ewing, 'The Resilience of the Political Constitution' (n 1) 2118.
[5] Ibid.
[6] For a critique of this defensive posture see M Goldoni and C McCorkindale, 'Three Waves of Political Constitutionalism' (2019) 30 *King's Law Journal* 74.
[7] Ewing, 'The Resilience of the Political Constitution' (n 1) 2118.
[8] JAG Griffith, 'The Political Constitution' (1979) 42 *MLR* 1.

Parliamentary sovereignty, because Ewing found it difficult to see how a political constitution could operate without it.[9] Indeed, Griffith's only explicit reference to the principle in that lecture was to deny – *contra* contemporaneous challenges[10] – that the sovereignty of Parliament was amongst the constitutional vices of the time.[11]

The second claim that Ewing makes for the political constitution is offered in a recent paper on the constitution of social democracy. There, Ewing (rightly) said that 'Keynsian economics needs different kinds of constitutional arrangements than neo-liberal economics,' observing wryly that 'the constitutional preconditions and priorities of Marx are different from those of Hayek.'[12] However, the reference here – to Marx's *The Civil War in France*[13] – is telling. It was, after all, the reflections documented there about the experience of the Paris Commune that caused Marx to reconsider his view, expressed in *The Communist Manifesto,* that 'the first step in the revolution by the working class is to raise the proletariat to the position of ruling class to win the battle of democracy';[14] that, in other words, the working class must win, and then put to use, the ready-made apparatus of the state, and in particular the legislature, to *their* ends. Instead, the experience of the Commune, 'when, for the first time, the proletariat held political power for a two-month period,'[15] taught Marx – and later editions of *The Communist Manifesto* were prefaced with this reflection – that 'the working class cannot rest content with taking possession of the existing machinery of the State in order to place it in the service of its own aims,' but that a radical reorganisation of political power would be required if that power was not to be abused once more against them.[16]

The tension, then, (at least as I see it) is that the former claim – that faith ought to be shown to the principle of Parliamentary sovereignty as a *sine qua non* of the political constitution – may well be the most significant restraint upon the radical potential of the latter. Put differently, the dynamic that has traditionally defined the political Constitution has been two-fold. First, an attack against the effectiveness of Parliament as an institution, and against its legislative supremacy, from those conservative forces[17] who have favoured stronger legal and judicial checks on the exercise of political power. Second, a response by political constitutionalists *in defence of* 'actually existing democracy'[18] – a re-examination *in defence of* Parliament's record[19] – that (precisely because the posture is a defensive one) leaves untouched the core assumptions (the sovereignty of Parliament foremost amongst them) that underpin the political Constitution.

[9] Ewing, 'The Resilience of the Political Constitution' (n 1).

[10] Amongst the targets of Griffith's ire were Lord Hailsham's *The Dilemma of Democracy: Diagnosis and Prescription* (London, Collins, 1978) and Lord Scarman's *English Law – The New Dimension* (London, Stevens, 1974).

[11] Griffith (n 8) 18.

[12] Ewing, 'Jeremy Corbyn and the Law of Democracy' (n 3) 343.

[13] K Marx, *The Civil War in France* (first published 1870–71, Moscow, Progress, 1948).

[14] K Marx and F Engels, *The Communist Manifesto* (first published 1848, New York, Modern Reader, 1968) 93.

[15] See F Engels, 'Preface to the English edition' in K Marx and F Engels (eds), *The Communist Manifesto* (1888) (first published London, New York, Verso, 1998).

[16] Ibid.

[17] As well as Hailsham and Scarman (n 10) political constitutionalists have reacted to the later work of, eg, Sir J Laws, 'Law and Democracy' [1995] *Public Law* 2 and TRS Allan's *Law, Liberty and Justice: The Legal Foundations of British Constitutionalism* (Oxford, Clarendon Press, 1993) and *Constitutional Justice: A Liberal Theory of the Rule of Law* (Oxford, OUP, 2001).

[18] See R Bellamy, *Political Constitutionalism: A Republican Defence of the Constitutionality of Democracy* (Cambridge, CUP, 2007).

[19] See A Tomkins, 'In Defence of the Political Constitution' (2002) 22 *OJLS* 157 and *Our Republican Constitution* (Oxford, Hart Publishing, 2005).

In this chapter I want to challenge political constitutionalism from a different angle. This is not a challenge from law: that the political Constitution must be constrained by law in order to guard against the effects of political hyperactivity (that, as Lord Denning said, left unchecked the powers of the Welfare State lead to the Totalitarian State).[20] Rather, this is a challenge from politics: that the core of the political Constitution tends – indeed, tends *by design* – to *undermine* the potential of, and for, meaningful political action. Parliamentary sovereignty, this is to say, monopolises the public space because (understood in own terms) it is from there, through there and against there that the political legitimacy of all else either flows or is contingent. In order to embrace the potential of political action – action that, as Ewing has said, 'is not just about removing "them" but also,' and *truly*, 'about empowering "us"'[21] – political constitutionalists (certainly political constitutionalists *of the left*)[22] must think beyond the unitary implications of sovereignty (whether Parliamentary or popular) and instead embrace those fundamental principles of constitutionalism which may constitute, maintain and augment the *plurality* of spaces from which that power might be generated, *and which in the performance of that task carry their own legitimacy.*

In support of this claim, let us return to a period of constitutional history that has been a rich source of thought for contemporary political constitutionalists: the constitutional tumults of seventeenth century England.[23] Through a detailed examination of King Charles I's demand for ship money – a form of extra-parliamentary taxation levied on coastal towns by prerogative writ in order to maintain a naval fleet in times of war, that controversially was expanded inland by the King during peacetime – and of the famous response made by Parliament's chief propagandist, Henry Parker, we will see that the case for Parliament's supremacy, as it emerged from (and asserted itself in) conflict with still prevailing claims of Royal absolutism, both invoked *and immediately sought to contain* that active and constitutive power of the people themselves. If the legacy of this double move has been (intentionally) to obscure that constituent power, in order to preserve a new order with Parliament's supremacy at its core, then what is at stake here in recognising and exposing that move is the opportunity once more to think radically about the virtues of politics and of the plurality of constitutional spaces within which those virtues might best be nurtured.

II. The Demand for Ship Money

The Crown's right to requisition both ships and men in time of emergency has long been accepted 'in the widest manner'.[24] It was, however, '[t]he attempt made by Charles I to use

[20] Sir A Denning, *Freedom Under the Law* (Hamlyn Lectures) (London, Stevens and Sons, 1949) 126.

[21] Ewing, 'The Resilience of the Political Constitution' (n 1) 2117.

[22] Whilst in recent times political constitutionalism has most closely been associated with the political left, recent work by Graham Gee has sought to recover the link between political constitutionalism and the political right – see G Gee, 'The Political Constitution and the Political Rights' (2019) (30) *King's Law Journal* 148.

[23] See, eg, M Loughlin, 'Constituent Power Subverted: From English Constitutional Argument to British Constitutional Practice' in M Loughlin and N Walker (eds), *The Paradox of Constitutionalism: Constituent Power and Constitutional Form* (Oxford, OUP, 2007) and Tomkins, *Our Republican Constitution* (n 19).

[24] W Holdsworth, 'The Power of the Crown to Requisition British Ships in a National Emergency' (1919) 35 *LQR* 12, 12–13.

his prerogative over ships and shipping to raise a permanent extra-Parliamentary revenue by means of ship-money' which roused the suspicions of his subjects.[25] Having dissolved Parliament on 2 March 1629, following a 'disorderly scene' in the Commons, when the Speaker, John Finch, had been forcibly held in his chair to receive a stinging remonstrance against the Crown's taking of tonnage and poundage without the consent of the Parliament,[26] Charles would wait eleven years before calling another. In the meantime, however, the Crown's need to generate income was undiminished.[27] By 1634 it was thought that England's fleet would struggle to keep up with its expanding and improving French and Dutch counterparts. Whilst the law would allow Charles to requisition private ships, however, it would not allow him the money to fit his own. As Glenn Burgess observed, '[the law] allowed [the king] to do what he did not need to do, but did not allow him to do what he needed to do.'[28] To be sure, ship money of sorts was nothing new. As late as 1619, James I had raised nearly £50,000 from seaport towns in lieu of ships for war against Algiers.[29] In that case, the country was on a war footing and the danger to the Commonwealth was both immediate and visible. In 1634, however, Charles issued a writ requisitioning ships, or money in lieu thereof, directly from his people against the widely held suspicion that no such threat was in fact imminent.

The writs of 1634, commonly attributed to the Attorney General, William Noy, were carefully drafted to conform to old precedents: restricted in application to the maritime counties and seaport towns and asking first for ships and not for money.[30] The initial collection which followed was relatively successful, 79,589 pounds having been collected from assessments totalling 80,609. However, having invested some 88,000 pounds on their fleet, the Crown required yet more income and so, by 4 August 1635, a second levy was charged which not only renewed the previous maritime levy, but which extended the tax inwards, to the inland counties.[31] '[T]his burden of defence[32] which touches all,' the writ explained, 'ought to be borne by all.'[33] Accordingly, the writ was accompanied with an instruction to those sheriffs charged with collection to levy – instead of a ship – a specified sum of money.[34]

Charles had fully anticipated the unpopularity of the revised policy, and, anticipating the difficulties in collection which surely followed, sought to counteract his subjects'

[25] Ibid, 26.

[26] FW Maitland, *The Constitutional History of England* (Cambridge, Cambridge University Press, 1908) 314.

[27] On the contribution of the Crown's 'poverty' to the eventual outbreak of civil war see, generally, G Burgess, *The Causes of the English Civil War: The Ford Lectures Delivered in the University of Oxford 1987–1988* (Oxford, Clarendon Press, 1990) esp ch 7.

[28] Ibid, 183.

[29] R Tanner, *English Constitutional Conflicts of the Seventeenth Century 1603–1689* (Cambridge, Cambridge University Press, 1928) 76.

[30] See 'Specimen of the first Writ of Ship-money' in SR Gardiner (ed) *Documents of the Puritan Revolution 1625–1660* (Oxford, Clarendon Press, 1889) 105.

[31] MD Gordon, 'The Collection of Ship-Money in the Reign of Charles I' (1910) 4 *Transactions of the Royal Historical Society* 141, 143.

[32] For the record, the danger spelled out in this writ was virtually identical to that of the first.

[33] Quoted in RL Noble, 'Lions or Jackals? The Independence of the Judges in Rex v. Hampden' (1962) 14 *Stanford Law Review* 711, 715.

[34] Tanner (n 29) 77.

displeasure with the support of his judges. Thus, having already offered his support for the initial writs, the royalist judge, Finch, urged his colleagues to subscribe to an extra-judicial opinion maintaining the legality of the policy. This they did, to the effect that:

> (1) … where the benefit of naval defence was more particularly felt by the coastal districts, they alone should contribute to the cost; (2) that the King was sole judge of whether the danger extended to the country as a whole; and (3) that where he judged that it did so, the burden of defence fell on all alike.[35]

To this (unpublished) opinion Hutton did not subscribe, and Croke offered a separate opinion.[36] Frustrated by continued problems of collection, Charles returned for a further opinion, this time to be made public. Therein, the scope for collection was widened still: 'explicitly stating that the King could command contributions from his subjects and coerce the refractory.'[37] Again, Croke and Hutton disagreed. This time, however, it was urged 'that the lesser number must submit to the major, although they varied in opinion,' and the opinion did as if it was unanimous, published as the 'resolution of "all the judges of England".'[38] With the opinion of the judges (seemingly) behind them, the Crown felt confident that the legality of ship money could withstand judicial scrutiny, and brought proceedings against the politician and noted opponent of the King, John Hampden, for his refusal to pay.[39]

III. 'A Controversy Like No Other'

The substitution of the King's judgment with that of Parliament was not original to Parker's famous response to the majority in *Hampden*. As with the majority opinion of Jones, for Croke the courtroom was an inappropriate forum for the resolution of such fundamental questions as the constitutional relationship between the monarch and his subjects. However, in stark contrast to Jones – who left 'divines' to such determinations – for Croke, the question was best resolved neither by divines nor by the court, but in 'a public Assembly of the whole State.'[40] This early attempt to locate a constitutive power – one which embraces *radical* disagreement about the very distribution of power within the state – in (an assembly of) the people met with the monarch's rebuke, and Croke duly obeyed Charles' demand for the case to be heard. It was, furthermore, a position upon which Croke stood alone. The language of the bench was, quite naturally, that of fundamental laws, of the ancient Constitution, of the monarchic history and traditions of the English Constitution, but by employing this language the law kept closed the emergence

[35] DL Keir, 'The Case of Ship-Money' (1936) 52 *LQR* 546, 555.

[36] Noble (n 33) 716.

[37] Keir (n 35) 555.

[38] Noble (n 33) 716. It was alleged that in order to procure support for the King from all the judges Finch had used bribes and threats to secure their signatures: see WJ Jones, *Politics and the Bench: The Judges and the Origins of the English Civil War* (London, George Allen & Unwin Ltd, 1971) 127.

[39] *R v Hampden* (1637) 3 State Tr 826.

[40] Ibid at 146 per Croke.

of subjects as citizens: of the people as an active rather than a passive political, legal, and constitutional force. Nevertheless, his opinion, albeit delivered by reason of obedience, was one which remained rooted to an idea of the people (at least as constituted in Parliament) as the Commonwealth's constituent power and legitimising authority. Having failed to replace the judgment of the court with that of the 'whole nation', Croke's opinion called for the no less revolutionary substitution of Parliament for the King as the repository of *salus republicae*. 'We have a pious King,' he said, 'and he will not [abuse his power, by declaring an emergency where none exists], but the law looks into the inconvenience.'[41] The law in other words must *assume* at least the possibility that the monarch (or rather, in his caution, some future monarch) may either abuse their power personally, or use it unnecessarily on the basis of misinformation. Safer, therefore, to trust 'the judgement of Parliament', and neither the monarch nor their counsel, in the assessment of any such emergency. This proposition, rejected explicitly in the majority opinion of Finch,[42] was doubted even by Croke's allies in the minority.

Throughout the 1630s, a decade of government without Parliament, the public's perception of the latter was somewhat mixed. To some, and in this we can include Croke, Parliament was a council comparable to the Roman Senate, in which the King:

> … could hear advice important to him and to the realm. He could insure that his subjects understood his needs, demonstrate his concern for them by hearing their grievances, and avoid embarking on a course of action for which he would find it difficult to obtain their support.[43]

In Parliament, in other words, opinions could be exchanged, tested and formed, and, more than that, imparted to the King, influencing his own opinion. It was also variously seen as a supporter in war, a maker of laws and a granter of taxes. Yet, Cope has argued that in its absence 'few individuals expressed either regret … or desire that one be called.'[44] Thus it was the view of Parliament as 'a turbulent assembly where overzealous subjects poured out grievances and aspired to assume authority over matters which they did not understand and which belonged to the royal prerogative'[45] which found the strongest support amongst the judiciary in *Hampden*.

In the context of early Stuart England, where (cosmic or divine) order was revered, the charge of *disorder* made against Parliament, initiated by the Crown and reaffirmed by the majority of the judges in *Hampden*, was a potent one. In an instant, however, Parker turned those very claims back upon the judiciary, opening his *Case of Shipmony* with wonder at the 'strange contradiction' that existed 'amongst the pleaders, and dissent amongst the Judges, even in those laws which are most fundamental, that we are left in a more confused uncertainty of our highest privileges, and those customs which are most essential to Freedom than we were before.'[46]

[41] Ibid.
[42] Ibid at 203 per Finch.
[43] ES Cope, 'Public Images of Parliament during Its Absence (1982) 7 *Legislative Studies Quarterly* 221, 226.
[44] Ibid, 222.
[45] Ibid, 225.
[46] H Parker, *The Case of Shipmony Briefly Discoursed, According to the Grounds of Law, Policy, and Conscience, and Most Humbly presented to the Censure and Correction of the High Court of Parliament* (London, 1640) 1–2.

Parker's prescription was made with gusto; the publication of *The Case of Shipmony*, timed to coincide with the opening of the Long Parliament, stating with clarity and precision that:

> To remove ... this uncertainty, which is the mother of all injustice, confusion, and public dissent, it is most requisite that [Parliament] (of which none ought to think dishonourably) would take these Arduis Regni, these weighty and dangerous and dangerous difficulties, into ferocious debate, and solemnly end that strife, which no other place of Judicature can so effectually extinguish.[47]

As Michael Mendle has said, the 'intellectual and political task of *The Case of Shipmony* ... was to re-establish order amidst the confusion' engendered by the judgement.[48] It was the near unanimous verdict of the judges in *Hampden* that the case was the most significant constitutional dispute to come before an English court. And yet, for Parker, the astonishing fact betrayed by their various opinions was that the 'greatest Sages of our Law'[49] had *no* firm idea of the constitutional fundamentals upon which the King's (undisputed) power to compel aid in times of emergency in fact, as well as in theory, was grounded. At times the judges argued upon grounds of natural law. That 'since the King is head, and bound to protect, therefore he must have wherewithal to protect.' Some argued from the prerogative, yet Parker was left unsure as to the exact nature of that prerogative: 'whether [it be the] Prerogative natural of all Kings, or the Prerogative legal of the Kings of *England*.' Some argued that 'by Law there is natural allegiance due to the King from the subject,' by which the monarch could not be denied the grant of aid; whilst others argued from the very opposite: that by law man had a right in his property, 'and it doth not stand with that property, that the King may demand of them without consent.' Finally, it was argued that the King's prerogative could not be used to create injustice, from the starting assumption 'that to levy money without consent is unjust.'[50] To rest the prerogative on such uncertain ground was, for Parker, '[t]o introduce ... such a Prerogative ... as destroys all other Law, and is incompatible with popular liberty.'[51] Echoing the contributions made by Peard, Seymor and St John in the debates of the Short Parliament, the decision to uphold Charles' policy on such a basis stripped the subject of more than his right to property. '[I]f we grant Ship money upon these grounds with Ship money we grant all besides.'[52] That is to say we grant to the King not *only* our property, but – in conceding to so broad a discretion – we surrender also our status as free subjects.[53]

Thus where law is no longer made in co-ordination between prince and people – wherein each is capable of wooing the opinion of the other, or at least to modify one's own in light of it – but instead where the mere will of the King is law, where *Rex* is indivisibly *lex*, the people are no less miserable in their subjection to the King, as is the slave

[47] Ibid, 2.
[48] M Mendle, *Henry Parker and the English Civil War* (Cambridge, CUP, 1995) 35.
[49] Parker, *The Case of Shipmony Briefly Discoursed* (n 46) 2.
[50] Ibid, 3–4.
[51] Ibid, 2.
[52] Ibid.
[53] Ibid, 4.

to his master.[54] This, Parker observed, was precisely the danger which lurked in the majority's support for the charge of ship money:

> … as sole judgement is here ascribed to the King, he may affirm dangers to be foreseen when he will, and of what nature he will: If he say only, Datum est nobis intelligi,[55] as he does in his Writ … to his sole indisputable judgement it is left to lay charges as often and as great as he pleases. And by this means if he regard not his word more than his profit, he may in one year drain all the Kingdom of all its treasure, and leave us the most despicable slaves in the whole world.[56]

What concerned Parker was not merely the use by the King of his prerogative to violate the property rights of his subjects *in this instance*, rather it was the very existence of that prerogative, which might be exercised at any indeterminate time, by any indeterminate means, which left Charles' subjects in so dire a predicament. Parker, in Quentin Skinner's estimation, therefore became Parliament's 'most lucid and resourceful supporter,'[57] for his ability to articulate this condition of uncertainty: by which the people 'possess [no] such liberties, since the very existence of such prerogative powers reduces us to a level below that of free subjects.'[58] No person, this was to say, could reliably act upon their freedom because no person could be certain that the liberties that they enjoyed today would endure tomorrow. In this way, the very essence of virtue was at stake:

> Those who live at the mercy of such rulers learn to curb the very qualities that need to be given freest rein if civic greatness is to be achieved. The alternative … is to learn from experience that under tyranny the possession of outstanding qualities is a 'capital crime'. With virtue effectively proscribed, we are condemned to living in a servile society in which flatterers and time-servers flourish unopposed.[59]

It was amidst this uncertainty that Parker sought to establish an island of predictability and, with that, a forum for the expression of civic greatness in the institution of Parliament.

IV. Parliament's Privado

More, then, than an acid analysis of the majority opinion in *Hampden*, Parker's *Case of Shipmony* would lay the key-stone for a full blown account of Parliamentary absolutism. For Parker, the divine constitution in which the King had sat as God's lieutenant on Earth had proven itself *by the king's own actions* to be inadequate:

> Divines of late have been much to blame here in preaching one universal form of government, as necessary to all Nations [that being monarchic rule by divine right], and that not the moderate and equal neither, but such as ascribes all to Sovereignty, nothing at all to popular liberty.[60]

[54] Ibid, 5.
[55] 'It is given us to be understood'.
[56] Parker, *The Case of Shipmony Briefly Discoursed* (n 46) 11.
[57] Q Skinner, *Visions of Politics, Volume II: Renaissance Virtues* (Cambridge, Cambridge University Press, 2002) 293.
[58] Ibid, 288.
[59] Ibid, 290.
[60] Parker, *The Case of Shipmony Briefly Discoursed* (n 46) 8.

It was 'not sufficient,' he said, for Jones, in his majority opinion, to determine that Kings might lawfully raise money without the consent of their subjects, 'unless he first prove that such Prerogative be good and profitable for the people.'[61] It was, moreover, insufficient for the majority to hold that, in so proving, 'it is contrary to presumption of Law to suspect falsity in the King.'[62] In support of his counter-proposition Parker offered examples which must have shocked his audience: that even England's 'best Kings, King Charles, King James, Queen Elizabeth … have done undue illegal things,' having been misinformed by their Ministers.[63] Whilst at this stage Parker was either unwilling or unprepared to make the more explicitly republican argument that monarchs ought to give account before the people for the 'illegal things' done unto them, he nevertheless hinted as much in his stated refusal to 'condemn any Nation as unjust' who had, for the most part throughout Christendom, displaced the absolute monarch and 'given [themselves] to republics or to conditional and restrained forms of government.'[64]

If it was just, in the last place, for the people to rise up against their monarch; if some have chosen republics, or other restrained governments, where once they had submitted to monarchy, then Parker must at this point in time have understood the further implication that *in* the political community itself was to be found the original (that which *forms* the shape of government) and the final (that which *contests* the shape of government) *locus* of political power. Parker did not, here, follow his arguments to the conclusion that monarchy had no place in the English Constitution. However, his claim that by the Constitution all Kings, good or bad, should act only and always in Parliament was no less revolutionary. Such a King, he advised, 'which is potent in Parliament, as good as any King may, is as it were so ensconced in the hearts of his subjects, that he is almost beyond the trains or aims of treason and rebellion at home, nay foreign hostility cannot pierce him, but through the sides of all his people.'[65] As Mendle has said, to give Parker's words their due 'is to come close to asserting Parliamentary control of executive power.'[66]

That Parker attributed the 'undue' and 'illegal' acts committed even by virtuous monarchs to the 'misinformation' offered by their counsel speaks to two possible lines of criticism, each challenging the appropriateness of the monarch's right to act as the sole judge of the common good. On the one hand it is probable that Parker himself did not believe Charles to be one of England's 'best Kings,' as he had said, but that, aware of the consequences of making a direct claim for Charles's incompetence or, worse still, nefarious designs, Parker found it strategically advantageous to level those claims instead at the King's trusted advisors.[67] In addition, however, is the underlying implication that such misinformation as did make its way to the King might itself have been symptomatic of the suffocation

[61] Ibid, 6.
[62] Ibid, 21.
[63] Ibid.
[64] Ibid, 7–8.
[65] Ibid, 38.
[66] M Mendle, 'The Ship Money Case, The Case of Shipmony, and the Development of Henry Parker's Parliamentary Absolutism' (1989) 32 *The Historical Journal* 513, 526.
[67] Mendle notes that as a 'pure, freestanding printed political tract [*The Case of Shipmony*] was not a natural mode of expression' at that time. Rather it stood out for '[taking] a current issue and [discussing] it in a way that led to practical prescription … as well as to a broader political vision' Mendle, *Henry Parker and the English Civil War* (n 48) 32–33.

of virtue under subjugation; that the slide to 'slavish servility', to 'cowardice' and 'sloth', of which those Roman authorities such as Sallust and Tacitus had warned, could easily translate, in the minds of contemporary Englishmen, to those who had so ill-informed Charles throughout his reign.[68] Discouraged from the heroic virtues of political action by their King, Englishmen could rely only on a small circle of 'cowards', 'time servers' and 'flatterers' to advise their monarch. No wonder, then, Parker's observation that 'it is more probable and natural, that evil may be expected from good Princes, than good from bad.'[69] Because the state suffers equally whether that 'evil' springs forth from the King's malice or from his ministers' bad (or slavish) advice, the law must, he said – contrary to the majority opinion in *Hampden* – allow the King's actions to be scrutinised. '[I]f we must presume well of our Princes,' he asked, 'to what purpose are Laws made.'[70] Parker's claim was not that Charles would falter, although the implication was there. '[I]t is enough,' was his point, 'that we all, and all that we have are at his discretion.'[71]

If the King had shown by his actions the limits of the divine Constitution, Parker was equally clear that the sovereignty of *law*, personified by the judges and expressed in their judicial opinions, was an incapable alternative. Laws are made; they are as rules; and, whilst they exist to limit the discretion of executive power, this could not manifest as the sovereignty of law. This was because laws are always subject to exception:

> God dispenses with many of his Laws, rather than *salus populi*[72] shall be endangered; and that iron-law, which we call necessity itself, is but subservient to this Law: for rather than a Nation shall perish, anything shall be held necessary, and legal by necessity …[73]

It was clear, to Parker, that the King was an unsatisfactory judge of so extraordinarily powerful a state of exception, because of his exposure to private interest and bad counsel. However, the judges fared no better – for it was they who (amongst others) provided that counsel. Insurrections, suggested Parker, served to warn Kings not to 'overstrain their Prerogatives too high.' He continued, however, that they served equally 'to warn all wise Princes … not to give ear to such Counsellors as some of our Judges are, who affirm the King's Prerogative to be in all points unalterable, and by consequence not depending upon Law at all.'[74] For Parker, the decision of the majority to uphold the taking of ship money without the consent of Parliament was worthy itself of punishment. Thus, closing his argument, he recommended that 'some dishonourable penalty may be imposed upon the Judges which ill advised the King herein, and the argued as Pleaders, not as Judges.'[75] The judges themselves had, in Parker's estimation, acted as a branch of the Crown and not as an impartial and fair arbiter between the King's prerogative and the subject's liberty. By placing the prerogative power beyond the reach of the court that power, in Parker's view, tended to the de facto destruction of *all* laws. 'If,' he said, 'a King should shut up the Courts of ordinary

[68] Skinner (n 57) 290.
[69] Parker, *The Case of Shipmony Briefly Discoursed* (n 46) 21–22.
[70] Ibid, 22.
[71] Ibid.
[72] That 'the health of the people is the supreme law'.
[73] Parker, *The Case of Shipmony Briefly Discoursed* (n 46) 7.
[74] Ibid, 9.
[75] Ibid, 47.

Justice, and prohibit all pleadings and proceedings between man and man, and refuse to authorize Judges for the determination of suits, he would be held to do a most unkingly thing,'[76] and yet, the effect of the judges' slavish support for the King's policy – whose 'necessity has been answered, and disproved already'[77] – was almost the same.

In Parliament, on the other hand, the case of necessity would be the subject of ferocious debate, demanding of the very virtues suffocated by subjection to monarchic rule: wisdom, sincerity, and greatness.

Wisdom, said Parker, could not be expected from the King nor from his few advisors, for 'all private single persons may deceive and be deceived.' It was inconceivable, however, that 'an inconsiderable number of Privados should see or know more than whole Kingdoms,' as, 'all cannot deceive one, nor one all.' In Parliament, however, was to be found a public forum in which the great controversies of the day were openly and freely debated from a multiplicity of perspectives that tended against duplicity. It was, then, 'a just law, that no private man must be wiser then Law publicly made.'[78] The very assembly, the public assembly, of the 'whole kingdom', as it was put, had endowed the institution of Parliament with wisdom; such wisdom as the King, in the privacy of his counsel, could never achieve. The *sincerity* of Parliament's advice is attributed, by Parker, to the presence of God amongst the assembled, and yet remained at the same time inherent in the people. Blessed by God 'so their ends cannot be so sinister,' the 'common body can effect nothing but the common good, because nothing else can be commodious for them.'[79] The contrast of course was with the King. Not only, *contra* Jones, *could* the King do wrong, all Kings, great and tyrannous alike, *had* done wrong; their private interests, or those of their closest advisors bringing 'common calamity' to the nation.[80] Parliament, on the other hand, could do no wrong to the kingdom because *it was* the kingdom. Any course other than the common good could therefore *only* be against its, and inextricably the public's, interests.[81]

By tapping into the wisdom and sincerity of Parliament the King would achieve true *greatness*; this because more than wisdom, more than sincerity, Parliament offered a public space into which heroic action could be seen and be remembered in the 'hearts of the people': hearts, Parker said, which beat with such force for the public welfare that any King 'potent in Parliament … is [put] almost beyond the [the fate] of treason and rebellion' which had befallen so many tyrants.[82] Such hearts the King's few ministers simply could not carry, even if their counsel was both wise and sincere. For sure, it was possible to argue that the advice given to the Crown regarding the need for and implementation of ship money was legally defensible. In the hearts of the people, however, the argument was lost: the sharp collapse of the policy that immediately followed the judgment was evidence itself that the view of Charles as an 'arbitrary' and 'absolute' monarch had formed in the minds of his subjects:[83]

[76] Ibid.
[77] Ibid, 44.
[78] Ibid, 35.
[79] Ibid, 35–36.
[80] Ibid, 36.
[81] R Zaller, 'Henry Parker and the Regiment of True Government' (1991) 135 *Proceedings of the American Philosophical Society* 255, 258.
[82] Parker, *The Case of Shipmony Briefly Discoursed* (n 46) 36.
[83] G Burgess, *The Politics of the Ancient Constitution: An Introduction to English Political Thought 1603-1642* (Pennsylvania, Pennsylvania State University Press, 1992) 202.

'no Tyranny is more abhorred,' said Parker, 'than that which has a controlling power over all Law, and knows no bounds but its own will.'[84]

James I in word, and Charles I in deed, had established their accountability to no other authority than God himself by tracing the origins of their temporal office to divine sanction from heaven: to the divine right of Kings to rule on Earth. For Parker to claim that the King must find greatness in Parliament, or risk bringing tumult upon his reign, required more than a challenge to the fiction of divine right, but the discovery of a new founding principle upon which the authority of that Parliament could rest. In *The Case of Shipmony* a case was tentatively made that it was by the people themselves that political power was conferred upon the King. From Charles' own maxim, that 'the peoples liberty strengthens the Kings prerogative, and the Kings prerogative is to maintain the peoples liberty ', Parker inferred not only that prerogative and liberty were compatible, but that the former, which exists purely for the sake of the latter, must be subordinate; that by nature 'more favour is due to the liberty of the subject, then to the Prerogative of the King, since the one is ordained only for the preservation of the other.'[85] As Zaller has said, this was more than the mere restoration of balance following constitutional rupture. Rather, 'it was a decisive alteration in the equation';[86] a new form of government, it might be said, of world-historic importance. For sure James I had advised his heir that the king was ordained for his subjects, and not his subjects for the king. Contrary to the claims of divine right however, the question which followed was not 'what liberty the Kings absoluteness or prerogative may admit' but instead, 'must be, what prerogative the peoples good and profit will bear.'[87] In Parliament, it would seem, Parker had found the means by which the limits of the people's forbearance could be measured. Implicit was the message that the King had been created by the people, his prerogative for their welfare; that therefore the people, or a manifestation thereof, best knew the limits of both. What was implicit in *The Case of Shipmony* would soon be made explicit: Parker beginning his *Observations* of July 1642[88] with the powerful assertion that:

> Power is originally inherent in the people, and it is nothing else but that might and vigour which such or such a society of men contains in itself, and when by such or such a Law of common consent and agreement it is derived into such and such hands.[89]

From the divine sanction of God to the constituent power of the people, the prescription which would become Parker's epitaph was that in Parliament's hands was *salus republicae*, that supreme law, safest, because Parliament itself *was* the people in whom political power naturally inhered.

However, if we revisit, for a moment, the story of Ship Money, we can see the emergence, if even for a fleeting moment, of an active, a real people, resisting the King and calling his authority into question. Moreover, it was this initial moment of local resistance which opened the space within which Parliament – most conspicuously through Parker – could re-invent the nation's constitutional foundation.

[84] Parker, *The Case of Shipmony Briefly Discoursed* (n 46) 22.
[85] Ibid, 4–5.
[86] Zaller (n 81) 257.
[87] Parker, *The Case of Shipmony Briefly Discoursed* (n 46) 5.
[88] H Parker, *Observations upon some of his Majesties late Answers and Expresses* (London, 1642).
[89] Ibid, 1.

V. The People Out of Doors: Ship Money Re-visited

If the extension of Ship Money to the inland counties caused contemporaneous controversy, its value remains contested even to this day. Kevin Sharpe has called Ship Money the 'great success story' of personal rule. 'It is significant,' he argues, 'that when the writ was extended from the maritime counties to the country at large, the point at which the legality [of the policy] might have been questioned, only 2½ per cent of the sum requested failed to come in, and the amount raised, £194,864, was never exceeded.'[90] On the other hand, Lamar Hill ascribes 'failure to the six years of Ship Money collection which ended in 1640.' Despite the immediate success of the policy – the per annum average of £107,000 (even allowing for the virtual non-collection of the final year) amounted to 'the highest peace-time direct tax receipt ever recorded' – for Hill the policy 'failed utterly in the long run and was a major divisive element in the build up to civil war.'[91] Certainly, the effect of *Hampden* on the success of collection suggested at best a temporary and limited victory for the Crown. Despite the 7–5 majority decision in the King's favour, the narrowness of that victory, and the articulation of strong dissenting opinions, preyed on the suspicions of the people at large that the charge being asked of them was illegal. As Cromartie said, '[f]rom a practical political perspective, the only thing that mattered was that virtually all England [already] believed that the payments demanded were indefensible.'[92] Thus, in the months between the hearing of the arguments and the delivery of the judgment a number of people opted to withhold payment in anticipation of the policy being held to be illegal. If large numbers continued to pay, and this (in the very short term at least) they did, their doing so seemed to be an act of compliance rather than an act in support of the Crown's authority. How else to explain that not defeat but a narrow victory for the Crown saw 'by 1638 a falling off and by 1639 only a fraction' of successful collection?[93] The judges, it was said, had acted 'upon such grounds and reasons as every stander-by was able to swear was not law,'[94] and this, coupled with the quick and influential spread of the minority verdicts, soon precipitated the collapse of the entire policy. As early as May in 1638 it was noted that '[t]he King's moneys come in a great deal more slowly than they did in former years, and that to a very considerable sum.'[95] Reporting on the difficulties of collection, Clarendon was clear in his opinion that the spread of the judgments had the paradoxical effect of strengthening Charles's subjects in their resolve to resist collection,[96] as a 'considerable' deficit shortly gave way to 'extraordinary public [and on occasion violent] hostility,' and a collection of almost nil.[97] As Cressy concluded, 'Ship money became uncollectable, even before Parliament declared it illegal.'[98]

[90] K Sharpe, *Politics and Ideas in Early Stuart England: Essays and Studies* (London, Pinter Publishers, 1989) 115.

[91] LM Hill, 'County Government in Caroline England, 1625-1640' in C Russell (ed), *The Origins of the English Civil War* (Basingstoke, Palgrave Macmillan, 1973) 83.

[92] A Cromartie, *The Constitutionalist Revolution: An Essay on the History of England, 1450-1642* (Cambridge, Cambridge University Press, 2006) 239.

[93] Jones (n 38) 128.

[94] Clarendon's *History of the Rebellion*, quoted in Tanner (n 29) 78.

[95] Letter of Laud to Wentworth, quoted in Tanner, ibid 79.

[96] Jones (n 38) ch 5.

[97] C Russell, 'Parliament and the King's Finances' in Russell (ed) (n 91) 109.

[98] D Cressy, *England On Edge: Crisis and Revolution 1640-1642* (Oxford, Oxford University Press, 2007) 355.

In spite of, indeed following Clarendon it is surer to say because of, the Crown's victory in *Hampden*, the very prerogative of the Crown to act as it saw fit in the face of a perceived threat to the state seemed to lose its binding force. That this was no petulant strike against authority, no individual objection by men of means to the confiscation of their property, but a resistance which took place in that grey area between the letter and the spirit of the Constitution, a resistance to law in the name of legality, is supported by the fact that the occurrence of disobedience was sporadic and rare, until it had become clear that the legal process had failed in its rights protecting function. What is more, it was the strength of the dissenting opinions which had emboldened that resistance and 'had increased the difficulties of collection.'[99]

This moment of resistance is both significant, and largely ignored, in *constitutional* interpretations of this period, which focus on the Parliament's invocation of the people in the abstract – the mere substitute for a King who, before his Fall, had reigned over the whole nation. So, Loughlin says that 'the conviction that governmental authority was rooted in the opinion of the people' was employed 'to strengthen the Parliamentary case'; whilst Morgan takes it even further, calling the sovereignty of the people 'an instrument by which representatives raised themselves to the maximum distance above the particular set of people who chose them,' shedding their specific local connections in doing so.[100] Yet, before those claims could be made, it was in the (as we look back) somewhat obscured realm of local politics that the resistance to the Crown had taken shape. This may have reached its apogee in a national institution, when John Hampden's case was heard by the Court of Exchequer, but it had begun in the counties, where the extension of Ship Money had sharpened even the most introspective localities to the emergence of an urgent threat to their liberties.[101] Indeed, in the county of Kent, feeling the pinch of the levy more than most,[102] leading families had come together in their objection, circulating amongst themselves the preparation of a Book of Arguments against the policy, which centred on their perception of its illegality.[103] Thus, amongst their number, the Historian and (later) Member of the Short Parliament, Sir Roger Twysden, having first accepted the necessity of the levy, became, after due study of the precedents, convinced that it could not be defended in law; their concerns filtering down to the townsfolk and farmers who 'bitterly complained' of the tax's iniquity.[104] So, when Hampden – himself born of one of the leading families in his own home county of Buckinghamshire – was brought before the court for his steadfast refusal to give up that which had been demanded of him, he was more than the representative of a people in the abstract threatened by the King's recklessness, but of the people as a working reality in their various counties, sharing – in the exchange of their grievances – something of a unifying cause. To create a Book of Arguments against the policy, to challenge the legitimacy of the

[99] Jones (n 38) 128.

[100] ES Morgan, *Inventing the People: The Rise of Popular Sovereignty in England and America* (New York, Norton, 1988) 50; M Loughlin, 'Constituent Power Subverted: From English Constitutional Argument to British Constitutional Practice' in M Loughlin and N Walker (eds), *The Paradox of Constitutionalism: Constituent Power and Constitutional Form* (Oxford, Oxford University Press, 2007) 33–35.

[101] See A Fletcher, *The Outbreak of the English Civil War* (London, Edward Arnold, 1981) xxvi.

[102] Gordon (n 31).

[103] A Everitt, *The Community of Kent and the Great Rebellion 1640-60* (Leicester, Leicester University Press, 1966) 63–64.

[104] Ibid, 64.

King's writ in the court room, to withhold payment, actively to resist those sheriffs sent for collection: each of these acts opened and maintained a space – between law's letter and law's spirit – into which the people could emerge in a spirit of deed and of action. More still, this space simply could not co-exist with a conception of monarchy which held the King accountable to no human authority. As such it demanded both the knocking down of government as Stuart Royalists had known (or at least, had told) it, and the building up of a new form of government, capable of harnessing that spirit.

VI. *Jus Populi* and The Lost Treasure

It was not until he was freed from his obligations to Parliament that Parker himself followed the logic of the claim that power inhered in the people to his most radical conclusion: that sovereignty *itself*, and not merely the divine variety, was unpolitical. In one of his final, but less explored, political tracts, (the anonymously published) *Jus Populi*, Parker set out to dispel the royalist claim that political power was at all hierarchical in nature. Finding agreement with his opponents that domination inheres in private relationships – that the father properly is possessed of a natural authority over his son,[105] that the husband is naturally possessed of a contractual authority over his wife[106] – the boldness of *Jus Populi* lay in detaching political power and public interests from any analogy with private power and personal interests. For one, whilst the son, wife and household stood to benefit from their submission (and I will leave for elsewhere a critique of domination in private relationships),[107] the condition of 'servitude' created by 'absolute, arbitrary' government 'professes no justice in itself.'[108] Indeed, he said to the contrary that such rule encourages injustice: 'arbitrary government does not only rob slaves of that natural interest which they have in themselves, and states of their public interests … but it is often a very strong incentive to cause an abuse of that usurped interest.'[109] For another, government itself (arbitrary or otherwise; monarchic or democratic) was created in the exercise of (what then must be a political) freedom, and neither by nature (father/son) nor necessity (husband/wife). Thus, he said: 'I conceive that freedom being in itself good, and acceptable to Nature, was preferred before government, which was also good,' with the consequence that prior to any government was the freedom to create that government. If government was not to 'abuse the usurped interests' of its citizens, it was important for Parker that under the weight of government 'man be left free and not abridged of his own consent [and note the positive/political connotation of freedom as consent here, surely more demanding than, say, (negative/private) liberty] or forced by any Law of God to depart from his freedom.'[110] For Parker, arbitrary

[105] H Parker, *Jus Populi* (London, 1644) 33–34.
[106] Ibid, 35–36.
[107] Note, however, that for Parker the powers of father over son, husband over wife, whilst ordered hierarchically did not amount to 'jurisdiction' or to 'coercive' control: disputes therein were properly to be settled not by the father/husband's will but by 'an impartial judicator' or other 'public authority' (ibid, 32).
[108] Ibid, 36.
[109] Ibid, 38.
[110] Ibid, 5–6.

or absolute or sovereign authority obscured the reality that political power inhered in the community of (plural) men. Following this, when Parker declared 'horrid, unnatural, and altogether … damnable' those who denounced resistance – 'for hereby it is plainly averred that either government was erected for subversive ends, or else that general subversion may conduce malevolent ends'[111] – it would seem that his reassertion of that reality in an act of *dissent* against constituted power was the surest way to rein in domination.

Here, however, is the rub: and the trick which has remained with us since. What Parker said in *Jus Populi* was undoubtedly radical. Yet the force of the argument was lost with the immediate proviso that 'Parliament is … nothing else, but the very people itself; that the two [Parliament and people] ought not, in honour, in majesty, in commission … to be divided, or accounted different.'[112] Put differently, having proclaimed that government must not abridge the peoples' consent, lest it be encouraged to nefarious ends, Parker immediately exchanged the real world for an imaginary one: with the fiction that Parliament *was* the people, that the consent of Parliament was indivisible with and gave expression to the consent of the people. The importance of this is not to be underestimated. If the people consent to government, they can legitimately confront it in an act of dissent. If the people *created* Parliament in an act of consent, then the people might legitimately *dissent* where Parliament abuses its power. However, to say that Parliament *was* the people was to deny any prior constitutive act, and therefore any right to revoke or to re-order that act. That there was no public realm outwith Parliament's walls, no space of appearance in which opinions could be exchanged and formed – let alone the sort of resistance encouraged and praised when directed against the King. As it was put in one anonymously authored pamphlet: '[Parliament's] judgement is our judgement, and they that oppose the judgement of Parliament oppose their own judgement.'[113] Thus, for Parker, there was nothing 'horrid, unnatural, and altogether … damnable' about advocating non-resistance *to Parliament*: indeed, he said, 'there can be nothing … which can be more perfidious and more pernicious in the people,' than resisting the acts of that institution.[114] Another of Parliament's most prominent spokesmen, Charles Herle, was even more clear:

> A … question begged [by the Royalist, Henry Ferne] is that in case the king and Parliament should neither discharge their trusts, the people might rise and make resistance to them both, a position which no man I know maintains. The Parliament is the people's own consent, which once passed they cannot revoke … the people have reserved no right in themselves from themselves in Parliament.[115]

Having set out in *Jus Populi* to demonstrate that there was 'no sufficient rule, precedent, or authority, for arbitrary power,' indeed, having brilliantly done so, Parker immediately lay the foundations for the most arbitrary power of all, imagining a world in which others simply did not exist: Parliament *was* the people; there *were* no others. Parliament, in the most royalist of language, could 'do no wrong.'[116]

[111] Ibid, 56.
[112] Ibid, 18.
[113] Anon, *Plain Dealing With England* (London, 1643) 2.
[114] Parker, *Observations upon some of his Majesties late Answers and Expresses* (n 88) 16.
[115] C Herle, *A Fuller Answer to a Treatise Written by Dr Ferne* (London, 1642).
[116] J Marsh, *An Argument or Debate in Law* (London, 1642) 15.

VII. Conclusion

The story of ship money captures the legacy of the era: a period when, as Loughlin has said, 'a "constituting power" located in "the people" [first emerged] not simply as a rhetorical symbol but as an active force emerges for the first time,'[117] only to be repressed by those 'seeking to manage the unfolding English revolution.'[118] This paradox is the fault line upon which the political Constitution rests: the realisation by the Parliament men that there was no greater threat to the stability of the new order that they sought to establish than the revolutionary spirit harnessed by them in order to bring it into being, caused the question of constituent power to be obscured. To escape this paradox let us return to where we started – with Marx, and with what Ewing has described as being perhaps the purest form of political constitutionalism.[119]

The constitutional preconditions established by Marx in *The Civil War in France* are grounded in two principles that – as we have seen – are incompatible with the construction of the political Constitution on the 'bedrock'[120] of Parliamentary supremacy. The first is that the people, according to Marx, register – constitutionally speaking – as a working reality and neither merely as a latent power ('[i]nstead of deciding once in three or six years which member of the ruling class was to misrepresent the people in Parliament,' Marx said, 'universal suffrage was to serve the people, constituted in Communes')[121] nor, as in Parker's defence of Parliament, as a foundational myth. The second – and the key to understanding Marx's late writing on politics – is the turn to political organisation in spontaneous form. What Marx came to realise – and what, in the end, has drawn Ewing so tantalisingly towards this work – is that to contain politics (as accounts predicated on Parliamentary sovereignty do and indeed must) within a unitary and particular institutional form is to undermine the activity – and in so doing to undermine the *power* – of politics itself. It is no wonder then that Ewing – a labour lawyer for whom political action in alternative spaces such as within the trade union movement carries its own justification – has come to see the turn from power (to constitute political spaces anew) to accountability (within the already existing constitutional apparatus) as being little more than 'an indulgence and a distraction.'[122]

What Marx saw in the Paris Commune was a new form of government that had emerged in reaction to, and in so doing that had unsettled, long standing assumptions both about the constitution of power and about the ends to which that power ought to be directed. A highly democratic form of government, the Commune was:

> … formed of the municipal councillors, chosen by universal suffrage in the various wards of the town, responsible and revocable at short terms. The majority of its members were naturally

[117] Loughlin (n 23) 28.
[118] Ibid, 47.
[119] Or, so he said in the email exchange that inspired this chapter!
[120] *Jackson v Attorney General* [2005] UKHL 56, [2006] 1 AC 262 [9] per Lord Bingham.
[121] Marx (n 13) 25.
[122] Ewing, 'Jeremy Corbyn and the Law of Democracy' (n 3) 350. Indeed, it is a curious omission that political constitutionalists have had a great deal to say about the protection of rights under the Human Rights Act 1998 and the balance between judicial power and the central executive/legislature but have had almost nothing to say about the creation of alternative, and sometimes rival, sites of political power in the devolved legislatures or in local government and about the dynamics that drive their relations with the centre.

> working men, or acknowledged representatives of the working class. The Commune was to be a working, not a parliamentary body, executive and legislative at the same time. Instead of continuing to be the agent of the Central Government, the police was at once stripped of its political attributes, and turned into the responsible, and at all times revocable, agent of the Commune. So were the officials of all other branches of the administration. From the members of the Commune downwards, the public service had to be done at workman's wage. The vested interests and the representation allowances of the high dignitaries of state disappeared along with the high dignitaries themselves. Public functions ceased to be the private property of the tools of the Central Government. Not only municipal administration, but the whole initiative hitherto exercised by the state was laid into the hands of the Commune.[123]

For sure, Marx was alert to what he saw as being the failings of the Commune, most significantly its 'good nature' in avoiding a more direct conflict with a bourgeoisie who then in turn would crush it. Overwhelmingly, however, he was inspired by what it had achieved during its short life-span: the abolition of conscription; the separation of church and state, measures (albeit short of enfranchisement) for the betterment of women; the abolition of night work for bakers; the development of plans to re-open factories under the control of labour, and more besides.[124] But – and this is the point – the Commune, for Marx, marked a 'new point of departure of world-historic importance'[125] not only because of what it was and what it had achieved but also because of what it represented: the discovery of 'a working class government, the product of the struggle of the producing against the appropriating class, the political form at last discovered under which to work out the economical emancipation of labour.'[126]

So where does this leave us? '[T]he *polis* properly speaking,' wrote Hannah Arendt, a critic of Marx who nevertheless shared his fascination with politics in this spontaneous and communal form, 'is not the city-state in its physical location; it is the organization of the people *[wherever] it arises* out of acting and speaking together.'[127] Political institutions, as Marx came laterally to recognise, might *favour* the creation of political power, but they are not a necessary *precondition* for its emergence. Political action, wherever it arises, however it registers, carries its own legitimacy and is not contingent upon constitutional form. Indeed, the reverse is true: to take seriously what is *political* about the political constitution is to expose Parker's work of fiction, that Parliament *is* the people and therefore can do no wrong, and instead to recognise that constitutional form is always contingent upon the appearance and the expression of political power.

[123] Marx (n 13) 25.

[124] For commentary see P D'Amato, 'The Paris Commune' (The Socialist Worker, 10 December 2002) https://socialistworker.org/2002-2/433/433_10_ParisCommune.php and P Dorn, 'Two Months of Red Spendor: The Paris Commune and Marx' Theory of Revolution' www.runmuki.com/paul/writing/marx.html.

[125] Karl Marx in correspondence with Ludwig Kugelmann, April 17 1871, reproduced in *Marx-Engels Correspondence* (New York, International Publishers, 1968), available at www.marxists.org/archive/marx/works/1871/letters/71_04_17.htm.

[126] Marx (n 13) 27.

[127] H Arendt, *The Human Condition* (Chicago, University of Chicago Press, 1958) 198 (emphasis added).

7

Enhancing Parliamentary Democracy: The European Court of Human Rights' Scrutiny of National Parliaments' Exercise of Disciplinary and Internal Order Powers

ALASTAIR MOWBRAY*

Professor Ewing has long advocated the importance of Parliament as a major body for securing constitutional reform leading to his vision of democratic socialism. Over twenty years ago he elaborated that 'the sovereignty of the people exercised through elected representatives is the primary source of constitutional authority … Parliament is thus the institutional vehicle for realising the political sovereignty of the people'.[1] Subsequently he contended that the 'solution to the problem of liberty lies not with rights, lawyers or judges, but with power, procedures and politicians'.[2] He considered that, '[i]n a parliamentary democracy it is the job of Parliament first and foremost to protect the liberty of the individual from the ambitions of the government'.[3] He noted how historically the UK Parliament had secured the core political rights of universal suffrage, freedom of trades unions to form a political party and fair rules governing elections. However, he then identified many examples of Parliament failing to constrain the granting of excessive powers to the executive from the enactment of the Official Secrets Act 1911 to the Civil Contingencies Act 2004. Overall he felt, '[t]here is thus every reason to be scornful of Parliament's role under Conservative and Labour governments'.[4] His solutions were reform of the electoral system and the creation of a partially or wholly elected second chamber to replace the current House of Lords. A revitalised Parliament with consequent enhanced democratic legitimacy should engage in rigorous scrutiny, building upon the work of the existing Joint Committee on Human Rights, of proposed legislation to ensure the latter respected basic rights encompassing both first generation, civil and political, and second generation, economic and social, rights.

* Many thanks to my fellow participants at the Colloquium for their valuable comments on my oral paper and to the Editors for their insightful comments on my draft chapter.

[1] KD Ewing, 'Democratic Socialism and Labour Law' (1995) 24 *Industrial Law Journal* 103, 105–6.

[2] KD Ewing, *Bonfire of the Liberties: New Labour, Human Rights and the Rule of Law* (Oxford, OUP, 2010) 266.

[3] Ibid.

[4] Ibid, 269.

More recently, writing after 'the unexpected surge of support for a Labour Party standing on its most progressive manifesto since 1983',[5] he has analysed some of the constitutional implications that might arise for a future government elected on a commitment to promote social democracy. In such circumstances he would now focus on the powers of the second legislative chamber/House of Lords rather than its composition. He also supports the important function of non-parliamentary bodies in securing the achievement of progressive policies; 'the essence of social democracy, which is the recognition of the legitimacy of collective power and the authority of organisations, operating alongside- but independently of- parliamentary procedures'.[6]

Examining the respective roles of the courts[7] and Parliament in the Article 50 Brexit notification saga, Professor Ewing has observed that the Supreme Court judgments in *Miller*[8] reflected a strong reassertion of the traditional Diceyian concept of parliamentary sovereignty and yet '[i]f anything Parliament was demeaned rather than enhanced by the litigation, revealing itself to be a rather cowed sovereign body'.[9]

Professor Bellamy has developed the concept of the 'political constitution' from that of Professor Griffith's seminal description of the British Constitution in the late 1970s,[10] and which Professor Ewing noted had placed limited restrictions on socialist (and other) governments,[11] to a universal theoretical model applicable to other constitutional systems.[12] The latter theory advocates that:

> the very democratic mechanisms through which the people authorize their political and legal representatives and hold them to account comprise the constitution of a polity. They prioritize a parliamentary model of rights review and a 'weak' form of rights-based judicial review, in which a declaration of incompatibility by the appropriate court is either advisory or can be overridden or put aside by the legislature.
>
> … a democratic political system, involving regular elections for the legislature and executive between competing parties on the basis of one person, one vote and majority rule, offers the most legitimate and effective mechanism for constraining governments so they rule in the interests of the governed, including by ensuring they protect and promote rights.[13]

[5] KD Ewing, 'Jeremy Corbyn and the Law of Democracy' (2017) 28 *King's Law Journal* 343.

[6] Ibid, 362.

[7] On the High Court judgment see KD Ewing, 'Editor's Introduction' (2016) 27 *King's Law Journal* 289, 296.

[8] *R (Miller) v Secretary of State for Exiting the European Union* [2017] UKSC 5, [2018] AC 61.

[9] KD Ewing, 'Brexit and Parliamentary Sovereignty' (2017) 80 *MLR* 711, 724.

[10] JAG Griffith, 'The Political Constitution' (1979) 42 *MLR* 1. For a contemporary analysis of the historical context and subsequent, distorted, use of Griffith's lecture/paper see M Loughlin, 'The Political Constitution Revisited' *LSE Law, Society & Economy Working Papers* 18/2017. RB Taylor advocates a 'mixed constitution' model which embraces elements of the political, common law and legal concepts of the British Constitution in, 'The Contested Constitution: An Analysis of the Competing Models of British Constitutionalism' [2018] *PL* 482. See also Professor Gee's contribution to this book and his earlier article distinguishing between Griffith's descriptive usage of the phrase 'the political constitution' and others' (including Professor Bellamy) normative utilisation of the concept: G Gee and GCN Webber, 'What Is a Political Constitution?' (2010) 30 *OJLS* 273.

[11] Ewing, 'Democratic Socialism and Labour Law' (n 1) 104.

[12] R Bellamy, 'The Democratic Legitimacy of International Human Rights Conventions: Political Constitutionalism and the European Convention on Human Rights' (2014) *European Journal of International Law* 1019.

[13] Ibid, 1021 and 1024.

Clearly this model has a number of similarities with Professor Ewing's views noted above. Bellamy then examines how the universal model can be applied to international human rights systems established by voluntary associations of democratic states:

> Such an association offers a "two level" political constitution, whereby a political constitution at the international level renders an International Human Rights Convention and International Human Rights Court subject to the democratic authorization and accountability of the representatives of the contracting democratic states, who are in turn democratically authorized and accountable to those they represent through a political constitution at the domestic level.[14]

He continues to analyse whether the regional system of human rights protection established under the European Convention on Human Rights[15] (hereinafter the ECHR or the Convention) can be assessed as being in conformity with this contemporary model of a two level political constitution. Signatory states have to meet basic democratic standards and the Committee of Ministers of the Council of Europe which, inter alia, supervises the execution of judgments of the European Court of Human Rights (hereinafter the Court or the ECtHR), is composed of Foreign Ministers (or their diplomatic representatives). There is also the Parliamentary Assembly of the Council of Europe, comprising representatives from national parliaments, which has the final say in the election of judges to the Court. The Court applies its long-established margin of appreciation doctrine and Protocol 15 to the ECHR will add references to the doctrine and the principle of subsidiarity to the Preamble of the ECHR.[16] However:

> the ECtHR does not adopt weak review. Under Article 46 of the Convention its judgments have binding force on the High Contracting Parties, and once a final ruling has been given by a Grand Chamber there are no further grounds of appeal. Still, it does not disapply national laws- they remain in force until the relevant domestic legislature changes them and can only offer a remedy in international not domestic law. To that extent, the ECtHR could be described as applying a 'soft' version of strong review.[17]

Therefore, Bellamy concludes that overall the ECHR system 'largely conforms' to the requirements of a two level political constitution.[18]

From the above writings we have seen the importance placed by Ewing and others on the leading role of national parliaments in seeking to safeguard basic rights with the ECtHR having a secondary role. Nevertheless, Ewing has acknowledged that: 'the ECtHR has continued to be an indispensable institution for the protection of personal liberty, despite the enactment of the Human Rights Act'.[19] Now we shall focus on how the ECtHR has sought to enhance the effectiveness of national parliamentary processes which underpin the national and international concepts of a political constitution.

[14] Ibid, 1033.
[15] Convention for the Protection of Human Rights and Fundamental Freedoms, ETS No 005 (1950).
[16] See, A Mowbray, 'ECtHR: May 2013-April 2014' (2014) 20 *European Public Law* 579.
[17] Bellamy (n 12) 1037.
[18] Ibid, 1042.
[19] Ewing, *Bonfire of the Liberties* (n 2) 265.

I. Parliamentary Exercise of Disciplinary Powers Over Non-members

The original Court scrutinised a national Parliament's attempts to punish a journalist who wrote a satirical review of a parliamentary debate in *Demicoli v Malta*.[20] The applicant was the editor of a political satirical magazine in which he wrote a commentary on a televised debate in the Maltese House of Representatives. The applicant described one Member of Parliament's (MP) (Mr Debono Grech) performance as that of trying to 'play the clown' and another MP (Mr Bartolo) of 'talking rubbish'. In his satire the applicant wrote that the debate had caused him to boo so loudly that his neighbours considered that he had suffered an epileptic fit. The two MPs referred the article to the House as an alleged breach of privilege. A few weeks later the Speaker ruled that he considered the article to constitute a prima facie case of breach of privilege. The same day the House, on a motion by Mr Debono Grech, passed a resolution that it considered the article amounted to a breach of its privileges, contrary to section 11(1)(k) of the House of Representatives (Privileges and Powers) Ordinance. A couple of weeks later the House considered a motion, seconded by Mr Debono Grech, to summon the applicant to appear before the House at a specified time to 'state why he should not be found guilty of breach of privilege'. After debate the motion was passed. The applicant thereupon began an action in the Civil Court of Malta contending that the House of Representatives proceedings against him were penal and violated his constitutional right to trial before an independent and impartial court. Before the Civil Court ruled on the applicant's claim he and his lawyer appeared, for three days, before the House of Representatives. The Speaker determined that the case against the applicant should not be suspended until after the Civil Court delivered its judgment. The applicant refused to state whether he was guilty of breach of privilege. The House threatened him with further proceedings for contempt and then followed the practice of criminal courts where a defendant refuses to plead by assuming a plea of not guilty. The applicant's article was read out to the House and the two MPs who had been referred to were invited by the Speaker to express their views. The MPs stated that they believed they had been ridiculed both as members of the House and in their personal lives. The House then found the applicant guilty of breach of privilege. The question of punishment was adjourned by the House. Two months later the Civil Court determined that the proceedings against the applicant were not criminal, as no criminal court had been involved and sanctions imposed by the House were not criminal penalties. However, the Civil Court held that it was necessary under the Ordinance for a court to make the initial determination of whether a defamatory libel had occurred and if that was found then the House could bring contempt proceedings. Subsequently the Constitutional Court overruled the Civil Court, determining that the Constitution empowered Parliament

[20] *Demicoli v Malta* (1992) 14 EHRR 47. In the enlightening discussion on my paper at our colloquium Professor M Ford noted the Court's review of a Parliament's exercise of disciplinary powers over a Supreme Court judge in *Oleksandr Volkov v Ukraine*, (2013) 57 EHRR 1. In that judgment the unanimous Chamber noted the growing importance of the notion of the separation of powers, between the political organs of government and the judiciary, in the Court's jurisprudence (para 103). Furthermore, the applicant's dismissal, in breach of Articles 6 and 8 of the ECHR, 'could be viewed as a threat to the independence of the judiciary as a whole.' (para 205). I have analysed other aspects of this case in 'An Examination of the European Court of Human Right's Indication of Remedial Measures' (2017) 17 *HRLR* 451.

to enact laws establishing its privileges and immunities and that consequently the contempt proceedings against the applicant had not infringed his right to a fair hearing before an independent court. Thereupon the House summoned the applicant to appear before it for the determination of his punishment. Through his lawyer the applicant stated that he had nothing to say except that he would comply with the decision of the House. The named MPs participated in the proceedings until the death of Mr Bartolo. The applicant was fined 250 Maltese liri and ordered to publish the House's finding of contempt against him in his journal. He did not pay the fine and no enforcement action was taken against him.

Demicoli then lodged an application with the European Commission of Human Rights alleging breaches of Article 6(1) of the Convention as the House of Representatives proceedings against him amounted to the determination of a 'criminal charge' by a body that was not an 'independent and impartial tribunal' and Article 6(2) because those proceedings also violated the presumption of innocence. The Commission, unanimously, expressed the opinion that there had been a breach of Article 6(1) and that no separate issue arose under Article 6(2). The Commission referred the case to the Court.

Before the Court the government argued, inter alia, that under domestic law the proceedings against the applicant were disciplinary and not criminal, therefore Article 6 was inapplicable. The applicant and the Commission disputed that view. The Court noted that it had already held that the concept of a 'criminal charge' under Article 6 had an autonomous meaning and the Court was not bound by domestic classifications. Therefore, the Court applied its well-established criteria from *Engel and Others v the Netherlands*,[21] to determine how the parliamentary proceedings should be categorised. Regarding the 'nature of the offence' the Court observed that:

> Mr Demicoli was not a Member of the House. In the Court's view, the proceedings taken against him in the present case for an act of this sort done outside the House are to be distinguished from other types of breach of privilege proceedings which may be said to be disciplinary in nature in that they relate to the internal regulation and orderly functioning of the House. Section 11(1)(k) potentially affects the whole population since it applies whether the alleged offender is a Member of the House or not and irrespective of where in Malta the publication of the defamatory libel takes place. For the offence thereby defined the Ordinance provides for the imposition of a penal sanction and not a civil claim for damages. From this point of view, therefore, the particular breach of privilege in question is akin to a criminal offence[22]

As to the severity of the punishment the Court noted that the maximum punishment applicable to the proceedings against the applicant was imprisonment for up to 60 days. This was sufficiently serious to justify classifying the offence as criminal under the ECHR. Consequently, the Court held that Article 6 of the Convention was applicable to the parliamentary proceedings brought against the applicant.

Regarding his claim under Article 6(1) the applicant submitted that he had not received a fair hearing before an independent and impartial tribunal as the MPs he had written about participated in the House of Representatives' proceedings as victims, accusers, witnesses, and judges. The government responded that the House was independent of the executive and the parties and that was sufficient to exclude any legitimate doubt about its impartiality.

[21] *Engel and Others v the Netherlands* (1979–80) 1 EHRR 647.
[22] *Demicoli* (n 20) para 33.

Furthermore the two MPs ridiculed in the applicant's article had intervened to defend the dignity of the House not just their personal reputations. The Commission considered that the House was not a court nor did it meet the independence and impartiality requirements of Article 6(1). The Court determined that:

> According to its case-law, "a 'tribunal' is characterised in the substantive sense of the term by its judicial function, that is to say determining matters within its competence on the basis of rules of law and after proceedings conducted in a prescribed manner … It must also satisfy a series of further requirements – independence, in particular of the executive; impartiality; duration of its members' terms of office; guarantees afforded by its procedure – several of which appear in the text of Article 6 para. 1 itself" (see the *Belilos* [*v Switzerland*] judgment of 29 April 1988, Series A no 132, p. 29, para. 64).
>
> 40. In the circumstances of the present case the House of Representatives undoubtedly exercised a judicial function in determining the applicant's guilt. The central issue raised in this case is whether the requirement of impartiality was duly respected. For the purposes of Article 6 para. 1 (art. 6-1) this must be determined according to a subjective test, that is on the basis of the personal conviction or interest of a particular judge in a given case, and according to an objective test, namely ascertaining whether the judge offered guarantees sufficient to exclude any legitimate doubt in this respect. In this context even appearances may be of a certain importance, particularly as far as criminal proceedings are concerned …
>
> 41. The two Members of the House whose behaviour in Parliament was criticised in the impugned article and who raised the breach of privilege in the House participated throughout in the proceedings against the accused, including the finding of guilt and (except for one of them who had meanwhile died) the sentencing. Already for this reason, the impartiality of the adjudicating body in these proceedings would appear to be open to doubt and the applicant's fears in this connection were justified …[23]

Therefore, the united Court found a breach of Article 6(1) and decided that it was not necessary to consider other elements of the Convention's fair hearing requirements. Likewise the Court considered it unnecessary to examine the applicant's complaint under Article 6(2) of the ECHR. The Court went on to reject the applicant's claims for pecuniary just satisfaction (he had not paid the fine nor had enforcement measures been taken against him) and non-pecuniary compensation (any distress he had suffered as a result of the parliamentary proceedings against him had received adequate redress by the Court's finding of a breach of the Convention).

This was a momentous judgment for the Court in the context of its relationship towards national parliaments exercising purported disciplinary powers over non-members. The Court reached its own assessment of whether those proceedings fell within the ambit of the procedural guarantees enshrined in Article 6(1) of the Convention. We should welcome the robust way in which the Court evaluated the 'criminal' nature of the privilege proceedings by considering their application to a journalist regarding his work outside of the Parliament and the potential severity of the sanctions facing him (imprisonment). Perhaps the Court was too restrictive in limiting its ruling to the issue of the impartiality of the House of Representatives' proceedings rather than also addressing the other breaches

[23] Ibid at paras 39–41.

alleged by the applicant (including the matter of whether the House had already prejudged his guilt and thereby violated his right to be presumed innocent under Article 6(2) of the Convention). But, the Strasbourg review did not replicate the deferential approach to the parliamentary proceedings demonstrated by the Constitutional Court's judgment. The judgment in *Demicoli* clearly revealed that Article 6, ECHR could be successfully invoked by members of the public subject to punitive disciplinary proceedings and sanctions by parliaments. This was a positive protection against the type of inherently unfair and biased process inflicted on Demicoli. Given that he was working as a journalist in a society subject to the Convention requirements of tolerance towards critical political expression, the leading Strasbourg judgment in *Lingens v Austria*[24] having been delivered three months before the Maltese Constitutional Court's judgment and five months before the House of Representatives imposed its punishment on Demicoli, the conduct of the Parliament toward him was even more egregious.

II. Parliamentary Exercise of Physical Force on Non-members

An even more dramatic and coercive use of physical force by parliamentary officials against journalists reporting on parliamentary matters was examined by the Court in *Selmani and Others v The Former Yugoslav Republic of Macedonia*.[25] The six applicants were journalists accredited to report from the national parliament. On Christmas Eve in 2012 the applicants, together with other authorised journalists, were in the gallery (above the parliamentary chamber) observing a tense debate on the state budget. There was extensive public and media interest in the debate. Opposing groups had gathered outside the Parliament and, according to the government, several people were injured in clashes between those groups. Disorder also developed in the parliamentary chamber with some opposition MPs approaching the Speaker and slapping his table. Officers, from the parliamentary security service, entered the chamber and pulled the Speaker out of the chamber. Then the officers began forcibly removing the opposition MPs. According to a press release issued by the Speaker, a couple of days later, he had exercised powers under section 43 of the Parliament Act to authorise the parliamentary security service to ensure the proper working of Parliament. The applicants claimed that whilst opposition MPs were being removed from the chamber, four security officers entered the gallery and ordered all the journalists to leave for security reasons. The other journalists left but the applicants refused as they claimed the public had the right to be informed of the escalating disorder in the chamber. Thereupon the security officers physically removed the applicants from the gallery. In his subsequent press release the Speaker explained that the parliamentary security service had decided the gallery should be cleared in order to avoid a larger scale incident. He expressed regret regarding the action taken against the journalists. The Association of Journalists (of which the first applicant was President) wrote to the Ministry of the Interior's Department for Control

[24] *Lingens v Austria* (1986) 8 EHRR 407. More generally see, A Mowbray, 'The Role of the ECtHR in the Promotion of Democracy' [1999] *PL* 703.

[25] *Selmani and Others v The Former Yugoslav Republic of Macedonia* (2018) 67 EHRR 8.

and Professional Standards complaining about the treatment of the evicted journalists and alleging a breach of Article 10 of the ECHR. The Department replied that the journalist had been asked to leave the gallery until order was restored in the parliamentary chamber and when the applicants resisted acceptable force had been used by the security officers. Some months later the state President established a commission of inquiry, including observers from the European Union, to investigate the events in the Parliament on Christmas Eve. The commission's report was critical of the lack of appropriate guidelines governing how the media should be dealt with in a crisis situation and found that the treatment of the journalists violated their rights to freedom of public information and publicity regarding the workings of Parliament.

The applicants brought a constitutional complaint, alleging a breach of their rights under Article 10, ECHR, before the Constitutional Court. Against the request of the applicants the Constitutional Court declined to hold a public hearing on the applicants' complaint. Subject to one dissent, the Constitutional Court dismissed the applicants' complaint on the grounds that the physical removal of the applicants from the gallery, necessitated by the chaos and disorder in the Parliament, had the aim of protecting the journalist and not restricting their freedom of expression or preventing them from undertaking their role in public information.

After the above judgment the applicants lodged an application at Strasbourg contending that they had suffered a violation of Article 6(1) of the Convention due to the failure of the Constitutional Court to hold an oral hearing and, more importantly from our perspective, a breach of Article 10. The Court, unanimously, found a breach of Article 6 as the right to a public hearing generally requires an oral hearing before a first and only instance court. Regarding their Article 10 complaint the applicants argued that their physical removal from the gallery had neither been 'in accordance with the law', given the lack of foreseeability of the national legislation, nor justified by a 'pressing social need' as required by Article 10(2) ECHR. Whilst the government accepted that the physical removal of the applicants had amounted to an interference with their freedom of expression it sought to justify the actions of the security officers as falling within the state's margin of appreciation. The officers had been seeking to protect the physical integrity of the journalists and their physical removal was a measure of last resort after the applicants had refused to leave voluntarily.

The Court was unanimous in concluding that the physical removal of the applicants constituted an interference with their right to freedom of expression under Article 10(1). Turning to paragraph two of that Article the Court applied its well-established tripartite methodology and examined whether the interference was 'prescribed by law'.[26] The Court found that the Parliament Act and the official Rules of Procedure of Parliament provided a sufficiently foreseeable domestic legal basis for the actions of the Speaker and the parliamentary security officers to meet this Convention requirement. The Court also accepted the government's submission that the interference was for the legitimate aims of protecting 'public safety' and the 'prevention of disorder'. The final element was for the Court to decide if the security officers' actions met the test of being 'necessary in a democratic society'. After citing its recognised jurisprudence that this requires the respondent state to demonstrate a 'pressing social need', whilst allowing the state a margin of appreciation in the determination

[26] See, A Mowbray, *Cases, Materials & Commentary on the ECHR*, 3rd edn (Oxford, OUP, 2012) 700–730.

of that matter, the Court additionally emphasised the crucial role of the media in democratic societies of providing the public with information about matters of public interest. The Court held that:

> the disorder in the parliamentary chamber and the way in which the authorities handled it were matters of legitimate public interest. The media therefore had the task of imparting information on the event, and the public had the right to receive such information. In this connection, the Court refers to its case-law regarding the crucial role of the media in providing information on the authorities' handling of public demonstrations and the containment of disorder, which likewise applies to the circumstances of the present case. It reiterates that the "watch-dog" role of the media assumes particular importance in such contexts, since their presence is a guarantee that the authorities can be held to account for their conduct *vis-à-vis* the demonstrators and the public at large when it comes to the policing of large gatherings, including the methods used to control or disperse protesters or to preserve public order. Any attempt to remove journalists from the scene of demonstrations must therefore be subject to strict scrutiny (see *Pentikäinen* [*v Finland*[27]] …). This applies even more so when journalists exercise their right to impart information to the public about the behaviour of elected representatives in Parliament and about the manner in which authorities handle disorder that occurs during Parliamentary sessions.[28]

Turning to the factual assessment of whether the physical removal of the applicants from the gallery was necessary the Court noted that the Constitutional Court had not examined the extent to which the protests outside the Parliament building had threatened the safety of persons inside the Parliament. Furthermore the applicants had been removed from the gallery not the building itself despite the alleged threat to the security of Parliament. Regarding the disorder caused by some MPs:

> During the disturbance in the chamber, the applicants were passive bystanders who were simply doing their work and observing the events. The Government conceded that they had neither contributed to nor participated in the disturbance in the chamber … Accordingly, they did not pose any threat to public safety, order in the chamber or otherwise.[29]

The Court considered that it was significant that the security officers had removed the applicants as the parliamentary security service believed there was a risk to the applicants' lives and physical integrity if they remained in the gallery. But, the applicants did not feel threatened. Furthermore:

> the Court finds no indication that the disorderly behaviour of the MPs in the chamber would have put the applicants' lives and physical integrity in danger. It was not presented with any evidence that the disturbance in the chamber had been violent and that anyone, in the chamber or elsewhere, had sustained an injury as a result of that disturbance. The only relevant element on which the Constitutional Court based its finding that the applicants had not been safe was that "objects were thrown in the chamber – some in the direction of the gallery". However, the Court notes that no further explanation was provided as to the type and number of objects thrown and whether any of them had reached the gallery, which as noted above, was situated above the chamber.[30]

[27] *Pentikäinen v Finland* (2017) 65 EHRR 21.
[28] *Selmani* (n 25) para 75.
[29] Ibid at para 8.
[30] Ibid at para 83.

Finally, the parties had submitted divergent accounts of whether the applicants had been able to follow what had been occurring in the chamber, via live television broadcast, after they had been removed from the gallery. The Court concluded that:

> the applicants' removal entailed immediate adverse effects that instantaneously prevented them from obtaining first-hand and direct knowledge based on their personal experience of the events unfolding in the chamber, and thus the unlimited context in which the authorities were handling them … Those were important elements in the exercise of the applicants' journalistic functions, which the public should not have been deprived of in the circumstances of the present case.[31]

Therefore, the Court, unanimously, decided that the respondent State had failed to establish 'sufficient' reasons to justify the removal of the applicants as being 'necessary in a democratic society'. Consequently, there had been a breach of Article 10 of the ECHR and each applicant should be awarded €5,000 as compensation for their non-pecuniary damage.

The Court's judgment discloses a protective stance towards the vital role of the media in reporting not only the decision-making of Parliaments but also the manner in which members of those institutions behave in their Parliaments and the actions of parliamentary staff in the workings of those organisations. Clearly in a democracy, voters, and others (such as interested younger persons not yet eligible to vote), have a legitimate interest in being informed if some of their parliamentarians are disrupting proceedings and how the parliamentary authorities have responded. Such information will enable citizens to make up their own minds about the desirability of voting for (or where constitutionally available recalling) particular candidates or political parties. Furthermore, citizens also need to be informed by journalists of the circumstances and means by which parliamentary authorities use physical force within parliaments. Otherwise there is the danger that ruling/majority parties might be able to suppress critical views by the physical removal of their opponents from parliamentary proceeding without media representatives being able to witness and report on such actions.

III. Parliamentary Exercise of Disciplinary Powers Over Members

A former MP and Cabinet Minister, who was a qualified lawyer, complained to the Court that disciplinary proceedings and sanctions taken against him by the House of Commons violated several of his Convention rights in *Hoon v UK*.[32] After announcing his retirement from Parliament, but whilst still an MP, the applicant was secretly recorded by an undercover journalist (who the applicant believed to be a representative of an American communications company) stating that after he left Parliament he wished to 'translate my knowledge and contact about the sort of international scene into something that, bluntly, makes money'.[33] He also told the undercover journalist that he could help her (fictitious) company's clients gain insights into the government's Defence Review as 'I know some people on the team

[31] Ibid at para 85.
[32] *Hoon v UK* (2015) 60 EHRR SE6.
[33] Ibid at para 4.

in the Ministry of Defence who are working on this, because they brief me about this'.[34] The applicant also appeared to offer to inform a private equity fund, purportedly represented by the undercover journalist, about the relationship between NATO and the UK's National Defence Policy. Extracts from the journalist's secret recordings of the applicant were published in the *Sunday Times* newspaper and broadcast on a Channel 4 television documentary. Subsequently an opposition MP made a formal complaint about the applicant's behaviour to the Parliamentary Commissioner of Standards (appointed by the House of Commons to investigate and report on complaints made against MPs).

The Parliamentary Commissioner sought and obtained the applicant's comments on the complaint and questions raised by the Commissioner's investigation. Some months later the Commissioner produced his finding of facts and this document was sent to the applicant for his observations. The Commissioner then produced his final report containing his findings of fact and conclusions which was given to the Standards and Privileges Committee of the House of Commons. The Commissioner rejected the applicant's contention that the Code of Conduct for MPs, approved by the House in 2009, did not apply to the applicant's dealing with the undercover journalist as he was merely discussing his future actions as a private person.

The Commissioner looked at whether the applicant had breached the Code in ten distinct ways. He concluded that two breaches had been established on a balance of probabilities. First, by offering to brief the fictitious company's clients about the MoD's United Kingdom Strategic Defence and Security Review, he breached the Code in that he at least gave the impression that he would draw on what he had learnt in his meeting with officials who were working on the review. This was deemed a serious breach of the rules of the House of Commons because it brought the House into disrepute. Secondly, he breached the Code when he suggested that he could draw on his access to information about the NATO defence review and the United Kingdom's Strategic Defence and Security Review for the benefit of the private equity fund. In this way he was giving the impression that he was offering an inside track on defence strategy to the fund. This was also found to be a breach of the rules of the House of Commons because it brought the House generally into disrepute.[35]

The applicant submitted written and oral comments to the Standards and Privileges Committee repeating his view that the Code of Conduct did not apply to a private conversation about his future once he left Parliament. The Committee rejected this argument finding that the Code applied to the applicant's meeting with the undercover journalist as he was an MP and public figure at that time and he made numerous references to his public life experiences when talking to the journalist. The Committee also agreed with the Commissioner's findings in his report and recommended that the applicant apologise to the House of Commons, through the Committee, for his conduct and that his parliamentary photopass (which enables former MPs privileged access to parts of Parliament) be suspended for five years. The applicant sought to involve the Speaker of the House of Commons in the disciplinary proceedings but the Speaker informed the applicant he could not intervene on his behalf. Subsequently the House of Commons approved the Committee's report on the complaints against the applicant.

[34] Ibid at para 5.
[35] Ibid at para 13.

At Strasbourg the applicant first contended that the Parliamentary disciplinary proceedings against him violated Article 6(1), ECHR and that Article 9 of the Bill of Rights 1689 prevented him challenging those findings in the ordinary courts. However, the unanimous Court held that:

> According to well established case-law, the right to stand for election and to keep one's seat is a political right and not a "civil" one within the meaning of Article 6 § 1 (see *Christian Estrosi v. France*, no. 24359/94, dec. 30 June 1995, D.R 82-B, p. 56 and *Pierre Bloch v. France*, 21 October 1997, § 50, Reports of Judgments and Decisions 1997 VI for cases concerning candidates' obligation to limit their election expenditure). Accordingly disputes relating to the arrangements for the exercise of a parliamentary seat lie outside the scope of that provision.
>
> 30. Therefore, the parliamentary proceedings in question, which were concerned with investigating possible breaches of the Code of Conduct of Members of Parliament, did not attract the application of Article 6 § 1 of the Convention, since they did not determine, or give rise to, a dispute as to the applicant's "civil" rights for the purposes of Article 6 § 1. Accordingly this part of the application, including the complaint relating to lack of access to court to challenge the legality of the parliamentary proceedings, is incompatible *ratione materiae* with the provisions of the Convention within the meaning of Article 35 § 3 and must be rejected pursuant to Article 35 § 4.[36]

The applicant then claimed that the disciplinary proceedings had violated his right to respect for his private life guaranteed by Article 8 ECHR. The Court agreed that the protection of a person's reputation fell within that right and the publicity given to the Commissioner's and Committee's reports on the applicant amounted to an interference with his right to respect for his private life. But those disciplinary proceedings could be justified under Article 8(2), ECHR. They were 'in accordance with the law' as they were provided for in the Standing Orders of the House of Commons. The 'legitimate aim' under Article 8(2) had been to protect the rights and freedoms of others by enabling the public to know of the outcome of the Parliamentary investigation into the conduct of an MP. As to whether those proceedings had been 'necessary in a democratic society' the Court found that the applicant had been given a 'fair opportunity' to defend himself during the disciplinary procedure.[37] The immunity of British parliamentary proceedings from review by the ordinary courts had previously been upheld by the Court (in *A v UK*)[38] as protecting free speech in Parliament and the separation of powers between the legislature and the judiciary. Therefore the UK authorities had remained within their margin of appreciation and the applicant's complaint under Article 8, ECHR was manifestly ill-founded. Finally the Court dismissed the applicant's complaint of a breach of Article 13, ECHR, because it was not engaged as the Court had already found he had no valid claims under Articles 6 and 8 that required determination by a domestic remedial body.

The complete rejection of the applicant's complaints in *Hoon* by a united Court at the admissibility stage of Strasbourg proceedings can be seen as a supportive response by the Court to national parliaments having the primary responsibility for exercising disciplinary powers over their members. Indeed those powers can extend to activities outside of

[36] Ibid at paras 29–30.

[37] Ibid at para 39.

[38] *A v United Kingdom* (2003) 36 EHRR 51 and see Mowbray, *Cases, Materials & Commentary on the ECHR* (n 26) 398.

Parliament by a current member where they have a sufficient link to the member's public role and the reputation of the Parliament. Whilst not expressly mentioning the principle of subsidiarity,[39] the decision in *Hoon* applied the margin of appreciation doctrine, which has origins in the former,[40] when assessing if the domestic authorities had violated the applicant's rights under the Convention. Nevertheless the Court noted that the parliamentary disciplinary proceedings against the applicant had accorded him sufficient opportunities to defend his conduct and reputation. So there was a symmetry in recognising the wide disciplinary powers of national legislatures over their members provided that fair procedures were followed.

In the later joined applications of *Karácsony and Others v Hungary*,[41] the Court was faced for the first time with parliamentarians challenging the imposition of disciplinary punishments on them for their conduct and expression in the legislature. During a session of the Hungarian Parliament the first and second applicant (MPs for an opposition party) placed a large placard next to a government Minister, who was responding to a speech from another opposition MP, displaying the words 'FIDESZ [the governing party] You steal, you cheat, and you lie.' Despite the Speaker's request to the applicants to remove their placard they then moved it next to the Speaker's pulpit. He then ordered parliamentary staff to remove the placard from the Chamber. A week later the Speaker proposed to Parliament that the applicants should be fined the equivalent of €170 and €600 as he considered that their behaviour had been gravely offensive to parliamentary order. Parliament approved the Speaker's proposed punishments without a debate. A couple of weeks later, during a parliamentary vote on tobacco legislation the third and fourth applicants (MPs from the same opposition party) displayed a large banner in the centre of the Chamber stating 'Here Operates the National Tobacco Mafia.' The Speaker informed the applicants that their conduct was a grave disruption of proceedings and they should hand the banner to an usher. They refused to do so, but subsequently left the Chamber. After a few days the Speaker proposed that each of these applicants should be fined €240 and that was approved by Parliament without debate. The other three applicants were MPs from another opposition party. A month after the above disruptions these applicants displayed a banner in the Chamber, during a vote on legislation concerning agricultural land, proclaiming 'Land distribution instead of land robbery!' One of them used a megaphone to speak to fellow MPs and the final applicant placed a small ornamental wheelbarrow filled with soil on the table in front of the Prime Minister. The Speaker subsequently proposed that these applicants be fined €430 and €510 with Parliament approving the penalties without debate.

Subsequently the applicants complained to Strasbourg alleging that the imposition of the disciplinary fines on them constituted a breach of their right to freedom of expression

[39] See A Mowbray, 'Subsidiarity and the European Convention on Human Rights' (2015) 15 *Human Rights Law Review* 313. For the views of a senior judge at Strasbourg on this topic see, R Spano, 'The Future of the ECtHR-Subsidiarity, Process-Based Review and the Rule of Law' (2018) 18 *Human Rights Law Review* 473.

[40] Mowbray, 'Subsidiarity and the European Convention on Human Rights' (n 39) 321 where I examined H Petzold's elaboration that the 'margin of appreciation thus stems directly from the principle of subsidiarity as it applies within the Convention system.' (H Petzold, 'The Convention and the Principle of Subsidiarity' in R St J Macdonald, F Matscher and H Petzold (eds) *The European System for the Protection of Human Rights* (Alphen aan den Rijn, Kluwer, 1993) 59).

[41] *Karácsony and Others v Hungary* (2017) 64 EHRR 10.

guaranteed by Article 10, ECHR and, as they had no effective domestic remedy to challenge the penalties, they had suffered a violation of Article 13 of the Convention. A Chamber, unanimously, upheld those complaints. The respondent government then sought an Article 43 rehearing by the Grand Chamber.

After rejecting the government's submission that the applicants had failed to exhaust domestic remedies by bringing a constitutional complaint before the Constitutional Court, because the Grand Chamber held that remedy could not have redressed the applicants' complaints, the Grand Chamber focused on the Chamber's finding of a breach of Article 10. The Chamber classified the applicants' conduct as constituting political expression and the interference with it had not been justified by a compelling reason as the applicants' behaviour had not been shown to have seriously disrupted order in the Hungarian Parliament. Therefore, the disciplinary punishments imposed on them had not been 'necessary in a democratic society' as required by Article 10(2) of the Convention. The applicants argued that the governing coalition controlled over two-thirds of the votes in Parliament and had used that majority to reduce the opposition's participation in policy-making. The applicants unusual, but not offensive or dangerous, symbolic forms of expression in the Parliament were the only ways they had of showing their opposition to government policy. Consequently, the fines imposed on them had been disproportionate interferences with their political expression. The respondent government rejected the applicants' view of the health of parliamentary democracy in Hungary and asked the Court to evaluate the sanctions imposed on the applicants in the context of harsher penalties (including exclusion or suspension of an MP) applied in other European states. In the submission of the government, states should be accorded the widest possible margin of appreciation regarding the operation of national Parliaments. The limited punishments imposed on the applicants (not all the fines had been at the maximum level) had been for the legitimate aims of 'protection of the rights of others' and the 'prevention of disorder', as recognised by the Chamber, and proportionate given the serious disruption to parliamentary proceedings. The Czech Government submitted third-party written comments outlining disciplinary proceedings in the national Parliament. The UK Government likewise provided a lengthy written submission on the disciplinary powers of the Westminster Parliament. MPs were restricted to the use of 'reasoned oral argument' in the House of Commons, but could engage in symbolic forms of political expression outside of Parliament.[42] In the opinion of the UK Government 'a proportionate but dissuasive penalty' was necessary to ensure that parliamentary debates took place without being disrupted by banners and megaphones etc.[43]

The Grand Chamber noted that the parties did not dispute that the fines imposed on the applicants constituted an interference with their right to freedom of expression. Whist the parties disagreed on whether the interference met the Article 10(2) requirement of being 'prescribed by law', the Grand Chamber found that the Hungarian Parliament Act satisfied that Convention condition. The Grand Chamber also determined that the interference pursued the Article 10(2) legitimate aims of 'preventing disorder' by seeking to prevent disruption to the work of the Parliament and protecting the 'rights of others' (ie the other MPs). The main focus of the Grand Chamber was on whether the disciplinary punishments

[42] Ibid at para 117.
[43] Ibid.

of the applicants were 'necessary in a democratic society'. Existing case-law identified the freedom of expression of MPs as being 'political expression *par excellence*'.[44] Furthermore:

> There can be no doubt that speech in Parliament enjoys an elevated level of protection. Parliament is a unique forum for debate in a democratic society, which is of fundamental importance. The elevated level of protection for speech therein is demonstrated, among other things, by the rule of parliamentary immunity. The Court has acknowledged that the long standing practice for States generally to confer varying degrees of immunity on parliamentarians pursues the legitimate aims of protecting free speech in Parliament and maintaining the separation of powers between the legislature and the judiciary. Different forms of parliamentary immunity may indeed serve to protect the effective political democracy that constitutes one of the cornerstones of the Convention system, particularly where they protect the autonomy of the legislature and the parliamentary opposition … The guarantees offered by both types of parliamentary immunity (non-liability and inviolability) serve to ensure the independence of Parliament in the performance of its task. Inviolability helps to achieve the full independence of Parliament by preventing any possibility of politically motivated criminal proceedings (*fumus persecutionis*) and thereby protecting the opposition from pressure or abuse on the part of the majority … The protection afforded to free speech in Parliament serves to protect the interests of Parliament as a whole and should not be understood as protection afforded solely to individual MPs[45]

But Article 10(2) empowered parliaments to respond when members engaged in disorderly conduct hindering the normal working arrangements. The Grand Chamber distinguished between:

> States – or indeed Parliaments themselves – should, in principle, independently regulate the time, place and manner of speech in Parliament, and that, correspondingly the Court's scrutiny in this respect should be limited. By contrast, States have very limited latitude in regulating the content of parliamentary speech. However, some regulation may be considered necessary in order to prevent forms of expression such as direct or indirect calls for violence.[46]

The former type of regulation could be characterised as 'the jurisdictional autonomy of Parliament' and the Council of Europe's European (Venice) Commission for Democracy through Law had found that the majority of democratic parliaments have disciplinary sanctions which can be applied to members. Regarding the Court's scrutiny of those procedures:

> In principle, the rules concerning the internal functioning of national parliaments, as an aspect of parliamentary autonomy, fall within the margin of appreciation of the Contracting States. The national authorities, most notably parliaments (or comparable bodies composed of elected representatives of the people), are indeed better placed than the international judge to assess the need to restrict conduct by a member causing disruption to the orderly conduct of parliamentary debates and which may be harmful to the fundamental interest of ensuring the effective functioning of Parliament in a democracy.[47]

Given that a comparative-law survey of 44 Council of Europe states, conducted by the Court's Research Department, found a diverse range of disciplinary sanctions available to

[44] Ibid at para 137.
[45] Ibid at para 138.
[46] Ibid at para 140.
[47] Ibid at para 143.

different parliaments when dealing with members' disruptive behaviour the Grand Chamber held that:

> where the underlying purpose of the relevant disciplinary rules is exclusively to ensure the effectiveness of Parliament, and hence that of the democratic process, the margin of appreciation to be afforded in this area should be a wide one.[48]

Nevertheless, parliaments should exercise their internal disciplinary powers in a manner that reflects the concept of an 'effective political democracy' referred to in the Preamble to the ECHR. In the view of the Grand Chamber this meant that:

> the rules concerning the internal operation of Parliament should not serve as a basis for the majority abusing its dominant position vis-à-vis the opposition. The Court attaches importance to protection of the parliamentary minority from abuse by the majority. It will therefore examine with particular care any measure which appears to operate solely, or principally, to the disadvantage of the opposition.[49]

Applying the above principles to the facts of the present complaints the Grand Chamber considered that displaying a banner or placard in a parliament was not a normal manner of expression by MPs and the use of a megaphone clearly disrupts parliamentary proceedings. Furthermore the punishments imposed on the applicants were in respect of their behaviour not the views they were expressing. The Grand Chamber then focussed on whether there had been adequate procedural safeguards for the applicants. The Court accepted the respondent government's distinction between the scenarios of the immediate imposition of disciplinary sanctions by parliamentary authorities on an MP who was disrupting proceedings and the *ex post facto* imposition of punishments (as happened to the applicants). The Grand Chamber held that where a grave disturbance of parliamentary proceedings occurred the immediate imposition of disciplinary sanctions should normally be preceded by a warning. 'With regard to *ex post facto* disciplinary sanctions, the Court considers that the procedural safeguards available to this effect should include, as a minimum, the right for the MP concerned to be heard in a parliamentary procedure before a sanction is imposed.'[50] Additionally, the Grand Chamber held that this type of disciplinary decision 'should state basic reasons, thus not only enabling the MP concerned to understand the justification for the measure but also permitting some form of public scrutiny of it.'[51] However, the principle of parliamentary autonomy meant that MPs who had been subjected to parliamentary disciplinary process were not generally entitled to an external remedy to challenge such sanctions. Here the applicants had not been given an opportunity by the Hungarian parliamentary authorities to be heard nor did the Speaker's proposed fines/adoption by the Parliament provide any reasons why the applicants' conduct was considered to be gravely offensive to parliamentary order. Consequently the applicants had not been accorded any procedural safeguards. This failure meant that the sanctions imposed on them had not been proportionate and therefore failed to satisfy the 'necessary in a democratic society' element of Article 10(2). Consequently Article 10 had been violated. Given that finding, the Grand Chamber held that it was not necessary to examine separately the applicants' complaint of

[48] Ibid at para 146.
[49] Ibid at para 147.
[50] Ibid at para 156.
[51] Ibid at para158.

a violation of Article 13, ECHR. Each of the applicants was awarded pecuniary damages equivalent to the fine imposed on her/him.

The above unanimous judgment of the Grand Chamber embodied a subtle balancing of the interests of parliaments and their members and the role of the Court in scrutinising the disciplinary relationship between the former. The Court accepted the primary role of parliaments in regulating the conduct of their members during parliamentary proceedings. However, the Court elaborated essential procedural safeguards when either immediate or *ex post facto* disciplinary sanctions were being considered for imposition on a member. Realistically time considerations meant that the procedural safeguards were more extensive in the case of *ex post facto* disciplinary sanctions. Nevertheless, even where immediate sanctions were being contemplated by the parliamentary authorities the relevant member should be accorded a prior warning regarding her/his disruptive behaviour and the consequences of its continuance. By elaborating these protective measures the Grand Chamber was seeking to promote the effective operation of parliaments with safeguards for members facing disciplinary action in respect of their conduct in parliament.

IV. Conclusions

We have ascertained that this is a developing area of the Court's jurisprudence. The Court has recognised the wide ambit of national parliaments' disciplinary authority over their members extending from conduct during parliamentary debates (*Karácsony*) to external behaviour reflecting adversely on the Parliament (*Hoon*). The relevant national authorities have a wide margin of appreciation when exercising such powers and if complaints are made to Strasbourg the Court's role is a subsidiary one. Nevertheless, the Court has required basic procedural fairness to be followed, under both Articles 8 and 10 of the ECHR, by parliaments when exercising disciplinary powers over members. Indeed, as we have seen in *Karácsony* the unanimous Grand Chamber found a violation of Article 10 due to the failure of the Hungarian Parliament to observe these procedural obligations.

Both the original and current Court have protected journalists commenting and reporting on parliamentary proceedings from the abusive application of disciplinary proceedings and internal order powers by parliaments. In *Demicoli* the Court mandated the observance of fair hearing obligations in respect of serious disciplinary proceedings reaching the threshold of a 'criminal charge' under Article 6(1), ECHR. Whilst more recently the Court applied a 'strict scrutiny' approach when determining if the physical exclusion of the journalists observing disorder in the parliamentary chamber violated Article 10 of the Convention in *Selmani*.

These judgments have helped to foster the proper and effective functioning of national parliaments and journalistic coverage of parliamentary proceedings. In doing so the Court has contributed towards the Council of Europe's vision that 'National parliaments are the institutions which embody diversity of opinion within a society. Their role is to manage and defuse tensions and to maintain balance between competing claims. This in turn creates a sense of fair process, social cohesion and solidarity.'[52] Values entirely consistent with the views of Professor Ewing.

[52] *State of Democracy, Human Rights and the Rule of Law: Report by the Secretary General of the Council of Europe* (Strasbourg, May 2018) 71.

8

Employment Status in the Social Democratic Constitution: Law and Politics

ALAN BOGG*

I. Social Democracy and Employment Status: The Curious Incident of the Dog in the Night-time

In recent times, the field of labour law has been dominated by the legal issue of employment status. The question of whether a work relation is one of employment is often treated as the fundamental issue of labour law. To be characterised as an employee or worker entitles the individual to claim a range of fundamental rights against the employer. It is the principal mechanism whereby those engaged in work are accredited with normative agency, demanding recognition and respect as bearers of rights. Its importance has led to employment status being fetishised in certain quarters. It is as if the fate of decent work for all depended upon the quest for a perfect definition of employee. A steady stream of appellate cases has issued forth on a multitude of technical legal points: personal work and substitution clauses, the meaning of 'mutuality of obligation', the nature of control in work relations, and so forth. For some scholars, this body of case law is a kind of *corpus mysticum*, and the task of the scholar-acolyte is to divine hidden doctrinal wisdom in the ancient common law, derived from the scattered pronouncements of judge-priests.[1] Over the last 40 years, many leading scholars in the field have been associated with a particular terminology or doctrinal position on the issue of employment status: Mark Freedland on the 'personal employment contract';[2] Bob Hepple on the 'employment relationship';[3] Lord Wedderburn on the 'elephant test' for a contract of employment;[4] or Hugh Collins on 'vertical disintegration'.[5] Indeed, this may be regarded as one of the 'badges of membership' of the club of labour law luminaries.[6]

* I would like to thank Serena Crawshay-Williams for excellent research assistance in preparing this chapter. Thanks to my co-editors and to Michael Ford QC for helpful comments on an earlier draft, and to Keith Ewing for modestly hinting at his own role in the Homeworking select committee inquiry. I am very grateful to the Leverhulme Trust for its ongoing support of my work through the Leverhulme Prize.

[1] For the avoidance of doubt, this is a self-portrait.

[2] M Freedland, *The Personal Employment Contract* (Oxford, Oxford University Press, 2003).

[3] B Hepple, Restructuring Employment Rights (1986) 15 *Industrial Law Journal* 69.

[4] Lord Wedderburn, *The Worker and the Law*, 3rd edn (London, Penguin, 1986) 116.

[5] H Collins, 'Independent Contractors and the Challenge of Vertical Disintegration (1990) 10 *OJLS* 353.

[6] On 'badges of membership' as an employment status test, see ibid 380.

During this period, Keith Ewing has been a leading figure in the fields of comparative, international, European, and UK labour law. His work displays a range and mastery of topics that is probably unrivalled. Yet despite having produced many leading scholarly contributions on the common law contract of employment,[7] there is no distinctive Ewing 'take' on the legal definition of employment status. This is the curious incident of the dog in the night-time, and it is the subject of this chapter.

It would seem rather ungracious in a work celebrating Ewing's scholarly contribution to identify a lacuna as the subject of a chapter. On closer investigation, the lacuna is apparent rather than real. I want to suggest that we can understand Ewing's engagement with the issue of employment status through Ewing's orientation as a democratic socialist public lawyer. Ewing's identity as a public lawyer is bound up with his identity as a labour lawyer. One cannot understand one without the other. This was evident in one of his most famous papers, 'Democratic Socialism and Labour Law'.[8] His social democratic perspective on the Constitution is developed more fully in his recent paper, 'The Resilience of the Political Constitution'.[9] In it he recognised the complex interplay between the legal and the political in constitutional arrangements. According to Ewing, 'the infusion of law does not remove so much as compound the politics. It simply opens up a new arena of political contestation.'[10]

While these reflections are focused upon the interplay between political and legal modes of accountability in the Constitution, they are highly pertinent to employment status. Whether X is an employee and so entitled to certain statutory rights is a legal question. Indeed, it is often treated as *the* preeminent legal question in labour law. Yet it is also a political question. When precarious workers – homeworkers, casual workers, gig workers – go to court to seek recognition as employees or workers, this is a political act. Beneath the bristling legal technicalities is an assertion of one's status as a bearer of rights under conditions of democratic equality. Could any legal question be more political than that?

Ewing's work is testament to the political character of employment status. While there is a paucity of high scholarship on the definition of employee in Ewing's oeuvre, there is no paucity of political engagement with those same issues. In 1981, a young Dr K D Ewing acted as special adviser to a select committee inquiry into homework.[11] It was an early example of the unity of scholarship and activism that came to define him as a labour lawyer. It was also a vivid example of how *thinking politically* about employment status, in political fora, might be different to *thinking legally* about employment status in the courts. The most recent and dramatic example of this has been Ewing's leading role in drafting *A Manifesto for Labour Law*,[12] which formed the basis to the Labour Party's policy platform and had the potential to transform UK labour law if enacted.

In this chapter, I will explore these issues by focusing on the role of select committees in labour law, as a specific example of political engagement. In section II, I will explain how Chantal Mouffe's democratic socialist conception of politics, agonistic politics, could provide a distinctive political perspective on employment status. This political way of

[7] See, eg, KD Ewing, 'Remedies for Breach of the Contract of Employment' (1993) 52 *Cambridge Law Journal* 405.
[8] KD Ewing, 'Democratic Socialism and Labour Law' (1995) 2 *Industrial Law Journal* 103.
[9] KD Ewing, 'The Resilience of the Political Constitution' (2013) 14 *German Law Journal* 2111.
[10] Ibid, 2136.
[11] Employment Committee, *Homeworking* (HC 1981–82, 1).
[12] KD Ewing, J Hendy and C Jones, *A Manifesto for Labour Law* (London, IER, 2016).

thinking provides an alternative to the legal framing of employment status that has now become so dominant in public discourse. Once the distinctive contours of the political way of thinking are identified, we begin to see the value of political institutions (such as select committees) in engaging with employment status. This can complement the legal perspective on employment status, which characterises judicial engagement in courts. In section III, I will trace the scholarly development of employment status through the work of Kahn-Freund, Wedderburn, and Davies and Freedland. I will argue that this development can be understood as a movement from a legal to a political perspective on employment status. In section IV, I will compare the treatment of homeworkers in the courts and in the select committee report, as a way of understanding the distinctions between legal and political approaches to employment status. In section V, I will examine the recent engagements of select committees in the context of employment status in the gig economy. I shall argue that there has been a reassertion of dominance by the legal perspective, and a corresponding marginalisation of the political. This involves a significant democratic cost, and we need to be clear sighted about that. In the final concluding section, I will set out some thoughts on how and why this happened, and what might be done to reinvigorate an agonistic politics.

II. An Introduction to Agonistic Politics: How to Think Politically about Employment Status

In *Hegemony and Socialist Strategy* Ernesto Laclau and Chantal Mouffe developed an account of the 'political' in social democratic theory and practice.[13] According to Laclau and Mouffe, the future of social democracy needed to be understood as a struggle to expand and deepen the principles of democratic equality. The social democratic project is furthered where the principle of democratic equality is taken beyond the state into the economy and civil society. This is carried forward by the mobilisation of groups. This mobilisation requires a shift in consciousness, so that certain relations of 'subordination' come to be seen as sites of 'oppression'.[14] This occurs 'when the democratic discourse becomes available to articulate the different forms of resistance to subordination' so 'that the conditions will exist to make possible the struggle against different types of inequality'.[15] This struggle will be formulated as an assertion of rights against the oppressor, and a demand that those rights be respected under conditions of democratic equality.

This account of the political provides an important new perspective on the issue of employment status in labour law. Laclau and Mouffe's framework identifies the employment contract as a key site of the 'political'. The employment contract sits at the intersection between 'subordination' and 'oppression'. On the one hand, it establishes the employer's prerogative to control the labour process through the constitution of disciplinary powers, and so provides the legal underpinning to domination and inequality. On the other hand, it also provides a public platform for asserting fundamental social rights implemented

[13] E Laclau and C Mouffe, *Hegemony and Socialist Strategy* (London, Verso Books, 1985).
[14] Ibid, 137–138.
[15] Ibid, 138.

through employment legislation.[16] In its public function, it operates as a legal mechanism for oppressed groups to assert their rights against the employer. It is unsurprising, therefore, that the *legal* question of employment status has become a *political* battleground in the modern era. The 'contract of employment' has become legal shorthand for the fight for democratic equality by precarious workers seeking respect and recognition in the workplace.

Workers' struggles for democratic equality will often be inflected by different dimensions of political identity: migration status, race, age, gender, sexual orientation. Indeed, the narrative texture of many of the leading cases on employment status reveals precisely this kind of heterogeneity. For example, the claimants in *Nethermere (St Neots) Ltd v Gardiner* were women engaged in homework on a part-time and casualised basis, thereby displaying multiple markers of precarity that was typical of that type of working arrangement.[17] More recently, the decision in *Kalwak & Ors v Consistent Group Ltd and Welsh Country Foods* involved claims of employment status by Polish migrant workers whose labour was being supplied through agency arrangements.[18] The claimants had limited language skills and were engaged in low paid precarious work in the food processing sector. Beneath the surface of the unitary legal categories of employment status are diverse and distinctive forms of political struggle for recognition as rights-bearing agents.

What does it mean to think politically about legal categories such as the contract of employment? The juridical context to employment disputes in courts will generate its own internal constraints. Judges must be faithful to statutory language, the binding nature of precedent, and be guided by the principles of legality. In this way, the legal may be expected to impose restrictions on the political when judges are being called upon to interpret and develop the law. In later work, Mouffe explores the institutional arrangements that could facilitate agonistic political engagement in the circumstances of pluralism. This is centred upon the recognition of agonistic conflict as the fundamental basis of a healthy democratic polity, examining the features of the agonistic constitution. It indicates a different kind of approach to employment status. Political institutions should not simply mimic the legal reasoning in the leading employment status cases. They can bring a distinctive perspective to bear on the boundaries and categories of personal work status.

First, the political is concerned with the creation of *collective* identities, and these identities reflect a distinction between an 'us' and a 'them'. Conflict is ineradicable from the political. As Mouffe argues, 'the political is from the outset concerned with collective forms of identification … there can only be an identity when it is constructed as difference … any form of social objectivity is ultimately political and … it must bear the traces of the acts of exclusion that govern its constitution.'[19] The determination of the frontiers of identity is central to employment status, whether it be at the boundary between 'employer' and 'employee', or the boundary between 'employee' and the 'self-employed'. As such, pluralism 'cannot be envisaged only in terms of already existing subjects and restricted to their conceptions of the good. What must be addressed is the very process of constitution of the subjects of pluralism.'[20] Furthermore, every construction of a political identity is an act of

[16] *R (on the application of Unison) v Lord Chancellor* [2017] UKSC 51, [2017] 3 WLR 409.
[17] *Nethermere (St Neots) Ltd v Gardiner* [1984] ICR 612.
[18] *Kalwak & Ors v Consistent Group Ltd and Welsh Country Foods* [2008] EWCA Civ 430, [2008] IRLR 505.
[19] C Mouffe, *Agonistics* (London, Verso Books, 2013) 4.
[20] C Mouffe, *The Return of the Political* (London, Verso Books, 1993) 149.

power that has exclusionary effects on those who are positioned on the outside. The division between labour market insiders and outsiders has been one of the central and perennial themes of employment status. Courts are ill-equipped to deal with collective identities. The court is focused on the individual dispute between the parties. Consequently, courts struggle to adjust to the more collective idea of 'gig workers' or 'homeworkers' or 'zero hours' workers', even though this is how identities may be conceived by the workers themselves.

Secondly, the frontiers of political identity should always be regarded as contingent rather than naturalised. There is no objective essence that goes to the constitution of identity, and the boundaries of the political should always be open to contestation and challenge: 'every social order is a contingent articulation of power relations that lacks an ultimate rational ground.'[21] Admittedly, politics necessitates decisions, and decisions require the specification of an order. Labour law could not dispense with relational boundaries and 'personal scope'. Where there are rights to be allocated, there are boundaries to be demarcated. Yet those allocative decisions should never be regarded as final and conclusive. There must always be legal and political mechanisms that enable the boundaries of inclusion/exclusion to be open to contestation and challenge by new groups seeking democratic equality. This should make us particularly suspicious of discourses that fixate on 'clarity'. This often conceals a fairy tale belief that there is a perfect boundary awaiting discovery in the world, one that could quieten discord definitively.

Thirdly, Mouffe is suspicious of theories of liberal legalism that operate as forms of closure to stifle political conflict. She argues that there is now an increasingly 'marked tendency to privilege the juridical field and to expect the law to provide the solutions to all types of conflict. The juridical sphere is becoming the terrain where social conflicts can find a form of expression'.[22] This privileges the judiciary as constitutional actors. Deep political conflicts are reconfigured as interpretive disputes over the meaning of legal concepts. The privileging of courts in agonistic democracy is problematic because it fails to provide a democratic outlet for the passions as vital constituents of political engagement.[23] For example, Lizzie Barmes has drawn attention to the 'chilling, eerie quality to the bland recounting' of narratives of precarious and marginalised work in judicial discourse.[24] This moral sanitisation of judicial language, and the translation of political claims (eg 'respect me as an agent, respect my rights') into legal categories (eg did this break in employment constitute a rupture to 'continuity' or was it a 'temporary cessation' in accordance with the statutory definition?'), reflects the distinctive demands of legal reasoning in public courts. Where there are legal disputes, there will be a need for courts and judicial determination. However, the agonistic constitution would also make space for political approaches to contested questions like employment status. These political approaches should allow for the expression of anger, indignation, and the struggle against oppression. This could lead to fundamental structural changes to the organisation and governance of labour markets, in ways that transcend our existing conceptual apparatus ('contract of employment', 'worker') entirely.

[21] Ibid, 131.

[22] C Mouffe, *The Democratic Paradox* (London, Verso Books, 2000) 116.

[23] Mouffe, *Agonistics* (n 19) 8.

[24] L Barmes, 'Learning from Case Law Accounts of Marginalized Working' in J Fudge, S McCrystal and K Sankaran (eds), *Challenging the Legal Boundaries of Work Regulation* (Oxford, Hart Publishing, 2012) 318.

Finally, Mouffe develops a distinction between 'agonistic' and 'antagonistic' relations. The political is always vulnerable to the deep fissuring characteristic of the 'friend'/'enemy' distinction, which is a form of 'antagonism' that can erupt into violence and the will to annihilate one's opponent.[25] By contrast, 'agonism' describes a political situation where the possibility of conflict is given appropriate recognition, but where the organisation of political community is based upon a 'conflictual consensus'.[26] Constitutions must be designed so as to steer conflicts away from antagonistic forms of expression, while giving ample scope for agonistic confrontation. Political institutions such as select committees could provide a forum whereby conflicts about rights and employment status could be ventilated in agonistic ways, thereby defusing the potential for antagonistic conflicts.

According to Mouffe, the most significant risk in the design of political institutions and structures at the current time is in the suppression of conflict. Mouffe identifies these tendencies in theories of deliberative democracy, the rise of 'third way' politics that purport to have transcended the left/right distinction, and the juridification and judicialisation of political conflict. She advocates a strategy of engagement with existing parliamentary institutions, connecting extra-parliamentary mobilisation in civil society with established parliamentary structures and representative democracy, as a basis for securing structural changes that will extend the reach of democratic principles.[27] The political dimension of employment status means that a range of political institutions, in addition to courts, should also have an important role in setting (and resetting) the frontiers of employment protection. This process should never be viewed as the exclusive preserve of the courts. And no boundary should ever be viewed as final, definitive and conclusive.

In the next section, I will trace the historical development of scholarly discourse around employment status. I shall argue that it originated in a highly juridical frame in the seminal labour law literature of the early post-war period, in the work of Kahn-Freund. It was only during the 1980s that scholars began to recognise the political dimensions of employment status, and the scope for political institutions, such as select committees, to provide a distinctive input into the debates around personal scope. However, in this context as in others, the conceptual structure developed by Kahn-Freund has been persistent and enduring.

III. Historical Perspectives on Employment Status: From Law to Politics

A. Kahn-Freund and the Depoliticisation of Employment Status

In historical terms, the contract of employment was depoliticised as an organising category in labour law. It sat at the centre of the discipline, but as an axiom embedded in the timeless common law resting in the hands of the lawyers and judges. We shall examine its intellectual

[25] This framing of the political is obviously based on the work of Carl Schmitt, a thinker who Mouffe has engaged with critically in her own Left account of the political. See C Schmitt, *The Concept of the Political* (Chicago, University of Chicago Press, 2007).

[26] Mouffe, *Agonistics* (n 19) xii.

[27] Ibid, 109–119.

development through the work of some leading labour lawyers in the second half of the twentieth century who were, broadly speaking, approaching these issues from within a social democratic tradition. We begin, of course, with the work of Otto Kahn-Freund. For Kahn-Freund, the contract of employment represented a toxic conjunction of fictitious bargaining equality and legally enforced servitude through the contractual integration of Master and Servant norms. As Freedland has noted, Kahn-Freund's conceptualisation of the contract of employment was dynamic, and it took on an air of despondency in his later work.[28] In all this theorising, however, there is a continuous thread that runs through Kahn-Freund's work on the contract of employment. The contract of employment is treated as a legal enquiry to be undertaken by the courts applying ordinary common law principles. The personal boundary of 'labour' is taken as a pre-political given, rather than an object of political contestation.

Kahn-Freund's first major intellectual engagement with the contract of employment came in his 1954 essay, 'Legal Framework'.[29] It was here that he described the contract of employment in terms that have become enduring: 'For the lawyer … the individual relationship between employer and employee is the corner-stone of the edifice. Everything hinges upon what is called the "contract of employment" or "contract of service"'.[30] In the structural division of topics in 'Legal Framework', 'The Contract of Employment' comes first before other topics that would seem more fitting candidates for priority in the theory of collective laissez-faire, such as 'Collective Bargaining and the Law' or 'Industrial Conflict and the Law'. At first sight, the analytical centrality of the contract of employment in this essay, a manifesto for collective laissez-faire in Kahn-Freund's famous 1950s troika of essays,[31] is puzzling. After all, did not collective laissez-faire accord priority to the role of autonomous collective bargaining, and of voluntary over legal methods in the industrial sphere? And did the 'principle of contractual equality as between the individual employer and the individual employee' in the English common law not obscure the subordination and inequality that was inherent in the employment relationship?[32]

For Kahn-Freund, the centrality of the contract of employment was based in its functional importance as a conduit for worker-protective norms. Sometimes this occurred where legislative norms were 'grafted upon the common law by legislation',[33] as with minimum wage laws, the Truck Acts, or legislation on hours of work. More often, it occurred through the incorporation of norms from collective agreements into individual contracts of employment, brilliantly rationalised by Kahn-Freund through the concept of 'crystallized' or 'codified' custom.[34] Kahn-Freund also noted how some worker-protective techniques bypassed the contract of employment entirely, such as the use of tort law in the sphere of

[28] M Freedland, 'Otto Kahn-Freund, the Contract of Employment and the Autonomy of Labour Law' in A Bogg et al, *The Autonomy of Labour Law* (Oxford, Hart Publishing, 2015) 38–41.

[29] O Kahn-Freund, 'Legal Framework' in A Flanders and HA Clegg, *The System of Industrial Relations in Great Britain* (Oxford, Basil Blackwell 1954).

[30] Ibid, 45.

[31] See also O Kahn-Freund, 'Labour Law' in M Ginsberg (ed), *Law and Opinion in England in the 20th Century* (London, Stevens, 1959) and O Kahn-Freund, 'Intergroup Conflicts and their Settlement' (1954) 5 *British Journal of Sociology* 193.

[32] Kahn-Freund, 'Legal Framework' (n 29) 46.

[33] Ibid, 46.

[34] Ibid, 49.

worker health and safety. Here, the legal duty was imposed on the employer as occupier of premises rather than as party to the contract of employment. Where the vindication of these basic tort rights was at stake, the question of employment status was immaterial to the existence of the legal right.

The most striking feature of this examination of the contract of employment in 'Legal Framework', however, is that the identity of the contract of employment, and its division from the contract of service, is entirely absent from the discussion. It is a non-issue. This is most surprising viewed from the vantage point of today, when we sometimes talk of little else. This aspect of contractual identity was addressed in another less well-known piece of writing from the 1950s, a *Modern Law Review* case note, where Kahn-Freund provided an analysis of *Cassidy v Ministry of Health.*[35] Indeed, it is one of the rare instances where the issue of 'personal scope' was treated at any length by Kahn-Freund. In fact, *Cassidy* was not really an employment case at all. It was addressing vicarious liability in tort, and the circumstances in which a hospital authority could be liable for the negligence of its medical staff. For the majority in the Court of Appeal, the scope of vicarious liability turned upon the distinction between 'servants' working under a contract of employment and 'independent contractors' providing work under a contract for services. The note is still remembered for its critique of the 'control' test in defining an employee, given the growing proportion of the labour force with professional skills of a technical character. In these circumstances, an employer could not conceivably be viewed as exercising control over the performance (the 'how') of work. The control test 'was based upon the social conditions of an earlier age: it assumed that the employer of labour was able to direct and instruct the labourer as to the technical methods he should use in performing his work.'[36] Its anachronism was especially vivid within the context of the employed medical professionals in *Cassidy* itself. Kahn-Freund treated *Cassidy* as based upon an 'organisation' test rather than the traditional 'control' test, asking whether the permanent medical staff were integrated into the bureaucratic structure of the employing entity. He also observed parallel jurisprudential developments in France and Germany, which he described as 'another example of the similarity of developments in common law and "civil law" systems which are simply enforced by the irresistible power of economic necessities.'[37]

These two interventions, though rather slender, provided a stable and enduring framework for theorising the identity of the contract of employment through to the third and final edition of *Labour and the Law*, published posthumously in 1983. It was a framework that was strongly antithetical to the political view of the employment contract outlined in the previous section. In some respects, this reflected the character of employment status case law during the heyday of collective laissez-faire. The leading cases on the 'contract of service' during this period tended not to be claims for the vindication of rights against the employer. *Cassidy* was a case on vicarious liability rather than employment protection. The seminal decision in *Ready Mixed Concrete (South East) Ltd. v Minister of Pensions and National Insurance*, on the correct legal test for a 'contract of service', concerned a determination by the Minister of Social Security for an employer's liability for national insurance payments

[35] *Cassidy v Ministry of Health* [1951] 1 All ER 574, noted by O Kahn-Freund, 'Servants and Independent Contractors' (1951) 14 *MLR* 504.

[36] Ibid, 505.

[37] Ibid, 508.

under the National Insurance Act 1965.[38] The legal context of these judgments no doubt obscured the political character of employment status. This dimension was far more evident where social rights were being claimed, using the contract of service as a platform.

Kahn-Freund continued to under-estimate the political dimension of the contract of employment even after the statutory 'floor of rights' had been enacted in the mid-1970s. In 'Blackstone's Neglected Child', based upon a 1977 lecture, he described the 'atrophy' of the contract of employment as a legal category.[39] This 'atrophy' reflected the fact that 'the growth of a legal relation is stunted if it does not appear in the courts'.[40] Litigation on the contract of employment was so rare because 'the bulk of labour law, and especially the bulk of legislation for the protections of workers, developed until our own century and partly still develops outside the frame of the contract of employment … The normal pattern of protection was through the law of tort or through special statutory rights unconnected with the contract of employment.'[41]

For Kahn-Freund, this separation of statute and contract was reflected in the fact that statutory rights were not usually integrated into the contract itself. They had a juridical existence that was independent of the contract. So, they were enforced in special tribunals rather than ordinary courts, the substantive content of the rights was rooted in statute, and so forth. In retrospect, it seems to me that Kahn-Freund attached undue emphasis to this feature of the interface between contract and statute. It is not clear that this weak integration had a significant effect on the substantive level of worker protection. He also gave insufficient attention to the boundary between employment and self-employment, and its pivotal role in the allocation of statutory entitlements.

His earlier essay, 'A Note on Status and Contract in British Labour Law', can be read as a protean outing for the themes developed in the 1977 Blackstone lecture.[42] In the earlier essay, he emphasised the distinction between *ius dispositivum* and *ius cogens*, optional norms and mandatory norms, and of how English contract law had been hobbled by its failure to develop a body of mandatory norms to regulate contracts. Kahn-Freund recognised the existence of mandatory statutory provisions that 'presupposed the existence of a contract of employment'.[43] But neither here nor in the later Blackstone lecture did he recognise the profound significance of this for the politics of employment status. Mandatory statutory norms could be effectively transformed into optional norms by employers where the contractual arrangement was configured to present the relation as one involving an 'independent contractor'. The 'floor of rights' legislation in the Employment Protection Act 1975 would bring this political dimension to the fore, but it was something of a blind spot for Kahn-Freund even in 1977. By contrast, in his contemporary analysis of the 'individual aspects' of the 1975 legislation, Mark Freedland observed that some of the legislative changes 'will place still further weight upon the distinction between employees … and self-employed persons'.[44] That observation would prove to be highly prescient.

[38] *Ready Mixed Concrete (South East) Ltd. v Minister of Pensions and National Insurance* [1968] 2 QB 497.

[39] O Kahn-Freund, *Blackstone's Neglected Child* reprinted in O Kahn-Freund, *Selected Writings* (London, Stevens, 1977) 524–528.

[40] Ibid, 526.

[41] Ibid, 524.

[42] O Kahn-Freund, 'A Note on Status and Contract in British Labour Law' (1967) 30 *MLR* 635.

[43] Ibid, 640.

[44] Ibid, 564.

The primacy of legal thinking was reflected in three features of Kahn-Freund's framework. First, the legal perspective on the contract of employment tended to individuate work relations. As Kahn-Freund said in 'Legal Framework', 'The law thus refuses to look upon the workers in a factory as one entity. It dissolves the existing workshop community in a series of individual contracts.'[45] This individuating frame of reference, characteristic of the legal viewpoint, obscured the role of *collective* identities in work relations. Whereas workers might regard themselves in collective terms as 'homeworkers' or 'gig workers', the courts are apt to emphasise the individuated nature of the enquiry into the specific contracts at issue in the case.[46]

Secondly, Kahn-Freund's Note on *Cassidy*, which described the development of legal doctrine 'enforced by the irresistible power of economic necessities',[47] presented a materialist view whereby legal norms were determined by economic relations and the organisation of production. This materialist picture of superstructural legal norms simply mirroring an economic base failed to acknowledge the contingency of legal boundaries,[48] and the fact that these shifting political frontiers reflected the strategic choices and power relations between employers, workers, and judges.

Thirdly, and perhaps most surprisingly given his more general scepticism about law and legal norms, Kahn-Freund placed remarkable faith in lawyers to salvage the contract of employment from its 'atrophy'. In his 1969 Sidney Ball Lecture, 'Industrial Relations and the Law – Retrospect and Prospect', Kahn-Freund was fiercely critical of the failure of the law to perform its regulatory function, to provide a clear legal code of substantive rights and obligations for individual employees.[49] Kahn-Freund envisaged nothing less than a systematic codification project for individual employment law.[50] This was a public task 'for a new generation of lawyers' who could be entrusted with the drafting of 'comprehensive and systematic legislation and for courts that can apply it.'[51]

The effect of giving lawyers and courts such a pivotal role in reform was to transform political questions about the normative content and boundaries of personal work relations into technical legal questions. Kahn-Freund's treatment of the contract of employment reflected what Mouffe has described as a 'tendency to privilege the juridical field and to expect the law to provide the solutions to all types of conflict.'[52] Yet the question of which relations should be within the protective domain of social rights, and how those relations should be regulated, are inescapably political. One wonders how far Kahn-Freund's professional origins as a labour court judge shaped his intellectual framework on this set of issues. It contrasts sharply with his wider scepticism about the legal viewpoint in industrial relations in his general theory of collective laissez-faire.

It is important to remember that Kahn-Freund's work reflected the pressing regulatory issues of the day. These pieces were written before the great set piece battles of employment

[45] Ibid, 50.
[46] See, eg, Underhill LJ in *Pimlico Plumbers Ltd v Smith* [2017] EWCA Civ 51, [2017] 2 WLUK 293.
[47] Kahn-Freund, 'Servants and Independent Contractors' (n 35) 508.
[48] On this materialist feature of Kahn-Freund's work, see H Collins, 'Against Abstentionism in Labour Law' in J Bell and J Eekelaar (eds), *Oxford Essays in Jurisprudence* (Oxford, Clarendon, 1987).
[49] O Kahn-Freund, 'Industrial Relations and the Law – Retrospect and Prospect' (1969) 7 *British Journal of Industrial Relations* 301.
[50] Ibid, 313.
[51] Ibid, 316.
[52] Mouffe, *Democratic Paradox* (n 22) 116.

status, such as *O'Kelly v Trusthouse Forte*,[53] had been fought out in the courts. In that case, it may be recalled, casual waiters on 'zero hours' contracts were unprotected from trade union victimisation because the court concluded that they were not employees. In *Labour and the Law*, there is some recognition that the constitution of the subjects of labour law is difficult and contested.[54] 'Management' and 'labour' are described as 'abstractions'.[55] Furthermore, Kahn-Freund acknowledged that it is not 'possible neatly to separate these two categories of persons … A production manager or the head of one of a chain of stores is "management" if seen from below and "labour" if seen from above.'[56] There are still heavy traces of his materialist analysis of *Cassidy* from the 1950s, with the conceptual fuzziness of 'labour' and 'management' a reflection of technological and organisational changes in the labour market. Nevertheless, there are also perceptive discussions of the changing composition of 'labour', for example the growing number of women workers.[57] There is also a discussion of the growth in white collar employment, and the expanding relational scope of protective legislation to encompass these new groups of workers.[58] Still, and even allowing for the fact that *Labour and the Law* was focused on collective labour relations, there was little to suggest that employment status was about to rupture into one of the principal sites of legal and political conflict in the labour field.[59] The expanding scope of protective legislation appears in *Labour and the Law* as a rational reflex response to certain features of newly emerging employment forms, such as its subordinate quality. The crucial dimension of workers' agency in agitating for recognition as bearers of rights is scarcely acknowledged. The account of pluralistic conflict in Kahn-Freund's work was thus heavily circumscribed, confined to the 'distribution of the social product between consumption and investment',[60] while treating the *subjects* of pluralism as a pre-political given.[61] Thus, even in Kahn-Freund's final reflections on the personal scope of employment law published in 1983, very little had in fact changed since his work in the early 1950s. The law's construction of identity in work relations, and its creation of 'insiders' and 'outsiders', is ingrained in common law categories that seem to exist beyond the scope of political challenge. The lawyers and the judges are still very much in charge.

B. Law Gives Way to Politics: Wedderburn and Davies and Freedland

How enduring was Kahn-Freund's depoliticised framing of the employment contract? During the 1980s, there was a bifurcation in the genre of worker-protective labour law scholarship.[62] On the one hand, scholars such as Lord Wedderburn could be viewed

[53] *O'Kelly v Trusthouse Forte* [1984] QB 90.
[54] P Davies and M Freedland (eds), *Kahn Freund's Labour and the Law*, 3rd edn (London, Stevens, 1983).
[55] Ibid, 15.
[56] Ibid, 16.
[57] Ibid, 38.
[58] Ibid, 49.
[59] Of course, *O'Kelly* itself was an employment status case that involved trade union rights. It was thus as much a matter of collective labour law as it was individual labour law.
[60] Davies and Freedland (n 54) 27.
[61] See the critique in R Hyman, 'Pluralism, Procedural Consensus and Collective Bargaining' (1978) 16 *British Journal of Industrial Relations* 16.
[62] H Collins, 'Labour Law as a Vocation' (1989) 105 *LQR* 468; R Dukes, *The Labour Constitution* (Oxford, OUP, 2014) ch 5.

as standing in the direct lineage of Kahn-Freund, developing and refining the tenets of collective laissez-faire in the face of new political and economic challenges.[63] On the other hand, Paul Davies and Mark Freedland were developing a new paradigm of the 'law of the labour market' which involved a reorientation around a wider set of normative goals, including economic policies such as control of inflation, productivity, and competitiveness; and a corresponding widening of disciplinary scope to include matters such as job creation, training, and labour market policy.[64]

To what extent did this bifurcation lead to divergent treatment of the issues around personal scope? The answer to this is rather complex. The political dimension of employment status emerges very strongly in Wedderburn's work. The contract of employment does not represent a natural boundary in the world, awaiting discovery through the formulation of an appropriately scientific method. It is a site of conflict and exclusion, and it must be understood as political in nature. Wedderburn also emphasises the importance of Parliament and legislative intervention, alongside the traditional role of the courts. By contrast, Davies and Freedland place their faith in a more scientific and objective method based in dispassionate economic analysis. This involves a negation of the agonistic dimension. However, like Wedderburn, they also place emphasis on Parliament's role in addressing the emerging labour market problems of atypical and insecure work. In this respect, the political is recognised at the institutional level, even though the possibilities for a distinctively political way of thinking is obscured by the attachment to scientific objectivity.

Let us start with Wedderburn. In an important essay on Kahn-Freund's legacy in 1983, Clark and Wedderburn described the contract of employment as exemplifying 'a deeply rooted crisis in … legal concepts and beyond them in the wider society.'[65] Given the foundational role of the contract of employment, this crisis 'is of the most profound moment for the whole of our labour law.'[66] For Clark and Wedderburn, this 'pathological eruption in the law',[67] reflected in an anarchy of legal tests and unpredictable outcomes of judicial characterisation of work relations, was of relatively recent origins and was a product of both legal and social factors. The legal factor was the strong attachment of the English judiciary to notions of subordinated service. It was natural, given the centrality of subordination in the common law imagination, for judicially formulated tests to fixate on issues of 'control'. We might also note the deep incongruence between the common law ideology of master and servant and the newly emerging statutory ideology of employees as bearers of rights in the employment relation.

For Clark and Wedderburn, this crisis in the contract of employment was more strongly rooted in social and economic factors. The changing composition of the workforce, and the diversification of work arrangements across multiple axes differentiated by time (part-time, casual work, fixed term work, task contracts), space (homework) and payment mechanism (piecework), generated tectonic strains on the binary divide between employees and independent contractors. The anarchic disintegration of the employment contract was

[63] R Dukes, 'Wedderburn and the Theory of Labour Law' (2015) 44 *Industrial Law Journal* 357.
[64] Dukes, *The Labour Constitution* (n 62) 96–97.
[65] Lord Wedderburn, 'Modern Labour Law: Problems, Functions, and Policies', in Lord Wedderburn, R Lewis and J Clark (eds) *Labour Law and Industrial Relations: Building on Kahn-Freund* (Oxford, Clarendon, 1983) 144.
[66] Ibid, 145.
[67] Ibid, 151.

exacerbated by 'freedom of contract', and the scope for manipulation of contractual terms to present work arrangements as ones of 'self-employment' to courts. Clark and Wedderburn also note the increasing importance of Parliament in intervening to resolve the difficulties of personal scope through legislation, in areas such as the regulation of temporary agency work. This was an important recognition of the political character of employment status, at least at the institutional level. This provided a welcome corrective to the tendency to focus on the judiciary and case law. Overall, however, there is an air of despondency in this essay, and the authors seem agnostic on the capacities of legal regulation to respond to the dramatic social and economic forces that had been unleashed in the post-war period.

In *The Worker and the Law*, Wedderburn provided a more positive reconstructive approach to the profound problems identified in the 1983 essay with Jon Clark.[68] The chapter that deals with this material, on 'The Employment Relationship', is very deliberately located within a rights-based paradigm.[69] As Wedderburn notes, the 'floor of rights' had been constructed around the contract of employment.[70] The political and legal significance of the binary divide, therefore, is in its role as constituting workers as agents asserting rights-based claims against their employers. Wedderburn is still critical of the disorder in judicial tests of employment status.[71] Indeed, he famously put forward his 'elephant-test' for the contract of employment: 'an animal too difficult to define but easy to recognize when you see it.'[72] However, Wedderburn is also astute to the policy dimension to the employment status enquiry: 'the semantic tests are less important than the social policy pursued by the court in respect of each issue: qualification for unfair dismissal, category for national insurance purposes, vicarious liability of the employer and so on.'[73] This appears to describe a purposive approach to employment status, recognising that the boundary is sensitive to the purpose for which it is being drawn. Where protective rights are being claimed, this would necessitate an approach 'that protects the worker who is a part of the enterprise, wherever the work is done, without the same definition necessarily applying to legal principles devised for other purposes, such as vicarious liability.'[74] Wedderburn's arguments also suggest that certain rights, such as the right not to be discriminated against, are so fundamental that they warrant an especially wide personal scope.[75] He is also explicit in identifying an important role for Parliament:

> what seems to be needed is an intervention by Parliament that can use flexible machinery … to protect those in a subordinate – or "para-subordinate" – relationship doing certain types of work … Labour law cannot have lost its touch for inventing different types of "workers" for different purposes; it cannot muddle on in the pretence that the common law "contract of service" is a formula for all seasons.[76]

In this way, Wedderburn's work exposes the political character of employment status. Courts should not be accorded an exclusive or privileged institutional role in setting the boundary.

[68] Lord Wedderburn, *The Worker and the Law*, 3rd edn (London, Penguin,1986).
[69] Ibid, ch 2.
[70] Ibid, 107.
[71] Ibid, 112–116.
[72] Ibid, 116.
[73] Ibid.
[74] Ibid, 132.
[75] Ibid, 124.
[76] Ibid, 132.

At its core, the employee concept is the gateway into the domain of worker-protective rights. Where judges are called upon to interpret and apply the relevant legal principles, they should do so purposively by acknowledging the dimension of fundamental rights. Moreover, there is nothing natural or inevitable about the common law boundary developed by the courts. The boundary should be regarded as contingent: it can be made (and remade) for different purposes, perhaps differentiated according to the specific rights being claimed, and it is an exercise in creative political judgement. Since employment status was within the domain of the political, Wedderburn argues that Parliament should take a strong and interventionist role in the constitution of work relations. However, he is also realistic about the prospects for such legislative intervention in the mid-1980s, recognising that a more modest strategy of judicial clarification of employment status might be more achievable in securing tangible improvements for workers. Significantly, however, clarification is regarded very much as a second-best strategy, a reflection of harsh political realities rather than an ambitious reform aspiration.

In Davies and Freedland's *Labour Law: Text and Materials*, there is a similar recognition of the crisis in legal concepts.[77] The authors describe the 'tautology' into which the judicial tests 'so readily descends',[78] as they invoke notions of consistency with a 'contract of service' without elaborating the identifying attributes of this work relation.[79] Like Wedderburn, there is also a sophisticated differentiation of the multiple ways in which work contracts have fragmented across the dimensions of time, place, and payment method. In order to move beyond casuistry, the authors propose an economic frame of reference for developing the judicial approach. An economic analysis of the distribution of risks and incentives in work arrangements could provide a 'better chance of leading to a scientific rather than intuitive and impressionistic method of classification'.[80] This economic approach would be 'a relatively objective, meaningful and informative way of distinguishing' employees from independent contractors.[81] The authors also reject the purposive approach to employment status, where differentiation is sensitive to the legal point of the enquiry, 'because that again would discredit the claim of the process of definition to be an objective one, and such a claim is necessary to give the internal strength with which alone the rather shaky edifice can be supported.'[82] This appeal to a 'scientific' or 'objective' basis, and its assignment to a technical exercise in economic theory, stands in rather sharp contrast to the political characterisation of employment status in Wedderburn's work. It also fails to do justice to the vital conflictual nature of employment status, as a site where political identities are constructed and where agency is exercised by groups of workers.

At the institutional level, however, Davies and Freedland emphasised that a focus on judicial intervention 'is too narrow a perspective', and that legislative intervention should be given more prominence in accounts of the employment relationship.[83] To this end, their chapter examines the legislative treatment of new forms of work, such as labour-only

[77] P Davies and M Freedland, *Labour Law: Text and Materials* 2nd edn (London, Weidenfeld & Nicolson, 1984).
[78] Ibid, 87.
[79] Ibid, 85.
[80] Ibid, 89.
[81] Ibid.
[82] Ibid, 93.
[83] Ibid.

sub-contractors, temporary and casual workers, part-time workers, and home workers. It also examines the variety of legislative options available, including the extension of employment protection legislation to a wider scope of work relationships as with sex and race discrimination laws.

Across both genres of worker-protective labour law, therefore, there was an important recognition that an exclusive focus on the courts was unduly limiting. The complex and polycentric character of the issues around employment status, and the conflictual nature of its politics, might sometimes be better addressed through parliamentary intervention. However, Davies and Freedland's work is an important reminder that it is possible to approach employment status politically in institutional terms, while denying the agonistic quality of the issues at an analytical level.

In recent years, select committees have made some high-profile interventions in public deliberation about employment status in the gig economy. In the next section, the role of select committees as labour law actors will be examined. In institutional terms, of course, select committees represent a form of political engagement. It remains to be seen whether the engagement of select committees as labour law actors is 'political' in the agonistic sense elaborated by Mouffe. As we shall see, the intense activity of select committees presents something of a mixed picture when it is examined from the perspective of agonistic democracy. Overall, this story is one of missed political opportunities, and the capture of the political by the legal.

IV. An Introduction to Select Committees on Employment Status: The Case of Homeworkers

The modern structure of select committees was based in the 1978 report by the Select Committee on Procedure, whereby select committees were linked to the relevant government departments to provide a mechanism of government accountability.[84] During the late 1970s and early 1980s, at a time when rudimentary computers still occupied large rooms and Gig work was a distant prospect, homeworking was an intense focus of regulatory attention in the courts and in Parliament. This reflected concerns about the exploitation of homeworkers, and an inadequate legal framework to enforce their basic rights such as health and safety and the payment of adequate wages in accordance with relevant wages council norms.[85] In cases such as *Airfix Footwear Ltd v Cope*[86] and *Nethermere (St Neots) Ltd v Gardiner*,[87] the courts had considered the entitlement of homeworkers to claim unfair dismissal protection, which depended upon a finding of employee status. These cases would still be well known to employment lawyers today. Another important intervention during that period, though far less likely to be remembered now, is the First Report of the Employment Committee

[84] Select Committee on Procedure, *Proposals for a new system of Select Committees* (HC 1978–79, 588-1) chs 5–7, cited A Bradley, KD Ewing and C Knight, *Constitutional and Administrative Law* (London, Pearson, 2014) 215–216.

[85] KD Ewing, 'Homeworking: A Framework for Reform' (1982) 11 *Industrial Law Journal* 94.

[86] *Airfix Footwear Ltd v Cope* [1978] ICR 1210.

[87] *Nethermere (St Neots) Ltd v Gardiner* [1984] ICR 612.

Session 1981–82 on 'Homeworking'.[88] The select committee's deliberations were supported by one Dr KD Ewing, then a young lecturer in public law at the University of Edinburgh and special adviser to the committee. The contrast between the Court of Appeal's approach in *Nethermere* and the Employment Select Committee's approach suggests some parameters for understanding the differences between legal and political approaches to employment status. This enables us to identify the distinctive *political* contribution that select committees might make to public deliberation about the regulation of work. Given his vision of public law and the 'Political Constitution', it should not surprise us that the young Dr Ewing was associated with the political dimension of employment status.

Nethermere involved a claim for unfair dismissal by homeworkers, following a determination by the Industrial Tribunal that the claimants were employees. The majority of the Court of Appeal concluded that the tribunal's original decision did not involve a misdirection in law or a decision that was perverse. According to Stephenson LJ, there must 'be an irreducible minimum of obligation on each side to create a contract of service.'[89] Although Stephenson LJ regarded the evidence of such mutual obligations as 'tenuous',[90] he was prepared to accept that the tribunal had been entitled to reach its conclusion that they were employees. In an important statement of principle, he went on to observe that 'I cannot see why well founded expectations of continuing homework should not be hardened or refined into enforceable contracts by regular giving and taking of work over periods of a year or more.'[91] This was supported by Dillon LJ who concluded that a contract of employment may be 'inferred from a course of dealing'.[92]

From an agonistic political perspective, there are four features of *Nethermere* that should be emphasised. First, the judgment is highly individuating in its framing of the relevant issues. Although this was a case concerning homeworkers, a group within the labour market with distinctive needs and vulnerabilities, the Court of Appeal was keen to stress that it was focused on the specific contracts of Mrs Taverna and Mrs Gardiner. According to Stephenson LJ, 'there was just enough material to make a contract of service a reasonably possible inference … I follow Slynn J. in *Airfix Footwear Ltd. v. Cope* [1978] I.C.R. 1210 *in refusing to say anything about the general position of outworkers*'.[93] The form of legal judgment thus struggles to accommodate the agonistic notion that identities might be collective, in this case their identities as homeworkers, focusing instead on the specific contracts of the individual claimants.

Secondly, the legal enquiry is highly technical and formalistic. Each of the judgments in *Nethermere* contains a set of sophisticated legal reflections on the nature of 'mutuality of obligations', the distinction between questions of law and mixed fact and law, the formation of obligations through courses of dealing, and the distinction between umbrella contracts and discrete contracts of service. The emotional texture of the dispute, and what is at stake for the protagonists themselves, all but disappears in the judgment. It is a forum of legal reason rather than passion. The technical analysis of mutuality takes on a life of its

[88] Employment Committee (n 11).
[89] *Nethermere* (n 87) 623.
[90] Ibid, 626.
[91] Ibid, 626–627.
[92] Ibid, 634.
[93] Ibid, 627 (emphasis added).

own, a *pas de deux* between clever lawyers, and it becomes detached from the underlying substantive question whether these homeworkers experienced vulnerabilities that warranted their inclusion within the scope of protective employment rights.

Thirdly, the court adopts a sequential formulation of the legal enquiry that separates it into two stages. The court treats the question of whether the individuals are 'employees' as a preliminary jurisdictional point, and a threshold for examining the substance of the unfair dismissal claim itself. While in legal terms this distinction makes logical sense, the formal detachment of jurisdiction from substantive right obscures the purposive dimension of the employment status enquiry. Reading *Nethermere* it is possible to forget entirely what was at stake for the employees, which is whether they had been unfairly dismissed by their employer. Finally, legal judgments are particularised rather than holistic. The legal dispute is bipolar, focused on the specific contractual arrangements between the claimants and defendant, and abstracted from the wider regulatory context to homework. We do not know from the Court of Appeal judgment whether these individuals are covered by a wages council, the level of remuneration, the health and safety conditions in the homes of outworkers, the gender dimension of homework, and the number of homeworkers working in the garment sector. There is limited scope for the court to consider social science data and to contextualise its individuated legal enquiry.

The identification of these elements should not be read as a criticism of the courts. There are certain features of legal reasoning, and of the constitutional responsibilities of courts, that mean that this approach to employment status is appropriate to its context. Courts are required to apply the law dispassionately to the facts, to focus on the position of the parties in the case, to be guided by authoritative legal reasons, to be faithful to statutes and binding precedents, and so forth. However, it does mean that judicial approaches to employment status have certain limitations from an agonistic perspective. They need to be supplemented by political approaches. And political approaches should not be hobbled by the formal constraints of legal reasoning.

In this respect, the political intervention of the Employment select committee on Homeworking reveals a distinctive approach to employment status. The first point of contrast is that work identities are conceived in a less individuated way. Thus, in its section on 'The Nature and Extent of Homeworking', the committee contextualises the practice of homeworking drawing upon the social science evidence submitted to it. It examines the sectoral distribution of homeworking, the economic explanation for its use by employers, the gendered nature of homework, levels of unionisation, and the distinctive vulnerabilities of homeworkers.[94] In this way, despite real differences in the work experiences of homeworkers, it is nevertheless meaningful to demarcate 'homeworkers' as a collective identity and as a focus of regulatory action.

The second is the holism of the committee's approach. The issue of employment status is located within a wider consideration of the regulatory problems of homework: weak enforcement mechanisms for health and safety law, illegal underpayment of wages, limited coverage of Wages Councils, and difficulties with the enforcement of schemes for the registration of homeworkers. This is an important corrective to overly compartmentalised

[94] Employment Committee (n 11) [5]–[8].

reasoning, where we lose sight of the basic matter of *why* employment status is important. It also prevents the fetishising of employment status: it is not enough to have a clever and workable legal definition of employment status in circumstances where basic rights are practically unenforceable.

The third is the rejection of a naturalised view of the employment status boundary, that 'employee' represents something real in the world separately from its legal construction as an identity in law. For example, the report identifies a range of possible reasonable definitions of homework, identifying the exclusionary effects of certain definitions.[95] On employment status, there is an important recognition of the difficulties with aligning employment protection and social security considerations. In particular, the intermittent nature of homework might mean that employee status would bring with it a liability to pay social security contributions without a reciprocal entitlement to claim unemployment benefits.[96] On the other hand, the committee observed that 'Homeworkers should enjoy the same employment protection as other workers. Indeed, because of their vulnerability to exploitation, the Committee feel that homeworkers have a greater claim than most other workers to be included within the scope of this legislation.'[97] The report gets beyond technicalities to focus on the substantive social and economic characteristics of homework, and the corresponding substantive need for employment protection. It also invites a more purposive approach to employment status, with boundaries sensitive to the purposes for which they are being drawn. In his reflections on the report, Ewing suggested that 'it seems reasonable to state specifically that homeworkers are to be treated as employees for the limited purpose of employment protection and common law remedies arising from that employment.'[98] This could be consistent with a different boundary for tax and national insurance purposes.

In the next section, the role of select committees in relation to gig work will be examined. As we shall see, the role of the select committees has become curiously depoliticised and dominated by a more legalistic approach to the issues around employment status.

V. Select Committees and the Gig Economy: From Politics Back to Law

A. Introduction

In recent years, the phenomenon of work in the gig economy has dominated academic, popular media and public policy conversations in labour law. Admittedly, the term is often deployed with an appearance of conceptual solidity that does not stand up to critical scrutiny. Many disputed employment status cases are described as 'gig economy' cases in the national media when they are no such thing.[99] Furthermore, the numbers involved in

[95] Ibid, [2]–[4].
[96] Ibid, [11].
[97] Ibid, [10].
[98] Ewing, 'Homeworking: A Framework for Reform' (n 85) 109.
[99] O Bowcott, 'Gig economy: heating engineer wins claim against Pimlico Plumbers' *The Guardian* (London, 13 June 2018); see *Pimlico Plumbers Ltd v Smith* [2018] UKSC 29, [2018] 4 All ER 641; O Bowcott, 'Employment tribunal hears cases against National Gallery' *The Guardian* (London, 16 July 2018).

'gig economy' work are still small relative to its total capture of the political and legal imagination.[100] Nevertheless, it is undeniable that gig work has been a site of intense regulatory activity by both political and legal institutions, with much of that focus on issues of employment status. It is also undeniable that, for all its imprecision, gig work has provided a collective basis for work identity, providing some loose identifying attributes of identity based upon common needs and vulnerabilities. It therefore provides an excellent contemporary case study in the politics of employment status.

Currently, there is ongoing litigation around the legal category of 'worker' in *Deliveroo* and *Uber*, with *Uber* set for a high noon showdown in the United Kingdom Supreme Court in July 2020.[101] The legal issues in these cases are in fact rather distinct, reflecting important differences in the contractual arrangements and the nature of the rights being claimed. For example, the appeal in *Deliveroo* is concerned with substitution clauses, the obligation of personal work, and the fundamental right to collective bargaining under Article 11 of the ECHR. None of these issues arise in *Uber*. There has also been significant political focus on employment abuses in the Gig economy. In October 2016, Matthew Taylor was appointed to lead a review of employment practices in the modern economy, and this led to a report published in July 2017.[102] Much of this report was concerned with problems of enforcement, especially in Gig economy work, and it produced a series of proposals which included proposals on employment status. While some of those proposals have now been adopted and implemented by the government,[103] others are still under active consideration.

Amid this frenetic legal and political activity, select committees have also emerged as influential constitutional actors. In particular, the Scottish Affairs Committee, the Work and Pensions Committee (WPC), and the Business, Energy and Industrial Strategy Committee have each made important interventions in the public debate. Sometimes those interventions have resulted from joint work by the committees. The changing context to the work of select committees has no doubt contributed to their growing presence in the sphere of labour law reforms. As Christopher Johnson has explained, the modern era of select committees instituted in the 1970s reforms was implemented to strengthen Parliament's scrutiny of the executive.[104] More recently, that role has evolved 'into the territory of public inquiries, investigating wrong-doing and scandal in both public and private sectors.'[105] The inquiry into employment practices at Sports Direct provides a particularly vivid example of this type of engagement,[106] but there have been others too.[107] In part, this development is

[100] See J Prassl, *Humans as a Service* (Oxford, OUP, 2018).

[101] *R (on the application of Independent Workers Union of Great Britain) v Central Arbitration Committee* [2018] EWHC 3342 (Admin), [2019] IRLR 249; *Uber BV v Aslam* [2018] EWCA Civ 2748, [2019] 3 All ER 489.

[102] M Taylor et al, 'Good work: the Taylor review of modern working practices' (July 2017) www.gov.uk/government/publications/good-work-the-taylor-review-of-modern-working-practices.

[103] See, eg, The Conduct of Employment Agencies and Employment Businesses Regulations 2003 was amended to include Reg 13A that requires employers to provide agency workers with a 'Key information document'. The amendment was made under Reg 3 of the Conduct of Employment Agencies and Employment Businesses (Amendment) Regulations 2019. The provision will come into force on 6 April 2020; ibid 36.

[104] C Johnson, 'Select Committees: Powers and Functions' in A Horne, G Drewry and D Oliver (eds), *Parliament and the Law*, 2nd edn (Oxford, Hart Publishing, 2018) 118.

[105] Ibid, 118.

[106] Business, Innovation and Skills Committee, *Employment practices at Sports Direct* (HC 2016–17, 219).

[107] See for example the joint select committee inquiry into the collapse of Carillion: Business, Energy and Industrial Strategy and Work and Pensions Committees, *Carillion* (HC 2017–19, 769).

attributable to the inherent flexibility of the working practices of select committees, which has lent itself to shifting priorities.[108] It has also been driven by the provision for direct election of committee chairs, removing control from the party whips.[109] Where committee chairs have an interest in issues such as employment protection and welfare reform, for example Frank Field MP as chair of the Work and Pensions Select Committee, the independence imbued by direct election may lead to those issues having particular prominence in the select committee's work focus. In this way, the select committees have been concerned with holding private power to public account, which is an important dimension of the new institutional landscape of labour law.

Before examining the 'gig economy' inquiry work of these committees, there are three general points of importance. First, while the work of select committees operates in the political sphere, it does not follow that their mode of operation is always agonistic. For example, the achievement of consensus and a deliberative approach to inquiries is often characteristic of the select committee approach. Mouffe has been critical of deliberative models of democracy in limiting the opportunities for confrontation between opposed political positions, and the risk that consensus-based models can suppress agonistic conflicts.[110] To the extent that select committees encourage the deliberative building of consensus across party political lines in their inquiries, the resulting neutralisation of agonistic confrontation may undermine their political role in a social democratic constitution. Secondly, there are also challenges in formulating criteria for evaluating the effectiveness of select committees. Russell and Benton have undertaken important work on select committee inquiries, and their research reveals that select committees have been relatively successful in producing recommendations that are accepted by the government leading to changes in law and policy.[111] The report also sets out the ways in which select committees can have non-quantifiable influence, which includes the shaping of policy debates, spotlighting issues and altering policy priorities, brokering in policy disputes, unearthing new evidence, holding the executive and powerful private actors to public account, public exposure of wrongdoing, and prompting anticipatory changes through the fear of select committee attention.[112] In evaluating the performance of gig economy inquiries, therefore, there are a broad range of measures of 'success'.

Finally, the issue of employment status in the gig economy has been a focal point for legislators, courts, select committees, independent inquiries, academics, think tanks, and trade unions. This overlapping of institutional work raises important questions about coordination across multiple constitutional sites. For example, how should the select committees relate to the work of the independent inquiry into modern working practices? Should this take the form of an agonistic confrontation between the select committees and Matthew Taylor? Or should it be a team effort to build momentum for specific legislative proposals? And should select committee proposals seek to clarify and codify existing legal principles developed by the courts, or should they reject the straitjacket of existing legal classifications

[108] Johnson (n 104) 118–119.
[109] Liaison Committee, *Rebuilding the House: Select Committee Issues* (HC 2009–10, 272) [80].
[110] Mouffe, *Agonistics* (n 19) 6–7.
[111] M Russell and M Benton, 'Selective Influence: The Policy Impact of House of Commons Select Committees' (*UCL Constitution Unit*, 2011) www.ucl.ac.uk/constitution-unit/sites/constitution-unit/files/153.pdf.
[112] Ibid, 79–90.

and begin afresh to think *politically* about the construction of collective identities in the labour market? It is possible to distinguish three types or characters of select committee engagement. Over time, the agonistic dimension has been squeezed out, and it has been displaced by a legal perspective on employment status. This represents a lost opportunity to think politically about employment status.

B. Telling Stories: Sports Direct and City Link

As Russell and Benton have argued, the public exposure of wrongdoing is one of the important ways in which select committees can generate impact in their inquiry work. Where this narrative is constructed around a specific event or employer, and where the inquiry is focused on the human impact of egregious employment practices, the resulting outrage and media attention can be very potent. There are two examples of this kind of inquiry.

The first is the Business, Innovation and Skills Committee inquiry, 'Employment practices at Sports Direct'.[113] This inquiry was prompted by significant media coverage into appalling practices at Sports Direct, particularly centred on its warehouse facilities at Shirebrook in Derbyshire. This had been the focus of investigations by the BBC, Channel 4 Dispatches, and *The Guardian* newspaper. The Scottish Affairs Committee had also taken evidence on employment practices at Sports Direct in 2015.[114] As such, the BIS Committee inquiry was responding to existing public anger about Sports Direct, contributing to a mobilisation of public opinion that was already well underway. The conduct of the inquiry contained passages of high public drama, with the head of Sports Direct Mr Mike Ashley testing the limits of the select committee's legal powers to compel attendance.[115] There was also controversy around the evidence provided by one of the employment agencies used by Sports Direct to provide workers for its warehouses, Transline, with the report alleging that witnesses from Transline had deliberately misled the committee.[116] The dramatic context to the inquiry proceedings undoubtedly elevated the public attention given to the inquiry, which magnified the impact of its findings.

The inquiry provided a detailed and harrowing account of working life at Sports Direct. The employment contracts provided to the committee were highly imbalanced, with minimal obligations on Transline to provide work and extensive obligations on workers to be available and 'on call'.[117] The inquiry also set out a highly punitive regime of discipline, underpayment of national minimum wage as a result of lengthy unpaid queuing to undergo intrusive security searches when leaving work, serious concerns about health and safety, and a reluctance to engage with independent trade union representatives. The inquiry took evidence from both management and trade union representatives from UNITE, although there was no doubt that the inquiry view was aligned with those of UNITE. The BIS inquiry

[113] Business, Innovation and Skills Committee (n 106).

[114] Scottish Affairs Committee, 'Sports Direct: employment practices and the sale of USC inquiry' (March 2015) www.parliament.uk/business/committees/committees-a-z/commons-select/scottish-affairs-committee/inquiries/parliament-2010/usc-and-sports-direct-inquiry/.

[115] Business, Innovation and Skills Committee (n 106) [8].

[116] Ibid [55].

[117] Ibid [14].

is an exemplar of agonistic politics. The language in the report is often emotive and highly charged, and there is a genuine sense of confrontation between the select committee and Sports Direct.

Despite these agonistic features, Mouffe's reflections on the political also identify some problems with the general approach of the inquiry. The outrage is often directed at specific personalities, such as Mike Ashley or the witness from Transline, rather than the legal and economic structures that enable such business practices. Much of the focus of the report is on improving the business practices at Sports Direct, and encouraging genuine engagement with the trade union, rather than reflecting on the legal restrictions that impeded effective trade union action. As Mouffe has argued, 'It is commendable to give voice to the outrage against the financial system, but this must be done in a political way, targeting the ideological, economic and political forces that structure this system. Otherwise there is a real danger that the current protests will operate in the register of morality, on the basis of a good/bad dichotomy.'[118] Nevertheless, the inquiry should not be taken in isolation. For example, the inquiry observed that 'there is a risk that this model – which has proved successful for Mr Ashley – will become the norm. We will be considering the full implications of this business model in the context of our broader inquiry into the labour market.'[119] It is valuable for political critique to use scandalous episodes like Sports Direct as a basis for exposing the legal structures that facilitate wrongdoing, and for pursuing deep systematic change. Select committees are less apt as surrogate collective bargaining mechanisms for securing the improvement of terms and conditions in individual firms.

Another example of 'telling stories' is the joint report of the BIS and Scottish Affairs Committees, 'Impact of the closure of City Link on Employment'.[120] The inquiry was prompted by the controversial circumstances of the closure of City Link, which went into administration on Christmas Eve, 2014. This led to hardship and anxiety for the staff and contractors who worked for City Link. The inquiry examined a range of legal issues arising out of the closure, such as the scope for alternative outcomes, shortcomings in communication once the administration order had been issued, and the effectiveness of sanctions for breach of redundancy consultation obligations. The inquiry also identified problems with false self-employment of contractors, given the reduced protection available for self-employed contractors under the Insolvency Act 1986 regime.[121] The law on protection of creditors in insolvency provided an important perspective on self-employment, which had tended to focus on the tax and employment protection aspects. The inquiry referred to the earlier work of the Scottish Affairs Committee on zero hours contracts in Scotland,[122] and it used the specific example of City Link to renew its call for legislation to tackle false self-employment. Like the Sports Direct inquiry, the human scale of the tragedy in City Link is powerful in mobilising affective anger at the injustice experienced by the self-employed drivers. However, the affective tone is tempered by a tight focus on the wider regulatory

[118] Mouffe, *Agonistics* (n 19) 116.

[119] Business, Innovation and Skills Committee (n 106) [34].

[120] Business, Innovation and Skills and Scottish Affairs Committees, *Impact of the closure of City Link on Employment* (HC 2014–15, 928).

[121] Ibid [63]–[69].

[122] Scottish Affairs Committee, *Zero hours contracts in Scotland: Interim Report*' (HC 2013–14, 654).

structures regulating redundancies and insolvency, and the specific ways in which those legal structures might be reformed.

C. Deliberative Inquiries into General Labour Market Challenges

Another mode of select committee engagement is a more general examination of areas of concern in labour law. We shall focus on two examples. The first is the Scottish Affairs Committee inquiry, 'Zero hours contracts in Scotland: Interim Report'.[123] Strictly speaking, this was not a gig economy inquiry. It was, however, focused upon a form of collective work identity that had been rather ubiquitous before the phenomenon of gig work became dominant: the zero hours contract worker. It is included in this analysis because some of its legal recommendations would later be echoed in the Taylor Review where the focus was more explicitly on the regulatory problems of gig work. In this respect, it was an important early strand in the rather complex set of policy developments that were to follow.

The report reveals the variety of ways in which collective identities can be constructed. 'Zero hours' work encompasses a wide variety of different contractual arrangements, working conditions, and sectors, the report nevertheless draws upon social science evidence to build up a picture of its forms, its labour market distribution, and the particular needs and vulnerabilities that appear common to zero hours' contract workers. Thus, chapter 1 provides a contextual picture of the labour market statistics, a breakdown of their use in different sectors, and survey evidence drawn from different sources on employee satisfaction with zero hours arrangements. The report is highly critical of their use where there is no compelling business justification for doing so, given the corrosive effects of uncertainty on the capabilities and well-being of workers. The report details the many problems that flow from income uncertainty, such as financial planning, housing, and Jobseekers' allowance.[124] The report also provided a holistic perspective on the specific problems with employment status for zero hours' workers. These regulatory problems relate to the enforcement of basic employment rights. The report detailed the underpayment of national minimum wage for care workers on zero hours contracts which, in powerful affective language, the report labelled 'a disgrace'.[125] The report also highlighted problems with health and safety enforcement, particularly in light of the risks of victimisation where employers simply fail to offer further work to workers seeking to raise grievances in employment tribunals.[126] As the report demonstrated rather vividly through its evidence base, the economic repercussions of 'market forces' are disastrous for those living precarious lives in the permanent shadow of uncertainty.

The issue of employment status was also addressed by the report in chapter 2, which was entitled 'Employment rights: confusion and abuse'. Some of the legal discussion around employment status is rather problematic. For example, the chapter opens with the following statement: 'Workers on zero hours contracts are not defined as "employees" and as a result

[123] Ibid.
[124] Taylor et al (n 102) 41–44.
[125] Ibid, 22.
[126] Ibid, 39.

can lose out on employment rights'.[127] This claim is simply wrong as a matter of law. There is no legal reason why workers in zero hours contract arrangements cannot be employees during periods of work, even if the factual circumstances sometimes militate against finding a contract of employment.[128] Ultimately, this will depend upon the characteristics of the work arrangements. Zero hours arrangements often militate against qualifying for certain employment rights, but this will usually be attributable to problems of continuity of employment where there is a statutory qualifying period, as with the two years' continuous employment requirement for unfair dismissal. Even then, there are statutory techniques available that can allow casual employees to build up continuity in intermittent work arrangements.[129] Later in the chapter, the report acknowledges that the courts may find that the casual is an employee 'if the day-to-day reality of the work suggests a relationship of employment'.[130] However, there is no explanation of the relevant legal principles, and this sits uneasily with the rather categorical and misleading opening to the chapter.

From a legal perspective, the discussion of employment status in chapter 2 is inadequate. This highlights a deeper problem where there is an overlap between political and legal perspectives on employment status. Where political institutions are examining the legal dimensions of employment status, there are real difficulties around institutional expertise. While select committees are not as well-placed as courts or law reform bodies to address legal questions, it is obviously important that the legal principles are accurately encapsulated in political inquiries.[131] A more fundamental problem is the apparent displacement of political thinking around employment status in the inquiry, and its capture by the legal. It is implicit in much of the discussion that employment status is a naturalised boundary, and it is one that is demarcated by the existing legal boundary. Thus, the inquiry made the following proposal:

> Denying workers rights that are legally due to them, whether it is through confusion, abuse or even a failure to determine an individual's employment status, is unacceptable. Employers must make clear from the outset an individual's employment status. In addition, all workers should be legally entitled to a written contract setting out the terms and conditions of their employment.[132]

There is no sense here that the setting of the boundary between employees and other types of work contract is a creative political act. The task of the law is to ensure that the existing boundary is clear and transparent to the parties. This clarity will be facilitated by a right to written statement of terms, conditions and employment status. This denial of a more political view of employment status, that it is an artificial boundary amenable to disruption by political choices, provides a conceptual worldview that would prove highly influential in the later inquiries.[133]

[127] Ibid, 15.

[128] See, eg, *Carmichael v National Power Plc* [1999] 1 WLR 2042.

[129] *Cornwall CC v Prater* [2006] EWCA Civ 102, [2006] 2 All ER 1013; Employment Rights Act 1996, ss 210–212.

[130] Taylor et al (n 102) 17.

[131] Select committees can and often do engage expert advisers to assist them in their inquiry work. My excellent colleague Professor Michael Ford QC has been engaged frequently in such a role.

[132] Taylor et al (n 102) 19.

[133] The Taylor Review proposed a right to written statement from day 1 for all workers, which has now been adopted. The Scottish Affairs Committee also proposed a right to request a contract for guaranteed work after a specified period of time (53), a proposal which was also echoed in the later recommendations of the Taylor Review, Taylor et al (n 102) 48.

The second example is the report of the Work and Pensions Committee, 'Self-employment and the gig economy'.[134] Again, the report seeks to construct a collective identity, on this occasion around self-employment. The significance of self-employment as a form of collective identity in work is linked explicitly to the gig economy.[135] The chair of the Work and Pensions Committee, Mr Frank Field, has a deep interest in welfare reform, and the issues of employment status were examined through this regulatory lens. For example, the report recommends that the national insurance contributions of the self-employed should be equalised with employee contributions, given that the entitlements are now aligned.[136] The report also sets out a range of imaginative proposals on entrepreneurial support for the self-employed and auto-enrolment in pensions contributions.[137] There is also a discussion of employment status. The report rejects the shibboleth of some business lobbyists that self-employment/employment maps neatly onto flexibility/rigidity. As the report notes, 'this is a fiction. Self-employment is genuinely flexible and rewarding for many, but people on employment contracts can and do work flexibly; flexibility is not the preserve of poorly paid, unstable contractors. Profit, not flexibility, is the motive for using self-employed labour in these cases.'[138] To this end, the report recommended a default of worker status, which is effectively a legal presumption of entitlement to statutory employment rights.[139] Unlike the Scottish Affairs Committee report on zero hours contracts, the naturalised view of the employment boundary is less prominent. The shifting default of worker status would effectively move the boundary in favour of inclusion, which involves a political choice to shift the frontier. This proposal would be echoed in the Taylor Review's recommendations.

D. After Taylor: Coordination and Alignment

The Taylor Review was not focused solely on employment status, though this aspect of the review's work attracted the most attention. The dominant concern in the review was the lack of clarity in the current law.[140] This reflected a deeper alignment with a view of employment status as embodying a naturalised boundary.[141] In order to achieve 'clarity', the review envisages a more prominent role for a comprehensive statutory definition, particularly as regards the intermediate category of 'worker'. The codification of the multiplicity of legal principles will lead to greater transparency of rights. In terms of what should be codified, the review observes of the current case law that 'if the Government believes these to be an accurate reflection of what they consider to be the main characteristics of a status, legislation should be updated to reflect this.'[142] There is very little in this to suggest that Taylor

[134] Work and Pensions Committee, *Self-employment and the gig economy* (HC 2016–17, 847).
[135] Ibid, 4.
[136] Ibid, 6.
[137] Ibid, 15–18.
[138] Ibid, 13.
[139] Ibid, 14.
[140] Taylor et al (n 102) ch 5.
[141] For further discussion, see K Bales, A Bogg and T Novitz, '"Voice' and 'Choice' in Modern Working Practices: Problems With the Taylor Review' (2018) 47 *Industrial Law Journal* 46, 58–63.
[142] Taylor et al (n 102) 34.

regards the existing legal boundary as much awry. It should be recognised that the review does not simply recommend a mechanical transposition of the existing corpus of legal rules and principles on employment status into statute. For example, there is a valuable proposal to remove personal work as a necessary requirement of worker status.[143] Furthermore, the review also pursues the proposal in the earlier WPC report on self-employment to legislate for a presumption of employment status, in order to promote more effective enforcement.[144] However, the emphasis on 'clarity' and juridical precision undoubtedly reflects a conservative disposition which largely maintains the status quo in the distribution of employment rights. There is no sense that this boundary should be altered radically. This was no doubt shaped by the absence of trade union input into the report. This removed an important source of political contestation and challenge to the current set of legal demarcations. In an inquiry of this kind, perhaps a once-in-a-generation opportunity to reconstitute political identities in work, these fundamental questions should have been addressed. Instead, the overwhelming spirit of the review's contribution to employment status is simply a refinement of existing legal principles. A form of legal restatement, if you like, giving law priority over politics. This was a frame of reference that was already visible in the Scottish Affairs Committee report on zero hours contracts. Yet the constitution of the Taylor review meant that it was not well-placed to engage in a systematic process of legal reform unlike, say, the Law Commission or some other body with significant legal expertise.

This priority of law over politics was reflected in some of the specific proposals in the Taylor review. For example, Taylor proposed a 'day 1' right for both employees and workers to a written statement of basic employment information, in order to promote clarity of status and greater transparency of rights.[145] It also proposed an 'online tool' which could be used to indicate employment status using 'the advantages of digitalisation and machine learning'.[146] This technocratic dream of the eradication of human judgement from the process of deciding on employment status is very revealing. It is somewhat redolent, perhaps, of the earlier 'law of the labour market' faith in economic tools to provide an objective and scientific measurement for employment status. The effort in Taylor to purge the exercise of human judgement and sensitivity to factual circumstances represents a denial of the political in demarcating the perimeter of rights. There is significant concern about the accuracy of the current HMRC online tool for employment status,[147] which may reflect broader difficulties with the operation of algorithms in contexts requiring wise situational judgement.

The Taylor Review was followed by two significant select committee reports, a joint report from the Work and Pensions Committee and the Business, Energy and Industrial Strategy Committee and a report from the Scottish Affairs Committee. The joint report, 'A framework for modern employment', was explicit in regarding its role as weighing behind the Taylor Review recommendations. In its own words, it 'sought to maintain the momentum created by the Taylor Review and to support Government in implementing its most

[143] Ibid, 34.
[144] Ibid, 62.
[145] Ibid, 39.
[146] Ibid.
[147] S Spicer, 'HMRC employment status test tool not working properly' (*Small Business*, 6 February 2019) https://smallbusiness.co.uk/hmrc-employment-status-test-tool-not-working-properly-2546629/.

transformative recommendations.'[148] The joint report provided a strong endorsement of 'clarity' and the primacy of legislation in defining employment status.[149] It also endorsed the Taylor Review's identification of 'control' as the distinguishing feature of the intermediate worker category. The joint report also produced a rather hastily drafted Bill where it sought to model the Taylor approach in primary legislation. Much of that legislative definition in section 1 of the draft Bill was simply a restatement of existing principles in the case law. Other specific Taylor proposals related to 'clarity', such as the 'day 1' right to a written statement for all workers, was also endorsed by the committees.[150] The Scottish Affairs Committee, in 'The future of working practices in Scotland', also saw its own role as reinforcing the convergent approach of the Taylor Review and the joint report 'A framework for modern employment' in focusing on legislative clarification of the boundary between different categories of employment.[151] In this way, the distinctively political perspective on employment status was lost in these select committee engagements, with the select committees providing support to a rather modest exercise in legal restatement of existing principles set out in Taylor.

VI. Concluding Thoughts: Select Committees in the Social Democratic Constitution

There has been significant political energy invested in reforming employment status. This has been reflected in the intensive activity of the various select committees on these regulatory problems, especially in the gig economy context. To what extent can these interventions be adjudged a success? The answer to this is rather complex. Compared with courts, the select committees have had the benefit of social science evidence informing their deliberations; they have conceived of work identities in more collective and less individuated ways, constructing identities around various markers ('gig workers', 'self-employed workers', 'homeworkers', 'zero hours workers'); and they have examined issues around employment status in a more holistic frame, considering issues of precarity and the non- or under-enforcement of basic labour rights. All these elements contribute to thinking about employment status in a more political way, something for which the courts are less suitable.

Nevertheless, the sheer number of different select committee interventions is very striking. Sometimes these interventions were coordinated, resulting either in joint committee reports or single committee reports which referenced and built upon the relevant work of other committees. Nevertheless, one wonders whether this diffusion of resources and dispersal of focus might sometimes have contributed to rushed work and a lack of preparation on some of the more complex legal issues in employment status.[152] It is possible that if a future Labour Government were to create a Ministry of Employment Rights, with

[148] Work and Pensions and Business, Energy and Industrial Strategy Committees, *A framework for modern employment* (HC 2017–19, 352) 6.
[149] Ibid, 10.
[150] Ibid, 18.
[151] Scottish Affairs Committee, *The future of working practices in Scotland* (HC 2017–19, 449).
[152] See more generally Russell and Benton (n 111) 92–93.

a corresponding select committee on Employment Rights, there might be a stronger and more directed focus on the relevant issues surrounding employment status. Nevertheless, it should also be acknowledged that there has been value in the multiple viewpoints on employment status generated by the current variety of committees. Employment status has not been viewed solely from the perspective of employment protection: other reports have focused on its role in tax and welfare and the priority of creditors in insolvency situations.

There is also complexity in selecting the relevant metrics for measuring the 'success' of select committee interventions, as set out in Russell and Benton's analysis of select committee work. One measure of success might be whether the government accepted a select committee recommendation. In this respect, the convergence of the Taylor Review and various select committees reports on a 'day 1' right for all workers to a written statement could be adjudged a success. Moreover, if there is eventually a statutory definition of employment status that 'clarifies' the boundaries of work relations, this would also look like a 'win' for the select committees. Against that view, the acceptance of a legislative reform on employment status by a Tory government may well reflect its inertness as a legal reform. It might be better for select committees to seize the political opportunity and to produce radical political alternatives to the status quo, even where that means failing heroically. Indeed, one wonders whether the select committees' alignment with the Taylor Review, and the rush to produce a draft Bill, was being driven by a desire to be seen to have achieved something tangible on the statute book. The softer metrics around 'spotlighting issues' and 'exposure',[153] prominent in 'Sports Direct' and 'City Link' inquiries, provide examples where the select committee interventions had a very powerful impact on the tone and content of public dialogue on work, even if they did not lead to a specific legislative change.

Where do select committees fit in the agonistic constitution of social democracy? In certain respects, there could be a disjunction between the practices of agonistic politics and the consensual and deliberative mode of select committee business. The weakening of party-political influence over select committee membership may well have contributed to a further weakening of the partisan conduct of committee business. Of course, an agonistic constitution does not depend upon every element of its constitutional order performing agonistically. Indeed, it is very important that this is not the case. Agonistic constitutions must also perform an integrative role, otherwise there is a danger that democratic 'adversaries' will become 'enemies', with politics configured around a Schmittian confrontation between the 'friend' and the 'enemy'.[154] Select committees could provide a constitutional site where conflicts are channelled into procedures that defuse those conflicts in constructive ways. It is also important to note that select committee inquiries are not monotypic, and the gig economy reports exemplify a diverse democratic ecology of approaches. Different select committee reports sometimes pursue more agonistic and confrontational approaches, sometimes more deliberative and consensual, and this pluralistic approach could be a democratic virtue.

While our judgements must be cautious given these nuances, the overall endpoint of the select committee reports on employment status in gig work was disappointing from an agonistic perspective. First, in the range of public institutions engaged in deliberation on

[153] Ibid, 83–88.
[154] Mouffe, *Agonistics* (n 19) 7.

gig work – courts, Taylor Review, select committees – none of them was really operating in agonistic mode. For the courts, this is as it should be. The constitutional responsibility of the court is to apply the existing law, and to develop it coherently and incrementally within existing doctrinal parameters. The absence of the agonistic perspective was particularly problematic for the Taylor Review. No provision was made for trade union representation in its membership, and this negated a contestatory voice in the formulation of its proposals. As the select committees converged on the Taylor Review proposals, and consensus on a narrow policy agenda became entrenched, there were very serious agonistic deficits. Matthew Taylor was not subjected to searching interrogation in select committee questioning. There was no constitutional mechanism through which the Taylor Review was being held to account. Indeed, the only conceivable institution that could have done this was the select committees.

Secondly, it is remarkable how political perspectives on employment status (which workers or work relations should have their normative agency respected through the provision of enforceable rights?) were displaced by legal perspectives (what is the most rational restatement of the existing corpus of norms on employment status?). Yet none of the main players had the time or expertise to do the legal restatement exercise well.[155] Both the select committees and the Taylor Review often proceeded based on simplistic or misguided understanding of the relevant law. If the purpose of the exercise was simply law reform, it would have been far better for those questions to have been allocated to a body with the relevant expertise, such as the Law Commission or even a Royal Commission with appropriate membership and logistical support. Neither the select committees nor the Taylor Review were well placed to do this job, and this showed in many of the resulting proposals.

Finally, the fixation on 'clarity' reveals a depoliticised understanding of what is fundamentally at stake in the employment status debates. Clarity can be achieved in many ways, and it could be consistent either with the contraction or expansion of the protective boundary of labour law. The contraction or expansion, *that* is the political question – how should we construct collective identities that confer rights-based agency on groups that warrant social protection? Clarity goes to the technical finesse by which the political determination is implemented in law.[156] In elevating control as the marker for workers, it is arguable that 'clarity' has been achieved, albeit that the protective perimeter of the intermediate category has contracted and is less generous than the current 'integration' approach in *Bates van Winkelhoff*.[157]

The obsession with a statutory definition and 'clarity' may also be based upon a misguided view that political contestation around employment status can be eliminated once and for all by a clever draftsperson. Of course, there must be decisional closure from time to time on 'who is in' and 'who is out.' The work of the world must be done, and this will

[155] For a full criticism of the main legal problems with the Taylor proposals on employment status, see Bales, Bogg and Novitz (n 141) 57–64.

[156] Though not merely technical. Clarity is also a moral value, connected as it is to legality and the rule of law. See generally L Fuller, *The Morality of Law* (New Haven, Yale University Press, 1969).

[157] *Bates van Winkelhof v Clyde & Co LLP* [2014] UKSC 32, [2014] 1 WLR 2047. Compare *Jivraj v Hashwani* [2011] UKSC 40, [2011] 1 WLR 1872 where the UKSC adopted a subordination test for the personal scope of the Equality Act. This was subjected to trenchant criticism in M Freedland and N Kountouris, 'Employment Equality and Personal Work Relations – A Critique of Jivraj v Hashwani' (2012) 41 *Industrial Law Journal* 56.

require decisions to be made and implemented in legislation. From an agonistic perspective, however, no determination of this kind can ever be treated as final and conclusive. The ingenuity of capital to transform itself will always be matched by the ingenuity of new 'outsider' groups in the labour market who assert their normative agency and demand their rights. Such conflict is healthy in a pluralistic democracy. Employment status will *always* be a site of political contestation, and any such boundary should be regarded as contingent and open to political challenge. The agonistic perspective gives this political dimension its appropriate due. Its retrieval in the law and politics of employment status would be a fitting testament to the work of the young select committee adviser Dr KD Ewing who – characteristically – saw this so clearly before many of the rest of us did.

PART III

Democracy in the Social Democratic Constitution

9

The Law of Electoral Democracy: Theory and Purpose

GRAEME ORR

This chapter explores the question of 'theory' within the law of electoral democracy, by considering what it would mean for such a theory to exist given the contested nature of democracy itself. The chapter begins with a brief survey of the terms in question, including the emergence of this area of law as a field of study and its under-theorised state. It is quickly shown that, outside of a narrow and minimalist conception of a free election as one where votes are cast and counted, there is little agreement on the norms that should determine the law in this area, even on some fundamental concrete questions.

Normative coherence however can be demonstrated within competing approaches to the law. A social democratic theory of law is seen to provide salutary reminders. Reminders that democratic politics is collective more than individualist and that electoral democracy is not the whole of democracy. Within that tradition, the distinctive contribution of Keith Ewing to political finance – which he configures as party finance, and his defence of labourism within that – is discussed. Finally, a four-sided functionalist account of the purposes of the law is then offered. The aim of the functionalist account is to show that whilst normative approaches may be sharply contested, we are not lost at sea: theory can help set the parameters of the ongoing debate over the shape of the law.

I. Electoral Law: Its Scope and Intellectual History

A. Definitions

The law of electoral democracy encompasses the law and institutions governing representative elections (at whatever level), political parties, political finance and referendums. As a commonplace shorthand, 'electoral law' will be used in what follows. Occasionally, jostling for attention, people have tried on the term 'the law of democracy'.[1] But that is either too grandiose or too diffuse. Even to proponents of parliamentarianism and popular sovereignty,

[1] Eg, S Issacharoff et al, *The Law of Democracy: The Legal Structure of the Political Process*, 5th edn (New York, Foundation Press, 2016).

electoral democracy may be the pinnacle, but it is just the pinnacle of an iceberg.[2] For thoroughgoing social democrats such as Keith Ewing, electoral democracy is nestled within a wider constitutional project of economic and social democracy marked by industrial and liberation movements.[3]

By electoral law 'theory', I mean primarily to explore questions about 'purpose'. Purpose as telos, in the sense of prescriptive or normative aims. But also, especially later in the chapter, purpose in the more descriptive sense of functions of the law.

B. A Brief Intellectual History[4]

It is commonplace to claim that electoral law only emerged as an area of study in its own right in the past three decades. But there has been electoral law since time immemorial: in statute since at least 1275 in England.[5] And, for all the proliferation of books on electoral law lately, across common law domains such as the US,[6] UK,[7] and Australia,[8] the field still pales compared to the Victorian era. In the nineteenth century, the Great Reform and electoral corruption questions generated more, and more contentious, case law, practitioner works, and parliamentary and public interest in reform than exists today.

What then does it mean to say that electoral law has emerged as a field in recent decades? Two things are implied. One is about modernity. The Victorian era was a long transitional moment: representative democracy did not truly take off until full female suffrage and the emergence of strong parties in the first few decades of the twentieth century. The other implication is that electoral law had to emerge from the shadow of constitutional law. It has done so in two senses. In an existential sense: electoral law is not just a dusty prelude to parliamentary or legislative studies. And in a methodological sense: electoral law is not determined by a few abstract constitutional principles. It has an 'affinity with' but 'separable

[2] KD Ewing, 'Democratic Socialism and Labour Law' (1995) 24 *Industrial Law Journal* 103, 105–06.

[3] KD Ewing 'Jeremy Corbyn and the Law of Democracy' (2017) 28 *King's Law Journal* 343.

[4] For a potted history in the US see ED Mazo, 'Introduction: The Maturing of Election Law' in JA Douglas and ED Mazo, *Election Law Stories* (New York, Foundation Press, 2016) 7–11.

[5] Section 5 of the first Statute of Westminster (3 Edw I) is an edict that no-one 'by force of arms, nor by malice, or menacing shall disturb any to make free election'.

[6] DH Lowenstein et al, *Election Law: Cases and Materials*, 6th edn (Durham, Carolina Academic Press, 2017); S Issacharoff et al (n 1); MR Dimino et al, *Voting Rights and Election Law*, 2nd edn (Durham, Carolina Academic Press, 2015); JA Gardner and G Charles, *Election Law in the American Political System*, 2nd edn (New York, Wolters Kluwer, 2017); EB Foley et al, *Election Law and Litigation: The Judicial Regulation of Politics* (New York, Wolters Kluwer, 2014). There are even supporting texts in the form of a primer and a casebook, respectively: DP Tokaji, *Election Law in a Nutshell*, 2nd edn (St Paul, West Academic, 2016) and MR Dimino et al, *Understanding Election Law and Voting Rights* (Durham, Carolina Academic Press, 2017).

[7] HF Rawlings, *Law and the Electoral Process* (London, Sweet & Maxwell, 1988); N de Silva and R Price, *Parker's Law and Conduct of Elections* (London, LexisNexis, 1996); R Blackburn, *The Electoral System in Britain* (London, Macmillan, 1995); B Watt, *UK Election Law: a Critical Examination* (London, Glass House Press, 2006). On specific sub-fields see KD Ewing, *The Cost of Democracy: Party Funding in Modern British Politics* (Oxford, Hart Publishing, 2007) and C Morris, *Parliamentary Elections, Representation and the Law* (Oxford, Hart Publishing, 2012).

[8] G Orr, *The Law of Politics: Elections, Parties and Money in Australia*, 2nd edn (Sydney, The Federation Press, 2019). On specific sub-fields see J Tham, *Money Politics: The Democracy We Can't Afford* (Sydney, UNSW Press, 2010) and A Gauja, *Political Parties and Elections: Legislating for Representative Democracy* (Farnham, Ashgate/ Routledge, 2010).

and unique character' from constitutional law.[9] Elections are steeped in statutory law and administration, the affairs of parties and associations governed by agreements and anti-discrimination law, and a residue of common and parliamentary law dealing with issues as diverse as defamation and disputed election returns.[10] By 2010 a leading US scholar could confidently state that election scholarship had 'declared [its] independence from constitutional law in a bloodless revolution'.[11]

C. Theorising Electoral Law

Opening his book *Election Law and Democratic Theory*, David Schultz observed that 'election law is an endeavour in search of a political theory'.[12] This echoes Samuel Issacharoff's quip that that the myriad rules that govern elections have 'all the allure of city council debates on garbage pick-up routes, with few of the immediately observable benefits'.[13] Issacharoff was being self-deprecating (he has spent half a lifetime immersed in the field). The broader point is that in an under-theorised realm we risk losing the forest for the trees.

Befitting a political scientist who sees election law as mired in the 'parochialism' of 'case law and doctrine', Schultz seeks to connect a 'rudderless' law to democratic theory.[14] Being from the US, his account is embedded in a culture that sees electoral law contentions in terms of 'the answers provided by the Supreme and other courts'.[15] Such appellate-courtitis is a long-standing feature of a constitutional Bill of Rights and a politicised judiciary. Regardless of disciplinary background or national context however, Schultz's broad complaint holds water. The field of electoral law may have 'declared its independence from constitutional law', but at the cost of being accused of disintegrating into technicalities.

The search for overarching, guiding principles however, may prove elusive. We could seek to induce a 'theory' of election law, from the raw matter of legislative rules, institutional practices and customs, and case law. But there is a morass of such material, and even the more prominent sources like appellate court opinions are episodic and confined. Alternatively (as Schultz suggests) we could seek to deduce principles from democratic theory, and see constitutional, statutory and administrative law in the area as nested within the crucible of political philosophy.[16]

Such a deductive process however founders on one inescapable rock. There is no agreed or agreeable conception of democracy, or even electoral democracy. To see this one need look no further than the ideal of 'representation', on which representative democracy rests.

[9] H Green, 'Fixing Democracy's Rules: Statutes and Elections in the Constitution' (2017) 28 *King's Law Journal* 173, 174.

[10] This is obvious in the UK and NZ where constitutional law is subsumed within public law, but is hardly less true elsewhere since few written constitutions seek to set electoral law in stone.

[11] HK Gerken, 'Keynote Address: What Election Law has to Say to Constitutional Law' (2010) 44 *Indiana Law Review* 7, 7.

[12] D Schultz, *Election Law and Democratic Theory* (Burlington, Routledge/Ashgate, 2014) 1.

[13] S Issacharoff, 'The Constitutional Logic of Campaign Finance Regulation' (2009) 36 *Pepperdine Law Review* 373.

[14] Schultz (n 12) 38. He complains (at 43) of 'rulings [that look as if they] are simply edicts'.

[15] Schultz (n 12) 1.

[16] Schultz (n 12) 270–71.

Beyond vaguely tautological, even Heideggerian phrases such as 'representation means making present that which is absent', all Hannah Pitkin's classic work *The Concept of Representation* could do was reveal the multiple, often competing, conceptions of what it might mean to be a 'representative' in a plural society.[17]

And indeed, within election studies we find a singular lack of agreed metrics, outside one basic aspect. That aspect – the exception to the rule – involves a fairly minimalist conception of the catch-phrase 'free and fair elections'. As Bill Mackenzie observed, in his ground-breaking *Free Elections*, that term boils down to the principle that 'the election depends on the voters' choice'.[18] Elections should consist of a ballot that is tolerably open to a variety of candidates or parties, where everyone entitled to vote can do so free of intimidation, and all votes are counted. To say this is a technocratic imagining of elections as an aggregative contest, administered impartially, is not to understate its importance. Many countries that aspire to democratic status (including parts of the US) struggle with voter suppression, polling day chaos and so on. Mackenzie concluded his search for generalisable principles with the warning:

> There is no right way of conducting elections, but there are a number of ways which are clearly wrong: wrong in the logical sense that they apply the machinery of elections to negate the declared objects of the machinery.[19]

To adapt a medical metaphor, there is no ideal healthy electoral democracy, rather there are many pathologies that may need to be treated in practice.

II. A Social Democratic Electoral Law?

Before exploring the interaction of social democratic thought with electoral law we might reflect on its boundaries. Social democracy is not the same as democratic socialism; flipping the adjective and noun matters. Ewing's second major work on political finance opens with this breath-catching epigraph:

> Wealth is almost invariably selfish and lacking in moral principle. Its interests are often diametrically opposed to sound public policy.[20]

This could be a cri de coeur of democratic socialism. It goes beyond the standard process-focused view that wealth in elections needs regulating lest it corrode democratic process by tilting campaigns and legislators against the egalitarian spirit of one person, one-vote. It expresses a deeper substantive aversion to the interests of wealth per se.

[17] H Pitkin, *The Concept of Representation* (Berkeley, University of California Press, 1967). 'There are many views of what fair representation is – geographic representation, descriptive representation, ideological or party political representation': The ACE Electoral Knowledge Network, 'Electoral Systems: Guiding Principles' <aceproject.org/ace-en/topics/es/introduction/es20>. This is not to say that we cannot chart, historically and sociologically, the evolution of different forms of representation: see, eg, B Manin, *The Principles of Representative Government* (New York, CUP, 1997).

[18] WJM Mackenzie, *Free Elections* (London, Allen & Unwin, 1958) 12.

[19] Mackenzie (n 18) 169.

[20] KD Ewing, *Money, Politics and Law: A Study of Electoral Campaign Finance Reform in Canada* (Oxford, OUP, 1992) v.

Social democracy on the other hand is a less demanding philosophy than democratic socialism. (Compare John Rawls vacillating between 'market socialism' and 'property-owning democracy' in his final 'restatement' of his theory of justice).[21] Whilst lacking democratic socialism's concern for equality of outcomes, it goes beyond the welfare liberal's concern with enhancing equal opportunity of individuals. Social democrats thus share with democratic socialists a distaste for liberalism's reduction of the world to individuals.[22] They recognise that humans are embedded in groups and that the social whole is not blindly evolving through competitive forces but is a vehicle for enhancing the common good. Admittedly, the forms of human flourishing are diverse, so that there is not a single conception of 'the good life'. Yet, regardless of whether 'democracy' is used adjectively or as a noun, the two philosophies share a creed: electoral democracy must seek to underpin forms of representative practice that recognise the connectedness and equal worth of everyone.[23]

A. Purpose as Norms: Concretising the Search for Guiding Principles

To flesh out the quest for electoral law theory, we need to concretise the topic. To do this, let us briefly consider three basic and perennial questions in electoral democracy. These are: the franchise, in the sense (a) who votes, and (b) what a vote is worth; plus (c) the voting system. I have chosen these as they are first order issues of the sort that are often thought to have been definitively settled a century ago. But, as we shall see, they are in significant part still normatively open and contested.

i. Who Votes

It's now an axiomatic principle of liberal democracy that the suffrage should be universal. Of course it has not always been that way: chartists and other social democrats had to win that battle in the nineteenth century against conservative forces. The latter feared 'ir'responsible government if the economically dependent (workers, women) had the same franchise as propertied men. But the battle was eventually won, with most women finally gaining a vote in the UK a century ago.[24]

Yet as to what 'universal' means in practice, there remain disagreements. Should citizens resident abroad vote, or should non-citizen permanent residents vote? Here there is

[21] J Rawls (edited by E Kelly), *Justice as Fairness: a Restatement* (Cambridge Mass., Harvard University Press, 2001) 138–39. In his earliest work on political finance, Ewing invoked Rawls to argue against political parties being dependent on wealthy interests: KD Ewing, *The Funding of Political Parties in Britain* (Cambridge, CUP, 1987) 175–76.

[22] Ewing, 'Jeremy Corbyn and the Law of Democracy' (n 3) 361–62.

[23] But compare J Rowbottom, 'Political Finance and the Constitution of Social Democracy' (ch 10), reasoning that there is limited room for a distinctly social democratic electoral law, given that this law must be primarily a procedural enterprise acceptable to a wide range of political perspectives.

[24] In 1918, albeit at a higher age than men: irrationally, given older women were more likely to be married/economically dependent. Full equality did not come about until the Representation of the People (Equal Franchise) Act 1928 (UK).

fundamental disagreement. To social democrats, there is a preferred answer. 'No' to expatriate voting, but yes to permanent residents.[25] This flows from the progressive idea of substantive interests, over liberal valorising of citizenship per se or a conservative idea of birthrights.[26]

So far, so good. There is in-principle agreement on the universality of the franchise, and a social democratic position on citizenship versus residency. But what of the obvious next question: is voting to be voluntary, or compulsory? Here, one might think social democrats would embrace compulsion. Compulsory turnout is a shibboleth of the centre-left in Australia, and compulsory enrolment likewise in New Zealand. Compulsion seeks to maximise voice and it may nudge policy towards more substantively egalitarian outcomes, say its proponents.[27] Yet such rules have not spread to other common law democracies. In the UK, compulsory turnout attracted some support from within the Labour Government in the mid-2000s, leading to a Ministry of Justice green paper canvassing a statutory 'duty' to vote but without any sanctions to enforce it.[28] But the proposal went nowhere. Of course inertia favours the status quo, but compulsory voting is a classic example of a fundamental issue where liberty and equality norms collide intractably.

ii. The 'Weight' of Each Vote

One-vote, one-value may seem to be a no-brainer today, as a correlative of a universal franchise. And yet … witness its long absence from the distribution of seats in Westminster, and the limited interest of social democrats in implementing it. It would be too easy to suggest that allowing smaller enrolments for 'regional' seats in the UK is a partisan redoubt (Labour being historically stronger in Wales and Scotland than the epicentre of southern England). There are principles at play as well. In contrast, for American progressives the fight has all been the other way. In 'easily the most important case in the [US] law of politics canon',[29] they won a strict one-vote, one-value rule by convincing the Supreme Court to imply it from the Bill of Rights and the '*equal protection* of the laws'.[30]

There are counter-arguments, from a different view of representation, that votes need not be weighted equally if power and wealth is disproportionately centred in one region. Take London and the 'home' counties of England, within the UK. Devolution may help

[25] G Orr, 'Citizenship, Interests, Community and Expression: Expatriate Voting in Australian Elections' in S Bronitt and K Rubenstein (eds), *Citizenship in a Post-National World: Australia and Europe Compared*, Law and Policy Papers (Sydney, Federation Press, 2008) 24.

[26] By this token prisoners should vote; but not all social democratic parties wish to expend political capital on a cause affecting a small minority and whose symbolism triggers socially conservative values. Despite enjoying a sizeable parliamentary majority for five years after the European Court of Human Rights ruled against UK prisoner disenfranchisement in *Hirst v UK* (No 2) (2006) 42 EHRR 41, the Labour Government kicked the issue into the long grass. Only 13 years later, under a Conservative Government, has reform partly harmonised the UK franchise with European rights law.

[27] J Brennan and L Hill, *Compulsory Voting: For and Against* (New York, CUP, 2014) especially ch 6.

[28] S Birch, 'The Case for Compulsory Voting' (2009) 16 *Public Policy Research* 21, 22.

[29] GE Charles and L Fuentes-Rohwer, 'Reynolds Revisited' in JA Douglas and ED Mazo (eds), *Election Law Stories* (St Paul, Foundation Press, 2016) 21, 57.

[30] US Constitution, 14th amendment. Emphasis added. See, eg, *Reynolds v Sims* 377 US 533 (1964) which was a challenge to gross malapportionment in Alabama. Chief Justice Warren, who led the court to adopt strict one-vote-one-value had curiously, in his earlier career as Governor of California, defended vote weighting for regional counties: Charles and Fuentes-Rohwer (n 29) 49–50.

redress the power imbalance amongst the nations of the UK, but the south of England remains wealthier than regions adjusting to the post-industrial economy, key constituencies for Labour's socio-economic project. One-vote, one-value is more than a mere a 'slogan or political catchcry' (as it was once dismissed by an Australian Chief Justice);[31] however it is not a universal principle. At different times and places conservatives *and* social democrats have recognised that equity of treatment and voice is not always the same as mathematical equality of votes. Does this suggest agreement over an underlying principle of substantive equality? Not necessarily. But what it does reveal is that even within an ideal like 'political equality', different notions of 'equality' exhibit strong tension.

iii. The Voting System

Here, there are a smorgasbord of models, each with profound differences for the degree of electoral choice and for the make-up of parliaments and government. To name just the three most prominent clusters of options in use, there are forms of proportional representation (PR), majoritarian run-offs (including the preferential or alternative vote (AV)), and the old stand-by of first-past-the-post or plurality voting. Even in countries with similar Westminster lower houses, common law and party systems, the room for principled difference is profound.

Given the chance in a referendum in 2010, the British Labour Party declined to embrace AV. Part of its reason was a preference for strong, responsible party government, an artefact of a view of popular sovereignty that is wary of bicameralism let alone coalition government.[32] Labour prefers to take its chances on the bipolar pendulum rather than risk further fracturing of the left-of-centre vote. Preferential voting, after all, was a system introduced in Australia to diminish the effect of any split in the conservative vote between parties of the right. But it is an article of faith on the left in Australia. Australia's most progressive Prime Minister since WW2 even went as far as to praise optional preferential voting, as the one system that allows electors to express indifference to options on the ballot.[33] Further abroad, in much of continental Europe, PR is seen as a necessary social democratic position, expressing the diversity principle of representation and reflecting a sense of the value of multi-party jostling and co-operation.

III. Political Finance: A Search for Norms

The most pressing electoral law question, for some decades, has been money in electoral politics.[34] This is the case across the 'developed' democracies. The area has proved febrile as regulators, legislators and courts shift between liberal, via egalitarian then onto integrity

[31] *Attorney-General v Commonwealth; ex parte McKinlay* (1975) 135 CLR 1, 17.
[32] Compare Ewing, 'Jeremy Corbyn and the Law of Democracy' (n 3).
[33] EG Whitlam, *The Whitlam Government 1972–1975* (Ringwood, Viking, 1985) 679.
[34] Money in politics is 'arguably the biggest threat to democracy worldwide' according to the Secretary-General of International IDEA: E Falguera et al (eds), *Funding of Political Parties and Election Campaigns: A Handbook of Political Finance* (Stockholm, IDEA, 2014) v.

positions, and back again. Here, then, is an area where we can divine no overarching theory or set of nested principles to direct regulation.

It is nigh on impossible to imagine consensus on aims between those who see democracy as about individual expression and those who see it as protecting collective interests, as the endless US debate makes clear. Perhaps this is unsurprising. As Anika Gauja explained in her search for international norms on the regulation of political parties:

> significant normative disagreements exist surrounding the desirability of parties as electoral actors, qualifications upon freedoms of association, the extent to which parties should be supported by the state, the nature of party competition, and the extent to which equality interferes with the freedoms of political expression and association (and vice versa).[35]

Her conclusion was that outside some quite minimal liberal principles – parties have a right to exist to contest elections – the search for consensus was fruitless.[36] Instead, '[d]etermining and defining the parameters of the debate, rather than advocating for a universal policy solution' was the role for any theoretical systematisation.[37] In similar fashion, International IDEA has avoided trying to define a theory for political finance regulation, since 'there is no form of democratic governance that is preferred everywhere'.[38] At best there are broad but competing goals that may express themselves differently in different political systems and contexts.

But can we diagnose a core, social democratic position on regulating money in electoral politics? We can, although it is partial rather than holistic and more an axiomatic tendency than a manifesto. This approach is guided by the sentiment, expressed by Ewing (above), that wealth in itself is corrosive of democracy. Money and monied interests put at risk the social democratic (and democratic socialist) promise of electoral democracy – equal respect and voice. To the social democrat the value of electoral democracy is as a counterbalance to a marketplace which, for all its dynamism and efficiency, is not built on humane values and reinscribes social and economic inequality

A. 'Party Finance': The Distinctive Ewingian Focus[39]

Political finance is the area of electoral law in which Keith Ewing has made his greatest contribution. It is no exaggeration to say he has been the most prolific and influential scholar in this area in the common law world beyond the US. His dedicated books include three research monographs and four edited volumes. Whilst his monographs focus on the

[35] A Gauja, 'The Legal Regulation of Political Parties: Is there a Global Normative Standard?' (2016) 15 *Election Law Journal* 4, 4.

[36] Gauja (n 35) 17. Even then, militant liberals embrace rules banning parties that oppose the liberal democratic order: eg German Basic Law, Art 21(2).

[37] Gauja (n 35) 6.

[38] Falguera et al (eds) (n 34) 16.

[39] See also Rowbottom, 'Political Finance and the Constitution of Social Democracy' (n 23) on Ewing's account of money in politics as one based on the importance of pluralist competition between organised forces, especially parties, unions and corporations.

UK and Canada,[40] his edited works span Europe, north America and Australasia.[41] Here, by way of sample, are the essential elements of their titles: 'The Funding of Political Parties in Britain', 'The Funding of Political Parties: Europe and Beyond', 'The Challenge of Party Political Funding', 'Party Funding and Campaign Financing in International Perspective', 'Party Funding in Modern British Politics', 'The Funding of Political Parties'.

One thing shines from that list. In Ewing's framing, what others label 'political finance' or 'campaign finance' is, at root, a question of the fair and proper funding of *political parties*. This emphasis on party is pragmatically rooted in the idea of responsible party government. It would make less sense in a country like the US, with its directly elected chief executives and its candidate-centred primary elections. But it is also expresses an ideological variant of social democracy.[42]

Ewing's 'Political Party Finance – Themes in International Context' is instructive here.[43] It is not just a neat summation of the value of his 'party finance' orientation, it is as close to a generalised statement about the norms that ought shape, and methods that might manage, the regulation of money in politics, as anyone has given anywhere. On the all important normative side, Ewing lists three 'guiding principles':

> The first concern … is the need to ensure that parties have adequate funding. … The second concern is … to ensure that this occurs by means that do not expose them to the dangers of corruption and conflict of interest. … The third concern [is that] we need also to ensure there is fair competition between them.[44]

The last two concerns are familiar.[45] Anti-corruption or integrity concerns are shared even by a body as liberal as the US Supreme Court. 'Fair competition' can be parsed as a parity of arms conception of equality, where the focus of the parity is between parties as the chief agents within modern parliamentary government. Where, a liberal might ask, is 'liberty', the concern for electoral and expressive freedoms? Is its literal absence some blindness or malevolence on the part of social democracy? That would be odd, as the championing of civil liberties – including freedoms of political protest – in another strand of Ewing's work can attest.[46] Rather, Ewing's concern is not with individual electoral freedoms in the abstract.

[40] Ewing, *The Funding of Political Parties in Britain* (n 21), Ewing, *Money, Politics, and Law* (n 20) and Ewing, *The Cost of Democracy* (n 7).

[41] KD Ewing (ed), *The Funding of Political Parties: Europe and Beyond* (Bologna, CLUEB, 1999); KD Ewing and NS Ghaleigh (eds), *The Challenge of Party Political Funding: Comparative Perspectives* (Bologna, CLUEB, 2001); KD Ewing and S Issacharoff (eds), *Party Funding and Campaign Financing in International Perspective* (Oxford, Hart Publishing, 2006) and KD Ewing, J Rowbottom and J Tham (eds), *The Funding of Political Parties: Where Now?* (Abingdon, Routledge, 2012).

[42] 'We begin with the party …': Ewing, 'Jeremy Corbyn and the Law of Democracy' (n 3) 347 and following.

[43] K Ewing, 'Political Party Finance: Themes in International Context' in J Tham et al (eds), *Electoral Democracy: Australian Prospects* (Melbourne, MUP, 2011) 143.

[44] Ewing, 'Political Party Finance: Themes in International Context' (n 43) 147–49.

[45] Indeed under the headings 'institutional accountability' (of parties and donors) and 'fair rivalry' they were the heart of Ewing's analysis at the conclusion of *The Funding of Political Parties in Britain* (n 21) 178–87.

[46] See KD Ewing and W Finnie, *Civil Liberties in Scotland: Cases and Materials*, 2nd edn (Edinburgh, W Green & Son, 1988); K Ewing and C Gearty, *Freedom under Thatcher: Civil Liberties in Modern Britain* (Oxford, OUP, 1990); K Ewing and C Gearty, *The Struggle for Civil Liberties: Political Freedom and the Rule of Law in Britain, 1914–1945* (Oxford, OUP, 2001) and KD Ewing, *Bonfire of the Liberties: New Labour, Human Rights and the Rule of Law* (Oxford, OUP, 2010) especially ch 4 of the latter on 'Freedom of Assembly and the Right of Public Protest'.

It is with the ability for parties, as the collective voice of different interests, to participate in a roughly fair competition.

Having laid down three guiding 'principles', Ewing addresses the question 'how can we implement these principles?' He offers 'no single bullet', but a 'menu' of 'three dishes':

> The starter is transparency, which is now fully recognised as [a] prerequisite … The main course [consists of] contribution caps or spending limits. … [T]he sweet course [is] in the form of public or state funding.[47]

This summation of principles isn't just the work of a mature systematiser: it was echoed 20 years earlier in Ewing's book on Canadian political finance. (The one work, perhaps because it had a more north American audience, or perhaps because Canada was even then beginning to look at third parties, where the organising term was not 'party finance'.) In that book, we learn that 'the case for control [of money in politics] starts with the principle of political equality … at the heart of the system of government in the liberal democratic tradition'.[48]

This overarching principle – which is social democratic rather than liberal democratic, unless 'liberal' is inflected with a north American accent – itself comprises two foci. One on fair competition or 'the right of equal opportunity to secure election'; the other on 'equal representation'.[49] The fair competition or campaign principle involves ensuring three things. First that 'each of the candidates or parties representing major strands of opinion should have enough money to effectively fight an election [and] maintain an organization between elections'. (Note how candidates are mentioned, but the focus is still on parties as collective, organized interests). Second, that these players should 'have access to the major instruments of communication' (essentially the media). And third that 'no party or candidate should be permitted to spend more than its rivals by a disproportionate amount' (ie spending limits).[50]

The equal representation principle, for its part, combines integrity and fair government concerns. Again, Ewing breaks this down into a triad. First, electors should be encouraged to contribute, to reduce dependency on big donors (this is a nod to Canada's attempt to use tax credits to encourage small, citizen donations). Second, those who contribute should be accountable. In this, disclosure is key. Third, 'the influence of the economically powerful should be restricted by controlling the amount of money they contribute'. This seems to point to caps on donations. But, as we shall now see, donations by corporations and the rich are in the sights, rather than contributions from civil society groups like unions.[51]

B. Supply, Demand and Trade Union Money in Politics

Earlier we noted that, unlike classical liberals or libertarians, social democrats are concerned to restrain money in politics and to do this by law, rather than leave it to ethics or custom. Indeed, this might be a sine qua non or litmus test for social (electoral) democracy.

[47] Ewing, 'Political Party Finance: Themes in International Context' (n 43) 151–53. This typology is echoed in Falguera et al (eds) (n 34) 21–30.
[48] Ewing, *Money, Politics and Law* (n 20) 13.
[49] Ewing (n 20), 14, 17.
[50] Ewing (n 20), 17–18.
[51] Ewing (n 20), 22.

But a desire to restrain money is a vague principle, not a regulatory scheme. Amongst social democratic positions there are those, like Ewing, who focus on the demand side; that is, on expenditure limits. Then there are those who focus on the supply side; that is, on donation limits. The supply-siders include US progressives who, for over a century, have been concerned with busting the power of big corporations and cartels, and countervailing it with citizen-based action and contributions.

These different approaches can, in part, be rationalised as forms of path dependency, driven by concerns rooted in differing times and contexts. As early as 1883, the UK initiated expenditure limits – then on candidates – with good reason. The initiative was part of a wider war on electoral corruption, then emblemised by outright electoral bribery. In tamping down on expenditure, a broader aim was to relieve pressure on existing MPs and parties by reducing the arms' race. A happy by-product of this was making electoral contests more accessible to less well-to-do candidates. In contrast, under the pervasive influence of First Amendment doctrine and values, the concern in the US was to avoid industrial strength 'purchasing' of influence over legislators or directly elected executives. To this day, the UK has expenditure limits, but not donation caps; the US has the reverse.

Besides these factors, there have also been pragmatic arguments about the enforceability of donations limits and expenditure limits. Donations occur in private, and so are harder to monitor than campaign publicity, which rivals and regulators can monitor.[52] This administrative insight is, however, becoming less convincing as campaigning moves into the dark arts of targeted, online advocacy, including e-campaigning contracted via companies located offshore.[53] Money is fluid and slippery, whether being given or spent.

Beyond these national contexts and enforceability factors, there is a deeper question for social democrats. To the likes of Ewing, social democracy still very much means mobilising collective interests. This has chiefly been through labourism and a parliamentary party tied to the labour movement.[54] It follows then that social democracy may shoot itself in the foot if it caps all donations, since unions ensure the Labour Party survives during droughts in opposition and keep it tethered to its roots. Consistent with this vision, other scholars like Joo-Cheong Tham and Jacob Rowbottom – who Ewing has mentored – have argued in detail that the participatory and collective nature of unions distinguish them from business groups and for-profit corporations when it comes to making political contributions.[55] This is not to say that dependence on institutional donations (say from a small number of big unions) is not a risk: 30 years ago Ewing recognised the importance of transparency and membership approval of such contributions. But, in practice, that risk has reduced since the advent of a more corporate-friendly Labour Party in the last 20 years.[56] Above all, for Ewing, any significant cap on union contributions would be a deprivation of freedom of

[52] For other practical arguments against donation limits see Ewing, *The Funding of Political Parties in Britain* (n 21) 176–78.

[53] There is also the co-ordinated spending problem, where sympathetic groups or parties effectively magnify the spending limit for 'their' side of a campaign.

[54] KD Ewing, 'The Trade Union Question in British Political Funding' in Ewing, Rowbottom and Tham (eds), *The Funding of Political Parties: Where Now?* (n 41) 54 and Ewing, 'Jeremy Corbyn and the Law of Democracy' (n 3) 347–49.

[55] Tham (n 8) 108–19 and J Rowbottom, 'Institutional Donations to Political Parties' in Ewing, Rowbottom and Tham et al (eds), *The Funding of Political Parties: Where Now?* (n 41) 11.

[56] Ewing, *The Funding of Political Parties in Britain* (n 21) 173.

association. Not just in a practical sense by denying a key funding source but by rendering 'unlawful the existing constitutional structure of the Labour Party'.[57]

We should pause here, to note how Kahn-Freund's ideal of collective laissez-faire in labour relations has resonance for action in the electoral arena, where a self-reliant labour/Labour movement is pitted against more conservative antagonists.[58] This realisation can explain not just the rejection of supply-side, donation caps by British Labour, but also their absence in NZ and most of Australia.[59] Conversely, where parties of the centre-left are less enmeshed with the labour movement, as in Canada and the US, donation caps covering all types of donors (for-profit corporations, unions and other groups, and individuals alike) are staples of the regulatory menu. The idea of collective self-reliance can also explain why state support for political parties has not been a focus of social democratic reformers in the UK,[60] the way it has in Australia and continental Europe. In parts of those more statist jurisdictions, the bulk of party electioneering and even administrative costs are met from public funds.[61]

IV. Purpose as Function

So far, I have described the problems inherent in seeking to theorise any coherent, singular set of purposes for electoral law, where purpose is understood as normative aims. There is, of course, another way of understanding purpose, as function. Here I want to briefly sketch, and recommend, a functionalist conspectus of electoral law theories.

There are various functionalist approaches to law. The best known is Karl Llewellyn's 'law jobs' theory.[62] Llewellyn's concern was with the 'how' of law, which he dubbed 'juristic method'.[63] To him, the ultimate 'why' of the law revolved around settling disputes without

[57] KD Ewing, 'The Disclosure of Political Donations in Britain' in Ewing and Issacharoff (eds), *Party Funding and Campaign Financing* (n 41) 57, 75–76. See also Ewing, *The Funding of Political Parties in Britain* (n 21) 176 and Tham (n 8) 116–19. Even in despair with 'New Labour' and its reliance on big donors, Ewing opposed legislated caps on donations, offering instead the idea of parties setting 'their own limits [overseen] by the Electoral Commission': *The Cost of Democracy* (n 7) 248.

[58] Note here how Ewing's voluminous work on labour and trade union rights bleeds into his work on electoral law, meeting in the middle as early as KD Ewing, *Trade Unions, the Labour Party and the Law – a Study of the Trade Union Act 1913* (Edinburgh, Edinburgh University Press, 1982) and 'Trade Union Political Funds – the 1913 Act Revisited' (1984) 13 *Industrial Law Journal* 227.

[59] This can lead to regulatory stalemate, since conservative and liberal interests object to one-sided caps allowing union, but not business donations, as hypocritical or functionally unfair. As a halfway house, the Australian jurisdictions of New South Wales and Victoria cap all donations, but permit collective bodies like unions to join parties and pay fees based on the number of members they affiliate.

[60] Ewing, *The Funding of Political Parties in Britain* (n 21) 136 and 150 reasoned that 'arguments against public funding are powerful [but] not necessarily persuasive nor conclusive' and that '[i]f there is to be state aid' it should reflect electoral support. Such cautious consideration features in his later writing. So funding remains a 'vexed' idea, embraced simply as a way 'to fill at least part' of the gap between parties' needs and their ability to meet those from non-corrupting, fully disclosed private sources: *The Cost of Democracy* (n 7) 279.

[61] G Orr, 'Full Public Funding: Cleaning Up Parties or Parties Cleaning Up?' in J Mendilow and E Phélippeau (eds), *Handbook of Political Party Funding* (Northampton, Edward Elgar, 2018) 84.

[62] Most comprehensively stated in K Llewellyn, 'The Normative, the Legal, and the Law-Jobs: the Problem of Juristic Method' (1940) 49 *Yale Law Journal* 1355.

[63] See the gloss by Llewellyn's academic biographer: W Twining, 'The Idea of Juristic Method: a Tribute to Karl Llewellyn' (1993) 48 *University of Miami Law Review* 119.

repressing human creativity or flourishing. In mentioning Llewellyn in a discussion of election law, I don't mean to invoke his concepts of juristic method or dispute settlement. As we saw at the start of this chapter, electoral law is not predominantly about litigation or the negotiation of conflict under the umbrella of the law. On the contrary, as a key element in the ordering of the political domain, it is a *precursor* to government and hence law-making and dispute resolution on substantive issues. Rather, I mean to invoke the simpler insight that the 'purpose' of a domain like electoral law can be considered in terms of the functions it might fulfil or fail to fulfil.

Here, in diagrammatic form, is my functionalist mapping of election law theory. Space precludes a lengthy summary,[64] but I will briefly explain the layout and grouping of concepts in turn.

Figure 9.1 A Typology of Election Law Theories

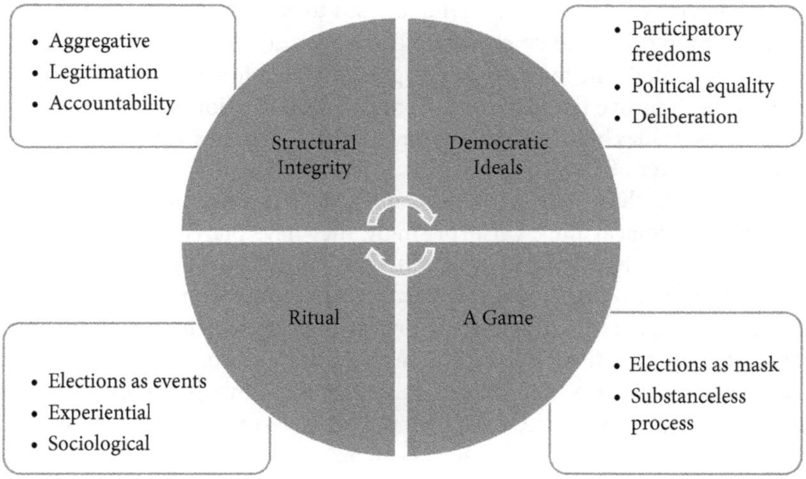

The top half of the diagram identifies the two most common, and instrumental, approaches to election law. The 'structural integrity' theme, at root, is captured in the old saying about electoral democracy being the least worst system of government. This conception is developed in Joseph Schumpeter's 'realist' account of electoral democracy as a realm of elites.[65] This is not an empty metaphor of politics as a mere mechanism to populate legislatures.[66] It encompasses the goal of fair elections in the fundamental sense of counting all the votes, and applying rules of the contest impartially. Independent electoral administration and law enforcement are critical, lest 'regulation [become] public deception'.[67] Ultimately it also encompasses elections as a crude accountability mechanism, where governments and

[64] See further Orr, *The Law of Politics* (n 8) ch 1 and G Orr, *Ritual and Rhythm in Electoral Systems: a Comparative Legal Perspective* (Farnham, Ashgate/Routledge, 2015) 6–10.

[65] J Schumpeter, *Capitalism, Socialism and Democracy*, 2nd edn (London, Allen & Unwin, 1947) chs 21–23.

[66] Though Green (n 9) is right to object to that instrumentalist caricature.

[67] M Mietzner, 'Indonesia' in P Norris and A Abel van Es (eds), *Checkbook Elections? Political Finance in Comparative Perspective* (New York, Oxford, 2016) 84, 84.

legislators are opened up to regular electoral judgment. In this conception, voting boils down to hiring and firing decisions as candidates and parties seek to gain or renew a mandate.[68]

This will still feel like a minimalist conception. To say our rulers are answerable to 'the people', rather than God, family or oligarchical backers, is a negative rule rather than a model of representation. But, in the course of human history, the ability to turnover those in power, bloodlessly yet without limiting the rulers to a bloodline, has proven a precious thing. This conception also then speaks to a variety of regulatory questions: stressing the importance of independent electoral authorities, access to the ballot and ballot box, the regularity of elections and laws to minimise the risk of quid quo pro corruption.

The top right of the diagram, in contrast, captures the more questing aims of electoral law in most democratic traditions.[69] These include the prominent normative purposes discussed earlier: political liberty and political equality. Without these two wings the bird won't fly. But there is tension not only between those two purposes, but within them. There are different approaches to liberty (collective or individual), and to equality (formal or substantive, and party, interest group or candidate centred). There are also other liberal values which have tended to be sublimated. The most obvious is good deliberation: to what extent can electoral law and processes improve the quality of debate and information?[70] Realists, for their part, do not reject these values but see them as 'romantic', 'folk theories' that can obscure as much as they limit the power of elites.[71]

These two approaches – the structural integrity and the liberal democratic – both express several teleological aims. Unsurprisingly, they have played an explicit role in shaping the law. But there is a third view which sees electoral democracy as, in a sense, an end in itself. This, as I've explained elsewhere, is the conception of elections as rituals.[72] Not rituals in the empty sense, but in the everyday sense in which any patterned, recurrent and meaningful human activity is lived out. In this more sociological approach, however we stage elections under law we should be cognisant of the symbols and experiences that are generated. Should we, for instance, vote in schools or government buildings, and on a single polling day or across weeks? These questions can be analysed in terms of instrumental goals (maximising turnout for the sake of legitimacy and participation). But they also need to be understood as choices that shape the social experience and understanding of an election as the one occasion that truly brings together a secular society.

Finally, in the bottom right quadrant, lies the realm of the deep sceptic. In this view, elections are just a game, in the hollow sense of the word. This approach differs from the other three, which each assume a commitment to the enterprise, whilst differing in

[68] J Buchler, *Hiring and Firing Officials: Rethinking the Purpose of Elections* (New York, OUP, 2011).

[69] Compare A Geddis, 'Three Conceptions of the Electoral Moment' (2003) 28 *Australian Journal of Legal Philosophy* 53, discussing 'liberation', 'egalitarian' and 'deliberation' as core values for election law. Any theory of electoral authoritarianism (if that is not an oxymoron) belongs elsewhere.

[70] See R Levy and G Orr, *The Law of Deliberative Democracy* (Abingdon, Routledge, 2016). Contrast J Gardner, *What are Campaigns For? The Role of Persuasion in Electoral Law and Politics* (New York, OUP, 2009), arguing that elections are irredeemably agonistic and that, in the US at least, the law ought just focus on getting the aggregative dimension, of letting everyone vote and counting each vote, right.

[71] CH Achen and LM Bartels, *Democracy for Realists: Why Elections Do Not Produce Responsive Government* (Princeton, Princeton University Press 2016).

[72] Orr, *Ritual and Rhythm in Electoral Systems* (n 64). See further S Coleman, *How Voters Feel* (Cambridge, CUP, 2013).

their portrayal of the 'jobs' that elections perform. By contrast, in the 'it's a game' view, paying too much heed to building good electoral institutions and laws risks obscuring the possibility that elections function as a mask. This sentiment is most easily distilled in the catchcries 'whoever you vote for a politician always wins' and 'if voting changed anything, it would be illegal'. Variants of those slogans have been attributed to everyone from political activists to the literary wag Mark Twain. Long usage of such sayings, without obvious source, attest to their popularity. Less cynical are critiques that nuance satirical detachment with commitment to alternatives to liberal democracy. Most obvious are Marxism and anarchism. Emblematic of this is Emma Goldman's essay doubting the value of suffragism: 'Our modern fetich [sic] is universal suffrage. … Woe to the heretic who dare question that divinity!'[73] Market-oriented libertarians, also deeply sceptical of government, sometimes also echo this view.

There is even a related strand of neo-conservative thought, which doubts the value of elections precisely because electoral law is concerned with (hollow) proceduralism. Thus, in Irving Kristol's account, elections are games that we manage in the name of legitimising a self-perpetuating system:

> Democracy is a "political system" … reduced to its mechanical arrangements … nothing but a set of rules and procedures whereby majority rule and minority rights are reconciled.[74]

In other words, liberal electoral democracy lacks a conception of the good, or any sense of virtue or character, values required to avoid politics becoming the terrain of self-serving apparatchiks. Democratic socialists would not completely disagree. After all, equal dignity and respect are hardly to be achieved if electoral democracy boils down to a utilitarian calculus where everyone votes in their own interest. If that happens, electoral outcomes may be procedurally utilitarian, but substantively unfair for vast numbers. Ultimately, the outsider critique of elections as a game is of little use to regulators. But it serves as a reminder that democracy cannot be reduced to the rules of electoral democracy. To a social democrat, industrial democracy for instance is no less a constitutional value than parliamentary democracy.

V. In Conclusion

To explore any area of law in the hope of finding a 'theory' for it, in the sense of a set of guiding principles, is heroic. At a generous level of generality, some regulatory domains can be captured in a succinct set of aims in search of a balance. So environmental law has a grundnorm of sustainability, within which it juggles deep-green or precautionary principles with approaches which give more weight to human demands. The essence of taxation law can be captured in the need to collect public revenues to address social aims like redistribution and promoting desirable activity, without strangling economic incentive. Labour law,

[73] E Goldman, 'Woman Suffrage' in *Anarchism and Other Essays*, 2nd edn (New York, Mother Earth Publishing Association, 1911) 201.

[74] I Kristol, *Reflections of a Neo-Conservative: Looking Back, Looking Ahead* (New York, Basic Books, 1983) 50–51.

for its part, has existed in a state of perpetual tension between its governing ideal of protecting employees and wider economic forces. In recent times its scope has been stretched, almost unrecognisably, into an inter-connected 'law of work', paid and unpaid.[75] (Others in this volume will seek to redefine a protective and social democratic vocation for labour law amongst the complexities of twenty-first century.)

Why then can't a seemingly niche domain like electoral law be so neatly contained? We began by noting that electoral law has been under-theorised, and asking if it were possible to synthesise a set of normative purposes to guide it. The answer is 'perhaps': try political liberty, equality and deliberation. But the tension between those norms is often irreconcilable and, expressed with such generality, concepts like political 'liberty' and 'equality' are indeterminate. Ultimately, the contested nature of representative democracy ensures we will struggle to find any nested set of normative guidelines to guide electoral law. This is the case even allowing for different political contexts. Yes, principles may express themselves in different answers to the same question across different historical and social contexts (hence shifts in the minimum voting age for instance). But context cannot explain away more basic differences (say over voluntary versus compulsory voting, or over the role of money in politics).

All is not normative randomness however. Social democrats share a conception of electoral democracy that can guide reform in that mould – even allowing that, within social democratic theory, we see distinctive inflections of the principle of social equality and the collective nature of society. A good example of that is Ewing's work on money in politics, with its framing of the law around 'party funding', recognising the desirability of a certain parliamentary and party system and emphasising labourism.

Electoral law is special in that it is constitutive, of the politics and governments that in turn create law in other, more substantive domains.

> The key insight of election law is that laws regulating the political process are not "neutral" … Politics is therefore a "game" – not in the sense that its outcomes are trivial, but in a sense that the winners and losers are determined by the strategic decisions and actions taken within … a system of rules. Election law is about the creation and implementation of those rules.[76]

To social democrats and conservatives alike, this is not something to be lamented. The design of the law is less a search for platonic ideals and more a contest of values and worldviews. In other words, there is no 'theory'; rather there is a variety of clashing, normative theories. Ewing's contribution stands unashamedly in this tradition. He advances a particular, pragmatic version of a social democratic view of politics and constitutionalism. As Jacob Rowbottom observes, his approach is 'consistent with social democratic values' in seeking 'to ensure that political rights can be exercised in practice and are not dependent on levels of wealth' but 'does not seek to re-design the system [but rather] defends the

[75] Eg, R Owens and J Riley, *The Law of Work* (South Melbourne, OUP, 2007). And see how shifts in nomenclature, from 'master and servant', through 'industrial' and 'labour', onto 'employment' and 'workplace relations' law embody these ideological and disciplinary shifts: G Orr, 'The Fair Work Act and other Names of Shame' (2009) 16 *Australian Journal of Administrative Law* 74.

[76] Dimino et al (n 6) [preface]. Compare D Rae, *The Political Consequences of Electoral Laws* (New Haven, Yale University Press, 1967).

existing institutions as providing a rough approximation to an inclusive system that best fits [his country's] political history.'[77]

To appreciate that there is no overarching 'theory' of electoral law does not, however, condemn us to conceptual chaos. In a contested domain like electoral law, theory can play a systematic role by setting a framework for debate. The value of this approach is to set parameters for discussion and to help frame syntheses, critiques or reform proposals about the law, both in academia and policy-making. This is where a functionalist typology, like the one I have offered, fits in. Being taxonomic, a functional approach need not weigh-in on normative disputes between different social democratic or libertarian traditions. Its weakness is that its dispassion can seem rudderless or anti-theoretical, like the 'garbage can' theory of mixed or pluralist jurisprudence.[78] But without some parameters, debates are likely to become blinded to the variety of questions in play, or worse, mired in particularities and pure partisanship.

[77] Rowbottom, 'Political Finance and the Constitution of Social Democracy' (n 23).
[78] Criticism levelled, eg, at C Sampford, *The Disorder of Law: a Critique of Legal Theory* (Oxford, Blackwell, 1989).

10

Political Finance and the Constitution of Social Democracy

JACOB ROWBOTTOM*

This chapter will examine Professor Keith Ewing's contribution to the law of political finance. In doing so, it will look at several key features that have defined his work, in particular the role of trade unions as a vehicle of mass representation and the central role played by political parties in representative democracy. Ewing offers a model for regulating political finance that seeks to provide realistic opportunities for political rights to be exercised and to counter the influence of very wealthy and non-representative bodies. As will be discussed, his approach emphasises the importance of the link between trade unions and the Labour Party. That approach does not demand a radical rewrite of the political system and fits with the traditional model of British politics. However, Ewing's model relies on the traditional institutions of representative democracy, which have increasingly come under attack in recent years. Before examining Professor Ewing's work on political finance, the following section will consider what it means to discuss elections and political parties within a constitution of social democracy.

I. Political Finance and Social Democracy

The democratic aspects of a constitution focus on the procedures to manage disagreement within society and arrive at collective decisions. Consequently, the law of elections (and related processes) should set out the rules of the game that are acceptable to all political perspectives. If the results of an election are to secure legitimacy, then the basic rules of the process should be as acceptable to socialists, social democrats, liberals, conservatives and libertarians. As such, the democratic part of a constitution should not be designed in a way that aims to produce outcomes in line with a particular political outlook. A constitution is therefore not to entrench social democratic policies. According to this view, a distinctly social democrat framework for election law may struggle to secure legitimacy among those different political outlooks.

The rules underpinning an electoral process will, however, reflect certain substantive values. That much is inevitable, and the choices made when designing a system will not be

* With thanks to Alan Bogg for comments on an earlier draft.

politically neutral. The choices include the voting system and the rules on the conduct of elections. If a social democrat has a distinct view on what constitutes a fair and just society, then that will in turn colour the assessment of what a fair political process requires. Accordingly, if a social democrat believes that social justice demands some fair distribution of resources, then a social democrat will be attracted to a substantive account of political rights, which demands not only the absence of formal restraints, but also meaningful opportunities to exercise those rights. This means that political freedoms have a positive aspect, which requires access to certain resources (whether information, education or the means of communication). A significant element can also be stated in the negative – namely that it is important to constrain the use of economic power in the political sphere to prevent an unfair advantage in the process or domination of the electoral debate.

Of course, a process that is consistent with a social democratic outlook will not necessarily produce the results favoured by social democrats. A system in which people have roughly equal political resources may vote parties into power that are strongly pro-free market, and defend cuts to various public services. In a constitution that is consistent with social democratic values, such an outcome would be democratically legitimate (even if opposed by the social democrat). Moreover, one can accept rules of a political system that are consistent with social democracy without being a social democrat.[1] Along these lines, a person could disapprove of the use of vast sums of money in the electoral process, but nonetheless have fewer qualms about inequality of wealth more generally. The presence of a fair electoral process may be necessary to legitimate an economic system that produces inequalities in wealth.[2] Accordingly, people can apply different rules of distribution within the political and economic spheres.[3] The account of political finance that follows can be regarded as part of the constitution of social democracy in a fairly thin sense, as a framework that ensures political rights can be exercised in practice and that inequalities in wealth should not be a major barrier or advantage in the process.

II. Professor Ewing's Contribution

There are many ways that a political system can be designed to be consistent with the social democratic values outlined above. Professor Ewing's work on political finance provides one particular approach, and this chapter will discuss his work on election law to identify some of the key elements. Ewing's approach has developed over several decades, and to assess his contribution this chapter will primarily focus on three major books on political finance that are representative of his work. The first is *Trade Unions, the Labour Party and the Law*, which was published in 1982 and based on his PhD thesis (supervised by Patrick Elias).[4]

[1] Eg, a liberal could support constraints on money in politics as a way to secure political equality.

[2] See J Cohen, 'Money, Politics and Political Equality' in A Byrne, R Stalnaker and R Wedgwood (eds) *Fact and Value* (Cambridge Mass, MIT Press, 2001) 53.

[3] See M Walzer, *Spheres of Justice: a Defence of Pluralism and Equality* (Oxford, Blackwell, 1983). See discussion in J Rowbottom, *Democracy Distorted* (Cambridge, Cambridge University Press, 2010) 27–28.

[4] KD Ewing, *Trade Unions, the Labour Party and the Law: a study of the Trade Union Act 1913* (Edinburgh, Edinburgh University Press, 1982).

The book is grounded in the political history of the relationship between trade unions and the Labour Party. The book examines the workings of the law governing trade union political activity and compares the way other jurisdictions address similar questions and makes some suggestions for future reforms. As a contribution to the field early on in Ewing's career, the book sets out some key themes that can be found in his later work on party funding.

Five years after the study of trade unions and the Labour Party saw the publication of Ewing's second book on the subject. The *Funding of Political Parties in Britain* looked at the system of political finance as a whole, including the role of companies, political parties and the framework for the regulation of political expenditures. The work identified a number of gaps that had emerged in the system of regulation. At the time, political parties were not legally required to disclose sources of income.[5] Election spending was regulated only at the local level, but not at the national level. Consequently, the election spending law seriously missed its target and failed to constrain the most important areas of political expenditure.[6] In the years following the publication of the earlier 1982 study, the Thatcher Government imposed further controls on the operation of union political funds under the Trade Union Act 1984. Professor Ewing contrasted this system of regulation with the lack of comparable controls on company political activities.[7]

While the two early books on political finance were published during the Thatcher years, which saw a sustained attack on trade union political activity, Ewing's *The Cost of Democracy* was published in a very different political climate two decades later.[8] That book reviewed the workings of the Political Parties, Elections and Referendums Act 2000. That Act was a major overhaul of UK election finance law, which was enacted by the Blair Government following a review by the Committee on Standards in Public Life. The statute required political parties to disclose donations above a threshold amount and imposed limits on election spending by (and in support of) political parties (which had been advocated in Ewing's earlier work). The book was also published in the aftermath of a spate of political finance scandals that had come to light under the new law. The work built on his earlier analysis and set out the main objectives for regulating political finance, providing a conceptual framework. The book also argued that any future reforms need to respect the diversity of party structures and organisations.[9]

From these three works, there are several key features to be found in Ewing's treatment of political finance. The first is that he takes an approach to political finance that is consistent with social democratic values, seeking to ensure that political rights can be exercised in practice and are not dependent on levels of wealth. However, he does not seek to re-design the system to assign equal political resources to each citizen. Instead, he defends the existing institutions as providing a rough approximation to an inclusive system that best fits with the UK's political history and practice. This leads to the second key feature in Ewing's work, in which trade unions are seen as a vehicle for the organisation, mobilisation and

[5] *R v Tronoh Mines* [1952] 1 All ER 697.

[6] KD Ewing, *Funding of Political Parties in Britain* (Cambridge, Cambridge University Press, 1987) 79.

[7] Ibid, 47–48, 69, 73, 184.

[8] KD Ewing, *The Cost of Democracy: Party Funding in Modern British Democracy* (Oxford, Hart Publishing, 2007).

[9] Ibid, 35.

representation of working people. While the union-Labour link provides just one means for trade unions to secure representation, the link is defended with reference to political history in the UK and the right to freedom of association.

The third key feature is that emphasis is placed on certain representative institutions and groups as the primary political actors. This is an approach that reflects a model of political pluralism, in which various organised interests (including companies) balance one another to enable a system of fair representation. The approach is also rooted in the traditional Westminster model of representative politics. The fourth key feature follows from the third, that political parties provide a central channel for participation and translate political preferences into government action.[10] Accordingly, elections should enable a level of 'fair rivalry' between the leading parties.[11] To achieve this, the main parties require an adequate and stable level of resources. Political parties should also enjoy autonomy and the state should not prescribe any specific organisational model.

The issues surrounding political finance are key to understanding Ewing's overall body of scholarship, in so far as it provides a link between his work on constitutional law and labour law. Following his approach to constitutional law, his work on political finance emphasises the importance of political participation through representative institutions. Throughout his career, Ewing has resisted calls for a stronger role for the judiciary to act as a check on the other branches of government (and his background in labour law also shapes this general suspicion of judges). Instead, social change is best pursued through political means. For this reason, particular emphasis is given to the fairness of the electoral system and for people to enjoy real opportunities to influence collective decisions. The latter point provides the link with Ewing's work on labour law, in which trade unions are viewed as a practical means to ensure mass representation of working people in the UK. Ewing's work is therefore not simply a critique of judicial review with no alternative prescribed. His work on political finance helps to sketch a model for how political channels should operate. In the following discussion, the key features of Ewing's work will be explored in greater depth, and the long-term prospects for his model of political finance (and politics generally) will be considered.

III. The Union-Labour Link

At the heart of Professor Ewing's work on political finance is a defence of the link between trade unions and the Labour Party. Under this arrangement, a number of trade unions are affiliated with the Labour Party. Members of an affiliated union pay money into the trade union's political fund, which is then used to pay an affiliation fee to the Party. In practice, this means that trade union political funds make significant contributions to the finances of the Labour Party on a regular basis. The affiliated trade unions are then represented on the Party's decision-making bodies, for example with a number of seats on the National Executive Committee being reserved for trade union representatives. The arrangement creates a unique institutional connection between an interest group and a political party. A trade

[10] Ewing, *Funding of Political Parties in Britain* (n 6) 1.
[11] Ibid, 182–3.

union's political fund is not, however, limited to political donations and can be spent on a wide range of political activities (such as a lobbying or publicity campaigns on political issues).

Ewing's analysis of the trade union-Labour Party link is rooted in political history. The 1982 book, *Trade Unions, the Labour Party and the Law*, begins with the history of trade union political activity, outlining the early alliance between some trade unions and the Liberal Party in the late Victorian era, and the limits of that alliance. At the time, trade unions faced a number of challenges, notably from the courts imposing criminal liability in relation to industrial action.[12] Consequently, there was a need for trade unions to seek support in Westminster, to secure legislation to reverse the hostile rulings. The practice of trade unions sponsoring MPs developed during this period, leading to the formalisation of the arrangement under the Labour Representation Committee, which in turn evolved into the Labour Party at the turn of the twentieth century. The emphasis on history in Ewing's work is used to show how the link with trade unions goes to the essence of the Labour Party and the reason for its foundation.

By starting with the political history, Ewing's defence of the union-Labour link is based on political realities and on what is possible, rather than on abstract principles. While a formal link between trade unions and a political party is not the most obvious way to facilitate participation if a political system were being designed from scratch, Ewing is concerned with what can be realistically achieved. The link is thereby justified as a practical way of ensuring that working people are represented and that political rights can be meaningfully exercised. As Ewing wrote in 2007:

> In the case of the British Labour Party, the party was formed in order to facilitate the political representation of working-class and trade union interests, and to ensure that working people were represented in Parliament. The continuing trade union link can be defended on the ground that it allows for the formal representation of working people in the political system, and for providing an institutional forum for their voices to be heard.[13]

While there are other (more radical) methods to distribute political resources that could provide working people with a chance to influence collective decisions, the trade union-Labour link is long established in the UK and does not require large scale reform of the political system.

In defending the union-Labour link, Ewing's analysis rests on a view of trade unions as political organisations. In Ewing's view, political activity undertaken by trade unions primarily aims 'to protect the liberties of unions and members' and provides a 'means of promoting industrial interests'.[14] While a trade union can protect the interests of its members at the workplace through the processes of collective bargaining with employers, that is not the sole means for protecting those interests. Some changes may be achieved more appropriately through legislation. Where that is the case, the political activities of the trade union will advance its interests in the legislature. Moreover, political pressure is important as a way to secure the conditions that enable effective collective bargaining (along with other ways to negotiate with management). According to this view, political action is not extraneous

[12] Eg, *Temperton v Russell* [1893] 1 QB 715 and *Quinn v Leatham* [1901] AC 495.
[13] Ewing, *The Cost of Democracy* (n 8) 37.
[14] Ewing, *Trade Unions, the Labour Party and the Law* (n 4) 140.

to the ordinary activities of the trade union, but is 'a second string to the union bow' that provides an important tool to advance the interests of its membership.[15]

To Ewing, political activity is at the core of the trade union's function. The union is therefore not simply a neutral conduit that facilitates the political choices of its members. That can be seen in Ewing's criticism of proposals made in the 1980s to allow union members to choose which political party their contribution to the political fund should go to.[16] Under that proposal, when paying into the political fund, union members would be able to say whether a proportionate share of the fund should go to Labour, the Conservatives, Liberal Democrats, etc. Ewing's criticism of the proposal was that it failed to treat the trade union as a political actor in its own right.[17] For Ewing, the emphasis is therefore on the rights of the union as a collective actor, rather than as a mere agent for individual preferences. As stated, the political activity is primarily to pursue the union's goals about the best way to protect its members' rights. A trade union should therefore not be under any obligation to supply money to a party that is opposed to that union's own interests (even if some of its members support that party).[18]

Finally, Ewing's defence of the union-Labour link reflects a view that 'internal' representation is necessary to supplement 'external' representation. Under an internal model of representation, the trade union secures influence through the internal procedures within the Party. By providing affiliation fees on behalf of its members, representatives of the affiliated union are given some say in the Party's decision-making procedures. That can be contrasted with an 'external' model, in which the union influences political actors through strategies such as lobbying (which has always been an element of union activity), publicity campaigns, and the supply of information and research to decision makers. Under an external model, a group seeks to influence a political party without formal affiliation or membership. In his 1982 book, Ewing also noted that along with other pressure groups, trade unions seek to influence government externally and are often consulted at various stages of the political process.[19] The book was published at the tail end of the era of corporatism, when trade unions were routinely included in the process of economic decision-making, and retained considerable influence over policy. Ewing nonetheless found that such inclusion did not render the internal party funding role redundant, especially as processes of consultation can be 'empty' gestures in which views are heard but given little weight.[20] By having a place within the Labour Party itself, the unions were in a powerful position that allowed them to 'veto' any policies that would harm their position in industrial relations.[21]

IV. The Role of Interest Groups

Ewing's discussion of the trade union-Labour link reveals a view in which interest groups play an important role as vehicles for representation. This role is not limited to trade unions.

[15] Ibid.

[16] Proposed by the SDP MP William Rodgers in 'Ten Million with a Right to Choose' *The Times* (London, 7 January 1982). Discussed in Ewing, *Trade Unions, the Labour Party and the Law* (n 4) 205–6.

[17] Ewing, *Trade Unions, the Labour Party and the Law* (n 4) 206.

[18] Ibid.

[19] Ibid, 144.

[20] Ibid, 145.

[21] Ibid, 149, citing the reaction to the White Paper, *In Place of Strife*.

Accordingly, Ewing accepts that political donations from various institutions and unincorporated associations are legitimate and ensure that political parties have adequate levels of funding.[22] While such donations are often viewed with suspicion, Ewing argues that such collective contributions are an exercise of rights of association:

> In Britain it has long been recognised that freedom of association permits an interest group to seek to realise its goal through representation in Parliament, whether by working through the established parties or by presenting its own candidates for election.[23]

Not only are such institutional donations an exercise of association rights, Ewing also argues that there is no principled objection to an external body having a formal link with a political party. To Ewing, what is important is that such institutional activities are transparent and supported by citizens:

> so long as people are willing to endorse the platform of a special interest which is financing the activities of a political movement it is hard to see why such conduct should be discouraged or prohibited, provided that the organisation makes clear, and does not conceal the fact, that it promotes the cause of a particular sectional interest or is supported by a particular sectional group.[24]

The institutional connection is thereby seen to provide a channel through which a representative can be made responsive and accountable to certain groups of citizens. However, this account can be challenged on the grounds that a formal link or sponsorship privileges a particular institution's relationship with an MP. While the MP is accountable to that institution, that could undermine the independence of the MP or lead to the prioritisation of the funding group's interests above those of other citizens.

Institution donations are, in Ewing's view, to be valued in creating a balance in political influence. Trade union political activity is seen to provide a counter to the activities of corporations:

> Individual wage-earners acting alone are powerless in a system in which one individual can write a cheque for £5m, and in which newspaper proprietors and transnational corporations have great political authority.[25]

Such comments are consistent with an account of pluralism in politics, in which interests are represented through organised and collective activity. In such a system, it is important that no particular interest dominates or has a clear advantage over the other, and that various sets of interests can counter one another.

The type of balance outlined above reflects a traditional view of politics in the post-war Westminster model, in which political issues were often structured in terms of disputes between management and labour, right versus left. The funding of political parties by companies and trade unions was thought to (largely) track such divisions. One question for the future is how this model is affected by changes to the political culture in recent decades. The division between right and left (and economic interests) does not play such a central role in certain political disputes. The point is often made that coalitions can form

[22] See Ewing, *Funding of Political Parties in Britain* (n 6) ch 8.
[23] Ibid, 176.
[24] Ibid.
[25] Ewing, *The Cost of Democracy* (n 8) 37.

around distinct issues. The cross-party divisions over Brexit provide one such example. This could have two implications for the model of politics outlined above. First, it could potentially weaken the case for an institutional link between the unions and the Labour Party. Under this view, the union may be one voice among many in the political landscape and not the defining voice for the political movement. As noted earlier, the present arrangements privilege a particular type of organisation. If the old divisions between political parties have truly broken down, a trade union may wish to retain the option to support other political parties, rather have a formal attachment to one party. The second implication is that the balance between political interests outlined above may be disturbed. For example, there was a period in the 2000s when Labour became successful in attracting donations from wealthy individuals and companies, in addition to trade unions. As a result, it gained a significant financial advantage. Greater fluidity in politics means that the traditional sources of institutional funds do not always generate a balance of interests.

V. The Legal Regulation of Trade Unions

While Ewing defends the union-Labour link as a method for a union to advance its interests and as a practical way to facilitate political representation, the link has long been subject to legal regulation. Much of Ewing's work criticises some of the legal controls regulating union political activities and opposes calls for further regulations. For example, he extensively critiques the judicial attack on trade union political activity that took place in the early part of the twentieth century. In *Osborne*, the House of Lords ruled that it was ultra vires and thereby illegal for a trade union to impose a levy on members to secure representation in Parliament.[26] In that case, the Amalgamated Society of Railway Servants had registered under the Trade Union Act of 1871. The rules of the union provided for members to pay a levy to enable the union to pay a salary or maintenance allowance to Labour MPs. The arrangement therefore provided a way for those without independent means to take up a seat in Parliament. Osborne challenged the arrangement on the grounds that it was outside the purposes of a trade union and thereby ultra vires.

In finding for Osborne, the House of Lords' decision rested on the interpretation of the Trade Union Act of 1871. That statute provided a definition of a trade union as a combination 'for regulating the relations between workmen and masters' or 'for imposing restrictive conditions on the conduct of any trade or business'.[27] The majority concluded that the purposes of a trade union were to be found within that statute, and any other purposes (such as financially supporting MPs) were prohibited. Lord Halsbury stated that 'it is impossible to uphold this power of taxing the members beyond the purposes for which the trade union exists'.[28] In his analysis of the case, Ewing criticised the reasoning of the decision both in terms of the interpretation of the statute and for treating registered trade unions as analogous to corporations.[29] The discussion above explains why, in Ewing's view, such political

[26] *Amalgamated Society of Railway Servants v Osborne* [1910] AC 87.
[27] As amended in 1876.
[28] *Amalgamated Society of Railway Servants v Osborne* [1910] AC 87, 93.
[29] Ewing, *Trade Unions, the Labour Party and the Law* (n 4) 26.

activities should be regarded as part and parcel of a union's core functions, and not ultra vires. More broadly, Ewing has criticised the decision for disrupting the balance of political power and the representation of working people, starving the Labour Party of funds:

> it undermined the ability of British citizens without private means to stand for election to Parliament, and would have deprived British electors of the right to be represented in Parliament by the person of their choice.[30]

The decision is remembered as a further judicial attack on the trade union movement, which would have had a devastating effect on the Labour Party and trade union political activities (and can partly explain the suspicion of the courts on the left in the following years).

The ruling in *Osborne* was, however, reversed by the Trade Union Act of 1913, which permitted political expenditures by trade unions, subject to certain conditions. The central condition was that such expenditures were not to be made out of the general funds of the trade union, but from a separate political fund. A political fund could only be established following approval by a ballot of members. Once those conditions were met, special protection had to be made for dissenting members that did not want to make payments to the Labour Party. The protection of the dissenting member reflected Lord Atkinson's concern expressed in *Osborne*, that compelled payments are 'unjust and oppressive'.[31] Lord Atkinson reasoned that the system of compelled payments meant that union members faced either a restriction on 'freedom of opinion' by being required to contribute to political parties of which they may disapprove, or face expulsion from the union (and thereby be deprived of the benefits of union membership).[32] To address this, the legislation gave union members a right to opt-out of paying into the political fund by notifying the union.

However, once that legislation was in place, it became vulnerable to further changes and opened the door to restrictions on union political activity. Ewing notes that the 1913 Act created a 'fragile settlement' that was subject to attack from Conservatives, in particular with allegations about the difficulties in exercising the right to opt-out.[33] The General Strike of 1926 was followed by legislation in 1927 that amended the 1913 Act to require trade union members to 'opt-in' to the political fund.[34] The change placed the burden on the union to convince members to agree to pay an additional levy for the political fund. The 1927 reforms were later repealed by the Attlee Government, which restored the 1913 settlement and the 'opt-out' provisions. That has not been the end of the matter and further changes to the political fund rules were implemented by the Thatcher Government, requiring a ballot on the existence of a political fund every decade.[35] More recently, in 2016 the Conservative Government under David Cameron once again imposed a requirement for trade union members to opt-in to paying into a political fund (but with a minor compromise that retained the opt-out model for existing trade union members).[36]

[30] Ewing, *The Cost of Democracy* (n 8) 30.

[31] *Amalgamated Society of Railway Servants v Osborne* [1910] AC 87, 105.

[32] Ibid.

[33] Ewing, *Trade Unions, the Labour Party and the Law* (n 4) 50–51.

[34] Trade Disputes and Trade Unions Act 1927.

[35] Trade Union and Labour Relations (Consolidation) Act 1992, s 73.

[36] Trade Union Act 2016, s 11, amending the Trade Union and Labour Relations (Consolidation) Act 1992. See A Bogg, 'Beyond Neo-Liberalism: The Trade Union Act 2016 and the Authoritarian State' (2016) 45 Industrial Law Journal 299. There is some evidence that the change in the law is having an impact on trade union political funds,

At first sight, the question of whether the interests of dissenting members are best protected through an opt-in or opt-out requirement may appear to be a largely technical matter, albeit one that has very important strategic consequences for the political parties. Inertia among members means that an opt-out rule will lead to over-payments into the political fund, with non-Labour supporters paying the levy simply because they have not got around to requesting the opt-out. The reverse is true for opt-in. Either approach may seem defensible in the abstract, and political parties thereby argue for a default rule in line with their strategic interests. However, setting the default rule is important and there are issues of principle. Much depends on the relationship between the political activities and the other functions of the trade union. As was noted earlier, in Ewing's view political activities are simply one tool to promote the union's general objectives, and under that view the act of joining a union may signal the member's authorisation of those activities. The employee is thereby faced with a basic choice of whether to join a union (and contribute to its package of activities), rather than having an a la carte choice of whether to support each area of activity undertaken by the union. In so far as political activities are more sensitive matters on which people should have greater choice, the view outlined above suggests that an opt-out model offers a sufficient level of protection and that the onus should be on the individual to object.[37] That view, however, stands in contrast to the opt-in arrangement now being implemented under 2016 Trade Union Act.

The legal controls on union political activity are also criticised for a creating a lopsided system of regulation that challenges the balance assumed in a pluralist model. Ewing has frequently noted that no other institution is subject to controls equivalent to those imposed on trade unions. Companies, for example, do not have to set up a separate political fund. The issue was only partly addressed by a reform enacted in 2000, which requires companies to gain authorisation from company members before political expenditures are incurred.[38] This requirement does not allow shareholders to approve any specific donations or political parties. Moreover, the rules fall far short of anything equivalent to the more restrictive regime that has long been in place for trade unions.

VI. The Role of Political Parties

So far, the discussion has focused on the role of institutions in supplying funds to political parties. Ewing's work on election law also emphasises the importance of political parties in the constitutional system. While much constitutional scholarship is often critical of political parties, for example in eroding the independence of MPs, such institutions play a central role in the UK's representative democracy.[39] Political parties enable candidates to stand on a national policy platform, and allow an elected government to implement its platform with

see J Pickard, 'Labour's biggest donor hit by legislation on political funds' Financial Times (London, 16 September 2019).

[37] By contrast, if the political activity were taken to be an additional activity largely extraneous to its other activities, then we can see why simply joining the union does not provide such authorisation.

[38] Companies Act 2006, s 366.

[39] For an overview of the criticisms and rebuttal stressing the importance of parties, see NW Barber, *The Principles of Constitutionalism* (Oxford, Oxford University Press, 2018) ch 6.

the necessary support from Parliament. Accordingly, Ewing described the British system as one where parties compete by setting out different ideologies and policies, and the party that secures enough seats to form a government can 'claim to translate into positive law the policies which it presented to the electorate'.[40] Party discipline enables those laws to pass through Parliament without being diluted and distorted by amendments to appeal to the various interests of individual MPs. In Ewing's account, parties also play a continuous role in connecting the public with the formal institutions of government. Accordingly, Ewing wrote in 2007:

> They provide a channel for political participation, they provide for the collective representation of citizens views, and they provide the personnel of government and opposition.[41]

There are other broader functions performed by political parties. For example, Nancy Rosenblum argues that political parties 'stage the battle' by organising interests and views into conflicting groups, which 'create the lines of division over social aims, security, and justice'.[42] Such division is no bad thing. It promotes a system for the framing of issues for public debate and for those in power to be held to account. Moreover, organisation into a party means that the losers of the most recent election maintain hope of capturing power in the future, and so remain committed to the system.[43]

There are two central themes in Ewing's work in relation to political parties. The first is the need for fair competition between the leading parties. Such competition is necessary in a healthy system, if voters are to be presented with a genuine choice and for all arguments to be properly scrutinised. Fair competition can, however, be jeopardised by unequal spending power. The 'fair rivalry' between political parties[44] means 'no party should have an unfair advantage because it has greater financial resources than its rivals'.[45] In addition, a competitive system requires that parties have sufficient funds to draw up policies, communicate and organise, as well as enjoy a level of financial stability. Consequently, fair rivalry does not mean that the health of a party's finances should simply be proportionate to its level of support among the public. Instead, the fair rivalry requires that parties have a level of resources to perform their constitutional function effectively and to challenge the other leading parties. As such, the focus is on protecting the institution itself. As noted earlier, under this view donations from trade unions and companies could work to create an approximate equilibrium between the two leading political parties. Such an equilibrium has, however, been disrupted where one side has received far higher levels of funds than the other.

The concern for fair rivalry explains why Ewing supports a legal cap on election spending, which was introduced in the PPERA 2000. That cap means that no matter how much money is raised by the political party, there are constraints on how those resources can be converted into an electoral advantage. There are limits to what such a law can achieve, as the

[40] Ewing, *Trade Unions, the Labour Party and the Law* (n 4) 139.
[41] Ewing, *The Cost of Democracy* (n 8) 29. See also 174.
[42] N Rosenblum, *On the Side of the Angels* (Princeton, Princeton University Press, 2008) 456–7.
[43] Ibid, 363.
[44] Ewing, *Funding of Political Parties in Britain* (n 6) 182–3.
[45] Ewing, *The Cost of Democracy* (n 8) 28.

cap will not cover all spending by a political party, but only those on election campaigns. The effectiveness of that cap thereby depends on how election material is defined, and whether it can be separated from the other operational costs of a political party. The UK laws are also complex in so far as different spending limits are applied to the political party and to candidates spending locally during the same election. While a spending cap is important in constraining the use of resources, it does not eradicate the advantages secured through higher levels of income.

In addition to a spending cap, Ewing endorses greater state support for political parties. Such support would not aim to make parties independent of companies, trade unions and individuals. Instead state funding would reduce the potential for donors to apply pressure on parties, by making the party less dependent on external sources of funding.[46] Such money would reflect the importance of political parties and ensure a level of financial stability. State support would also help to ensure a level of 'fair rivalry' between the parties, so that the ability to compete in an election does not depend solely on attracting private donors.[47] One possible system of extended state funding would provide grants to political parties along the lines suggested by the Houghton Committee, which proposed to provide money to national parties based on the number of votes received in the previous general election.[48] Ewing has supported such an approach, although he argued that the state funds should be conditional on the party incentivising the recruitment of members.[49] In Ewing's view, this is to be preferred to other schemes such as matching grants (where the state matches private donations) or voucher schemes (where the state gives each individual voter a fixed sum to donate to a party of their choice).[50] While such schemes assign a greater role to the individual voter, the Houghton proposals ensures a greater level of stability, so that party funds are less vulnerable to the fluctuation of voter preferences. Again, Ewing's preference for a system of grants in which sums are fixed over a longer period reflects the interest in protecting the political party as the primary player in an election campaign.

The provision of state funds to political parties could be seen as the logical course of action for a social democratic constitution. Where certain actors do not have the means to raise political finance, it is then for the state to provide the resources. As a result, state funding can be vulnerable to characterisation as a type of 'welfare state' for politicians. Moreover, there are questions about why the state needs to finance a private organisation. That objection can easily be met, on the basis that parties themselves perform a key function in the democratic system, which would not function as well if the parties had no resources. State funding is an important step in ensuring that political parties can remain viable without a wealthy donor. In any event, the reforms proposed by Ewing are not for the state to finance all of a party's activities, but to supplement the private sources of income. The bigger challenge in proposals for state support lies in deciding which parties should be eligible for funds. In the current political landscape, there are multiple parties that could claim entitlement. Most of the proposals address this by requiring some threshold of support or level of parliamentary representation to qualify. While there is much sense in

[46] Ewing, *Funding of Political Parties in Britain* (n 6) 177.

[47] Ibid, 182–3. Noting also that such state support might also address the unfairness towards the Alliance under the arrangements in place at the time.

[48] Ewing, *Funding of Political Parties in Britain* (n 6) 139.

[49] Ibid, and on the incentives see Ewing, *The Cost of Democracy* (n 8).

[50] Compare B Ackerman and I Ayres, *Voting with Dollars* (New Haven, Yale University Press, 2002).

that requirement, it could nonetheless help to entrench the existing successful parties that are likely to receive funds and generate a disadvantage for newer political parties.

Aside from the issues of funding, a second key point in Ewing's treatment of political parties is the autonomy of the organisation. Traditionally, such autonomy has been respected in the UK and the internal affairs of political parties are not subject to comprehensive direct state regulation.[51] This does not mean that political parties enjoy 'privileges', and they are largely subject to the ordinary law.[52] In so far as there are legal controls, Ewing notes that 'the courts have expressed reluctance about being drawn into rule-book disputes, preferring the parties themselves to resolve internal conflicts'.[53] That much reflects the status of parties as private organisations. However, as the constitutional importance of political parties has been recognised, demands to impose regulations have grown. For example, political parties are now required to register with the Electoral Commission. Parties now have a legal identity, which allows the organisation to be liable for breaking certain election rules.[54] Political parties are also required to disclose the source of donations above a certain threshold.

While there are good reasons for such regulations, in 2007 Ewing wondered if such steps towards financial accountability will pave the way for further regulations, which could potentially infringe the autonomy of political parties.[55] The potential could arise if regulations were to demand that political parties meet uniform standards in organisation and fundraising. Such an issue would most obviously arise if a cap were to be imposed on the amount of money that any source can donate to a political party. If applied uniformly to individuals and institutions alike, such a cap would break the longstanding link between trade unions and the Labour Party, as the affiliation fees would be prohibited. A special rule to permit larger union donations (as an aggregate on individual subscriptions) may provide one route around that problem, but Ewing has noted that such a position may not be politically acceptable to other political parties.[56] Ewing's opposition to a donation cap rests on a view that it legally compels a change in the traditional structure of the Labour Party.[57] Again, Ewing's argument rests on respect for the political histories of different political parties, which have adopted radically different organisational structures. According to this view, there is no one organisational model that can secure legitimacy.

In terms of money in politics, Ewing's preference is to leave political donations unlimited, subject to rules on permissible sources and transparency. Concerns about the role of money in politics are better addressed through limits on election spending. The reasoning suggests that what goes into the political party is its own affair, and the appropriate target for regulation is the output of those resources (however they are acquired). The approach also fits with emphasis on fair rivalry between political parties, as opposed to attempts to secure equality among individual citizens (as potential donors).[58] According to this view, a large donation may be desirable, in so far as it helps a party compete with a better financed rival. On this point, there are shortcomings to Ewing's position. While the overall recorded

[51] Ewing, *The Cost of Democracy* (n 8) 67.
[52] Ibid, 74.
[53] Ibid, 67.
[54] Ibid, 85.
[55] Ibid, 86.
[56] Ibid, 49.
[57] Ibid, 49 and 231.
[58] Ibid, 47 and 228.

spending on national election campaigns tends to be relatively modest, the modern day scandals tend to focus on large donations to political parties. There is a suspicion that very large donations can help to acquire access to politicians and influence over decisions (even if that is difficult to prove in any case). More broadly, the large donation gives the wealthy individual or organisation a disproportionate voice in deciding which parties should be competitive.[59] Finally, while the history of a political party is important, it does not provide a compelling reason to respect arrangements that can be considered damaging to the current practice of democracy.

The issue of party organisation goes beyond funding and raises questions about the relationship a political party has with its members. Ewing notes that parties can function as 'elite' institutions that do not have mass membership, but which offer candidates and policies.[60] It is often noted that some methods of campaigning (such as media campaigns) no longer depend on having an active membership, but merely require a healthy bank balance. However, Ewing argues that it is through public participation that parties gain their legitimacy.[61] Such a reliance on participation faces a number of challenges. In the long-term, there has been overall decline in the number of people joining a political party, though there has been some resurgence in Labour Party membership in recent years.[62] Tormey has noted that in contemporary politics citizens are no longer satisfied with the vertical hierarchies found in traditional political parties, with a sharp division between the leadership and members.[63] As people have more ways to make their voices heard through digital communications, there is less patience with the traditional indirect opportunities to influence politics through a party.

Political parties have sought to respond to this change by strengthening internal party democracy. Political parties thereby secure legitimacy not only through votes or membership, but by giving party members some say in the party's decisions. In recent years, UK parties have moved in this direction. For example, the Labour Party abandoned its old rules for electing a party leader under an 'electoral college' (consisting of blocs of members, MPs and trade unions) and adopted a process in which nominated candidates (with support from a proportion of the parliamentary party) are put to a vote among party members, affiliated supporters and registered supporters.[64] The Conservative Party has adopted a two stage system for choosing a leader, in which MPs select two candidates, who are then put to a vote of party members on a one member one vote basis.[65] Such moves have been adopted voluntarily by the political parties as a way of making the organisations more democratic and responsive. In his later work, Ewing also supported such moves to empower party members. While such changes should not be mandated by law, he argued

[59] See Rowbottom (n 3).

[60] Ewing, *The Cost of Democracy* (n 8) 32.

[61] Ibid, 33.

[62] Membership of political parties in the UK reached a historic low of 0.8% of the electorate in 2013. This increased to 1.6% in 2018. See L Audickas, N Dempsey and R Keen, 'Membership of Political Parties' (House of Commons Library Briefing Paper SN05125, 2018) https://researchbriefings.parliament.uk/ResearchBriefing/Summary/SN05125.

[63] S Tormey, *The end of representative politics* (Cambridge, Polity, 2015) 94.

[64] N Johnston and L Maer, 'Leadership Elections: Labour Party' (House of Commons Briefing Paper, September 2016) https://researchbriefings.parliament.uk/ResearchBriefing/Summary/SN03938.

[65] N Johnston, 'Leadership elections: Conservative Party' (House of Commons Briefing Paper, December 2018) https://researchbriefings.parliament.uk/ResearchBriefing/Summary/SN01366.

that internal party democracy could be incentivised through a system in which state funding for political parties is conditional on the adoption of a Charter of member's rights. The Charter would give members a say over certain decisions.[66]

The case for a Charter reflects the view that political parties are not like an ordinary private organisation, which also explains why such a requirement would be attached to state funds. Ewing's proposal nonetheless leads to greater regulation of a party's internal affairs, albeit in a fairly modest form of incentivised self-regulation. A more fundamental challenge is to query the wisdom of the moves to internal party democracy. In other words, are stronger rights for members really something that should be incentivised? Ewing finds that the legitimacy of the party is derived from its membership and so the logic follows that legitimacy can be strengthened by giving members greater voice.[67] However, in a defence of the traditional Westminster model of politics, Rosenbluth and Shapiro argue that the move to empowering party members risks damaging the system.[68] The argument runs that party members and supporters tend be more extreme in their political beliefs than the average voter. However, the party leader has to appeal to the average voter to secure votes. A party leader that is more responsive to the extremes is unlikely to gain office. Internal party democracy is thereby seen to place political leaders in a difficult position, which is likely to generate division between MPs (who will seek to appeal to the average voter) and party members. As a result, the job of governing is made harder.[69]

The changes in the election of party leaders has had significant effects. Most obviously, the new rules in the Labour Party leadership elections paved the way for the rise of Jeremy Corbyn (and his victory in a second leadership contest). Corbyn's tenure saw considerable tensions between the Party leadership and the Parliamentary Labour Party. One response is that internal party democracy is not supposed to make anyone's life easier. The cohesion between MPs and party leadership defended by Rosenbluth and Shapiro was achieved by limiting the voice of members. However, there are concerns that internal democracy could result in a tension with the other goals of the party system. For example, if parties become captured by more extreme members, it could lead to MPs leaving a political party (as a small number did under Corbyn) and the fragmentation of parties into smaller groups. That in turn would undermine the basic idea of a political system composed of two larger parties competing for election, balancing one another and seeking to translate its mandate into policy. However, internal party democracy is only one issue in a broader range of challenges to the traditional party system, which will be considered in the concluding section below.

VII. The Future of the Social Democratic Constitution

The discussion has outlined some of the key features of Ewing's work on political finance. Ewing's approach values the social democratic commitment to substantive equality in

[66] Ewing, *The Cost of Democracy* (n 8) 246–48.
[67] Ibid, 33.
[68] FM Rosenbluth and I Shapiro, *Responsible Parties: Saving Democracy From Itself* (New Haven, Yale University Press, 2018) 81–89.
[69] Ibid, 89.

political rights, but in his view such a goal is best realised through representative institutions that have a long and established history in the UK. Rather than advocating the introduction of elaborate schemes to distribute (and redistribute) political money, Ewing sees trade unions and political parties as offering opportunities for political participation and representation. So while Ewing values participation, it is not the type of participation envisaged by radical democrats, but a more arms-length engagement with representative institutions. The proposal for state funding to political parties would provide a major extension of the existing public support currently on offer, but would supplement rather than replace private sources.

The approach taken has the benefit of working within the existing political framework. However, there are a number of criticisms that could be made. This first line of argument is to challenge whether trade unions are the true vehicle for public representation that Ewing's account suggests. One version of the criticism runs that the political decisions are largely made by the union leadership, which is not truly accountable to its members. One response to this criticism is to point out that the political activities of trade unions are already more heavily regulated than other organisations that make political contributions. Moreover, trade unions are membership organisations, so there is a framework for accountability to members. A more fundamental challenge to Ewing's model lies in the long-term decline of trade union membership.[70] As a result, the union-Labour Party link does not provide a channel for the participation and representation of the majority of workers.

A second line of criticism is that Ewing's approach does not adequately address the problem of large donations. Large donations from a single source have been one of the biggest controversies in political finance for the last two decades. Despite the potential for negative publicity, contributions of hundreds of thousands of pounds and sometimes in excess of a million pounds continue to be made. Those individuals making large donations become treated as party grandees, whose views on the party are regularly treated as being newsworthy. Ewing's resistance to a cap on large donations is based on the desire to protect large union donations from further restriction. There are possible routes out of this impasse, such as exceptions for membership organisations with political funds. There are risks and challenges in a donation cap, but the status quo is also deeply problematic. In 2007, Ewing proposed that political parties should be expected set their own limits on the size and source of permissible donations.[71] While that offers flexibility, it is not clear that the major parties would have any incentive to set those limits at the levels necessary to address the public concern at the heart of the scandals.

A broader question lies with the future of Ewing's model to political finance, in so far as it relies on political traditions that are coming under increasing challenge. Recent years have seen a number of commentators lament the decline in some traditional political institutions, in particular of political parties and the mass media.[72] The changes in political communication and activity represent a fundamental shift in the nature of the democratic system.

[70] Though trade union membership is significant. Government figures show that in 2017 around 6.2 million UK employees were members of a trade union. Department for Business, Energy and Industrial Strategy, 'Trade Union Membership 2017' (May 2018) www.gov.uk/government/statistics/trade-union-statistics-2017.

[71] Ewing, *The Cost of Democracy* (n 8).

[72] There is a wide body of literature, see, eg, P Mair, *Ruling the Void: The Hollowing of Western Democracy* (London, Verso, 2013); Y Papadopoulos, *Democracy in Crisis* (Abingdon, Routledge, 2013) ch 1.

The shift is sometimes described as 'post-representative'. Accordingly, traditional parties are increasingly fragile. The sections of society from which Labour and Conservatives traditionally drew support no longer represent the main divisions in society. Moreover, such parties are tainted by past failures and subject to widespread scepticism. Against this background, newer parties are likely to arise and become real contenders for government. Examples often cited from overseas include the Five Star Movement or Podemos. It remains to be seen if the UK will produce a new centrist party, or if parties will divide in response to Brexit. There is also the rise of the 'party within a party' in which factions within a political party become increasingly organised. This trend can be seen with the rise of Momentum within the Labour Party, but less formal examples might be the inter-party plotting that takes place among factions of MPs via WhatsApp groups.

More fundamentally, the criticism runs that much of politics takes place outside of the formal political institutions. Political campaigning is conducted through networks which include interest and advocacy groups, bloggers and social media campaigners, think tanks and alternative news sources. John Keane talks about the emergence of non-elected representatives.[73] Such politics can be conducted outside of elections, with organisations using digital communications to mobilise and apply pressure on political actors at any time. People are less reliant on the traditional representative institutions when they can contact a politician directly via social media or organise into informal groups with like-minded individuals. Many people are also engaged in political movements that respond to events or mobilise through a sense of injustice.[74] The 'Me Too' movement provides one example of the way individuals can make their voices heard outside of formal politics. Elections, of course, remain important,[75] but may not provide the definitive democratic moment. Such a view suggests that the traditional model of representative democracy (associated with Westminster), around which the rules of political finance are focused, are being supplemented through other means of representation and direct activity. To the champions of the new politics, the changes may represent a redistribution of the means required to participate meaningfully. While the results are seen to have facilitated a more polarised and aggressive political landscape, the response may simply be that this is what a democracy looks like and that nobody said it would be good mannered.

Not everyone greets such changes with enthusiasm. Minimal democrats query whether the increased levels of participation are really desirable. Under this view, there are limits to what mass democracy can really achieve and democratic participation can provide a very blunt signal of the public's priorities. The limited and remote model of traditional representative democracy may be the closest thing to a functioning democracy on a mass scale. One does not, however, have to be a minimal democrat to express some scepticism about the changes in political campaigning. For present purposes, any conclusion that the new politics is truly egalitarian should be resisted.[76] The new opportunities to participate via digital communications depend on a handful of US technology firms, which can control the terms on which people debate, what content is likely to be seen, and have access to

[73] J Keane, *Democracy and Media Decadence* (Cambridge, Cambridge University Press, 2013).
[74] Tormey (n 63) 87.
[75] Keane (n 73).
[76] See M Hindman, *The Internet Trap* (Princeton, Princeton University Press, 2018), Rowbottom (n 3).

the vast amounts of user data. Money can still secure advantages in the system, whether through advertising, through ownership of media outlets or the sponsorship of research organisations (to name a few methods). Various lobbying organisations spend significant sums on social media advertisements (although this may occur outside the context of an election), for example in encouraging people to contact their MP.[77] Moreover, the skills required to participate in the alternative forms of political activity (whether on or offline) are not equally distributed.[78] This raises a significant challenge for political finance. The question is not simply a matter of who funds political parties, but also who finances the various other political actors. As the range of political actors has become more diffuse and decentralised, the activities are harder to monitor and scrutinise.

Regardless of one's view of such changes, the system of election finance law is in need of a major update.[79] For example, there is a need to ensure the identity of political campaigners on the digital media is transparent.[80] There is also a need for greater transparency in the categories of parties' campaign spending.[81] The Electoral Commission has called for greater clarity on rules prohibiting foreign organisations spending money on elections and referendums.[82] More broadly, it is also not clear how well the existing regulations capture and identify the money spent by the various third parties in an election campaign. There are further issues about the acquisition and use of data to engage in practices of microtargeting. While the old problems have not gone away, elections can no longer be characterised as a competition between the two main parties, supported by a set of reliable donors to provide an approximate balance in resources.

Moreover, the 'post-representative' diagnosis does not have to be accepted as inevitable. While the forms of political communication are changing, political parties still play a significant role, given that elections provide the means for accessing and controlling state power. For all the talk of declining party membership in recent years, Jeremy Corbyn's leadership has done much to revive Labour Party membership levels.[83] Moreover, steps could be taken to restore the position of traditional representative institutions. Along such lines, the state funding of political parties may be more important than ever, to ensure that political organisations enjoy a level of stability in the face of such changes. Matching grants attached to donations to political parties could incentivise people to give money to political parties, as opposed to other organisations. While there is much merit in such proposals, fully restoring the political settlements that emerged in the mid-twentieth century is not an option. The challenge for a constitution of social democracy is to ensure that changes do not upturn a system that in practice enables political rights to participation and representation to be exercised regardless of wealth.

[77] See A Hern, '£250,000 ad campaign urges voters to oppose May's Brexit plan' *The Guardian* (London, 20 October 2018) and J Waterson 'Facebook Brexit ads secretly run by staff of Lynton Crosby firm' *The Guardian* (London, 3 April 2019).

[78] Papadopoulos (n 72) 33 and 36.

[79] See Electoral Commission, 'Digital campaigning: Increasing transparency for voters' (June 2018) www.electoralcommission.org.uk/media/1831.

[80] Ibid, 9.

[81] Ibid, 12.

[82] Ibid, 18.

[83] In 2018, the Labour Party was reported to have 540,000 members, see Audickas, Dempsey and Keen (n 62).

11

The Abolition of Class Government

TIMOTHY K KUHNER*

It is a critical time to discuss the resurrection and possible entrenchment of social democracy, although it might not seem like it at first. Since 2014, the need to stop liberal democracy from sliding into authoritarianism has appeared much more urgent. Progressives and social democrats expected growing popular dissatisfaction with the failures of liberal democracy – including rising inequality, global trade inequities, systemic corruption, and political responsiveness to elites. But, rather than gains for labour and the left, popular dissatisfaction has led to a resurgence in racism, sexism, xenophobia, vehement nationalism, religious intolerance, disdain for the rule of law, and 'strongmen' type leaders. With illiberal populists on the extreme right outperforming electoral expectations, undoing their nations' democracies from within, the fate of liberal democracy has become the most salient issue of the day.

The fate of social democracy, by contrast, has appeared to be sealed for some time. In 1993, Cambridge University Press published a new translation of Eduard Bernstein's 1899 work *The Preconditions of Socialism*, probably the seminal book on social democracy. Citing the end of communism, a reviewer noted that it was an opportune time to consider the viability of social democracy.[1] But the outcome of that moment of history soon became a matter of public record. The globalisation of democracy that occurred in the 1990s turned out to be, for the most part, synonymous with the globalisation of capitalist democracy – commodification, privatisation, deregulation, austerity, and the like. As of the turn of the century, a consensus emerged that social democracy had ended, at least outside of Scandinavian countries.[2] The record reflects social democracy's golden age from roughly 1945 to 1970 and its status as an endangered political species shortly thereafter.

Under these circumstances, however, social democracy's decline bodes in its favour. Neoliberalism rose to power as social democracy fell, and now illiberal populism and authoritarianism are rising thanks to the socio-economic injustices of neoliberalism. If there were ever a political reason to reinfuse democracy with its social content, one would

* For comments, the author thanks Treasa Dunworth, Keith Ewing, Caroline Foster, Anna Hood, John Ip, Janet McLean, Jane Norton, Scott Optican, Arie Rosen, Nicholas Thoburn, Warren Swain, Hanna Wilberg, David Williams, and Edward Willis. For editorial assistance, the author thanks Scott Yang.

[1] V Geoghegan, 'The Preconditions of Socialism: Eduard Bernstein', edited and translated by Henry Tudor (Cambridge, Cambridge University Press, 1993); (1996) 22 *History of European Ideas* 153, 153–4.

[2] See, S Berman, 'The Roots and Rationale of Social Democracy' in EF Paul, FD Miller Jr, and J Paul (eds), *After Socialism* (New York, Cambridge University Press, 2003) 113.

not have to look past these trends to find it. But of course an urgent matter of political ecology bodes in social democracy's favour as well, namely the game of 'chicken' playing out between government in the private interest and catastrophic climate change.[3] Social democracy could prove itself liberalism's rightful heir by deposing neoliberalism and illiberalism, and begin a new era by creating a green economy and responding to climate change.

And yet, even Jeremy Corbyn as Prime Minister, Bernie Sanders as President, Alexandria Ocasio Cortez as Senate Majority Leader,[4] and a global reversal of all offending laws and policies might make little difference in the medium to long term. That is because of the elephant in the room: social democracy's track record of succumbing to everything from revolutionary Marxism to economic libertarianism. That colossal failure of the ideology, the movement, and the associated political parties to identify and entrench their own foundational principle within the constitutional order would have to be remedied. Otherwise there is no realistic scenario in which social democracy could endure.

By 'foundational principle,' I mean a core structural prescription about how the economy and the state are supposed to operate. Take the abolition of private control of the means of economic production and the establishment of communist party control over the means of political production – those foundational principles define Marxism and communism. Or consider the abolition of public control of the means of economic production and the consolidation of private control of the means of political production – those foundational principles define capitalist democracy. If it ever wishes to be resuscitated and entrenched, I believe social democracy must define its own foundational principle.

In this chapter, I propose a foundational principle for social democracy: the abolition of private control over the means of political production, including elections and appointments, campaign and party finance, rights of popular participation, and legislative and policy-making processes. Or, for short, the abolition of class government.

To alter a foundational principle is to move from one political system to another, and to alter history in the process. That is what social democracy began to do when it revised orthodox Marxism by eschewing violent revolution in favour of enhanced democracy and regulating capitalism in the public interest instead of expropriating private property and nationalising industries. And social democracy began to alter history once more when it revised capitalist democracy by securing labour rights, safer working conditions, a minimum wage, public health care, public education, pensions, and other social programs and entitlements. But, social democracy failed to prevent Stalinism, Maoism, and Soviet Communism. Similarly, it failed to prevent Reagan's and Thatcher's conservative revolutions, and the neoliberal global order that followed. For all its success in revising the foundational principles of other political systems, social democracy never seemed to identify and entrench its own.

There are many seemingly foundational arrangements that fall short of being definitive in the way I have in mind. Take, for example, such legal foundations as a parliamentary system, a presidential system, a common law system, a civil law system, a full separation of powers, voting systems such as mixed member proportional or first past the post, or

[3] Neither appears prepared to swerve – not the fossil fuels oligarchs and their allies in government, nor atmospheric chemistry. The former will be dead and out of office, while the latter thrashes and torments posterity for millennia if not a mega-annum.

[4] (Until she's old enough to be President.)

even a written constitution. However entrenched and influential, such arrangements are not definitive of the political system on the whole. Political systems are defined by matters of authority and power, which depend, at base, on control of economic production (supply of goods, services, and ultimately wealth) and control of political production (supply of office-holders, law, policy, and ultimately authority). Pharos, emperors, kings, queens, theocrats, and dictators all knew that effective political authority depended on control over economy and state – perhaps that is why such rulers merged them and did not dare emancipate either one from vertical compulsion. Systems of political rule on the basis of divine favour, royal birth, and military control are all based on entrenched power structures.

Private control of the means of economic production is exactly that: a power structure (underlying capitalism); the same goes for state control of economic production (underlying Marxism). Social democracy's balance between the two is just a compromise between power structures, not an actual political system. And it leads to incessant rent seeking – constant pressure from short-term vested interests (over and above diffuse and long-term interests) for favourable laws and policies. The question is, what would stop wealthy pressure groups from tipping the balance and controlling the political economy (to the effect of producing today's levels of inequality, precarity, cultural backlash, and carbon emissions)?

Social democracy opposed the abolition of private control over the means of economic production, and wisely so. But it failed to pair that stance with its necessary corollary: an unbending insistence on the abolition of private control over the means of political production. I refer to the entrenchment of a popular power structure in the form of a political sphere that is autonomous from the economic sphere, and thus insusceptible to financial capture. This is a necessary structural condition for obtaining the fruits of that abolition of private government: political rule on the basis of consent, participation, responsiveness, representation, accountability, and ultimately sovereignty, all of a popular variety. Or to put it yet another way, the foundational principle to be guaranteed is freedom, equality, and self-governance for all, regardless not just of race, sex, religion and the like, but also property (or wealth).

The *constitution* of social democracy represents the proper framing of the issue today, but it does not invite a law and policy wish list. Rather, it invites the entrenchment of social democracy's own native power structure. Although the abolition of class government requires a strong constitutional baseline spanning the law of democracy and anti-corruption law, this chapter does not analyse present-day trends in those fields or undertake a comparative analysis of their laws. Its tasks are more rudimentary: identifying this foundational principle in the definition of social democracy, highlighting its relevance to democratic backsliding (past and present), and noting its current articulation in political theory and international agreements. I see these as the first steps on the path to a constitution of social democracy.

I. What is Social Democracy?

Social democracy is commonly defined as the things that it does, not what it is inherently. For example, it is famous for achieving certain differences in degree with liberal democracy: more regulation of the economy in the public interest, less privatisation; more social provisions by government – such as universal health care and free education all the way through the university level; greater benefits for the poor and the elderly; greater empowerment for workers and greater rights and protections for unions; and a social democratic political party (usually under the guises of labour) that achieves a greater presence in government. Every democracy in the world could be mapped along these lines, forming a multidimensional spectrum. But at some point and in certain moments in history, such differences in degree correspond to an autonomous philosophy, movement, party formation, and political system. Keating and McCrone's definition, a 'third way between revolutionary Marxism and unbridled capitalism,'[5] raises preliminary issues.

Let us begin with social democracy's relationship with Marxism, which is the focus of Sheri Berman's definition:

> [T]he movement and ideology that emerged from the democratic revisionism that Eduard Bernstein and others espoused in the late nineteenth and early twentieth centuries, which itself is best understood not as an updated version of orthodox Marxism (as most accounts would have it), but as a fundamental rejection of some of its most important principles.[6]

One such principle was historical materialism – that supposed inevitability of class conflict and capitalism's collapse. When Bernstein's papers were collected after his death, there surfaced an envelope with handwritten notes on the back: 'Peasants do not sink; middle class does not disappear; crises do not grow even larger; misery and serfdom do not increase'.[7] Economic progress in the Germany of Bernstein's day seemed to disprove Marx's mid nineteenth-century fatalism. Social democrats believed that universal suffrage could change history, further contradicting scientific socialism's determinism. The proletariat could gain representation, regulate the economy, and improve their lot. Eventually, 'The Marxist view of democracy as a "bourgeois façade" was abandoned'.[8]

Making room for human agency within the existing economic and political panorama led social democrats to abandon another core Marxist principle: revolutionary struggle. Bernstein wrote that democracy 'is a weapon in the struggle for socialism' and 'the form in which socialism will be realised'.[9] Like other types of socialists, Bernstein wholeheartedly agitated for 'the transition from the modern social order to a higher one,' but he added the words 'without compulsive upheavals'.[10] 'Social democracy,' he emphasised, 'has no enthusiasm for a violent revolution'.[11]

That brings us to the second issue, social democracy's relationship with capitalism. Two of the reasons why social democracy does not resort to violent revolution pertain to this relationship: first, a belief in 'the necessity and instrumental value of the market'[12] and, second, a belief in the efficacy of regulation, what Andrew Levine describes as 'reforms designed to mitigate capitalism's worst features'.[13]

[5] M Keating and D McCrone, 'The Crisis of Social Democracy' in M Keating and D McCrone (eds), *The Crisis of Social Democracy in Europe* (Edinburgh, Edinburgh University Press, 2013) 1–2.

[6] Berman (n 2) 114.

[7] Geoghegan (n 1) 154.

[8] 'Social Democracy' (*Encyclopaedia Britannica*) www.britannica.com/topic/social-democracy.

[9] E Bernstein, *The Preconditions of Socialism* (H Tudor trans, Cambridge, Cambridge University Press, 1993) 142.

[10] Ibid, 145.

[11] Ibid, 158.

[12] Keating and McCrone (n 5) 3.

[13] A Levine, 'The Political Theory of Social Democracy' (1976) 6 *Canadian Journal of Philosophy* 183, 192.

Implementing such reforms, social democracy brings about social capitalism, which Clauss Offe calls 'organized,' 'embedded' and 'regulated' capitalism.'[14] Informed by 'the precepts of a social market economy,'[15] Offe contrasts social capitalism with liberal capitalism – or European capitalism versus Anglo-American capitalism. Though this may be a coarse distinction, it highlights a series of key juxtapositions, including:

> equality versus efficiency, collective bargaining versus individual contracting, cooperation versus conflict, rights versus resources, wage moderation versus distributive conflict, ... social partnership versus class conflict, ... associational collectivism versus individualism, social security versus competitiveness, [and] politics versus markets.[16]

Opting for the first choice in the pairings above, social democracy seeks to prevent profit-maximising behaviour from leading to domination by concentrated capital. It also seeks to enable ordinary people to benefit from economic freedoms and, collectively, create an economic system consistent with their needs and values (the economic system being embedded in politics and culture, after all).

Implementing such reforms, social democracy demonstrated that government could usefully regulate the market. But what could make such regulations long-lasting? Durability could only come from social democracy's prescriptions for the political system itself – the motor for producing and, later, protecting social democracy's policies.

Through critical of social democracy, Frederick Engels and Karl Kautsky pointed to its political requirement. Engels wrote:

> One could imagine the old society peacefully growing into the new in those countries where a national assembly represents social power and is free to implement what it wants, in accordance with the majority of the people.[17]

Today, however, the notion of a representative legislative body is practically laughable. Campaign and party finance, lobbying, conflicts of interest, corruption, and the decline of countervailing power are among the structural obstacles to the kind of peaceful transformation referenced by Engels.

Also writing before Bernstein, Karl Kautsky referred to the same overarching issue of popular responsiveness and representation:

> Whenever the proletariat engages in parliamentary activity as a self-conscious class, parliamentarism begins to change its character. It ceases to be a mere tool in the hands of the bourgeoisie. [Such organized political participation] is the most powerful lever that can be utilized to raise the proletariat out of its economic, social and moral degradation.[18]

But why would Kautsky assume that engagement and participation by the proletariat would lead to changes? What legal conditions would be required in order for participation by the

[14] C Offe, 'The European Model of 'Social' Capitalism: Can It Survive European Integration?' (2003) 11 *The Journal of Political Philosophy* 437, 447.

[15] Ibid, 447.

[16] Ibid, 441.

[17] Engels, quoted in MB Steger, *The Quest for Evolutionary Socialism: Eduard Bernstein and Social Democracy* (Cambridge, Cambridge University Press, 1997) 144.

[18] K Kautsky, *The Class Struggle (Erfurt Program)* (WE Bohn trans, Chicago, Charles H. Kerr & Company, 1910) 188.

lower social classes to be a powerful lever? Just two pages earlier, Kautsky admitted that '[t]he influence of a class within a parliament depends, in the first place, on the nature of the electoral law in force;'[19] or, more broadly, it depends on the field now known as the law of democracy.[20]

In the preface to the 1909 English translation of his *Evolutionary Socialism* (also translated under the title *The Preconditions of Socialism*), Bernstein ably summed up the overall point that I think Engels and Kautsky meant to communicate:

> I strongly believe in the socialist movement, in the march forward of the working classes, who step by step must work out their emancipation by changing society from the domain of a commercial land-holding oligarchy to *a real democracy* … guided by the interests of those who work and create.[21]

A subsequent translation of the same book in which Bernstein wrote his 1909 preface contains the key phrases for what 'real democracy' would entail. Here we have the foundational principle for social democracy: 'the abolition of all laws which limit the universal equality of rights,' the '*absence* of class government,'[22] and the '*abolition* of class government'.[23] These formulations are shorthand for structural safeguards against oligarchy and structural guarantees for good government.

Major episodes of democratic backsliding show the urgency of those safeguards, as well as the difficulty of ever obtaining them. The episodes I have in mind feature false consciousness and fascism, historically, and their modern-day equivalents in rising populism of the illiberal and authoritarian variety. Today's authoritarianism was preceded by class government, that is, government by and for such industries as banking and finance, fossil fuels, agribusiness, and pharmaceuticals. And despite today's rising populism, neoliberalism persists across most countries that hold elections, making it still the main obstacle to social democracy. But if Karl Polanyi was right that a similar devotion to the needs of capital caused the rise of fascism in the 1920s, then we may have a historical pattern on our hands. That is an additional problem that social democracy would be uniquely positioned to solve.

II. Old-school Backsliding

The Revolutions of 1848 swept through much of Europe and even parts of South America. They induced the Prussian King to join in and forced the resignation of Klemens von Metterich, the First Chancellor of the Austrian Empire.[24] Workers asserted their socioeconomic interests so vigorously that it appeared as though monarchies had really been

[19] Ibid, 186–7.

[20] See KD Ewing, TK Kuhner, and J Tham, 'Editors' Preface' (2017) 28 *King's Law Journal* 161, 161–2.

[21] E Bernstein, 'Preface to the English Edition' in *Evolutionary Socialism: A Criticism and Affirmation* (EC Harvey trans, London, Independent Labour Party, 1909) xxii–xxiii.

[22] Bernstein, *The Preconditions of Socialism* (n 9) 140.

[23] Ibid, 143.

[24] See P Jones, *The 1848 Revolutions*, 2nd edn (New York, Routledge, 2013) 3–4. I include the 1848 Revolutions in the category of socialist movements even though the revolutionary regimes ultimately disagreed about the desirability of adding social and economic rights to civil and political ones. The Revolutions 'aroused workers into defending their social and economic interests.' 17 Arising out of a major economic crisis, the impetus was social even though the immediate results were primarily liberal.

defeated, popular constitutions firmly established, and democracy placed on the path to consolidation. But that impression was brief. As Jones notes, 'If a survey for a political map of Europe had been carried out in 1845 and then repeated ten years later it would have revealed few differences'.[25]

The revolutionary democratic freedoms that had just been established led to an apparently popular counterrevolution. As Rapport notes, 'the public was carefully "managed" by appeals to monarchy, patriotism, religion and property against the spectre of "anarchy", "communism" and "terror"'.[26] Once conservative and counter-revolutionary forces gained the upper hand, 'Europe experienced a decade of iron-fisted rule which made the pre-revolutionary conservative order seem positively lax'.[27] This turn of events helps explain Jones' conclusion: at the end of the day, the Revolutions 'destroyed the idealistic, almost mystical, belief that universal suffrage would bring with it social equality'.[28] That, perhaps, was the longest-lasting impression created by the 1848 Revolutions.

France was a particularly vexing case. While the February Revolution of 1848 did succeed in ending the July Monarchy of Orleans, the June Days uprising that followed was violently repressed by the military, signalling that France would not become a democratic and social republic after all. Louis-Napoleon Bonaparte's election later that year and 'self-coup' three years thereafter confirmed the point. Napoleon III's 17-year reign as the Emperor of the French is hardly what the revolutionaries had in mind. And yet, consistent with the impression that universal male suffrage was no panacea, a large portion of the public supported a military end to the June uprising, Bonaparte won his 1848 election by a large margin, and his 1851 coup was met by public apathy, even support.[29]

This outcome was all the more damning in light of the dictatorship and empire that followed the French Revolution (of 1789). Bernstein wrote that 'the modern socialist movement, as well as its theoretical expression is … the product of the great French Revolution and of the conceptions of right which, through its general influence, gained general acceptance in the wages and labour movement'.[30] But writing in 1899, Bernstein could surely see, like Marx, that 1848 ultimately stood as a farcical repetition of the eventual outcome of 1789. What the modern socialist movement really had to wrestle with was counterrevolution and its own failure to entrench itself.

In Ann-Sophie Chambost's articulation, the failure of France's 'bold experiment in popular sovereignty … call[ed] into question the same "people" which European radicals had sought to make sovereign ever since the French Revolution'.[31] Such conservative 180-degree shifts in revolutionary trajectory ushered in the original *What's the Matter with Kansas* literature, the attempt of Marxists, mostly, to account for all the citizens outside

[25] Ibid, 98.

[26] M Rapport, '1848: European Revolutions' in B Isakhan and S Stockwell (eds), *The Edinburgh Companion to the History of Democracy* (Edinburgh, Edinburgh University Press, 2012) 282–92, 19–20 of pre-publication version, available at http://eprints.gla.ac.uk/78871/1/78871.pdf.

[27] Ibid, 20.

[28] Jones, *The 1848 Revolutions* 102.

[29] See A Chambost, 'Socialist Visions of Direct Democracy: The Mid-Century Crisis in Popular Sovereignty and the Constitutional Legacy of the Jacobins' in D Moggach and GS Jones (eds), *The 1848 Revolutions and European Political Thought* (Cambridge, Cambridge University Press, 2018) 112.

[30] Bernstein, *The Preconditions of Socialism* (n 9) 160.

[31] Chambost (n 29) 112.

the bourgeoisies who lacked class consciousness. A large part of the blame for socialism's fragility fell on them.

For Marx, the 'Lumpenproletariat' was a 'nebulous, disintegrated mass' of wide-raging elements, including 'roues … ruined and adventurous offshoots of the bourgeoisie … vagabonds, discharged soldiers, discharged jailbirds, escaped galley slaves, swindlers … tricksters, gamblers [and] brothel keepers'.[32] And according to Marx it was here, in this non-class that Louis Bonaparte, 'the chief of the lumpenproletariat', found his 'kindred element'. Together, they proceeded to 'benefit themselves at the expense of the laboring nation'.[33] Marx's description of the Lumpenproletariat as a ragged bunch of drunks and knaves was one part observation, one part hostility – the latter inspired first from the odious fact that these elements of society allowed the tragedy of Napoleon I to repeat itself in the form of Napoleon III and, second (perhaps), from the fact that the successful counter-revolutionary movement that they supported contradicted Marx's historical method.

The lack of class consciousness was a key element in explanations of such counter-revolutionary outcomes. Nicholas Thoburn highlights a central aspect of Marx and Engels' explanation. A key to the lumpenproletariat's deplorable orientation to revolutionary change lay in its existence 'outside of productive relations,' a status that spanned Engels' description of 'those who do not wish to work' as lumpenproletariat and Marx's description of the financial aristocracy as 'the lumpenproletariat reborn at the pinnacle of bourgeois society'.[34] The July Monarchy that preceded the French Revolution of 1848 was, in Marx's words, 'nothing more than a joint-stock company for the exploitation of France's national wealth' characterised by 'the same prostitution, the same blatant swindling, the same mania for self-enrichment – not from production but by sleight-of-hand with other people's wealth'.[35] Writing of crony capitalists and backstreet swindlers uninterested in serious judgments about productive relations, Marx and Engels highlighted the difficulty of initiating and maintaining popular revolutions.

Analysing Mussolini's ascent to power, Leon Trotsky grouped 'the declassed and demoralized lumpenproletariat' together in the same category with the petty bourgeoisie as 'human beings who finance capital itself has brought to desperation and frenzy'.[36] In the rise of fascism against the Italian proletariat, Trotsky saw much more than the counter-revolutionary turn of the 1848 Revolutions – much more than the conservative's ability to benefit from popular sovereignty through manipulative appeals to patriotism and warnings of communism and revolutionary terror. Instead, Trotsky described the use of terror to dismantle the gains made by peasants and laborers. He wrote that as of September 1920 'the seizure of factories and industries by the workers' made the dictatorship of the proletariat 'an actual fact' and that consolidation would have been possible through better organisation and analysis. But instead, 'social democracy took fright and sprang back'. And then, just two months after the revolution paused, the Blackshirts began their terrorist campaign, murdering social democratic councilmen and labour leaders, destroying the offices of the organisations they abhorred, and intimidating the general population.[37]

[32] Marx, quoted in N Thoburn, *Deleuze, Marx and Politics* (New York, Routledge, 2003) 53.
[33] Marx, quoted at ibid, 53.
[34] Ibid, 57.
[35] Marx, quoted at ibid, 57.
[36] L Trotsky, *Fascism: What It Is and How to Fight It* (London, Pathfinder Press, 1996) 9.
[37] Trotsky describes these events of 21 November 1920 at ibid, 10.

Could any form of constitutional entrenchment have saved Italian socialism from Mussolini's 'voluntary militia for national security'? There was not time for entrenchment, which was partly the fault of revolutionary socialism itself. The more the Italian socialists caused large landowners and industrialists to panic and the more they alienated former soldiers, the less time they had had for consolidation. But if Trotsky was right about 'the fascist agency … utilizing the petty bourgeoisie as a battering ram'[38] and then 'strangl[ing] it within the vise of the bourgeois state,'[39] then 1920s Italy was not just an example of revolutionary over-reaching or false consciousness on the part of the lumpenproletariat. It was, rather, one of several notorious examples of a tyrannical union between industrialists, landowners, the military, and a charismatic authoritarian leader.[40] Trotsky alleged that once fascism prevails 'finance capital directly and immediately gathers into its hands, as in a vise of steel, all the organs and institutions of sovereignty'.[41]

Everyone interested in modern-day backsliding should take note of Trotsky's emphasis on a manipulative form of class conflict. He does not malign the lumpenproletariat like Marx and Engels did. Rather, he sympathises with it as having been 'entirely ruined by big capital' and laments that '[i]ts dissatisfaction, indignation, and despair are diverted by the fascists away from big capital and against the workers'.[42]

Regarding this dynamic, Karl Polanyi believed that Von Mises and Hayek's successful overtures against popular economic input gave way to rising fascism.[43] In summary, advocates of a self-regulating market produce 'weakened and unresponsive democracies … vulnerable to attack by extremist leaders bent on imposing authoritarian solutions'.[44] This mirrors Trotsky's description of a strategic use of class conflict in the service of class government: 'big capital ruins the middle classes and then, with the help of hired fascist demagogues, incites the despairing petty bourgeois against the workers'.[45] (Perhaps he had been watching Fox News and reading Breitbart.)

These historical examples are about as far as one can get from Bernstein's 'real democracy' or Kautsky's description of a politics that 'raises the proletariat out of its economic, social and moral degradation.' They provide the playbook for today's illiberal populists, a way to turn neoliberalism into a gateway for modern-day authoritarianism.

III. Modern-day Backsliding

After its 30-year 'golden age' commencing after the Second World War,[46] social democracy faltered during the 1970s and 1980s. Explanations for this decline range from a rather

[38] Ibid, 9.

[39] Ibid, 12.

[40] See M Casson, 'A Cultural Theory of Industrial Policy' in JF Peck and G Federico (eds), *European Industrial Policy: The Twentieth Century Experience* (Oxford, Oxford University Press, 1999), 404 (stating that this union was common to Hitler's and Franco's power configurations as well).

[41] Trotsky (n 36) 9.

[42] Ibid, 34.

[43] See FL Block and MR Somers, *The Power of Market Fundamentalism: Karl Polanyi's Critique* (Cambridge, Massachusetts, Harvard University Press, 2014) 42.

[44] Ibid, 35.

[45] Trotsky (n 36) 34.

[46] See B Jackson, 'Social Democracy' in M Freeden and M Stears (eds), *The Oxford Handbook of Political Ideologies* (Oxford, Oxford University Press, 2013) 352–3.

innocent complacency bred of success to a more nefarious combination of economic downturn and 'feisty neoliberal and right-wing populist challenges'.[47] In this section, I focus on neoliberalism and populism, which are the most relevant factors today.

In 1995, KD Ewing proposed a programme of constitutional reform based on 'fundamental goals and principles' belonging to social democracy. Those were: popular sovereignty as the basis for constitutional authority; the social, economic, and cultural welfare of citizens as the principal purposes for the exercise of state authority; and the requirement that the state's socio-economic objectives be realised in a manner consistent with individuals' civil liberties and political freedom.[48] The 1990s featured an astounding wave of globalisation, which could have made good on those goals and principles. On the surface level at least, democracy went from a minority position in 1989 to a dominant position by the turn of the century, present in two thirds of all countries. But deeper down, the spread of elections was accompanied by a form of systemic corruption unique to the democratic context.

Writing during this time period, Alexander and Rei noted that 'incredibly large monetary contributions … have permeated the world of politics in most continents'.[49] A 2003 global survey by the United States Agency for International Development (USAID) backed up this conclusion, finding that '[p]ayback of campaign debts in the form of political favors breeds a type of corruption that is commonly encountered around the world'.[50] By USAID's estimation, 65 per cent of the 118 democracies surveyed had low or virtually no political transparency.[51] All of this suggested a tremendous influx of private wealth into political processes with insufficient safeguards, which would naturally serve to oppose Ewing's public-spirited goals and principles.

That is the context for understanding the major initiatives of the time, such as the North American Free Trade Agreement (NAFTA), the World Trade Organisation (WTO), and international lending throughout the developing world. While free trade raised concerns for labour, the environment, and underdeveloped countries, international financial institutions magnified those concerns by insisting on austerity and 'structural adjustment'. And even before the consolidation of these initiatives, Ralf Dahrendorf and Anthony Giddens had announced, respectively, the impossibility of reviving any of socialism's variants and social democracy's 'defensive' if not 'moribund' status.[52] Ewing's willingness to push the envelope of a constitution of social democracy in the mid-1990s amounted to an effort to change these realities. But his recommendations were not followed and the problem grew.

In his 2015 exposé *The Death of Social Europe*, Ewing wrote that '[t]he contemporary focus is on new economic governance arrangements and the subordination of labour rights generally'.[53] He noted that European guidelines and treaties increasingly emphasised 'international competitiveness,' rather than a social market or social justice.[54] He characterised

[47] Berman (n 2) 114.
[48] KD Ewing, 'Democratic Socialism and Labour Law' (1995) 24 *Industrial Law Journal* 103, 105.
[49] HE Alexander and R Shiratori, 'Introduction' in HE Alexander and R Shiratori (eds), *Comparative Political Finance Among the Democracies* (Boulder, Westview Press, 1994).
[50] Office of Democracy and Governance, *Money in Politics Handbook: A Guide to Increasing Transparency in Emerging Democracies* (United States Agency for International Development (USAID), Washington D.C, 2003), available at www.usaid.gov/our_work/democracy_and_governance/publications/pdfs/pnacr223.pdf.
[51] Ibid, 2.
[52] Quoted in Berman (n 2) 113.
[53] KD Ewing, 'The Death of Social Europe' (2015) 26 King's Law Journal 76, 87.
[54] Ibid, 88.

European Commission guidelines as evaluating 'the right framework conditions for wage bargaining' in terms of 'competitiveness,' which Ewing called 'a prescription for collective bargaining deregulation by a technocratic process about which most citizens in most member states are largely unaware'.[55] He justified that claim by documenting a deregulatory trend in minimum wage and collective bargaining in Romania, Greece, and Ireland,[56] and significant deregulatory pressure in Italy, Spain, Belgium, and Portugal.[57]

The Death of Social Europe was well complemented by another recent assessment, Michael Keating and David McCrone's edited volume *The Crisis of Social Democracy*. Their diagnosis is stated in the broader terms of a 'transformation of capitalism … undermin[ing] many social democratic ideas and practices,' the '[o]ld class divisions no longer mak[ing] sense and the idea of a 'working class' [being] ever more elusive, creating problems for those parties … which rested on it,' the decline in trade union membership and the manufacturing industry creating 'a "missing middle" in the class spectrum,' the political right exploiting the divisions created by the welfare state, neoliberal ideology, global free trade and a 'race to the bottom'.[58]

In light of these reports of a social democratic crisis and even more damning analyses, such as Wendy Brown's 2015 work on the defeat of social-democratic commitments around the world by neoliberalism,[59] Ewing's 1995 prescription should be considered prophetic. He framed a constitution of social democracy as 'a possible restraint to future governments trying to turn back the clock of social democratic progress.'[60] Contemplating the return of 'Thatcher-like governments,' Ewing raised the strategically important issue of entrenchment:

> [W]hether democratic socialism in power should make more responsible use of the constitutional machinery of the State to protect its gains from such easy erosion.[61]

That use of constitutional machinery never came to pass in most countries, but easy erosion did – indeed, widespread programmatic erosion, as those 2015 analyses made clear. And that *death of social Europe, crisis of social democracy*, and *undoing of the demos* was only the beginning.

Since 2015, eulogies for social democracy have been drowned out by high-decibel calls to save liberal democracy, which turns out not to have entrenched itself either. Rising illiberal populism is most obvious in the cases of Brazil, the US, Turkey, Poland, Hungary, Italy, India, Austria, and, some would say, Brexit, but Pippa Norris' 2017 analysis points to a broader phenomenon. Illiberal populists occupy three times the number of parliamentary seats in Europe than they did in the 1960s.[62] Norris' estimation of a sustained threat – that populist-authoritarian growth 'threatens liberal democracy …. by challenging the core values of pluralism, social tolerance, rule of law, human rights, and

[55] Ibid (emphasis omitted).
[56] Ibid, 90.
[57] Ibid, 89.
[58] Keating and McCrone (n 5) 6–7.
[59] W Brown, *Undoing the Demos: Neoliberalism's Stealth Revolution* (Cambridge, Massachusetts, The MIT Press, 2015).
[60] Ewing (n 48) 107.
[61] Ibid, 107.
[62] P Norris, 'Is Western Democracy Backsliding? Diagnosing the Risks' (2017) *Harvard Kennedy School Faculty Research Working Paper Series* 10, accessed 22 August 2019.

freedoms' – is constantly repeated.[63] Bookshelves now groan under the weight of the new literature – including *The Populist Explosion, The Global Rise of Populism, How Democracies Die, and Fascism: A Warning.*[64] Is it time to stop grieving for social democracy and begin defending liberal democracy exclusively?

Actually, a brief review of the causes of rising illiberal populism suggests that social democracy is the solution and the effort to save democracy ought to be focused there. Surveying the literature on those causes, Tom Ginsburg, Aziz Hug, and Mila Versteeg home in on economic instability, the 'growing gap between the rich and the poor globally,' disruptive aspects of economic globalisation, and the 'subordinat[ion] of democratic constitutionalism to geopolitical ends' by the American, Russian, and Chinese empires.[65] Institutional diagnoses, such as Samuel Issacharoff's discussion of 'the accelerated decline of political parties and other institutional forms of popular engagement[,] the paralysis of the legislative branches[,] the loss of a sense of social cohesion[, and] the decline in state competence,'[66] might simply be parsing the effects of the deeper social and economic changes highlighted by Ginsburg et al., Keating and McCrone.[67]

Kim Lane Scheppele, meanwhile, brings such institutional factors together with their social and economic precursors. She lays the blame for illiberalism and 'autocratic legalism' not just on '[r]adical political polarization[,] increasingly bad electoral choices[, and] party systems [that cannot] handle shifts in voter preferences,' but also on 'fallout from traumatic economic shocks[,] corrupt agreements among political elites[, and] voters who become cynical after too many failed promises … who already voted repeatedly for moderate change only to get no change at all.'[68] The latter part of Scheppele's diagnosis and the better part of Issacharoff's and Ginsburg's could have been lifted from a socialist or social democratic pamphlet, and yet these authors are academic observers writing from within the American liberal establishment.

The connection between social democratic thought and mainstream diagnoses of liberal democratic backsliding is even clearer in Rosalind Dixon and Julie Suk's analysis.[69] They speak of 'the extremes of economic inequality that have become commonplace in liberal democracies throughout the world[,] poverty … on the rise *in the developed world*[, and] the stagnation of wages and economic insecurity.'[70] They bring this description to life through intuitive reasoning about what it means '[w]hen individuals who are born poor cannot become rich, and vice versa.'[71] In Dixon and Suk's estimation, that status quo

[63] Ibid, 10.

[64] JB Judis, *The Populist Explosion: How The Great Recession Transformed American and European Politics* (New York, Columbia Global Reports, 2016); B Moffit, *The Global Rise of Populism: Performance, Political Style, and Representation* (Stanford, California, Stanford University Press, 2016); S Levitsky and D Ziblatt, *How Democracies Die* (New York, Crown, 2018); and M Albright, *Fascism: A Warning* (New York, HarperCollins, 2018).

[65] T Ginsburg, A Hug, and M Versteeg, 'The Coming Demise of Liberal Constitutionalism?' (2018) 85 *The University of Chicago Law Review* 239, 245–6.

[66] S Issacharoff, 'Democracy's Deficits' (2018) 85 *The University of Chicago Law Review* 484, 488.

[67] Keating and McCrone (n 5).

[68] KL Scheppele, 'Autocratic Legalism' (2018) 85 *The University of Chicago Law Review* 545, 579–580.

[69] R Dixon and J Suk, 'Liberal Constitutionalism and Economic Inequality' (2018) 85 *The University of Chicago Law Review* 369. For a US-centric analysis along similar lines, see G Sitaraman, *The Crisis of the Middle-Class Constitution: Why Economic Inequality Threatens Our Republic* (New York, Vintage Books, 2017).

[70] Dixon and Suk (n 69) 371–3 (emphasis added).

[71] Ibid, 373.

discredits liberalism's claim about 'the freedom of individuals to determine their own fates' and demonstrates 'that society is an aristocracy'.[72]

As their diagnosis progresses, it is increasingly clear that Dixon and Suk lay the blame for the crisis of liberal democracy on the demise of social democracy. They claim that '[p]olitical legitimacy, in a liberal constitutional order, depends on there being, at a minimum, substantive equality of opportunity and substantively equal forms of political participation'.[73] Dixon and Suk are mostly referring to the effects of financial power on political power, which goes to one of Rawls' most important claims in 1971. Rawls: 'The liberties protected by the principle of participation lose much of their value whenever those who have greater private means are permitted to use their advantages to control the course of public debate'.[74] Dixon and Suk: 'When disparate economic power enables disparate political power, the situation is not only at odds with democracy; it is also resented'.[75]

This brings us back to Trotsky's description at the end of the previous part of this chapter: the middle classes are ruined by big capital's domination of the economic and political spheres; their indignation and despair are then diverted (with the help of hired fascist demagogues) against the most vulnerable segments of the population and sympathetic elites; and, all the while, their loyalties are captured by those who are either most responsible for their predicament to begin with or the political predators who are best positioned to exploit it. By claiming to solve problems of inequality, corruption, elitism, and neoliberal hegemony, illiberal populism has stepped into the role that social democracy should occupy.

IV. Articulating the Abolition of Class Government

Bernstein's foundational 1899 work considers that different forms of society are identified not by 'their technological or economic foundations but according to the basic principle of their legal institutions'.[76] Bernstein uses the words 'feudal, capitalist [and] bourgeois' to describe the basic principles available for a legal system,[77] thus recognising that the law is shaped to meet economic prerogatives. Bernstein contrasts social democracy with the principles of feudal, capitalist and bourgeois legal orders by positing 'the idea of cooperation as its starting point'.[78] He then goes on to characterise socialism as 'a movement towards, or the state of, a cooperative order of society'.[79] Adding to the principle of cooperation, Polanyi defined socialism in terms of 'the principle of social protection aiming at the conservation of man and nature as well as productive organization'.[80] Economic and political relationships would have to be structured on the basis of these principles in order for them to

[72] Ibid.

[73] Ibid, 374.

[74] J Rawls, *A Theory of Justice* (Cambridge, Massachusetts, Belknap Press, 1971) 224–225.

[75] Dixon and Suk (n 69) 374.

[76] Bernstein, *The Preconditions of Socialism* (n 9) 98.

[77] Ibid.

[78] Ibid.

[79] Ibid, 99.

[80] K Polanyi, *The Great Transformation: The Political and Economic Origins of Our Time*, 2nd edn (Boston, Massachusetts, Beacon Press, 2001) 138–9.

manifest. The question is how to move economics and politics away from hierarchical and exploitative principles, and towards collaborative and protective ones.

Orthodox Marxism does not frame or answer that question the same way Bernstein does, because for social democrats '[d]emocracy is both means and end[--]a weapon in the struggle for socialism, and … the form in which socialism will be realised'.[81] Beyond a basic legal principle for moving towards and maintaining a cooperative and protective social order, Bernstein searched for a legal principle that would do so democratically.

That is where Bernstein's definition of democracy comes in. Asking, 'what is democracy?' he disqualifies the standard answer of '"government by the people" [as] only a very superficial and purely formal definition'.[82] He faults this definition for allowing 'the oppression of the individual by the majority'.[83] In opposition to that superficial, formal, and potentially oppressive definition of democracy, Bernstein defines the term 'as the absence of class government[--]a state of society in which no class has a political privilege which is opposed to the community as a whole'.[84] He specifies within democracy 'an idea of justice[:] equality of rights for all members of the community'.[85]

To elucidate this idea, Bernstein posits as a central distinction between democracy and other political systems 'the absence of laws which create or sanction exceptions on the grounds of property, birth, or religious confession'.[86] Though he admits that democracy may involve laws that limit individual rights, Bernstein insists that it requires 'the abolition of all laws which limit the universal equality of rights, the equal right of all'.[87] And he later changes his initial definition of democracy from 'the *absence* of class government' to 'the *abolition* of class government' (but 'not yet the actual abolition of classes').[88]

Still, returning to Bernstein's claim that each society is identified by the basic principle of its legal system, the abolition of class government would not take us into the realm of a 'socialist legal system'. Socialist law, a recognised legal tradition, served the Communist Party and such power structures as the dictatorship of the proletariat and state ownership of the means of economic production.[89] But between the second and third editions of Merryman and Pérez-Perdomo's *The Civil Law Tradition*, socialist law disappeared.[90] Naturally, Bernstein was beginning to elaborate a basic, foundational principle for social-democratic law instead.

Although the abolition of class government has yet to be constitutionally entrenched in any jurisdiction that I am aware of, it has been developed into a political theory and a human right since Bernstein's death. Bernstein's terms regarding the absence of class

[81] Ibid, 142.
[82] Ibid, 140.
[83] Ibid, 141.
[84] Bernstein, 'Preface to the English Edition' (n 21) 140.
[85] Ibid, 141.
[86] Ibid, 141.
[87] Ibid, 141–2.
[88] Ibid, 143.
[89] See generally Z Kuhn, 'Development of Comparative Law in Central and Eastern Europe' in M Reimann and R Zimmermann (eds), *The Oxford Handbook of Comparative Law* (Oxford, Oxford University Press, 2006).
[90] The second edition identifies socialist law alongside civil law and common law as a legal tradition. But the third edition does not include it in the same list. See JH Merryman and R Pérez-Perdomo, *The Civil Law Tradition: An Introduction to the Legal Systems of Europe and Latin America*, 3rd edn (Stanford, California, Stanford University Press, 2007).

government are well expressed by the 'fair value of political liberties,'[91] stipulated to nearly 100 years later by John Rawls. In 1996, Rawls wrote, 'the worth of the political liberties to all citizens, *whatever their social or economic position*, must be approximately equal, or at least sufficiently equal, in the sense that everyone has a fair opportunity to hold public office and to influence the outcome of political decisions'.[92] Bernstein's terms also ought to remind us of Rawls' 1971 prescription, which focused more specifically on constitutional entrenchment:

> [T]he constitution must take steps to enhance the value of equal rights of participation for all members of society .... [T]hose similarly endowed and motivated should have roughly the same chance of attaining positions of political authority irrespective of their economic and social class.[93]

A political theory such as this ought to be the first step towards the entrenchment of our foundational principle, but in this case it came after a human right based on the same concerns.

Adopted in 1948, 100 years after the Communist Manifesto and the 1848 Revolutions, the Universal Declaration of Human Rights could be called a Bill of Rights for social democracy. Had it been binding and enforced, something far more comprehensive than the New Deal would have taken effect in the United Nations Member States that cast their votes for it. (Eleanor Roosevelt did chair the drafting committee, after all.)

Article 21(3) of the Declaration elevates popular sovereignty and elections to a universal standard for governmental legitimacy:

> The will of the people shall be the basis of the authority of government; this will shall be expressed in periodic and genuine elections which shall be by universal and equal suffrage[.][94]

Complimenting and operationalising this standard, the Declaration announced not only rights of free expression, free assembly, and association, but also rights to equal access to public service and political participation.[95] Indeed, the two sections of Article 21 make popular sovereignty a demanding and meaningful proposition:

> (1) Everyone has the right to take part in the government of his country, directly or through freely chosen representatives.
> (2) Everyone has the right of equal access to public service in his country.[96]

These provisions imply that the Declaration is serious about political participation, but is it serious about eliminating class-based distinctions therein?

Though rarely stated, the answer is more socialistic than one might think. The very next article states that 'Everyone, as a member of society ... is entitled to realization ... of the economic, social and cultural rights indispensable for his dignity and the free development of his personality'. The second generation rights immediately following Article 22 include

[91] J Rawls, *Political Liberalism* (New York, Columbia University Press, 1993) 327.
[92] Ibid.
[93] Rawls, *A Theory of Justice* (n 74) 224–5.
[94] Universal Declaration of Human Rights (adopted 10 December 1948) UNGA Res 217 A(III) (UDHR), art 21(3).
[95] Ibid, arts 19 ('Everyone has the right to freedom of opinion and expression; this right includes freedom to hold opinions without interference and to seek, receive and impart information and ideas through any media and regardless of frontiers') and 20(1) ('Everyone has the right to freedom of peaceful assembly and association.').
[96] Ibid, art 21(1-2).

the right to work and free choice of employment, equal pay, leisure, education, an adequate standard of living including food, housing and medical care, and participation in cultural life. If guaranteed in practice, such rights would reduce the class divide considerably. In the kind of society envisioned by the Declaration, even mere formal equality of political rights would be a relatively egalitarian proposition.

But the Declaration goes far beyond formal equality. Building on its impressive panoply of civil, political, economic, social, and cultural rights, Article 28 states that 'Everyone is entitled to a social and international order in which the rights and freedoms set forth … can be fully realized'. The full realisation of all such rights for everyone in society would imply a serious degree of substantive equality. And, like the Declaration's provisions for social and economic rights, that would make socio-economic class far less rigid and inequality less steep.

Despite the breadth and potential power of these provisions, the most direct path to eliminating class-based distinctions in political participation is to be found elsewhere, in Article 2. The inclusion there of one of the most important words in liberal and social democracies' lexicons – property – has sweeping implications.

> Article 2. Everyone is entitled to all the rights and freedoms set forth in this Declaration, without distinction of any kind, such as race, colour, sex, language, religion, political or other opinion, national or social origin, property, birth or other status.[97]

As qualified by Article 2's reference to property, Article 21 should be interpreted as abolishing class government.

Even in their unqualified form, universal suffrage and open standing for public office threaten the role of economic power in the political sphere by affording each citizen a say in electoral outcomes and the possibility of launching their own political campaign. Still, corporate special interests and wealthy individuals make up for lost ground by influencing elections and law-making through political donations to parties and campaigns, political expenditures, and lobbying. The overall regime of private control of the means of political production premises the financial viability of parties and campaigns on their ability to appeal to wealthy sectors of the population – including corporate and foreign interests. To that undemocratic constellation, we must add rampant conflicts of interest, trading in influence, and pro-capital media bias as a result of corporate consolidation and dependence on advertising for revenue. The intersection between Articles 2 and 21 should be read as prohibiting such plutocratic distortions of elections and political rights, because money is a form of property, not to mention a function of property.[98]

This equivalency between property and financial power is supported by other versions of the Declaration. Instead of property, the French version of the Declaration uses the word 'fortune,' while the Spanish version uses the words 'posición económica,' literally 'economic position,' but better translated as 'socio-economic status'.[99]

[97] Ibid, arts 1–2.

[98] Assets that can be converted into cash include real property, tangible personal property, and intangible property, such as stock options. All are protected by property law.

[99] Déclaration universelle des droits de l'homme G.A. Res. 217 (III) A, U.N. Doc. A/RES/217(III) (Dec. 10, 1948), available at www.un.org/fr/documents/udhr/index2.shtml and Declaración universal de derechos humanos, G.A. Res. 217 (III) A, U.N. Doc. A/RES/217(III) (Dec. 10, 1948), available at www.un.org/es/documents/udhr/.

The resulting principle for a constitution of social democracy can be stated in two ways: Leading with Article 21, *The right to take part in the government of one's country directly or through freely chosen representatives, and the right of equal access to public service may not be amplified for the rich or diminished for the poor through the operation of property, fortune, or socio-economic status.*[100] Or, following Article 2's framing, *Everyone is entitled to equal access to public service, political participation and representation without distinctions on the basis of property, fortune, or socio-economic status. And the state must ensure these rights through the necessary guarantees and prohibitions.*

Since Articles 2, 22, and 28 frame the entire instrument, it is clear that the Declaration is in reality a rights-based articulation of social democracy. So, why focus on the intersection between Articles 2 and 21 in particular? The resulting basic principle provides the democratic means for producing and entrenching social democracy, thus making the social and international order articulated in Article 28 a genuine possibility. That principle stands as the legal articulation of the non-hierarchical, non-class-based democracy for which Bernstein advocated in 1899. A democracy in which all citizens have an equal chance to affect political outcomes and even to hold political office, regardless of wealth and regardless of socio-economic class – that is Rawls' prescription in the flesh 23 years before *A Theory of Justice* and 48 years before *Political Liberalism*.

Articles 2 and 21 of the UDHR were incorporated into a legally binding instrument, the International Covenant on Civil and Political Rights (ICCPR), ratified by the world's democracies. Even so, the common-sense textual reading of these articles along Bernstein's lines has not been taken seriously. The reasons for this are embodied in Bernstein's own failure.

V. Democratic Integrity must be Entrenched

While Bernstein's theory and principles are pioneering, they are modest when it comes to entrenchment. Rather than designing a political tradition with certain core constitutional features, Bernstein wrote of the differences between countries like a bromide-encrusted professor of comparative law. He cited varying stages of 'economic, political, intellectual, and moral development,' and '[p]eculiarities of geographical situation, rooted customs of national life, inherited institutions, and traditions of all kinds [that] create ideological differences'. Although Bernstein granted the possibility of 'general political principles of Social Democracy which could claim universal validity', his sensitivity to national variations led him to deny the possibility of 'a programme of action which would be equally valid for all countries'.[101] That sensitivity is well placed when it comes to framing a nation's priorities and the specific laws and policies it wishes to adopt. But insofar as it prevents the framing of an essential constitutional baseline for self-government, it morphs into insensitivity, an insensitivity to danger.

[100] This is an exercise in reading art 21 in light of art 2, an exercise which art 2 itself demands by stipulating that '[e]veryone is entitled to *all the rights and freedoms set forth in this Declaration, without distinction of any kind*.' See above n 94 at art 2 (emphasis added).

[101] Bernstein, *The Preconditions of Socialism* (n 9) 159.

Bernstein considered the Bourgeoisie a 'reactionary mass because all of its elements feel themselves to be … threatened by Social Democracy … in their material [and] ideological interests,'[102] but he concluded that 'this is no longer necessary[, because] Social Democracy does not threaten all equally, and it threatens nobody personally[…]and it has no enthusiasm for a violent revolution.'[103] Was violent revolution ever the only sufficient cause of upper-class opposition to real democracy? Even without violent revolution or threatening all members of the Bourgeoisie equally, social democracy emphatically threatened the class-based political privileges upon which every liberal democracy stood at the time. And it continues to threaten the same privileges upon which capitalist democracies and the neoliberal global order stand today. In the end, Vincent Geoghan's 1993 criticism of Bernstein's *Preconditions of Socialism* seems accurate: it does seem to have 'lack[ed] awareness of the true nature of the social opposition to socialism.'[104]

To the extent that is the case, I would argue that Bernstein's insensitivity to opposition came from a good-natured faith in liberals' ability to avoid or transcend the dogmatic militancy and determinism associated with Marxists. Writing nearly 50 years after Bernstein, Karl Polanyi saw more clearly how 'economic liberalism burst forth as a crusading passion, and laissez-faire become a militant creed.'[105] He also saw more clearly how 'the content of our cultural beliefs now reflects the core ideas of Western liberalism [including,] belief in the sovereignty of the self-interested, materially-motivated individual, and the sacred status we effectively attribute to a rapidly developing economy.'[106] The key words here are 'creed' and 'sacred' – classical economic precepts went from the realm of assumption, theory, and policy prescription to the realm of belief, faith, and theology.[107]

Because that free market theology has persisted for 40 years (leading to the consolidation of neoliberalism, the rise of illiberal populism, and probably catastrophic climate change), there is reason to suspect that CB Macpherson supplied the last word on the future of democracy back in 1977. Asking whether liberal democracy would endure, Macpherson wrote that everything depended on what was meant by the term. In liberal democracy he located two very different types of societies: first, 'the democracy of a capitalist market society' and, second, 'a society striving to ensure that all its members are equally free to realize their capabilities.'[108] If the first kind of society prevailed and democracy continued to guarantee the 'freedom of the stronger to do down the weaker by following market rules,' then Macpherson's answer was no, democracy was doomed. If the second kind of society prevailed and democracy was reshaped to guarantee 'equal effective freedom of all to use and develop their capacities,'[109] then his answer was yes, democracy would flourish and endure.

In today's times, when democracies are trapped between *homo economicus* on the one hand and *homo exosus, indignans, et iracundus* on the other, it is essential that social

[102] Ibid, 158–9.
[103] Ibid, 158.
[104] See Geoghegan (n 1) 154.
[105] Polanyi, *The Great Transformation* (n 80) 143.
[106] Block and Somers, *The Power of Market Fundamentalism* (n 43) 30.
[107] See generally RH Nelson, *Reaching for Heaven on Earth: The Theological Meaning of Economics* (Savage, Maryland, Rowman & Littlefield Publishers, 1991); and P Goodchild, *Theology of Money* (Durham, North Carolina, Duke University Press, 2009).
[108] CB Macpherson, *The Life and Times of Liberal Democracy* (Ontario, Oxford University Press, 2012) 1.
[109] Ibid.

democracy finally spell out its own foundational principle and power structure as a political system. Of course it would revise neoliberalism by rejecting government of, by, and for the wealthy, and revise illiberal populism by rejecting discrimination, fear, and hatred, as well as rejecting violations of the rule of law and human rights. But more deeply, social democracy would reject the ideological and psychological bases of these systems, which propose that problems of law and society can be solved by all-knowing markets or national greatness – that is by belief in something above and beyond a political community engaged in conscious action on the basis of freedom, equality, and self-governance for all.

In order to make that equality of rights effective and produce a state of society in which no class has a political privilege opposed to the community as a whole, social democracy would have to do more than guarantee rights to political participation (including passive suffrage) regardless of socio-economic status. It would also have to erect a democratic power structure in the form of a political sphere that is autonomous from the economic sphere. That much would be required to enable and guarantee popular participation and representation – *real democracy*. I refer back to the abolition of private control of the means of political production, which would require more than discrete legal reforms in the areas of bribery, trading in influence, political finance, lobbying, and conflicts of interest. Stricter rules in these departments, plus improvements in monitoring and enforcement, would be required, and those new provisions could not remain dispersed in separate areas, such as anti-corruption law, election law, administrative law, and ethics rules. Rather, they would have to be centralised, interlaced, and consolidated at the very beginning of a democratic constitution in the form of a structural feature: the abolition of class government and the entrenchment of democratic integrity.

Let us think back to the first two of Ewing's 1995 goals and principles: popular sovereignty as the basis for constitutional authority; and the social, economic, and cultural welfare of citizens as the principal purposes for the exercise of state authority.[110] Ewing noted the assumptions upon which these depended, including that universal suffrage would effectively promote the interests of the masses, and that elected officials would not only heed the goals of their constituents but be transformed into public servants.[111] What warrants such assumptions? Surely the deeper constitutional baseline derived earlier from the UDHR and ICCPR: *Everyone is entitled to equal access to public service, political participation (including suffrage, speech, association, assembly, and petitioning) and to political representation without distinctions on the basis of property, fortune, or socio-economic status. And the state must ensure these rights through the necessary guarantees and prohibitions.* Naturally, that constitutional baseline, and therefore Ewing's goals and principles for a constitution of social democracy, would all require strict, carefully crafted, and dutifully enforced provisions on the role of wealth in the political process. Together, such provisions on the financing of political campaigns and political parties, corporate political spending and special interest groups, lobbying, trading in influence, and conflicts of interest would be required in order to establish social democracy and protect it from undemocratic opposition.

It is certainly the case, as Ewing stated, that '[t]hose drafting a constitution must ask themselves what type of society they wish to live in and draft accordingly'.[112] I believe

[110] Ewing (n 48) 105.
[111] Ibid.
[112] Ibid.

the conviction at the heart of social democracy today is that one must have the rule of law, a strong, sustainable economy, and the full panoply of human rights, but that neither hegemonic global markets nor authoritarian leaders will produce or tolerate such things. To abolish class government would be to take society seriously, which would entail remedying the political powerlessness that produces illiberal populism and overcoming the economic domination at the heart of neoliberalism. In terms of what constitutional drafters must decide, this amounts to choosing a social order instead of an anti-social one, and making that choice binding, not merely symbolic. It amounts to carving out inviolable space for a community of political equals to work out its own destiny, within liberalism's venerable limits of course.

PART IV

Social Justice in the Social Democratic Constitution

12

The Liberal Socialist Tradition in UK Labour Law

RUTH DUKES*

I. Introduction

Professor Sir Otto Kahn-Freund (1900–1979) was once one of the leading scholars of law in the UK, an authority on such diverse topics as comparative law, family law and international private law. Today, it is for his contribution to labour law that he is best remembered. Indeed, it is not unusual, even today, for scholarly consideration of a question arising in that field to begin with a moment's reflection on what Kahn-Freund thought, or might have thought, the answer to be. Given that such reflection must necessarily involve interpretation of written texts, this is not always a straightforward, or uncontroversial, exercise. Disagreement, mostly tacit, has arisen over the years between those who have characterised him as a liberal at heart, casting his views accordingly, and those who have sought instead to emphasise the socialist or social democratic intent that they discern in his academic endeavours. A source of particular controversy has been the principle of 'collective laissez-faire', elaborated by Kahn-Freund during the 1950s to explain what he understood to be the particularities of the British system of industrial relations and labour law throughout the greater part of the twentieth century. In substance, the system involved industry level collective bargaining and dispute resolution between trade unions and employers' associations. On the face of it, at least, the label 'collective laissez-faire' appeared to imply that these practices were somehow insulated from government intervention: that this was a sphere of action which the state left alone.

In an important article from 1998, Keith Ewing revisited Kahn-Freund's notion of collective laissez-faire, interpreting it to imply above all the relative insignificance of law, and legal sanctions, in industrial relations.[1] Ewing's central argument was that, as such, the principle provided an incomplete picture of the role of the state in that field.

> The state has been a much more active player in the building of collective bargaining and other institutions than a concentration on legal regulation would tend to indicate, thereby reflecting the

* I'm grateful to Mark Freedland and Alan Bogg for comments on an earlier draft.

[1] KD Ewing, 'The State and Industrial Relations: 'Collective Laissez-Faire' Revisited' (1998) 5 *Historical Studies in Industrial Relations* 1–31 [SIR].

> fact that legal regulation is only one method of intervention, but that there are others – sometimes less formal yet not necessarily less effective.[2]

In fact, Ewing suggested, the British system of industrial relations had been characterised by 'active and legally grounded intervention by the state', directed chiefly at encouraging the spread of collective bargaining across sectors, and at ensuring its effectiveness as a means of regulating terms and conditions of employment.[3] In order to reject collective laissez-faire in this way as offering an accurate description of the British system, Ewing first characterised it as strongly resonant with 'social liberalism' of the type expounded by Leonard Hobhouse and Ernest Barker. Its 'essence', he wrote, was 'by definition one of political indifference, in the sense that while the state may remove the impediments which prevent trade unions from operating, it is largely indifferent to the success or failure of trade union organization'.[4] As such, collective laissez-faire could be contrasted with social democratic theories of labour law and industrial relations which envisaged a much more proactive role for the state: the harnessing of state power to achieve particular political and economic ends.

In this chapter, I give extended consideration to Ewing's characterisation of collective laissez-faire as more or less synonymous with 'social liberalism'.[5] My focus lies specifically with collective laissez-faire as expounded by Kahn-Freund, and with Kahn-Freund's political views, and not with more widely held notions of voluntarism or abstentionism. As an aid to interpretation of the key texts, I consider Kahn-Freund's personal experiences of living and working as a judge in the Weimar Republic, and of moving to the UK as a refugee from Nazism, building here on recent biographical research which adds important detail to our existing knowledge of those experiences.[6] I also look briefly at work written by Kahn-Freund before and after his 'collective laissez-faire' publications, and at what he himself had to say about his scholarship and his political opinion in later life.

As is the case with any writer, biographical and bibliographical knowledge are important to an evaluation of Kahn-Freund's writing. We should read him as an academic trained in specific scholarly traditions, whose interventions in contemporary issues were conditioned both by his own preoccupations and by the possibilities embodied in definite institutional forms.[7] On that understanding, I argue in this chapter that there is in fact little disagreement between Ewing and Kahn-Freund as to the nature and extent of state, and legal, intervention in industrial relations during the first decades of the twentieth century, and little to distinguish Ewing's social democracy from Kahn-Freund's purported 'social liberalism'. If the latter accorded less *significance* to state and legal intervention than Ewing shows to be justified, then this was likely due in part to his own knowledge and lived experience of industrial relations and labour law in the Weimar Republic; of their tragic fate. In describing the British system as one of 'collective laissez-faire', Kahn-Freund's primary concern was to

[2] Ewing, SIR (n 1) 2.

[3] Ibid.

[4] Ibid 5.

[5] Drawing on previously published work, especially: R Dukes, 'Otto Kahn-Freund and Collective Laissez-Faire: an Edifice without a Keystone' (2009) 72 *MLR* 220; R Dukes, *The Labour Constitution: the Enduring Idea of Labour Law* (Oxford, OUP, 2014) ch 4; R Dukes, 'Otto Kahn-Freund: a Weimar Life' (2017) 80 *MLR* 1164.

[6] H Ludyga, *Otto Kahn-Freund (1900–1979) Ein Arbeitsrechtler in der Weimarer Zeit* (Berlin, De Gruyter, 2016).

[7] K Tribe, *Reading Weber* (Abingdon, Routledge, 1989) 3.

emphasise, with approbation, the measure of autonomy from the state which trade unions (and employers' associations) enjoyed in the UK, in comparison to the Weimar Republic and other jurisdictions. There is no basis here, I suggest, for concluding that he was a liberal or even a 'social liberal'. 'Liberal socialist' might be a more accurate label, but only if it is understood in the context of the time, and as equally applicable to writers like Hugo Sinzheimer and Harold Laski.

II. Ewing, the State and Industrial Relations

In his 1998 article, 'The State and Industrial Relations: "Collective Laissez-Faire" Revisited', Ewing's main purpose was to argue that the British state's role in the institution and maintenance of a system of collectivised industrial relations was routinely underestimated. In part, this error sprang from the tendency of commentators – and especially those with legal training – to focus unduly on the relevant law and to overlook or underappreciate the extent and significance of non-legal (administrative) intervention by state bodies.[8] Taken alone, the legal framework could indeed be interpreted as 'neutral' on questions of industrial relations: it removed common law impediments to unionisation, collective bargaining and, especially, industrial action, but stopped short of creating duties on employers to participate in collective bargaining, and to desist from firing or otherwise disciplining union members by reason of their membership or participation in strike action.[9] From the time of its creation in 1916, however, the Ministry of Labour had taken a range of steps to encourage employers rather more actively to recognise trade unions for the purposes of collective bargaining. Where effective collective bargaining was not possible, it had created alternative machinery for the setting of terms and conditions of employment with application across whole sectors.[10] In consideration of the Ministry of Labour's activities throughout the inter-war years, Ewing concluded, then, that:

> contrary to received wisdom, what we have in the British system is in fact active and legally grounded intervention by the state, which did not use legal instruments as the chosen means of intervention, though it was prepared to do so as the need arose.[11]

In the scheme of Ewing's argument, Kahn-Freund's notion of collective laissez-faire figured as a particularly influential expression of the 'received wisdom' that required to be debunked. While analysis of Kahn-Freund's work was not Ewing's primary aim, he did refer to it specifically, characterising it, as we have seen, as representative of the 'social liberal position' on industrial relations.[12] The essence of this position, according to Ewing, was that there was an imbalance of power between employers and employees which could be addressed only by intervention on the part of the state. Such intervention could take one of two forms, the first being to accept the role of voluntary institutions which would help to redress that balance

[8] Ewing, SIR (n 1) 7.
[9] Trade Disputes Act 1906, discussed Ewing, SIR (n 1) 7.
[10] Eg, Trade Boards Acts 1909, 1918, Catering Wages Act 1943, Road Haulage Wages Act 1938, discussed in Ewing, SIR (n 1).
[11] Ewing, SIR (n 1) 2.
[12] Ibid, 3–5.

of power, and the second being to intervene in order to ameliorate its worst consequences. While legislation setting a minimum level on matters such as pay and working conditions might also be contemplated, the essence of the social liberal position – of 'collective laissez-faire' – was by definition, 'one of political indifference': workers would be accorded the freedom to join trade unions, and trade unions and employers the freedom to engage in collective bargaining, but the matter of whether or not to exercise those freedoms would be regarded as one of free – 'voluntary' – choice on the part of the actors involved.[13]

On this reading of collective laissez-faire and of the relevant works by Kahn-Freund, Ewing noted three points of disagreement between the two authors. The first, already mentioned and returned to in part 3 below, was that collective laissez-faire did not provide an accurate description of the role of the state in industrial relations. Focusing unduly on the legal framework alone, Kahn-Freund had failed to recognise the progression that had taken place during the twentieth century, from government neutrality towards trade unionisation and collective bargaining to active encouragement of it, in a variety of ways.

The second and third points of disagreement related to the question, *why* industrial relations and labour law had taken the form that they had in the UK: why did labour law only facilitate and not encourage or require unionisation and collective bargaining? According to Kahn-Freund, it was highly significant in this respect that trade unions had developed in Britain at a point in time prior to the enfranchisement of working class men; before, therefore, those men were in a position to press for greater legal protections of their interests. As Ewing pointed out, however, at the time of the extension of the franchise in 1884 'almost all the way to universal male suffrage', only around 5 per cent of the labour force was organised in trade unions.[14] This first part of Kahn-Freund's explanation could therefore be easily dismissed.

Ewing also doubted Kahn-Freund's suggestion that industrial relations and labour law had been shaped primarily by the strength of British trade unions, their independence from the state and their reluctance to rely on legal rights in furtherance of their members' interests. 'Trade union "recognition" was achieved in this country by purely industrial as distinct from political and legislative action', Kahn-Freund had written: 'The proud edifice of collective labour regulation was built up without the assistance of the "law"'.[15] Trade unions did not campaign to be granted positive legal rights, so the argument seemed to go, because they preferred to rely on their own industrial strength to be recognised by employers, and to negotiate with employers improved terms and conditions of employment, and methods of dispute resolution.[16] When legislating to allow trade unions lawfully to engage in industrial action, the Liberal governments of the beginning of the twentieth century had agreed, apparently, that industrial disputes ought to be kept out of the courts insofar as was possible: hence the use of statutory immunities, and not positive rights, to create a freedom to strike.[17]

[13] Ibid 5.

[14] Ibid, 12.

[15] O Kahn-Freund, 'Collective Agreements under War Legislation' (1943) 6 *MLR* 112–4. See also O Kahn-Freund, 'Labour Law' in M Ginsberg (ed), *Law and Opinion in England in the 20th Century* (London, Stevens, 1959) 224; P Davies and M Freedland (eds), *Kahn Freund's Labour and the Law*, 3rd edn (London, Stevens, 1983) 52–3.

[16] Davies and Freedland (n 15) 53.

[17] Kahn-Freund, 'Labour Law' (n 15) 232.

As Ewing argued, however, review of the historical sources revealed that this account was misleading.[18] There might be some truth to the claim that at the turn of the century some trade unionists sought a legal settlement which would keep industrial disputes out of the *courts*. But evidence also suggested that a significant section of the labour movement wished for greater legal rights as a prop to assist them in securing recognition; that they argued, for that reason, for the introduction of a legally defined system of compulsory arbitration along the lines of those in force in New Zealand and Australia.[19] Others doubted the potential of a system of collective liberalism, built upon statutory immunities, to facilitate furtherance of the common interest.[20] In 1906, of course, it was the stronger trade unions' wishes for a wide 'freedom from the law', which came to be reflected in the terms of the Trade Disputes Act. Nonetheless, the assertion made by Kahn-Freund that trade unions preferred to rely on their own industrial strength rather than state-granted legal rights was not true of all unionists, and not at all times.

A further weakness of Kahn-Freund's explanation of the emergence and persistence of the system of collective laissez-faire was its failure to give adequate consideration to employer interests and motivations. The implication was that employers recognised trade unions because the unions were in a position to require them to do so, threatening and organising strike action as necessary. Allan Flanders famously disputed such accounts of what he called 'bootstrap voluntarism', arguing, instead, that it had often served the employers' own interests to recognise trade unions: to involve the unions in managerial control, and in the regulation of work and wages, in order to gain employee consent and cooperation; or to secure the unions' assistance in reducing wage competition.[21] Governments, too, had played an important role in promoting union growth, not least through the impact which they had had on employer attitudes and organisation.[22] '[T]he crude notion that British unions have dispensed with any external assistance in obtaining their growth' concluded Flanders, 'is greatly at odds with the facts.'[23]

III. Kahn-Freund, the State and Industrial Relations

What he called the 'principle' of collective laissez-faire was first developed by Kahn-Freund in a trilogy of works published between 1954 and 1959.[24] In his earliest writing on trade union law in the UK, he had interpreted the relevant provisions through the lens of his existing knowledge of German law, concluding that collective agreements between trade

[18] See, eg, C Howell, *Trade Unions and the State: The Construction of Industrial Relations Institutions in Britain, 1890–2000* (Princeton, Princeton University Press, 2007); H Pelling, 'Trade Unions, Workers and The Law' in *Popular Politics and Society in Late Victorian Britain: Essays* (London, Macmillan, 1979).

[19] A Flanders, 'The Tradition of Voluntarism' (1974) 12 *British Journal of Industrial Relations* 352, 354. See also S Webb and B Webb, *The History of Trade Unionism*, 2nd edn (London, Longmans, 1911) 320; Pelling (n 18) 72–8.

[20] Pelling (n 18) 80–1. See also S Webb and B Webb, *Industrial Democracy* (London, Longmans, 1902) xlii ff.

[21] Flanders (n 19) 355.

[22] Ibid.

[23] Ibid, 356.

[24] O Kahn-Freund, 'Legal Framework' in A Flanders and H Clegg (eds), *The System of Industrial Relations in Great Britain* (Oxford, Basil Blackwell, 1954); O Kahn-Freund, 'Intergroup Conflicts and their Settlement' (1954) 5 *British Journal of Sociology* 193; Kahn-Freund, 'Labour Law' (n 15).

unions and employers' associations were contractual in the legal sense.[25] In the 1950s trilogy, he placed at the centre of his analysis his belated recognition that collective agreements were *not* legally binding contracts, for the reason that the parties to them routinely lacked contractual intent.[26] Though it was possible for the normative terms of collective agreements to be made legally binding through incorporation into individual contracts of employment, the matter of incorporation was consensual and non-compulsory.[27] Since they were not legally binding, the interpretation, application and enforcement of collective agreements fell to the collective parties themselves, and not to the courts or other state authorities.[28] Nor were those parties under any generally applicable legal obligation to bargain collectively with one another in the first place. At the end of the nineteenth and beginning of the twentieth century, a series of legislative steps had been taken to create a legal freedom to organise and to take industrial action. Limitations had been placed on that freedom, signifying 'the limits within which the community is willing to tolerate warfare and peacemaking by the autonomous forces of industry'.[29] In addition, as Kahn-Freund discussed at great length, a wide variety of legal and non-legal methods had been used, since the beginning of the twentieth century, to encourage employers and unions to enter into collective bargaining arrangements with one another.[30] From a comparative point of view, then, what was remarkable about British industrial relations, according to Kahn-Freund, was not that there was an *absence* of law or state intervention – he was quite clear that there was no such absence – but rather that legal intervention in the UK tended to be indirect, aimed at persuading, rather than requiring, trade unions and employers to negotiate terms and conditions of employment and to resolve disputes peacefully.[31]

While each of the three published works in the trilogy dealt with the same body of law and analysed it in a similar way, only the third actually employed the term 'collective laissez-faire': a book chapter which began life as a public lecture.[32] By way of a definition of his term, Kahn-Freund juxtaposed the notion of *collective* laissez-faire with laissez-faire approaches to economic regulation. In doing so, he seemed to wish to suggest that, contra the great English jurist AV Dicey, there was nothing 'radical' or foreign to the British legal and political system about collective industrial relations.[33] Such practices reflected well the liberal understanding of the economy as a site where individuals could meet and bargain freely with one another, resulting in the 'free play of market forces'. To develop a normative

[25] Kahn-Freund, 'Collective Agreements' (n 15).

[26] Kahn-Freund, 'Legal Framework' (n 24) 57–58.

[27] Ibid, 58–61.

[28] Ibid, 44. See also Kahn-Freund, 'Intergroup Conflicts' (n 24) especially 202–210.

[29] Kahn-Freund, 'Intergroup Conflicts' (n 24) 215.

[30] Kahn-Freund, 'Legal Framework' (n 24) 101. In 'Legal Framework', there is discussion in particular of compulsory arbitration (83–101), of a range of statutory provisions intended to make the terms of collective agreements legally binding (58–65), 'Minimum Wage legislation' (65–75), fair wages clauses (75–83).

[31] See, eg, Kahn-Freund, ‚Legal Framework' (n 24) 65–6. In 'Labour Law' he describes the volume of statute law and subordinate legislation passed during the first half of the twentieth century as 'gigantic', and proceeds to explain why it was nonetheless 'subsidiary' to collective bargaining: Kahn-Freund 'Labour Law' (n 15) 245, 250. See also O Kahn-Freund, 'Industrial Relations and the Law – Retrospect and Prospect' (1969) 7 *British Journal of Industrial Relations* 301, 304 in which he refers to the relevant legislative measures, institutions, and administrative practices as constituting a 'statutory framework for organised persuasion'.

[32] Kahn-Freund, 'Labour Law' (n 15).

[33] Ibid, esp. 224.

underpinning for industrial relations in the UK, all that was required was that the notion of the freedom of the *individual* to bargain be replaced with that of the freedom of the *collective* to bargain: that individual *laissez-faire* be replaced with collective *laissez-faire*.[34] 'Dicey's antithesis of laissez faire and collectivism', concluded Kahn-Freund, 'was too simple.'[35]

Reading these passages today, one can understand why Kahn-Freund's exposition of labour law and industrial relations in the UK might have resonated strongly, for some, with liberalism of the British variety.[36] In critiquing the principle of collective laissez-faire in 1981, for example, Roy Lewis suggested that its key weakness was its failure to acknowledge the importance of class conflict, and the role of the state in mediating such conflict. In place of 'class struggles waged between movements with conflicting ideologies', wrote Lewis, Kahn-Freund had postulated 'reconcilable conflict between pressure groups'.[37] The notion that the state maintained an equilibrium between the opposed social forces through *legal abstention*, meanwhile – inherent, on Lewis' reading, in collective laissez-faire – was 'simply a myth'.[38] Characterising Kahn-Freund similarly as a dyed in the wool liberal, but to a rather different end, Collins and Mantouvalou suggested as recently as 2013 that he would likely have endorsed 'the strongest liberal position' espoused by the European Court of Human Rights in the case of *Redfearn v UK*: that the right to freedom of association for members of political parties ought to be defended against interference by an employer, even if those political parties held racist beliefs and opposed fundamental principles of the Convention.[39]

Alternative readings of collective laissez-faire placed greater emphasis on its socialist or social democratic nature. Lord Wedderburn was famously quite emphatic, in his later years, in insisting that collective laissez-faire had *not* been intended to imply a blanket rejection, or disapproval, of state intervention in industrial relations, legal or extra-legal.[40] The term had been coined by Kahn-Freund to describe, and to signal approval of, the 'primacy' of voluntary collective bargaining in British industrial relations, especially as compared with other countries: as a strong statement of advocacy, in other words, of trade unionism and industrial democracy.[41] While it could be understood broadly to convey a specific kind of non-intervention or neutrality on the part of the state, it was certainly not synonymous with state abstentionism straight-forwardly understood.[42] Collective laissez-faire meant that the state should – and did, for the most part – remain neutral as to the *outcomes* of

[34] T Ramm 'Epilogue' in B Hepple (ed), *The Making of Labour Law in Europe: A Comparative Study of Nine Countries up to 1945* (London, Mansell, 1986) 277.

[35] Kahn-Freund, 'Labour Law' (n 15) 223.

[36] See, eg, A Bogg, *The Democratic Aspects of Trade Union Recognition* (Oxford, Hart Publishing, 2009) ch 1.

[37] R Lewis, 'Kahn-Freund and Labour Law: an Outline Critique' (1979) 8 *Industrial Law Journal* 202, 218.

[38] Ibid.

[39] *Redfearn v UK* [2013] ECHR 1878; H Collins and V Mantouvalou, 'Redfearn v UK' (2013) 76 *MLR* 909. The authors' suggestion is implicit, communicated through the juxtaposition of an assertion that it was Kahn-Freund's belief that, in a democratic society, dismissal of an employee by reason of her membership of the Communist Party must be automatically unfair, with a description of the Court of Human Rights decision in *Redfearn*. See discussion of the 'Radio case' below.

[40] For an extended discussion see R Dukes, 'Wedderburn and the theory of labour law: building on Kahn-Freund' (2015) 44 *Industrial Law Journal* 357.

[41] Lord Wedderburn, 'Change, Struggle and Ideology in British Labour Law' in Lord Wedderburn, *Labour Law and Freedom: Further Essays in Labour Law* (London, Lawrence & Wishart, 1995) 6–7.

[42] Ibid, 10, 21.

collective bargaining and arbitration procedures.[43] It captured well the existence of a preference on both sides of industry for voluntary collective bargaining, and for forms of dispute resolution that did not involve the courts. And it described and advocated a system of industrial relations which involved, or reflected, state respect for those preferences.[44] But it did not mean that there should be, or had been in the UK, no labour law.[45] The picture painted by Kahn-Freund of British industrial relations, even in the 1950s, had *not* been one of 'unrelieved "abstention"; the "gloss" on voluntarism which we saw added by legislation was on the contrary intervenient'.[46] As had been explained by Kahn-Freund himself in his 1950s publications, a variety of legislative provisions and mechanisms had then existed which acted as a prop or support to collective bargaining. And compulsory arbitration of one form or another had remained a central feature of British labour law from the 1940s until 1980, 'in war and peace'.[47] Taking all this into account, Wedderburn concluded that it was perhaps regrettable that Kahn-Freund had ever used the term 'abstention' in his analysis of UK labour law, since this had allowed for the erroneous interpretation and premature rejection of collective laissez-faire by some other scholars.[48]

In previously published work, I have argued along similar lines to Wedderburn that collective laissez-faire was intended by Kahn-Freund to emphasise the fact that legal intervention in industrial relations in the UK tended to be indirect, aimed at reinforcing the autonomy of the collective parties in respect both of the negotiation of terms and conditions of employment and the resolution of collective disputes. If certain phrases or passages written by Kahn-Freund can seem, when taken out of context, to suggest that collective laissez-faire was intended to denote a complete absence of law or state intervention – for example, 'the retreat of law from industrial relations and of industrial relations from the law' – then these should be excused as rhetorical flourishes, intended to give force to his in fact rather more sophisticated argument.[49] Reading around these passages – reading also what Kahn-Freund wrote before and after the 1950s – we get a better understanding of collective laissez-faire as intended to emphasise what he understood to be particular, and admirable, about the British system *in comparison to others*: the degree of independence, or autonomy, from the state which the collective parties enjoyed.[50] As for the charge that he focused unduly on the law, this may be so – legal scholars, at the time, certainly tended to do so, and he likely saw it as his remit to explain the 'legal framework', rather than the administrative activities of the Ministry of Labour. A close reading of his work reveals that he was well aware of these, however, as he was of the indirect support afforded to trade unions and collectivisation by full-employment and other economic policies.[51]

[43] Ibid, 11, 15.
[44] Ibid, 22.
[45] Ibid.
[46] Ibid, 10.
[47] Ibid, 11.
[48] Ibid, 21–22.
[49] Kahn-Freund, 'Labour Law' (n 15) 225.
[50] For a similar reading of the principle of collective laissez-faire see S Deakin and F Wilkinson, *The Law of the Labour Market: Industrialization, Employment and Legal Evolution* (Oxford, Oxford University Press, 2004) 200 ff.
[51] Kahn-Freund 'Intergroup Conflicts' (n 24) 202, 199.

What of our finding in part 2 above, that Kahn-Freund's explanation of the emergence and persistence of the system of collective laissez-faire was not wholly borne out by the facts; that it was focused too narrowly on a postulated union preference for freedoms above rights that only ever accorded with the preferences of some trade unions in respect of some types of state intervention; that it accorded too little significance to employer and government preferences for industry level collective bargaining? Here, it must be borne in mind, I would suggest, that with his elaboration of the principle of collective laissez-faire, Kahn-Freund was writing as a scholar of law, of comparative law, and of the sociology of law, and *not* as an historian. As such, he was not immediately concerned to explain the nature of the political compromises involved in the drafting and adoption of collective labour legislation, or the policy priorities of the governments of the time. His aim was rather to analyse the provisions of the legislation then in force such that they fit with his normative vision of collectivised labour bargaining collectively with management, free from state control. Judged against that aim, the elaboration of the principle of collective laissez-faire was successful; as an account of the history of industrial relations and labour law in this country, it was less so. In what follows, I seek support for this reading of collective laissez-faire in the dramatic narrative of Kahn-Freund's life story, and in his own reflections on his work as an older man.

A. A Weimar Life

The broad sweep of Kahn-Freund's biography is well known.[52] Born in Frankfurt in 1900, he attended the *Goethe* grammar school in that city, and while still a school boy, in the summer of 1917, attended a peace rally, at which he heard Hugo Sinzheimer speak for the first time. Sinzheimer was the German-Jewish scholar, legal practitioner, and politician, who was later to become the principal architect of labour law in the Weimar Republic. Following graduation with a law degree in 1923, Kahn-Freund completed a PhD under the older man's supervision, and a legal traineeship in his chambers.[53] In 1928, he became a judge in the Charlottenburg district court in Berlin, and from 1929, in the Berlin labour court.[54] There he worked until 1933, when he was forced to flee what was by then Nazi Germany. He settled in London and embarked on a new course of study, of English law, at the London School of Economics: the first step in what was to become a long and highly distinguished second career. In 1936, he qualified as a barrister in the Middle Temple and became an assistant lecturer at the LSE, rising to Professor in 1951, and remaining there until 1964, when he took up the Chair of Comparative Law at the University of Oxford.[55] In 1976, he was knighted for 'services to Labour Law'.

[52] M Freedland, 'Otto Kahn-Freund' in J Beatson and R Zimmerman (eds), *Jurists Uprooted: German-Speaking Émigré Lawyers in Twentieth-Century Britain* (Oxford, Oxford University Press, 2004); O Kahn-Freund, 'The Study of Labour Law – Some Recollections' (1979) 8 *Industrial Law Journal* 197; O Kahn-Freund, 'Postscript' in R Lewis and J Clark (eds), *Labour Law and Politics in the Weimar Republic* (Oxford, Blackwell, 1981); BA Hepple, (1979) 8 *Industrial Law Journal* 193; Lord Wedderburn (1979) 42 *MLR* 609.

[53] O Kahn-Freund, 'Autobiographische Erinnerungen an die Weimarer Republik. Ein Gespräch mith Wolfgang Luthardt' (1981) 14 *Kritische Justiz* 183, 185.

[54] Freedland (n 52) 304.

[55] Ibid, 306–308.

Because of the times and the places in which he lived, Kahn-Freund's Jewishness assumed a significance to him that can hardly be overstated.[56] Born into a liberal, cosmopolitan, 'bourgeois' family, his first instinct had been to assimilate; to be simply German.[57] As support for the Nazis grew, however, throughout the 1920s and early 30s, his Jewishness came increasingly to define him in the eyes of others, to inform his own choices and actions, and eventually his own sense of self.[58] In March 1933, shortly after the Nazis had seized power, he bravely agreed to hear the so-called 'radio case' involving an employment law claim by three radio technicians who had been dismissed by reason of their suspected Communist Party membership and presumed readiness to sabotage a broadcast by Hitler to the nation.[59] In fact, the case was more or less thrust upon him by his colleagues:

> One or the other had perhaps thought that the judge Kahn-Freund could burn his fingers on this case as he had anyway not much to lose; as a Jew, outsider, oppositionist, was it not the case that he would in any case sooner or later not be able to sustain his position anymore, regardless of whether he decided the radio-case or not?[60]

Having found in the technicians' favour, Kahn-Freund was interrogated and placed under surveillance by the Gestapo. His own expulsion from the judiciary followed almost immediately thereafter, pursuant to the Civil Service Restoration Act (*Gesetz zur Wiederherstellung des Berufsbeamtentums*), which provided that all 'non-Aryan' and politically 'unreliable' civil servants be dismissed.[61] None of his colleagues on the bench protested.[62] After a short stay in Frankfurt, he left Germany for good in June 1933, but not without having first been required to pay a 'tax', or fine, for 'fleeing the Empire' (*Reichsfluchtsteuer*).[63] The horror of leaving his homeland in such circumstances stayed with Kahn-Freund throughout his life. Whenever I have nightmares, he said as an old man, I find myself in Frankfurt or Berlin.[64]

Of importance, too, to Kahn-Freund's sense of self was his identification as a socialist or social democrat. As a young man, his association with Sinzheimer brought him into close contact with a number of socialist lawyers and intellectuals: Ernst Fraenkel, Franz Neumann, Carlo Schmid (later a minister in the Federal Government of West Germany) and Hans Morgenthau. Through Sinzheimer or otherwise, he also became acquainted with Franz Oppenheimer, Otto Kirchheimer, and Hermann Heller. From 1922, Kahn-Freund was a member of the *Sozialistische Partei Deutschlands*, and from 1926 of the *Reichsbanner Schwarz, Rot, Gold*, one of the first groups actively to oppose Nazism. With Fraenkel, Neumann and Oppenheimer he taught during the early 1920s at the 'Labour Academy' at the Goethe University, established by Sinzheimer and Eugen Rosenstock-Huessys to provide higher education to workers who did not have a grammar school education (*Abitur*).[65]

[56] Ludyga (n 6) 75; O Kahn-Freund, 'Autobiographische Erinnerungen' (n 53) 195.

[57] Ramm (n 34).

[58] Ludyga (n 6) 10–11.

[59] Lewis and Clark, 'Introduction' in Lewis and Clark (n 52) 5; U Mückenberger, 'One Last Demonstration of Judicial Independence … Otto Kahn-Freund's Judgment in the "Radio Case"' (2015) *MLR* 1.

[60] Mückenberger (n 59) 10.

[61] Ludyga (n 6) 48.

[62] Ibid, 52.

[63] Ibid, 57.

[64] Ibid, 73.

[65] Ibid, 22.

In 1928, Heller offered him a postdoctoral position, but he decided at that point against an academic career – possibly because he was aware that his socialist political activities would have made career progression difficult.[66] As a judge, from 1928, he was conscious that his political leanings put him in a small minority amongst the otherwise deeply conservative judiciary.[67] For friendship, and political and intellectual debate, he turned again to Frankel and Neumann, among others, the former working together by then in Berlin as trade union lawyers.

Following his escape to England in 1933, Kahn-Freund participated in the external resistance movement, undertaking a range of activities aimed at hastening the defeat of Nazism, and paving the way towards the creation of a new socialist state in Germany.[68] From 1940 he chaired a committee which advised the Labour Party on propaganda matters, and with the same group of emigrants who constituted that committee, set up a pirate radio station to transmit socialist propaganda into Germany.[69] Financed and supervised by the British secret service, the station broadcast from London and then Bletchley until June 1942, encouraging German workers to acts of sabotage and passive resistance. Politically, its line was revolutionary socialist, agitating for an end to capitalism, militarism, imperialism and nationalism in all European nations and for their replacement with a united Europe under the leadership of the working classes. From 1943, Kahn-Freund also worked to set up the organisation, *German Educational Reconstruction*, which aimed to assist teachers and social workers with preparing for the work of reconstructing Germany.[70] It developed plans for the education of young people after the War, and informed the British public, through publications and lectures, about the current situation in Germany. At the War's end, it provided classes in history, economics, philosophy and sociology to German prisoners of war.[71]

In 1941, Kahn-Freund co-authored a short book with Fritz Eberhard, Walter Auerbach, Hilde Meisel and Kurt Mandelbaum: *The Next Germany: a Basis of Discussion on Peace in Europe*.[72] Wishing at the time to remain anonymous, neither he nor his co-authors were anywhere credited; however, the work is recognisably Kahn-Freund's in places, for example, where he quotes, without reference, a phrase that he elsewhere ascribed to Sinzheimer: 'Peace, Freedom, Bread'.[73] Writing with one voice, as a 'small circle of socialists', the authors argued passionately for the desirability of a proletarian revolution in Germany as the most effective means of bringing a lasting end to militarism, nationalism and imperialism, and ensuring a lasting peace in Europe.[74] In the short term, they envisaged the creation, from the grassroots up, of a council-based system of democracy to be replaced eventually by a centralised national government.[75] Workers' councils should play a particularly important

[66] Ibid, 26.
[67] Ibid, 31–3.
[68] Ibid, 61–72.
[69] Ibid, 61–7.
[70] Ibid, 69–72.
[71] Ibid, 71–2.
[72] L de Brouckere, *The Next Germany. A Basis of Discussion on Peace in Europe* (Harmondsworth, Penguin, 1943).
[73] Ludyga (n 6) 19; Kahn-Freund, 'Autobiographische Erinnerungen' (n 53) 185. My translation.
[74] de Brouckere (n 72) 6.
[75] Ibid, 38–40.

role in the new order, they believed, bearing a political, economic and social function both throughout the transitional period and thereafter.[76] As an only partly developed answer to the 'great issue' of the day – whether economic planning was compatible with political democracy – the circle proposed the involvement in economic planning of a number of interest associations: trade unions, peasants' cooperatives, craftsmen's cooperatives, and consumers' organisations.[77] The exercise of influence by individuals upon the decisions of a 'planning government' through the casting of a vote was 'not enough'.

> We must leave room for freely-formed social organs which operate on the spot and in the daily activities of which the citizen can take his part, and which materially influence his own well-being.[78]

At the war's end, Kahn-Freund dismissed a suggestion that the book be published in its original German language version.

> It was written on the presumption that there would be revolution in Germany. That presumption proved to be false.[79]

His position in this respect was representative of a much wider-reaching decision taken at the end of the War to desist from any further involvement in German politics or law. As he explained in an interview in the late 1970s:

> There is one thing that I have made a cast-iron principle, that in this life I shall never again interfere with anything German. I can talk about the past, but not about the present or the future … The past is too strong, the emotional influence of the past is too strong.[80]

He could never understand, as he went on to say, the decision of friends, including Fraenkel and Neumann, to return to the Federal Republic after the War's end. 'After we left Germany, I became completely immersed in English things'.[81]

B. Socialist, Liberal, or Liberal Socialist?

While there is disagreement among scholars on the correct interpretation of collective laissez-faire, it is generally acknowledged that, in later life, Kahn-Freund argued more unambiguously for certain types of state intervention in the regulation of industrial relations. In the context of full employment and relatively high levels of union membership and industrial action in Britain in the 1970s, he advocated the use of legislation to address what he considered to be abuses of trade union power: the control by the unions of access to some sections of the labour market, and the 'flying' and mass pickets organised by unions during the miners' strike of 1972.[82] To his famous dictum – 'the main object of labour

[76] Ibid, 62–8.
[77] Ibid, 55–8.
[78] Ibid, 56.
[79] Ludyga (n 6) 68, citing a letter from Kahn-Freund to Auerbach, 13.12.1945.
[80] Lewis and Clark (n 52) 201.
[81] Ibid, 200.
[82] O Kahn-Freund, 'Trade Unions, the Law and Society' (1970) 33 *MLR* 241; O Kahn-Freund, 'The Industrial Relations Act 1971 – Some retrospective reflections' (1974) 3 *Industrial Law Journal* 186.

law has always been, and we venture to say will always be, to be a countervailing force to counteract the inequality of bargaining power which is inherent and must be inherent in the employment relationship' – he added the arguably contradictory statement that 'the principal purpose of labour law, then, is to regulate, to support and to restrain the power of management and the power of organised labour.'[83] In discussing what he believed to be the 'inevitable' existence of conflicts of interest between labour and management, he characterised, 'management's interest in planning production and in being protected against its interruption' as the *exact equivalent* of the 'worker's interest in planning his and his family's life and in being protected against an interruption in his mode of existence'.[84] 'All this is palpably obvious', he continued, 'except for a person blinded by class hatred either way'.[85]

How might we square these opinions expressed by the older Kahn-Freund with what we know of his experiences in the Weimar Republic, his decidedly socialist beliefs and political engagement before and during the Second World War, and his analysis of UK labour law in the 1950s in terms of collective laissez-faire? It would be wrong, I think, to jump too quickly to the conclusion that he moved further to the right of the political spectrum as he got older. Notwithstanding some apparent changes of opinion over the years, there is also a deep vein of continuity, for example, between Kahn-Freund's first published work on labour law – his criticisms of the Weimar State's intervention in industrial relations – and his later elaboration of collective laissez-faire.[86] As I have endeavoured to show elsewhere, his belief that trade unions and employers' associations ought to enjoy a wide measure of autonomy in the regulation of industrial relations was formed in the Weimar Republic and continued to influence his scholarship throughout his life.[87] For him, trade union autonomy was a question of democracy: of guarding against the possibility of pernicious levels of centralised state power and the possibility, ultimately, of a descent into totalitarianism. During the 1940s, he was critical of the German trade unions and their failure to use their social power to resist Nazism, in a way which illustrates his thinking well.

> It was the fate of our Weimar trade unions that they messed around too much with labour law, allowing their fighting spirit thereby to be stunted.[88]
>
> The function of legal institutions is secondary. It is the social power of the trade unions that is primary. Social power has to do not only with mere membership figures and institutions but also with the spirited participation of the individual. This may be a truism, however, truisms have a tendency to be forgotten.[89]

There are clear echoes – or rather the anticipation – here of the opening passages of *Labour and the Law*, first published in 1972; the pronouncement that,

> in labour relations legal norms cannot often be effective unless they are backed by social sanctions as well, that is by the countervailing power of trade unions and of the organised workers asserted

[83] Davies and Freedland (n 15) 18, 15.

[84] Ibid, 66.

[85] Ibid.

[86] See, eg, *Das Soziale Ideal des Reichsarbeitsgerichts*, a short monograph from 1931, and 'Der Funktionswandel des Arbeitsrechts', an article from 1932, published in translation as 'The Social Ideal of the Reich Labour Court' and 'The Changing Function of Labour Law' in Lewis and Clark (n 52).

[87] Dukes, 'Otto Kahn-Freund' (n 5).

[88] Ludyga (n 6) 47 citing letter from Kahn-Freund to Auerbach, 8.4.1940, my translation.

[89] Ludyga (n 6) citing O Kahn-Freund, *Beiträge zum Neuaufbau des deutschen Arbeitsrechts*, London 1944, my translation.

> through consultation and negotiation with the employer and ultimately, if this fails, through withholding their labour.[90]

In a 1978 interview, or 'conversation' with the German scholar Wolfgang Luthardt, Kahn-Freund considered the possibility that there may have been a shift in his political views over the years. He began with a statement of his opinion that collective labour law required a certain balance of power between the representatives of the labour movement and the employers.[91] If someone had said that to him when he was a young man, he then reflected, he would perhaps have protested that this was an indefensible position; that the working classes had to rise to a position of power. Whether he would even then have only been paying lip-service to such objections, however, he was not anymore in a position to say.[92]

It emerges from the record of the Luthardt conversation that Kahn-Freund was never a member of the communist party, in Germany or the UK. In contrast to Fraenkel and Neumann, he was never an 'orthodox' Marxist either, he explained, at least not with respect to his political beliefs.[93] Clearly, his scholarship was strongly influenced by Marxist analysis:[94] his world view, or ideology, as he put it, less so.[95] He regarded himself as having stood a little to the 'right' of Fraenkel and Neumann, during their student years and later within the SPD.[96]

> My critical starting point was not an integral-Marxist but a democratic one … I always regarded myself as a liberal, more in the American than the German sense, with a small "l". The idea of individual freedom had greater weight for me than for my more strongly Marxist-oriented friends at that time.[97]

When we read these remarks today we must take care to understand them in the political context of the time. In the 1930s, 'liberalism in the American sense' meant, presumably, Roosevelt and the New Deal. A further indication of what Kahn-Freund intended by identifying himself as a 'liberal' is provided by his characterisation of both Sinzheimer and Laski as liberals too.[98] For each of these scholars, as for many others on the left, the 'Gretchen' question of the day was how to reconcile socialism with democracy. The answer – for Kahn-Freund, as for Sinzheimer, and Laski – lay with pluralism of a sort that would safeguard the autonomy of societal organisations from the state, and against the transformation of pluralism into corporatism of a 'fascist' variety.[99] If we are to attach the label of 'liberal socialist' to Kahn-Freund, then we must define our terms accordingly.

At the same time, of course, we ought not to overlook any differences of opinion that existed between Kahn-Freund and Sinzheimer, especially on the question of the role of the state in industrial relations. That the two were not wholly in agreement in this respect is

[90] Davies and Freedland (n 15) 20.
[91] Kahn-Freund, 'Autobiographische Erinnerungen' (n 53) 195.
[92] Ibid, 196.
[93] Ibid, 187, 189.
[94] Kahn-Freund, 'Postscript' (n 52) 195.
[95] Kahn-Freund, 'Autobiographische Erinnerungen' (n 53) 189.
[96] Ibid, 187, 189.
[97] Ibid, 189, my translation.
[98] Ibid, 190–192.
[99] Kahn-Freund, 'Autobiographische Erinnerungen' (n 53) 195–6.

discernible both from their writings of the late 1920s and early 30s, and from a comparison of collective laissez-faire with Sinzheimer's conception of the labour constitution.[100] Whereas collective laissez-faire posited collective bargaining as a process decidedly private to the collective parties engaged in it, the idea of the labour constitution was constructed upon an outright rejection of the 'bourgeois' notion of the economy as a private domain, and an insistence instead on the public nature of the economy. The very purpose of the labour constitution was to ensure that the economy was managed in furtherance of the common good and not in the interests of any particular individuals or interest groups. While Sinzheimer certainly emphasised time and again the importance of the autonomy of economic actors from the state, he also believed it to be undesirable that those actors should be afforded *absolute* freedom of action. The state was not only of the architect of the system of collective administration of the economy, it was also the ultimate guarantor of the public interest. A balance had always to be struck, in Sinzheimer's view, between the autonomy of the economic actors (fundamental to democracy), and state intervention. The state should not assume the task of regulating the economy, and collective actors should not be regarded as instruments of the state. Therein lay the path to totalitarianism.

In his work on Weimar labour law, it is striking that Kahn-Freund eschewed Sinzheimer's terminology of the 'labour constitution', and spoke instead of 'collectivism' as the dominant ideology.[101] Collectivism was then defined by him so as to emphasise the desirability of union and employers' association autonomy from the state:

> The characteristic feature of the collectivist ideology of law is that it transfers the main emphasis in social policy from the political to the social sphere … The state recognises as law the result of the social conflicts between collectively organised employees and collectively organised employers, and makes available all its resources of power in order to enforce the law thus created … The state relinquishes any claim to determine the legal situation as it affects social policy; on the contrary, it gives full scope to the social development of the law and endorses its outcome at any given time.[102]

In two important publications from 1931 and 1932, Kahn-Freund directed his analysis at demonstrating how the function of the originally collectivist legislation had changed while the content of the 'written law' remained the same. For him, the principal flaw in the Weimar system of labour law was that it allowed for too great a measure of involvement of the state. Like Sinzheimer, Kahn-Freund believed that too much state intervention would result in totalitarianism. Where they differed was precisely upon the question of how much amounted to too much.

IV. Conclusion

In recent work co-authored with John Hendy, Ewing has added to the historical evidence presented by him in 1998 to demonstrate the importance of government support – legal

[100] Dukes, *Labour Constitution* (n 5) 23–30.

[101] O Kahn-Freund 'The Social Ideal of the *Reich* Labour Court' and 'The Changing Function of Labour Law' in Lewis and Clark (n 52).

[102] Kahn-Freund, 'Changing Function' (n 101) 168.

and non-legal – to the British system of sectoral collective bargaining and dispute resolution during the first half of the twentieth century.[103] While other accounts published in recent years tell a similar story to Ewing, he is probably quite correct to argue that the state's role in industrial relations was and still is routinely underestimated, especially by those who begin their analysis from the notion of 'voluntarism' or 'abstentionism'.[104] To categorise Kahn-Freund as among those who made such an error, however, is not entirely warranted. It is not warranted, in my opinion, to characterise collective laissez-faire as, 'in essence', a principle of 'political indifference'.[105] Even on the face of it, the principle of collective laissez-faire suggested the *fundamental inversion* of laissez-faire, so that it was not the individual but the collective which enjoyed freedom of action in the economic sphere. As is clear from his writing on the subject, including the key publications from the 1950s, Kahn-Freund was not only aware of the range of legal and non-legal methods used to support collective bargaining and dispute resolution in the UK, he approved of them. He approved, in other words, of a range of measures designed specifically to override the wishes of the individual, as was necessary in any particular case, in the name of collectivisation, and the furtherance of collective interests.[106] Intended quite decidedly as descriptive of such measures, collective laissez-faire was not an expression of 'political indifference', nor of 'social liberalism'.

Criticism of Kahn-Freund's account of the emergence of the British system of industrial relations seems to me, in contrast, to be justified given his understatement of the importance of government policy and action, and employer preferences, in the construction of that system. As I suggested above, this error can perhaps be explained with reference to Kahn-Freund's preoccupations as a scholar of law, rather than of history. His primary concern was to analyse the provisions of the law then in force such that they fit with his normative vision of collectivised labour bargaining collectively with management, free from state control. He was less focused, I think, on uncovering the nature of the political compromises involved in the drafting and adoption of collective labour legislation, or the policy priorities of the governments of the time. A further explanation of Kahn-Freund's hesitance to ascribe much importance to the state as the architect of collective industrial relations in the UK lies with his experience of living and working as a labour court judge in the Weimar Republic. Already, in the early 1930s, Kahn-Freund wrote about labour law in a way which revealed his growing mistrust of an over-strong state and his belief in the importance of allowing for the autonomous regulation of industrial relations by collective parties. During the 1940s and 50s, it was his mistrust of too much intervention by the state, in particular, which informed his initial admiration for English industrial relations and his development of the principle of collective laissez-faire. Kahn-Freund's preference for a wide conception of trade union autonomy, formed already by the time of his arrival in England, seemed to fit with the realities of English society as he encountered them: with the liberal preference for small government and with the English pluralist 'tradition' of allowing all interested parties

[103] KD Ewing and J Hendy, 'New Perspectives on Collective Labour Law: Trade Union Recognition and Collective Bargaining' 46 *Industrial Law Journal* 23.

[104] D Brodie, *A History of British Labour Law: 1867–1945* (Oxford, Hart Publishing, 2003); Howell (n 18).

[105] Ewing, SIR (n 1) 5.

[106] Though see the discussion of Kahn-Freund's cautious approval of the 'individualist tradition' in UK labour law: A Bogg, '"Individualism" and "Collectivism" in Collective Labour Law' (2017) 46 *Industrial Law Journal* 78.

a say. In his enthusiasm for 'English things', he overemphasised the extent to which the autonomy of trade unions from the state was the primary explanatory factor of the particular characteristics of British industrial relations.[107]

None of this would seem to me to justify the characterisation of Kahn-Freund as a liberal, or even a 'social liberal'. In his youth and midlife, he was active in socialist organisations and resistance work, campaigning from England for socialist revolution in Germany. As a legal academic, in his 50s and 60s, he continued to argue in favour of free trade unionism and a wide conception of freedom of association, which included both the right to strike and to conclude closed shop agreements. If he moved further to the right of the political spectrum as an older man (and this would remain to be established, in my opinion), then he remained nonetheless committed to free trade unionism and the collective regulation of employment relations as matters of democracy. When he described himself as a 'liberal' in later life, he meant, I believe, that he was – like Laski and Sinzheimer – a liberal socialist, rather than a socialist of the revolutionary or Marxist variety. Today we would likely describe him simply as a social democrat, albeit one who was particularly concerned with questions of individual as well as group freedom.

[107] Lewis and Clark (n 52) 200.

13

Protecting Vulnerable Workers, Fairness and State Intervention

MARILYN J PITTARD*

I. Social Justice Purpose of Labour Law

In his stimulating 1995 article, Professor Keith Ewing argues that:

> … the purpose of labour law is to develop the express or implied constitutional objective of promoting social and economic equality, or social and economic equity, or whatever the redefined objectives of democratic socialism might be. As such, labour law is concerned with two general issues, one being the economic and social security of the individual within the community and the other being the way in which the workplace is governed.[1]

Within that overall purpose, including its constitutional element, Keith Ewing identifies a social justice purpose of labour law of providing employment conditions which meet certain minimum standards, derived from the concept that it is a duty of government in a democratic socialist community, to provide the standards which are necessary 'if people are to participate in political decisions as full and equal citizens and are [to be] able generally to enjoy the benefits of citizenship and "all that that entails"'.[2]

In addition, it is possible for social rights and social justice to be delivered through the indirect mechanism of collective bargaining, again to help make full citizenship possible.[3] Thus, through labour law, the state can ensure a framework of collective bargaining from 'a base of expanding social protection',[4] to help ensure the social justice purpose of collective bargaining, without thereby being relieved of the responsibility for regulation of working conditions.[5] To fulfil the social justice purpose of labour law in the democratic socialist

* I acknowledge the research assistance of Elizabeth Hicks and the feedback of the editors.

[1] KD Ewing, 'Democratic Socialism and Labour Law' (1995) 24 *Industrial Law Journal* 103, 131.

[2] Ibid, 111. For example, the 'right to reasonable hours of labour exists to ensure that 'the citizen may have leisure for creative tasks' ibid, 111, referring to the formulation of HJ Laski, *A Grammar of Politics*, 4th edn (Abingdon, Routledge, 1941) 110.

[3] Ibid, 113. For example, by enabling workers to play a part in the rule-making process of the enterprise through their trade unions, ibid, 118.

[4] Ibid, 116.

[5] Ibid, 114.

model, as defined by Ewing, structures for collective bargaining are to be established by the state and those structures should also provide for regulation of outcomes. In addition, the state should provide for the scope of the bargaining process, both as to the range of workers covered and the issues in relation to which bargaining takes place.[6]

In several places, the 1995 article refers to aspects of the Australian labour law model which exemplify how it has dealt over its history. To a degree, Australia has achieved the social justice purposes of these goals – in some respects almost by accident rather than by design, and not necessarily for the reasons or purposes that Keith Ewing has elucidated. In this chapter, I discuss the origins of the labour relations power in the Australian Constitution that paved the way for a continuing high degree of state intervention in workplace relations and safety nets of minimum wages and conditions for employees. The chapter considers the foundations on which these safety nets are built, following a major High Court decision endorsing the use of the corporations' power in the Constitution to enact laws with respect to employment generally.

As the events in 2005 to 2007 under a Conservative Government showed, the state intruded in a way that was detrimental to workers – the Federal Parliament legislated to dismantle protections. The political influence on employees and unions was profound. It took another political influence – a change of government in 2009 – to restore some balance in the legislative framework for the collective employment relationship. I analyse the extent to which the protections for vulnerable workers in the current legislation are insulated from politics and changes in government.

Bearing in mind that the Commonwealth of Australia is a federation of states, this chapter considers the extent to which the law in Australia – at the national (ie Commonwealth) level – achieves the social justice objectives or purposes of labour law, as articulated by Ewing. In considering these purposes, it is beyond the chapter's scope to deal with the diversity and complexity in the Australian system, arising from the various state systems of labour law. Each of these systems has, until relatively recent times, provided separate mechanisms for dealing with, or providing, comprehensive minimum wages and conditions of those employees who historically have been within the scope of state laws and have not been provided with protections under national, Commonwealth law. Despite the recent general referral[7] of the legislative powers of the states on matters relating to labour relations to the Commonwealth Parliament,[8] determination of some conditions of employment has remained in the bailiwick of state law (such as long service leave).[9] Similarly, some employees in a state (such as employees or public servants of a state) remain outside the scope of the minimum statutory conditions of employment established in the national system.[10]

[6] Ibid.

[7] In 2009. See A Lynch, 'The Fair Work Act and the Referrals Power – Keeping the States in the Game' (2011) 24 *Australian Journal of Labour Law* 1.

[8] Eg, Fair Work (Commonwealth Powers) Act 2009 (Vic). Upon referral, the Commonwealth Parliament then has legislative power in respect of the referred matters: see Australian Constitution, s 51(xxxvii).

[9] Eg, Long Service Leave Act 2018 (Vic).

[10] The referral of legislative powers by the States to the Commonwealth Parliament excluded some employees of the state.

II. Determining Minimum Standards – The Origins and Development of the Protective System in Australia

In the last decade of the nineteenth century, prior to the federation of the Australian colonies to become the Commonwealth of Australia in 1901, there had been some tentative steps towards providing mechanisms for ensuring minimum standards and conditions of employment under the laws of some of the Australian colonies.[11] These tentative and limited steps, at the level of the individual colony, arose in the context of significant labour disputes and economic depression in the 1890s.[12] They did not go very far in protection of minimum conditions of employees; employers sought to use various avenues to support their view of 'freedom to contract'.[13] However, the efforts to support minimum conditions continued, both locally and nationally. The colonial controls provided the backdrop for indirect but broader establishment of powers to provide mechanisms to resolve disputes concerning wages and conditions of employment as a significant element of the debates leading to federation of the colonies and ultimately the content of the constitutional arrangements for federation.

From its initial form in 1904 to the late 1990s, the legal framework for labour relations in Australia resulted in minimum wages and conditions being determined by an independent tribunal – through industrial awards[14] made by the tribunal – and collective bargaining could take place for improved wages and conditions through collective agreements. Individual bargaining saw payments, above the minimum specified in an applicable industrial award,[15] negotiated and agreed through the employment contract. This framework occurred as a result of what is arguably a fluke of history which led to the Commonwealth of Australia's Constitution containing a provision which conferred on the new Federal Parliament the power to make laws about labour relations, indirectly, through a power to provide for conciliation and arbitration, to prevent and settle industrial disputes extending beyond the limits of any one State of the Commonwealth.[16] While several influences were at play in the inclusion of this legislative power, the nationwide disputes in the early 1890s in the maritime and pastoral industries 'undoubtedly contributed' to the perception that a national approach was needed to deal with industrial conflict which could readily arise

[11] See, eg, Factories and Shops Act 1896 (Vic). This Act provided for special Boards (constituted by representatives of employers and employees) to be established to provide minimum rates of pay for certain activities (in clothing and footwear manufacture, furniture, and bread baking). This legislation built on prior laws relating to factories and shops which covered shop opening hours and other matters relating to working conditions such as provisions for sanitation and cleanliness. Other colonies experimented with or adopted somewhat different approaches. See, eg, Conciliation and Arbitration Act 1899 (NSW), which was to deal with the prevention and settlement of trade disputes.

[12] B Creighton, 'One Hundred Years of the Conciliation and Arbitration Power: A Province Lost?' (2000) 24 *Melbourne University Law Review* 839, 843.

[13] Ibid, 860.

[14] An industrial award was usually operative in relation to defined categories of employees in a defined group of employers in an industry (such as the *Metal Engineering and Associated Industries Award 1998*) or in relation to a defined group of employers who engaged labour of a particular type (such as the *Clerical and Administrative Employees Award 2004*).

[15] Commonly referred to as 'over-award payments'.

[16] Australian Constitution, s 51(xxxv) confers on the Commonwealth Parliament the power to make laws with respect to 'conciliation and arbitration for the prevention and settlement of industrial disputes extending beyond the limits of any one State'. The 'fluke' of history was the narrow majority support for such power, after putting the motion more than once.

beyond the limits of a single state in the new federation.[17] In addition, factors such as the inadequacies of the mechanisms for voluntary conciliation which had been demonstrated in the 'industrial chaos' of the 1890s[18] were encouraging a new approach.

The clear basis for achieving social justice, as perceived by the supporters of legislation establishing conciliation and arbitration of industrial disputes, was colourfully (and perhaps optimistically) articulated by Alfred Deakin in 1903 as follows:

> No measures ever submitted to any legislature offer greater prospects of the establishment of social justice and of the removal of inequalities than those which are based upon the principle of conciliation and arbitration.[19]

The vision of two of the constitutional founding fathers, Henry Bournes Higgins and Charles Kingston, and the nature of that constitutional power as interpreted by the courts, ultimately supported a system that provided not only protection to weaker and vulnerable employee groups but also conferred a collective voice on employees through the recognition and registration of trade unions. Associations of employers were also recognised; and corporate legal status was conferred on each type of organisation.

The vision was given effect through several key elements of the 1904 legislation. Both unions and employer associations could submit industrial disputes to the Commonwealth Court of Conciliation and Arbitration ('Arbitration Court').[20] The use of compulsion in the legislation as to both conciliation and arbitration of an industrial dispute acted to encourage agreement on wages and employment terms and conditions.[21] Provision for making any collective agreement legally binding upon the parties to the agreement (usually a union, or unions, and an employer or an association of employers), once the agreement was 'certified' by the Arbitration Court, formed part of the framework from the inception of the legislation.[22] The agreement did not become part of the individual employment contract.[23]

The Arbitration Court could also 'take cognizance' of a dispute which was not brought to its attention by an organisation of employers or a union.[24] These provisions were not redundant; but from reported instances they were used relatively rarely.[25]

[17] Hon Justice M Kirby, 'Industrial Conciliation and Arbitration in Australia: A Centenary Reflection' (2004) 78 *Australian Law Journal* 785, 785. See also R Naughton, *The Shaping of Labour Law Legislation: Underlying Elements of Australia's Workplace Relations System* (London, LexisNexis, 2017) para 2.11.

[18] See Naughton, ibid, para 2.14.

[19] Commonwealth, *Parliamentary Debates*, House of Representatives, 30 July 1903, 2858 (Alfred Deakin) cited in O de R Foenander, *Industrial Conciliation and Arbitration in Australia*, 1st edn (Sydney, Law Book Company of Australasia, 1959) vi.

[20] Conciliation and Arbitration Act 1904 (Cth) s 19.

[21] There was also a power for the Arbitration Court to refer a dispute temporarily to a conciliation committee (with equal representation of employers and employees) to endeavour to settle a dispute amicably: Conciliation and Arbitration Act 1904 (Cth), s 34.

[22] Conciliation and Arbitration Act 1904 (Cth), s 24(1).

[23] Section 24 of the Conciliation and Arbitration Act 1904 (Cth) deemed the agreement to be an award and was enforceable through mechanisms provided by the Act (Part IV). There were later debates whether an award clause prohibiting unfair dismissal by employers was automatically incorporated into the contract of employment: see M Pittard and R Naughton, *Australian Labour and Employment Law* (London, LexisNexis Butterworths, 2015) ch 5. The High Court resolved the question in *Byrne v Australian Airlines* (1995) 185 CLR 140, ruling that award terms were not automatically implied or incorporated into contracts of employment. Awards and contracts are separate sources of employment obligations.

[24] Conciliation and Arbitration Act 1904 (Cth), s 16.

[25] See, eg, *Federated Engine-Drivers and Firemen's Association of Australasia and The Maxwell's Gold Mining Company* [1914] CthArbRp 29, (1914) 8 CAR 205. This dispute was not resolved in conference and was submitted

If the employee and employer representatives were unable to find mutual grounds for agreement to resolve the industrial dispute, the Arbitration Court could determine the dispute and provide an arbitrated award which was binding upon the parties.[26] In the hope that the relations of employers and employees was a 'new province for law and order',[27] the 1904 legislation included a 'quid pro quo' of restriction of labour (and employer) rights in other ways – including a prohibition of strikes and lock outs.[28]

From these beginnings – including specific roles for representative organisations of employers as well as unions – compulsory conciliation and arbitration became defining characteristics of the Australian system. An additional defining characteristic from the beginning was the availability of a clear mechanism for employers and unions to enter into legally enforceable collective agreements. Indeed, both for conciliation and arbitration, and for making of agreements, the effective operation of the system depended upon the recognition, legality and operation of trade unions.[29]

Despite the Australian Constitution being devoid of labour rights that might feature in the constitutions of some other countries – freedom from slavery, the right to associate, freedom from discrimination, for example – the legislation enacted pursuant to the constitutional labour relations power established a system of conciliation and compulsory arbitration, which exhibited a relatively high degree of state regulation in labour relations. This intervention gradually became more extensive, despite the legislation itself being unable to include provisions which directly determined actual or minimum wages and conditions of employment.

What the constitutional forefathers may not have foreseen was the High Court of Australia's role in establishing a system that was broad in coverage, far beyond perhaps the original expectations that the system would be limited to significant interstate issues such as those that had arisen in the 1890s, that is, those disputes that would be beyond the capacity of any one state to settle.

Generally, an interstate industrial dispute could be validly established by a union serving a 'log of claims' (or demands) upon various employers in two or more states, through the so-called 'paper dispute', and the employers not responding to, or refusing, those demands.[30]

to the Court under s 19 (see n 20 above). There were a number of separate agreements certified as a result of these proceedings which varied somewhat, as between employers. For a single agreement between a union and numerous employers, see: *Federated Liquor Trade Employees Union of Australasia, and Tooth and Company Limited* [1914] CthArbRp 17, (1914) 8 CAR 93.

[26] Conciliation and Arbitration Act 1904 (Cth), s 24(1). For the first reported example of the exercise of this power to make an award, see: *Merchant Service Guild of Australasia v The Commonwealth Steam-Ship Owners Association* [1905] CthArbRp 1, (1905) 1 CAR 1. This award, made by the President of the Court, covering the ship's masters and officers, included a disputes settlement procedure in cl 17.

[27] H Bournes Higgins, 'A New Province for Law and Order: Industrial Peace through Minimum Wage and Arbitration' (1915) 29 *Harvard Law Review* 13, 14: '… the process of conciliation, with arbitration in the background, is substituted for the rude and barbarous processes of strike and lockout. Reason is to displace force; the might of the State is to enforce peace between industrial combatants as well as between other combatants; and all in the interest of the public'.

[28] Conciliation and Arbitration Act 1904 (Cth) Pt II. This prohibition was repealed by the 1930s but strikes were limited by the possibility (and occasional use) of the common law proceedings in the economic or industrial torts against unions, their officials and/or employees. The practice of industrial tribunals too in resolving industrial disputes giving rise to strike action through conciliation and arbitration was important.

[29] See generally Naughton (n 17).

[30] Callinan J explained the history of this 'legal fiction' in his judgment in *New South Wales v Commonwealth* (2006) 229 CLR 1 (Work Choices case) 344–350.

In essence, the High Court's interpretation of the definition of 'industrial dispute' and how in this way disputes could arise and be 'interstate' in nature (on paper) gave the system a great boost in its early days. This expansive interpretation covered these and other elements of the constitutional provision, with some ebbs and flows over the years in the willingness of the Court to adopt a narrower or more expansive interpretation.[31] In addition, no technical interpretation was to be given to the term 'industrial dispute'; rather it had then an ordinary meaning as understood by the 'man in the street', and was initially at least broadly interpreted.[32] For example, in the 1983 *Australian Social Welfare Union Case*,[33] it was argued that neither the project officers employed by various Community Youth Support Scheme Committees, nor their employers, were engaged in or in connection with an industry, so that an 'industrial dispute' could not arise out of the non-acceptance of a log of claims served by the Union on the Committees, relating to their pay and conditions. The High Court of Australia disagreed, finding that the phrase 'industrial disputes' in the relevant constitutional head of power included all disputes between employees and employers about terms of employment and conditions of work, and was not confined to disputes in productive industry and organised business carried on for the purpose of profit.[34]

Overall, the interpretation meant that disputes were more easily brought to the Court of Conciliation and Arbitration as established in 1904 (and its court and tribunal successors over the following years[35]) for settlement; that industrial awards in settlement of disputes could perform the protective role of laying down minimum conditions that could not lawfully be departed from;[36] and that 'weaker' groups had a voice through their union and before the court or tribunal.[37] With no legislated terms and conditions of employment, the full impact of collective bargaining could potentially have been disadvantageous to weaker groups of workers. However, the legislative framework softened this impact with the award system effectively providing the safety net for workers, particularly as an award as a general rule applied to all workers engaged by the employer or employers who were parties to and bound by the award, whether they were members of the union or not. And this system was one which successive governments supported, though not without attempts to curtail

[31] Kirby (n 17) 785. See also Justice Giudice, '*The Constitution and the National Industrial Relations System*' (Australian Law Journal 80th Anniversary Conference, Sydney, 15 March 2007) paras [29]–[43] www.fwc.gov.au/documents/documents/speeches/giudicej150307.htm.

[32] Pittard and Naughton (n 23) ch 9; *R v Coldham; Ex parte Australian Social Welfare Union* (1983) 153 CLR 297, 312 (Gibbs CJ, Mason, Murphy, Wilson, Brennan, Deane and Dawson JJ). See also *Re Australian Education Union; Ex parte Victoria* (1995) 184 CLR 188, 236–237 (Mason CJ, Brennan, Deane, Toohey, Gaudron and McHugh JJ); Work Choices case (n 30) 184 (Kirby J).

[33] *R v Coldham* (n 32).

[34] Ibid, 312. See also Giudice (n 31) [37]–[38].

[35] In the initial phases of the system, the appointees to the Commonwealth Court of Conciliation and Arbitration were judicial in nature and included judges of the High Court of Australia. The nature of the Commonwealth tribunal dealing with interstate industrial disputes changed in 1956, as a result of a decision of the High Court of Australia (*R v Kirby; Ex parte Boilermakers' Society of Australia* (1956) 94 CLR 294; the *Boilermakers' Case*), which determined that the judicial power of the Commonwealth could not be vested in a tribunal that also exercised non-judicial functions. Consequently, through the Conciliation and Arbitration Act 1956, the Commonwealth [later Australian] Conciliation and Arbitration Commission was established as the tribunal to exercise powers of conciliation and arbitration, and the Commonwealth Industrial Court was established to deal with matters such as legal proceedings to enforce awards of the Commission.

[36] Wages and conditions more beneficial to employees were possible, and did occur, as the system was concerned to determine minima.

[37] Pittard and Naughton (n 23) 12–18.

discretion of the court (and later the tribunal) and to 'tinker' in various ways with the underlying legislative framework. Throughout however, the awards of the tribunal provided the means by which minimum wages and conditions were determined in the Commonwealth jurisdiction.

In time, by way of contrast, from the mid-1940s the states used their broad legislative powers to set some minimum conditions directly in legislation, although in limited fields of entitlement such as leave.[38] This broad division of approach as between the Commonwealth and the states, which was derived from the perceived limits on Commonwealth legislative power, persisted for the latter six decades of the twentieth century and only changed with the dramatic re-working of the legislation in the first decade of the twenty-first century.

Despite the absence of any explicit reference to rights in the initial federal labour relations legislation, the concept of fairness underpinned the regulatory framework for workplace relations in Australia, long before the word 'fair' was either expressly used in the name of the federal workplace relations legislation or included as a goal in that legislation. The legislative framework established in 1904, and much varied since, created ultimately a legacy of protection in the form of minimum wages and conditions of employment for employees.

In a varied form, this legacy survived even the major systemic changes from the conciliation and arbitration legislative model to an enterprise bargaining model being provided for in detail in the Commonwealth legislation. Although collective bargaining was always available and used, and indeed had become common, until the 1990s the legislative underpinnings for it were slight.[39]

The shift to a greater emphasis in the legislation on collective bargaining at the enterprise level commenced in the early 1990s and continued more significantly in the 2005 revisions of the Workplace Relations Act 1996 (Cth) and further under the Fair Work Act 2009 (Cth) (Fair Work Act).

Since 2006, the legacy of protection of minimum standards can be seen in the presence of certain minimum conditions of employment in the legislation itself,[40] with other minimum conditions of employment now contained in some 122 awards covering specified industries or occupations, with minimum rates of pay determined by the statutory Australian Fair Work Commission, as a 'safety net' for employees.[41] The legislative structure is built on the basis that actual terms and conditions above these minima will be determined by collective bargaining at the enterprise level. Bargaining at the industry level is not provided for by the legislative scheme, and that absence has been the subject of criticism.[42] Individual bargaining

[38] Eg, Annual Holidays Act 1944 (NSW). As noted earlier, separate state legislative schemes established industrial tribunals to determine minimum wages and terms and conditions of employment for employees within that state. These awards, and awards made by the Commonwealth tribunal, tended to operate in distinct spheres.

[39] The revision of the Commonwealth legislation in 1988 continued the traditional focus on conciliation and arbitration with provision for tribunal approval of certified (collective) agreements, which prevailed over an award, being dealt with primarily in the Industrial Relations Act 1988 (Cth), ss 115–117.

[40] This aspect of the current legislation is based on the constitutional power to make laws in respect of trading and financial corporations (see below text to nn 69 and 70).

[41] According to the 2017–2018 Annual Report of the Fair Work Commission, as at 30 June 2018 there were 122 industry and occupational modern awards operating across Australia. The report notes that, in addition, there were 33 modern awards covering specific enterprises or state public sector bodies that are part of the national workplace relations system: Fair Work Commission, 'Fair Work Commission Annual Report 2017–18' (*Commonwealth of Australia*, 2018) 55.

[42] See, eg, J Isaac, 'Why Are Australian Wages Lagging and What Can Be Done About It?' (2018) 51 *The Australian Economic Review* 175.

or market forces may also lead to more beneficial wages and conditions being provided above the minima.

III. The Shift Towards a Focus on Enterprise Bargaining

In an environment in which changes in labour relations were being sought by business towards greater decentralisation of determination of employment conditions, increased flexibility and less rigidity of awards,[43] a number of changes were made towards a degree of decentralisation of determination of employment conditions in the 1990s.[44] These changes started with the Industrial Relations Reform Act 1993 (Cth) which created a specific focus on, and promotion of, enterprise bargaining,[45] consistent with a move away from conciliation and compulsory arbitration in dispute resolution.[46]

The changes were made by the Labor Party Government at the time to adhere to the principles of fairness which had traditionally been part of the system for nigh on a century,[47] but nonetheless marked a move away from reliance on compulsory arbitration whilst seeking to ensure vulnerable workers were not disadvantaged. Agreements remained at the collective level. Moreover, the industrial tribunal (then to be called the Australian Industrial Relations Commission, or 'AIRC')[48] continued to be empowered to approve collective agreements between employers and unions. Unions broadly maintained their traditional rights to represent specific categories of employees in an industry or occupation.

An innovation in the 1993 legislation was the provision for collective agreements to be made at the enterprise level (called then 'enterprise flexibility agreements', or 'EFAs') without union involvement, and without the need for a pre-existing industrial dispute.[49] Significantly it was a Labor Government that championed the non-union stream of bargaining (that is a collective agreement could be made with a group of employees and a union need not be involved in negotiations). This was a policy move that ran counter to the ILO's concept of collective bargaining which very clearly envisages collective agreements to be between unions and employers or their organisation.[50] As a protective measure, an EFA was not operative until it was approved by the AIRC in accordance with a range of conditions, including that employees were not disadvantaged by the terms of the EFA.[51] In summary,

[43] Creighton (n 12) 848.

[44] Pittard and Naughton (n 23) 18–25.

[45] Reflected in the revised s 3 and pt 5 of the Industrial Relations Act 1988 (Cth).

[46] Naughton (n 17) paras 4.1–4.2.

[47] Ibid, para 4.3.

[48] This change, replacing the former Australian Conciliation and Arbitration Commission, occurred as a result of the passage of the Industrial Relations Act 1988 (Cth).

[49] The Australian Council of Trade Unions was sufficiently assured by the protections in the legislation and system to accept this fundamental shift made by a Labor Party government: see T Pallas, 'The IR Reform Act 1993. A Union Perspective: Labouring Towards Workplace Reform (*ACTU*, 8 June 1994) www.actu.org.au/actu-media/archives/1994/the-ir-reform-act-1993-a-union-perspective-labouring-towards-workplace-reform.

[50] See, eg, International Labour Organization (ILO), Convention concerning the Promotion of Collective Bargaining (adopted 3 June 1981, entered into force 11 August 1983) C154, art 2, which defines 'collective bargaining' as negotiations taking place 'between an employer, a group of employers or one or more employers' organisations, on the one hand, and one or more workers' organisations, on the other …'.

[51] Industrial Relations Act 1993 (Cth) s 170NC.

the legislation shifted emphasis from a state-sponsored system for resolution of disputes to more direct negotiations between the parties at the enterprise level. The role of the tribunal became more supervisory in nature and less determinative.[52] However its approval was fundamental to the implementation and enforcement of the agreement. Critically however, there was as yet no attempt to enable agreements with individual employees to supplant or override conditions provided by an award of the industrial tribunal, or an approved collective agreement or an approved EFA. Significantly, too, the legislation brought into Australia law certain ILO Conventions including protection against unfair dismissal, a limited right to strike and freedom of association.[53]

IV. The Chilling Effect of Changes in the Political Winds

Despite these significant changes, further legislative emphasis on the decentralisation of determination of minimum wages and conditions of employment was pursued, following the election of a Liberal-National Party Coalition Federal Government in 1996, in the new Workplace Relations Act 1996 (Cth), which came into operation in 1997. For its constitutional foundation, it relied on the traditional 'conciliation and arbitration' head of legislative power but also significantly relied on the 'corporations power' in the Constitution to broaden coverage of non-union agreements to corporate employers. It also nonetheless made substantial changes to the legal framework, largely based on the principal object of achieving 'a framework for cooperative workplace relations which promotes the economic prosperity and welfare of the people of Australia by' (amongst some 13 stated purposes):[54]

> (d) ensuring that, as far as possible, the primary responsibility for determining matters affecting the employment relationship rests with the employer and employees at the workplace or enterprise level; and
>
> (e) enabling employers and employees to choose the most appropriate form of agreement for their particular circumstances …

The Workplace Relations Act 1996 (Cth) also continued provisions from the 1993 amendments of the Industrial Relations Act 1988 (Cth) which provided for some limited minimum standards for employees within the scope of the legislation.[55]

In addition to limiting the historical scope of the content of awards (through the introduction of a specific definition of 'allowable matters' outlining matters that could be included

[52] Creighton (n 12) 849.

[53] M Pittard and R Naughton, 'The Right to Strike: Australia' in Bernd Waas (ed), *The Right to Strike: A Comparative View* (AH Alphen aan den Rij, Kluwer Law International, 2014) 95–120.

[54] Workplace Relations Act 1996 (Cth), s 3. This Act, which repealed the Industrial Relations Act 1988 (Cth) in its entirety, came into operation on 1 January 1997. The change in terminology in the title of the legislation itself sought to emphasise the nature of the fundamental changes brought about by it, by removing 'industrial relations' (with its suggestion of the importance of the collective interests) and substituting 'workplace relations' with its terminological emphasis on the individual workplace and individual work relationships between employer and employee.

[55] Including equal remuneration for equal work, termination of employment, and parental leave: see Workplace Relations Act 1996 (Cth) Pt VIA, as at 20 January 1997.

in awards),[56] thereby diminishing the importance of awards, the 1996 Act, in its pursuit of the individualisation of workplace relations, introduced a completely new form of individual agreement, the Australian Workplace Agreement ('AWA').[57] This radical innovation, going far beyond the union and non-union but collective EFAs under the prior legislation, was a form of agreement which could be made by an employer with an employee, and when lodged with a statutory officer, overrode the application of an award or the application of a collective agreement,[58] provided that the AWA satisfied a 'no disadvantage overall' test.[59] This AWA mechanism fundamentally altered the previous legal position that an employer and employee could not – at least in a way which was legally enforceable by either party – agree to any terms and conditions which did not satisfy the minimum applicable conditions of an award or collective agreement.[60] A minimum condition provided by the award could be overridden (that is, not be strictly complied with) if 'overall' the employee was not disadvantaged by the AWA. In effect, the AWA was supposed to include some benefits which overcame the loss of some other minimum entitlement under an award or agreement, so that there was 'no disadvantage overall'.

Other changes worked towards the same objective of increased emphasis on individualism in employment relations: they included significant changes such as union preference clauses and closed shop provisions being prohibited in awards and collective agreements,[61] restrictive changes to union entitlements in respect of a right of entry to workplaces in connection with breaches of awards and agreements and in relation to an opportunity to meet with employees,[62] and the creation of an entitlement for an employee to not join a union just as much as historically there had been (and there remained) protection of an employee's right to join a union.[63]

Even so, some traditional elements of the former system remained. There continued to be a role for collective bargaining, as well as powers for the AIRC to make awards in settlement of industrial disputes.

The legislation continued to be tinkered with after 1996; changes were made in each year after 1996, in a diverse array of areas.[64] There were also concerted attempts to reduce the protection of unfair dismissal by exempting small businesses, though these were largely unsuccessful due to the government not having the necessary majority in the Senate (the upper house of Parliament) to support the passage of the legislation.[65]

[56] Workplace Relations Act 1996 (Cth), ss 513–519, 525.

[57] A type of statutory contract of employment.

[58] Naughton (n 17) 168; M Rimmer, 'The Workplace Relations Act 1996: An Historical Perspective' (1997) 23 *Australian Bulletin of Labour* 69, 73.

[59] See Workplace Relations Act 1996 (Cth) Pt VIE, s 170VPB, as at 20 January 1997. Amendments were later made to these requirements.

[60] See *Byrne and Frew v Australian Airlines Ltd* (1995) 131 ALR 422,427, citing *Kilminster v Sun Newspapers Ltd* (1931) 46 CLR 284. The award operates with the force of statute to secure its conditions.

[61] G Patmore, 'A Voice for Whom? Employee Representation and Labour Legislation in Australia' (2006) 29 *University of New South Wales Law Journal* 8.

[62] Union right of entry was governed now by the legislation.

[63] The concept of freedom of association was endorsed; however, it was expanded to include the right not to join a union, thereby introducing an individual right into a collective labour law concept.

[64] See Pittard and Naughton (n 23) 18–25, chs 10, 13.

[65] M Pittard, 'Unfair Dismissal Laws: The Problem of Application to Small Businesses' (2002) 15 *Australian Journal of Labour Law* 154.

V. The Revolutionary Work Choices Legislation – Individualism to the Fore with Diminished Job Security

The most dramatic and extensive changes came into effect in 2006,[66] following the re-election of a Liberal-National Party coalition Government, under Prime Minister Howard, in 2004. These changes were in an historical and constitutional sense revolutionary, not only in their content but also and more particularly in their reliance on constitutional powers of which only limited use had been made previously. Justice Paul Munro, a former Senior Deputy President of the Australian Industrial Relations Commission, described it as a 'counter-revolutionary reversal of egalitarian and collectivist values institutionally embedded since Australian Federation'[67] and a 'servant of market ideology and anti-collectivist tendencies'.[68]

Amongst its many changes to the prior legislative framework for the conduct of industrial relations and the relations of employees and employers, the Work Choices legislation (enacted in 2005) in large part relied on heads of legislative power (other than the conciliation and arbitration power) to establish specific entitlements for employees within the scope of the legislation. In doing so, in particular the 2005 legislation relied on the power to make laws in relation to trading and financial corporations formed in Australia – called 'constitutional corporations' (the 'corporations power').[69] This relatively novel use of the corporations power was upheld by the High Court of Australia despite the dissents, on distinct grounds, from their Honours, Justice Kirby and Justice Callinan.[70] The abandonment of general use of the 'conciliation and arbitration' power also resulted in very limited powers of arbitration being left to the AIRC.

The legislation included a departure from prior Commonwealth legislative practice (by way of contrast to long-established practice in the use of legislative powers by the states to legislatively determine minimum conditions of employment),[71] by establishing actual minimum conditions of employment for all employees within the scope of the legislation as statutory entitlements.

These entitlements included provisions for minimum rates of pay, maximum ordinary hours of work, annual leave, parental leave and personal leave. There were other changes too – including the establishment of the Australian Fair Pay Commission whose function was to undertake wage reviews and determine minimum rates of pay, removing that function from the AIRC – which continued in existence but with reduced functions and powers, as national minimum rates of pay had become the province of the Australian Fair Pay Commission.

From one perspective, these provisions directly ensured that some dimensions of a social justice purpose of labour law were served, since the vast majority of employees in Australia

[66] Workplace Relations Amendment (Work Choices) Act 2005 (Cth) (the Work Choices legislation).

[67] P Munro, 'Changes to the Australian Industrial Relations System: Reforms or Shattered Icons? An Insider's Assessment of the Probable Impact on Employers, Employees and Unions' (2006) 29 *University of New South Wales Law Journal* 128, 128.

[68] Ibid, 133; Naughton (n 17) para 6.5.

[69] Australian Constitution, s 51(xx).

[70] Work Choices case (n 30).

[71] See above text to n 38, also nn 7–10.

gained the benefit of a small number of statutory minimum conditions of employment (largely reflecting prior conditions contained in awards and/or collective agreements and known as the Australian Fair Pay and Commission Standards), although minimum rates of pay remained outside the ambit of specific legislation as noted above.[72]

Despite that, the other structural changes diminished the 'social justice' purpose of establishing the framework for collective bargaining. This was reflected in characteristics of the bargaining framework, including the limited circumstances in which the tribunal was able to arbitrate when bargaining did not achieve an agreed outcome, the prohibition (except in limited circumstances) of collective bargaining at the industry or sector level and the virtual elimination of effective unfair dismissal protections, though retained in name for employees of 'large' employers which engaged 101 or more employees.[73] The impact on terms and conditions of employment was significant for the weaker groups and for those who lost previously won conditions through the changed framework for individual agreements and loss of what were incorrectly labelled 'protected' award conditions. This was a predicted outcome, and became quickly apparent in the year after the operation of the Work Choices.[74]

The historical acceptance of fairness and protection to vulnerable employees was all but gone under this phase of intervention by the state. This loss and the shift to individualism proved politically dangerous for the Conservative Government and it was voted out of office by the electorate in an election campaign that rested largely on industrial relations. The new Labor Government swiftly took steps to reverse the impact of Work Choices, but the pendulum had swung too far– and for reasons that no doubt included political caution on the part of the newly elected Labor Government, the tried system of conciliation and arbitration was not to be reinstated.

VI. Fair Work Act – The Return to Fairness and Protecting Vulnerable Employees and the Move Away from Individualism

This section focusses on the changes in the federal system since the enactment of the Fair Work Act 2009 which provided protection of workers and minimum conditions of employment – but in a somewhat patchwork way.

Enterprise bargaining is intended by the legislation to be the main way of determining actual employment conditions, subject to the independent tribunal's[75] approval, hence the third party supervision is vital to protecting standards and to assisting to overcome the

[72] The industrial tribunal too was by-passed for determining wages – this was given to a new body, the Australian Fair Pay Commission, no doubt in an attempt to avoid the rulings of what the government had perceived as a body that favoured employees over employers.

[73] M Pittard, 'Back to the Future: Unjust Termination of Employment under the Work Choices Legislation' (2006) 19 *Australian Journal of Labour Law* 225; M Pittard, 'Fairness in Dismissal: A Devalued Right' in J Teicher, R Lambert and A O'Rourke (eds), *WorkChoices: The New Industrial Relations Agenda* (Sydney, Pearson, 2006) 74.

[74] D Peetz, 'Assessing the Impact of "Work Choices" One Year On', Report for Industrial Relations Victoria (Department of Innovation, Industry and Regional Development Industrial Relations Victoria, 2007); D Peetz, 'How Wide is the Impact of Work Choices?' in K Abbott and others (eds), *Work Choices: Evolution or Revolution* (Melbourne, Heidelberg Press, 2007) 23–42.

[75] The Fair Work Commission. For a period, it was called Fair Work Australia.

common, indeed usual, occurrence of an imbalance of bargaining power as between an employer and an individual employee. Unfair dismissal protection was reintroduced with an exception for true small business employers;[76] the right to strike was maintained for the purposes of bargaining to reach an enterprise agreement,[77] with powers to deal with strikes in essential services;[78] freedom of association applying to the right *not* to join a union was maintained; and importantly the individual form of agreement, the Australian Workplace Agreement, was abolished.[79]

A. Safety Net of Conditions and Enterprise Bargaining

Adopting and adapting the concepts inherent in the Australian Fair Pay and Conditions Standard under Work Choices and reflecting previous decisions of the tribunal on labour standards,[80] there are now legislated minimum standards for various types of leave and for maximum hours of work, public holiday entitlements, notice of termination and redundancy pay,[81] which apply generally across the board (other than to state public servants etc who are not within the scope of the legislation). These National Employment Standards ('NES'), when combined with the modern awards which prescribe minimum pay in industries (or, in some cases, occupational groups) and deal with some other matters, form the safety net of minimum conditions.

Enterprise bargaining can achieve better conditions and can derogate from some award standards[82] where the tribunal is satisfied that *each and every employee* will be better off under the agreement compared to the award.[83] The safety net functions of minimum employment conditions through the NES and the Federal Minimum Wage and, where applicable, award conditions, when combined with the requirement that any bargaining must provide employees with conditions which are 'better off overall' certainly go a long way towards satisfying the social justice purpose of labour law, as set out in the goals identified by Keith Ewing.[84] Interestingly, it is a combination of laws on the one hand enacted by Parliament (the NES), with Parliament largely adopting the previous decisions of the industrial tribunal in determining basic employment standards[85] and on the other hand decisions of the tribunal in ruling and updating modern awards which provide the

[76] M Pittard, 'Protection From Unfair Dismissal: Fairness and the Fair Work Act' in C Ozich (ed), *Employment Rights Now: Reflections on the Australian Charter of Employment Rights* (Victoria, Hardie Grant Books, 2015) 83–95; M Pittard, 'Fair Process in Unfair Dismissal Claims: Changing Landscape Under the Fair Work Act' (2010) 17 *Australian Journal of Administrative Law* 199. Even then, small businesses should comply with a checklist which incorporates that a valid reason is needed and there should be fair process for dismissal.

[77] See Pittard and Naughton (n 23).

[78] R Naughton and M Pittard, 'Australia' in M Mordehai Mironi and M Schlachter (eds), *Regulating Strikes in Essential Services: A Comparative 'Law in Action' Perspective* (The Netherlands, Wolter-Kluwers 2018) 53–87.

[79] In the sense that no new AWAs could be made but the existing AWAs were to be phased out.

[80] M Pittard, 'Reflections on the Commission's Legacy in Legislated Minimum Standards' (2011) 53 *Journal of Industrial Relations* 698.

[81] Fair Work Act 2009 (Cth), Pt 2.2.

[82] Ibid, s 172.

[83] Ibid, ss 186(2)(d), 193(1). See also *ALDI Foods Pty Limited v Shop, Distributive and Allied Employees Association* (2017) 350 ALR 381.

[84] Ewing (n 1) 111.

[85] See M Pittard, 'Reflections on the Commission's Legacy in Legislated Minimum Standards' (2011) 53 *Journal of Industrial Relations* 698.

yardstick for the approval of enterprise agreements. Thus, both Parliament and tribunal currently have an on-going role in setting basic standards. Parliament can of course take away or erode that role of the tribunal, as we saw in the 2005 Work Choices legislation, so Conservative governments have not been shy in legislating to tilt the balance towards employers.

How well the legislation has achieved this goal is not clear. The most recent published survey data from the Australian Bureau of Statistics, dealing with methods of setting pay (not industrial instrument coverage generally), suggests that as of May 2018, 58.9 per cent of employees had their actual terms and conditions of employment determined by an award or a collective agreement. As between awards and collective agreements, the estimates data indicates that in May 2018, 21.0 per cent of all employees are reliant on awards for their conditions of employment ('award only' employees), with some 36.4 per cent being reliant on a collective agreement.[86] Employees paid by individual arrangement – that is, above the applicable award rate – account for 37.3 per cent of all employees,[87] with the remaining 3.8 per cent of employees being owner managers of incorporated enterprises. Despite limitations with the data,[88] it appears that between 2012 and 2018 there has been an increase in the proportion of all employees and non-managerial employees who are paid on an 'award only' basis (from 16.1 per cent to 21.0 per cent).

These collective agreements are made with the involvement of bargaining agents on behalf of the employees, who will generally be the relevant union (or unions) with rights under the Fair Work Act 2009 to represent the industrial interests of those employees. Any agreement must be approved by a vote of the employees who are to be covered by the agreement. That protection of the interest of employees is not of course absolute, provided each employee is better off overall; some groups may do relatively better in the result than others since the assessment under the BOOT is 'overall', not on a line-by-line comparison of the relevant award with the agreement.[89]

In practice, almost all agreements are approved by the Fair Work Commission.[90] However, the tribunal has not always been satisfied that an agreement meets the 'better off overall' test,[91] so in that way the interests of the employees are being protected by it. But on

[86] Although there are some difficulties of comparability of the data, as noted by the Australian Bureau of Statistics so that the data only provides high level, broadly (not directly) comparable estimates, it appears that there has been a decline (from 42.0% to 37.9%) in the proportion of employees whose conditions are determined by collective agreements in 2018 compared to 2012. See Australian Bureau of Statistics, *Employee Earnings and Hours, Australia, May 2018* (Catalogue No 6306.0, 22 January 2019); Australian Bureau of Statistics, *A Guide to Understanding Employee Earnings and Hours Statistics, Australia, May 2018* (Catalogue No 6306.0, 13 February 2019) App 1.

[87] This figure includes employees whose earnings are not covered by an award or a collective agreement; for this group, earnings are determined by the Federal Minimum Wage (determined by the Australian Fair Work Commission) and conditions by the National Employment Standards – that is, they are paid at the minimum legal level. See Australian Bureau of Statistics, *A Guide to Understanding Employee Earnings and Hours* (n 89).

[88] See n 86.

[89] See, eg, the decision of Deputy President Colman, *BOC Limited* [2019] FWCA 5544, 12 August 2019.

[90] See Fair Work Commission, 'Annual Report 2017–2018', ch 2.9, Table 20. In that year, the Commission approved 3,658 single enterprise agreements (of which 1,159 were approved without undertakings, and 2,499 were approved with undertakings), 42 were dismissed and 776 were withdrawn. The Commission cannot approve an agreement with an undertaking (usually from the employer), if the effect of accepting the undertaking is likely to cause financial detriment to any employee covered by the agreement, or result in substantial changes to the agreement.

[91] See, eg, *Armacell Australia Pty Ltd* [2010] FWAFB 9985.

other occasions the initial favourable determination by the tribunal about an agreement (which was made with a union as the bargaining agent) has been successfully challenged within the tribunal's appeal processes,[92] again therefore protecting the interests of employees, at least within the scope of the legislative framework.

The problem of movement in a collective agreement away from minimum standards as provided by the relevant award, and in that respect the social justice purpose of labour law as reflected in the award, arises from a combination of factors. On the one hand, we have the perceived necessity provided for in the legislation to allow for different arrangements to be negotiated by employers and represented employees than are provided by the award. On the other hand, we have the practical difficulty of applying a 'better off overall test' which is inherently potentially both objective and subjective in nature, given that not all benefits or detriments in an agreement are objectively measurable, at least in money terms. The Fair Work Commission itself noted the requirements and difficulties in its 2017–2018 Annual Report:

> The BOOT [the 'better of overall' test] requires an overall assessment. The Commission must identify the terms in the proposed agreement that are both better and worse for an employee and make an overall decision about whether the employee is likely to be better off under the proposed agreement. While this decision is generally mathematical for wages, it is more complex where the proposed clauses concern benefits not directly related to money, benefits accessible at the employee's choice, or financial benefits which rely on specific events occurring.[93]

Although this judgement can involve considering various elements, some of which are more readily determined on an objective basis, whereas others are more subjective in nature,[94] the persons making those judgements on an objective basis as members of the Fair Work Commission in the course of proceedings have the benefit of submissions from the parties to the agreement on these issues. Moreover, for many years, members of the tribunal have been appointed from a diversity of backgrounds and have possessed a range of skills, knowledge and experience of industrial and employment matters – union officials, employer organisation officers or employer human resources officers, public servants, lawyers (both barristers and solicitors), academics, economists, and others.

Whilst some of the members of the tribunal have judicial status, they are not exercising judicial power when considering approval of the agreement. Although the balance of the backgrounds of appointees varies over time and is sometimes criticised as favouring the employer side, or the union side, the nature and composition of the tribunal, as well as its statutory obligations, provide some confidence that these 'better off overall' judgements will be made on the whole reasonably, with the possibility of unreasonable application of the legislation being mitigated by the availability of an appeal.

[92] The necessary judgements can be difficult to make, given the different types of benefits (payments and non-monetary benefits; see, eg, *Hart v Coles Supermarkets Australia Pty Ltd and Anor* [2016] FWCFB 2887.

[93] Fair Work Commission, 'Annual Report 2017–2018', ch 2.9: 'Significant decision – will every worker be better off overall?' referring to *Loaded Rates Agreements* [2018] FWCFB 3610.

[94] See, eg, the decision of Deputy President Colman, *BOC Limited* [2019] FWCA 5544, 12 August 2019, in which the collective agreement for which approval was sought provided employees with better terms in remuneration, but did not provide for 'lifestyle' entitlements, such as time off in lieu of overtime and rostered days off. The Deputy President considered that the BOOT required an objective test; the requirement is to consider the objectively verifiable benefits or detriments provided to each employee, compared to the underlying award, not 'subjective and unquantifiable matters'.

So, with core minimum standards established by legislation (through the NES) and enforceable under that legislation, achieving the additional benefits available for employees – above wages and conditions established by awards – involves not only effective use of the enterprise bargaining provisions, but also strong understanding and application of the role played by the tribunal in ultimately approving an enterprise agreement.

VII. Challenges to Achieving Social Justice

There are some weaknesses however; the Fair Work Act has gaps in its protections. The minimum standards set out in the NES are not comprehensive, although they are significant, and their protections are a safety net only.

Mostly, the NES set particular objective standards, some of which are set on standards of former award conditions (for example, severance or redundancy pay and the period of annual leave). Others are of a more subjective character.

One of the NES provides a maximum full-time work week of 38 hours. However, the employee may be required to work 'reasonable additional hours',[95] so the set objective and maximum standard is a maximum in name only. The extra hours are limited by that elusive notion of reasonableness. An employee covered by an award or enterprise agreement may be entitled to overtime or penalty rates for time worked in excess of the maximum, which will vary according to that award or agreement. By way of contrast, an employee who is not covered by an award or a collective agreement may be required to work reasonable additional hours (in addition to the 38 hours per week, for a full time employee), but is not entitled under the NES to receive a higher rate of pay for that overtime work; there is no NES coverage of pay for overtime hours or additional rate of pay if the work is outside usual working hours in the industry or at other times (such as at weekends). In each case, whether the hours are reasonable is not always easy to determine, given the flexibility inherent in the term 'reasonable additional hours' which the employer may require the employee to work.

Although an employee may refuse to work the required additional hours, if these are unreasonable,[96] she or he does so at risk of termination of employment if the judgement of reasonableness later turns out to be wrong. The legislation does set out a range of ten factors[97] to be considered in determining whether additional hours which an employer requires are 'reasonable'. These reflect factors relevant in some cases to employer concerns[98] and in other cases to employee concerns.[99] The legislation therefore calls for a balancing of the factors relevant in a particular case in order to determine what is 'reasonable' in that case, but it may not always be easy for an employee to be certain in advance that the hours are indeed unreasonable.[100] Further the legislated standard of additional hours is not

[95] Fair Work Act 2009 (Cth), s 62(1).
[96] Ibid.
[97] Including 'any other relevant matter': Fair Work Act 2009 (Cth), s 62(3)(j).
[98] Eg, the needs of the workplace and the usual pattern of work in the industry: Fair Work Act 2009 (Cth), ss 62(3)(c), 62(3)(g).
[99] Eg, the employee's family responsibilities: Fair Work Act 2009 (Cth), s 62(3)(b).
[100] See, for an example of the application of these factors, *Elwin v Edwards Motors Pty Ltd* [2015] FCCA 334.

related to pay – penalty or shift rates may come from other sources (awards or collective agreements), but not from the legislated standard.

Moreover, where the legislation does set a specific standard (such as the various obligations in respect of leave and severance or redundancy pay), these are minimum entitlements only.

Actual conditions are left to the vagaries of enterprise negotiations, which are less common than would have been anticipated when the system was introduced. Unionised industries tend to have enterprise agreements, compared to non-unionised industries and to those sectors where there are many small employers. Modern trends have seen a decline in enterprise agreements and parties falling back on minimum award conditions, partly because of the legal emphasis on the need for each and every employee to be better off under the agreement. Greater divergence as between sectors may result; and there is divergence too within industries given that bargaining occurs at the enterprise level.

Given the increasing proportion of workers whose minimum conditions are award based (rather than enterprise agreements), these workers are closer to the safety net; and arguably they are less able to have 'adequate wage' and fair conditions.

In addition, contemporary challenges to the provision of an adequate wage and minimum conditions, that is to fair conditions, come from the uneven application of awards which do not apply uniformly, both in substance and as a matter of law, because of a number of factors discussed below.

(i) Employees Outside the Scope of the Fair Work Act

Partly for constitutional reasons, some employees are not within the scope of the Fair Work Act. Employees who are not included in the scope of the legislation include, for example, those who work for a state public service at senior levels, and some Western Australian employees as that state has not wholly referred its industrial relations law-making powers to the Commonwealth. There are some exclusions, too, from eligibility to claim unfair dismissal, for example, true casual employees who are not regularly or systematically employed by the employer; employees who are engaged for less than six months (or 12 months in the case of small businesses); and employees who are not covered by awards and whose salary exceeds the 'high income threshold'.

(ii) Awards do not Apply to all Employees of Employers who are Within the Scope of the Fair Work Act

Not all types of employment are covered by awards. For types of employment which are 'not traditionally covered by awards',[101] no award can be made. This includes, for example, employees in the broad information technology sector (unless the employees fall within the traditional scope of an award which applies in a particular industry).

For these employees, there are therefore no relevant minimum conditions of employment other than those in the NES (eg their minimum rate of pay is determined by the Federal Minimum Wage and there is no legislation requiring a higher rate of pay for overtime work). Pending any legislative change to overcome this limitation, the classes of workers in this area of minimal legislated protection are, to this extent, frozen in time.

[101] See Fair Work Act 2009 (Cth), ss 143(7), 143A.

(iii) Independent Contractors

Individual workers engaged as independent contractors form a significant component of the total workforce – currently around 8 per cent of the Australian workforce.[102] Perhaps surprisingly, there is no special definition of 'employee' in the Fair Work Act,[103] because the common law meaning of 'employee'[104] is applied to determine whether a person is an employee (and therefore potentially covered by an award). This legal status of the workers determines the application of the Fair Work Act, its protective conditions, and awards and agreements made under it. Although the common law factors used to determine the legal status of a worker are well known,[105] difficulties in application to particular factual circumstances occur relatively frequently, as illustrated by the degree of litigation in such areas. Consequently, another factor limiting the protection of the legislation is the increased use of independent contractors in circumstances in which the correct legal characterisation may be that of an employee. There are some mechanisms to prevent or control abuse,[106] but these can be difficult to apply and enforce.[107]

(iv) The Pool of Vulnerable Workers

Workers who might previously have enjoyed the protection and safeguards of the legislation may find that they are now at risk of little or no protection. Linked to (iii) above, the impact of the gig economy, where models of engagement of labour services label the workers as 'contractors' to deliberately by-pass protections given to employees, is now significant. Whilst there have been rulings on the status of these new gig economy workers, their status commonly remains in doubt, which is not aided by the piecemeal approach to obtaining rulings to clarify their status.[108] There is no appetite, it seems, to legislate to clarify the position of gig economy workers, though state legislatures have endeavoured to deal with labour hire issues.[109] There is also uncertain status of some workers, eg 'nannies' and au pairs, where they might not truly be employees but utilise this nanny/au pair status to gain entry to the country on working holiday visas.[110]

[102] Australian Bureau of Statistics, *Characteristics of Employment, Australia, August 2018* (Catalogue No 6333.0, 29 November 2018).

[103] The concept of the status of a person as an 'employee', fundamental to the operation of the legislation, has been left to be resolved in accordance with the common law definition from the beginnings of the national system, from the first Conciliation and Arbitration Act in 1904, despite the manifest difficulties of determining the characterisation under the common law principles, at least at the significant margins.

[104] See, eg, *Hollis v Vabu Pty Ltd* (2001*)* 207 CLR 21; Pittard and Naughton (n 23) ch 4.

[105] Some legislation has endeavoured to overcome these difficulties by 'deeming' workers in certain circumstances to be 'employees'.

[106] See the Independent Contractors Act 2006 (Cth) and the 'sham contracting' provisions of the Fair Work Act 2009 (Cth), ss 357–359 where it an offence to misrepresent the relationship as principal and worker when at law it is that of employer and employee.

[107] As the constitutional basis of the legislation is now the corporations' power (section 51(xx) of the Constitution), there is no constitutional reason to prevent the legislation providing more directly for minimum conditions for independent contractors, especially contractors who are individuals.

[108] Unlike in the UK in *Uber BV v Aslam* [2018] EWCA Civ 2748, [2019] 3 All ER 489, there has not been a definitive superior court ruling in Australia on the status of Uber workers. For some recent rulings, see *Pallage v Rasier Pacific Pty Ltd* [2018] FWC 2579; *Kaseris v Rasier Pacific V.O.F* [2017] FWC 6610; cf *Klooger v Foodora Australia Pty Ltd* [2018] FWC 6836.

[109] See, eg, Labour Hire Licensing Act 2018 (Vic); and Labour Hire Licensing Act 2017 (Qld).

[110] L Berg and G Meagher, 'Cultural Exchange or Cheap Housekeeper? Findings of a National Survey of Au Pairs in Australia' (*Migrant Worker Justice Initiative*, 2018) https://static1.squarespace.com/static/593f6d9fe4fcb

Whilst the Fair Work Act deals with vocational employment and has certain controls and safeguards on work experience for students, a person classified as an 'intern' to gain experience as a pathway to more permanent employment is also at risk of reduced labour rights, as evidenced in recent cases.[111] Volunteers may also have dubious status and be used as a method of avoiding the operation of the minimum protections in the Fair Work Act.

Even where the status of workers is clear and their entitlements to protection under the Fair Work Act not in doubt, exploitation in employment of international students and other visa holders with effectively no or limited work rights in practice has emerged as a major issue of concern within the economy. Where the visa holder depends on the employer's goodwill to continue in employment in order to lawfully remain in the country, the employee is at risk of exploitation. An inquiry into international students, backpackers and temporary migrants found that 'Almost a third (30%) of survey participants earned $12 per hour or less. This is approximately half the minimum wage for a casual employee in many of the jobs in which temporary migrants work.'[112] Particularly egregious instances of exploitation have occurred with international students which led to a report and many legal proceedings in an attempt to rectify the exploitation.[113]

A. Enforcement of Minimum Entitlements – Issues of Compliance

Enforcement of minimum conditions presents challenges. Difficulties in the path of ensuring that employers comply with legal obligations commonly arise, particularly (but by no means exclusively) in relation to small business employers such as those who operate as franchisees[114] where we have seen failures to provide minimum conditions and wages: the business structure of franchising resting in many cases on exploitation of labour in order to yield profit to the franchisee. There is a dedicated government funded regulator to ensure

5c458624206/t/5bfcd3040ebbe858997ee1f7/1543295760802/UTS0001+Au+Pairs+in+Australia+Report_final.pdf. The report estimates there are 10,000 au pairs and nannies, many of whom work excessive hours for little pay.

111 See, eg, *Fair Work Ombudsman v Crocmedia Pty Ltd* [2015] FCCA 140; *Fair Work Ombudsman v Aldred* [2016] FCCA 220; *Fair Work Ombudsman v Her Fashion Box Pty Ltd* [2019] FCCA 425. See also A Stewart and R Owens, 'The Nature, Prevalence and Regulation of Unpaid Work Experience, Internships and Trial Periods in Australia: Experience or Exploitation?' (*Fair Work Ombudsman*, 2013) www.fairwork.gov.au/about-us/access-accountability-and-reporting/research-reports.

112 L Berg and B Farbenblum, '*Wage Theft in Australia: Findings of the National Temporary Migrant Work Survey*' (Migrant Worker Justice Initiative, 2017) 5 www.mwji.org/highlights/2017/11/14/report-released-wage-theft-in-australia-findings-of-the-national-temporary-migrant-work-survey. The participants in the survey were '4,322 temporary migrants across 107 nationalities of every region in the world, working in a range of jobs in all states and territories' (see pages 12–13 of the report by Berg and and Farbenblum). See also Industrial Relations Victoria, 'Victorian Inquiry into the Labour Hire Industry and Insecure Work' (*State of Victoria*, 2016) https://engage.vic.gov.au/inquiry-labour-hire-industry-and-insecure-work.

113 Fair Work Ombudsman, 'A Report of the Fair Work Ombudsman's Inquiry into 7-Eleven: Identifying and Addressing the Drivers of Non-compliance in the 7-Eleven Network' (*Commonwealth of Australia*, 2016). For a case where employers were fined and ordered to pay back pay owing, see, eg, *Osorio v Sprint Telco Pty Ltd* [2017] FCCA 1061.

114 See Fair Work Ombudsman's Report, ibid, revealing significant underpayment of employees by franchisees occurring in the franchising model utilised by the 7-Eleven Network.

compliance and enforcement, meaning that it is no longer the province solely of unions or employees themselves. Both limited resourcing of the external regulator/enforcer (the Fair Work Ombudsman)[115] compared to the need, and reduced union resources (lower density) mean less effective enforcement, so that there is arguably an increasing divergence between the appearance of social justice and the reality. Unions are empowered under the statute to instigate legal enforcement proceedings, but they can face significant challenges in enforcement,[116] despite this apparent advantage. By way of example, the fact or extent of underpayment may escape notice by the union because the union is not present in the workplace. In relatively recent times, for example, major issues of underpayment have emerged in various sectors, including the restaurant[117] and retail sectors,[118] predominantly but not exclusively amongst small employers. Many of these employers are franchisees and, as individual employers, would generally have no or relatively few union members amongst their employees and little or no immediate union representation in the enterprise.[119] Consequently, union 'presence' in the enterprise and capacity to represent staff and check that employees are being paid correctly appears to have suffered from the traditional and recognised problems with union organising – large numbers of employers, small numbers of employees in each enterprise, and small enterprises which are frequently geographically dispersed.

Employees of small businesses have longer minimum employment periods to satisfy before they are eligible for unfair dismissal protection – the lack of security during this time may inhibit their bringing forward complaints about not meeting minimum standards.

B. Wages – Low Wages Growth

Enterprise bargaining in Australia has produced low wages growth. This feature of the outcome of bargaining puts at risk the social function of labour law of providing an adequate wage. Emeritus Professor Joe Isaac's analysis of this phenomenon in his scholarly

[115] On its face the Fair Work Ombudsman ('FWO') has been a fierce enforcer of employment rights and is well resourced. However, there is commentary and research which suggests that this is inadequate in relation to the size of the non-compliance and exploitation problem. See, eg, Australian Council of Trade Unions, 'FWO Report Barely Scratches the Surface of Wage Theft' (*ACTU*, 8 November 2018) www.actu.org.au/actu-media/media-releases/2018/fwo-report-barely-scratches-the-surface-of-wage-theft; B O'Connor, 'Morrison and his Liberals Fail to Stop Exploitation of Workers' (*Australian Labor Party*, 8 November 2018) www.brendanoconnor.com.au/news/latest-news/morrison-and-his-liberals-fail-to-stop-exploitation-of-workers; M Baldwin, 'FWO Report Shows There is Much to be Done' (*Kott Gunning*, 11 December 2018) www.kottgunn.com.au/updates/employment-law/fwo-2018-report-lessons. On the other hand, the deterrence effect of FWO enforcement activities should not be underestimated, see, eg, J Howe and T Hardy, 'Creating Ripples, Making Waves? Assessing the General Deterrence Effects of Enforcement Activities of the Fair Work Ombudsman' (2017) 39 *Sydney Law Review* 471.

[116] See, eg, I landau and J Howe, 'Trade Union Ambivalence Toward Enforcement of Employment Standards as an Organizing Strategy' (2016) 17 *Theoretical Inquiries in Law*; and 'Trade Unions and Enforcement of Minimum Employment Standards in Australia' (*Centre for Employment and Labour Relations Law*, 2014).

[117] See, eg, Fair Work Ombudsman, 'MADE Establishment Enforceable Undertaking'(July 2019) www.fairwork.gov.au/about-us/our-role/enforcing-the-legislation/enforceable-undertakings/2019-2020-enforceable-undertakings.

[118] See Fair Work Ombudsman, 'A Report of the Fair Work Ombudsman's Inquiry into 7-Eleven Identifying and addressing the drivers of non-compliance in the 7-Eleven network' (April 2016) www.fairwork.gov.au/about-us/access-accountability-and-reporting/inquiry-reports#7-11.

[119] Eg, union density in retail trade has declined from 23.3% to 11.4 % between 1994 and 2016, and in accommodation and food services it has declined from 19.3% to 2.4% over the same period: see: www.aph.gov.au/About_Parliament/Parliamentary_Departments/Parliamentary_Library/pubs/rp/rp1819/UnionMembership#_Toc527380733.

article, generally attributes the reasons to the change in the balance of power between employer and employee due to legislative change, and identifies several underlying factors including low union density, and the legislative framework in which lawful industrial action is permitted in limited circumstances of negotiating a new enterprise agreement only.[120] Amongst other steps, he advocates for a return to some features of earlier legislation to rectify this slow wage growth – this would include tilting the balance back towards employees, returning to industry or multi-employer bargaining, increasing union power by inter alia allowing union preference clauses in awards and greater powers to the industrial tribunal to bring parties together.

C. Wages – The Gender Gap

There are challenges though that seem to transcend the system. One of those is the gender pay gap – 'the difference between women's and men's earnings, expressed as a percentage of men's earnings'.[121] A substantial pay gap between female and male employees persists, despite the system providing for equal pay for equal work through the present provision of powers to the Fair Work Commission to make orders to ensure: 'equal remuneration for men and women workers for work of equal or comparable value'.[122] In some cases, these provisions have been successfully used to help reduce the gap,[123] but they are not necessarily a panacea for resolution of the differences.[124]

The gender pay gap has been slowly diminishing,[125] but it is still substantial: as at February 2019, the difference in pay between male and female workers is 14.1 per cent for full time employees on average or $239.80 per week.[126] According to the Workplace Gender Equality Agency,[127] this gap is influenced by a range of factors, which include:

- discrimination and bias in hiring and pay decisions;
- women and men working in different industries and different jobs, with female-dominated industries and jobs attracting lower wages;

[120] Isaac (n 42).

[121] See Workplace Gender Equality Agency, 'What is the Gender Pay Gap?' (*Commonwealth of Australia*, 2019) www.wgea.gov.au/data/fact-sheets/australias-gender-pay-gap-statistics; S Charlesworth and M Smith, 'Gender Pay Equity' in A Stewart, J Stanford and T Hardy (eds), *The Wages Crisis in Australia* (Adelaide, University of Adelaide Press, 2018) 85. See also G Gilfillan and C McGann, 'Trends in Union Membership in Australia' (*Parliament of Australia*, 15 October 2018) www.aph.gov.au/About_Parliament/Parliamentary_Departments/Parliamentary_Library/pubs/rp/rp1819/UnionMembership#_Toc527380733.

[122] Fair Work Act 2009 (Cth) Pt 2–7. For a detailed analysis of the legislation and cases up to 2013, see R Layon, M Smith and A Stewart, 'Equal Remuneration under the Fair Work Act 2009: A Report for the Pay Equity Unit of the Fair Work Commission' (*Commonwealth of Australia*, 2013) www.fwc.gov.au/documents/documents/payequity/er-report-6-dec-2013.pdf.

[123] See, eg, *Australian Municipal, Administrative, Clerical and Services Union* [2011] FWAFB 2700; *Australian Municipal, Administrative, Clerical and Services Union* [2012] FWAFB 1000. See also F Macdonald and S Charlesworth, 'Equal Pay under the Fair Work Act 2009 (Cth): Mainstreamed or Marginalised?' (2013) 36 *University of New South Wales Law Journal* 563.

[124] See the rejection of the union application for an equal remuneration order in *Application by United Voice and the Australian Education Union* [2018] FWCFB 177. At time of writing, an application for an equal remuneration order by the Independent Education Union of Australia is pending.

[125] Workplace Gender Equality Agency (n 121).

[126] Workplace Gender Equality Agency, 'National Gender Pay Gap Hits Record Low' (*Commonwealth of Australia*, 2018) www.wgea.gov.au/newsroom/media-releases/national-gender-pay-gap-hits-record-low.

[127] A statutory body established by the Workplace Gender Equality Act 2012 (Cth).

- women's disproportionate share of unpaid caring and domestic work;
- lack of workplace flexibility to accommodate caring and other responsibilities, especially in senior roles;
- women's greater time out of the workforce impacting career progression and opportunities.[128]

In addition, industries in which wages are more award-reliant tend to have a higher concentration of female employees.

Similar factors also contribute to the so-called 'super gender gap'.[129] Australia has a comprehensive system to provide superannuation (or a retirement pension) from superannuation plans to which employers must contribute, generally in respect of all employees, other than limited exceptions. However, women retire on average with 37 per cent less superannuation than men.[130]

Having said that, Australian labour law has, as yet, failed to bring changes to deal comprehensively to remove the gender gap with provision of fair wages and comparative wage justice for workers in industries, such as aged care and child care, despite a mechanism for equal remuneration in sectors which predominantly employ women.

VIII. Shifting Minimum Standards to Parliament – The Political Realm?

Whilst some core labour standards are now legislated in the NES, it is a trite observation to say that what Parliament can give, Parliament can take away – or at the very least, vary adversely. Hence labour conditions remain firmly in the political domain with changes in minimum conditions for workers generally subject to the party political and parliamentary process.[131] The shift away from the independent tribunal determining some conditions to the Parliament legislating the standards risks attacks on these conditions, especially with some decline in the labour movement and rise of populist 'third party' influences. So far this has not happened; but equally no appetite to improve these conditions has been shown. The result could be stagnation of legislated standards over time[132] as well as increasing future disparities between groups of employees. Over time, those disparities may increasingly reflect structural factors such as differences in bargaining power between those groups, the

[128] Workplace Gender Equality Agency, 'Gender Pay Gap' (n 126).

[129] B Coates, 'What's the best way to close the gender gap in retirement incomes?' (2018) Grattan Institute Working Paper No 2018-01 https://grattan.edu.au/wp-content/uploads/2018/02/899-Best-way-to-close-gender-gap-retirement-incomes.pdf.

[130] Australian Bureau of Statistics, *Gender Indicators, Australia, Sep 2017* (Catalogue No 4125.0, 21 November 2017).

[131] Bodies such as the peak federation of trade unions, the Australian Council of Trade Unions, would need to agitate through the parliamentary process to effect legislative change compared to bringing a claim before the industrial tribunal as was the case under the system of conciliation and arbitration.

[132] The recent history of substantial changes to long service leave, which is dealt with by state law, might however indicate that improvement of minimum conditions is possible, if not common. See, eg, Long Service Leave Act 2018 (Vic) which included several changes, including a capacity to take leave after 7 years of continuous employment (in place of the former 10 years).

lack of a general power of the Fair Work Commission to arbitrate disputes,[133] the system's reliance for actual wages and employment conditions above the minima on enterprise bargaining in sectors where bargaining is either absent or minimal (as many employers are small to medium in size, with relatively few employees),[134] and the continuing historical decline (overall) in union density.[135]

Short of a political will and successful parliamentary activity to amend the NES to improve them (eg in respect of severance or redundancy payments), general improvements in basic labour conditions now depend upon the outcomes of enterprise bargaining and the limited powers of the Fair Work Commission to extend the scope and/or content of awards beyond their current content and/or to vary current awards.[136]

Put broadly, the Australian tradition since 1904 has been that improvements in terms and conditions of employment for employees as a whole have come about from gradual changes in arbitrated awards,[137] through the federal or state industrial tribunals, although enterprise bargaining has also contributed in some areas. As the transfer of a range of minimum conditions of employment from awards (determined by the tribunal comprised of judges in the early days) to Commonwealth legislation[138] has occurred only relatively recently, the extent to which the Commonwealth Parliament will be willing to enhance legislated minimum conditions is a matter of speculation.[139] We are in new territory – it remains to be seen how the elected Parliament can deliver or advance social justice and whether the trust that Professor Ewing placed in Parliament in his 1995 article will be realised. However, the NES have been amended favourably to employees on occasion since their introduction – including in relation to family and domestic violence leave.[140]

[133] Fair Work Act 2009 (Cth), Pt 2–5.

[134] The concept of 'small and medium enterprises' is defined variously for different purposes: see, eg, Australian Securities & Investments Commission, 'Small Business' (*ASIC*, 2 May 2019) https://asic.gov.au/for-business/small-business.

[135] See, eg, Gilfillan and McGann (n 121); G Griffin and S Svensen, 'The Decline of Australian Union Density – A Survey of the Literature' (1996) 38 *Journal of Industrial Relations* 505.

[136] Fair Work Act 2009 (Cth) Pts 2–3, as to matters which can be included in awards (eg an industry-specific redundancy scheme), and significant matters that are forbidden (eg right of entry for union officers to workplaces, and long service leave). As to limited powers of arbitration available to the Fair Work Commission, see Fair Work Act 2009 (Cth) Pts 2–5.

[137] Recently, for example, the Fair Work Commission has provided a standard of five days' unpaid family and domestic violence leave. See Fair Work Commission, *4 yearly review of modern awards – Family and Domestic Violence Leave*, [2019] FWCFB 767 and [2019] FWCFB 5144. This supplemented a change to the NES to provide for 5 days unpaid family and domestic violence leave: Fair Work Amendment (Family and Domestic Violence Leave) Act 2018 (Cth).

[138] Leave entitlements have traditionally been an area of active legislative determination at the state level. These are now mainly provided by the NES. However, one area of employee entitlements left to the states, to set minimum conditions, is long service leave. Victoria, for example, has recently extended legislative entitlements for long service leave based on portability of service between employers, in an expanded list of industries: see Long Service Benefits Portability Act 2018 (Vic.). These entitlements are an extension of long service leave entitlements based on service with a single employer under the Long Service Leave Act 2018 (Vic.).

[139] In its 2019 Platform, the Australian Labor Party proposed limited changes to the NES – to introduce 10 days paid Domestic Violence leave, to work to achieve a national minimum standard for long service leave, and to review the operation of the NES to clarify any issues which have arisen since their introduction. Ch 5, paras 44, 57 and 76. See Australian Labor Party, 'A Fair Go for Australia: National Platform' (2018) www.alp.org.au/media/1539/2018_alp_national_platform_constitution.pdf.

[140] See, eg, amendments referred to in n 137 above and also the Fair Work Amendment Act 2013 (Cth) which extended the right to request flexible work, conferred by the NES in the Fair Work Act 2009, to a broader group of

The safety net, whilst reasonably fair, is not immune from erosion with consequences for continuing social justice.

IX. Concluding Comments

Returning to the concept of social justice espoused by Professor Ewing, the Australian model has shown a high degree of state intervention to provide protection for employees. It was Parliament which enacted the framework legislation in which conciliation and arbitration operated, and the federal Parliament, constrained by the limit on its constitutional powers, initially left the determination of conditions to the tribunal. In the early days, the conciliation and arbitration system entrenched collective bargaining against the backdrop of awards prescribing minima; and frequently these awards, notably made then by Judges of the Court of Conciliation and Arbitration, were the main protection, with bargaining in the background. The state was concerned to provide framework legislation for bargaining and awards, but over time the nature of the state intervention changed to include a greater degree of legislation providing directly for minimum conditions of employment. State intervention has generally been aimed at fairness (but with notable exceptions), landing today on an enterprise bargaining model supported by a safety net of modern awards and legislated standards, with intervention and supervision by an independent tribunal. This goal of fairness is left in the hands of both judges (using that word in a broad sense to embrace the tribunal members) and the Parliament. The social justice aspects of the framework legislation, which is the province of Parliament, is at risk of attack. Such a risk was realised in 2005 with the drastic erosion or reduction of workers conditions and rights in the Work Choices legislation enacted by a conservative government holding the balance of power in both Houses of Parliament. Whilst generally a better balance has been achieved with the Fair Work Act, following the Forward with Fairness policy initiative,[141] there are challenges, however, with some workers remaining vulnerable, despite the expressed overarching aim of fairness; and there are issues in enforcement and compliance that require constant vigilance. The gains to employees, ironically and at odds with Professor Ewing's view of how social justice could be promoted, do not seem to have been achieved through enterprise bargaining, at least in the way the Australian system has conceived and implemented collective bargaining under the Fair Work Act.

employees and outlined criteria for determining what are reasonable business grounds for an employer's refusal of a request for flexible work.

[141] Forward with Fairness was the policy blueprint of the Labor opposition (Kevin Rudd and Julia Gillard) which was elected to power and immediately set up eliminating the worst features of Work Choices and enacted the Fair Work Act.

14

There is Power in a Union? Revisiting Trade Union Functions in 2019

MICHAEL FORD QC AND TONIA NOVITZ*

In an important and influential article written in 2005, shortly after the conclusion of the Warwick Agreement between the New Labour Government and the trade unions and just before the third election victory of Tony Blair, Keith Ewing provided an overview of how five key functions of trade unions had been moulded and affected by recent government policies and laws.[1] The functions he identified were (i) a service function, seen as how unions provide benefits and services to their members; (ii) a workplace representative function, meaning both representing individuals and collective consultation and bargaining within an individual enterprise; (iii) a regulatory function, by which he meant the degree to which unions were involved in making rules which extended beyond members (and others) working for a single employer, exemplified by sectoral collective bargaining and the system for its legal extension in some European countries; (iv) the governmental function, encompassing the representation of the interests of working people in the political process and in order to channel state power; and (v) the closely-related public administration function, in which trade unions were actively involved in the delivery of government policies on the ground. We use Ewing's categorisation as a starting point to analyse how, in 2019, trade unions have responded to changes in the political and legal environment and their reactions to the emergence of what has been termed the 'gig economy'.

Although Ewing talked of five 'functions' of trade unions, his principal focus was on the purposes of trade unions. Functions, of course, are not identical with purposes, though at times Ewing treats them as indistinguishable.[2] The acceptance of the legitimacy of unions in advanced capitalist states across political parties, including by those on the Right, has often been attributed to their function in defusing social conflict, as a significant body of Marxist literature attests.[3] Operating behind the backs of social actors, these wider functions are the

* We would like to thank the participants at the King's College workshop held in honour of Professor Keith Ewing for their comments, including those from Professor Ewing himself. We are also very grateful for the observations and information provided by, Professors Alan Bogg, Ruth Dukes and Alison Young. All errors and omissions are our own.

[1] KD Ewing, 'The Function of Trade Unions' (2005) 34 *Industrial Law Journal* 1.

[2] Ibid, 20, referring to the 'principal purposes' of trade unions.

[3] K Marx, 'Value, Price and Profit' in K Marx and F Engels (eds), *Collected Works*, Vol 20 (New York, International Publishers, 1985) 146. Cf. R Cox, 'Labor and hegemony' and 'Labor and Hegemony: A reply' in R Cox and TJ Sinclair (eds), *Approaches to World Order* (Cambridge, CUP, 1996).

subject of critical sociology; they did not figure on Ewing's list because his analysis proceeded from an assumption of how unions would themselves characterise their purposes at the time he was writing. Nor did he consider, at that juncture, how radically the constitution of the workforce would change. Already in 2005, Leah Vosko had begun to identify the decline in a 'standard employment relationship', especially in relation to women's work,[4] even if Guy Standing's more radical pronouncement regarding the emergence of a 'precariat' would only gain widespread attention in 2011.[5] The process accelerated with the emergence of what has become known as the 'gig economy', probably attributable not only to the developments in digital technology to which it is often ascribed, but also to forms of task-based work which became more frequent in the wake of the financial crisis.[6] Confronting fresh challenges in organising, recruiting and bargaining in such conditions, unions have adjusted their functions in response.

There is an implicit hierarchy in Ewing's functions, signalled by his dismay at the limited support given to collective bargaining by New Labour in 2005. Elsewhere, drawing on the work of TH Marshall[7] and Bernstein,[8] Ewing explained the two critical functions performed by collective bargaining in democratic socialism, seen as an essential means of delivering full citizenship.[9] To begin with, collective bargaining is one of the principal means of achieving social justice. Without an adequate wage or reasonable hours of work, genuine equal citizenship is impossible, and collective bargaining has a central role to play in delivering these goods. In addition, the process of collective bargaining is an aspect of industrial citizenship, supplementing political citizenship, and the primary means by which social democracy extends to the economic sphere. The state retains a residual role in steering the procedures of collective bargaining and ensuring the outcomes do not fall below minimum standards; but free collective bargaining alone delivers both elements of citizenship. The other functions of unions alluded to by Ewing are means to this end or second-best strategies, adopted as a process of downwards preference adjustment where what he refers to as the 'regulatory role of collective bargaining' is hampered or blocked.

A further key assumption of Ewing's article is a common feature of much labour law writing. He takes it for granted that unions represent their members and will seek to deliver their members' interests by means of collective bargaining, representation, political or other means. Unions and their members on this conception form a single, unified agency when they confront the outside environment, of which law is part, and their actions result in

[4] L Vosko, *Temporary Work: The gendered rise of a precarious employment relationship* (Toronto, University of Toronto Press, 2000); and L Vosko, *Precarious Employment: Towards an improved understanding of labour market insecurity* (Montreal, McGill-Queen's University Press, 2006). Her best-known book being LF Vosko, *Managing the Margins: Gender, Citizenship and the International Regulation of Precarious Employment* (Oxford, OUP, 2010).

[5] With publication of his book, G Standing, *The Precariat: The new dangerous class* (Oxford, Bloomsbury Academic, 2011). See previously, G Standing, 'Work and Occupation in a Tertiary Society' (2009) 19 *Labour & Industry: A journal of the social and economic relations of work* 49; and G Standing, *Work After Globalization: Building Occupational Citizenship* (Cheltenham, Edward Elgar, 2009).

[6] DE Guest and K Isaksson, 'Temporary employment contracts and employee well-being during and after the financial crisis' (2019) 42 *Economic and Industrial Democracy* 165; also making this link are R Costa and S Machin, 'Real Wages and Living Standards in the UK' (*CEP Election Analysis*, 2017) http://cep.lse.ac.uk/pubs/download/ea036.pdf?utm_content=buffer11cd5&utm_medium=social&utm_source=twitter.com&utm_campaign=buffer.

[7] TH Marshall, *Citizenship and Social Class* (Cambridge, CUP, 1950).

[8] E Bernstein, *The Preconditions of Socialism* (Cambridge, CUP, 1993).

[9] KD Ewing, 'Democratic Socialism and Labour Law' (1995) 24 *Industrial Law Journal* 103.

delivering wider social goods. This assumption may result in paying insufficient attention to how the formation and preservation of a collective agency via unions is an achievement which itself is always vulnerable to fragmentation, including by law. For example, in a 'gig economy' setting, crowd-workers with heterogeneous interests in what they need or want from work may compete for short-term contracts to perform tasks on online platforms or via apps accessed individually and privately, presenting a challenge to the formation of a collective agency.[10] Yet unless members can generate ideas of solidarity and collective identity which transcend their narrow, individual economic interests, the capacity of unions to mobilise members, ultimately in strikes, will be weakened or non-existent.[11]

Some elements of Ewing's analysis imply, of course, that the law can disrupt the ability of a union to organise itself, to constitute itself as a collective agency, an issue on which he has written extensively elsewhere.[12] But this aspect receives little attention in his article on the five functions – probably a result of his starting point, that unions are already-constituted agents seeking strategic success through the exercise of their five functions. Potential tensions between the union bureaucracy and members, or between the heterogeneous interests of different groups of members, are consequently ignored. Nor is this problem restricted to the relationships within unions. To the extent that unions are engaged in representing or delivering benefits for wider groups, highlighted by the regulatory, governmental and public administration functions, the potential for a gap between the interests of the union's bureaucracy and the underlying constituency is further enhanced. The proposals for sectoral collective bargaining advanced by the Institute of Employment Rights and the Labour Party under Jeremy Corbyn suggested that those functions are only in abeyance and may be revived in future.[13] Our general point, however, is that the constitution of the union as an agency has important and often unpredictable consequences for Ewing's five functions.

Claus Offe has explained, for instance, how unions face a tension between size and power, echoing that between bureaucracy and democracy.[14] Active participation is more easily generated in small unions with a homogeneous membership, whereas larger size produces greater resources which enhance the capacity of the union's bureaucracy to provide services, to support members, to act as an effective executive and ultimately to survive. These two ends pull in opposite directions, with no optimal resolution: mergers which arrest membership declines and guarantee funds for service provision are also liable to increase the heterogeneity of members' interests and the gap between members and the union bureaucracy. The apparent stability of institutional forms across time can disguise this latent instability, only revealed in times of crisis.

[10] V De Stefano, 'The Rise of the "Just-in-Time Workforce": On-demand work, crowd work and labour protection in the "Gig-Economy"' (ILO Working Paper, January 2016) www.ilo.org/travail/whatwedo/publications/WCMS_443267/lang--en/index.htm. See also J Prassl, *Humans as a Service: The Promise and Perils of Work in the Gig Economy* (Oxford, OUP, 2019) ch 1.

[11] See C Offe, 'Two Logics of Collective Action' in his *Disorganised Capitalism* (Cambridge, Polity Press, 1985) 175.

[12] See, especially, his analysis of the democratic rhetoric surrounding the earlier industrial action and political fund balloting rules in ch 5 of P Elias and K Ewing (eds), *Trade Union Democracy: Members' Rights and the Law* (London, Mansell, 1987).

[13] K Ewing, J Hendy and C Jones (eds), *A Manifesto for Labour Law* (London, IER, 2016). See too the Labour Party election manifesto for 2017, *For the Many, Not the Few* (Labour Party, London, 2017) and for 2019, *It's Time for Real Change* (Labour Party, London, 2019) available at: https://labour.org.uk/manifesto/.

[14] See Offe (n 11).

As one means of overcoming the dilemma, unions may engage in what Offe calls 'opportunism': a strategy in which they attempt to make the survival of the union's bureaucracy increasingly independent from the members' willingness to act. For Offe, the principal means of achieving this is for the union to seek external, legal guarantees of support (legal rights to consultation and so on) in place of members' willingness to act and, at the same time, increasingly to provide services to members for their individual benefits (legal services and so on). In this way, the existence of the bureaucracy is increasingly disassociated from support below. There are no doubt other forms of opportunistic behaviour. The increased use of 'leverage' action and other forms of symbolic or visible protests which do not require significant mobilisation of the membership may be another example.[15] It can be interpreted as a form of bureaucratically-organised protest, a simulacrum of the strong collective agency based on the articulation of common interests needed to engage in traditional strikes and which consequently is not so costly in terms of mobilising members.

But the resort to legal guarantees in place of members' willingness to act comes with a particular risk of its own:[16]

> once relative independence of the organization from its members "willingness to act" is achieved and internal guarantees are substituted by external ones, the organisation no longer has any capacity to resist attempts to withdraw external support and the externally provided legal and institutional status. In other words, the organisation itself becomes incapable of guaranteeing the guarantees.

The consequence is that laws which apparently improve the legal powers of the union *qua* bureaucratic agent can paper over weakness at grass roots' level. Removal of legal support in times of political opposition to unions or corporatism exposes the underlying power vacuum. Streeck has traced just such a process in Germany from the 1990s onwards.[17] As the state began to withdraw support for the political status of trade unions – what Streeck calls the 'logic of influence' – unions were increasingly forced to resort to the 'logic of membership' in order to retain social power.[18] A declining membership and conflicts between heterogeneous groups of workers meant unions were unable to mobilise sufficient resistance when employers began to defect from industry-wide agreements. The result was the relatively rapid destabilisation of what appeared to be secure sectoral collective bargaining and an accompanying increase in wage differentials and hence inequality.[19]

The UK environment, of course, has been more hostile to unions than Germany and for a longer period.[20] Any union functions going beyond a stripped-down individual service model have been the direct target of government action. From 1979 unions met a perfect storm of a monetarist economic policy, a declining manufacturing sector, the abandonment

[15] Discussed in M Ford and T Novitz, 'An Absence of Fairness? Restrictions on Industrial Action and Protect in the Trade Union Bill 2015' (2015) 44 *Industrial Law Journal* 522, 545–547.

[16] Offe (n 11) 218.

[17] W Streeck, *Re-forming Capitalism* (Oxford, OUP, 2009), especially Pt 1.

[18] Ibid, ch 4.

[19] L Hayes and T Novitz, *Trade Unions and Economic Inequality* (London, CLASS/Institute of Employment Rights, 2014).

[20] Though since 2010 Germany has gone further down the same line: see A Tooze, 'Which is Worse' (2019) 41 *London Review of Books* 19.

of corporatist political arrangements, rising unemployment, privatisations, the curtailment of public sector collective bargaining and the removal of legal props for collective bargaining.[21] The law also played a central role in fragmenting membership solidarity and unions' capacity to resist once forced back on the 'logic of membership', exemplified by the rules on internal union democracy and the procedural and substantive restrictions on calling strike action now found in Part V of the Trade Union and Labour Relations (Consolidation) Act 1992 (TULRCA). The new ballot thresholds for strikes in the Trade Union Act 2016 (TUA)[22] demonstrate that this policy goal has still not exhausted its appeal to the right of the Conservative Party, despite the very low levels of industrial action in the UK.

No-one should underestimate the difficulty of mapping the empirical effects of legislative programmes, based on the responses and strategies of multiple actors. As an obvious example, laws directed at fragmentation of collective solidarity may have the opposite effect, of strengthening internal democracy, as illustrated by some of the findings of Jane Elgar and Bob Simpson in relation to how unions responded to strike ballot laws.[23] The vulnerability of unions' agency adds a further complicating factor. Offe's thesis is just one example of a plausible short-term strategy unions may adopt with potential long-term risks; Streeck's historical narrative shows how the sometimes dysfunctional responses of institutions to changes in law, economy and politics may only be explicable with the benefit of hindsight, not *a priori*. The big question in this context is whether and how the law could reverse the decline in unions' regulatory functions we have witnessed in the UK (and other European countries) since the 1980s, an issue thrown under the spotlight by the Labour Party's endorsement of the proposals for sectoral collective bargaining in the IER's *Manifesto for Labour Law*.[24]

Ewing's valuable article illustrated how the law, at a critical time in the New Labour administrations, affected the five principal functions of unions acting *qua* agents in the external world. As has been observed elsewhere, it was very much an analysis of its time, for 'typologies of functions … undergo constant change and evolution depending on the external political and economic conditions and environments to which trade unions must adapt'.[25] The advent of the Conservative – Liberal Democrat coalition Government in 2010 and the successor Conservative administrations of David Cameron and Theresa May did not lead to any intentional enhancement of the functions of trade unions. Even the service function was targeted in the TUA 2016, in the provisions regarding facility time; unions' representation function has been ignored or undermined (though the laws on compulsory recognition remain intact); probably the last remnant of a regulatory function enshrined in legislation, the Agricultural Wages Board, was abolished in 2013; and what was left of unions' role in government and public administration has significantly decreased. Unions

[21] Such as curtailing the role of wage councils in the Wages Act 1986. For the history, see P Davies and M Freedland, *Labour Legislation and Public Policy* (Oxford, Clarendon Press, 1993) chs 9–10.

[22] R Dukes and N Kountouris, 'Pre-strike Ballots, Picketing and Protest: Banning industrial action by the back door?' (2016) 45 *Industrial Law Journal* 337.

[23] See J Elgar and B Simpson, *Industrial Action Ballots and the Law* (London, Institute of Employment Rights, 1996) ch 3, discussed further below.

[24] See n 13 above.

[25] R Zahn, *New Labour Laws in Old Member States: Trade Union Responses to European Enlargement* (Cambridge, CUP, 2017) 18.

were mostly notable by their absence in the programme of reform set in motion by the Taylor Review commissioned by the May Government.[26] It would be very surprising if anything changes under the premiership of Johnson.

But unions have not been passive by-standers to these changes or the shifts in the labour market. We consider in this context the responses of larger established and smaller emergent trade unions determined to address the contemporary problems posed by the gig economy and a hostile legislative environment. Examples include the creative use by unions of their legal services function, engaging in what Trevor Colling once identified as 'legal mobilisation' in order to secure collective goals.[27] We suspect that the GMB could not have achieved its notable collective agreement for Hermes couriers,[28] for example, without prior successes in the employment tribunal regarding 'worker' status.[29] These responses are in sharp contrast to Ewing's 2005 snapshot at a time of relative political stability, when unions could still seek some legal props and government support for their functions. We are writing, however, at the beginning of this process, not the end, though we hope that the five functions continues to provide a useful device for a preliminary analysis of how unions are shaped by, resist and mould the very different legal and labour market in 2019.

I. The Service Function

Keith Ewing described the 'service function' of a trade union as 'the activity of a fledgling and immature organisation'.[30] This historicist claim arose from the trade union experience in the UK in which 'the provision of services and benefits to members' was offered by early 'friendly societies'.[31] Nascent trade unions operated lawfully only as clubs which offered forms of insurance, their collective representative function being seen as a form of civil and even criminal conspiracy.[32] But Ewing also acknowledged the recent revival and transformation of this function in the form of 'professional services' – 'legal advice and representation to help with problems at work, accidents on the way to work, or problems unrelated to work'.[33] The ebb in the regulatory or public administrative role of trade unions meant they no longer laid down the ground rules for work relations but instead increasingly turned to assisting individual members to enforce legislation passed by Parliament.[34]

Ewing saw the re-emphasis on the service function of trade unions as a consistent theme of both Conservative and Labour Governments from 1979, all part of an attempt

[26] M Taylor et al, 'Good work: the Taylor review of modern working practices' (July 2017) www.gov.uk/government/publications/good-work-the-taylor-review-of-modern-working-practices. For discussion, see K Bales, A Bogg and T Novitz, '"Voice" and "Choice" in Modern Working Practices: Problems with the Taylor Review' (2018) 47 *Industrial Law Journal* 46.

[27] T Colling, 'Court in a Trap? Legal Mobilisation by Trade Unions in the United Kingdom' (Warwick Papers in Industrial Relations, No 91, June 2009) https://warwick.ac.uk/fac/soc/wbs/research/irru/wpir/wpir_91.pdf.

[28] Available at: GMB Union, 'Hermes and GMB in ground breaking gig economy deal' (4 February 2019) www.gmb.org.uk/news/hermes-gmb-groundbreaking-gig-economy-deal.

[29] *Leyland v Hermes Parcelnet Ltd* [2018] 6 WLUK 464 (ET, 22 June 2018) www.leighday.co.uk/LeighDay/media/LeighDay/documents/Employment/1800575-17-Hermes-PH-Judgment.pdf.

[30] Ewing, 'The Function of Trade Unions' (n 1) 3.

[31] Ibid.

[32] See H Pelling, *A History of British Trade Unionism* (Harmondsworth, Penguin, 1973) ch 2.

[33] Ewing, 'The Function of Trade Unions' (n 1) 3.

[34] Ibid.

to tame and control the movement which he connected to the 'open membership rules' under section 174 of TULRCA.[35] On this view, unions were intended to become 'universal service providers' who would struggle to reject even members fundamentally opposed to their objectives, such as BNP members, as illustrated by the litigation in *ASLEF v Lee*.[36] Exhibiting a similar aim of channelling unions away from strikes or politics and towards a role as sanitised providers of services in a market were the provisions on unjustified discipline in sections 64–67 of TULRCA, owing their origin to the Employment Act 1988. Thus section 64(2)(d) includes as an instance of discipline the deprivation 'to any extent of, or of access to, any benefits, services or facilities which would otherwise be provided or made available to him by virtue of his membership of the union', and unjustified discipline includes taking action because a member failed to support a strike or proposed to resign from the union.[37]

Running in parallel with the legislative rules were changes in union practice. Ewing wrote of 'an apparent increase' in the 'trade union service function',[38] explaining that expansion of benefits can operate as a recruitment tool where traditional collective bargaining seems ineffective. The trend has continued, even if there is little evidence that it has improved recruitment.[39] Trade unions now offer free legal advice, discount car insurance, and even welfare protection for members in sectors which have been especially devastated.[40] UNISON and even the University and College Union (UCU) advertise such services on their websites, presumably as a recruitment device.[41] There is also some fleeting recognition of the significance of service provision in legislation insofar as trade union discrimination provisions introduced by New Labour prevent detriment or dismissal for access to trade union services,[42] though these provisions were largely enacted to comply with the spirit of ruling of the European Court of Human Rights (ECtHR) in *Wilson and Palmer*.[43]

A. Open Membership as Reinforcing the Service Function?

Ewing stated that the 'only explanation' for the retention of open-membership rules in section 174 was an acceptance of their rationale, as reinforcing the service function. This is questionable. A formal individual right to join a union (and the linked rights not to be expelled) could be based on a view of membership *à la* service model, in which members

[35] Ibid, 5.

[36] *ASLEF v Lee* [2004] All ER (D) 209; EAT/0625/03/RN.

[37] See TULRCA 1992, s 65(2)(a)(b) and (g) and the discussion in *UNISON v Kelly* [2012] IRLR 442 (EAT). UNISON received permission to appeal to the Court of Appeal, after which the case was presumably settled.

[38] Ewing, 'The Function of Trade Unions' (n 1) 6–7.

[39] R Gumbrell-McCormick and R Hyman, *Trade Unions in Western Europe: Hard Times, Hard Choices* (Oxford, OUP, 2013) 47–8.

[40] Ibid and Ewing, 'The Function of Trade Unions' (n 1) 7.

[41] See '7 reasons to join UNISON' (UNISON) https://joining.unison.org.uk/reasons-join-unison/. which include legal services, financial assistance, and even 'savings on holidays through the UNISON travel club, plus discounts on home, car, pet and travel insurance, dental and health plans, cashback on mortgages'. The UCU offers 'UCU Law Extra' (Legal help for you and your family: family law services • wills online • probate and estate administration • lasting powers of attorney • property (including conveyancing and landlord & tenant) • road traffic defence • professional negligence • medical negligence') as well as financial advice and insurance: www.ucu.org.uk/ucuplus.

[42] Employment Relations Act 2004, s 31, amending s 146 and s 151 of TULRCA 1992.

[43] *Wilson and Palmer v United Kingdom* (2002) 35 EHRR 20.

simply purchase individualised economic benefits from the union *qua* market actor; but it could also be based on a 'thicker' conception of membership, involving individual participation within the union. We think *both* aspects can be traced in the legislation.[44] Rights to join (and corresponding restrictions on expulsions) were part of a set of measures by which dissenting members were meant to become involved in the union's decision-making and thereby constrain the union executive in all its activities, as Ewing has analysed elsewhere.[45] Supplementing this aim was a vision of the legitimate role of unions as politically-neutral service providers. Subject to the logic of the market, unions would compete for members and would be unable to exclude those individuals who viewed membership as a purely market transaction. Unions would thus find themselves with a membership whose orientation to the union was instrumental, who would be difficult to mobilise for solidarity action and who, if they did participate in internal affairs, would act as a restraining influence. The overriding goal, however, was to regulate and disrupt the union's internal self-constitution and its capacity to act as a collective agent.[46]

The reinforcement of the service function was therefore part and parcel of a wider strategy aimed at depoliticising and internally fragmenting unions. To the extent the legislative measures succeeded, they may well have the effect of causing unions to retreat into their service functions. Both points – legal goals and union response – were foreshadowed in Ewing's analysis, though he was agnostic as to the causal role of legislation. The position has hardly become clearer since he wrote in 2005.

One supplement to his analysis arose from the use of human rights' litigation, which itself might be characterised as an aspect of the service function. The potential conflict of domestic law with Article 11 of the European Convention on Human Rights (ECHR) highlighted by Ewing was resolved by judgment of the European Court of Human Rights (ECtHR) in *ASLEF v UK* which tempered universal access in a helpful way, allowing expulsion of BNP members and leading to some (if not sufficient) control on which individuals trade unions were required to accept as members.[47] The ECtHR's background conception of trade unions was very different from the vision of them as service providers in a market which underpinned the domestic legislation. For the ECtHR, they were organisations formed by individuals 'espousing particular values or ideals [who] intend to pursue common goals'.[48] Thus (our emphasis):[49]

> Historically, trade unions in the United Kingdom, and elsewhere in Europe were, and though perhaps to a lesser extent today are, commonly affiliated to political parties or movements,

[44] M Ford, 'Citizenship and Democracy in Industrial Relations: The Agenda for the 1990s' (1992) 55 *MLR* 241. However, cf. the limited aspirations of the Conservative Governments post-1979 and New Labour, for which see respectively Davies and Freedland, *Labour Legislation and Public Policy* (n 21) and P Davies and M Freedland, *Towards a Flexible Labour Market* (Oxford, Clarendon Press, 2007).

[45] See Elias and Ewing (n 12).

[46] Regarding the 'licence to poach' and the goal of undermining the Bridlington Principles and broader TUC solidarity, see B Simpson, 'The TUC's Bridlington Principles and the Law' (1983) 46 *MLR* 635; and J Elgar and B Simpson, 'A Final Appraisal of "Bridlington"? An evaluation of TUC Disputes Committee decisions 1974–1991' (1994) 32 *British Journal of Industrial Relations* 47.

[47] See *ASLEF v UK* (2007) 45 EHRR 34 and TULRCA 1992, s 174(4A)-4H) TULRCA as amended.

[48] *ASLEF* (n 47) para 39.

[49] Ibid, para 50.

> particularly those on the left. *They are not bodies solely devoted to politically-neutral aspects of the well-being of their members, but are often ideological, with strongly held views on social and political issues.*

The restriction on the expulsion of BNP members was, accordingly, a disproportionate interference with ASLEF's freedom of association. The amendments made to TULRCA as a result were rightly criticised by Ewing,[50] trade unions still have to act with caution when disciplining members in terms of their access to services and some forms of disciplinary action are ruled out *in limine*.[51] But, still, the ruling in *ASLEF* provides an important, if imperfect, corrective to a legal vision of unions as no more than universal service providers and, so long as the UK is a signatory to the ECHR, a brake on future legislative interferences with their autonomy.

The more difficult question is how unions and members have responded to the legislation. Broader internal access rights may actually have the unintended consequence of promoting the external scope and perceived legitimacy of trade union action. Indeed, it may be that trade unions, when presented with new forms of work, have sought to broaden their membership to include those not traditionally thought to be encompassed by the sectors or professions that they tend to represent. In this we see some older more established unions taking a cue from the small Independent Workers Union of Great Britain (IWGB), pushing to widen the pool of eligible members beyond those ordinarily seen as workers.[52] Already, Unite the Union is offering 'community membership' to those out of work (for just 50p a week) offering benefits advice and debit counselling, while campaigning on broader issues such as the bedroom tax.[53] On the one hand, through these methods trade unions may be able to increase social solidarity beyond the confines of their traditional membership, characterised by full-time permanent employees. On the other, they then face the need to accommodate an increasingly heterogeneous membership, which may require setting new goals and strategies. These issues do not only relate to services, but to all facets of access to trade union representation and membership, and warrant further research.

B. Reinvigorating the Service Function?

Ewing saw the service function as increasingly occupying the space left vacant by a retreat from the regulatory function. There is no doubt that 'professional services' in the form of legal advice on workplace disputes and representation in tribunals has been one of the key methods by which unions have attracted and served members in recent times. But union-backed litigation has expanded beyond the confines of legal assistance on the insurance

[50] KD Ewing, 'Employment Act 2008: Implementing the ASLEF Decision – A Victory for the BNP?' (2009) 28 *Industrial Law Journal* 50.

[51] Most notably disciplinary action against those who break strikes or who assert that the union has acted unlawfully: see TULRCA 1992, s 65(2)(a)-(c), containing provisions originally enacted in s 3 of the Employment Act 1988.

[52] Even though the attempt to set up new unions to represent those previously not deemed 'workers' has not always been successful, as in the case of professional foster carers. See *National Union of Professional Foster Carers (NUPFC) v Certification Officer* [2019] IRLR 860 (the case is subject to an outstanding appeal).

[53] D Foster, 'The striking Ministry of Justice cleaners know their worth – all power to them' *The Guardian* (London, 7 August 2018).

model, with no aims beyond obtaining compensation for the individual member's loss. The role has been increasingly used by trade unions for 'test' cases which can be seen as enhancing representative functions and, even, drifting towards a 'regulatory' or 'government' function. Such litigation has been and is being used to seek to set generally-applicable standards and to place strategic pressure on a Conservative Government to regulate, illustrated by the *ASLEF* case. By this means the service function can turn back to bite the hand that fed it.

The best example was the *UNISON* litigation that challenged the 2013 Fees Order, requiring the payment of substantial fees before bringing a claim in the employment tribunal and or appealing to the Employment Appeal Tribunal.[54] Undeterred by defeats in two separate Divisional Courts and in the Court of Appeal, the union (supported by the Equality and Human Rights Commission) ultimately succeeded in the Supreme Court, which found that the fees regime was an unlawful interference with the fundamental common law principle of access to the courts as well as being in breach of EU law and Article 6 of the ECHR.[55] The Government Review, published shortly before the Supreme Court hearing, showed that even on the government's own estimate fees deterred around 14,000 claimants each year from making tribunal claims.[56] The sharp and sustained increase in tribunal claims since the ruling suggests this was, if anything, a considerable under-estimate.[57]

On one view, the case is not related to the service function at all, so long as that is conceived as providing services for members' narrow individual economic interests, because UNISON already paid its members' fees when it supported them in tribunal cases. Indeed, on the kind of conventional costs-benefit analyses based on the prospects of success which guide the funding decisions of legal insurance providers, the case might well never have been brought at all. In fact, the case had much wider aims and effect. While the abolition of fees was no doubt of some benefit to UNISON and its members, the principal beneficiaries were workers in general, and perhaps especially those who are not union members, who do not benefit from union support or who bring claims for small sums of money (where fees were a powerful deterrent). The boundary between service and wider functions turns out to be rather porous.

Since the fees challenge, UNISON has been prominent in other public interest litigation, such as the claim for national minimum wage on behalf of carers during 'sleep ins'[58] and successfully intervening in litigation concerning the holiday rights of all 'term time' workers.[59] In the context of the 'gig' economy, it is probably the IWGB which has been

[54] The Employment Tribunals and Employment Appeal Tribunal Fees Order 2013, SI 2013/1893.

[55] *R (on the Application of UNISON) v Lord Chancellor* [2017] UKSC 51, [2017] 3 WLR 409. See for discussion, A Bogg, 'The Common Law Constitution at Work: *R (on the application of UNISON) v Lord Chancellor* (2018) 81 *MLR* 509; M Ford, 'Employment Tribunal Fees and the Rule of Law: *R (on the Application of UNISON) v Lord Chancellor*' (2018) 47 *Industrial Law Journal* 1.

[56] Ministry of Justice, *Review of the Introduction of Fees in the Employment Tribunal* (January 2017) www.gov.uk/government/consultations/review-of-the-introduction-of-fees-in-the-employment-tribunals.

[57] See Ministry of Justice, *Tribunals statistics quarterly: January to March 2019* (June 2019) table C.1 www.gov.uk/government/statistics/tribunal-statistics-quarterly-january-to-march-2019.

[58] *Royal Mencap v Tomlinson-Blake* [2018] EWCA Civ 1641, [2018] IRLR 932 (heard in the Supreme Court in February 2020).

[59] *Harpur Trust v Brazel* [2019] EWCA Civ 1402, [2019] IRLR 1012.

at the forefront of 'test' litigation on employment status and thereby public policy. Their support of the *Uber* litigation counteracted the assumption that all those hired through platform apps were to be treated as independent contractors rather than workers and therefore ineligible for the national minimum wage or holiday pay under the Working Time Regulations.[60] Similarly, it was the IWGB that supported the litigation which concluded in findings that 'gig work' *Citysprint*[61] and *Addison Lee* cycle couriers[62] (again hired through apps) were workers. This strategy is connected with attempts to enforce the representative function via collective bargaining, demonstrated by the, to date, unsuccessful application made by the IWGB to the Central Arbitration Committee (CAC) for trade union recognition on behalf of Deliveroo drivers.[63]

The GMB has also been very active, supporting the *Uber* case, successful claims that Hermes couriers were workers and current litigation being brought by delivery drivers against Amazon.[64] In common with the *UNISON* case, there is a spill-over of such litigation beyond the service function, since the cases have effects on all members employed by the relevant employers and no doubt influenced the Taylor Review and the associated legislative proposals.[65] The Hermes case also supplemented the representative function, since the resolution of the case led to union recognition and a novel collective agreement for all Hermes couriers, allowing them to opt for paid annual leave and other benefits, which may provide a model for other 'gig' economy workforces.[66]

At the end of his discussion of the 'service function' Ewing observed the concern of the then Department of Trade and Industry (DTI) in its Review of the Employment Relations Act 1999 to 'ensure there is adequate protection for employers against excessive or inappropriate use of work time by workers when accessing union services'.[67] Perhaps this signalled a nascent realisation that the promotion of trade union services was not having quite the debilitating effect on trade unions as was originally intended or anticipated. This proposal found a later echo in the Conservative Government's TUA of 2016 which aimed to curtail union officials' facility time, now targeting both the service function and the representative function. Thus the Act gave a power to the Secretary of State to require public sector employers to publish details of trade union facility time and its cost, and subsequently to

[60] *Uber BV v Aslam [2018]* EWCA Civ 2748, [2019] IRLR 252 (to be heard in the Supreme Court in 2020).

[61] *Dewhurst v CitySprint* [2017] 1 WLUK 16 (ET, 5 January 2017).

[62] *Gascoigne v Addison Lee* [2018] ICR 1826.

[63] Discussed below in relation to the representative function.

[64] See *Leyland v Hermes Parcelnet Ltd* (n 29) and GMB Union, 'Amazon firms face legal action' (4 June 2018) www.gmb.org.uk/news/amazon-firms-face-legal-action; cf. the earlier BBC documentary screened 11 November 2016 on treatment of Amazon drivers at: BBC News 'Amazon drivers "work illegal hours"' (11 November 2016) www.bbc.co.uk/news/uk-england-37708996.

[65] See the Taylor Review, Taylor et al (n 26); and See HM Government, *Good Work: A Response to the Taylor Review of Modern Working Practices* (February 2018) www.gov.uk/government/publications/government-response-to-the-taylor-review-of-modern-working-practices.

[66] See R Wright, 'Hermes couriers awarded union recognition in gig economy first' *Financial Times* (London, 4 February 2019); S O'Connor, 'Gig economy agreements promise a brighter future for trade unions' *Financial Times* (London, 26 February 2019) and the GMB news item at GMB Union, 'Hermes and GMB in groundbreaking gig economy deal' (n 28).

[67] Department of Trade and Industry, 'Review of the Employment Relations Act 1999' (2003) para 3.11 https://webarchive.nationalarchives.gov.uk/20060214214053/http://www.dti.gov.uk/er/erareview.pdf; cited by Ewing, 'The Function of Trade Unions' (n 1) 8.

make regulations limiting the amount of facility time.[68] The same legislation introduced provisions, not yet in force save for the purpose of making regulations, requiring unions to pay public sector employers reasonable sums in return for the benefit of check-off facilities.[69] The original aim of the provision was to abolish check-off in the public sector altogether.[70] It is difficult to interpret these provisions charitably: if the Conservative government's vision was that unions should concentrate on their function of service provision, still this did not prevent the adoption of legislation which hampered unions in performing it.

Nevertheless, the actions of trade unions such as UNISON, the IWGB and the GMB show that the exercise of the traditional service function, of providing legal services, can have aims or effects which extend far beyond offering services to individual members. Within the union, it may generate what Trevor Colling refers to as 'inspirational effects', in which it provides a means of mobilising members around a specific issue or injustice.[71] This in turn may generate 'radiating effects', in which the litigation may itself establish issues of public or workforce importance, which act as a springboard for collective bargaining or may influence policy in the political sphere. In a legal environment hostile to the regulatory and representative function, union strategies of mobilisation around legal issues, which have a long history in the US,[72] may become increasingly prominent in the UK. The GMB collective agreement with Hermes may be an early example of how such a pragmatic strategy can lead to collective agreements in areas from which they were traditionally absent. While such strategies have, of course, serious limitations, they show the elastic boundaries of the service function.

II. Re-shaping the Representative Function

Ewing's article was written at a time when there had been a significant strengthening of the workplace representative function by New Labour, most notably by the introduction of the right to statutory recognition and the right to be accompanied at disciplinary and grievances hearings, both introduced by the Employment Relations Act 1999. But he noted at least four important limitations to the law and policy. First, the provisions for compulsory recognition excluded small employers and were limited in their subject matter. Second, the model adopted was based on representation, not his concept of regulation, most obviously in the restriction of recognition to a bargaining unit within an employer. Third, both the government and the Trades Union Congress (TUC) had embraced the idea of a 'partnership' between business and unions, emphasising the pursuit of common objectives rather than conflict and opposition. Fourth, the continued legal restrictions on unions' ability to strike, which he interpreted as themselves expressing the representative function, often meant that unions had no effective means of imposing representation or partnership on a resistant employer.

[68] See TUA 2016, s 13 (creating TULRCA 1992, s 172A).

[69] See TULRCA 1992, s 116B introduced by TUA 2016, s 15 (the provision is not yet in force).

[70] For the compromise reached on this 'in principle' reform, see M Ford and T Novitz, 'Legislating for Control: The Trade Union Act 2016' (2016) 45 *Industrial Law Journal* 277, 290.

[71] Colling (n 27).

[72] See L Weinrib, *The Taming of Free Speech: America's Civil Liberties Compromise* (Cambridge, Harvard UP, 2016).

The representative function encompasses two distinct elements, foreshadowed in our introduction. One is the extent to which the law strengthens or weakens the union's ability to act as an agent representing its members externally, in particular with employers. The other concerns how the law steers the relationship between the individual member and the union internally: how far and by what mechanisms it seeks to ensure the union is 'representative' of the individual member. Owing to his focus on functions, Ewing tended to elide these two aspects and give less attention to the second; but we think it is useful to distinguish them. The second is important because, ever since the election of the coalition Government of 2010, unions are less able to rely on any form of government support for their external representative function, making the 'logic of membership' more important than ever.

A. Ignoring the Representative Function of Unions

Since Ewing wrote, and the New Labour Government was succeeded by a coalition Government and three further Conservative administrations, there have been no further steps to strengthen unions' external capacity to act in a representative capacity. The tide has now turned away from partnership with unions, and they are now peripheral to government policy, even if legal rights to information and consultation (mostly a product of EU law), the statutory provisions on compulsory recognition in Schedule A1 of TULRCA and the individual right of representation in disciplinary and grievance procedures have so far survived.

One small step to the detriment of legal rights of representation was taken when the coalition Government reduced the periods of consultation for collective redundancies in section 188 of TULRCA as part of the Employment Law Review which took place between 2010 and 2015.[73] If this small change was mostly a reflection of its policy of no 'gold plating' of directives,[74] the consultation nevertheless was revealing about how the government saw worker representation. According to the Foreword, penned by Norman Lamb MP, it was important workers were consulted over 'big issues' because this:[75]

> helps businesses to make better decisions. But it is not the role of the Government to dictate how that input should be sought. It is our role to create a flexible framework to support high quality consultation and to allow employers and employees' representatives to conduct it in a way that suits their unique circumstances.

Elsewhere in the document, the Department for Business, Innovations and Skills (BIS) emphasised how consultation could deliver better decisions and the importance of a positive relationship with employee representatives (in part to speed up the process).[76]

[73] See the Trade Union and Labour Relations (Consolidation) Act 1992 (Amendment) Order 2013, SI 2013/763.

[74] See HM Government, *Guiding Principles for EU Legislation* (April 2013) www.gov.uk/government/publications/guiding-principles-for-eu-legislation.

[75] BIS, *Collective Redundancies: Consultation on Changes to the Rules* (June 2012), Foreword, 4, https://assets.publishing.service.gov.uk/government/uploads/system/uploads/attachment_data/file/31361/12-808-collective-redundancies-consultation.pdf.

[76] Ibid, para 3.3, 15; para 3.6, 16.

But, consistent with the Foreword's distaste for legal intervention, the means of enforcing this was a non-statutory Code of Practice.[77]

The model in the BIS document was already one step backwards from New Labour's vision of partnership between unions and employers of which Ewing was critical. Other government consultations ignored both partnership with employee representatives and any role for trade unions in representing workers. For example, nowhere in the many proposals set out in the coalition Government's Employment Law Review which took place between 2010 and 2015 was there any reference to partnership with unions.[78] The new rhetoric was 'flexible', 'effective' and 'fair', found both in the Review itself[79] and on the title of a BIS publication in 2011.[80] According to the latter document, the fairness element ought to be restricted to a 'core of fundamental employment protections', but this 'should be limited to the minimum necessary'.[81] Passing uses of the fashionable phrase 'employee voice' meant, it seemed, only requests by individual employees, not collective representations or negotiations, demonstrated by the treatment of individual requests for flexible working as a manifestation of that 'voice'.[82] Unions had all but vanished from these policy documents.

The necessity for workers to have a 'voice' was naturally endorsed by the Taylor Review announced by Theresa May soon after she became Prime Minister.[83] But the contemplated voice, it turned out, was to be used in polite discussions with management rather than to make demands in circumstances of conflict. Any idea that trade union representation should be strengthened formed no part of the Review's recommendations because, according to Taylor, 'voice can and should be exercised even where there is little or no trade union organisation and representation'.[84] That a voice without a collective agency behind it might fall on deaf ears was passed over. Nothing was proposed to reverse the decline in trade union recognition, stabilised at 22 per cent. of workplaces with five or more employees since 2004 according to the Workplace Employment Relations Study (WERS).[85] The only proposals to improve workplace dialogue were, first, a feeble amendment to the ICE Regulations[86] and, second, a suggestion that government should work with Investors in

[77] See now the ACAS booklet, *Handling Large Scale Redundancies*, https://m.acas.org.uk/media/3650/Advisory-booklet---Handling-large-scale-collective-redundancies/pdf/Handling-large-scale-collective-redundancies-advisory-booklet.pdf.

[78] See, eg, BIS, *Employment Law Review- Annual Update 2012* (March 2012) https://assets.publishing.service.gov.uk/government/uploads/system/uploads/attachment_data/file/32146/12-p136-employment-law-review-2012.pdf and BIS, *Employment Law 2013: Progress on Reform* (March 2013) at https://assets.publishing.service.gov.uk/government/uploads/system/uploads/attachment_data/file/184892/13-P136-employment-law-2013-progress-on-reform2.pdf.

[79] See e.g. BIS, *Employment Law Review- Annual Update 2012* (n 78) para 1.5, 5.

[80] BIS, *Flexible, Effective, Fair: Promoting Economic Growth Through a Strong and Efficient Labour Market* (October 2011) https://assets.publishing.service.gov.uk/government/uploads/system/uploads/attachment_data/file/32148/11-1308-flexible-effective-fair-labour-market.pdf.

[81] Ibid, para 9, 4.

[82] See, eg, BIS, *Employment Law 2013: Progress on Reform* (n 78) paras 1.30, 1.36, 15–16.

[83] See Taylor Review, Taylor et al (n 26) ch 7.

[84] Ibid, 52.

[85] B van Wanrooy et al, *The 2011 Workplace Employment Relations Study* (Basingstoke, Palgrave MacMillan, 2013) 57–9.

[86] The Information and Consultation of Employee Regulations 2004, SI 2004/3426.

People, ACAS and unions 'to promote further the development of better employee engagement and workforce relations'.[87] Little surprise that the government felt able to accept both recommendations, even if was forced to acknowledge empirical evidence that the impact of the ICE Regulations has been 'limited'.[88]

To date, however, the government has advanced no proposals to repeal the existing recognition machinery in TULRCA. To that limited extent, the legitimacy of unions continues to be accepted across the political spectrum – provided, that is, they are sufficiently representative, only seek collective bargaining within an employer and confine themselves to discussions about pay, hours and holidays.[89] Still, the government could not resist adding elements to the TUA 2016, the ideologies of which have been well described elsewhere,[90] in order to chip away at trade unions in their representative activities. The provisions in the Bill ended up being watered down as Cameron's Government sought allies from other parties in the run up to the Brexit referendum. But the provisions in the Act aimed at disrupting existing arrangements for facility time and check off, discussed above, exhibit continuing hostility towards union partnership in the public sector, where union membership is at its most dense.[91] It is no exaggeration to say that government support for the representative function of trade unions, even in a tepid form of partnership, is all but dead.

Since Ewing wrote, the only significant legal development endorsing the representative function of unions has come not from the legislature but from the Courts. In *Wandsworth LBC v Vining* the Court of Appeal held that the right of UNISON to be consulted in collective redundancies was one of the essential elements protected by Article 11 ECHR, which the UK had a positive duty to respect.[92] In the absence of any justification explaining why parks constables were not included within the statutory regime,[93] their exclusion was a breach of the union's (and the individual constables') rights under Article 11.

But we are still a long way from a universal right to representation based on Article 11 ECHR. The *Deliveroo* case demonstrates that even where a union, the IWGB, was representative of those working in a bargaining unit, the legal device of a rarely-exercised substitution clause, deliberately inserted to prevent worker status, could stop the application for recognition in its tracks.[94] The ruling has been strongly criticised by Alan Bogg, and we await to see whether the Court of Appeal adopts a different view of the application of Article 11 to

[87] Taylor et al (n 26) 53.

[88] See HM, *Good Work: A Response to the Taylor Review of Modern Working Practices* (n 65) 43–44. According to the WERS, B van Wanrooy et al (n 85) 61, by 2011 Joint Consultative Committees had only been established at no more than 8% of workplaces with five or more employees; see too the evidence in BEIS, *Good Work: The Taylor Review of Modern Working Practices. Consultation on Measures to Increase Transparency in the UK Labour Market* (February 2018) 30–31, https://assets.publishing.service.gov.uk/government/uploads/system/uploads/attachment_data/file/679849/Consultation_-_Increasing_Transparency_-_070218__3_.pdf.

[89] TULRCA 1992, Schedule A1, para 3: 'References to collective bargaining are to negotiations relating to pay, hours and holidays'.

[90] See the Special Issue: The Trade Union Act 2016 (2016) 45 *Industrial Law Journal*.

[91] BEIS, *Trade Union Membership 2017: Statistical Bulletin* (May 2018), 12–13 https://assets.publishing.service.gov.uk/government/uploads/system/uploads/attachment_data/file/712543/TU_membership_bulletin.pdf.

[92] *Wandsworth LBC v Vining* [2017] EWCA Civ 1092, [2018] ICR 499.

[93] That is, TULRCA 1992, s 188.

[94] See the *Independent Workers' Union of Great Britain (IWGB) v RooFoods Ltd (t/a Deliveroo)* CAC decision [2018] IRLR 84 and the unsuccessful judicial review: *R (on the application of IWGB) v CAC* [2018] EWHC 3342 (Admin), [2019] IRLR 249. Before the CAC, the IWGB gave evidence that more than 50% of the workers in the bargaining unit had signed a petition asking for union recognition: see [6] of CAC decision.

circumstances which bear the hallmarks of an employment relationship.[95] In other contexts unions have used more traditional methods, divorced from Article 11, to achieve recognition in respect of gig economy workers. The outcome in *Deliveroo* can be contrasted with the success of the IWGB in bringing the NHS contractor 'The Doctors Laboratory' (TDL) to the bargaining table. The IWGB was successful in achieving statutory recognition from TDL,[96] which then refused to engage in any form of meaningful bargaining, a tactic which has long been observed to be a boon for opportunistic employers under Schedule A1 of TULRCA.[97] Finally, after two days of strike action in May 2019, on 21 June 2019, TDL entered into a collective agreement with the IWGB. The IWGB will continue with litigation assisting some 45 couriers in claiming holiday pay, indicating the symbiotic, mutually reinforcing role of collective and legal mobilisation.[98]

B. Resisting the Absence of Representation

The survival of the statutory recognition regime, warts and all, means it cannot be used to test Offe's hypothesis, that external legal guarantees offer a substitute for internal solidarity and willingness to act but when they are removed the organisation may well lack the power to resist.[99] Nevertheless, the replacement of New Labour's support for union partnership with the current government's hostility or apathy towards unions brings the issue into the foreground. Perhaps it also offers the opportunity for more determined struggle, once the fiction of respect for trade unions as institutions has been abandoned.

In his 2005 article Ewing had already raised the problem, arguing that unions were ill-equipped to enforce partnership on reluctant partners because of the law on industrial action, giving the examples of the requirements to ballot individual members before industrial action and the right of individuals not to participate in a democratic, lawful strike.[100] While he treated these laws as manifestations of the spread of the representative function into industrial action, we consider they are better analysed from the perspective of targeting union's internal self-organisation. Integral to a general strategy of empowering dissenting members and increasing conflict within unions in the hope that this would weaken the authority of the executive, the provisions have the potential detrimentally to affect the union's ability to constitute itself an effective agency in industrial action because of its reduced power to sanction defectors.[101] This is because section 65 of TULRCA prevents a union from disciplining a member for failing to participate in or support a strike even

[95] See A Bogg 'Taken for a Ride: Workers in the Gig Economy' (2019) 135 *LQR* 219. See too V De Stefano, 'Non-standard Work and Limits on Freedom of Association: A Human Rights-based Approach' (2017) 46 *Industrial Law Journal* 185.

[96] *IWGB v The Doctors Laboratory Limited* TUR1/1016 (2017) 28 February 2018.

[97] T Novitz and P Skidmore, *Fairness at Work: A Critical Analysis of the Employment Relations Act 1999 and its Treatment of Collective Rights* (Oxford, Hart Publishing, 2001) 102–118; A Bogg, *The Democratic Aspects of Trade Union Recognition* (Oxford, Hart Publishing, 2009) 273–282.

[98] See IWGB, 'IWGB reaches historic pay deal with NHS contractor TDL and calls off strikes' (21 June 2019) https://iwgb.org.uk/post/5d0c844ddd65b/iwgb-reaches-historic-pay-deal.

[99] Offe (n 11) 217–8.

[100] Ewing, 'The Function of Trade Unions' (n 1) 12 and see TULRCA 1992, ss 226 and 65.

[101] For discussion of policies behind the original legislation in the Employment Act 1988, see S Auerbach, *Legislating for Conflict* (Oxford, Clarendon Press, 1990) ch 8.

where the democratic mandate of the union was to call one – the exemplar of representative democracy – *and even where the individual member voted in favour of the strike* and hence was individually 'represented' by the union calling for industrial action.

The provisions are nonetheless relevant to the bigger question of unions' capacity to enforce representation, recognition or collective bargaining in a changed climate, with less support for voluntary partnership arrangements. In their research in the 1990s based on surveys of trade unions, Jane Elgar and Bob Simpson showed that, while the strike laws had many detrimental consequences on unions' ability to strike (including cost, delay and opportunities for legal challenge), the effects were not all to unions' disadvantage. Unions soon adjusted their practices to accommodate ballots, the processes strengthened unions' accountability and internal democracy, and successful ballot results (which most were) gave great strength to the union and members in negotiations with employers.[102] Legal duties aimed at increasing the effect of dissenting voices may thus have the opposite result, of strengthening strike campaigns and the ability to mobilise members. In the context of UCU industrial action in 2017, the determination to meet the 50 per cent turnout threshold introduced by the TUA 2016 arguably led to greater support for the strike.[103]

One can see an echo of the unpredictable consequences of legislation in how the labyrinthine rules on statutory recognition, which Ewing gently chided, played out in the recent Boots litigation. In *Pharmacists Defence Union v Boots Management Services*[104] the Court of Appeal accepted that the voluntary recognition of a non-independent trade union, the Boots Pharmacists Association, for extraordinarily limited purposes (facilities for officials and machinery for consultation) was nonetheless sufficient to block an application by an independent union, the Pharmacists' Defence Association, for recognition in relation to the core collective bargaining purposes, such as pay. The PDA, it appeared, *was* the genuine representative of the workers, because it had a substantial membership within the bargaining unit;[105] but this was trumped by the device of Boots recognising the BPA (the membership of which is not specified). The tortuous route for derecognising the non-independent union[106] was, according to the Court of Appeal, sufficient means of vindicating the rights of both the PDA and its members under Article 11 EHRC.[107] If matters had ended there, the workers would have been denied collective bargaining by the only independent union which represented them and Article 11 would have exhausted its effects. But, accepting the invitation of the Court of Appeal, the workers returned to the CAC and succeeded in their application for de-recognition of the BPA, following a ballot in which 87 per cent

[102] See Elgar and Simpson, *Industrial Action Ballots and the Law* (n 23) and J Elgar and B Simpson, 'The Impact of Law on Industrial Disputes Revised: A Perspective on Developments over the Last Two Decades' (2017) 46 *Industrial Law Journal* 6 22.

[103] See, eg, S Smyth, 'The UCU strikes: a battle for the future of Higher Education' (LSE Blog, 27 February 2018) http://blogs.lse.ac.uk/politicsandpolicy/the-ucu-strikes-a-battle-for-the-future-of-higher-education/; see also British Sociological Association, 'Sociology and the USS Strike' (March 2018) www.britsoc.co.uk/about/latest-news/2018/march/sociology-and-the-uss-strike/.

[104] *R (on the application of Boots Management Services Ltd) v Central Arbitration Committee* [2017] EWCA Civ 66, [2017] IRLR 355.

[105] In the application it claimed to have 2,100 members from 5,500 employees: see the CAC decision [6] [2013] IRLR 262.

[106] Summarised by Underhill LJ [57].

[107] A Bogg and R Dukes, 'Article 11 ECHR and the Right to Collective Bargaining: Pharmacists' Defence Association Union v Boots Management Services Ltd' (2017) 46 *Industrial Law Journal* 543.

of the more than 3,000 workers who voted supported de-recognition of the BPA.[108] The turnout was high – almost half of the workers in the bargaining unit. It is plausible that the result of this lengthy process has been to strengthen the PDA within Boots, and to enhance its capacity for collective representation, as evidenced by conclusion of a new voluntary recognition agreement announced on 11 July 2019.[109]

There are, of course, plenty of other examples of unions using effective campaigning or resistance to impose recognition or bring employers to the bargaining table, the IWGB being a prime example. But it would be naive to overlook how recent changes in the law have the potential to exert a very serious detrimental impact on the ability of unions to mobilise members in effective strikes. The revised balloting thresholds introduced by the Trade Union Act 2016 are likely to place insurmountable blocks in the way of much industrial action and, by the same token, reduce the negotiating power of the threat of a strike. The 50 per cent turnout on postal ballots will often prove impossible to achieve in an era when most post is junk mail which is thrown away unopened; the 40 per cent positive mandate required where a majority of the electorate are normally engaged in important public services represents a level of endorsement higher than that attained in any public elections.[110] The ballot rules and right of members not to participate in strikes raised by Ewing seem flimsy legal obstacles in comparison.

These changes throw a bright light on the horns of the dilemma on which unions presently find themselves. Any strategy of relying on legal rights of representation or consultation or voluntary partnership arrangements as substitutes for members' willingness to act now appears misplaced. First, apart from the legal rights to union recognition in TULRCA, many legal rights to consultation conferred on unions are derived from EU law and are open to repeal once Brexit takes effect.[111] Secondly, voluntary partnership with the exiting government, which is at best indifferent and at worst hostile to unions, is a fantasy. Thirdly, the effect of the legal recognition machinery is probably exhausting its potential, mostly based on the 'shadow' of the law.[112] Yet, at the same time, the legislation on strikes makes it increasingly difficult to mobilise members to force employers to the bargaining table, save where the electorate is extremely engaged (or perhaps highly homogeneous in its interests). Alternative forms of fashionable and visible 'leverage' action, less demanding in terms of the mobilisation of members than traditional strikes, also impose far less economic pressure on the employer.[113] Unions are thus placed in the unstable position of

[108] *Parker and others v BPA and Boots Management Services Limited*, Case no TUR6/003/2017, 11 June 2018.

[109] For the new agreement, see PDA, 'PDA Union and Boots UK sign historic recognition agreement' (11 July 2019) www.the-pda.org/pdau-boots-sign-recognition/.

[110] See TULRCA 1992, s 226(2)(a)(iiia) and s 226(2B)-(2F). For discussion and evidence, see R Darlington and J Dobson, *The Conservative Government's Proposed Strike Ballot Thresholds: the Challenge to Trade Unions* (Liverpool, Institute for Employment Rights, 2015); and Dukes and Kountouris (n 22).

[111] The notable exception are the Safety Representatives and Safety Committees Regulations 1977, based on the model of union involvement favoured by the Robens Committee and expressed in s 2(6) of the Health and Safety at Work Act 1974 (HSWA). Even these have been overwritten by Framework Directive on Health and Safety 89/391/EEC on health and safety, which also led to the Health and Safety (Consultation with Employees) Regulations 1996. For summary, see M Ford, 'Workers' Rights from Europe: The Impact of Brexit' (*TUC*, April 2016) paras 58–61 https://www.tuc.org.uk/research-analysis/reports/workers%E2%80%99-rights-europe-impact-brexit.

[112] See B van Wanrooy et al (n 85) 117–122.

[113] See, on this, Gumbrell-McCormick and Hyman (n 39) ch 5.

having greater need to mobilise their members precisely because alternative strategies are hampered (legal support, voluntary partnership) at just the time when the law has severely restricted lawful mobilisation.

Where this instability will lead is an open question. The election of a Corbyn Government would have fundamentally altered the legal environment because of the Labour Party's proposals to roll out sectoral collective bargaining, to repeal the TUA 2016, to guarantee unions a right to access to the workplace and to enforce rights to union representation.[114] Now that will not happen, little is predictable about how worker discontent will be channelled or the response of unions in sectors where strikes are, in effect, legally blocked because of the turnout thresholds in postal ballots. Once again, the surface stability of institutional forms can disguise the deep turbulence occurring below, and hide the social pathologies which threaten them in the long run.

III. The Continuing Eclipse of the Regulatory Function

Ewing's diagnosis that unions' regulatory function – the extension of collective bargaining beyond the immediate employer – had 'no public policy support'[115] is even truer today than when he wrote. One often unnoticed step, not requiring legislation, was the delegation of pay bargaining in government to individual departments in the period 1996–2001, ending a single set of terms across the civil service.[116] While Ewing drew attention to the persistence of some sectoral collective bargaining in the private sector, since 2005 the scope and coverage of collective bargaining has declined further. By 2011, multi-employer collective bargaining was used to determine pay at only 7 per cent of workplaces, down from 9 per cent in 2004; only 2 per cent of private sector workplaces used sectoral collective bargaining to fix pay; and in the public sector multi-employer pay bargaining fell sharply from 58 per cent of workplaces 2004 to 43 per cent in 2011.[117] Though there are exceptions, most notably Agenda for Change in the NHS,[118] the general trend has been to amplify what Ewing referred to as the 'paradox' in which state regulation, in the form of individual employment rights, increasingly supplants the regulatory role of collective bargaining. The same pattern is evident in other Western European countries, such as Germany, where national minimum wage legislation has increasingly supplanted collective bargaining as the effective minimum standard. In the UK, this process has generated its own legitimation crisis because of problems of individuals enforcing their legal entitlements, something highlighted by the Supreme Court judgment in *UNISON* and by the Director of Labour Market Enforcement.[119]

[114] See the Labour Party manifesto, *For the Many, Not the Few* (n 13) in the section 'rights at work'.
[115] Ewing, 'The Function of Trade Unions' (n 1) 14.
[116] Discussed in *Robertson v DEFRA* [2005] EWCA Civ 138, [2005] ICR 750, CA.
[117] B van Wanrooy et al (n 85) Table 5.5, 83.
[118] See the 'NHS Terms and Conditions Service Handbook' www.nhsemployers.org/tchandbook/part-1-principles-and-partnership/principles-and-partnership.
[119] See *UNISON* (n 55) and the report of Sir David Metcalf, *United Kingdom Labour Market Enforcement Strategy 2018–19* (*HM Government*, May 2018) 12–16 https://assets.publishing.service.gov.uk/government/uploads/system/uploads/attachment_data/file/705503/labour-market-enforcement-strategy-2018-2019-full-report.pdf.

At the time Ewing wrote, there was still one relic of legislative endorsement of a regulatory function for trade unions following the earlier abolition of the wage councils[120] – the Agricultural Wages Board, in existence in various forms since 1917, and which set pay, holidays and other terms and conditions for farm workers through a process of surrogate collective bargaining, involving union and employer representatives. In June 2013 it was abolished in England by section 72 of the Enterprise Regulatory and Reform Act 2013.[121] According to the preceding consultation document which gave less than one month for responses, the AWB was unnecessary owing to other employment rights, such as the national minimum wage; it would be easier for employers not to have to establish which workers fell within it; it dissuaded 'modern working practices' such as piece rates; and it was an unnecessary administrative burden which constrained flexibility between employers and employees and which was hard to understand.[122] Only 37 per cent of respondees supported abolition of the AWB, whereas 61 per cent opposed it.[123] But this counted for nothing: the AWB's extinction was the logical conclusion of 30 years of sustained assaults on sectoral collective bargaining.

Here, the ECtHR did not come to the rescue. In its application to Strasbourg, Unite argued (among other matters) that the abolition of the AWB in a sector dominated by small employers, almost all of whom fell below the 21-worker threshold for compulsory recognition in TULRCA,[124] was contrary to the right to collective bargaining enshrined in Article 11, ECHR as recognised by the Grand Chamber in *Demir*.[125] The application was dismissed as inadmissible by the Court.[126] Noting that the application had to be seen from the perspective of the UK's positive obligations, the ECtHR was not prepared to find that the exclusion of small employers was unjustified (even though the UK Government did not seek to offer evidence to justify it). Nor did Article 11 require a legal mechanism for compelling collective bargaining by employers, even in a context where the dispersal of workers among many small employers and the historical evidence showed voluntary bargaining was very unlikely to emerge.[127] A very long-standing practice of surrogate collective bargaining on behalf of around 140,000 workers was thus replaced overnight by statutory minimum rights to wages and working time, enforceable by individual applications in the employment tribunal.

No-one would expect a campaign of industrial action or resistance in a sector where, as the evidence before the ECtHR showed, employers are highly dispersed, workers are often seasonal or migrants, and consequently it was and is extremely difficult for unions to organise – as the official data confirm.[128] Nonetheless, the process of the abolition of the

[120] Finally ended by s 35 of the Trade Union and Employment Rights Act 1993.

[121] Though not in Wales: see *In re Agricultural Sector (Wales) Bill* [2014] UKSC 43, [2014] 1 WLR 2622.

[122] DEFRA, *Consultation on the Future of the Agricultural Wages Board for England and Wales* (October 2012) www.gov.uk/government/consultations/the-future-of-the-agricultural-wages-board-for-england-and-wales-and-agricultural-wages-committees-and-agricultural-dwelling-house-advisory-committees-in-england.

[123] See DEFRA, *Consultation on the Future of the Agricultural Wages Board for England and Wales, and Agricultural Wages Committees and Agricultural Dwelling House Advisory Committees in England: Summary of Responses* (2013) https://assets.publishing.service.gov.uk/government/uploads/system/uploads/attachment_data/file/182151/awb-consult-summmary-responses-130228.pdf.

[124] TULRCA 1992, Sch A1, para 7.

[125] *Demir and Baykara v Turkey* (2009) 48 EHRR 54.

[126] *Unite v United Kingdom* [2017] IRLR 438.

[127] DEFRA's final Equality Impact Assessment dated 19 December 2012 showed that only 1% of farm businesses employed more than ten workers.

[128] See BEIS, *Trade Union Membership 2017: Statistical Bulletin* (n 91) 7 showing that, for the only years when the sample size was sufficiently large (1995 and 2016) about 8% of employees in agriculture, forestry and fishing were

AWB and its aftermath is at least consistent with Offe's hypothesis. The legal structures in the AWB enabled a process akin to collective bargaining to occur for many years, maintaining a function for the union bureaucracy. When the legal rug was suddenly pulled away, and the legal challenge in the courts failed, the resistance turned out to be muted. While the Labour Party has announced that it will reinstate the AWB if elected, the outcome of the 2019 General Election renders that extremely unlikely in the immediate future.[129] The AWB process exemplifies the tendency identified by Ewing, in which the regulatory function increasingly depends on political campaigning and legislation rather than collective bargaining.[130] But it also illustrates the risks where a hitherto benign legal environment turns hostile, and the legal guarantees are not underpinned by the potential to mobilise members.

IV. The Governmental and Public Administration Functions

Ewing saw the governmental and public administration functions as 'both a recognition of the role played by trade unions and a reflection of their penetration', albeit as secondary to the primary functions: as he put it, unions 'need to engage with government in order to secure legislation that will enable them to perform their other functions'.[131] He viewed both, in their own distinct ways, as instrumentally enabling trade unions' regulatory function.[132] The difficulty he identified – the retreat of sectoral collective bargaining in the absence of mechanisms of legal support – has significantly worsened in the UK since 2005.[133] In that context, the governmental function perhaps increasingly came to be seen as the primary means of achieving union goals, almost an 'end in itself'.

Union involvement in government and public administration can entail 'the organised political representation of working people', both restraining the powers of the state and harnessing that power.[134] As Ewing noted in a later essay, '[p]olitical action is necessary not only to establish the structures within which trade unionism can operate, but also to deal with those questions that are unlikely to be dealt with effectively without some dedicated legislative support'.[135] Through their governmental and public administration functions, trade unions can be engaged in 'the development, implementation and delivery of government policy'.[136] This can range from assistance in the design and achievement of health and education policies to control of wage inflation.[137]

in a union (Table 1.8). In 2017, unions were present in only 11.9% of such workplaces and only 7.2% of employees in those sectors had their pay affected by a collective agreement (Table 1.10).

[129] See the Labour Party manifesto *For the Many, Not the Few* (n 13) 89. For further proposals for sectoral bargaining, see KD Ewing, J Hendy and C Jones, *Rolling Out the Manifesto for Labour Law* (Liverpool, IER, 2018) ch 4.

[130] Ewing, 'The Function of Trade Unions' (n 1) 15.

[131] Ibid, 4.

[132] Ibid, 5.

[133] See B van Wanrooy et al (n 85) Tables 5.1 and 5.2, at 79.

[134] Ibid.

[135] KD Ewing, 'The Importance of Trade Union Political Voice: Labour Law Meets Constitutional Law' in A Bogg and T Novitz (eds), *Voices at Work: Continuity and Change in the Common Law World* (Oxford, OUP, 2014).

[136] Ewing, 'The Function of Trade Unions' (n 1) 5.

[137] Ibid.

If links between the trade unions and New Labour were weaker than they had been prior to 1997, they were nonetheless still extant, as Ewing observed.[138] Trade unions were represented on the Health and Safety Executive (HSE), the Advisory Conciliation and Arbitration Service (ACAS) and the Low Pay Commission (LPC).[139] There is some anecdotal evidence that trade unions ceased to be the exclusive source of worker representation on tripartite bodies, as in the case of employment tribunals.[140] Yet mostly trade unions still tend to be evenly matched with employer side representation, while the independent members engaged in administration of the HSE, ACAS and LPC may not be unsympathetic to worker interests.[141] The problem is not so much with the absence of trade union connections in the governance of such institutions as the underfunding of the tripartite bodies and the difficulties this creates for their management. One interesting example was the threat of strikes by staff at ACAS affected by restructuring, which came at the very time that it was assisting UCU and Universities UK in resolving their 2018 strike over pensions.[142] Further, other institutions on which trade unions were represented, such as the AWB, have simply been abolished.[143]

There may have been diminished access of trade unions to policy-making in the Labour Party in 2005, which Ewing notes was illustrated by the non-implemented Warwick agreement of 2004 and the later proposals for reform by Ed Miliband.[144] Today, however, a clear fault line has emerged between the Labour Party, in which unions such as Unite are closely involved in policy-making, and their complete estrangement from the Conservative Party. An early sign of the determination of the Conservative Party in this regard was the introduction of the Transparency of Lobbying, Non-Party Campaigning and Trade Union Administration Act 2014 (also known as 'the Gagging Act') which, as Alan Bogg has noted, placed significant restrictions on the political activities of trade unions among other civil society actors, resulting in a 'disproportionate silencing effect on political challenges to an austerity agenda'.[145] In particular, Part 2 of that legislation (amending controls on expenditure under the Political Parties, Elections and Referendums Act 2000) places limits on the purpose and public nature of the expression of views by trade unions as well as other civil society organisations.[146]

This measure was soon followed by proposals in the original Trade Union Bill in 2016 which sought to change a trade union member's right to 'opt out' of participation in a

[138] Ibid.

[139] Ewing, 'The Function of Trade Unions' (n 1) 16–17.

[140] P Burgess and S Corby, 'Employee Lay Judges in Great Britain: For Decoration Only?' Presentation at the 11th European Regional Congress of ILERA, Milan. Vol 8. No 10. 2016.

[141] Regarding the HSE Board, see: Health and Safety Executive, 'HSE Board' www.hse.gov.uk/aboutus/hseboard/biographies/board.htm. For ACAS Council membership, see: ACAS, 'The Acas Council' www.acas.org.uk/index.aspx?articleid=1401. Regarding the LPC, see: HM Government, 'About us' www.gov.uk/government/organisations/low-pay-commission/about.

[142] This industrial action organised by PCS eventuated in May 2018. See the ACAS, 'Acas statement on PCS strike' (11 May 2018) www.acas.org.uk/index.aspx?articleid=6532 (accessed 18 July 2019). See also 'Conciliation service Acas faces strikes over workload and resources' *The Guardian* (London, 19 March 2018).

[143] See above at n 121.

[144] Ewing, 'The Importance of Trade Union Political Voice: Labour Law Meets Constitutional Law' (n 135) 293 and 296.

[145] A Bogg, 'Beyond Neo-Liberalism: The Trade Union Act and the Authoritarian State' (2016) 45 *Industria Law Journal* 299, 309; see also S Cavalier and R Arthur, 'A Discussion of the Certification Officer Reforms' (2016) 45 *Industrial Law Journal* 236, 373–4.

[146] Ewing, 'The Importance of Trade Union Political Voice: Labour Law Meets Constitutional Law' (n 135) 294–5.

political fund to an 'opt in' requirement: a measure designed to exploit the potential apathy of members and to reduce union funding of the Labour Party. The compromise eventually reached in the TUA 2016 was to apply the 'opt in' rule only to new members at the end of the transitional period, while requiring an annual reminder from unions of their members' right to opt out, somewhat softening the blow without ameliorating it entirely.[147]

Since then the dominant message of the Conservative Government has been that trade unions are now largely otiose and irrelevant. It is apparent that the very design of the Taylor Review process on 'modern working practices' established to respond to 'innovative forms of working'[148] was intended to exclude trade union voice. Led by Matthew Taylor, previously Director of Tony Blair's 'New Labour' No 10 Policy Unit and now CEO of the RSA, the rest of the 'Review team' consisted of: Greg Marsh (previously CEO of Onefinestay sold to Accor in 2016); Diane Nichol (a partner in Pinsent Masons specialising in employment law); and Paul Broadbent (the new head of the Gangmasters Licensing Authority, previously assistant chief constable of Nottinghamshire police). There were no representatives of trade unions as there had been in the Donovan Commission.[149] Even an early press release indicated that the Taylor Review would be oriented towards 'alternative forms of representation around the world', such as 'the Freelancers Union in New York which focuses on access to health insurance, or the California App Based Drivers Association which lobbies companies like Uber on behalf of drivers'.[150] Alt-labor organisations seem to have been deemed acceptable,[151] but not the engagement of traditional unions such as the GMB, UNISON or Unite, or new bottom-up organisations like the IWGB.

Actually, both the larger traditional trade unions and smaller newly formed collectivities have succeeded in making life difficult for employers. Forced to bypass political lobbying, in part due to how little they have been heard, unions have resorted to other means to exercise voice. UNISON used litigation, not political action, to reverse the pernicious fees regime. The government's attempted reinforcement of restrictive balloting requirements, through for example 'membership audit' under the 'Gagging Act', has been rendered irrelevant in practice by spontaneous or leverage action. Examples include that taken by so-called contracted out staff, whether in universities (organised by the IWGB)[152] or migrant workers in government departments such as the Ministry of Justice (organised by United Voices of the World).[153]

[147] See TUA 2016, s 11 and TULRCA 1992, s 84A. Note also the requirement under the new s 32ZB of TULRCA 1992 requiring that details of political spending be included in a union's annual return to the Certification Officer. See Cavalier and Arthur (n 145) 378–9 for the precise details, including confirmation of the notice given regarding the option to opt out.

[148] See Taylor et al (n 26) 7.

[149] As there had been in the Royal Commission on Trade Unions and Employers' Associations, *Donovan Commission Report* (1968); as discussed in Bales, Bogg and Novitz (n 26) 53.

[150] See RSA, 'Matthew Taylor to lead independent review of employment practices in the modern economy' (1 October 2016) www.thersa.org/about-us/media/2016/matthew-taylor-to-lead-independent-review-of-employment-practices-in-the-modern-economy.

[151] See for discussion of alt-labor as a mode of collective resistance, A Aloisi, 'Negotiating the digital transformation of work: non-standard workers' voice, collective rights and mobilisation practices in the platform economy' (*CADMUS*, 2019) 12 http://cadmus.eui.eu//handle/1814/63264.

[152] See Solidarity Federation, 'London cleaners strike – and win' www.solfed.org.uk/catalyst/london-cleaners-strike-and-win; and O Jones, 'The courage of the LSE's striking cleaners can give us all hope' *The Guardian* (London, 25 May 2017).

[153] D Foster, 'The striking Ministry of Justice cleaners know their worth – all power to them' *The Guardian* (London, 7 August 2018).

Yet the official line remains that trade unions are largely irrelevant to regulation, government or public administration, even in respect of the most extreme forms of labour exploitation. The inaugural *United Kingdom Labour Market Enforcement Strategy* issued for 2018/19 by the first Director of Labour Market Enforcement, David Metcalf, envisaged involving trade unions in the enforcement of wages and holiday pay,[154] and to improve areas of guidance that are ambiguous or difficult to apply.[155] While the TUC and a number of individual unions such as UNISON, Unite and USDAW sought greater access rights to workplaces to assist in securing employment rights enforcement,[156] Metcalf considered that 'it would carry me long past my remit to make such a proposal'.[157] Notably, the Conservative Government response made no such concession; instead only recognising the potential for trade union engagement briefly in two respects. The first mentioned consultation of trade unions regarding measures to be taken concerning non-compliance in supply chains.[158] This is a very sparse response to the already considerable campaigning conducted by the TUC on labour market enforcement in a supply chain context,[159] and indeed the extensive proposals in *Rolling Out the Manifesto* from the Institute of Employment Rights.[160] There is one further brief mention in the government response of the capacity of trade unions to act in partnership with the Employment Agency Standards Inspectorate, her Majesty's Revenue and Customs, National Minimum and Living Wage enforcement team, and the Gangmasters and Labour Abuse Authority,[161] without articulating any clearly defined role. Since then, Metcalf has announced his resignation, after only being in the role for two years and Matthew Taylor has been appointed in the interim.[162] Where trade unions succeed in generating collective action among a diverse or heterogeneous workforce (engaging more with the irregular working patterns of female workers, outsourced workers, migrant workers and others) and developing internal democracy, they are defying the meagre functions the present Conservative Government wish to allot to them.

V. Conclusions

Ewing's 2005 article was written at a time of relative stability in the development of trade union functions. The trends he identified – an absence of support for the regulatory

[154] See Metcalf, *United Kingdom Labour Market Enforcement Strategy 2018–19* (n 119) 5 and 43.

[155] Ibid, 37.

[156] See the compilation of consultation responses available at: HM Government, *Enforcement of employment rights recommendations* (February 2018) www.gov.uk/government/consultations/enforcement-of-employment-rights-recommendations.

[157] See Metcalf, *United Kingdom Labour Market Enforcement Strategy 2018–19* (n 119) iv.

[158] Available at: HM Government, *United Kingdom Labour Market Enforcement Strategy 2018/19: Government response* (December 2018) 27, para 104 https://assets.publishing.service.gov.uk/government/uploads/system/uploads/attachment_data/file/765124/dlme-strategy-government-response.pdf.

[159] See TUC, 'Shifting the risk: Improving enforcement of employment rights' (April 2018) www.tuc.org.uk/research-analysis/reports/shifting-risk.

[160] Also, Ewing, Hendy and Jones, *Rolling Out the Manifesto for Labour Law* (n 130) 54–60 (ch 9).

[161] See HM Government, *United Kingdom Labour Market Enforcement Strategy 2018/19: Government response* (n 158) Annex A, 3.

[162] This resignation was announced on twitter at 28 June 2019 at https://twitter.com/ukdirectorlme?lang=en. See for Matthew Taylor's role as interim Director of Labour Market Enforcement from 1 August 2019: www.gov.uk/government/people/matthew-taylor.

function, limited support for the representative function, a retrenchment of the service function and increased resort to the government and public administration functions – were well-established and, apart from the last, exhibited continuity with the policies of the previous Conservative Governments. His hope that a form of corporatist social policy, based on the Warwick agreement, might reinvigorate the regulatory function turned out to be misplaced. By the end of the New Labour Governments, in 2010, the same trends had continued. Nothing was done to increase trade unions' regulatory role and no changes were made to the laws on strikes which hampered any attempts to force employers to engage in collective bargaining.

The major piece of employment legislation enacted in the dying days of the New Labour, the Equality Act 2010, gave further emphasis to rights based on individual enforcement in tribunals, not involving unions. The Agency Worker Regulations 2010,[163] enacted by New Labour to comply with EU law,[164] exemplified the trend Ewing identified, of unions resorting to the government function *faute de mieux.* UK opposition to the Directive was withdrawn once the TUC and CBI reached an agreement in 2008 about the scope of the proposed protection of agency workers.[165] The means of protection was legal, via individual tribunal claims even though the UK social parties envisaged the then government consulting with them about the details of the final regulations. The Regulations marked the eclipse of collective bargaining by legal regulation and unions' engagement in that process.

But, following Streeck, the apparent stability of institutions, including law, across time can mask deep-rooted instabilities. Unions in the UK have long been in an unstable position owing to the tension between bureaucratic power and organisational power. The changes in union functions under New Labour in part reflected unions' responses to that instability, as they sought to draw on the 'logic of influence' to compensate for an environment, including the law, which made resort to the 'logic of membership' more difficult. Since the coalition Government of 2010, however, that environment has radically changed. Lawful strikes in many sectors are now often a practical impossibility owing to the high ballot thresholds in the TUA 2016. This is especially so where the strike involves more than one workplace, where union membership levels are low or where the membership is dispersed, heterogenous or difficult to contact. As a crude summary, one can say that lawful strikes are most easy to organise among more highly educated, professional, full-time employees in large workplaces where unions are recognised – which is where union membership tends to be concentrated.[166] Just as in relation to the enforcement of individual legal rights, the paradox is that those workers with the most need of union protection are least able to draw on it.

This is not to say, however, that the response of unions will be decline and death. New strategies are already evolving, such as novel forms of protest action and the use of important test-case ligation to achieve strategic goals, to affect legislation and to act as a means of recruiting and drawing together a wider and more diverse pool of members. At the same

[163] SI 2010/93.
[164] Directive 2008/104/EC on temporary agency work.
[165] The agreement was published as Annex C to the consultation by the then Department for Business, Enterprise and Regulatory Reform, *Employment Agencies: Implementation of the Agency Workers Directive: a Consultation Paper* (May 2009) https://assets.publishing.service.gov.uk/government/uploads/system/uploads/attachment_data/file/250625/0447.pdf.
[166] See BEIS, *Trade Union Membership 2017: Statistical Bulletin* (n 91) 9–11.

time, unions have successfully pressed for the Labour Party to reverse the strong distaste for the regulatory function exhibited by governments of all political complexions since 1979. But, in contrast to when Ewing wrote, we are writing at a time where the political environment is less predictable than at any time since the second World War, where very significant blocks on membership mobilisation have only just come into effect, and in which the legal environment could radically change almost overnight, quite apart from the changes in the nature of work itself. Radical instability is now the name of the game, and it will need much more empirical work and greater historical distance to see where the pieces are heading.

15

The Irrepressible Common Law: The Economic Torts and the Right to Strike

DOUGLAS BRODIE*

I. Introduction[1]

At common law, the economic torts have operated to regulate the conduct of trade disputes in the UK and it is of course the case that their impact has been hugely significant as well as controversial. The right to strike which is, of course, a fundamental right in a social democratic constitution has always been at risk of being undermined by this body of law. The capacity of trade unions to conduct industrial action is dependent upon the strength of the statutory immunities provided in contemplation or furtherance of a trade dispute. The current iteration of those immunities is contained in the Trade Union and Labour Relations (Consolidation) Act 1992. In 1979 Ewing published an article in the Industrial Law Journal on the judicial approach to construction of the immunities and drew attention to two ways in which they were being undermined.[2] First of all, vulnerabilities existed as they did not offer comprehensive protection against common law liabilities that might arise in the course of industrial action. The tort of inducing breach of statutory duty was given as an example. However, the main thrust of the article was the failure of the courts to give a purposive interpretation to the wording of the statute. Attention was drawn to the

> development of narrow and difficult distinctions and the gratuitous qualification of the statutory language by concepts of reasonableness, directness and remoteness have enabled the courts to assert a high level of discretion and control over the circumstances in which industrial action may lawfully be conducted.[3]

* I am extremely grateful to the editors for a number of very helpful comments and also to those who attended the symposium in Kings in September 2017. The usual disclaimer applies. I am even more grateful to Keith whose teaching in Edinburgh in 1981/2 instilled a lifelong passion for the study of labour law. I should also add that but for his kindness and encouragement I would not have had a career in academic life.

[1] There are a number of very helpful articles which provided a detailed review of the current state of the law on the economic torts. See, eg, H Carty, 'The modern functions of the economic torts: reviewing the English, Canadian, Australian, and New Zealand positions' (2015) 74 *CLJ* 261 and PS Davies and Sir P Sales, 'Intentional Harm, Accessories and Conspiracies' (2018) 134 *LQR* 69.

[2] KD Ewing, 'The Golden Formula: Some Recent Developments' (1979) 8 *Industrial Law Journal* 133.

[3] Ibid, 135.

Several years later in 1982, Ewing and Elias published a comprehensive review and analysis of the economic torts in the Cambridge Law Journal.[4] Their paper emphasised the common law's capacity to frustrate legislative intentions by ongoing doctrinal development in ways that were not always anticipated and in some instances could not have been. As might have been expected, the paper also stressed that matters were compounded by the judicial tendency to give a restrictive interpretation to the wording of the statutory immunities against common law liabilities. The paper drew attention to the difficulties faced by the legislature in providing adequate protection against a backdrop of doctrinal uncertainty. The decision in *Rookes v Barnard*[5] provides a notorious example:

> The judgment outflanked the statutory trade dispute immunity because the tort of intimidation had not been within the contemplation of Parliament in the drafting of the legislation. It was an act of judicial defiance, asserting the primacy of the common law over democratically enacted legislation.[6]

The article concluded with the provocative assertion that a system of positive rights should supplant the statutory immunities; a view which whilst remaining aspirational has at the same time proved to be highly controversial. Wedderburn vehemently claimed in response that 'Nothing is worse than the assumption that "positive rights" *necessarily* afford a wider area of industrial legality than a statutory "immunity". Both the historical and the comparative study of labour law systems prove any such assumption to be false.'[7] At least for the time being, less attention is being paid to the economic torts by labour lawyers than has traditionally been the case. Judicial creativity in the context of claims made in trade disputes cases has not been evident for some years. This of course is very much connected to the existence of a hugely restrictive statutory regime where the litigious employer is much more likely to object to, for instance, a breach of balloting requirements than seek to probe and challenge the boundaries of the common law.[8] This has prompted one leading judge, writing extra-judicially, to make the very significant claim that where the regulation of industrial relations was involved 'the economic torts have run their course'.[9] The validity of this claim is very much open to challenge and this chapter seeks to review its merits. It will be suggested that it would be a mistake to disregard the possibility that the economic torts might move at some point into an expansive phase where trade disputes are concerned. This chapter is firmly focussed upon the common law position; the judicial approach to statutory interpretation is not discussed other than to note that the treatment of the statutory constraints is now a matter of some significance. This chapter addresses in the main the issue of doctrinal uncertainty and the consequent challenge for Parliament. By so doing it is hoped that an assessment might be offered of the extent to which the concerns raised in the Cambridge Law Journal article remain valid.

[4] P Elias and KD Ewing, 'Economic Torts & Labour Law: Old Principles and New Liabilities' (1982) 41 *CLJ* 321.

[5] *Rookes v Barnard* [1964] AC 1129. And see KW Wedderburn, 'Intimidation and the Right to Strike' (1964) 27 *MLR* 257, 257.

[6] A Bogg, 'The hero's journey: Lord Wedderburn and the "political constitution" of labour law' (2015) 44 *Industrial Law Journal* 299.

[7] Lord Wedderburn, 'The New Politics of Labour Law: Immunities or Positive Rights?' in Lord Wedderburn, *Employment Rights in Britain and Europe* (London, Lawrence and Wishart, 1991) 90.

[8] *London & Birmingham Railway v ASLEF* [2011] ICR 848 is but one example.

[9] Lord Hoffmann, 'The Rise and Fall of the Economic Torts' in J Edelman, J Goudkamp and S Degeling (eds), *Torts in Commercial Law* (Sydney, Thomson Reuters, 2011) 113.

II. A Historical Perspective

The law of the economic torts has experienced previous spells of judicial abstention and comparison might be made with the period between the early 1920s and 1960s. The period was notable for the decision on lawful means conspiracy in *Crofter Hand Woven Harris Tweed v Veitch* where the defence of justification was extended to include the pursuit of legitimate trade union interests.[10] It should also be said that, for much of this time, unfavourable economic conditions constrained trade union activity and employers had little incentive to resort to litigation. *Crofter* and the earlier case of *Reynolds v Shipping Federation*[11] can be seen as demonstrating that the courts adopted a much more accommodating attitude to trade union interests in the post-first world war period. Kahn-Freund claimed that the *Crofter* case showed 'the acceptance by the courts of the principle of non-intervention in industrial disputes.'[12] The courts, for their part, acknowledged that non-intervention came at a price but that price was found to be worth paying:

> It is true that the advantage or benefit may be at the cost of another's injury, but in a world of commercial and industrial ruthlessness, whose morality still shows some traces of the jungle, our courts of Law have wisely refrained from prescribing counsels of perfection.[13]

Crofter made an important contribution to the development of the common law but it is worth noting a few of the unsuccessful arguments for the employer.[14] The pursuers had also argued without success that liability should arise on the basis of unlawful interference with contractual relations and liberty to exercise the right of trade. Employers would of course mount similar arguments in the years to follow and judges would prove to be very receptive. The House of Lords was only asked to consider arguments on the common law but the lower courts had also reached a conclusion on the applicability of the statutory immunities.[15] It must be said that, rather than vindicating trade union interests, a rather restrictive approach was taken over interpretation and application. The contrast between the approach to common law and statute is considerable and demonstrates that judicial acceptance of trade union interests is rarely unqualified.

With reference to *Crofter*, Wedderburn wrote in 1980 that 'Until 1979 it could be said that almost every major decision of the House of Lords … had not favoured or had failed to understand collective trade union interests since *Allen v Flood*. The one major exception, in war time, was *Crofter* (where the interests of the big union, coincided with those of the big employers)'.[16] What of Wedderburn's cynicism? In truth, neither of those elements

[10] *Crofter Hand Woven Harris Tweed v Veitch* [1942] AC 435.

[11] *Reynolds v Shipping Federation* [1924] 1 Ch 28. Liability did not arise in *Reynolds* as the closed shop agreement 'was entered into not from a malicious desire to inflict loss on an individual or class of individuals, but from a desire to advance the business interests of employers and employed alike by maintaining the advantages of collective bargaining and control, it was not unlawful, and no action for conspiracy was maintainable by the plaintiff'.

[12] O Kahn-Freund, 'Labour Law' in M Ginsberg (ed), *Law and Opinion in England in the 20th Century* (London, Stevens & Sons, 1959) 242.

[13] *Crofter Hand Woven Harris Tweed v Veitch* [1940] SLT 210, 219.

[14] See D Brodie, 'The Scottish Case: Crofter Hand Woven Harris Tweed v Veitch' in KD Ewing (ed), *The Right to Strike: From The Trade Disputes Act 1906 to a Trade Union Freedom Bill 2006* (London, Institute of Employment Rights, 2007).

[15] Ibid, 132–8.

[16] Lord Wedderburn of Charlton, 'Industrial Relations and the Courts' (1980) 9 *Industrial Law Journal* 65, 70 fn 22.

helps to explain the outcome in the case. The fact of the matter was that the law had moved firmly down a particular path; crystallised by the decision in *Sorrell v Smith* where liability in conspiracy did not arise against a trade association where the predominant purpose was to further their own interests and unlawful means had not been used.[17] It would have been impossible to have denied the defenders in *Crofter* the benefit of this approach. It is worth noting that the opinion in the Outer House was delivered before the War had started, and throughout the case the courts were consistent in believing that the union was entitled (belatedly) to the benefit of *Mogul Steamship v McGregor*.[18] *Mogul* was a commercial case which determined that a conspiracy (without recourse to unlawful means) did not give rise to liability as long as the predominant purpose was to further the commercial interests of the conspirators. It may be observed that, whatever the impediments generated by the common law, fidelity to doctrinal consistency imposed some constraints on the judicial role in trade disputes.[19]

A more recent instance of judicial caution over taking steps to regulate the exercise of collective power is provided by *Universe Tankships v ITWF* where the House of Lords addressed the application of economic duress to negotiation of collective agreements.[20] It appears that action that attracts the protection of the trade dispute immunities will not be viewed as illegitimate and therefore not give rise to a claim on the basis of duress. The statutory immunities

> afford an indication, which your Lordships should respect, of where public policy requires that the line should be drawn between what kind of commercial pressure by a trade union upon an employer in the field of industrial relations ought to be treated as legitimised despite the fact that the will of the employer is thereby coerced, and what kind of commercial pressure in that field does amount to economic duress that entitles the employer victim to restitutionary remedies.[21]

This is not an unreasonable position to take and avoids the court drawing the criticism that the position adopted by the legislature was being undermined. However, the real issue where trade unions are concerned is the extent of protection against liability in tort which, as is well known, is greatly diminished.

III. Restatement and the Supreme Court

As already discussed, it has been a considerable period of time since controversy over the scope of the common law has arisen in the context of a labour dispute. There have though been two major decisions of the House of Lords on the economic torts in recent years: *OBG v Allan*[22] and *Total Network v Revenue & Customs*.[23] The two cases are key to our

[17] *Sorrell v Smith* [1925] AC 700.
[18] *Mogul Steamship v McGregor* (1889) 23 QBD 598.
[19] I am indebted to Alan Bogg for this insight.
[20] *Universe Tankships v ITWF* [1983] 1 AC 366.
[21] Ibid, 385.
[22] *OBG v Allan* [2007] UKHL 21, [2008] 1 AC 1. And see the commentary by B Simpson (2007) 36 *Industrial Law Journal* 468.
[23] *Total Network v Revenue & Customs* [2008] UKHL 19, [2008] 1 AC 1174.

understanding of contemporary law. The speeches therein may also give some indication of the potential for the economic torts to enter a more interventionist phase. It must be said though that intervention comes naturally to the common law given that combatting abuse of power is a fundamental aim irrespective of the nature of the case. The decisions will be reviewed from a labour law perspective to allow an assessment of the extent to which trade unionists should remain concerned about the potential impact of the economic torts.

OBG involved conjoined claims and prompted a comprehensive review of the law by the Supreme Court. Much was said about the torts of inducing breach of contract and interference in business by unlawful means. The validity of the 'unified theory' which treated inducing breach of contract as one species of a more general tort of actionable interference with contractual rights was assessed. The theory was rejected and interference in business by unlawful means and inducing breach of contract were said to be two distinct heads of liability. Inducing breach of contract was said to treat

> contractual rights as a species of property which deserve special protection, not only by giving a right of action against the party who breaks his contract but by imposing secondary liability on a person who procures him to do so. In this respect it is quite distinct from the unlawful means principle, which is concerned only with intention and wrongfulness and is indifferent as to the nature of the interest which is damaged.[24]

OBG provided important guidance on demarcation lines but also clarified the pre-requisites of an action for inducing breach of contract and, in particular, that nothing short of an actual breach was required before a claimant had a right of action. Where the tort of interference in business was concerned Lord Hoffmann also advanced a restricted meaning of unlawful means which was accepted by a majority of the court:

> In my opinion, and subject to one qualification, acts against a third party count as unlawful means only if they are actionable by that third party. The qualification is that they will also be unlawful means if the only reason why they are not actionable is because the third party has suffered no loss.[25]

Underpinning this stance was the view that the rules of economic competition (whether in the sphere of labour disputes or otherwise) were primarily for Parliament.[26]

The highly forensic interrogation of the common law by the Supreme Court in *OBG* has resulted in some helpful clarification of the law. It is now clear that the tort of inducing breach of contract necessitates an actual breach of contract and not simply interference with performance. Lord Denning in the Court of Appeal in *Torquay Hotel v Cousins* had taken a different view,[27] which was later confirmed by the House of Lords in *Merkur Island Shipping v Laughton*, where it was said that all 'prevention of due performance of a primary obligation under a contract was intended to be included even though no secondary obligation to make

[24] *OBG* (n 22) [32].

[25] Ibid [49].

[26] It is important that Lord Hoffmann's view prevails given the wide variety of statutory provisions that could be relevant to a trade dispute. See, for instance, A Bogg, 'Taken for a Ride: Workers in the Gig Economy (2019) 135 *LQR* 219.

[27] *Torquay Hotel v Cousins* [1969] 2 Ch 106. The speeches in the Court of Appeal revealed somewhat different approaches. Russell LJ and Winn LJ were of the view that the exclusion clause in the case afforded 'only an immunity against any claim for damages; it could not bar a right to treat the contract as repudiated by continuing breach.' Denning MR took the view that a breach had not arisen but nevertheless a claim in tort could still be brought.

monetary compensation thereupon came into existence, because the secondary obligation was excluded by some force majeure clause.'[28] The extension of the tort to include interference falling short of breach was not only doctrinally controversial but also created considerable uncertainty over the boundaries of liability. Once one moved beyond the talisman of breach of contract and into the realm of protecting contractual expectations it became very difficult to say where liability was to end.[29] Shortly after *Torquay*, in *Midland Cold Storage v Steer*,[30] it was argued that there was a tort of wrongfully preventing a person from entering into a contract. This was rejected by Megarry J though I would suggest that the argument was not untenable in the wake of *Torquay Hotel*. Megarry J's assessment of the case law was reinforced by a concern over indeterminacy of liability: 'Unless hedged about with many restrictions, such a tort would have an extremely wide ambit that would be likely to work as much injustice as justice.'[31] Labour law historians would be likely to endorse this given that torts of wide and uncertain ambit have been responsible for much injustice. Against that backdrop, *OBG* provided a measure of clarity but, perhaps more significantly from a labour law point of view, signalled that a modest role for the economic torts was appropriate. This manifested itself most strongly doctrinally when it came to the question of the definition of unlawful means.

Prior to *OBG*, discussion of the fundamental principles in this area of law invariably involved the seminal decisions of the House of Lords in *Allen v Flood*[32] and *Quinn v Leatham*.[33] *Allen* had held that an act lawful in itself is not converted by a malicious motive into an unlawful act so as to make the doer of the act liable to a civil action. *Quinn* promptly diminished, to some extent, the impact of *Allen* by denying its applicability where the tort of simple conspiracy was concerned. A clear tension existed between the two decisions and they can be depicted as sitting on quite different points of an absentionist/interventionist spectrum. It is of course the case that they were separated in time by a mere three and a half years. Against that backdrop, the decision of the House of Lords in *Total Network* which arose less than twelve months after *OBG* deserves careful consideration. The issue in the case was whether the Commissioners could maintain a claim for damages under the tort of unlawful means conspiracy against a participant in carousel fraud. Three key questions needed to be considered. The first was whether it was open to the claimants to bring an action in damages as a means of recovering VAT from a person who has not been made liable for that tax by Parliament. It was held that the commissioners' claim was not a claim for tax or the levying of tax but a claim for loss caused by fraudulent conspiracy and therefore did not offend the fundamental constitutional principle enshrined in article 4 of the

[28] *Merkur Island Shipping v Laughton* [1983] 2 AC 570.

[29] In *Torquay Hotel* itself Winn LJ said, obiter, that 'it can at least be said, with confidence, that where a contract between two persons exists which gives one of them an optional extension of time or an optional mode for his performance of it, or of part of it, but, from the normal course of dealing between them, the other person does not anticipate such postponement, or has come to expect a particular mode of performance, a procuring of the exercise of such an option should, in principle, be held actionable if it produces material damage to the other contracting party.' Such an outcome would have involved a radical extension of the law and it is extremely surprising that the dictum could have been expressed 'with confidence.'

[30] *Midland Cold Storage v Steer* [1972] ICR 435.

[31] Ibid, 450.

[32] *Allen v Flood* [1898] AC 1.

[33] *Quinn v Leatham* [1901] AC 495.

Bill of Rights (1689) that no money should be levied for or to the use of the Crown except by grant of Parliament. The second and third questions have far greater relevance for the purposes of current discussion and may be stated as follows: (i) was it an essential requirement of the tort of unlawful means conspiracy that the conduct which is said to amount to the unlawful means should give rise to a separate action in tort against at least one of the conspirators?; (ii) did the enactment of the statutory VAT scheme excluded the possibility of a common law claim for damages?

It would be difficult to have sympathy for the position of the defendants and it should be said that there is an instant temptation to look for a way to impose liability when faced with avoidance of tax by corporate bodies. The transactions which led to the litigation had 'no economic purpose other than to cheat and/or defraud [the Commissioners] of revenue' and were entered into '… with intent to cheat [the Commissioners] of revenue and/or to defraud the Revenue.'[34] The Court of Appeal had looked to *OBG* and had held that it was an essential requirement of the conspiracy action that the unlawful means had to be independently actionable.[35] The House of Lords disagreed and arrived at an entirely different (and wider) view on what constituted unlawful means: 'a conspiracy is tortious if an intention of the conspirators was to harm the claimant by using unlawful means to persuade him to act to his own detriment, even if those means were not in themselves tortious.'[36] Lord Hoffmann's approach was not adopted though it might have been anticipated that a singular meaning of unlawful means would be arrived at given 'the obvious desirability of consistency and coherence'.[37] Nevertheless, the House of Lords was prepared to distinguish *OBG* for the purposes of a claim in unlawful means conspiracy. The contrasting approach between the two decisions speaks yet again to the volatility of the common law in this area and causes one to doubt that any period of abstention is likely to be prolonged. It would also be difficult to claim that the law was coherent and a lack of coherence is likely to be conducive to innovative arguments which will run the risk of unsettling the law should they be accepted. The latter problem is compounded by the fact that complex common law arguments may well arise in the context of interlocutory proceedings.

Concerns over coherence are reinforced by contemporaneous developments in other common law systems. The Canadian Supreme Court decision in *A I Enterprises v Bram Enterprises* had followed the lead of the majority in *OBG* and adopted the same approach to unlawful means.[38] The following justification for a similarly absentionist stance was offered:

> The scope of the unlawful means tort should be understood in the context of the broad outlines of tort law's approach to regulating economic and competitive activity. Several aspects of that

[34] *Total Network* (n 23) [52]. In the Court of Appeal ([2007] 2 WLR 1156) Ward LJ explained that 'carousel fraud' referred to a fraud 'consisting of a series of sales of taxable goods, of which sales the initial one is zero rated, under the next one the initial buyer sells the goods and receives VAT from its buyer but then disappears without accounting to the Revenue for the VAT it has received, and the third sale made by the buyer from the "missing trader", is a zero rated sale of the goods back to the original vendor. This seller, who has paid VAT to the "missing trader", then claims back from the Revenue as input tax the amount of the VAT paid to the missing trader. The invoices are all in order so the Revenue accepts the claim for repayment of the input tax but because the "missing trader" has not accounted to the Revenue for the VAT it had apparently received, the Revenue is out-of-pocket by the amount it has had to pay to the vendor under the third sale …'.

[35] *Customs and Excise Commissioners v Total Network SL* [2007] EWCA Civ 39, [2007] 2 WLR 1156.

[36] *Total Network* (n 23) [34].

[37] Ibid, 220.

[38] *A I Enterprises v Bram Enterprises* [2014] 1 SCR 177.

> approach support adopting a narrow scope for the unlawful means tort: the common law accords less protection to purely economic interests; it is reluctant to develop rules to enforce fair competition; it is concerned not to undermine certainty in commercial affairs; and the history of the common law shows that tort liability, if unduly expanded, may undermine fundamental rights.[39]

The last of the reasons adumbrated resonates very strongly with labour lawyers and the court in *Bram Enterprises* elaborated on this aspect of their reasoning:

> A final consideration supports a limited scope for this tort: the risk inherent in the economic torts generally that they will undermine legislated schemes favouring collective action in, for example, labour relations and interfere with fundamental rights of association and expression. At one time, the common law of tort was ready – and many would say overready – to intervene to prevent economic coercion in the context of industrial disputes.[40]

The foregoing candid appraisal notwithstanding, Canadian law contains the same inherent tensions as the UK as the same approach is taken where conspiracy to use unlawful means is concerned.[41]

OBG and *Total Network* were certainly capable of being distinguished (the absence of conspiracy in *OBG* provided a very easy route[42]) but it is striking just how quickly the courts can move from a restrictive to an expansive approach as exemplified by the change in definition of unlawful means. The possibility of liability arising in any individual case is thereby increased. *Total Network* also provides encouragement to those who would wish to make greater use of the economic torts in the commercial arena. Carty portrays the outcome as one which provides 'a wider common law control of commercial misbehaviour that intentionally causes economic harm to the claimant. Having been the poor relation of the economic torts, it is now revitalised as a commercial tort.'[43] It does not seem unreasonable to assume that the desire to impose 'commercial morality' is related to high profile corporate failures and scandals. In the process we are thereby reminded that common law doctrine is often hugely malleable in the hands of a court determined to find what is seen as a just outcome in a particular case.

Developments in the context of commercial litigation are likely to be applicable more widely and the fact that the common law continues to be looked to where the use of economic pressure is seen as objectionable is perhaps a little ominous. One is also left wondering to what extent the outcome in *Total Network* was influenced by the factual matrix. There would be few who would have sympathy for the defendants but judicial desire to bring about justice in individual cases has worked to the disadvantage of trade unions on numerous occasions. Almost 150 years ago, it was judicially observed that questions of fair competition should not depend on the 'idiosyncrasies of individual judges'.[44] Can we be sure that those 'idiosyncrasies' would not play a part in trade dispute cases in the future? I would doubt that we can.

[39] Ibid [29].

[40] Ibid [34].

[41] Carty (n 1) 274.

[42] The House of Lords (*Total Network* (n 23) [124]) highlighted Lord Hoffmann's stance in *OBG* that 'discussion of unlawful means' was limited to cases involving 'interference with the actions of a third party in relation to the plaintiff', and did not necessarily apply to 'a case of 'two party intimidation', which 'raises altogether different issues'.

[43] Carty (n 1) 277.

[44] *Mogul Steamship v McGregor* [1892] AC 25, 51.

However, perhaps most worryingly the element of combination played its part in judicial deliberations: 'it appears that the law of tort takes a particularly censorious view where conspiracy is involved'.[45] The latter dimension is explored in the next section.

IV. The Resilience of Conspiracy

From a trade union point of view, the fact that the element of conspiracy serves as the point of departure from *OBG* may be the principal concern. It has proved to be a very useful device for employers over the years in trade disputes cases. Conspiracy is a tort with very long tentacles and this can prove very advantageous to claimants in a variety of ways. It can, for example, act to increase the number of defendants where a breach of contract has been induced to include those who are not inducers as such.[46] More fundamentally, the very fact of the existence of a conspiracy is said to call for a more 'censorious view' and trade unions are only too well aware that historically this has been very much the case. Bowen LJ, in the 1880s, put forward the following justification for the treatment of a combination: 'The distinction is based on sound reason, for a combination may make oppressive or dangerous that which if it proceeded only from a single person would be otherwise.'[47] In the trade union context this is particularly worrying as it is not difficult to portray the organisation of industrial action as involving an element of combination; eg between a trade union and local activists. In some ways it is surprising that the distinction retains cogency as the courts now espouse a different view of the economic realities. It is accepted that it cannot be assumed that the existence of a combination gives rise to an unacceptable degree of economic power. It is also recognised that a corporation may be infinitely more powerful than a group of conspirators. Just short of 100 years after Bowen LJ's judgment Lord Diplock offered a very different perspective:

> But to suggest today that acts done by one street-corner grocer in concert with a second are more oppressive and dangerous to a competitor than the same acts done by a string of supermarkets under a single ownership or that a multinational conglomerate such as Lonrho or oil company such as Shell or B.P. does not exercise greater economic power than any combination of small businesses, is to shut one's eyes to what has been happening in the business and industrial world since the turn of the century and, in particular, since the end of World War II.[48]

Lord Diplock's views were endorsed by the House of Lords more recently in *Lonrho v Al-Fayed*.[49] The dicta just referred to would point towards an acceptance that adding

[45] *Total Network* (n 23) [221].

[46] In *Palmer Birch v Lloyd* [2018] 4 WLR 164, [2018] 4 WLR 164 [232] it was said that 'One might imagine a case where the number of persons conspiring to bring about a breach of the claimant's contract was greater than that made up of the contract-breaker and the inducer(s) properly so described. In such a case, some of the alleged conspirators might wish to argue they had not been guilty of any actual persuasion or inducement in relation to the breach of contract. However, proof that they were nevertheless party to a conspiracy that others should bring about the breach ought to result in liability, provided always that the claimant can show they had the requisite intention to harm him.'

[47] *Mogul* (n 18) 616.

[48] *Lonrho v Shell* [1982] AC 173.

[49] *Lonrho v Al-Fayed* [1992] 1 AC 448, 464.

allegations of conspiracy should add little to the strength of an economic torts case. *Total Network* confirms that this is not in fact true and it would seem that suspicion of combinations is deeply ingrained at common law.

V. The Wider Context

It is of course the case that the economic torts often play a key role in litigation which is not concerned with a trade dispute. This can be overlooked to some extent by labour lawyers but should not be as legal challenges in other spheres of activity may arise which will provoke common law changes. The stability and coherence of the law cannot be assessed purely by reference to trade disputes cases. Litigation over commercial relations for example has been very much at the forefront of the recent evolution of the law. Developments in that area may prompt the emergence of new or reconstituted torts which, in the fullness of time, may be looked to by employers to increase their chances of success in an action against a trade union.

The economic torts determine the appropriateness of the use of economic pressure in a wide range of situations. Judicial creativity and extension of the scope of the common law may be readily justifiable in some contexts. The economic torts may also enter employment relations in the context of competition between employers. In *Tullett Prebon v BGC Brokers* the claimant was an inter-dealer broker company who claimed against a rival company for conspiracy and inducing breach of contract in respect of brokers who had reneged on contractual commitments.[50] Such actions tend to attract little by way of controversy. It is also worth recalling that around the time *Rookes* was decided the Court of Appeal dealt with the contractual plea of economic duress in *DC Builders v Rees*.[51] The common law development which emerged in *Rookes* was that unlawful means for the purposes of the tort of intimidation was extended to include the threat of a breach of contract. *Rees* brought about an analogous development in the law of contract. The case concerned the making of a threat of a breach of contract to bring about a variation in contractual terms. The plaintiffs were builders who sought to recover the balance due for work done for the defendants. The latter had been reluctant to pay and, at a point when the plaintiffs were in desperate financial straits, the defendant offered to pay part of the amount due if the plaintiffs would accept it in full settlement. It was made clear that if the offer was not accepted no payment would be made. The plaintiffs told the defendants that they had no choice but to accept and they received partial payment in exchange for a receipt stating that the sum was received 'in completion of the account.'[52] On the plaintiff's successful claim for the balance it was held that payment by a debtor of a lesser sum than the amount of the debt was not a settlement of the debt which was binding at law on the creditor. The view was taken, given the element of economic duress constituted by the threat to pay nothing unless the cheque was accepted in settlement, that there was no true accord between the parties, and nothing to

[50] *Tullett Prebon v BGC Brokers* [2011] EWCA Civ 131, [2011] 2 WLUK 722.
[51] *DC Builders v Rees* [1966] 2 QB 617.
[52] Ibid, 622.

prevent the plaintiffs from recovering the full amount of the debt. The situation was seen as highly analogous to *Rookes*:

> She was making a threat to break the contract (by paying nothing) and she was doing it so as to compel the creditor to do what he was unwilling to do (to accept £300 in settlement): and she succeeded. He complied with her demand. That was on recent authority a case of intimidation …[53]

The case of *Rees* unlike *Rookes* was a two-party situation but both cases are concerned with the legitimacy of the threat of a breach of contract when used to gain an economic advantage. A limited number of reported cases in the *Rees* mould have arisen over the years but the decision does not appear to have been doubted. It also did not appear to create any kind of furore at the time. By way of contrast, it was said of *Rookes* that 'In 1964 … the House of Lords has invented a new extension of civil liability, and then reduced to insignificance the protections of the TDA, 1906, which should have been a protection against it.'[54]

VI. The Evolution of Economic Duress

Total Network provides a warning that the common law is unlikely to stand still. It also confirms that doctrinal developments may emerge which increase the likelihood of judicial intervention. A similar picture emerges when developments in the law of contract are taken on board. The common law's continued willingness to regulate the exercise of economic pressure is further demonstrated by developments in the contractual concept of economic duress since *Rees*. It has been recognised for a long time that the traditional concept of duress has limited relevance in modern society. Claimants are much more likely to be concerned with economic threats rather than ones of physical violence. The decision in *Rees* held that the threat of breach of contract could supply the requisite degree of illegality. However, in recent years the courts have touched upon the question of whether economic duress could occur even where there had been no unlawful behaviour. The question of whether a claim of lawful act duress could be maintained was explored by the Privy Council in *Borrelli v Ting* and the view was taken that unconscionable conduct could give rise to a claim.[55] At first glance this might herald a significant expansion in the scope of duress. However, it is by no means clear what the Privy Council meant by the term unconscionable. In *Borrelli* itself the impugned conduct included false evidence and forgery and, as a corollary, there was no need to explore whether the term unconscionable might extend to a much wider range of conduct than had hitherto been viewed as relevant. It remains the case that commercial pressure is not enough.[56]

The law remains somewhat uncertain whether lawful act duress exists and even more uncertain what the parameters might be. There are those who would confine it to a narrow range of situations by accepting no more than 'that a lawful threat may render a contract voidable because it is inextricably linked to previous unlawful conduct'.[57] Recent decisions

[53] Ibid, 625.
[54] KW Wedderburn, 'Intimidation and the Right to Strike' (1964) 27 *MLR* 257, 257.
[55] *Borrelli v Ting* [2010] UKPC 21.
[56] *Pao On v Lau Yiu Long* [1980] AC 614, [1979] 3 WLR 435.
[57] PS Davies, '"Lawful Act" Duress' [2018] 134 *LQR* 5.

had pointed to a more expansive view though, as we shall see, the Court of Appeal has recently turned its face against this.[58] In *Times Travel v Pakistan International Airlines* two travel agents brought claims against an airline alleging that the airline had pressured them into entering into new and less favourable agency agreements.[59] The previous agreement had been terminated by the giving of due notice. It was alleged that the airline had improperly pressured them to sign the new agreement, under which they gave up accrued claims for commission under the contractual arrangements previously in force. The claimants alleged that they had entered into the new agreement because of economic duress and/or misrepresentation.

In a bold judgment, Warren J held that the claimants had been subject to economic duress as, although respecting the terms of the contract, the airline had placed illegitimate pressure on them. There had been no adequate notice period and the claimants had had no practical alternative. They were therefore entitled to rescind the new agreement. The law was stated in the following terms:

The necessary ingredients for a successful economic duress claim are: (i) Pressure which is illegitimate. (ii) The pressure must be a significant cause inducing the Claimant to enter into the contract. (iii) The practical effect of the pressure is that there is compulsion on, or a lack of practical choice for, the victim.[60]

Times Travel was followed in the later recent decision in *Al Neyhan v Kent*[61] where it was accepted that a threat to commit an otherwise lawful act could be improper if coupled with a demand going substantially beyond what was legitimate. The decision had the potential to have a considerable impact on employment law given that employers routinely adopt the approach followed by the defendants in *Times Travel*. A proposal for a variation of contract which would be very much to the employee's detriment can be forced through in this way.[62] However, the Court of Appeal has now found for the defendants on appeal.[63] The theoretical difficulties in embracing lawful act duress have also been articulated by Beatson:

> it is ordinarily not duress to threaten to do what one has a right to do: to lawfully terminate a contract or to refuse to enter into a contract. The general rule is, moreover, based on good reasons. First, whereas in the developing body of public law principles of propriety of purpose, relevance, and rationality – *Wednesbury* reasonableness – limit the exercise of power, the basic position in private law is a Diceyan one. All that is not prohibited is permitted and there is no general doctrine of abuse of rights. If therefore a person is permitted to do something, he will generally be allowed to do it for any reason or for none.[64]

Economic duress is unlikely to assume a significant role where trade disputes are concerned. However, I would maintain that developments in that area are relevant. Judicial willingness

[58] R Ahdar, 'Contract doctrine, predictability and the nebulous exception' [2014] 73 *CLJ* 39.

[59] *Times Travel v Pakistan International Airlines* [2017] EWHC 1367, [2017] 6 WLUK 255.

[60] It may be noted that *Chitty on Contracts* (32nd edn) at 8-046 recognises the existence of lawful act duress: '… Threatening to carry out something perfectly within one's rights will not normally amount to duress; for instance, a party who relies on his existing contractual rights to drive a hard bargain is not, on that ground alone, guilty of economic duress. But there can be no doubt that even a threat to commit what would otherwise be a perfectly lawful act may be improper if the threat is coupled with a demand which goes substantially beyond what is normal or legitimate in commercial arrangements …'.

[61] *Al Neyhan v Kent* [2018] EWHC 333, [2018] 2 WLUK 528.

[62] See D Brodie, *The Employment Contract* (Oxford, Oxford University Press, 2005) ch 13.

[63] *Times Travel (UK) Ltd v Pakistan International Airlines Corp* [2019] EWCA Civ 828, [2019] 5 WLUK 157.

[64] J Beatson, *The Use and Abuse of Unjust Enrichment* (Oxford, Clarendon Press, 1991) 129.

to consider a significant expansion of the law of economic duress points to an appetite to take further control of the exercise of economic power. It also suggests that the courts may be willing to commit to a position of uncertain scope to achieve an appropriate outcome in individual cases. The decision of the Court of Appeal in *Times Travel* may not be the end of the matter; the Privy Council's referencing of unconscionability in *Borrelli* may yet stimulate common law developments.

VII. Statutory Constraints: A Johnson v Unisys Dividend?

Since the decision in *Rookes* the House of Lords has had to consider the impact of the creation of a statutory regime on the common law on a number of occasions.[65] The intervention of Parliament can mean that further common law development is foreclosed. In the field of employment law *Johnson v Unisys* decided that the statutory law of unfair dismissal meant that the implied obligation of mutual trust and confidence should not be extended to the process of termination.[66] In a similar vein *Marcic v Thames Water Utilities* held that the claimant could not being an action in common law nuisance given the existence of a detailed statutory scheme of regulation.[67] The question is said to be one of construction whether the existence of a statutory scheme excludes the possibility of a common law remedy. Where the statutory regime is comprehensive it is more likely that the conclusion will be drawn that there is no scope for the common law to play a role. However, in a wide range of situations where Parliament only occupies the field to a limited extent the common law will continue to expand. Sometimes this will be with a view to filling gaps or in some way supplementing the legislation. In *Total Network* itself it was argued that the statutory VAT scheme established exclusive remedies for the recovery of tax or for dealing with false input tax repayment claims and that these remedies could not be supplemented by a tortious action for damages. This argument was rejected and a common law action was held to be necessary to allow the claimants to recover damages that had been caused by illegal and fraudulent tax evasion.

The question arises whether the statutory immunities would be seen as analogous to the regimes in *Johnson* and *Marcic* and thereby be protected from common law advances. Bogg observes that:

> Had their Lordships in *Rookes* regarded the common law as Lord Hoffmann regarded it in *Johnson*, as subsidiary to democratically enacted legislation in the development of a composite body of employment law consisting of both legislation and common law, *Rookes* might well have been decided very differently.[68]

Can we assume that given the greater judicial elaboration of the relationship between the common law and statute that has taken place in the years since *Rookes* greater respect will be shown for 'democratically enacted legislation'? I would be far from confident that that would be the case. The courts operate on the basis that the legitimacy of common law

[65] See A Bogg, 'Common Law and Statute in the Law of Employment' (2016) 69 *Current Legal Problems* 67.
[66] *Johnson v Unisys* [2003] 1 AC 518, [2001] 2 WLR 1076.
[67] *Marcic v Thames Water Utilities* [2004] 2 AC 42, [2003] 3 WLR 1603.
[68] A Bogg and H Collins 'Lord Hoffmann and the Law of Employment' in PS Davies and J Pila (eds), *The Jurisprudence of Lord Hoffmann* (Oxford, Hart Publishing, 2015) 213.

development is assumed at least where private law is concerned.[69] In *Total Network* it was suggested that 'the statute must positively be shown to be inconsistent' with a mooted common law development before the latter is denied.[70] There is also an important difference between *Rookes* and *Johnson*. The latter was concerned with a common law obligation particular to the law of the employment contract (albeit it can be linked to more general obligations of good faith) and it was therefore relatively straightforward to conclude that an employment statute stood in the way of development. The content of the obligation mooted and the statutory scheme were found to cover the same ground. By way of contrast, any development in the law of the economic torts is much more likely to be of general application such as the modernisation of the tort of intimidation that took place in *Rookes*. For Lord Devlin, acceptance of the defendants' case in *Rookes* would have restricted the law's development more widely and such a position was viewed as unsatisfactory. Denial of the claim would 'hobble the common law in all classes of disputes lest its range is too wide to suit industrial disputes.'[71] I would not be surprised if the courts were to adopt a similar stance in the future and, as in *Rookes*, it is far from certain that the purposive interpretation likely to be required by way of protection would be forthcoming.[72]

Analysis of the relationship between common law and statute is rendered more difficult as 'no satisfying overarching principle has been identified to explain the relationship between statute and common law'.[73] The limits of common law intervention are also uncertain. Baroness Hale has pointed out that the judiciary '... must not overstep that indefinable line between the development and elaboration of existing principles and the making of brand new law which is unquestionably the province of Parliament'.[74] Undefinable lines by definition do not offer much by way of guidance. The extent of statutory regulation in any given area is likely to be significant. The fact that a statutory framework does not involve a codification of the common law may be regarded as leaving the door to judicial creativity very much open. There is though probably a tendency to regard legislative intervention as only partially pre-empting the scope for common law development.[75]

VIII. The Future

For the time being at least the economic torts play very much a secondary role in trade disputes given the levels of statutory regulation which currently exist. In *OBG* Baroness Hale saw a great deal of merit in an abstentionist approach at common law continuing:

> In the modern age, Parliament has shown itself more than ready to legislate to draw the line between fair and unfair trade competition or between fair and unfair trade union activity. This can

[69] The position may well be different in public law where judicial review cases display a good deal of caution in the face of statutory regulation. I am grateful to Alison Young for this insight.

[70] *Total Network* (n 23) [130].

[71] *Rookes* (n 5) 1218.

[72] It is conceivable that Art 11 of the ECHR may encourage a more purposive approach at common law. I am grateful to Alan Bogg for this observation.

[73] S McLeish, 'Challenges to the Survival of the Common Law' [2014] *Melbourne University Law Review* 818.

[74] *OBG* (n 22) 305.

[75] C Barnard and L Merrett, 'Winners and Losers: Edwards and the Unfair Law of Dismissal' (2013) 72 *CLJ* 313, 319.

> involve major economic and social questions which are often politically sensitive and require more complicated answers than the courts can devise. Such things are better left to Parliament. The common law need do no more than draw the lines that it might be expected to draw.[76]

Labour lawyers would undoubtedly endorse the view that the law of trade disputes is one for the legislature. Currently, maintaining a policy of judicial abstention is assisted by the fact that employers have little need to probe for new lines of argument at common law given the highly favourable legislative position they enjoy. Were a statutory framework to emerge which was more protective of collective rights, I would suggest that it is far from certain that judicial abstention would prevail.

Developments in the law of economic duress do not point to judicial passivity where the regulation of economic power is concerned. It is striking that just as the law of tort is taking a narrower view of unlawful means (where the tort of interference in business by unlawful means is concerned) the law of contract may be moving in the opposite direction through the acceptance of lawful act duress. Both contract and tort are concerned with constraining the illegitimate use of economic power. A requirement that an unlawful act take place is a way of limiting the scope of liability for economic duress but it also provides a measure of certainty. One of the challenges in accepting lawful act duress is in finding a way of delimiting liability but also in providing guidance as to what the law actually is. A term such as unconscionable tells us very little. It is also striking that the courts may well be willing to embark upon such unchartered waters given the difficulties they have had in establishing boundaries where the economic torts are concerned.

Academic critique of the judicial approach to labour dispute cases has often focussed on the failure to understand and give proper recognition to the interests of the collective. A greater appreciation of the collective interest would not necessarily prevent judicial intervention. The common law is wedded to achieving a just outcome in any individual case and this is reflected in the 'extreme reluctance on occasions to affirm an existing categorical rule.'[77] It is said by Ahdar that 'this reticence may be seen as another manifestation of the movement of late towards greater doctrinal flexibility and individualised justice.'[78] It is of note that this thesis was supported by reference to several contractual doctrines; one of which was economic duress: 'Making the test for lawful act duress dependent on social morality, as determined by the judges, hardly assuages the concerns of those already critical of the defence.'[79] It is true that Ahdar was writing with reference to the law of contract but I would suggest that his observations also apply to the law of obligations in general. It should be said that the common law temperament is not suited to inactivity and, for example the judiciary may not be minded to await parliamentary intervention:

> While the techniques of tax avoidance progress and are technically improved, the courts are not obliged to stand still. Such immobility must result either in loss of tax, to the prejudice of other taxpayers, or to Parliamentary congestion or (most likely) to both.[80]

[76] *OBG* (n 22) 306.
[77] Ahdar (n 58) 39.
[78] Ibid.
[79] Ibid, 47.
[80] *Ramsay v Inland Revenue Commissioners* [1982] AC 300, 326.

IX. Conclusions

Is Lord Hoffmann's assessment that the economic torts have run their course in labour disputes likely to be borne out? This is far from certain. The economic torts have taken on something of a new lease of life in the commercial context and may be seen as providing rules to ensure corporate morality. Developments arising in that arena will be just as applicable in trade dispute cases. We therefore need to reflect on the appropriate legislative response. In 1982 Ewing (along with Elias) took the view that there was merit in switching to a system of positive rights. In particular, it was suggested that a rights based system might mean that a right to strike 'could exist regardless of common law developments.'[81] In 2006 Ewing reminded us of the underlying problem that the Trade Disputes Act 1906 had been 'hobbled from birth by casting the freedom to strike in the form of an immunity rather than a right, and by creating an immunity from known liabilities, failing to anticipate the possibility that new liabilities would arise in the future.'[82] The merits of this analysis have been recognised beyond the academy by the Canadian Supreme Court in *Bram Enterprises*:

> This history draws attention to the risk that expanded liability for the economic torts may be used to undermine legislative choices and perhaps even constitutionally protected rights of expression and association … A narrow and clear definition of the scope of liability reduces this risk.[83]

Ewing has continued to advocate a new legal settlement containing a right to strike and his warnings over reliance on traditional approaches to statutory protection are as pertinent as ever. It would be unwise to assume that the possibility of the immunities being circumvented by new liabilities can be disregarded and attention needs to be paid to the form that statutory protection would take.[84]

[81] Elias and Ewing (n 4) 358.

[82] KD Ewing and C Jones, 'From the Trade Disputes Act to the Trade Union Freedom Bill' in KD Ewing (ed) *The Right to Strike: From The Trade Disputes Act 1906 to a Trade Union Freedom Bill 2006* (London, Institute of Employment Rights, 2007) 5.

[83] *Bram Enterprises* (n 38) [34].

[84] For an alternative view, see Wedderburn (n 7).

16

Corporatism and its Discontents: Pluralism, Anti-Pluralism and Anglo-American Industrial Relations, c. 1930–1970[1]

BEN JACKSON

We were pluralists, believing that a free society consists of a large number of overlapping groups, each with its own interests and objectives which its members are entitled to pursue so long as they do so with reasonable regard to the rights and interests of others. But we were also egalitarians, wishing to see a shift in the distribution of wealth toward those with lower incomes, and a shift of power over the conduct of their working lives and environment towards working men and women; and, for both these reasons, emphasising the importance of trade unions in industry, in the economy and in society. We therefore attached special importance to collective bargaining as the means whereby trade unions pursue their objectives.

Hugh Clegg[2]

I. Introduction

As the work of Keith Ewing reminds us, the strength of trade unions always stands in a complex relationship with state power and civil society mobilisation. While many distinguished observers of industrial relations have emphasised the latter rather than the former as the more significant driver of unionisation in Britain, Ewing has persuasively argued for the importance of the state in fostering collective bargaining at the high watermark of trade union influence during the mid-twentieth century. One of the most striking claims developed by Ewing is that a fully egalitarian model of labour law that seeks 'to extend the idea of democracy from the political arena to the workplace' specifically requires the state to empower unions rather than taking a more neutral stance that seeks merely to create the space in which unions may develop.[3] However, as Alan Bogg and Ruth Dukes have

[1] This chapter draws on material previously published in M Bevir, *Modern Pluralism: Anglo-American Debates Since 1880* (Cambridge, Cambridge University Press, 2012) 105–28.

[2] Quoted in D Kynaston, *Austerity Britain 1945–51* (London, Bloomsbury, 2007) 455.

[3] K Ewing, 'The State and Industrial Relations: "Collective Laissez-Faire" Revisited' (1998) 5 *Historical Studies in Industrial Relations*, 5 (1998) 1, 6; K Ewing and J Hendy, 'New Perspectives on Collective Labour Law: Trade Union Recognition and Collective Bargaining' (2017) 46 *Industrial Law Journal* 23.

shown, key figures in the fields of industrial relations and labour law in the middle of the twentieth century were heavily influenced by a pluralist philosophy that tended to downplay the significance of state intervention to trade union success, both as a matter of historical record and of normative desirability.[4] In this chapter I will build on this work by investigating the Anglo-American public debate on trade unionism between the 1930s and 1970s. My aim in doing so is in the first place to augment these existing accounts by documenting the pervasiveness of this pluralist account of industrial relations in wider political debate. Secondly, this chapter demonstrates the extent to which this pluralist stance not only indicated – as Ewing argues – a misunderstanding of the necessary role of the state in supporting trade unions but also marked a significant narrowing of the goal of 'economic democracy' itself by focusing on collective bargaining to the exclusion of other forms of democratic participation.[5] As I will show, by the 1960s and 1970s this left industrial relations pluralism vulnerable to critics from both the New Left and the neo-liberal right who sought to portray it as either insufficiently democratic or fundamentally illiberal respectively.

Clearly, there was much that distinguished the industrial politics of Britain and the US in this period, not least the fact that, in spite of their enormous growth, American unions were consistently weaker and less politically influential than their British cousins. Nonetheless, at an ideological level, it is striking that a broadly similar discourse of industrial relations pluralism exercised a powerful – although fleeting – grip on elite-level debates in both Britain and the US in the middle of the twentieth century. It was this now neglected tradition of Anglo-American corporatist pluralism that neo-liberals viewed with suspicion and sought to rebut.[6] The conclusion of this chapter will therefore be that while mid-century corporatism was in an important sense a pluralist doctrine, advocating the importance to a democratic society of vibrant, oppositional pressure groups, particularly labour organisations, neo-liberalism was in this respect anti-pluralist and regarded pressure group activity, particularly by unions, as inimical to the authority of the state.

II. Corporatist Pluralism in Depression and War

The leading sponsors of corporatism in this period espoused an intriguing mixture of ideas drawn from a variety of sources, including the earlier socialist pluralism of Harold Laski and GDH Cole and the emerging 'realist' and pluralist theories of democracy articulated by Joseph Schumpeter and Robert Dahl. But we should also note that the Anglo-American

[4] A Bogg, *The Democratic Aspects of Trade Union Recognition* (Oxford, Hart Publishing, 2009) 3–76; R. Dukes, *The Labour Constitution* (Oxford, Oxford University Press, 2014) 69–91.

[5] I therefore focus chiefly on the political rather than legal debate and leave to one side the important work of Otto Kahn-Freund, the quintessential legal pluralist, but whose theoretical contribution has already been perceptively reconstructed in Bogg (n 4) and Dukes (n 4).

[6] As Nelson Lichtenstein has pointed out, the word 'corporatist' would not have been used by the left in the mid-twentieth century because of its association with fascism. Nonetheless, the word can be seen in retrospect to capture an important aspect of the new social order envisaged by liberals and socialists at this time, namely the settlement of major social and economic decisions through bargaining between the state and economic interest groups, particularly business and unions: N Lichtenstein, 'From Corporatism to Collective Bargaining: Organized Labor and the Eclipse of Social Democracy in the Post-War Era' in S Fraser and G Gerstle (eds), *The Rise and Fall of the New Deal Order* (Princeton, Princeton University Press, 1989) 146 fn 6.

roots of this thinking encompassed other influences as well, and in particular drew on the early work of the leading British Fabians, Sidney and Beatrice Webb, and the American institutionalist economist, JR Commons. The detailed empirical studies of trade unionism undertaken by the Webbs and Commons led them to proclaim that the gradual emergence of organised labour as a powerful social actor signified the growth of mature democratic self-government on the part of the workers, and was the harbinger of a new model of economic organisation. Representative organisations drawn from both sides of industry would in future meet to negotiate agreements over pay and conditions, as well as other matters of mutual concern.[7]

With this eclectic range of sources in mind, a useful point of entry into the later period covered by this chapter is Walter Milne-Bailey's 1934 book, *Trade Unions and the State*. Milne-Bailey spent his career in the British trade union movement, culminating in a stint as head of research for the Trades Union Congress between 1926 and 1935, but he also retained an interest in more theoretical discussions. His book was clearly shaped by the problematic legacy of the 1926 General Strike in Britain, in particular by the challenge the strike had purportedly posed to the authority of the state, and by an enthusiasm for the pluralist political theory of Harold Laski. A quote from Laski's *Liberty in the Modern State* (1930) served as the epigraph of the book, while Milne-Bailey's preface paid tribute to Laski's 'brilliant and suggestive work' and his 'generous counsel throughout the writing of the book.'[8] This was not mere politeness on Milne-Bailey's part. By the 1930s the pluralist episode in British socialism was widely seen as having run out of steam, not least by its staunchest advocates, such as Laski and Cole. It was therefore of some interest that it was the pluralist language of associational autonomy that Milne-Bailey appropriated in order to characterise the relationship between unions and the state. Milne-Bailey based his analysis on the fundamental pluralist claim that free individuals must be guaranteed the opportunity to form and participate in diverse associations that stand independently of the state in order to enjoy liberty and self-government. 'Every interposition of such a voluntary group between the individual and the state must, unless the idealist position is adopted with all its implications, result on balance in an enlargement of freedom.'[9] Milne-Bailey argued that trade unions were spontaneous, organic associations that had developed among workers from their authentic individual desires for fellowship, solidarity, collective bargaining and greater control over their working lives. Trade unions, he continued, offered 'no clearer example … of the inherent vitality of a genuine group organisation having a common purpose and a vivid group aspiration.'[10]

Unsurprisingly, Milne-Bailey took the opportunity to criticise both communist and fascist societies for their failure to guarantee individuals a rich associational life independent

[7] S and B Webb, *The History of Trade Unionism* (London, Longmans, Green, 1894); S and B Webb, *Industrial Democracy* (London, Longmans, Green, 1897); RW Schatz, 'From Commons to Dunlop: Rethinking the Field of Industrial Relations' in N Lichtenstein and H John Harris (eds), *Industrial Democracy in America: The Ambiguous Promise* (Cambridge, Cambridge University Press, 1993) 97–100.

[8] W Milne-Bailey, *Trade Unions and the State* (London, George Allen & Unwin, 1934) 9, 11.

[9] Milne-Bailey (n 8) 242–5, 273, 356 (quote); for the roots of these ideas in pluralist theory, see D Runciman, *Pluralism and the Personality of the State* (Cambridge, Cambridge University Press, 1997) 89–194; M Stears, *Progressives, Pluralists and the Problems of the State* (Oxford, Oxford University Press, 2002) 88–123; M Grimley, *Citizenship, Community and the Church of England: Liberal Anglican Theories of the State Between the Wars* (Oxford, Oxford University Press, 2004) 65–102.

[10] Milne-Bailey (n 8) 96.

of the state, but he also observed that within the remaining mature capitalist democracies a clear social trend could be discerned: notionally 'capitalist' economies were in fact evolving into a hybrid of capitalism and socialism. Such economies, including Britain, the US and France, had abandoned laissez-faire in favour of greater state rationalisation and planning of economic activity, while the widely discussed split between ownership and control in capitalist enterprises had made the question of private versus social ownership less relevant than in earlier decades.[11] The real issue, Milne-Bailey argued, was how to secure greater democratic control over both private and public industrial organisations. He proposed, somewhat in the vein of guild socialism, that greater functional decentralisation was the answer, but he was also careful to stipulate that in his view it was necessary to chart a middle way between the industrial autocracy of capitalist business as usual and the grave economic inefficiency that would be precipitated by syndicalism. His middle way envisaged the use of much greater consultation between employers, the state and trade unions, which would yield the three-fold benefit of giving workers greater influence on decision-making; attenuating industrial unrest; and enhancing the legitimacy of democratic politics. This 'democratic view of industry' entailed greater use by Parliament of consultative and advisory bodies (including a new National Economic Council); union representation on the boards of publicly-owned industries; works councils in private industry; and a strong social commitment to collective bargaining as itself a mechanism of democratic government.[12] But Milne-Bailey also ruled out as impractical the 'crudest notions of democracy' advocated in earlier pluralist theory. Any stronger form of industrial democracy was classed as likely to impede efficiency and to require a degree of technical expertise that the 'untrained layman' lacked. Hence, even before the work of Schumpeter and Dahl, the meaning of industrial democracy had begun to be diluted in corporatist theory: certain managerial prerogatives were to be protected and direct self-government by workers in industry was seen as incompatible with the technical requirements of modern economic production.[13]

A similar interpretation of the meaning of 'industrial democracy' gained currency in the American labour movement around the same time as Milne-Bailey's book was published in Britain. The immediate industrial context in the US was of course rather different from Britain. Milne-Bailey had to contend with the gloomy aftermath of the historic defeat of the unions in the General Strike and an unsympathetic Conservative-dominated government. In contrast, theorists of industrial democracy in the US were inspired by a series of successful union mobilisations in the 1930s, and buoyed by a relatively pro-labour federal government led by the Democrats. The rise of this new and dynamic unionism was associated above all with the unions who worked together under the banner of the Congress

[11] The split between ownership and control referred to the tendency for firms to be run by a salaried managerial class rather than the owners of the enterprise, and for the owners to be a dispersed group of relatively passive shareholders. The classic diagnosis of this trend was A Berle and G Means, *The Modern Corporation and Private Property* (New York, Harcourt, Brace & World, 1932).

[12] Milne-Bailey (n 8) 322–3, 337–354, 360–84. This diagnosis was similar to the one outlined by John Maynard Keynes in *The End of Laissez-Faire*, with the significant difference that Keynes laid greater stress on a broadly elitist model of public corporations runs by experts and professional managers, whereas Milne-Bailey sought to temper this rule by experts with the active involvement of workers' representatives. See JM Keynes, *The End of Laissez-Faire* [1926], in *The Collected Writings of John Maynard Keynes Volume IX: Essays in Persuasion* (London, Macmillan, 1972) 288–91.

[13] Milne-Bailey (n 8) 359–60.

of Industrial Organizations (CIO) after breaking away from the American Federation of Labor in 1935.[14] However, in spite of this more promising industrial and political context, the particular understanding of 'industrial democracy' defended by the CIO was similar to that outlined by Milne-Bailey. Radical syndicalist proposals, of the sort articulated earlier in the century by the Industrial Workers of the World, were firmly rejected as impractical, and replaced by an emphasis on collective bargaining, social legislation, and consultation with worker representatives by both employers and the state. As CIO President Philip Murray put it, such measures were democratic because they introduced 'a system of rules' to 'supplant the arbitrary will of the employer.'[15] Murray drew on the American democratic tradition to substantiate this claim. In his view, liberal democracy was itself threatened by autocratic capitalism: 'The exploited casual labourers of California and the feudalistic bosses that exploit them are no part of a liberal democratic constitution. Neither are the unhappy serfs of the unorganised mills and factories.'[16] While the American Constitution was grounded on a federalist desire to pluralise political decision-making, and thus make it more accountable, said Murray, industrial decision-making remained the sole preserve of unaccountable dictators: 'the maximum of feasible home rule is as wholesome for industrial as it is for political democracy.'[17] Unions were therefore essential groups in industrial societies, formed organically out of the desire of workers to influence the conditions in their workplaces and thus enhance their freedom. Indeed, Murray suggested that greater worker involvement in industrial decision-making could only benefit political democracy in a larger sense, since it would help to teach workers about the virtues of democratic citizenship: 'There is little hope of interesting the average man in political ideas and practice when his political experiences are largely confined to voting at widely spaced elections. By contrast, his contacts with industry fill every hour of the working day.'[18]

In practical terms, this demand for industrial democracy chiefly amounted to a defence of collective bargaining as the principal means of introducing fair procedures to govern matters such as wages, working hours, health and safety, operational control of the workplace, discipline and promotion.[19] However, CIO leaders and theorists also attempted to push forward a broader, although somewhat inchoate, vision that would see unions take on the role of worker representatives in a corporatist political economy, through which unions would help to shape industrial planning and welfare state expansion. One version of this promoted by Murray, for example, envisaged the creation of a National Production Council including labour representatives to help plan economic growth, and industry-wide councils that brought together employers, unions and the state to plan production in their own particular field. These ideas also underpinned the influential but ultimately unsuccessful wartime plan proposed by the United Automobile Workers' Walter Reuther, which sought

[14] R Zieger, *The CIO, 1935–1955* (Chapel Hill, University of North Carolina Press, 1995) 22–41.

[15] M Cook and P Murray, *Organized Labor and Production: Next Steps in Industrial Democracy* (New York, Harper & Brothers, 1940) 188.

[16] Cook and Murray (n 15) 248.

[17] Cook and Murray (n 15) 88–89.

[18] Cook and Murray (n 15) 39–42, 49, 213–21, quote at 213–14. This was essentially the same argument that Carole Pateman would later press against elitist theories of democracy in her *Participation and Democratic Theory* (Cambridge, Cambridge University Press, 1970).

[19] Cook and Murray (n 15) 109–55; Zieger (n 14) 120.

to reorganise aircraft production under a tripartite production board.[20] All of this indicated the direction of travel in leftist political thought on both sides of the Atlantic before 1945: towards a pluralist corporatism which sought to ensure that the vogue for economic planning incorporated an important role for labour representation within it, but also rejected core elements of earlier, more radical pluralist thinking.

III. Post-War Pluralism: Collective Bargaining as Industrial Democracy

Milne-Bailey's book was influential on post-war British writers on industrial relations as they sought to theorise the new social settlement cemented into place by the peculiar conditions of total war. British academics such as Hugh Clegg and Allan Flanders (leaders of the so-called 'Oxford School' of industrial relations), alongside Labour politicians such as Anthony Crosland, followed in Milne-Bailey's foot-steps by setting out a social democratic programme that by-passed the familiar socialist focus on nationalisation and prioritised instead the promotion of greater material and social equality through fiscal policy, the welfare state, and collective bargaining.[21] A central component of this social vision was the associational autonomy granted to the trade unions to negotiate wages and conditions on behalf of the working class. Less radical, although roughly similar, views were also expounded after the Second World War in the US by an influential generation of labour economists and industrial relations scholars broadly sympathetic to the claims of organised labour, some of whom were taught or directly influenced by JR Commons. Leading figures in these fields, such as Clark Kerr, John Dunlop, Sumner Slichter and Richard Lester, characterised themselves as 'pluralist' in their commitment to promoting an inclusive and democratic society through the existence of diverse centres of contending social power, with unions allocated a key role in constraining the power of capital. Although these American authors were careful to describe themselves as 'liberal pluralists', and were anxious to effect a reconciliation between labour and capital, they nonetheless envisaged a legitimate and significant economic role for unions and for the state in co-ordinating the bargaining between interest groups.[22]

[20] P Murray, *CIO Re-Employment Plan* (Washington DC, CIO, 1945) 10; Lichtenstein, 'Corporatism to Collective Bargaining' (n 6) 125–7; A Brinkley, *The End of Reform: New Deal Liberalism in Recession and War* (New York, Alfred A Knopf, 1995) 203–9, 218; N Lichtenstein, *Walter Reuther: The Most Dangerous Man in Detroit* (New York, Basic Books, 1995) 154–74; Zieger (n 14) 141–7, 323–8.

[21] My understanding of the links between the Oxford School and Labour revisionism is indebted to P Ackers, 'Collective Bargaining as Industrial Democracy: Hugh Clegg and the Political Foundations of British Industrial Relations Pluralism' (2007) 45 *British Journal of Industrial Relations* 77; J Kelly, *Ethical Socialism and the Trade Unions: Allan Flanders and British Industrial Relations Reform* (London, Routledge, 2010). For the wider ideological context of revisionism, see B Jackson, *Equality and the British Left* (Manchester, Manchester University Press, 2007) 151–218.

[22] For further discussion of American industrial relations pluralism, see K van Wezel Stone, 'The Post-War Paradigm in American Labor Law' (1981) 90 *Yale Law Journal* 1509–80; B Kaufman (ed), *How Labor Markets Work* (Lexington MA, Lexington Books, 1988); Schatz (n 7).

This transatlantic discourse of pluralist corporatism was in the fortunate position of inheriting the social patriotism of the people's war. British and American authors alike emphasised the extent to which 'stable democracies', in essence the English-speaking nations and the Scandinavians, had developed a mature democratic culture in part because of the important democratising role played by labour organisations. A Whiggish story about the gradual growth of Anglo-American liberty and democracy was adapted to encompass the emergence of constitutional government in industry thanks to the union movement. The existence of such pressure groups, pluralists argued, helped to diffuse any potentially totalitarian concentrations of power, of the sort exhibited in Nazi Germany and the Soviet Union.[23] As Clegg put it:

> Stability is given to a democratic system by the articulation and independent organization of many interests whose pressure through the political institutions of the country provides an approximate equilibrium between all the forces with real power within the system, and therefore protects and gives stability to a free society.[24]

Of course, it was recognised that one influential analysis of the Weimar Republic was precisely that it had collapsed under the weight of sectional conflict between excessively powerful interest groups. But this was not taken very seriously as a possible outcome for 'stable democracies' that had a well-entrenched, widely-shared democratic culture of compromise and liberty, and that were enjoying the benefits of the post-war economic boom.[25]

Post-war pluralist writings therefore adopted the socialist pluralist emphasis on independent labour organisations as the primary mechanism by which economic life could be democratised, and stressed the authoritative democratic credentials of a political system that institutionalised the formal representation of unions in the policy-making process. J K Galbraith's famous phrase, 'countervailing power', which made its entry into political debate in 1952, was eagerly adopted by the post-war pluralists as crystallising their vision: a society where the power of capital was constrained and regulated by the state and by powerful civil society organisations such as unions and consumer groups.[26] According to this analysis, however, unions could only play their legitimate role in a pluralist democracy if they remained independent of both management and the state. Furthermore, on the basis of the experience of industrial relations in the nationalised industries in Britain since 1945, the ownership of industry was deemed largely irrelevant to the role and status of organised labour. Under both private and public ownership, pluralists argued, independent trade unions would be required to ensure the voices of workers were articulated. By analogy with political democracy, unions were portrayed as creating 'a two-party legislative system

[23] RE Schiller, 'From Group Rights to Individual Liberties: Post-War Labor Law, Liberalism, and the Waning of Union Strength' (1999) 20 *Berkeley Journal of Employment and Labor Law* 11–13.

[24] H Clegg, *A New Approach to Industrial Democracy* (Oxford, Blackwell, 1960) 115; the influence of pluralist political science is evident in this passage. This book was written by Clegg under the aegis of the Congress for Cultural Freedom, which had organised a conference in Vienna in 1958 on 'Workers' Participation in Management.' Both Clegg and Crosland had attended, and Clegg was commissioned to write-up the fruits of the discussion as a book. On the broader agenda of the Congress for Cultural Freedom, see F Stonor Saunders, *Who Paid the Piper? The CIA and the Cultural Cold War* (London, Granta, 1999).

[25] For a characteristically sanguine view, see C Kerr, 'Industrial Relations and the Liberal Pluralist' [1955], in his *Labor and Management in Industrial Society* (New York, Anchor Books, 1964) 8–14.

[26] JK Galbraith, *American Capitalism: The Concept of Countervailing Power* (Boston, Houghton Mifflin, 1952).

governing the life of the workplace. In their absence, the rules would be set exclusively by the employer.'[27] Crucially, though, it was the process of collective bargaining that was said to promote democracy and not direct worker participation in industrial decision-making. Through collective bargaining, rules and procedures could be agreed that would narrow the scope of arbitrary management decisions and hence grant protection and control to workers. Collective bargaining was therefore presented as introducing 'the "rule of law" in employment relations.'[28] Walter Reuther gave a flavour of the democratic rhetoric that framed this view after the War: 'Management has no divine rights. Management has only functions, which it performs well or poorly. The only prerogatives which management has lost turned out to be usurpations of power and privilege to which no group of men have exclusive right in a democratic nation.'[29]

The corollary of the emphasis on collective bargaining as democratic was that direct democratic control of industry by the workers was deemed unnecessary and undesirable; the role of labour organisations was to act as if they were a parliamentary opposition. In Clegg's famous phrase: 'The trade union is thus industry's opposition – an opposition which can never become a government.'[30] Like Milne-Bailey, the post-war pluralists ruled out the syndicalist or guild socialist dreams of earlier radicals. But they also took this argument further than Milne-Bailey and the CIO strategists of the 1930s by narrowing the definition of industrial democracy to such an extent that it became, to all intents and purposes, co-extensive with collective bargaining. Although union theorists of the 1930s had rejected as impractical the guild socialist form of industrial democracy sketched by Cole and Laski, mechanisms for formal worker representation in industrial decision-making remained an important part of their agenda, alongside collective bargaining, as a means of advancing a new form of economic citizenship. In the post-war period, pluralist theorists appropriated the notion of industrial democracy to characterise the status quo of the post-war settlement and as a motif of social conciliation rather than of the struggle to deepen democracy. In this sense, industrial relations pluralism had become oriented towards the problem of how to maintain order and discipline in the workplace at the expense of the desire to make democracy a lived reality for workers.[31]

IV. For and Against Industrial Democracy

Why did the post-war pluralists object to stronger forms of industrial democracy? Three reasons were offered, although they were never very clearly distinguished from one another.

[27] Kerr, 'Industrial Relations and the Liberal Pluralist' (n 25) 25.

[28] A Flanders, *Management and Unions: The Theory and Reform of Industrial Relations* (London, Faber, 1970) 41–2, 225 (quote). Flanders at times also supported 'joint consultation' between workers and management as a possible mechanism for direct worker participation that could supplement collective bargaining: see Kelly (n 21) 102–3, 120.

[29] W Reuther (1948), quoted by N Lichtenstein, 'Great Expectations: The Promise of Industrial Jurisprudence and its Demise, 1930–60' in Lichtenstein and John Harris (n 7) 130–1.

[30] H Clegg, *Industrial Democracy and Nationalization* (Oxford, Basil Blackwell, 1951) 22. This aspect of Clegg's view of industrial democracy was singled out for particular criticism by Pateman (n 18) 71–2.

[31] N Lichtenstein, 'Pluralism, Post-War Intellectuals and the Demise of the Union Idea' in SM Milkis and JM Mileur (eds), *The Great Society and the High Tide of Liberalism* (Amherst, MA, University of Massachusetts Press, 2005).

First, it was argued that formal worker involvement in the making of industrial decisions (as opposed to merely influencing them) would jeopardise the independence of trade unions. The pluralist analysis depended on the bracing democratic effects of independent groups – the state, business and unions – contending with one another; collusion between these groups, in particular between management and unions, was thought likely to undermine the union leadership in the eyes of its members. The suspicion of 'being in the boss's pocket', maintained Clegg, would inevitably attach itself to the union leadership if it was involved in making management decisions.[32] Second, pluralists believed that a more radical form of democratic self-government in industry was likely to be extremely inefficient and perhaps even impossible to render workable in practice. A clear functional division was said to exist between managers and workers. While workers could play a role in influencing management decisions, the technical requirements of modern industry, and its large-scale, meant that managers must nonetheless be granted the power to make the final decisions themselves.[33]

Third, pluralists argued that a radical model of industrial democracy offered a romanticised image of democratic self-government that failed to get to grips with the cutting-edge findings on this subject by social scientists. It is clear, for example, that the work of Schumpeter and Dahl had been read and absorbed by these authors.[34] From these sources they derived a 'realist' view of democracy, which was sceptical of the appetite and capacity of the average citizen when it came to engaging in detailed democratic deliberation, and emphasised bargaining between multiple pressure groups as the primary means of fostering democratic government. This realist theory was also extended to internal union democracy. Pluralists had low expectations of the degree of participation in union affairs that could be reasonably required from union members and saw the centralisation and professionalisation of union leaderships as inevitable.[35] Doubts were also expressed about the normative desirability of a more participatory democracy. Crosland, for example, argued on a number of occasions that it was empirically unrealistic to expect widespread participation in decision-making, since 'all experience shows that only a small minority of the population will wish to participate.' But he added to this piece of Schumpeterian political sociology the normative claim that this behaviour was entirely justifiable, since the bulk of the population would rightly 'prefer to lead a full family life and cultivate their garden.'[36] The importance of the individual being free to cultivate his or her garden was a theme that Crosland reprised on a number of occasions – as Stuart Hall observed, it was 'Mr Crosland's metaphor for happiness.'[37] In Crosland's view, liberty required that individuals should be free to opt out of public life:

> if we believe in socialism as a means of increasing personal freedom and the range of choice, we do not necessarily want a busy bustling society in which everyone is politically active, and fussing

[32] Clegg, *New Approach* (n 24) 22–3; CAR Crosland, 'Industrial Democracy and Workers' Control' in his *The Conservative Enemy* (London, Jonathan Cape, 1962) 218–19.

[33] Clegg, *Industrial Democracy* (n 30) 73–4; Flanders, *Management* (n 28) 145–6; C Kerr et al, *Industrialism and Industrial Man* (Cambridge, MA, Harvard University Press, 1960) 294–5.

[34] Ackers, 'Collective Bargaining' (n 21) 93.

[35] C Kerr, 'Unions and Union Leaders of their own Choosing' in his *Labor and Management* (n 25) 34–7; R Lester, *As Unions Mature* (Princeton, Princeton University Press, 1958) 21–34, 106–7, 149–53.

[36] CAR Crosland, 'Socialists in a Dangerous World' [1968] in his *Socialism Now* (London, Jonathan Cape, 1974) 65–6. See also the same point in his *Conservative Enemy* (n 32) 229.

[37] S Hall, 'A Sense of Classlessness' (1958) 5 *Universities and Left Review* 29.

> around in an interfering and responsible manner, and herding us all into participating groups. The threat to privacy and freedom would be intolerable.[38]

There was therefore some truth to EP Thompson's observation that, according to this social democratic revisionism, 'the main participation demanded of the people is to cross the ballot-paper 13 or 14 million times.'[39]

Of course, one further interpretation is that these three reasons for limiting direct worker participation in industry were themselves merely cloaks for an underlying desire on the part of Cold War pluralists to preserve or conciliate existing social relations rather than to transform them. Such at any rate was the view taken by the New Left as it emerged in Britain and the US in the 1950s and 1960s. Many of the key theorists associated with this movement promoted ideals of participatory democracy that invoked the heritage of an earlier, more radical socialist pluralism. C Wright Mills's first book, for example, was a detailed survey of the American labour movement and its leadership, *The New Men of Power: America's Labor Leaders* (1948), which concluded with a powerful plea for the democratisation of the productive process that was inspired by GDH Cole's guild socialism. According to Mills, unions should ensure that 'in every workshop or its equivalent the unionised workers would continually strive to encroach upon the functions now performed by owners of industry and their appointed managers.' For it was only through a thorough democratisation of the workplace that the goal of human freedom could be realised, by ensuring that workers had the opportunity to enjoy self-rule by participating in the making of every social decision that 'vitally affected' them.[40]

Similar ideas were also expressed by the British New Left as they digested the implications of the pluralist ideas expounded by the Oxford School and Labour revisionists such as Crosland. Raymond Williams's stress on the moral attractions of the politically assertive aspects of working-class culture was particularly influential. Williams powerfully evoked the creation of autonomous proletarian political institutions as sites of active resistance to the inequalities and individualism of capitalism. The proletarian way of life, 'with its emphases of neighbourhood, mutual obligation, and common betterment, as expressed in the great working class institutions, is in fact the best basis for any future English society.'[41] In their willingness to adjust to the apparent success of corporatist capitalism, Williams said, the Labour Party establishment had neglected the need to disseminate a new consciousness, 'a real feeling of community – the true knowledge that we are working for ourselves and for each other.' But the fundamental obstacle to this realisation was 'the plain fact that most of us do not own or control the means and product of our work.'[42] When Hugh Clegg's *A New Approach to Industrial Democracy* was dissected in the pages of *New Left Review*,

[38] CAR Crosland, 'A Social-Democratic Britain' [1971] in his *Socialism Now* (n 36) 89. Clegg added that perhaps the most dangerous feature of theories of participatory democracy was that, when applied outside of small groups, they could lapse into the advocacy of a 'mystical' general will that would lead to totalitarianism: *Industrial Democracy* (n 30) 34, 121–3.

[39] EP Thompson, 'Revolution' (1960) 3 *New Left Review* 6.

[40] C Wright Mills, *The New Men of Power: America's Labor Leaders* (New York, Harcourt, Brace and Company, 1948) 252–5, Cole cited at 253, 258, 310. On the appropriation of Mills's ideas by the American New Left, see M Stears, *Demanding Democracy: American Radicals in Search of a New Politics* (Princeton, Princeton University Press, 2010) 179–84.

[41] R Williams, 'Culture is Ordinary' in N MacKenzie (ed), *Conviction* (London, MacGibbon & Kee, 1958) 80.

[42] R Williams, *The Long Revolution* (London, Chatto & Windus, 1961) 301–5, 335.

Royden Harrison opened his review with a quote from GDH Cole's *Self-Government in Industry* (1917) and proceeded to rebut Clegg's argument that guild socialist-style workers' control was impractical and undesirable. Democracy, Harrison argued, did not depend on the existence of organised opposition to government, but on the capacity of the people to change governments. A democratic model of industry should therefore involve direct worker control over management. It was essential, Harrison continued, to set about creating an economy that mixed state ownership of large, strategically important industries (but with worker representatives on their Boards) with other industries owned and run as co-operatives or owned by the state but run by the workers themselves.[43]

Yet the New Left critique of post-war pluralism was a double-edged sword. While in one sense the New Left tried to radicalise corporatism in a direction similar to that sought by earlier guild socialists and syndicalists, in another the New Left helped to foster slogans and arguments that could be used against corporatism per se. Two examples seem particularly striking in retrospect. First, the New Left's critique of union leaderships and bureaucracies, and of the cordial relations between union leaders and corporate bosses, at times cultivated an image of unions as ossified, oligarchic institutions that stood in the way of individual freedom just as surely as large corporations.[44] Second, Reuel Schiller has argued that the New Left's dismissal of interest-group pluralism as a smoke-screen for rule by elites paved the way for an eventual reassertion of individual rights over the group rights enjoyed by unions under the pluralist dispensation. The pluralist model of industrial relations allowed unions a modicum of organisational autonomy to mobilise their members in collective action, even if union activities required individuals in the workplace to comply with decisions and actions that they did not personally consent to. However, the New Left's characterisation of unions as just another elite-dominated pressure group generated – particularly in the US – a powerful rhetoric that privileged the individual over the group. New Left writers at times suggested that union collective action simply reflected the interests of an elite class of labour leaders. The group rights enjoyed by unions were, on this New Left account, vulnerable to the claim that they did not in fact serve the interests of their membership. Given these assumptions, a discourse of individual rights guaranteed by the state began to hold greater appeal than the more traditional call for union-based solidarity.[45] Both of these strands of New Left thinking – the critique of unions as remote oligarchies and the trumping of group rights by individual rights – were to have a wide cultural resonance, in part because they intersected with another, much more hostile analysis of corporatism that rose to prominence in the same period.

V. Neo-Liberalism as Anti-Pluralism

This rival theoretical discourse to both pluralist corporatism and the New Left lurked on the margins of public debate in this period. As corporatist pluralists bestrode high-profile

[43] R Harrison, 'Retreat From Industrial Democracy' (1960) 4 *New Left Review* 32–8. For a similar New Left critique of Clegg and Crosland, this time invoking Tom Mann and the 1889 London Dock Strike, see K Coates and T Topham, *The New Unionism: The Case for Workers' Control* (London, Peter Owen, 1972) 18–29, 40–6.

[44] Wright Mills (n 40) 224–33; T Topham, 'Shop Stewards and Workers' Control' (1964) 25 *New Left Review* 3–16; L Williams, 'Ideological Parallels Between the New Left and the New Right' (1987) 24 *The Social Science Journal* 318–19.

[45] Schiller (n 23) 1–73; Lichtenstein, 'Pluralism, Post-War Intellectuals and the Demise of the Union Idea' (n 31).

Anglo-American academic and political debates like colossi, neo-liberalism began to take shape in more low-profile settings. Obscure professors and academic scribblers gathered at private conferences and well-appointed, centrally located sets of offices to hone their critique of the post-war settlement. Sympathetic policy organisations also began to emerge on to the political scene (notably the American Enterprise Association in 1943 and the Institute of Economic Affairs in 1955). These neo-liberals took much more seriously the parallels between the fate of the Weimar Republic, in their view destroyed by sectional pressure groups, and the trajectory of Western capitalism after 1945.

While neo-liberalism is often demotically presented as an ideology that favours the individual and is hostile to the state, more sophisticated analysts have long observed that neo-liberal theorists and politicians were perfectly well aware that a strong state would be required to restructure and police the boundaries of the market.[46] Neo-liberals placed great emphasis on the damage that would be inflicted on the state, the economy and the individual by the legal latitude afforded to pressure groups, especially trade unions, under corporatist social arrangements. However, this stance left neo-liberal theorists to finesse a tricky problem. According to pluralists, unions were voluntary associations, organically generated by the workers themselves, and an ineradicable feature of a free society. This account seemed to be a close cousin of the neo-liberal preference for 'spontaneous' voluntary activity in civil society over the coercive legislative actions of the state. How could neo-liberals maintain both a preference for voluntary associationalism and a desire for state action to reduce the power enjoyed by unions? This delicate balancing act was preserved by distinguishing between spontaneous and voluntary forms of association – which of course they strongly supported – and coercive forms of association that exercised dangerous levels of power over the individual – against which they sought to deploy the state.

Friedrich Hayek's work, for example, at times explicitly drew on the liberal pluralist tradition, notably by naming Tocqueville and Acton as inspirational classical liberal precursors and in stipulating that 'true individualism' was opposed 'only against the use of *coercion* to bring about organisation or association, and not against association as such.' The value of the family, the voluntary association, and local autonomy were all stressed by Hayek as crucial means of warding off state power over the individual and the pursuit of abstract egalitarian goals from the centre.[47] However, these voluntarist modes of association were sharply distinguished in Hayek's mind from the forms of working class organisation that were feted by his pluralist contemporaries as essential to a democratic society. Unions, Hayek and his neo-liberal allies believed, were coercive institutions that forced individuals into collective action that they did not support, and were artificially propped up by partisan pro-union labour legislation enacted by the social democratic state. In this sense, neo-liberals saw unions as neither voluntary nor spontaneous.

The power of organised labour was therefore a long-standing source of anxiety among free market revivalists. Ludwig von Mises's *Socialism* (1922), one of the earliest and most influential works in the neo-liberal canon, had got the ball rolling in the inter-war period

[46] A Gamble, *The Free Economy and the Strong State* (Basingstoke, Macmillan, 1994); P Mirowski, 'Postface: Defining Neo-Liberalism' in P Mirowski and D Plehwe (eds), *The Road From Mont Pèlerin: The Making of the Neo-liberal Thought Collective* (Cambridge MA, Harvard University Press, 2009).

[47] FA Hayek, 'Individualism: True and False' in his *Individualism and Economic Order* (Chicago, Chicago University Press, 1948) 16, 23, 28, 31 emphasis in original.

by rebutting the economic viability of guild socialism.[48] Two other early works laid out the neo-liberal approach in more detail.[49] One was WH Hutt's *The Theory of Collective Bargaining*, published in 1930 and, significantly, reissued in 1975 by the Institute of Economic Affairs. Hutt was a stalwart member of the Mont Pèlerin Society, the international discussion group convened by Hayek from 1947 onwards to revive market liberal ideas. The second early neo-liberal statement on trade unionism was by Henry Simons in a 1944 article entitled 'Some Reflections on Syndicalism'.[50] Simons was based at the Chicago Law School for most of his career and along with colleagues such as Frank Knight and Jacob Viner formed the earliest cohort of the 'Chicago School' of economics. The influence of both Simons and Hutt was long-lasting – it can be seen in Hayek's 1960 *Constitution of Liberty*, for example, and their work continued to form a key reference point in pamphlets issued by the Institute of Economic Affairs in Britain during the 1970s and 1980s.[51]

Hutt and Simons conceptualised unions as monopolies that sought to control the labour supply in order to charge a price for labour in excess of its competitive level. They argued that the monopoly gains reaped by union insiders should therefore not be seen as improving the position of labour as a whole but rather as increasing unemployment and income inequality, since unionised workers were simply advantaging themselves relative to lower-paid members of the working class. As Simons put it, unionism 'enables an aristocracy of labour to build fences around their occupations, restricting entry, raising arbitrarily the costs and prices of their products, and lowering the wages and incomes of those outside, and of the poor especially'.[52] Hutt and Simons further claimed that unions facilitated collusion between certain groups of employers and workers – bilateral monopoly – to the detriment of the consumer. Increased prices were the outcome, and since the majority of consumers were workers, they argued this too served to undermine working class living standards.[53]

Hutt and Simons were also appalled by what they regarded as the unacceptable violence used by unions to enforce their interests. Strikes, boycotts, closed shops, and other trade union tactics were, in their view, the use of private coercive power to impose an economic settlement on other workers, employers and consumers in a way that threatened the state's monopoly on the use of violence. 'Labour monopolies', said Simons, 'enjoy an access to violence which is unparalleled in other monopolies', rendering governments 'impotent' and enabling unions to 'deal with scabs in ways which make even Rockefeller's early methods seem polite and legitimate'. Unions therefore presented an unparalleled challenge to the liberal state: 'they are essentially occupational armies, born and reared amidst violence, led by fighters, and capable of becoming peaceful only as their power becomes irresistible'.[54] The use of metaphors comparing unionism to legalised piracy and banditry were widespread

[48] L von Mises, *Die Gemeinwirtschaft*, 2nd edn (Jena, Verlag von Gustav Fischer, 1932 [1922]) 230–4; translated as *Socialism: An Economic and Sociological Analysis* (New Haven, Yale University Press, 1951) 258–62.

[49] The following paragraphs draw on B Jackson, 'An Ideology of Class: Neo-Liberalism and the Trade Unions, c. 1930–79' in C Griffiths, J Nott and W Whyte (eds), *Classes, Cultures and Politics: Essays for Ross McKibbin* (Oxford, Oxford University Press, 2011) 263–81.

[50] The article was originally drafted in 1941: H Simons, 'Some Reflections on Syndicalism' (1944) 52 *Journal of Political Economy* 1 fn 1.

[51] See, eg, *Trade Unions: Public Goods or Public Bads? IEA Readings 17* (London, IEA, 1978) 25–6, 52.

[52] Simons (n 50) 12.

[53] WH Hutt, *The Theory of Collective Bargaining* (London, IEA, 1975) 66–73; Simons (n 50) 2, 15.

[54] Simons (n 50) 7, 21.

in both these texts, for what infuriated these authors was that industrial relations legislation in Britain and the US respectively had actually been designed to facilitate union activities: the 1906 Trade Disputes Act and the 1935 Wagner Act were prime examples of the state support for unions that they deplored. In spite of their great discontent, however, at this stage neither Hutt nor Simons actually mentioned any specific proposals for legislative reform. By the time Hutt's book was reissued in 1975, he was less reticent. 'Ideally', he wrote in a new epilogue, 'what is needed for the emancipation of labour is the enactment of the principle underlying the British Combination Acts of 1799 and 1800 adapted to the 1970s.'[55]

Later neo-liberal writers, including Hayek, followed Hutt and Simons in their analysis of trade unions. As the post-war boom got underway, a large and increasingly apocalyptic literature on industrial relations was produced by neo-liberal economists and allied think-tanks, the vast majority of it published in the US.[56] According to this literature, the enhanced power enjoyed by organised labour thanks to full employment, a generous welfare state, and pro-union legislation simultaneously undermined economic efficiency; threatened the legitimacy of the state; and coerced unwilling individuals into collective action. Neo-liberals devoted particular attention to the power exerted by unions over individuals who did not wish to join one (through institutions such as the closed shop) and over union members who did not wish to participate in industrial action. 'The real exploiters in our present society', wrote Hayek, 'are not egoistic capitalists or entrepreneurs, and in fact not separate individuals, but organisations which derive their power from the moral support of collective action and the feeling of group loyalty.'[57] On this account, solidaristic sentiments between groups of workers were to be viewed with fear and suspicion, for they threatened the sovereignty of the individual, and well-organised pressure groups were deemed to command dangerous, perhaps even totalitarian, concentrations of power. Although business organisations were arguably even more susceptible to these strictures than unions (as Mancur Olson, for example, argued), this was not the view of neo-liberals when confronted with the distributive politics of the post-war boom.[58] As Hayek remarked in *The Constitution of Liberty*:

> I believe I have myself in the past used the tactical argument that we cannot hope to curb the coercive powers of labour unions unless we at the same time attack enterprise monopoly. I have,

[55] Hutt, *Theory* (n 53). The British Combination Acts, a legislative response to fears about the seditious influence of Jacobin ideas on the working class, made it illegal for workers to combine for the purposes of improving their wages and conditions. The Acts were repealed in the mid-1820s.

[56] A useful list of this literature is cited in FA Hayek, *The Constitution of Liberty* (Chicago, Chicago University Press, 1960) 505–6 fn 8. Important examples included: J Viner and F Machlup, in *Wage Determination and the Economics of Liberalism* (Washington DC, US Chamber of Commerce, 1947); D McCord Wright (ed), *The Impact of the Union* (New York, Harcourt, Brace and Company, 1951); S Petro, *The Labor Policy of a Free Society* (New York, Ronald Press, 1957); EH Chamberlin, *The Economic Analysis of Labor Union Power* (Washington DC, American Enterprise Association, 1958); PD Bradley (ed), *The Public Stake in Union Power* (Charlottesville, University of Virginia Press, 1959); Hayek, *Constitution* 267–84; WH Hutt, *The Strike-Threat System* (New Rochelle NY, Arlington House, 1973). For a valuable account of how this neo-liberal discourse about trade unionism was hammered out, see Y Steiner, 'The Neo-Liberals Confront the Trade Unions' in Mirowski and Plehwe (eds), *Road From Mont Pèlerin* (n 46) 181–203.

[57] FA Hayek, *Law, Legislation and Liberty*, Vol III (London, Routledge, 1979) 89–90.

[58] M Olson, *The Logic of Collective Action* (Cambridge MA, Harvard University Press, 1965) 141–8; M Olson, *The Rise and Decline of Nations* (New Haven, Yale University Press, 1982) 143–4.

> however, become convinced that it would be disingenuous to represent the existing monopolies in the field of labour and those in the field of enterprise as being of the same kind.[59]

According to Hayek and his colleagues, the threat to freedom posed by unions was far more serious than that posed by the capitalist firm. Unions, they argued, were the beneficiaries of explicit state support that effectively exempted them from the scope of the rule of law, rendering them immune from prosecution for the exercise of private coercive power.

Two features of this neo-liberal analysis are worth stressing. First, neo-liberals were willing to deploy the coercive power of the state against labour organisations. They envisaged significant state regulation of the labour market in order to diminish the power and status enjoyed by unions, including such reforms as: the prohibition of picketing in numbers; the abolition of the closed shop; the prohibition of secondary action; the removal of social security entitlements from workers on strike; and the removal of the right of unions to make contracts that would subsequently bind those who did not voluntarily delegate this authority to the union.[60] Some of the fiercest critics of the unions, such as Hutt, took this analysis much further by arguing for the abolition of the right to strike itself by returning to the principles that underpinned the British Combination Acts. This was never a widely supported proposal in these circles but it certainly existed as a legitimate point of view (indeed, as a half-way house support did exist for a strike ban in essential services). However, many of the theorists involved in these debates did favour two further, more radical proposals: first, that unions should be subject to anti-monopoly legislation in exactly the same way as corporations (with a view to abolishing industry-wide unions); and second, that union legal immunities should be removed to render unions liable for damages in civil law.[61]

Second, neo-liberals consciously rejected the democratic role envisaged for unions by theorists of corporatism. Neo-liberals were suspicious of any union collective action that might interfere with the operation of efficient economic production or that relied for its efficacy on the coercion of individuals in the interests of a larger group. But this placed them in the curious position of commending various forms of association and collective action that were by no means obviously non-coercive or efficiency-enhancing – local government and large corporations for example – while at the same time singling out trade unions as uniquely coercive associations.[62]

[59] Hayek, *Constitution* (n 56) 265. As Hayek's remark suggests, earlier neo-liberal writings had stressed the need for action against *both* large corporations and trade unions. I have discussed this aspect of early neo-liberal theory in B Jackson, 'At the Origins of Neo-Liberalism: The Free Economy and the Strong State, 1930–47' (2010) 53 *Historical Journal* 142–5.

[60] See, eg, Petro (n 56) 235–47; Hayek, *Constitution* (n 56) 278–9; G Haberler, *Inflation and the Unions* (London, IEA, 1972) 45–7.

[61] Hayek, *Constitution* (n 56) 278; HG Lewis, 'The Labor-Monopoly Problem: A Positive Program' (1951) 59 *Journal of Political Economy* 277–87; M Friedman, *Capitalism and Freedom* (Chicago, Chicago University Press, 2002 [1962]) 132; Haberler (n 60) 47–8.

[62] The treatment of trade unions as uniquely coercive organisations in neo-liberal analysis has been stressed by Lord Wedderburn, 'Freedom of Association and Philosophies of Labour Law' (1989) 18 *Industrial Law Journal* 8. I have explored the weaknesses of the neo-liberal approach to unions in greater detail in Jackson, 'An Ideology of Class' (n 49) 277–81.

VI. Conclusion

As we have seen, mid-century Anglo-American corporatist pluralism was a mixture of diverse theoretical elements – in some ways a compromise between the contending economic philosophies of capitalism and socialism. Corporatist pluralists envisaged social democracy as not merely an exercise in redistributing economic resources (important though this objective was), but also as centrally concerned with the democratisation of economic life. They were strongly committed to the notion that employees should have greater control and agency in their working lives than would be permitted under unregulated capitalism. This was to be achieved by allotting a powerful role to unions in industry and politics, and in particular by prioritising collective bargaining as the primary means of representing and articulating workers' interests. However, the boundaries of this industrial democracy were drawn more narrowly than had been entertained by earlier socialist pluralists such as Laski and Cole. Some observers might well see this transition in pluralist thought as a welcome accommodation on the part of pluralist theory to the basic facts of industrial life – the institutional proposals of Laski and Cole were, after all, hardly beyond reproach. Nonetheless, as the New Left pointed out, one consequence of this narrowing of the pluralist horizon was that these corporatists incorporated within their theory of industrial relations an elitist view of democracy that to some extent stood in tension with their egalitarian and democratic commitments and promoted a democratic theory of trade unionism largely grounded on opposition to managerial power. It is certainly arguable that a more constructive and durable corporatist culture might have been constructed from an industrial relations system that established greater common ground between the management and the work-force, and experimented with worker involvement in industrial decision-making.[63]

While this latter suggestion offers a possible synthesis of the distributive politics of post-war pluralism with elements of the New Left participatory agenda that emerged in the 1950s and 1960s, we have also seen that there were tendencies within the New Left that were less hospitable to associational pluralism and that converged with certain currents within neo-liberalism.[64] The New Left shared with the neo-liberals a critique of contemporary trade union practices – the image of 'big labour' and so on – and had some difficulties with accommodating the associational rights of unions. These views were of course taken much further by neo-liberals, who were scathing about the coercion inherent in labour organisations and sought to exempt the sphere of economic production from the scope of democratic scrutiny. And it was this neo-liberal view that famously triumphed in Anglo-American public discourse and policy-making during the 1980s. But as I have shown in this chapter, it is too quick to categorise the ideological battle-lines of the mid-twentieth century as a confrontation between statist socialists or liberals and nascent neo-liberal individualism.

[63] This is not a grossly idealist claim. In Britain, industrial relations experts such as Clegg and Flanders were highly influential in public policy discussions, notably in the deliberations of the Donovan Commission in 1968, so their writings had a fairly clear impact on the institutional design of British industrial relations: for further discussion, see P Davies and M Freedland, *Labour Legislation and Public Policy* (Oxford, Oxford University Press, 1993) 238–74. US pluralists were similarly influential in the framing of public policy and active in advising industry: for example, John Dunlop was Director of the Cost of Living Council in 1973–74 and Secretary of Labor in 1975–76.

[64] For further discussion of the overlap between neo-liberalism and the New Left, see Williams, 'Ideological Parallels' (n 44); M Kenny, *The First New Left* (London, Lawrence & Wishart, 1995) 202–3; J Kelley, *Bringing the Market Back In* (Basingstoke, Macmillan, 1997) 96–100.

Mid-century British democratic socialism and New Deal liberalism were pluralist doctrines. They respected the associational autonomy of working class institutions; sought to deploy the state to accomplish the universal access to education, health and social security that the working class had been unable to accomplish on its own; and embraced the contest between contending interest groups as crucial to the democratisation of civil society and the state. Many criticisms might now be made of the theory that underpinned this vision, and of how far Democratic and Labour politicians were in practice willing to implement it, but from the vantage point of the twenty-first century it is apparent that socialist pluralist aspirations were in fact closer to becoming a lived reality in British and American workplaces in the mid-twentieth century than at any time before or since.

17

What is the UK's True Constitution?

EWAN McGAUGHEY*

I. Introduction

If flexibility is a primary virtue of the UK's uncodified Constitution, it is equally matched by opacity. Without any code to delineate what is in and what is out, the 'constitution' is often said to be everything that 'constitutes' the body politic,[1] or that the constitution is just 'what happens'.[2] This is partly justified if, like Blackstone, we see constitutional law as one branch of the law of persons.[3] A nation-state is like any other organic, social institution, where its members experience life both as part of the community and as individuals, 'intertwined in reality as an indissoluble unity … distinct only in our imaginations.'[4] Similarly, among many, many foundational contributions to our understanding of justice that Professor Keith Ewing has made, there is a recurring theme: a constitution that locks up gates at Downing Street, blockades Whitehall, or kettles Parliament Square, away from the wider world is weaker. Dividing civil and political freedom from economic, social and cultural rights enables state power to cultivate private oppression. Law constructs power, public or private, with property, contract, or any form of regulation.[5] Our economic constitution shapes our politics (not least in the freedom that unions,[6] or political parties,[7] have to influence the law) just as politics shapes our economy. This tradition of thought sees that, unless our social constitution is perceived as a whole, people in the supposed private sphere are left 'practically at the mercy of corporations and individuals wielding power under public authority'.[8]

* I am very grateful to Tarunabh Khaitan, Robert Craig, Vernon Bogdanor and Alan Bogg for discussion and comments. Please contact at ewan.mcgaughey@kcl.ac.uk or @ewanmcg for deliberative discourse at any time.

[1] Cf, W Bagehot, *The English Constitution* (London, Kegan Paul, Trench, Trubner & Co, 1894).

[2] JAG Griffith, 'The political constitution' (1979) 42 *MLR* 1, 19.

[3] W Blackstone, *Commentaries on the Laws of England* (Philadelphia, J. B. Lippincott & Co, 1753) Book I.

[4] O Gierke, 'The Social Role of Private Law' (1889) translated by E McGaughey (2018) 19(4) *German Law Journal* 1017.

[5] KD Ewing, 'The State and Industrial Relations: 'Collective Laissez-Faire' Revisited' (1998) 5 *Historical Studies in Industrial Relations* 1, 2–3 and 31.

[6] Eg, KD Ewing and P Elias, *Trade Union Democracy, Members' Rights and the Law* (London, Mansell Publishing, 1987).

[7] Eg, KD Ewing, *The Cost of Democracy: Party Funding in Modern British Politics* (Oxford, Hart Publishing, 2007).

[8] *Civil Rights Cases*, 109 US 3 (1883) per Harlan J and cf KD Ewing, 'Jeremy Corbyn and the Law of Democracy' (2017) 28 *King's Law Journal* 343, 361, 'democracy is about the equal participation of citizens (with all that that implies) and their representative institutions in making and administering the rules by which they are governed. This includes the rules made not only by those exercising public power, but also by those exercising private power as well.'

But without a codified document, how do we begin to answer 'what is the UK's true constitution?' One answer was given in a 2007 article by Professors Bogdanor, Vogenauer, and Khaitan, assisted by a group of politics students.[9] They drafted a UK constitution, claiming it to be 'as it actually is rather than as it might be or as it ought to be.' An admirably clear document of just eleven pages, their method drew on statute and personal understandings of a constitution's proper limits. It starts with territory and nationality, with the monarch as a sovereign.[10] Then come the Commons and the Lords,[11] the Prime Minister, executive power,[12] local government,[13] judicial review,[14] and last a human rights list that reflects a minimal reading of the European Convention on Human Rights,[15] without much case law. It also raises the idea of referenda for transfers of power to a constitutional principle.[16] The trouble is, it is doubtful that this *is* the UK Constitution 'as it actually is'. Instead, it was curiously similar to previous writings by Professor Bogdanor, particularly by elevating referendums to a supposed constitutional norm. Many of these arguments, particularly with the unprecedented 'Brexit' poll crisis, do not look great today.[17]

This chapter's purpose is to ask, what would an evidence-based understanding of our Constitution lead to? Its central argument is that it is impossible to justify a document asserting itself as the UK's true Constitution without a reasoned and evidential basis. Logically, evidence should include what government does, people's real social priorities, an historically informed account of enduring Acts of Parliament, and of consistent principles in case law. It argues that Parliamentary democracy, the rule of law, the social state, and international comity, are essential principles of the modern UK Constitution. An overlapping consensus in UK society recognises that constitutional rights include free public health, dignity in old age, universal education, social inclusion, fair taxation, protection for the environment and countryside, fair wages through voice at work, and transparent and accountable governance of finance and enterprise. Many further additions could be debated. But whatever one favours as a preferred list of constitutional norms and rights, an account of what our Constitution 'is' must not elevate, without evidence, the importance of some Acts of Parliament over others.

[9] V Bogdanor, T Khaitan and S Vogenauer, 'Should Britain have a written constitution?' (2007) 78 *Political Quarterly* 499.

[10] Bogdanor, Khaitan and Vogenauer (n 9) arts 1–4.

[11] Ibid, arts 5–11.

[12] Ibid, arts 12–22.

[13] Ibid, (2007) arts 23–25.

[14] Ibid, arts 26–35.

[15] Ibid, arts 36–58.

[16] Ibid, arts 1, 23 and 59(2).

[17] Eg, V Bogdanor, *The people and the party system: The referendum and electoral reform in British politics* (Cambridge, Cambridge University Press, 1981), V Bogdanor, 'Referendums in British politics' (1988) 2(4) *Contemporary Record* 12, D Butler and A Ranney (eds), *Referendums around the world: The growing use of direct democracy* (London, Palgrave Macmillan, 1994) ch 3. Professor Bogdanor tutored David Cameron, who staged three referendums, but said before Cameron seized the keys to number 10, 'David was one of the nicest and ablest students I ever taught. But I'm not responsible for his views.' C Arnot, 'Interview: Ruling Class' *Guardian* (London, 17 February 2009). On consequences of referenda used as a political instrument, see E McGaughey, 'Could Brexit be Void?' (2018) 29 *King's Law Journal* 331, and AJ Zurchner, 'The Hitler Referenda' (1935) 29 *American Political Science Review* 91, on crude, familiar strategies. See also C Sunstein, *Designing Democracy: What Constitutions Do* (Oxford, Oxford University Press, 2001) 7, 'Deliberative democrats emphatically reject the view that a government should be run on the basis of popular referenda.'

II. What Does 'Constitutional' Law Mean?

Before examining what the evidence suggests about the UK's true Constitution, it seems necessary to address a prior conceptual question: what does 'constitutional' law mean? To explain the Constitution 'as it actually is rather than as it might be or as it ought to be', there are a range of alternative methods, with differing strengths and weaknesses. Three main alternatives are (1) for experts to deliberate, (2) to conceptually distinguish 'constitutional' law based on a public/private law divide, and (3) to follow deliberative democratic debate, and do so without limit.

A. Expert Deliberation

A first alternative is to construct a constitution based upon expert deliberation. This fits closely with the methodology of Professors Bogdanor, Vogenauer and Khaitan, as they 'held a seminar at Oxford, at which students were asked to draft a constitution for Britain'.[18] This produced an exceptionally clear document.[19] Yet it is curious that what were said to be the 'many areas of unclarity' about our Constitution appeared resolved without appeal to any external sources. The authors were quick to concede that 'it is impossible to say whether the students' answers accurately reflected the present state of the constitution precisely because nobody knows what the constitutional position actually is.' However, this concession appeared mostly to relate to a small number of grey areas, with 'insufficient clarity', rather than their constitution's broad shape. To demarcate that broad shape a criterion of 'controversiality' was applied for what was in or out, so that if someone argued that a norm belonged to the realm of political debate, it would not be included: that became what the Constitution 'might be' or 'ought to be', not what it was. As a result, the Appendix was proclaimed as 'The Constitution of the United Kingdom, as of 1 January 2007'.

The central difficulty of this method is the absence of a documented process of reasoning. Because no reasoning can be discerned, any product becomes an appeal to authority, saying 'it is constitutional because I think it is'.[20] A criterion of excluding norms as 'constitutional' if they are controversial in a select group fails to see that the norms of most constitutions (successful or not) emerge precisely after the settlement of controversies, and indeed bitter conflict, revolution, collapse, crisis, dictatorship, or war,[21] including the constitution of international law, and the 'Magna Carta of all' people, itself.[22] Moreover,

[18] Bogdanor, Khaitan and Vogenauer (n 9).

[19] Significant credit – although certainly a shared project – was attributed in the drafting to Tarunabh Khaitan. But it appears that certain values, such as the constitutional importance of equality, were not accorded sufficient weight in the final draft. On the values of anti-discrimination law, see the pathbreaking work, T Khaitan, *A Theory of Discrimination Law* (Oxford, Oxford University Press, 2015).

[20] Contrast A Schopenhauer, *Die Kunst, Recht zu Behalten* (Nikol Verlagsgesellschaft mbH, Hamburg, 1831) #30 on appeal to authority, rather than reason.

[21] This is true, for example, of the US (post-Revolution), India (post-Independence), Germany (post-WW2), France (post-Revolution, Napoleon, WW2, etc), China (post-Mao under Deng Xiaoping), Brazil (post-dictatorship), Russia (post-Iron Curtain), South Africa (post-Apartheid), and the UK for large part of its own Constitution (Magna Carta, Bill of Rights, etc). These examples alone account for all of the UN Security Council, and about half the globe's population.

[22] See the United Nations Charter 1945 and the Universal Declaration of Human Rights 1948.

a controversiality threshold is likely to be illegitimately minimalist, if not reactionary, in much the same way that an overlapping agreement between Dicey, Raz and Dworkin on the meaning of the 'rule of law' would probably produce the barest bones of 'legality',[23] rather than include respect for international law and human rights.[24] Private expert deliberation cannot credibly establish what is 'constitutional' law and what is not, without disclosing reason and evidence.

B. Conceptual Distinction

A second alternative is to defend a conceptual distinction of 'constitutional' law based upon a public/private divide, or something related to it. The existence of equity, and British scholars' aversion to theory, means the notions of public and private law are not part of UK legal tradition.[25] Yet the divide has increasingly become popular for the purpose of demarcating time limits and the proper forum for judicial review,[26] the organisation of textbooks,[27] even some academic titles.[28] Going further back, it has also long been common to speak of the 'Constitution' as 'directed to certain fix'd Objects of publick Good' and how 'the Community hath agreed to be governed'.[29] This continues in a general view that the Constitution relates to the 'basic institutions of the state' and the relation of these to 'the individual'.[30] In European Union law the same idea of 'vertical direct effect' as opposed to 'horizontal' application of rights was introduced by British advocates.[31] On this view, to be constitutional, 'power-conferring' rules must be no more than one degree of separation from Parliament Square.[32] Constitutional law is 'public law' minus administrative and criminal law, while private law covers the law of persons, property and obligations. The lines may be 'blurry and wobbly',[33] but the distinction can be kept on track, by saying that all 'contextual' subjects that do not fit (like cyberspace law or labour law) are a mixture of public and private law.[34]

The difficulty with this view is that the public/private divide is philosophically empty, and it has long been constitutionally abused. Philosophically, the most robust defence for

[23] Cf, AV Dicey, *Introduction to the Study of the Law of the Constitution* 3rd edn (London, Macmillan, 1889) Pt II, ch IV, 189, J Raz, 'The Rule of Law and its Virtue' (1977) 93 *LQR* 195.
R Dworkin, *A Matter of Principle* (Oxford, Clarendon, 1985) 32.

[24] Cf, T Bingham, 'The Rule of Law' (2007) 66 *CLJ* 67 and see also T Bingham, *Rule of Law* (London, Penguin, 2008) 8.

[25] Cf, AW Bradley, KD Ewing and CJS Knight, *Constitutional and Administrative Law* (London, Pearson, 2018) 677, '*O'Reilly* relied heavily on the public law/private law distinction, despite the difficulties that this presents in English law.'

[26] *O'Reilly v Mackman* [1983] 2 AC 237, 255 per Lord Denning MR.

[27] Eg, A Burrows (ed), *English Private Law* (Oxford, Oxford University Press, 2017) and D Feldman, *English Public Law* (Oxford, Oxford University Press, 2017).

[28] The author was originally hired as a 'lecturer in private law', teaching one notable subject with a 'professor of public law'.

[29] Viscount Bolingbroke, *A Dissertation upon Parties* (1733) Letter X, 108.

[30] HL Committee on the Constitution (HL Paper 11, 2001–2) ch 2.

[31] Eg, *Marshall v Southampton and South West Hampshire Area Health Authority* (1986) Case 152/84, [1986] ECR 723.

[32] Cf, HLA Hart, *The Concept of Law* (Oxford, Clarendon, 1961) ch 5(3) on secondary rules, which recognise, change or adjudicate rule making power.

[33] See, eg, D Feldman and M Elliot, *The Cambridge Companion to Public Law* (Cambridge, Cambridge University Press, 2018) ch 1.

[34] Cf, FH Easterbrook, 'Cyberspace and the Law of the Horse' [1996] *University of Chicago Legal Forum* 207, 208.

a public/private divide seems to be that it is a 'conceptual' distinction, not a 'contextual' one.[35] The trouble is, the state itself is a contextual creature. It is one legal person among many, and remains so even when public/private advocates relegate the other persons to 'private' law.[36] It is naive to think the state pursues more 'public' purposes than companies or families, because (even ignoring cases where companies and families dominate states) historically this is just not true.[37] It might be argued that the state has a 'distinctive claim to the legitimate exercise of coercive force'.[38] But since 1919, international law and human rights have delegitimised that very exercise of coercive force by states over people,[39] and democracy emerged to replace coercive force with electoral consent, as violence became less legitimate in *any* case.[40]

Constitutionally, the public/private divide has routinely been abused. For instance, it was said in the US *Civil rights cases* that state 'intervention' in private property (an ostensibly pre-state thing) to protect ex-slaves from discrimination was unconstitutional.[41] In *Lochner v New York*, the US Supreme Court went further to strike down state 'interference' in private freedom of contract, which included a limit to a 60 hour week for bakers.[42] What followed were decisions striking down public pensions,[43] minimum wages,[44] union organising,[45] and even a ban on child labour.[46] This was wrong, and the better view was always that all law is social, not public or private, and no division between the two can justify normative consequences. The better view is that the 'concept of all law's unity' must be defended.[47] There is no conceptual reason why inter-individual or horizontal rights may not be constitutional issues, or even at the centre. All individual rights must ultimately reflect the public good, and the state must serve individual freedom.[48]

C. Deliberative Democracy

A third alternative is to say that what is 'constitutional' law depends upon the outcome of ongoing deliberative discourse. Putting a reflective equilibrium into real life,[49]

[35] P Birks, *Introduction to the Law of Restitution* (Oxford, Clarendon, 1984) 73.

[36] Blackstone (n 3) Book I.

[37] Eg, T Paine, *Rights of Man* (1791) part I, the 'national purse is the common hack which each [party insider] mounts upon'. Cf, Feldman and Elliot (n 33) ch 1, conclusion.

[38] Feldman and Elliot (n 33) ch 1, an idea taken from the pre-modern distinction of M Weber, *Politik als Beruf* (1919).

[39] Eg, UN Charter 1945, art 2(4) and Universal Declaration of Human Rights 1948, arts 3–5, which limit state powers of coercion. This means that international law, not solely the state, determines legitimate exercise of force, and justifiably claims to do so.

[40] Recently in the UK, see A Ashworth, 'What if imprisonment were abolished for property offences?' (London, Howard League for Penal Reform, 2013).

[41] *United States v Stanley* 109 US 3 (1883).

[42] *Lochner v New York* 198 US 45, 64 (1908).

[43] Eg, *State Board of Control v Buckstegge*, 158 Pac 837, 842 (1916).

[44] Eg, *Adkins v Children's Hospital*, 261 US 525 (1923).

[45] Eg, *Coppage v Kansas*, 236 US 1 (1915) and *Duplex Printing Press Co v Deering*, 254 US 443 (1921).

[46] Eg, *Hammer v Dagenhart*, 247 US 251 (1918) and *Bailey v Drexel Furniture Co*, 259 US 20 (1922).

[47] Gierke (n 4) 1037–8.

[48] Eg, Universal Declaration of Human Rights 1948, Preamble: 'recognition of the inherent dignity and of the equal and inalienable rights of all members of the human family is the foundation of freedom, justice and peace in the world'.

[49] Cf, J Rawls, *A Theory of Justice* (Oxford, Oxford University Press, 1971) ch 1.

'constitutional' can mean anything that emerges from the 'laboratories of democracy' – polities of all kinds – at any given moment in history.[50] As Frederic Maitland said, we must 'not get into the way of thinking of law as consisting of a number of independent compartments, one of which is labelled constitutional, another administrative, another criminal, another property … law is a body, a living body, every member of which is connected with and depends upon every other member.'[51] Historically, there is 'hardly any department of law which does not, at one time or another, become of constitutional importance'.[52] This simple truth, once acknowledged, liberates the constitutional mind, and so it is to this conception that we now turn.

III. What Does the Evidence Say about Our Constitution?

To understand the UK Constitution as it is today, it seems logical to look at evidence about what the different branches of government and the state do and say. The three main branches of government are, of course, the executive, legislature and judiciary. Each provide a wealth of data – financial, historical, jurisprudential – on the nature of the UK Constitution. If we are to codify the UK Constitution as it 'is', it makes sense to start with these.

A. Social Priorities and Spending

A starting guide to the UK's Constitution is found in what the UK state actually spends most time doing. From the annual budgets it is clear what the preoccupations of modern UK society, and the state, are. According to the Autumn budget of 2018, 60.5 per cent of government spending is taken up by social security, social care and health spending.[53] Education is 13.7 per cent of spending. Defence and public order are 11.5 per cent of spending. Debt interest (mostly paying money to banks) is 5.7 per cent, transport 4.9 per cent, industrial, agricultural and employment policy 3.3 per cent, and so on.

Almost none of these fields of spending – almost all of what government actually does, almost all of what (in the time before the 'Brexit' poll) preoccupies politics – is reflected in the Bogdanor Constitution. Passing mention was given to a minimal right that 'No person shall be denied the right to education' or 'a minimum right of health care and subsistence'.[54] The only people who appear to retire in this Constitution are judges, the Speaker of the Commons and the Lords, and even then it seems only judges get a pension.[55] Speaker retirement and judicial pensions are important norms. But when nearly one-third of all UK government revenue is directed at retirement pensions for the general public, it would seem difficult to maintain that the right to social security is not an important constitutional norm.

[50] *New State Ice Co v Liebmann* 285 US 262 (1932) per Brandeis J.

[51] FW Maitland, *The Constitutional History of England* (Cambridge, Cambridge University Press, 1919) Period V, J, 538–9 and cf Bradley, Ewing and Knight (n 25) ch 21, 591–2, on the 'deceptively simple' public and private law distinction.

[52] Maitland (n 51) Period V, J, 538.

[53] HM Treasury, *Autumn Budget* (October 2018) 4.

[54] Bogdanor, Khaitan and Vogenauer (n 9) 516, arts 53 and 56.

[55] Bogdanor, Khaitan and Vogenauer (n 9), 507–8 and 513, arts 6, 8 and 34–35.

Figure 17.1 Public sector spending (£bn) 2019–2020

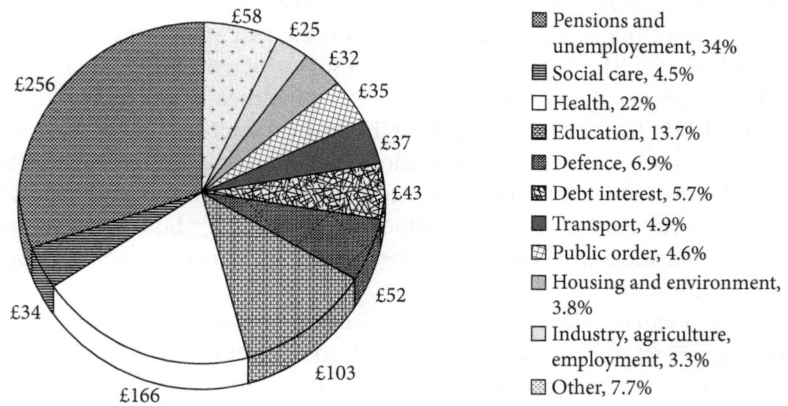

Source: Autumn Budget (2018) 4.

All fields of significant spending developed in response to the most important constitutional conflicts in modern UK history. First, the principles for the state pension and unemployment insurance are found in the Social Security Contributions and Benefits Act 1992.[56] This codifies the National Insurance system first set up through the Old-Age Pensions Act 1908 and the National Insurance Act 1911. There can be no doubt that the People's Budget, which also led to the Parliament Act 1911, was a constitutional crisis of a fundamental kind, resolved through Lloyd George threatening to pack the House of Lords, and the persuasion of the King to back His Majesty's government against the aristocracy.[57] The right to social security was therefore inextricably linked to the development of representative government.

Second, health and social care, 26.5 per cent of UK spending, developed through the National Health Service Act 1946, today found in the National Health Service Act 2006. The NHS is not (as the Bogdanor Constitution says is enough) a 'minimum right of health care and subsistence'. The NHS is a comprehensive, public service, free at the point of use.[58] It resulted from the Beveridge Report's determination to eradicate disease, alongside the welfare system's fight against want, squalor, idleness and ignorance.[59] Even critics of universal, public health care accept that the NHS is 'the closest thing the English people have now to a religion'.[60] It has become a political consensus, which hostile parties only question through guarded, surreptitious, or even covert remarks that are later qualified or denied.[61] It therefore seems prudent to suggest that free, public health care has constitutional value.

[56] Also the Jobseeker's Act 1995, and multiple revisions.
[57] MR Cohen, 'Property and Sovereignty' (1927) 13 *Cornell Law Quarterly* 8, 43, 'That which was hidden from Maitland, Joshua Williams, and the other great ones, was revealed to a Welsh solicitor who in the budget of 1910 proposed to tax the land so as to force it on the market ….'
[58] Department of Health, *NHS Constitution for England* (27 July 2015), arts 1(2) 'Access to NHS services is based on clinical need, not an individual's ability to pay ….'
[59] W Beveridge, *Social insurance and allied services* (1942) Cmd 6404.
[60] N Lawson, *The View from No. 11: Memoirs of a Tory Radical* (London, Bantam, 1992) 613.
[61] R Mason, 'Film shows Nigel Farage calling for move away from state-funded NHS' *Guardian* (London, 12 November 2014) a spokesperson saying for Farage, 'That was then and this is now. It doesn't stand up to say that's still his view.'

Third, education spending, particularly on schools, is structured by the School Standards and Framework Act 1998, tracing back to the Elementary Education Act 1870. The development of the school system was also intimately intertwined with UK constitutional development. The Second Reform Act 1867, which extended the right to vote to more working class people, was bitterly opposed by the then editor of *The Times*, Robert Lowe, a Liberal MP. Though Lowe lost the fight, he beat Walter Bagehot to be MP for the University of London, and became Chancellor of the Exchequer under Gladstone. Seeing he would be defeated in stopping the franchise extension, Lowe urged that because workers would have the vote, Parliament had to 'educate our masters'.[62] Like pensions and health, universal free education was one of the most significant constitutional developments in modern UK history.

Similar stories can be told for all fields of spending. The importance of national security and public order,[63] which cannot be understated, comes from the experience of revolution and war. The duty of the state to manage debt by providing financial stability, create employment, and control inflation,[64] comes from a long history, dating back to the contest between the Bank of England and the South Sea Company to be the banker of a fledgling united Britain. The collapse of the South Sea Company, which took on the national debt, led to the world's first stock market crash,[65] the incarceration of the Chancellor of the Exchequer in the Tower of London, and the development of the office of Prime Minister through the Tory Party's disgrace for a generation.[66] The rights to housing, accommodation, and a clean, safe, environment,[67] were essential to the welfare state's development, and public health, which all democratic movements fought for. Transport policy, and the right to services of general economic interest,[68] were not only essential to industrialisation and economic development, but at the centre of experiment with models of nationalisation, privatisation and socialisation of the means of production.[69]

That the UK's true Constitution is shaped by delivering better living standards (not just the power struggles between seventeenth century offices of state) is reflected in consistent public opinion.[70] Most notably, according to a 2006 survey of 2,231 people by ICM Research for the Joseph Rowntree foundation, 88 per cent thought the right to NHS treatment in a reasonable time should be included in any British Bill of Rights, just behind the right to a fair trial (89%) and even ahead of the right to privacy (82%), and freedom of assembly (73%).[71] The right to be housed was supported by 62% of Conservative voters,

[62] See previously, in opposing the Second Reform Act, 'You must take education up the very first question, and you must press it on without delay for the peace of the country.' Hansard HC Debs (15 July 1867) cols 1549–1550.

[63] See the Reserve Forces Act 1996, Armed Forces Act 2006 and the Police Act 1996.

[64] See the Bank of England Act 1998.

[65] Eg, Blackstone (n 3) Book IV, 117, referring to 'South-Sea project [that] had beggared half the nation'. A Smith, *The Wealth of Nations* (first published 1776, London, Penguin, 1999) Book V, ch 1, §119.

[66] See J Carswell, *The South Sea Bubble* (London, Cresset Press, 1960) and R Dale, *The First Crash: Lessons from the South Sea Bubble* (Princeton, Princeton University Press, 2004).

[67] Eg, Housing Act 1996, Environmental Protection Act 1990 and the Climate Change Act 2008.

[68] Eg, Railways Act 1993, Highways Act 1980, and Greater London Authority Act 1999, ss 141–188 and Sch 10.

[69] Eg, H Morrison, *Socialisation and Transport: Organisation of socialised industries with the particular reference to the London passenger transport bill* (London, Constable & Co, 1933).

[70] See also Ministry of Justice, *Rights and Responsibilities: Developing our Constitutional Framework* (2009) Cm 7577, para 1.11, suggesting the NHS is a constitutional 'landmark' like Magna Carta.

[71] ICM, 'State of the Nation 2006: Summary Results' (2006) question 15a, www.jrrt.org.uk/wp-content/uploads/2019/06/SoN-2006-summary-of-findings.pdf.

and 65% of people overall. Testament to the fact that most people do not distinguish the constitution of politics and the economy, 77 per cent of people thought the right to strike, and to be protected against unfair dismissal for it, is a fundamental right, as indeed it is in law.[72] Taken together, the evidence of people's social priorities through government spending and through dominant social opinion, suggests economic and social rights are at the core of the UK's true Constitution.

B. Enduring Acts of Parliament

A second main source of evidence about the UK Constitution's true nature must be what the legislature does. Social spending makes clear that the principles underpinning the welfare state and public services have been consistently reproduced through major Acts of Parliament. Yet the list of enduring Acts – and Acts that have been consistently recast and recodified – goes much further. Law constructs our most important economic and social institutions, in labour, capital, markets and land. Consistent empirical evidence shows law must do so on a lasting and stable basis to protect and advance human development.[73]

It is now generally accepted that some Acts have greater constitutional significance than others, but this leaves the difficulty of determining which should be which and why. In *R (HS2 Action Alliance Ltd) v Secretary of State for Transport*, Lord Neuberger and Lord Mance (with the whole house agreeing) posited that despite our Constitution being uncodified, we did have 'constitutional instruments'.[74]

> They include Magna Carta, the Petition of Right 1628, the Bill of Rights and (in Scotland) the Claim of Rights Act 1689, the Act of Settlement 1701 and the Act of Union 1707. The European Communities Act 1972, the Human Rights Act 1998 and the Constitutional Reform Act 2005 may now be added to this list. The common law itself also recognises certain principles as fundamental to the rule of law.

The Supreme Court went on to say that, it was 'certainly arguable' that 'fundamental principles' would not be construed as being abrogated by the UK's enactment of legislation to join international organisations.[75] The Supreme Court's list was hardly exhaustive. It did not mention, for example, the United Nations Act 1946, which is unquestionably fundamental to the UK's place in the post-war international order, as both a member of the UN General Assembly (which first met in London), and a permanent member of the

[72] See *Wilson v United Kingdom* (2002) 35 EHRR 20 and *Enerji Yapi-Yol Sen v Turkey* [2009] ECHR 2251.

[73] Eg, S Djankov, C McLiesh and R Ramalho, 'Regulation and Growth' (2006) 92 *Economics Letters* 395, and RE Hall and CI Jones, 'Why do some countries produce so much more output per worker than others?' (1999) 114 *Quarterly Journal of Economics* 83. There remains, however, some, albeit diminishing disagreement about the types of regulation that serve capital formation, economic and human development. See S Deakin, 'The contribution of labour law to economic development and growth' (2016) Cambridge Centre for Business Research Working Paper 478, www.cbr.cam.ac.uk/fileadmin/user_upload/centre-for-business-research/downloads/working-papers/wp478.pdf.

[74] *R (HS2 Action Alliance Ltd) v Secretary of State for Transport* [2014] UKSC 3, [2014] 1 WLR 324 [207]. Their Lordships adopted the colloquial expression 'unwritten constitution', though the constitution is written in statutes, caselaw and texts that describe conventions.

[75] *R (HS2 Action Alliance Ltd)* (n 74) [207]. On the facts, this meant that the requirements of the Environmental Impact Assessment Directive 2011 of public participation in planning decisions could not question internal Parliamentary procedure, and particularly a whipped vote to approve a high speed railway.

UN Security Council. The Supreme Court's point seems to be that while the UK enhances its sovereignty in global affairs by joining international organisations (like the UN, World Trade Organisation, and the European Union) it must do so based on the principles of democracy and human rights embedded in our Constitution.[76]

But on the Supreme Court's list alone, many rules and principles were entirely ignored by the Bogdanor version of the UK Constitution. For instance, Magna Carta set out, not just rights to a fair trial, Parliament, and principles for taxation, but also rights to share in common land and resources.[77] These rights to 'the commons' remained among the most important institutions through revolt and reformation,[78] and composed a whole body of jurisprudence up to Sir Edward Coke's time. The commons was a key to welfare, until (through the era of enclosure) it was transformed into institutions such as the poor law, and ultimately the welfare state.[79] The European Communities Act 1972, through its incorporation of the Treaty of Rome, did not just mean joining a supranational legislative structure, but made gender equality a general principle of law, even ahead of our own equal pay and sex discrimination legislation.[80] The Human Rights Act 1998, incorporating the European Convention on Human Rights, did not just entail civil and political rights, but because it is a living document, it is now clearly seen to contain the right to collectively bargain and to take collective action.[81] This is ultimately what guarantees, in the language of the Universal Declaration of Human Rights, the right to 'just and favourable remuneration'.[82] In eloquent reflection, in the International Covenant on Civil and Political Rights and the International Covenant on Economic, Social and Cultural Rights, the only three rights repeated in each document are the rights to 'freely dispose of their natural wealth and resources', to be free from discrimination, and the right of people 'to form and join trade unions for the protection of [their] interests'.[83]

The problem of which Acts are more constitutional than others can logically be resolved by analogy to constitutional conventions: if Acts consistently retain certain norms in substance, this founds a case for those principles to be regarded as constitutional. For example, Magna Carta and the Bill of Rights demonstrate how the right to a just system of taxation, based upon representative consent (the basis for a fair distribution of income

[76] This is a similar argument to that used by the German Federal Constitutional Court in the *Solange* judgments: see *Internationale Handelsgesellschaft mbH v Einfuhr- und Vorratsstelle für Getreide und Futtermittel* [1974] 2 CMLR 540, 549 and *Re Wünsche Handelsgesellschaft* [1987] 3 CMLR 225.

[77] Magna Carta 1215, cls 44–48. This was then transferred into the Charter of the Forest 1217, especially cl 9–12, signed at St Paul's in London on 6 November.

[78] See J Froissart, *Froissart's Chronicles* (First published 1385, London, F. C. and J. Rivington 1812) translated by GC Macaulay (1895) 251–252, on the Peasants' Revolt, and T More, *Utopia* (1516) Book I, translated by P Turner (London, Penguin, 2004) on sheep and enclosure.

[79] See S Deakin and F Wilkinson, *The Law of the Labour Market* (Oxford, Oxford University Press, 2005) chs 2 and 3.

[80] TFEU, art 157(1) and *Defrenne v Sabena (No 2)* (1976) Case 43/75, [10] 'this provision forms part of the social objectives of the community, which is not merely an economic union, but is at the same time intended, by common action, to ensure social progress and seek the constant improvement of the living and working conditions of their people'. The Equal Pay Act 1970, despite the year of its enactment, only took effect as the Sex Discrimination Act 1975 was passed.

[81] See *Enerji Yapi-Yol Sen v Turkey* (n 72).

[82] UDHR 1948, art 23(3).

[83] International Covenant on Civil and Political Rights 1966, arts 1, 22 and 26, International Covenant on Economic, Social and Cultural Rights 1966, arts 1, 2 and 8.

and wealth) has endured: no tax without Parliament.[84] The source of tax also highlights the UK's most important institutions that are constructed by legislation: that is the regulation of labour, capital, markets, land and the environment.

Within the tax base the Autumn Budget of 2018, first, projected that 41.3 per cent of revenue to be derived either from income tax, or national insurance: that is labour and capital income. Second, corporation tax stood at (after significant cuts) 7.4 per cent of revenue. Third, value added tax and excise duties – taxes on market transactions – were 25.3 per cent. Fourth, business rates and council tax – taxes on land – would generate 8.2 per cent of revenue. Under 'other taxes' are a growing number of environmental levies. Each tax base depends on the existence of stable legal institutions. Just like oppressive taxation before 1215 and 1688 led to constitutional revolutions, the stability of income and wealth distribution depends upon the stability of social institutions behind them, and the enduring patterns legislation that underpin them.

Figure 17.2 Public sector revenue (£bn) 2019–2020

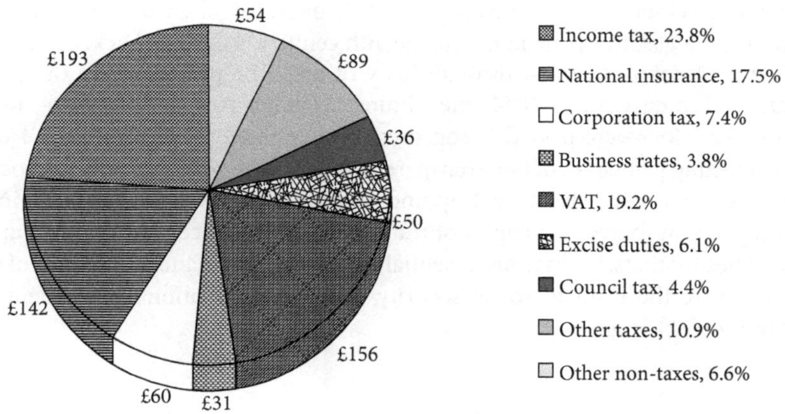

Source: Autumn Budget (2018) 5.

So first, what determines the structure of labour regulation? Four central statutes are the Employment Rights Act 1996, the National Minimum Wage Act 1998, the Trade Union and Labour Relations (Consolidation) Act 1992, and the Equality Act 2010. With many other norms,[85] these function like 'a charter protecting employees' rights'.[86] The principles, frequently the same words, go back to the Trade Disputes Act 1906, the Trade Boards Act 1909, and the race relations and sex discrimination legislation of the 1960s and 1970s. Over successive, even bewildering revisions,[87] even over intense political dispute, modern labour law has always advanced two principles.[88] First, it guarantees a minimum floor of

[84] Magna Carta 1215, cl 12 and Bill of Rights 1689, art 4. The right to representation is in itself is some guarantee of fairness, even if the principle of progressive taxation has wild loopholes.

[85] See H Collins, KD Ewing and A McColgan, *Labour Law: Text, Cases and Materials* (Cambridge, CUP, 2012) and E McGaughey, *A Casebook on Labour Law* (Oxford, Hart Publishing, 2018).

[86] *Gisda Cyf v Barratt* [2010] UKSC 41, [2010] 4 All ER 851 [37].

[87] See P Davies and M Freedland, *Labour Legislation and Public Policy* (Oxford, Clarendon, 1993).

[88] S Webb and B Webb, *Industrial Democracy* (London, Longmans, Green & Co, 1920) Part III, chs III(b) and (e).

rights through which nobody must fall. Second, to get fair wages and conditions beyond the minimum, it guarantees voice at work, through collective bargaining and direct voting rights. The balance of power has shifted forwards and back, but the principles of labour law have never been substantively questioned, because they are the essence of our constitutional structure. The march for the Tolpuddle martyrs, the meeting at Congregational Memorial Hall to overturn *Taff Vale* and organise the Labour Party, the fight of the Suffragettes, the Notting Hill riots and the first carnivals, the Dagenham strike for equal pay, were all moments of constitutional significance, producing lasting constitutional reform.[89]

Second, companies are essential to economic life, and structured by the Companies Act 2006, the Insolvency Act 1986, and the Financial Services and Markets Act 2000. As explained above, the South Sea Bubble of 1720 transformed the British Constitution, and also directly resulted in statute and case law on the accountability of fiduciaries in a governance structure,[90] their being bound by law, and their duty to avoid any possibility of conflicts of interest, which run through corporate regulation today.[91] The constitutional functions of these principles (to say nothing about the East India Company[92]) are also illustrated in the development of insolvency law. It is often forgotten that this was *the* single most important legislative issue in the nineteenth century.[93] Charles Dickens immortalised the problems of debtors' prison through his writing,[94] the period where the Joint Stock Companies Winding-Up Act 1844, the Limited Liability Act 1855, and the Joint-Stock Companies Act 1856 were passed.[95] Together these enabled social protection from insolvency, establishing principles of fair, transparent, and accountable winding up procedures.[96] Similarly after successive crises, and by understanding the Wall Street Crash in the US, financial regulation follows principles of transparency, prudence, and preventing conflicts in all securities markets.[97] These are essential to protect the financial integrity of the state, and to guarantee the right to social security, through occupational retirement schemes invested in the stock markets.[98]

[89] Though driven by the labour movement, they are as important as Peel's repeal of the Corn Laws, as Disraeli's piloting of the Second Reform Act 1867, as Baldwin's piloting of the Representation of the People (Equal Franchise) Act 1928, or as Thatcher's support for the Equal Pay Act 1970. See McGaughey (n 85) ch 1(3)(c).

[90] Bubble Act 1720 prohibited incorporation without Parliament, while *Attorney General v Davy* (1741) 26 ER 531 set the default rule to require that 50% plus one in the general meeting could do any corporate act, and thus exercise constitutional control.

[91] *Keech v Sandford* (1726) 25 ER 223, Lord King LC, and see today the Companies Act 2006, ss 175–177. Lord King LC was deliberately chosen to replace Lord Macclesfield LC, who before his disgrace over his role on the South Sea Company, decided in *Bromfield v Wytherley* (1718) Prec Ch 505 that a fiduciary was entitled to take money from a trust, invest it on their own behalf, and keep the profit, if they restored money to the trust. Macclesfield was impeached in the House of Lords, tried and found guilty of taking bribes in 1725.

[92] See S Tharoor, *Inglorious Empire* (London, Hurst & Co, 2018).

[93] See M Lester, *Victorian Insolvency* (Oxford, Clarendon 1995).

[94] C Dickens, *David Copperfield* (first published 1850, Oxford, Oxford University Press, 1997), *Hard Times* (first published 1854, Oxford University Press, 2008) and *Little Dorrit* (first published 1857, Oxford, Oxford University Press, 1979).

[95] The Debtors Act 1869 finally abolished imprisonment for debt.

[96] See further V Finch and D Milman, *Corporate Insolvency Law: Principles and Perspectives* (Cambridge, Cambridge University Press, 2017).

[97] Generally, N Moloney, E Ferran and J Payne (eds), *Oxford Handbook of Financial Regulation* (Oxford, Oxford University Press, 2017) ch 1.

[98] See E McGaughey, 'Participation in Corporate Governance' (PhD thesis, London School of Economics 2014) ch 6 and E McGaughey, 'Democracy in America at work: the history of labor's vote in corporate governance' (2019) 42 *Seattle University Law Review* 697, pt II.B.

Third, the market segment of the economy, the base for VAT and an array of duties and levies, derives from the laws of obligations and property, heavily codified through the Sale of Goods Act 1979, the Competition Act 1998, and the Consumer Rights Act 2015. These Acts recast principles from the Sale of Goods Act 1893, the Monopolies and Restrictive Practices (Inquiry and Control) Act 1948, and the Unfair Contract Terms Act 1977. They require that people have a right to run their business, and to do so according to the principle of fair competition, while guaranteeing consumers a high level of protection against unfair practices. A wealth of sector-specific legislation in markets which systematically fail – such as transport, electricity – also ensures that prices are fair, that universal service is provided, and that basic standards of service are adhered to.[99]

Fourth, land is the tax base for business rates and council tax, while the protection of the environment is the growing base for taxes like the climate change levy, landfill tax, petroleum revenue tax, air passenger duty, and vehicle excise. For land ownership, major statutes include the Land Registration Act 2002, the Compulsory Purchase Act 1965 and the Town and Country Planning Act 1990. Dating back to the Land Registration Act 1925, and the Town and Country Planning Act 1947, these enshrined (even if incomplete) the principles of transparency of land ownership, and that property carries responsibility to neighbours and the community. For the environment, the Environmental Protection Act 1990 and the Climate Change Act 2008 confront existential problems as scientific understanding has developed since the 1980s. They update what were the Public Health Acts of the nineteenth century and the Clean Air Acts in the post-war era. They put into practice the right to a clean environment.

While these categories of constitutional principle may appear tangential to narratives presented in some constitutional and public law books, they are central commitments made by the UK in international law, particularly the International Covenant on Economic, Social and Cultural Rights 1966.[100] This treaty, signed and ratified by 169 countries, recodified the Universal Declaration on Human Rights, the 'international Magna Carta' of humanity,[101] and binds the UK. Nearly all institutions summarised, and the rights that developed from them are also in the constitutions of other democratic European and Commonwealth countries, particularly the right to take collective action,[102] to run a business,[103] to consumer protection,[104] that property carries responsibility,[105] and the right to a clean environment.[106] It is true that fewer constitutions and human rights charters explicitly give space for fair competition,[107] or corporate and financial accountability, albeit that a growing discussion in international law is calling for business to be infused with human rights. Corporate and financial accountability is, however, an established part of the tradition of UK law, and fundamental to its constitutional development. In this way, it is also possible for the UK to be, not just a follower, but at the forefront of constitutional law and human rights.

[99] Eg, Electricity Act 1989, Water Industry Act 1991, Railways Act 1993, Communications Act 2003, etc.
[100] International Covenant on Economic, Social and Cultural Rights 1966, arts 6–15.
[101] E Roosevelt, *On the Adoption of the Universal Declaration of Human Rights* (9 December 1948).
[102] Eg, Charter of Fundamental Rights of the EU 2000, art 28.
[103] Eg, Grundgesetz, art 12.
[104] Eg, CFREU, art 38.
[105] Eg, Grundgesetz, art 14(2) dating back to the Weimar Constitution 1919, art 153(3).
[106] Eg, CFREU, art 37.
[107] Cf, FD Roosevelt, 'Eleventh State of the Union Address' (1944) on a Second Bill of Rights.

C. Principles in Case Law

A third main source of evidence about the nature of the UK's true Constitution is the case law of the judiciary. The *HS2* decision recognised this, as the Supreme Court stated that 'common law itself also recognises certain principles as fundamental to the rule of law.'[108] On the one hand, these principles could include the right against unjust discrimination,[109] the right against unfair competition and to take collective action,[110] or the right against environmental damage.[111] As well as common law, equity recognises fiduciary duties against conflicts of interest,[112] that property carries responsibility,[113] and the right against unjust dismissal.[114] But as anyone familiar with these lines of cases knows, such rights at common law and equity are, and can always be contested, qualified, refined or reversed. This is in the nature of case law. Any list, moreover, could be very long. On the other hand, case law recognises certain basic principles, which function at a higher level than other constitutional norms, either of structure, procedure, or rights, because they go to the mechanisms of construction. Four central principles can be identified.

First, our courts recognise the principle of representative, and deliberative democracy. While the path toward democracy was long,[115] and anything but inevitable, the principle of a democratic society pervades the legal system, and is the central legitimating factor in the sovereignty of Parliament. This is seen, first, in the construction of legislation relating to political spending. Magna Carta in 1215 proclaimed: 'To no one will we sell, to no one will we refuse or delay, right or justice'. Similarly, in the *Animal Defenders* case, Baroness Hale in 2008 stated that in the UK and Europe 'we do not want our government or its policies to be decided by the highest spenders. Our democracy is based upon more than one person one vote. It is based on the view that each person has equal value.'[116] Second, it is

[108] *R (HS2 Action Alliance Ltd)* (n 74) [207].

[109] Eg, *Kruse v Johnson* [1898] 2 QB 91 and *Constantine v Imperial Hotels Ltd* [1944] KB 693.

[110] Eg, *Mogul Steamship Co Ltd v McGregor, Gow & Co* [1892] AC 25, *Crofter Hand Woven Harris Tweed v Veitch* [1942] AC 435 and cf *OBG Ltd v Allan* [2007] UKHL 21, [2008] 1 AC 1 [56].

[111] Eg, *Rylands v Fletcher* (1866) LR 1 Ex 265 and most recently *Lungowe v Vedanta Resources plc* [2019] UKSC 20, [2019] 2 WLR 1051.

[112] Eg, *Keech v Sandford* (n 91).

[113] Summed up in the maxims *sic utere tuo ut alienum non laedas* (use of property should not harm) See *Wright v Simpson* (1802) 31 ER 1272, 1275. Also at common law, *ubi emolumentum, ibi onus* (where the benefits lie, so should the burdens): *Turberville v Stampe* (1697) 91 ER 1072, per Holt CJ, '… it being for the master's benefit.'

[114] Eg, *Dean v Bennett* (1870) LR 6 Ch 489 (finding in equity that a dismissal was unjust) and *Wilson v Racher* [1974] ICR 428 (holding that there is a common law duty of mutual respect, precluding wrongful dismissal at common law).

[115] The point at which the UK could claim to be a democracy was probably only with the Representation of the People (Equal Franchise) Act 1928, and even then such a point ignores the subjugation of political freedom in the Empire. On this view, when all of Her Majesty's citizens had the right to vote (with only limited exceptions, such as for prisoners), the UK was not democratic until the waves of independence in the late 1960s and 1970s. The disintegration of Empire therefore coincides with the UK's entry into the European Economic Community. There was never a point at which the UK was an 'independent', unconnected nation: see T Snyder, 'Brexit Is Not Going to Lead to the End of the EU. It Will Lead to Some Kind of Different Europe' (*Ukrayinska Pravda*, 1 July 2016) www.pravda.com.ua/eng/articles/2016/07/1/7113375/ 'there never was a moment when Great Britain was alone. It was an empire, and then it integrated into Europe.'

[116] *R (Animal Defenders International) v Secretary of State for Culture, Media and Sport* [2008] UKHL 15, [2008] 1 AC 1312 [48]. See also *R v Jones* [1999] 2 Cr App R 253, 255, per Lord Bingham CJ stating there is a need 'to achieve a level financial playing field between competing candidates, so as to prevent perversion of the voters' democratic choice between competing candidates within constituencies by significant disparities of local expenditure.'

seen in connection with the general principle, expressed in the *Simms* case, that 'Parliament must squarely confront what it is doing and accept the political cost. Fundamental rights cannot be overridden by general words', so as to prevent incursions passing 'unnoticed in the democratic process.'[117] Thus this principle forces greater deliberation in representative government. It opposes irrational executive action.[118] The democratic principle certainly does not include referendums, which in the UK context appear to frustrate the good administration of government.[119] By contrast deliberative, representative democracy must now be regarded as a norm whose weakening, let alone undoing, is unthinkable. 'Freedom once given cannot be taken away.'[120]

Second, the judiciary recognises the rule of law as an overriding constitutional norm. The rule of law was said by Lord Bridge to be 'as important in a free society as the democratic franchise'.[121] It applies to 'all persons and authorities within the state, whether public or private'.[122] In *R (Unison) v Lord Chancellor* this meant that fees for employment tribunals had to be regarded as ultra vires, Lord Reed stating that the 'constitutional right of access to the courts is inherent in the rule of law'. In this way, like other principles of construction, multiple rights can be developed by the courts out of the overriding norm.

Third, the UK's social welfare state is a general principle, used to construe both common law and statute. In *Gorringe v Calderdale MBC*, Lord Steyn said it was 'necessary' to view the law of negligence in the context of 'the contours of our social welfare state',[123] a necessity that can be observed across the law of obligations, property and through statute. In the landmark decision of *Gisda Cyf v Barratt*, Lord Kerr went as far as to say that the 'need to segregate intellectually common law principles relating to contract law, even in the field of employment, from statutorily conferred rights is fundamental'.[124] This meant, a standard rule of contract law that one is bound by a notice when one may reasonably be deemed to have seen it – not when one actually sees it – did not apply to an employment contract's termination. This meant that the three-month time limit for the employee to claim unfair dismissal only began once she actually knew she had been dismissed, not when a letter arrived at an empty home. Thus social principles, consistent with statutory rights, transform the nature of the common law. There is a fusion at work. As a principle of construction, statute and case law are read as a whole, in their context, to reflect the background of social expectations.[125]

[117] *R (Simms) v SS for the Home Department* [1999] UKHL 33, [2000] 2 AC 115, 131, per Lord Hoffmann.

[118] Arguably *R (Miller) v Secretary of State for Exiting the European Union* [2017] UKSC 5, [2018] AC 61 was an example of this.

[119] See further E McGaughey, 'Could Brexit be void?' (2018) 29(3) *King's Law Journal* 331, but contrast *Wilson v PM* [2019] EWCA Civ 304, [2019] 3 All ER 230. It seems likely that this judgment is far from the final word: contrast the Swiss Federal Court 'Heiratssrafe' (or Marriage Penalty) case of 10 April 2019, declaring a referendum invalid based on misrepresentation. The *ex tempore* judgment available at bundesgericht.simplex.tv, pending written reasons.

[120] *Blackburn v AG* [1971] EWCA Civ 7, per Lord Denning MR.

[121] *X v Morgan-Grampian Ltd* [1991] AC 1, 48, per Lord Bridge, 'The maintenance of the rule of law is in every way as important in a free society as the democratic franchise. In our society the rule of law rests upon twin foundations: the sovereignty of the Queen in Parliament in making the law and the sovereignty of the Queen's courts in interpreting and applying the law.'

[122] T Bingham, *Rule of Law* (London, Penguin, 2008) 8, 'all persons and authorities within the state, whether public or private should be bound by and entitled to the benefit of laws publicly made, taking effect (generally) in the future and publicly administered in the courts.'

[123] *Gorringe v Calderdale MBC* [2004] UKHL 15, [2004] 1 WLR 1057.

[124] *Gisda Cyf v Barratt* (n 86) [39].

[125] See further, *Johnson v Unisys Ltd* [2001] UKHL 13, [2001] 2 WLR 1076 [35]–[37] per Lord Hoffmann, and noting how 'statute and common law have proceeded hand in hand.'

Fourth, the principle of international comity transcends all common law and statute. In *R v Lyons*, Lord Hoffmann stated that 'there is a strong presumption in favour of interpreting English law (whether common law or statute) in a way which does not place the United Kingdom in breach of an international obligation.'[126] Similarly the Court of Appeal stated it 'is a principle of legal policy that the municipal law should conform to public international law.'[127] Again, this principle functions through construction, so that Parliament 'cannot be supposed merely by reason of its having used general words to be intending to do that which is against the comity of nations'.[128] For example in *Hounga v Allen*, the common law defence of illegality had to be construed in the light of the UN Convention against Transnational Organised Crime, 2000.[129] This resulted in enabling a young, undocumented migrant to claim race discrimination (and probably also to have succeeded in a wage deduction claim[130]) notwithstanding the fact that she had violated the Immigration Act 1971 by arriving to work in the UK. This is because international law requires that the victims of traffickers are protected from employers, not the other way around. Also dramatically, in *FHR European Ventures LLP v Cedar Capital Partners LLC* the Supreme Court held that profits resulting from a trustee's breach of fiduciary duty were held on constructive trust, and so elevated in insolvency priorities above secured creditors, despite fiduciary duties often being conceptualised as part of the law of obligations. This reversed long-standing common law precedent, and one of Lord Neuberger's own recent judgments,[131] because the Supreme Court took into account the UN Convention against Corruption 2003.[132] While the UK is yet to develop a full 'monist' system, it nevertheless has a powerful commitment in its principles of construction to ensure that the UK abides by international law.[133]

Together these four principles of construction – of democracy, the rule of law, the social state, and international comity – are so basic that they can be seen to pervade the interpretation of all statute and case law. They are usually unwritten assumptions, because ultimately they derive from a deep-seated consensus about the building blocks of a just society. They are maintained by the force of social opinion.[134] Of course, while social opinion can remain remarkably consistent and unmoved over time, it is possible to degrade it through concerted political action, and by attacking civil society and its institutions. This is why constitutional principles should be openly recognised, and defended, to ensure that

[126] *R v Lyons* [2003] 1 AC 976 [27]. He goes on to say 'As Lord Goff of Chieveley said in *Attorney-General v Guardian Newspapers Ltd (No 2)* [1990] 1 AC 109, 283: 'I conceive it to be my duty, when I am free to do so, to interpret the law in accordance with the obligations of the Crown under [the Convention]'.'

[127] *Saad v SS for the Home Department* [2001] EWCA Civ 2008, [2001] 12 WLUK 532 [15] Lord Phillips MR, quoting FAR Bennion, *Statutory Interpretation*, 3rd edn (London, LexisNexis, 1997) 630. Cf *R (SG) v SS for Work and Pensions* [2015] UKSC 16, [2015] 1 WLR 1449 [247]–[257] per Lord Kerr, advocating adopting monism.

[128] *Colquhoun v Brooks* (1888) 21 QBD 52, 57–58 per Lord Escher MR, and see also *Smith v East Elloe District Council* [1956] AC 736, 765, per Lord Reid, 'There are many cases where general words in a statute are given a limited meaning … they are limited so as not to conflict with international law'.

[129] *Hounga v Allen* [2014] UKSC 47, [2014] 1 WLR 2889.

[130] See *Patel v Mirza* [2016] UKSC 42, [2016] 3 WLR 399 [63]–[66] per Lord Sumption.

[131] *Sinclair Investments (UK) Ltd v Versailles Trade Finance Ltd* [2011] EWCA Civ 347, [2011] 3 WLR 1153.

[132] *FHR European Ventures LLP v Cedar Capital Partners LLC* [2014] UKSC 45, [2014] 3 WLR 535 [42] alongside the OECD Convention on Combating Bribery of Foreign Public Officials in International Business Transactions 1999 and the Bribery Act 2010.

[133] This may be termed the 'indirect effect' of international law.

[134] JS Mill, *On Liberty* (first published 1859, Oxford, Oxford University Press, 1991) ch 2, on the force of social opinion, and Hart (n 32) 56–57.

they are an irremovable part of the UK Constitution.[135] In this sense, it may be regarded as correct to say that judicial principles of construction are 'the ultimate controlling factor[s] on which our constitution is based.'[136]

IV. Conclusion

What is the UK's true Constitution? The answer must be that the true Constitution is democratic, social, and principled. By looking at what the UK Government actually does, the way that the state is constituted, it must be recognised that essential components of our Constitution include the right to social security, a universal, free and equal health system, free universal education, a right to social inclusion, fair taxation, protection for the environment and countryside, fair wages through voice at work, and transparent and accountable governance of finance and enterprise, at the least. The list is not closed. In the operation of law, our courts have consistently recognised core principles of construction, that must be regarded as indelible components of our constitution: the principles of democracy, the rule of law, the social welfare state, and international comity. So long as the judiciary exists, it would be unthinkable and maybe impossible to degrade or erase them through any act of the executive, or any Act of Parliament.[137]

What must be clear is that any theory about what the UK's uncodified Constitution 'is', not what we think it 'ought to be', must make its case with an appeal to evidence, and through reasoned argument. The oldest traditions of UK constitutional thought, from Blackstone or Maitland, and in modern contributions of Griffith or Ewing, adopt the preferable view that a constitution cannot be shackled within a public/private divide. History and society are not so compliant, and constantly remind us that the way we may organise our court procedures,[138] or may want to organise law school curricula,[139] for reasons of convenience, cannot determine our conceptions of constitutional law. Of course, law is not a natural science, where facts and causation in the physical word exist regardless of people's opinions. In the humanities, social sciences, and law, the force of people's opinions, the foundations

[135] See Y Roznai, *Unconstitutional Constitutional Amendments: The Limits of Amendment Powers* (Oxford, Oxford University Press, 2019).

[136] *R (Jackson) v Attorney General* [2005] UKHL 56, [2005] 3 WLR 733 [104] per Lord Hope. While the 'rule of law' may be argued, as Lord Hope suggested, to rank above Parliamentary sovereignty, it is harder to justify placing the rule of law above representative democracy. In truth, both are so heavily interconnected that it makes no sense to try awarding a first or second place.

[137] Nb. Plainly an Act of Parliament is the highest norm in our Constitution, and overrides all other sources of law. I have not, however, heard any credible argument that an Act of Parliament *could* abolish the courts, or restrict their independence. In a serious political crisis, of course, institutions are taken over through fear, coercion and then force, and depend upon a mass social movement for their defence, not merely the courts: see O Kahn-Freund, 'Autobiographical Memories of the Weimar Republic: A Conversation with Wolfgang Luthardt' (February 1978) original in (1981) 14(2) *Kritische Justiz* 183, translated into English by E McGaughey (2016) KCL Law School RP No 2016–34.

[138] Eg, *O'Reilly v Mackman* [1983] 2 AC 237, 255, per Lord Denning MR, on a private/public divide for judicial review time limits.

[139] Eg, P Birks, 'Before we begin: five keys to land law' in S Bright and J Dewar (eds), *Land Law: Themes and Perspectives* (Oxford, Oxford University Press, 1998) 457, 459, distinguishing between 'contextual' subjects like land law, and 'conceptual' subjects like those flowing from the public/private divide. See further, McGaughey (n 85) Preface.

of overlapping consensus, do create the reality being observed. A clear distinction between what 'is' and what 'ought to be' in law is conceptually impossible, if not absurd,[140] because the way we describe and explain the law contributes to shaping its very reality. Law, like all social institutions, like all of humanity's beliefs and conflicts, begins in the minds of women and men, and so it is in the mind that the foundations of justice must be constructed.[141] This is why it is important in matters of interpretation not easily to concede, and sometimes not at all, that the law 'is' what it is, even if it produces injustice. The UK's true Constitution is just.

[140] See Q Skinner, *Visions of Politics* (Cambridge, Cambridge University Press, 2002) vol 1, ch 2, and L Wittgenstein, *Philosophical Investigations* (first published 1953, London, Macmilan, 1968) §§23, 43 and 199–203.

[141] Cf, United Nations Educational, Scientific and Cultural Organization Constitution 1946, preamble, 'That since wars begin in the minds of men, it is in the minds of men that the defences of peace must be constructed'.

PART V

Frontiers of the Social Democratic Constitution

18

Constituting Social Democracy and the Challenge of National Isolation

MARK FREEDLAND

I. Introduction

This chapter seeks to explore a particularly fraught and difficult aspect of the task of realising an idea of Social Democracy in the UK in its current state and condition, namely that of dealing with the challenges of national isolation which are presented by the projected withdrawal of the UK from the EU originally due to take place in March 2019.[1] Drawing on an underlying notion of 'sustainable governance' which I have developed in other writings, the chapter addresses itself to the vision of the constitution of Social Democracy or Democratic Socialism which Keith Ewing has explicitly set forth in a series of key journal articles[2] and which in a larger sense informs the whole of his work in the fields of labour law and public law.

In this body of work Keith Ewing has identified some profound problems about how to situate the UK's national constitution of social democracy or democratic socialism, to or towards which he aspires, within a larger European legal and political order. Those problems remain crucially unresolved; and in the view of this writer they have since the Referendum of 2016 assumed the magnitude of a comprehensive threat that the UK will become nationally isolated from any mainstream body of the law and practice of social democracy in the European region. In developing and instantiating that thesis, the chapter will generally consider this threat of national isolation in terms both of public or constitutional law and of labour law, and it will focus in particular upon the need of the UK to formulate a body of labour migration law and policy which could conform to the ideals of social democracy and somehow align itself to or reconcile itself with the EU's regime of freedom of movement of workers.

The first stage of my argument will consist of describing, and positively endorsing, Keith Ewing's construction of an area of coalescence between constitutional law and labour law,

[1] A Postscript at the end of this chapter describes the chronology of its writing, and sets that in the context of the Brexit debate which is its essential subject.

[2] K Ewing, 'Democratic Socialism and Labour Law' (1995) 24 *Industrial Law Journal* 103, 'KDE 1995'; 'The Death of Social Europe' (2015) 26 *King's Law Journal* 76, 'KDE 2015'; 'Jeremy Corbyn and the Law of Democracy' (2017) 28 *King's Law Journal* 343, 'KDE 2017'; and 'Implications of the Post-Brexit Architecture' (2017) 28 *King's Law Journal* 403, 'KDE 2017(2)'

the creation and maintenance of which is in his view a precondition to the realisation of his ideal of social democracy or democratic socialism:[3] it is a view with which I strongly agree. At this stage I will seek to show how his view shifts from one in which, in earlier times, he was prepared to regard EU law as having a potentially positive contribution to make to the constituting of social democracy in UK law at that crucial point of convergence between labour law and constitutional law. I will consider the way in which, over time, he became deeply sceptical about whether EU law has any such positive contribution to make to this constitution of social democracy in UK law, thus eventually finding himself in a complex situation with regard to this aspect of the Brexit debate.

The second stage of my argument, while fully acknowledging the existence of these deep-seated problems, nevertheless contends that the constituting of social democracy within the UK is still and will remain dependent upon a high degree of conscious alignment with EU law in general and EU labour law in particular, warts and all. There are a number of different senses in which I believe this to be necessary, but my argument will home in on one of these. I foresee a particular continuing need for a considerable degree of accommodation between UK labour and social law and EU law in the area in which labour and social law intersect with migration law. This argument will be developed with reference to the ideas of sustainable governance and national isolation; those ideas culminate in a notion of 'the pathology of social law', which will be explained and explored.

II. Social Democracy and the EU – Keith Ewing's Developing Perspective

One of the major and recurring themes of Keith Ewing's scholarly work has consisted in the articulation of his vision of how social democracy, or democratic socialism, might best be constituted in the UK. This has formed a key point of convergence of his studies in the fields of constitutional law and of labour law especially in its collective aspect. In exploring this theme, he has regarded the British Labour Party as the essential agent for the realisation of social democracy in the UK, and he has measured the extent of its achievement primarily by reference to the changing fortunes and orientations of that political party.

At the same time, he has envisaged the development of social democracy in the UK as having a distinctively European dimension. This emerges clearly from his seminal article of 1995 on Democratic Socialism and Labour Law,[4] in which from the outset he indicates that he is working from the starting point of a partly Continental European paradigm of democratic socialism, for which he identified the Swedish Social Democratic Workers Party

[3] These are terms which Keith Ewing has treated as largely interchangeable, from KDE 1995 onwards; the equation is made in KDE 1995 (n 2) 103: '… [I]t is likely that Labour will remain in essence what the continental Europeans would identify as a social democratic party, a label which for obvious reasons would be inappropriate in the contemporary vocabulary of British politics. Alternatively then, Labour was and is likely to remain a democratic socialist party, performing the same function in our political system as say the *Socialdemokrtiska Arbetar partiet* in Sweden.' The 'obvious reasons' were that the social democratic terminology was still in 1995 in the UK strongly associated with the Social Democratic Party which had been formed in 1981 as a centrist breakaway from the Labour Party and later merged into the Liberal Democrats.

[4] KDE 1995 (n 2).

as a leading exemplar.[5] He pinpoints a key controversy in his own thinking as to whether the British Labour Party should be seeking to incorporate the European Convention on Human Rights into the constitutional law of the UK. Most pertinently to our present discussion, he correctly predicted that 'with regard to membership of the European Union … Labour in government would be a more committed participant, and much more willing to shape and embrace the social agenda of Brussels [than it had hitherto been]'.[6]

It is important, however, not to overstate the extent of Keith Ewing's orientation towards European labour law even at that juncture; in the Conclusion to that article, he was very clear that 'the principles of social democracy or democratic socialism, and the political purposes of labour law, do not lose their vitality and relevance simply because they are rooted in the social, economic and political history of the nation'.[7] Moreover, he was already expressing a real concern about the propensity of European formulations of fundamental human rights and freedoms to accord a greater priority to property rights and freedom to do business than it seemed to him was merited in a social democratic Labour constitution – his target at that point being the European Convention on Human Rights.[8] And for him it was still important to 'evaluate the direction' of the European Commission's White Paper on European social policy of 1994 according to the framework of social democratic principle which his article was designed to set up.[9]

From there I sense that Keith Ewing followed a winding and increasingly stony road of cautious entertainment of European labour law (in the sense of what we now think of as EU labour law) as a possible source of progress towards a state of social democracy in the UK. That path initially seemed to be heading towards some broad sunlit uplands, and I think Keith Ewing probably, in heyday of the Social Dialogue, shared some of the optimism of the late and lamented Brian Bercusson about the prospects for social democracy via European labour law.[10] But the way became more and more strewn with boulders, most conspicuously perhaps when the ECJ, in 2007 in the *Viking* and *Laval* complex of cases,[11] seemed to realise Keith Ewing's prescient fears about the potential for prioritisation of economic freedoms over fundamental social rights. From 2008 onwards, the institutions of the EU, and more particularly of its Eurozone, were visibly preoccupied with the aftermath of that

[5] KDE 1995 (n 2) 103, as quoted at fn 3 above.

[6] KDE 1995 (n 2) 103.

[7] Ibid, 132.We can see here a real connection with the late Brian Bercusson's work on European Labour Law, in which he framed European social law as generated by a strategy of ascent from national social democratic traditions across Europe; see generally B Bercusson, *European Labour Law*, 2nd edn (Cambridge, Cambridge University Press, 2009). See also below, fn 10 and text associated therewith.

[8] Ibid, 108: 'it remains to be seen whether this would be an appropriate item for democratic socialists to wear. There might be at least a measure of concern about the scope of the document, about the fact that liberal icons such as private property are expressly included (in the first protocol) and more seriously about the fact that it may be used by legal as well as by natural persons.' His stance on this point has also undergone changes over time, from his piece on the *Demir* case with John Hendy (KD Ewing and J Hendy QC, 'The Dramatic Implications of *Demir and Baykara*' (2010) 39 *Industrial Law Journal* 2) through to his more sceptical piece on the *RMT* case with Alan Bogg (A Bogg, KD Ewing, 'The Implications of the *RMT* Case' (2014) 43 *Industrial Law Journal* 221). In many ways, he has been on a parallel journey in his engagements with the EU and the Council of Europe.

[9] Ibid 132, referring to the European Commission White Paper, *European Social Policy: A Way Forward for the Union* (COM (94) 333), known as the Delors White Paper.

[10] Brian Bercusson's optimism was real, but at the same time he was vigilantly aware of the democratic pitfalls; compare his article 'Democratic Legitimacy and European Labour Law' (1999) 28 *Industrial Law Journal* 153.

[11] As to which, see generally M Freedland and J Prassl (eds), *Viking, Laval and Beyond*, (Oxford, Hart Publishing, 2014).

year's financial crisis and rapidly resiling from their earlier commitments to the maximisation of social progress in the Member States.

By 2015, Keith Ewing concluded that the end of that road of 'Social Europe' had been reached. Writing under the heading of 'The Death of Social Europe', he recounted the birth of that great initiative, as marked in Jacques Delors' famous speech as President of the European Commission to the British Trade Union Congress in September 1988, and its quite vigorous development in the ensuing 20 years.[12] He felt that, particularly with regard to the embedding of collective bargaining as a source of law, its integration as a regulatory process, and its recognition as a fundamental right, 'Jacques Delors kept his promise'.[13] He nevertheless concluded that Mario Draghi, as the head of the European Central Bank, had been all too accurate in his 'infamous announcement of the death of Social Europe in an interview in the *Wall Street Journal* in 2012',[14] and he went on to provide a long epilogue in the shape of an account of a process of deregulation, decentralisation, and destruction of collective bargaining which had in his view been in progress from 2008 onwards.[15]

All this, of course, was written before the Brexit Referendum of June 2016. This raises the question of what course he has subsequently felt that the UK should steer in relation to the European Union following the demise of Social Europe as he has thus identified it. His recent writings indicate that, while he has remained very doubtful of the capacity of the EU, while on its recent policy track, to contribute to the achievement of social democracy in the UK, he is nevertheless all too keenly aware of the process of demolition of social democracy in which the government of the UK seems currently to be engaged. The presence, and his increasing recognition, of those combining threats to social democracy in the UK have, I think, placed him in a quandary, eventually confronting him with a choice between almost equally sub-optimal modes of pursuit of social democratic goals for UK labour law, that is to say between remaining within and departing from the fold of EU labour law. (I use that terminology to denote the fact that, even on the assumption that the UK does leave the EU by 31 October 2019 as projected at the time of writing, there are still a number of possible permutations according to which the UK might remain at least partially adherent to the norms of EU labour law.)

I find that a slight shift can be discerned in Keith Ewing's thinking about and around this profound dilemma: it is visible in some differences of emphasis as between his articles on 'Jeremy Corbyn and the Law of Democracy' published in September 2017[16] and on 'Implications of the Post-Brexit Architecture'[17] which appeared online in February 2018. In the earlier piece, which is as its title implies primarily focused upon the prospects for the achievement of social democracy if a Labour government were to come to power under the leadership of Jeremy Corbyn, Keith Ewing seems steadfast in his conviction that EU labour law would have little to offer to that ameliorative process. He recognises it as an 'apparent irony' that 'a constitutional model for Labour's social democratic ambitions is to be found in the TEU, which we have voted in a Brexit referendum to reject'.[18] But for him a more

[12] KDE 2015 (n 2) 77–85.
[13] Ibid, 86.
[14] Ibid, 86–87.
[15] Ibid, 87–96.
[16] KDE 2017 (n 2).
[17] KDE 2017(2) (n 2).
[18] KDE 2017 (n 2) 358.

real and greater irony consisted in the way that 'those social democratic values, procedures and policies has been casually undermined by the steps taken under the Title VIII of the TFEU … to pursue a neo-liberal economic policy which is at odds with them'.[19] He experiences from the trajectory of EU labour policy 'the overwhelming sense that trade unions are to be agents in the management of their own demise and their own irrelevance to national and EU economies'.[20]

However, when Keith Ewing later returned to this set of questions in 'Post-Brexit Architecture',[21] we can sense that his predictions for, and his cost-benefit analysis of, Brexit upon UK labour law and social policy have somewhat changed. Less optimistic than before about the prospects, in any near future, for a Labour government with effective room for manoeuvre,[22] he is more preoccupied with the threat that the fashioning of all the terms and the outcomes of Brexit could easily fall into the hands of neoliberal policymakers, the least of whose concerns would be the keeping of Theresa May's promises to maintain the worker-protective legacy of EU labour law, still less that of building an edifice of social democratic labour law for the UK upon the foundations of those promises. He goes so far as to conclude that 'given the right-wing populism driving the Brexit process and the new economic architecture anticipated by its authors, there is … a risk of the *erosion* of EU-derived employment rights despite the government's promise to the contrary'.[23]

Leaving there for the moment my analysis of Keith Ewing's recent writings on the topic of UK and EU labour law, Brexit, and social democracy, I should offer two somewhat personal reasons for having engaged in such a close textual account of those writings. Perhaps indeed I should be offering *excuses* rather than reasons, since I am conscious of having been a bit presumptuous in so doing when Keith Ewing is entitled to speak for himself and is, I am sure, engaged upon the further development of this discourse. Anyway, my first reason or excuse for so doing has been the sheer fascination of following the thinking of a true master of the discipline, to my mind the most vigorous and effective of his generation of scholars at the interface of labour law and constitutional law.

My second reason or excuse for proceeding as I have done is a more immediately pertinent one. I realise in retrospect that as I was working my way through Keith Ewing's writings on this topic, I was more or less consciously seeking a point of convergence between his views and my own. For some time now his concerns in this area have been especially concentrated upon the shortcomings of EU labour law, particularly in its collective aspect, while mine have in the most recent years been more directed towards my fears about the rapid growth of extreme Euro-scepticism in the UK, which has culminated in the grand political and legal impasse which the national debate about Brexit now seems to have reached. It was therefore very significant to me to discover that, in the article on 'Post-Brexit Architecture', he had arrived at a position in which I could fully concur, and that he had articulated arguments which would enable me further to develop my own views on the topic. My perception of that important congruence is developed in the next part of this chapter.

[19] Ibid, 359.

[20] Ibid, 360.

[21] KDE 2017(2) (n 2).

[22] '[I]t remains to be seen of course whether Labour is ever elected to office to implement these policies, and if it is whether it meets the expectations of those who have invested so heavily in the current leadership.' KDE 2017(2) (n 2) 424.

[23] KDE 2017(2) (n 2) 413.

III. Brexit, the EU, and the Pathology of Social Democracy

As the previous section has shown, Keith Ewing and I have converged upon an understanding that very significant threats are posed to social democracy in the UK, or at least what remains thereof, both from the law and politics of the EU and from the law and politics of Brexit as currently pursued. In this section, while acknowledging the growth of the former threats, I nevertheless concentrate more especially on the latter. I attempt to theorise those threats, with some reference to Keith Ewing's writings but primarily by building upon some theoretical propositions which I have previously put forward. This development draws upon the notion of the 'pathology of legal systems' which is articulated in Herbert Hart's *Concept of Law*, and derives from it a different and more immediately applicable notion of the 'pathology of social democracy'. The current state of the law and politics of Brexit in the UK are represented as manifesting that pathology; and finally some possibilities are put forward for progress towards the reconstitution of social democracy in the UK, again alluding to Keith Ewing's writings.

A good point of entry into this more theoretical discussion is to be found in the idea of threats to the Rule of Law. In this context of constitutional theory, I discover further evidence of the convergence between Keith Ewing's analyses and my own. In 2015, he and John Hendy QC published an especially powerful paper castigating various EU Member States and the institutions of the EU itself for their growing disregard for the rule of law with respect to trade union rights.[24] Their central critique in that article is that while 'the proud provisions of the EU treaties [are] a hymn to social democratic values and achievements', including that of respect for the Rule of Law,[25] there is in their view a manifest contradiction between these high proclamations of EU Treaties and the actual institutional law-making and practice of the EU, the latter increasingly driven by an implicitly neoliberal ideology.[26] All of that said, Ewing and Hendy are the first to assert that the UK was already in the vanguard of EU member states in their march down that neoliberal road with regard to trade union rights.[27] Moreover, Keith Ewing in his 'Post-Brexit Architecture' article was ready to recognise the potentially negative implications of Brexit for the observance of the Rule of Law in the UK, especially with regard to the new genre of neoliberal bilateral trade arrangements which he viewed as Brexit's increasingly predictable outcome.[28]

For my part, I have been in recent times equally inclined to theorise current developments in the EU in general and in the UK in particular as representing various kinds of erosion of the Rule of Law; my special focus has been on the Brexit referendum of June 2016 and its aftermath. In one piece of writing,[29] I have argued that the threats posed to the Rule of Law by the current Brexit process can be envisaged as penetrating down into a deep sub-stratum of the political, constitutional and legal foundations upon which the respect for the Rule of Law in the UK is based. In that paper, I identified this sub-stratum as a

[24] K Ewing and J Hendy QC, 'The Eclipse of the Rule of Law: Trade Union Rights and the EU' (2015) 4 *Revista Derecho Social y Empresa* 80 ('KDE and JH 2015').

[25] KDE and JH 2015 (n 24) 84, referring in particular to TEU, art 2.

[26] Ibid, 84 et seq.

[27] Ibid, 81–84.

[28] KDE 2017(2) (n 2) 424.

[29] M Freedland, 'Brexit, the Rule of Law, and the Idea of Sustainable Governance' (2018) Oxford Legal Studies Research Paper No 5/2018 https://ssrn.com/abstract=3117471.

platform of 'sustainable governance', which when fractured destabilises the whole apparatus of observance of the Rule of Law itself.

In another piece of writing in a similar genre, I have homed in more closely on the intersection between public and labour law. Partly in order to identify the dangers of the path currently being taken towards Brexit, I have invoked the idea of 'the isolated worker in the isolated state'.[30] This notion is closely allied to that of the degradation of the Rule of Law, the linking factor being my perception that, in the present era especially, the legal and social rights of workers cannot realistically be realised or maintained in a society or a state which has distanced itself from or opposed itself to the international order to which it previously belonged, in the way that the current Brexit process seems to me to threaten to do.

These arguments can be illustrated or instantiated in many ways, perhaps in the most immediately relevant way by the apparent failure of the current politics of Brexit to generate a viable plan and set of policies for labour migration between the UK and the other EU Member States which will respect the acquired rights and legitimate expectations of EU citizens from other Member States to work and live in the UK, or, on the other hand, those of EU citizens from the UK to live and work elsewhere in the EU. At the moment of writing this chapter the UK Government is reported to be undergoing a major policy shift in this respect, whereby certain rights and expectations of the former group would be guaranteed by the UK Government upon Brexit regardless of whether the EU offers reciprocal arrangements to the latter group.[31] Motivated by a belated perception of the urgency of the UK's need for workers from other EU Member States, this unilateral concession would at the same time demonstrate a readiness if necessary to abandon the claims of UK citizens to comparable treatment in those other Member States after Brexit.

The particular issue of labour migration law and policy is centrally significant to the whole Brexit process; but its unresolved condition is only one symptom of a much more general set of problems with that process. The full and alarming sweep of those problems can perhaps best be displayed by a contemplation of some of the key features of the recently enacted European Union (Withdrawal) Act 2018,[32] and by pointing out the full extent of the threats which are posed by that Act to the Rule of Law and to the UK's substratum of sustainable governance. The government asserted that this legislation has the function of simply severing the direct input of EU Law into UK law at the moment of Brexit while in the short term at least retaining the norms of EU Law which applied in the UK and internalising them into UK domestic law insofar as that had not previously occurred:

> The Act repeals the European Communities Act 1972 (ECA) on the day the United Kingdom leaves the European Union [: it] ends the supremacy of European Union (EU) law in UK law, converts EU law as it stands at the moment of exit into domestic law, and preserves laws made in the UK to implement EU obligations.[33]

[30] M Freedland, 'Reinforcing the Philosophical Foundations of Social Inclusion – The Isolated Worker in the Isolated State' in H Collins and V Mantouvalou (eds), *The Philosophical Foundations of Labour Law* (Oxford, OUP, 2018).

[31] See, 'EU residents will be secure if no Brexit deal says Raab [Dominic Raab, the Minister for Exiting the European Union]' (*BBC News*, 21 August 2018) www.bbc.co.uk/news/uk-politics-45258343.

[32] The European Union (Withdrawal) Act 2018 ('EUWA 2018') received the Royal Assent and became law on 26 June 2018.

[33] 'European Union (Withdrawal) Act 2018 Explanatory Notes' prepared by the Department for Exiting the European Union ('EN 2018'), paras 1–2.

This enterprise of conversion was of course by no means a simple one in either a political or a legal sense, and even if it only went thus far, the Act would have created great areas of legal uncertainty. But right from the outset that ostensibly simple design was supplemented and qualified by two further sets of provisions which were deeply fraught with constitutional complexities. In the first such set of provisions, essentially those of Section 8 of the Act, the legislation endowed the government with ongoing powers, after Brexit has occurred, to modify and adapt the EU laws which have thus been internalised into UK law. As the Explanatory Notes put it:

> [The Act] also creates temporary powers to make secondary legislation to enable corrections to be made to the laws that would otherwise no longer operate appropriately once the UK has left, so that the domestic legal system continues to function correctly outside the EU.[34]

The granting of these powers to the government, for the two years following the UK's exit from the UK,[35] was cast in the most extensive terms, fulfilling the most pessimistic predictions of a 'Henry VIII' clause in this legislation. The power conferred by Section 8 to:'make such provision [by regulations] as the Minister considers appropriate to prevent remedy or mitigate … any deficiency in retained EU law arising from the withdrawal of the United Kingdom from the EU',[36] is elaborated but scarcely in any meaningful sense defined by the Act,[37] and seems to amount to the most swingeing delegation of the legislative powers of Parliament to have occurred in peacetime in the current or any recent century. The potential threat to the constitutional doctrines of the Separation of Powers and the Rule of Law could scarcely be greater.

The dangers presenting themselves from Section 8 of the 2018 Act to the stability and integrity of the UK Constitution after Brexit are thus considerable ones. However, an even more present and immediate danger arises from Section 9 of the Act, which, again according to the Explanatory Notes, gives the government 'a power to make secondary legislation to implement the withdrawal agreement … agreed between the UK and the EU under Article 50(2) of the TEU …'.[38] In this case, the danger consists not so much in the unrestricted nature of the delegation of legislative power[39] as in the almost impossibly uncertain and unpredictable timetable and set of contingent conditions which have been set for it to be exercised. On the one hand, the power is exercisable only down to Brexit day, that is to say only before 31 October 2019 at the latest as matters stand at the time of writing.[40] On the other hand, the power only arises once a withdrawal agreement has been made,[41] and

[34] EN 2018, para 2.

[35] EUWA 2018, s 8(8).

[36] Ibid, s 8(1). The whole section was set up as one gigantic 'Henry VIII clause' by the breath taking provision of s 8(5) that 'Regulations under subsection (1) may make any provision that could be made by an Act of Parliament.'

[37] EUWA 2018, s 8(2)–(4).

[38] EN 2018, para 136.

[39] In fact quite significant restrictions are imposed by s 9(3) – The power cannot be used to impose or increase taxation, make retrospective provision, create a relevant criminal offence, establish a public authority or amend, repeal or revoke the Human Rights Act 1998 (nor legislation made under it).

[40] EUWA 2018, s 9(4).

[41] Ibid, s 9(1) speaks of 'the withdrawal agreement', which can hardly be regarded as having come into existence until it has been struck between the EU Council and the UK Government – at which point it would also need to be ratified by the European Parliament.

apparently also once the UK Parliament has enacted a statute approving the final terms of the withdrawal of the UK from the EU.[42]

The window of time which is left open by those various constraints is by any stretch of the imagination already a narrow one, rapidly being closed by the growing prospect that no withdrawal agreement at all might be reached before Brexit day. This degree of uncertainty as to the nature of many of the legal, administrative, and regulatory arrangements which would apply to the UK and to its relations with the EU and the rest of the world after leaving the EU must be regarded as so profound as to call into question the prospects for the continuation of the sustainable governance of the UK, unless some as yet not apparent path can be found to take the country out of its present political impasse. In order to understand this point, we need to separate out two levels of discussion of this problem – on the one hand, the superficial level at which it has been presented by the UK Government, and on the other hand a deep level at which the legal and constitutional order of the UK is in serious jeopardy.

At the superficial and presentational level, Mrs Theresa May throughout her time as the UK Prime Minister and her allies within her government maintained that the Brexit process offered no serious threat to the prospects for sustainable governance of the UK because, they claimed, there were two viable courses of action which would safeguard those prospects. On the one hand, they contended that there was still the possibility of making and sufficiently implementing a withdrawal agreement before exit day, on the basis of what had become known as the Chequers proposal which the government put forward in July 2018.[43] On the other hand, they also started to maintain that if even no such agreement should be reached, the position of the UK following its withdrawal from the EU in 2019 would still and nevertheless be a viable and reasonably satisfactory one.[44] They began to publish a series of Technical Notes which were put forward as validating that contention.[45] Among them there was, for example, one on Workplace Rights which asserted that the UK Government would simply move to retain existing EU employment rights except with regard to certain aspects of the Insolvency Directive and the European Works Councils Directive, boldly concluding that 'In a "no deal" scenario, there are no expected financial implications or impacts for citizens or businesses operating in the UK (whether UK or EU-based) in regard to workplace rights'.[46]

[42] This seems to be the effect of the concluding clause of EUWA 2018, s 9(1); that is the view taken of that clause in the Explanatory Notes; see EN 2018, para 137.

[43] The Chequers proposal was the subject of a Statement from HM Government made at Chequers on 6 July 2018 reflecting an agreement within the Cabinet – which turned out to be a very short-lived one – as to the UK's position for the negotiation of a withdrawal agreement with the EU: https://assets.publishing.service.gov.uk/government/uploads/system/uploads/attachment_data/file/723460/CHEQUERS_STATEMENT_-_FINAL.PDF. The position was set out in greater deal in, Department for Exiting the European Union, *The future relationship between the United Kingdom and the European Union* (White paper, Cm 9593, 2018) www.gov.uk/government/publications/the-future-relationship-between-the-united-kingdom-and-the-european-union.

[44] See Department for Exiting the European Union, 'Secretary of State Dominic Raab's speech on no deal planning' (23 July 2018) www.gov.uk/government/news/secretary-of-state-dominic-raabs-speech-on-no-deal-planning.

[45] See Department for Exiting the European Union, 'Guidance, UK government's preparations for a no deal scenario' (23 August 2018) www.gov.uk/government/publications/uk-governments-preparations-for-a-no-deal-scenario, and its associated Collection of papers at www.gov.uk/government/collections/how-to-prepare-if-the-uk-leaves-the-eu-with-no-deal.

[46] Department for Business, Energy & Industrial Strategy, 'Guidance, Workplace rights if there's no Brexit deal' (23 August 2018) www.gov.uk/government/publications/workplace-rights-if-theres-no-brexit-deal/workplace-rights-if-theres-no-brexit-deal.

At a deeper level, the situation with regard to Brexit had become and has remained a much more fragile and fractured one. Three basic political stances are in seemingly irreconcilable contention with each other, so that there seems to be a complete absence of political consensus in favour of any one of them:

1. the 'Remain' position, which is that the UK should retain its membership of the EU;
2. the 'Deal' position, which is that the UK should leave the EU but make an agreement for some form of continuing partnership with the EU; and
3. the 'No-deal or 'Hard Brexit' position, which is that the UK should cleanly withdraw from the EU without retaining a special relationship with it.

I would argue that these three positions, between which the UK polity seems to have become deadlocked, actually represent not only three conflicting political stances, but also three competing visions of what the constitutional order of the UK itself should consist of. These are respectively:

1. a vision of the UK as having a constitutional order which is integrated into the EU, 'the EU-integrated constitutional order';
2. a vision of the UK as having a constitutional order which is not integrated into the EU but which is associated with it 'the EU-associated constitutional order'; and
3. a vision of the UK as having a constitutional order which is neither integrated into the EU nor associated with it 'the EU-rejecting constitutional order'.

The realisation from the three years following the Brexit Referendum, for me a painful one, has been of the extent to which the third vision has commanded a growing adherence as a normative view of the deep Constitution of the UK. Masked by a rhetoric of the UK as a 'global state', it is a view of the UK as ideally an autarky, that is to say an economically and politically self-sufficient state and society.

I would take this argument one stage further and contend that there are therefore in play, in the great Brexit controversy, very diverse perceptions, both analytical and normative, of the actual nature and the desirable nature of the legal order or legal system of the UK. Stated in those terms, the discussion seems to me to start to resonate with some elements of Herbert Hart's articulation of the Concept of Law,[47] in particular with his reflections upon the identity and recognition of legal systems and upon the pathology of legal systems.

Hart's general theory of the recognition of legal systems is too justly famous to require elaboration: it will suffice to recall his foundational formulation that:

> There are … two minimum conditions necessary and sufficient for the existence of a legal system. On the one hand, those rules of behaviour which are valid according to the system's ultimate criteria of validity must be generally obeyed, and, on the other hand, its rules of recognition specifying the criteria of legal validity and its rules of change and adjudication must be effectively accepted as common public standards of official behaviour by its officials.[48]

Less widely celebrated, indeed slightly receded from popular view, is his particular notion of 'the pathology of legal systems'. It is rooted in his idea of legal systems as having a life cycle: '… a legal system, like a human being, may at one stage be unborn, at a second not

[47] HLA Hart, *The Concept of Law* (Oxford, OUP, 1961) ('HCL').
[48] HCL (n 47) 116.

yet wholly independent of its mother, then enjoy a healthy independent existence, later decay and finally die'.[49] The idea of 'pathology' refers to a 'halfway stage between normal independent existence and death'; it is mirrored by a notion of 'embryology' which refers to the converse earlier halfway stage between birth and normal independent existence.[50] These halfway stages 'throw into relief the full complexity of what we take for granted when, in the normal case, we make the confident and true assertion that in a given country a legal system exists'.[51]

For Hart, the idea of the pathology of a legal system therefore identifies a complex and transitional phase in which its identity or integrity is in jeopardy to an extent which may, whether immediately or ultimately, be fatal to its very existence. He specifies various manifestations of such pathology of legal systems, the results of different 'disturbing factors' such as 'revolution', 'enemy occupation', 'anarchy', or 'the simple breakdown of ordered legal control in the face of anarchy or banditry'. These are extreme forms of pathology, clearly pointing to the morbidity of the legal system in question, and it may seem incongruous to imply that the Brexit controversy could be seen as placing the legal system of the UK in such a state.

However, Hart does emphasise that exact judgments about the extent or progress of the pathology of legal systems are essentially difficult ones, and moreover that 'The stage in which it is right to say in such cases that the legal system has finally ceased to exist is a thing not susceptible of any exact determination'.[52] Moreover, he says that

> we should notice other forms of partial failure of the normal conditions, the congruence of which is asserted by the unqualified assertion that a legal system exists. The unity among officials, the existence of which is normally presupposed when internal statements of law are made within the system, may partly break down. It may be that, over certain constitutional issues and only over those, there is a division within the official world ultimately leading to a division among the judiciary.[53]

Given this cautious and nuanced way in which Hart specifies his idea of the pathology of legal systems, I find it quite useful to consider the application of that idea to the present state of the Constitution of the UK as it struggles with its great Brexit controversy. It provides a way of understanding the extent of the challenges to the legal system of the UK which are posed by that controversy, and of asking whether that legal system is capable of surviving the strains under which it is placed. It identifies the fact that, when a national constitutional system is placed under extreme political pressure, divergent views of the nature and the ground-rules of its legal system tend to be placed in competition with each other. In such situations, different perceptions of 'the law of the land' are advanced and pursued, and both of Hart's minimum conditions for the existence of a legal system are subjected to stress-testing.

During the course of the great Brexit controversy which has raged in the UK from 2016 onwards, signs of pressure on Hart's first condition have already become evident. The

[49] Ibid, 112.
[50] See HCL (n 47) 112, 117, 119.
[51] Ibid, 112.
[52] Ibid, 118.
[53] Ibid, 121–122.

denunciation of the High Court judges in the *Miller* case[54] as 'enemies of the people' provides a potent example. More fundamentally threatening is an increasingly insistent political demand for explicit and complete excision from the constitutional and legal framework of governance of the UK of any element which can be seen as representing the continued supremacy of EU Law. There were significant formal concessions to this EU-rejecting political position in the Withdrawal Act of 2018;[55] but it is quite evident that this is not sufficient to appease political demands for a secession so absolute as to be very difficult to reconcile with an existing UK legal order which has over the past 45 years become deeply bound up with that of the EU itself.

As to Hart's second condition, that of acceptance by officials of the legal system's rules of recognition, of change, and of adjudication, it is equally clear that many in the junior ranks of the government, and many civil servants high and low, are subjected to intense contestation about the present and future impact of the Brexit process upon those rules. This must make them very uncertain of the character of the public administration which they are charged with maintaining, for example with regard to immigration into and residence in the UK of EU citizens from other Member States and their families.[56] It is debatable how far they have succumbed to those pressures, but the presence and heavy weight of them can scarcely be doubted. It is perfectly possible that both judicial and administrative officials could before long become engulfed in such controversies, particularly if those controversies became enmeshed in legal divergences and policy divergences between the regions of the UK and their partially devolved governments.

Thus we might feel tempted to conclude that the Brexit process has indeed placed or come close to placing the UK legal system in a pathological condition and that this exercise of testing for the 'pathology of a legal system' has indeed advanced our argument about the threats to the Rule of Law and to the maintenance of sustainable governance in the UK. However, some caveats must be entered, which will lead us to turn the argument in a slightly different direction. The first such caveat consists in a reminder that the assessment of the health, and the prospects for survival, of a legal system is a very difficult matter while it is in the midst of a constitutional crisis such as the Brexit controversy has unleashed. The diagnosis and prognosis for the patient undergoing such a crisis can only normally be confirmed from some distance of hindsight.

This difficulty is illustrated in a very perceptive article by Mark D Walters, highly pertinent to our present discussion, which was published in 1999,[57] and which deployed

[54] *R (on the application of Miller and another) v Secretary of State for Exiting the European Union* [2017] UKSC 5, [2018] AC 61. The judges in the High Court were castigated in this way by certain newspapers for their decision, upheld by the Supreme Court, that the government's notification of the withdrawal of the UK from the EU required prior authorisation by statute (which was shortly thereafter provided by Parliament in the shape of the European Union (Notification of Withdrawal) Act 2017).

[55] See (n 32) above; in particular the provision of s 5(1) (to which exceptions are then made) that 'The principle of the supremacy of EU law does not apply to any enactment or rule of law passed or made on or after exit day'.

[56] Compare T Colson, 'EU citizens could be the next victims of Theresa May's "hostile" immigration policy' (*Business Insider UK*, 24 April 2018) www.businessinsider.com/eu-citizens-theresa-may-hostile-environment-immigration-brexit-2018-4?IR=T.

[57] MD Walters, 'Nationalism and the Pathology of Legal Systems: Considering the *Quebec Secession Reference* and its Lessons for the United Kingdom' (1999) 62 *MLR* 371.

Hart's notion of the pathology of legal systems as the basis for an analysis of the outcome and implications of the *Quebec Secession Reference* to the Supreme Court of Canada.[58] While carefully avoiding exact predictions, Walters clearly regarded the legal system of Canada as struggling with the prospect of collapse under the strain of the movement for the secession of Quebec, and he contemplated the real possibility that the legal system of the UK might before long come under comparable separatist pressures, in particular from Scotland. Twenty years later, we would not regard him as having been totally mistaken in either of those analyses: but we would probably think that these two legal systems had survived those particular crises rather better than he was expecting. On the other hand, even three years ago, neither he nor we could have predicted that the grand secessionist crisis of Brexit would be threatening to rekindle separatist fires in Scotland and Northern Ireland.

There is, however, a second and perhaps even stronger reason to be cautious about deploying the notion of 'pathology of legal systems' in our present context. Not only are its diagnoses and prognoses descriptively difficult and uncertain, but they are also apt to be subjective and value-laden – perhaps more so than Hart himself might have cared to acknowledge, in view of his general concern to maintain his Concept of Law as a purely analytical one. A judgment that a legal system is in a 'pathological' condition inevitably carries stigmatic connotations of decay, neglect, and morbidity. Moreover, what appears to one person to be a legal system in that moribund state may seem in the eyes of another to be a different legal system in the course of being born or born again – especially if that other is animated by ideals of liberation and perceptions of tyranny, real or partly imagined.

These are not, in my view, reasons for regarding the 'pathology of legal systems' mode of analysis as irrelevant to our present discussion, but, instead, as a reason to choose a more openly normative and specifically focused criterion of assessment of the state of the UK's legal and constitutional system in the shadow of Brexit. By this route, I arrive at the idea of 'the pathology of social law' as an appropriate one within which to encapsulate the arguments which have been canvassed in the course of this chapter. I find it hard, for the reasons given, to be confident in pronouncing that the UK is experiencing the pathology of its legal system as a whole: but I do feel convinced that it is at least undergoing a pathology of a certain subset of its legal system, namely that of 'social law'.

In invoking this idea of the 'pathology of social law', I draw on a long-established idea of social law, but I use the terminology in a way which somewhat differs from the traditional usage. In that traditional usage, largely an importation from a continental European notion of *droit social, sozialrecht, diritto sociale, etc*, labour law is at the heart of social law but the concept extends outwards mainly in the direction of social security law or social welfare law. I am using the term with a different emphasis; labour law is still at the core of the idea of social law, but its extensions are more towards the area of the fundamental socio-economic rights of citizens and migrants, and towards the location of those rights in the basic constitution of the legal system in question.

[58] Reference by the Governor in Council, pursuant to s 53 of the Supreme Court Act, concerning the secession of Quebec from Canada [1998] 2 SCR 217.

Some may wish to think of this 'pathology of social law'[59] in the UK as a recent and rapidly progressing one, while others will prefer to see it as a long-term and gradual degradation.[60] Regarded as a new pathology, it is one for which the Brexit controversy is not the sole cause or origin, but of which it is certainly promising to be a major precipitating factor. As I have previously indicated, I regard this pathology as consisting particularly of a loss of political willingness for the legal association of the UK with other European nations in socially progressive forms of collaboration, and of the deterioration of such kinds of legal and social association between the citizens of those nations – especially their association as workers in various forms of collective bargaining, collective action, and collective representation.

Reverting to the introduction to this chapter, and to the conclusion of its first section, I make the point that the notion of the pathology of social law, as applied to the present condition of the UK while it is immersed in its great Brexit controversy, has the particular virtue and utility of identifying the point or area of convergence between my particular concerns in this field and those of Keith Ewing. His writings have emphasised that the pathology of social law in the UK, in the sense in which I am using that notion, has its sources both in domestic law and policy and in EU law and policy. Mine have concentrated especially upon what I regard as the socially dissolutive tendencies of UK law and policy which have culminated in the present political drive towards an EU-rejecting form or model of Brexit and post-Brexit international and internal relations. I like to think that both these discourses can sit alongside each other under the conceptual umbrella of the pathology of social law, and of social democracy in an even wider sense.

In the face of such over-arching concerns with a general pathology, it seems slightly incongruous to propose particular remedies for particular parts of the body politic. That said, I nevertheless perceive a special need for reconciliation between UK labour and social law and EU law in the area in which labour and social law intersect with migration law. This has of course been the most sensitive point of interaction, and indeed friction, between UK law and politics and those of the EU at large, as the UK polity has struggled to adapt to the EU law and practice of freedom of movement of workers – so far unsuccessfully, as all the experience of the 2016 Referendum result and its aftermath seem to attest. I argue that this is an adaptation which nevertheless has to be made, and now has to be made in almost the most difficult imaginable circumstances of negotiation of the UK's position vis-à-vis the rest of the EU.

In the absence of some such adaptation, it seems to me that the UK will find itself in a position of national isolation which will be inimical not only to the sustainable governance of the UK in general but also to any immediately likely prospect of realising the ideal of democratic socialism in the UK to which Keith Ewing has rightly attached such overriding importance in his scholarly work and his life in labour and constitutional law. Failing such an adaptation, the UK might indeed become the domain of the isolated worker in the isolated state, a dreary laboratory for researchers into the pathology of social law, and surely a land in which it would be curiously difficult to bring about the constitution of social democracy itself.

[59] I invoke this notion, rather than the narrower one of 'employment deregulation' to denote the degradation of the constitutional 'secondary' rules of social law, rather than simply the degradation of its 'primary rules'.

[60] Others yet might see it as never having arisen simply because fundamental socio-economic rights have never in any meaningful sense been part of the UK's constitutional order. Might Keith Ewing himself perhaps be sceptical of this thesis precisely on that account?

IV. Postscript

As was promised at the outset of the chapter, I am adding this Postscript (in November 2019) in order to explain the chronology of the writing and submitting of this chapter and to locate it within the larger chronology of the Brexit debate and process. I do this in the hope of justifying and sustaining my decision to write about Keith Ewing's position and my position in that debate, at a time when it is fully evident that anything one writes on this topic is all too likely, at one level, to be overtaken by political events and thus to appear to be inherently ephemeral.

My justification for taking this intellectual risk is two-fold: firstly, I feel that we should not, as legal scholars, be totally deterred by fear of ephemerality from writing about this subject even in works designed to have a medium-term or long-term relevance; if we were so deterred, a topic of paramount continuing importance might be paradoxically omitted from the enduring literature precisely because of the fast-changing character which is a function of its supreme significance.

Secondly, I feel that there is a positive value in writing and publishing papers which present snapshots of the state of the debate at particular moments: those snapshots so quickly appear to be faded sepia pictures of a psychologically distant past that it is important to remind ourselves of positions which presented themselves as reasonable and compelling and enduring ones even a short time ago.

It is in that spirit that I detail the chronology of this chapter: it was written in August/ September 2018; it was submitted in February/ March 2019 more or less in its original form and as speaking from its original date. In the intervening time, the challenges to Social Democracy which it describes have in my view assumed even more radical proportions. I have endeavoured to keep it up to date as far as possible during the production process of this book. I realise that this cannot be achieved in precise detail, and I acknowledge that it may not be possible to do justice to the fertile evolution of Keith Ewing's own thinking on this large topic. Even so, I believe that there is a real importance in trying to maintain an ongoing narrative and an ongoing critical conversation even when events are so fast-changing and detailed conclusions so difficult to draw.

19

The Narrowing Constitution: European Constitutionalisms, the Social Market Economy, and the Principle of Accommodation

NICOLA COUNTOURIS*

I. Introduction

Is the EU's constitutional envelope spacious enough to accommodate equally democratically legitimate, if (slightly) different, national variations of capitalism, including variants inspired to neo-Keynesian macroeconomic principles and the social democratic tradition? This is the fundamental question that this chapter seeks to address, primarily through an analysis of the EU's Economic and Social Constitutional discourses as emerging from the Court of Justice of the European Union's (CJEU) interpretation of selected areas of EU primary and secondary legislation, and from the EU's system of economic and monetary governance. Intuitively this is a question that could be answered positively and without hesitation, merely by observing the range of different social and economic models embodied by the 28 Member States of the EU, let alone by comparing the social and economic outcomes generated by these systems. Surely 'unity in diversity' is really what the process of European integration is all about. Or is it?

It has not gone unnoticed that, in the last two decades in particular, the EU has very much tightened its grip on the ways in which a growing number of EU Member States manage their own domestic economic, social, and ultimately political affairs. Since the notorious court decisions in *Viking* and *Laval* 'the fault lines that run between the single market and the social dimension at national level'[1] have been exposed in a rather dramatic fashion, reinforcing the perception that a narrow, free market oriented, EU 'microeconomic constitution' is increasingly asserting itself over long established national social institutions. In the last decade in particular, the EU's emerging 'macroeconomic constitution',[2] shaped by austerity and informed by the dogmas of tight public spending and macroeconomic

* I am grateful to the editors and to Keith Ewing, Mark Freedland, Jeff King, and Luca Ratti for comments and sharing their thoughts on earlier versions of this chapter. The usual disclaimer applies.

[1] M Monti, *A New Strategy for the Single Market* (Brussels, European Commission, 2010) 68.

[2] T Beuker, B de Witte, C Kilpatrick (eds), Constitutional Change through Euro-crisis Law (Cambridge, CUP, 2017).

and fiscal rigour, has had a profound impact on a large number of national constitutional traditions,[3] going as far as demanding some Member States to adopt specific constitutional reforms, effectively 'embedding' neo-monetarism as a constitutionally dominant economic theory. Keith Ewing's seminal article 'The Death of Social Europe'[4] has drawn together these two analytical threads, providing a caustic analysis of how a number of domestic collective bargaining and industrial relations systems have been put under growing strain by direct or indirect EU regulatory intervention.

On the other hand, it should not go unnoticed that some EU Member States, including some that retain a high degree of coordination of their respective economies and labour markets, with substantial levels of taxation and public spending, have been spared from the litany of Country Specific Recommendations requesting other states to engage in public spending cuts, wage bargaining decentralisation, and labour market deregulation. Countries like Sweden, for instance, have never been instructed by EU CSR/European Semester mechanisms to decentralise their collective bargaining regime, and the latest, 2019, Council Specific Recommendations,[5] remains primarily focused on correcting imbalances in the Swedish housing market, focusing investment in education, and ensuring the enforcement of anti-money laundering legislation. State intervention in the economy may well be frowned upon, and event drastically curtailed under EU State Aid and competition law rules, but the 2018 EU State Aid Scoreboard reveals that, somehow, state aid levels in Germany, Austria, and Denmark are four times higher than those in the UK, Italy, and Spain.[6] German company shareholders may well feel aggravated by the strictures of the national codetermination system, but the CJEU reassured the European public that the systems is unqualifiedly compatible with EU law.[7]

Against this mixed, and seemingly contradictory, backdrop the chapter suggests that the EU retains the potential to accommodate a range of national political, economic, and social systems, including relatively strong versions of the 'social democracy' variety. Its ability to do so is not without limits, and may have diminished in recent decades. In this respect it is arguable that the EU's Social and Economic constitutions are somewhat narrowing. But this potential is retained, the chapter argues, on the basis of the (loose) idea of '(highly competitive) social market economy' that the EU explicitly embraces in Article 3(3), TEU, a concept that ought to be used, by the Union, its institutions, and its Member States, to develop a 'principle of accommodation' between a relatively wide range of national political, social, and economic models (and democratic mandates) and the ever developing EU constitutional discourse. Not every model, and not every national mandate, will fit this narrowing constitution, and this is no doubt a matter of concern. But the constitutional envelope of the EU ought to be explored (and expanded) to its maximum effect, before suggesting that it is too tight and that it should therefore be torn apart.

[3] I Katsaroumpas, 'De-Constitutionalising Collective Labour Rights: The Case of Greece' (2018) *Industrial Law Journal* 465–503.

[4] KD Ewing, 'The Death of Social Europe' (2015) 26 *King's Law Journal* 76.

[5] Commission, 'Recommendation for a Council Recommendation on the 2019 National Reform Programme of Sweden and delivering a Council opinion on the 2019 Convergence Programme of Sweden' COM (2019) 527 final.

[6] European Commission, 'State Aid Scoreboard 2018' http://ec.europa.eu/competition/state_aid/scoreboard/index_en.html.

[7] Case C-566/15, *Erzberger v TUI AG* ECLI:EU:C:2017:562.

II. The 'Neutral Constitution' Revisited

The idea of 'constitutional neutrality' requires some further analysis. The concept has often been pronounced in high-sounding terms as evoking the view, rendered famous by Holmes J's dissenting opinion in *Lochner*, that

> a constitution is not intended to embody a particular economic theory, whether of paternalism and the organic relation of the citizen to the State or of laissez faire[8]

and that the democratic structures of the state are granted the broadest margin of appreciation in deciding national economic policies. There are numerous examples of courts deploying the 'concept of the economic neutrality of the constitution',[9] in some form or shape, both in Europe and in the US.

The reality of economic 'constitutional neutrality' is however, and arguably, slightly more nuanced than the term might suggest. All those twentieth century post-war, and anti-Fascist, constitutions that embraced and protected the fundamental right to private property, were in effect bound to exclude a priori command and centrally planned economies from the palette of possible future economic policy directions. And these constitutions typically contained long lists of civil and economic freedoms protected as fundamental rights.[10] Of course, most of these constitutions also embodied important constitutional social rights, including sometimes positive commitments to the idea of a 'social'[11] or a 'welfare' state. And most of them, while protecting 'private economic enterprise', also postulated that the latter 'may not be carried out against the common good or in such a manner that could damage safety, liberty and human dignity' asking the law to 'provide for appropriate programmes and controls so that public and private-sector economic activity may be oriented and co-ordinated for social purposes'.[12]

So, it is perhaps more accurate, looking at the vast majority of post-WW2 national European constitutions to speak of varieties of 'broad', rather than 'neutral', constitutions that sought to render totalitarianism, collectivism, but also paleo-liberalism incompatible with the emerging European political landscape, and promoted instead a broad range of social state models. As summarised by Ewing (by reference to Italy, but the point could be applied more generally), in his much more comprehensive comparative constitutional overview on economic rights:

> What emerges here is the presence of some fairly liberal principles in a social democratic wrapping: the right to private property, and the right to compensation if the property is appropriated.

[8] *Lochner v New York*, 198 U.S. 45 (1905), Mr Justice Holmes dissenting.

[9] J Baquero Cruz, *Between Competition and Free Movement The Economic Constitutional Law of the European Community* (Oxford, Hart Publishing, 2000) 34–35.

[10] Article 33 of the 1978, post-Franchist Spanish Constitution expressly protected '*el derecho a la propiedad privada y a la herencia*', while stating that '*La función social de estos derechos delimitará su contenido*'. Similarly, since 1975 Art 17 of the Hellenic Constitution has placed the right to private property under the protection of the state, while providing that the right cannot be exercised against 'the general interest'.

[11] J King, 'Social Rights, Constitutionalism, and the German Social State Principle' (2014) 1 *e-Pública Revista Eletrónica de Direito Público* 19. It was only in 1986 that Art 25(1) of the Greek Constitution was modified to include an express reference to a '*Κοινωνικό κράτος δικαίου*' or 'social rule of law', cf, Ι. Ιγγλεζάκης, *Κοινωνικό κράτος δικαίου* (Εκδόσεις Σάκκουλα, 2005).

[12] Article 41 of the Italian Constitution, adopted in 1948. See also the Preamble to the French Constitutions of 1946 and 1958 recalling Art 17 of the *Déclaration des droits de l'homme et du citoyen de 1789*, which expressly protected private property as '*un droit inviolable et sacré*' that can only be limited '*lorsque la nécessité publique, légalement constatée, l'exige évidemment, et sous la condition d'une juste et préalable indemnité*'.

> Although there is a formal recognition of free enterprise, there is also a notable formal recognition of the social function of private property.[13]

Often perceived or described as mixed-economic systems, the majority of post-WW2 Western European nations pursued a range of economic policies that Ewing described as falling within a renewed social-democratic tradition,[14] that saw a considerable involvement on the part of the state in managing the economy. Some of this involvement fell squarely within the Keynesian recipe of public investment for the sake of stimulating growth, demand, and employment.[15] It was what in a recent article on Social Europe Sidelsky referred to as Keynes' idea of socialising investments, noting that socialising or 'nationalising the capital stock' was not necessarily part of Keynes original idea.[16]

But some European states went well beyond that and actually decided to put or retain into public hands a substantial part of the economic infrastructure, including key components of the natural industrial and service base.[17] This type of public spending and involvement was not just anti-cyclical in nature, but was, or purported to be of a more structural character, seeking – in countries like Italy, the UK, and France – to place into 'public ownership … many of the important means of production, distribution and exchange'.[18] Some of them went as far as excluding the possibility that certain services described as public could end up falling into private hands,[19] although more recent constitutional amendments may have somewhat reduced the original rigour and scope of such provisions.[20]

We know, because Ewing has explained it to us on a number of occasions, that in that respect, the UK Constitution was particularly broad:

> The constitution was a means through which democratic socialist governments governed without serious impediment or restraint, with a wide range of recognisably democratic socialist initiatives being implemented by legislation between 1945 and 1951 in particular.[21]

This was pretty much the context in which the macroeconomic constitutions of Western European states operated for a large part of the second half of the twentieth century. But, as we all know, from 1957 national constitutions were tasked with interacting with an emerging 'new legal order of international law', the law of the European Communities.

[13] K Ewing, 'Economic Rights' in M Rosenfeld and A Sajó (eds), *Oxford Handbook of Comparative Constitutional Law* (Oxford, OUP, 2012) 1036, 1042–1043.

[14] Ibid, 1041.

[15] L Pasinetti and B Schefold, *The Impact of Keynes on Economics in the 20th Century* (Cheltenham, Edward Elgar, 1999); PA Hall, *The Political Power of Economic Ideas Keynesianism across Nations* (Princeton, Princeton University Press, 1989).

[16] Sidelsky, R, 'Keynes and Social Democracy' https://www.project-syndicate.org/commentary/keynes-and-social-democracy-today?barrier=accesspaylog.

[17] See IT Berend, *An Economic History of Twentieth-Century Europe – Economic Reguumes from Laissez-Faire to Globalisation*, 2nd edn (Cambridge, CUP, 2016) esp ch 5; Contra see F Sejersted, *The Age of Social Democracy: Norway and Sweden in the Twentieth Century* (Princeton, Princeton University Press, 2011) esp ch 1.

[18] KD Ewing, 'Democratic Socialism and Labour Law' (1995) 24 *Industrial Law Journal* 103.

[19] Eg, Art 87 of the German Grundgesetz see K König, 'Developments in Privatisation in the Federal Republic of Germany' (1988) 54 *International Review of Administrative Sciences* 517.

[20] M Sah and D Daintith, 'Privatisation and the Economic Neutrality of the Constitution' [1993] *Public Law* 465.

[21] Ewing, 'Democratic Socialism and Labour Law' (n 18) 104.

III. The European Economic Constitution from Rome to Lisbon

The coming into force of the Treaty of Rome in 1958 was not the constitutional game changer we now rightly recognise in the EU Treaties, at least in the area of labour and social rights. This is because, as explored by authors such as Scharpf, Giubboni, and others,[22] the establishment of the EEC was very much premised on a clear constitutional decoupling between the operation and regulation of supranational market freedoms and the activities of national welfare and social states. So it was for the EEC and its institutions to make sure that its microeconomic constitution ruled on market freedom and on creating and maintaining the conditions for undistorted competition, but it remained the exclusive prerogative of Member States to decide on their welfare policies, on social expenditure and of course on labour law (though of course from the 1970s the EEC would begin to intervene in this last area, albeit very incrementally).

Of course part of the idea of having a common market with undistorted competition was that Member States would not distort it themselves through unlawful state aid. But we should not think that this prevented Member States that sought to pursue ambitious nationalisation processes from doing so. As all those who have read *Costa v ENEL*[23] know, Italian socialist governments were still proceeding with nationalising the national energy sector well into the 1960s, unhindered by EEC Law, just as the UK (a non EEC country) was placing again under public ownership its steel industry, in 1967.

To be clear, the British post-WW2 welfare state (and to a certain extent other European social states) was built on high levels of public spending and public borrowing during years where the levels of national debt already exceeded 200 per cent of the nation's gross domestic product.[24] Elsewhere in Europe, and throughout the 1960s, Keynesian policies (and the public purse) were used, for instance, to assist the development of the Italian Mezzoggiorno, at a time where 'economic policy was directed towards the achievement of a welfare state'.[25]

It would be naïve to suggest that nothing much changed between the Treaty of Rome and the Treaty of Maastricht in terms of the monetary and macroeconomic ideologies, institutions, and arrangements shaping the European continent. Those were indeed the decades where the post-WW2 economic boom was starting to falter, where the first creeks in the Bretton-Woods armoury started becoming apparent, where 'stagflation' would manifest itself as a product of the excesses of Keynesian policies,[26] and where the New Right would rise on the back of new economic ideologies. And not solely in the US or Britain.

[22] S Giubboni, *Diritti e solidarietà in Europa: I modelli sociali nazionali nello spazio giuridico europeo* (Bologna, Il Mulino, 2012) esp ch 1; F Scharpf, 'The European Social Model: Coping with the Challenges of Diversity' (2002) *Journal of Common Market Studies* 645.

[23] Case C-6/64 *Costa v ENEL* [1964] ECR 593.

[24] M Kepp, 'Government borrowing, debt and debt interest: historical statistics and forecasts' (House of Commons Library, Briefing Paper Number 05745, 4 September 2019) 5 https://researchbriefings.parliament.uk/ResearchBriefing/Summary/SN05745 reports that in 1946/1947 public sector net debt amounted to 259% of the UK's GDP.

[25] P Bini, 'Keynesianism in Italy' in RW Dimand and H Hagemann, *The Elgar Companion to John Maynard Keynes* (Cheltenham, Edward Elgar, 2019) 613.

[26] Though see JA Zinn, 'Stagflation and the Rejection of Keynesian Economics: A Case of Naïve Falsification' MPRA Paper No 50536/2013 https://mpra.ub.uni-muenchen.de/50536/.

In the German election campaign of 1972, Helmut Schmidt, then still a Federal Minister for Economics under the charismatic Willy Brandt, 'made the famous statement, "better 5 per cent of inflation than 5 percent of unemployment" … [h]owever with mounting inflationary pressures in the 1970s and a strong increase in unemployment in the 1974–75 recession, Keynesian ideas lost ground in [German] economic theory and policy'.[27]

But for the purposes of the argument this chapter is trying to develop, it may be possible to suggest that the major change was arguably, and with hindsight, the introduction, in 1972, of the so-called European 'currency snake' (eventually institutionalised in 1979 as the European Monetary System, the EMS), a European post-Bretton Woods arrangements that sought to link most EEC countries' national currencies in order to prevent large fluctuations, by containing them within a band around +/- 2 to 6 per cent. Soon, the German Mark (the currency of the eventually unified Germany) emerged as the reference currency within the EMS, and it became clear, in the best neo-institutionalist tradition, that the development of an embryonic monetary system required the adoption of further and more institutionalised policies in order to reach the originally anticipated objectives.

The Delors EMU Report of 1989[28] is arguably worth reading as a prime example of the functioning of this type of 'spill-over' policy effect. There we can find the first example of a structured policy thinking around the idea of 'avoid[ing] unsustainable differences between individual member countries in public-sector borrowing requirements and place binding constraints on the size and the financing of budget deficits'.[29] An idea that would eventually develop into the (in)famous 'Maastricht Criteria' outlined by article 109j.1 of the Maastricht Treaty, and the attached Protocol on the Convergence Criteria and Protocol on the Excessive Deficit Procedure, and eventually shape what is now known as the European Monetary Union, EMU, a process eventually leading to the adoption of the Eurocurrency.

A central argument of this chapter is that, inevitably, all these institutional (but also fundamentally ideological) developments determined a progressive narrowing of the spectrum of national economic and fiscal policy options. In a way, they also determined a narrowing on the once broad, or broader, national constitutions.

Admittedly, and unsurprisingly, the post-Maastricht period also coincides with a phase of marked ideological shifts in Western Europe, with profound effects on the very foundations of social-democracy, and the dominant emergence of Third Way/Neue Mitte ideologues,[30] that – as noted by Fredman – 'caricature social democracy by portraying the state as suffocating and interventionist and equality as conformist'.[31] But this ideological confluence between neomonetarism and the Third Way, no doubt also determined some of the design flaws of the EMU.

[27] H Hagemann, 'Keynesianism in Germany' in RW Dimand and H Hagemann, *The Elgar Companion to John Maynard Keynes* (Cheltenham, Edward Elgar, 2019) 599.

[28] J Delors, 'Report on economic and monetary union in the European Community' (*EU Commission*, 17 April 1989) http://aei.pitt.edu/1007/.

[29] Ibid, para 19.

[30] T Blair and G Shroeder, 'Europe: The Third Way/Die Neue Mitte' (Friedrich Ebert Foundation, June 1998) http://library.fes.de/pdf-files/bueros/suedafrika/02828.pdf.

[31] S Fredman, 'The Ideology of New Labour Law' in C Barnard, S Deakin and G Morris (eds), *The Future of Labour Law* (Oxford, Hart Publishing, 2004) 39.

The EMU is premised on a very unstable policy framework, and right from its inception it was criticised, left and right, as offering a rather fragile framework for Europe's macroeconomic constitution. One of its key fragilities arises from the inherent asymmetries that afflict it. On the one hand the ECB enjoys an exclusive monetary policy competence (printing currency, deciding interest rate and lending terms). But on the other the EU only has a limited competence to *coordinate* national economic policies, it has no common fiscal policy or redistribution mechanism (in fact there is even a 'no bail-out/write off' clause in Articles 123–125, TFEU, which Member States have had to circumvent and which has been subject to major constitutional litigation in Karlsruhe)[32] and therefore essentially relies on controlling national budget deficits through fiscal rigour and arrangements such as the Stability Pact introduced in Amsterdam to avoid or mitigate what economists refer to as 'asymmetric shocks' within the EMU area. As pointed out by Joerges, 'What the President of the Bundesbank Helmut Schlesinger had argued in the Maastricht litigation is, by now, common wisdom: the separation of monetary policy from fiscal and economic policy, which the Treaty of Maastricht established, is a design failure'.[33] But there was nothing technocratic about this design flaw: 'the EMU was understood as a political project, albeit one that was to be shielded strictly from the influence of daily politics, and entrusted to the medium of law instead, and to a strictly politically independent institution',[34] the European Central Bank. Successive treaty reforms enshrined this ideological shift in the constitutional documents of the EU. Title VIII of what is now the TFEU is the embodiment of this visible constitutionalisation of neo-monetarist ideology.

A recent 'Research Briefing'[35] produced for the European Parliament perfectly illustrates this neo-monetarist drift, and locates it primarily in the prerogatives of the institutions regulating the EMU. 'The independent status of the ECB towards national governments, but also its monetary transmission mechanism and price stability goal are in line with Monetarist principles',[36] the document begins. It continues by noting that:

> While other central banks, e.g. the Federal Reserve, have a threefold mandate to achieve high employment, price stability and maintain moderate long-term interest rates, the ECB follows only one overarching macroeconomic goal. According to Article 127.1 and Article 282.2 of the Lisbon Treaty on the Functioning of the European Union (TFEU), the primary objective of the European System of Central Banks (ESCB) is price stability.[37]

It is worth noting – cursorily at this point as this issue is further addressed in the following sections – that just as the EU macroeconomic constitution was developing in such an unsatisfactory manner, its micro economic constitution was also starting to impinge more and more visibly on national labour law systems in particular. EU law became a

[32] BVerfG, Judgment of the Second Senate of 07 September 2011 – 2 BvR 987/10, www.bundesverfassungsgericht.de/SharedDocs/Entscheidungen/EN/2011/09/rs20110907_2bvr098710en.html.

[33] C Joerges, 'Social Justice in an Ever More Diverse Union' Zentra Working Papers In Transnational Studies, No 62/2015, 12 https://ssrn.com/abstract=2697440.

[34] C Joerges, 'The European Economic Constitution and its Transformation through the Financial Crisis' ZenTra Working Paper in Transnational Studies No 47/2015, 10 https://ssrn.com/abstract=2560245.

[35] C Karakas, 'The ECB and the financial crisis Rigid theory vs a pragmatic approach' (*European Parliamentary Research Services Briefing*, July 2015) www.europarl.europa.eu/RegData/etudes/BRIE/2015/565876/EPRS_BRI%282015%29565876_EN.pdf.

[36] Ibid, 4.

[37] Ibid.

tool facilitating the privatisation processes that had already begun at a national level in most Member States, eventually developing its own internal logic.[38] The *Viking* and *Laval* saga in 2007 are the primary example of this process, with the emergence of the spectre of maximum harmonisation in the areas of European labour and social law, and what is worse that of 'maximum harmonisation' shaped by market integration priorities.[39]

But of course 2007 also coincides with the beginning of the financial and economic crisis, a crisis that would go on to engulf the EU for the decade to come. The EU's initial response to this crisis was the introduction of increasingly stringent EU level controls over national budget deficits through measures from such as the Stability and Growth Pact; the European Semester; Six Pack; the Fiscal Compact (requiring national Parliaments to balance their national budgets and to avoid government deficits exceeding 0.5 per cent of the national GDP). These reforms created the policy context for further and more targeted measures directed to particular Member States whose macroeconomic imbalances were such as to warrant specific financial assistance programmes. These programmes were typically accompanied by stringent conditionality requirements driving both economic policy reforms and, at times, constitutional reforms.

IV. The Crisis, Austerity, and the Narrowing National Constitutions

In the aftermath of the 2008 crisis, and with the increasingly dogmatic emergence of austerity driven policies backed by a number of EU institutions and by the IMF, the shrinking EU macroeconomic constitution eventually begun to influence the very letter of the national (once broad) constitutions. Germany led by example in 2009, by amending its own Constitution to introduce *Schuldenbremse*, a debt brake that even the Economist rightly depicted as a 'fiscal straitjacket' but also a possible model for other European national constitutions.[40] Under its provisions, the federal government was required to cut its structural deficit to 0.35 per cent of GDP by 2016 and the Länder must eliminate theirs entirely by 2020.

In 2011 Spain also tweaked with Article 135 of its Constitution so as to give constitutional status to the principle of budgetary stability. This was no spontaneous reform. 'This amendment was initiated a few days after Zapatero received a letter from the European Central Bank in August 2011 urging him to "take bold measures to ensuring the sustainability of public finances"'.[41]

[38] J Clifton, J Comin and D Diaz, 'Privatizing public enterprises in the European Union 1960–2002: ideological, pragmatic, inevitable?' (2006) 13 *JEEP* 736; J Clifton, J Comin, D Diaz Fuentes, *Privatisation in the European Union – Public Enterprises and Integration* (Boston Mass., Springer, 2013).

[39] There is a vast literature on the topic. Cf, M Freedland and J Prassl, *Viking, Laval and Beyond* (Oxford, Hart Publishing, 2014) offering a compelling analysis and a comprehensive coverage of references up to 2014.

[40] 'Germany's debt brake – Tie your hands, please – Is Germany's fiscal straitjacket an example for others?' *The Economist* (London, 10 December 2011).

[41] L Diez Sanchez, 'Spain: Dealing with the Economic Emergency through Constitutional Reform and Limited Parliamentary Intervention' in T Beukers, B de Witte and C Kilpatrick (eds), *Constitutional Change through Euro-Crisis Law* (Cambridge, CUP, 2017) 201.

In 2012, the Italian Constitution was formally amended with the introduction of a new obligation in its Article 81, essentially constraining the ability of the Italian state to borrow and run government deficits outside certain parameters. This reform was also triggered by a stern letter drafted, a year before, by the incoming ECB President Mario Draghi, to the then Italian PM Silvio Berlusconi, and successively leaked to Italian newspaper *Corriere della Sera*.[42] The letter demanded structural reforms ranging from the decentralisation of sectoral collective bargaining to large scale privatisation, and crucially requested '*una riforma costituzionale che renda più stringenti le regole di bilancio*'.

V. The Labour Constitution within the 'Narrowing Constitution'

Ewing rightly notes that 'So far as economic rights are concerned, it is in relation to the economic rights of labour that social democratic constitutions make what is their most distinctive contribution'.[43] If this is so, then it is possible to argue that the EU narrowing constitution has not just constrained the ability of Member States to relax the public purses in times of economic crisis, but has also chipped away substantial room of manoeuvre in terms of embracing particular models of industrial relations and, to a certain extent, labour protection systems.

In 'The Death of Social Europe'[44] Ewing ascribed 'the displacement of social democracy by neo-liberalism' in Europe to 'the subordination of labour rights generally – and … collective bargaining specifically – to more closely coordinated national economic policies'[45] developing under the auspices of the Europe 2020 agenda as reinforced by financial assistance packages. It was a painstakingly meticulous deconstruction of the nefarious influences of the EU macroeconomic constitution on national labour constitutions. A tale of Recommendations, Guidelines, and Memoranda of Understanding encouraging and at time effectively imposing the rapid decentralisation of wage setting mechanisms and, in practice, the eventual demise of centralised collective bargaining structures, in countries as diverse as Belgium, Portugal, Ireland, Romania, and Greece.

A repeat of the systematic enquiry lead by Ewing in 2014 on the same sources would reveal that not much has changed in the last half decade. With the exception of two countries, Germany and Sweden, all other EU Member States still endowed with centralised sector level systems of collective bargaining and wage setting have continued to receive encouragements to deregulate and decentralise. Hopes were raised by the adoption of the European Pillar of Social Rights in 2017, and in particular its Principle 8, that expressly 'encouraged [the social partners] to negotiate and conclude collective agreements'. All 2018 Country Specific Recommendations, expressly referred to the European Pillar of Social Rights, but

[42] 'C'è l'esigenza di misure significative per accrescere il potenziale di crescita' (*Corriere della Sera*, 5 August 2011) www.corriere.it/economia/11_settembre_29/trichet_draghi_italiano_405e2be2-ea59-11e0-ae06-4da866778017.shtml?refresh_ce-cp.

[43] Ewing, 'Economic Rights' (n 13) 1043.

[44] Ewing, 'The Death of Social Europe' (n 4).

[45] Ibid 76 and 87.

six of them (the ones addressed to Bulgaria,[46] France,[47] Croatia,[48] Italy,[49] Romania,[50] and Finland[51]), continued to request action on wage setting mechanisms and collective bargaining. The latest 2019 CSRs offer similar or renewed advice to Bulgaria,[52] Croatia,[53] Cyprus,[54] Italy,[55] and Romania.[56]

VI. Contestation, Coexistence, and Reversibility

The previous paragraphs have illustrated a bleak picture of the European economic constitution, and its impact on national social and labour constitutions. This section seeks to add to that picture and shed some light on some contrasting phenomena that could prima facie appear as inconsistent with the dominant vision depicted so far. It will be argued that while these phenomena do not act as a countervailing force capable of reversing recent policy trends, they offer hope for a possible accommodation between fairly diverse national constitutions and the (admittedly) narrowing European one. This accommodation is often premised on a robust contestation dynamic where national regimes simply reject some of the constraints seemingly imposed to satisfy supranational demands or expectations. Sometimes it is premised on a tacit coexistence between seemingly antithetical policy and regulatory paradigms.

[46] Commission, 'Recommendation for a Council Recommendation on the 2018 National Reform Programme of Bulgaria and delivering a Council opinion on the 2018 Convergence Programme of Bulgaria' COM (2018) 402 final.

[47] Commission, 'Recommendation for a Council Recommendation on the 2018 National Reform Programme of France and delivering a Council opinion on the 2018 Stability Programme of France' COM (2018) 409 final.

[48] Commission, 'Recommendation for a Council Recommendation on the 2018 National Reform Programme of Croatia and delivering a Council opinion on the 2018 Convergence Programme of Croatia' COM (2018) 410 final, 'Lack of coherence in the wage-setting frameworks in the public administration and public services impede equality of treatment and government's control over the public wage bill'.

[49] Commission, 'Recommendation for a Council Recommendation on the 2018 National Reform Programme of Italy and delivering a Council opinion on the 2018 Stability Programme of Italy' COM(2018) 411 final, suggesting that 'bargaining at firm or territorial level remains limited, also due to the prevalence of small firms in Italy. This may prevent wages from adapting swiftly to local economic conditions'.

[50] Commission, 'Recommendation for a Council Recommendation on the 2018 National Reform Programme of Romania and delivering a Council opinion on the 2018 Convergence Programme of Romania' COM (2018) 422 final.

[51] Commission, 'Recommendation for a Council Recommendation on the 2018 National Reform Programme of Finland and delivering a Council opinion on the 2018 Stability Programme of Finland' COM (2018) 425 final, 'Wage setting practices are changing and moving towards sectoral and local level bargaining. … this should allow more wage differentiation between firms, ensuring that real wage increases are in line with productivity growth'.

[52] Commission, 'Recommendation for a Council Recommendation on the 2019 National Reform Programme of Bulgaria and delivering a Council opinion on the 2019 Convergence Programme of Bulgaria' COM(2019) 502 final.

[53] Commission, 'Recommendation for a Council Recommendation on the 2019 National Reform Programme of Croatia and delivering a Council opinion on the 2019 Convergence Programme of Croatia' COM(2019) 511 final.

[54] Commission, 'Recommendation for a Council Recommendation on the 2019 National Reform Programme of Cyprus and delivering a Council opinion on the 2019 Stability Programme of Cyprus' COM(2019) 513 final, 'The containment of the public-sector wage bill, which has been a significant factor in fiscal consolidation in Cyprus, warrants continuation'.

[55] Commission, 'Recommendation for a Council Recommendation on the 2019 National Reform Programme of Italy and delivering a Council opinion on the 2019 Stability Programme of Italy' COM(2019) 512 final.

[56] Commission, 'Recommendation for a Council Recommendation on the 2019 National Reform Programme of Romania and delivering a Council opinion on the 2019 Convergence Programme of Romania' COM(2019) 523 final.

And on occasion it is premised on a residual 'reversibility' option that remains, and ought to remain, on the plate of a democratic Europe.

It may be opportune to begin by reminding ourselves that, similarly to Spain and Italy, other EU Member States were pushed into embracing constitutional reforms embedding fiscal rigour as a structural element of domestic economic policy. But some resisted the urge or temptation to do so and, as noted by Ginsburg, 'The EMU suggestion for constitutional amendment seems to have been ignored entirely in other member states'.[57] A number of Member States placed budgetary constraints in (easily reversible) primary legislation, other appearing to have taken no action at all.[58]

No less importantly, some Member States that had implemented such reforms, partly reframed them, often by means of judicial intervention at the hands of their supreme or constitutional courts. An exemplary case is the Italian Constitutional Court decision that, in 2015, reversed the public sector pay freeze produced by the suspension of collective wage setting mechanisms introduced with Decree Law No 98 of 6 July 2011, aptly headed 'Urgent provisions on financial stabilisation'.[59] In the hearing, the government had argued that the pay freeze 'was responding to the objective of respecting a balanced budget (Article 81 of the Constitution) adopting policies projected in a timeframe that necessarily surpassed a single year'. But the Court reached the conclusion that

> The now systematic nature of this suspension has thus crossed the line, thereby now striking an unreasonable balance between trade union freedom (Article 39(1) of the Constitution), … and the requirements relating to the rational distribution of resources and control of spending within a coherent financial programme (Article 81(1) of the Constitution).[60]

While the 2017 Social Pillar initiative does not appear to have been a turning point for the Commission's Recommendations, the 2019 CRS also summoned Germany for its persistently stagnating wages, the document noting that 'Strengthening the conditions to promote wage growth would support domestic demand and contribute to euro area rebalancing'.[61] A similar encouragement was offered to the Netherlands.[62] It also worth noting that Sweden, a country renowned for its highly coordinated system of industrial relations and centralised bargaining, has survived some two decades of Recommendations completely unscathed. In its latest National Reform Programme, the Swedish Government boasted:

> The social partners are responsible for wage formation on the Swedish labour market, and they safeguard their autonomy as a party. The fundamental components of the model include trade unions with a high organisation rate, employer organisations with broad membership, the strong status of collective agreements, workplace representatives with a mandate to negotiate, as well as the independence of the social partners from central government. […] At present there are

[57] T Ginsburg, 'Balanced Budget Provisions in Constitutions' in T Ginsburg, MD Rosen, G Vanberg (eds), *Constitutions in Times of Financial Crisis* (Cambridge, CUP, 2019) 62.

[58] Ibid.

[59] Sentenza 178/2015 (ECLI:IT:COST:2015:178).

[60] Ibid, para 17.

[61] Commission, 'Recommendation for a Council Recommendation on the 2019 National Reform Programme of Germany and delivering a Council opinion on the 2019 Stability Programme of Germany' COM (2019) 505 final, para 18.

[62] Commission, 'Recommendation for a Council Recommendation on the 2019 National Reform Programme of the Netherlands and delivering a Council opinion on the 2019 Stability Programme of the Netherlands' COM (2019) 519 final.

about 680 central collective agreements on wages and general terms and conditions of employment in Sweden.[63]

So there is perhaps more to the complexities of the EU's macroeconomic constitution, and its relationship with the domestic labour constitutions, than meets the eye, and there is certainly more to elaborate on in order to appreciate fully the complexities of the relationship between the narrowing European constitution (and there is no doubt cast in this chapter in respect of its constant narrowing) and national constitutions. There may be more examples to be summoned through systematic research in support of the suggestion that pockets of social-democratic experimentation are still achievable within the EU and compatible with the idea of a 'highly competitive social market economy' enshrined, but not explained, in Article 3(3), TEU. There may be more examples of successful contestation to be identified in the interstitial spaces of national jurisprudential traditions and even administrative practice.

Perhaps most importantly there may be further attempts to test the 'reversibility' of the counter-revolutionary reforms (to borrow another expression from Ewing's work)[64] depicted, admittedly with a very broad brush, in the previous sections of this chapter. Will Greece, for instance, be able to turn the clock back on the reforms implemented under the terms of the Memoranda of Understanding?[65] It is worth noting that some of the most egregious restrictions to collective bargaining introduced during the austerity years, had been partly or wholly reversed by the previous, left-leaning, Greek executive.[66] Another opportunity to test the reversibility of the obsessive deregulatory focus of the EU institutions vis-à-vis national wage setting mechanisms could emerge from the latest social agenda presented by the newly appointed Commission, instructing the new Commissioner-designate for Jobs to 'put forward a legal instrument to ensure that every worker in our Union has a fair minimum wage. This can be set through collective agreements or legal provisions, depending on each country's traditions'.[67]

VII. The 'Social Market Economy' and the Principle of Accommodation

In his recent article on 'Jeremy Corbyn and the Law of Democracy'[68] Ewing identifies a crucial contradiction within the EU Treaties' constitutional set up, exemplified by the

[63] Regeringskansliet, 'Sweden's National Reform Programme 2018 – Europe 2020 – the EU's strategy for smart, sustainable and inclusive growth' (2018) 46 https://ec.europa.eu/info/sites/info/files/2018-european-semester-national-reform-programme-sweden-en.pdf.

[64] Ewing, 'The Death of Social Europe' (n 4) 76.

[65] Papadopoulos appears to suggest this might not be the case until at least 2022, though the recently elected centre-right government is unlikely to want to test this proposition. See N Papadopoulos, 'Austerity-based labour market reforms in Greece vs fundamental rights in the aftermath of the European debt crisis: An analysis of supranational & national bodies' jurisprudence' (2019) *European Public Law*, forthcoming.

[66] Cf, ΝΟΜΟΣ ΥΠ' ΑΡΙΘΜ. 4475 ΦΕΚ Α 83 – 12.06.2017, in particular Άρθρο 5 -Ελεύθερες συλλογικές διαπραγματεύσεις.

[67] European Commission, 'Ursula von der Leyen, President-elect of the European Commission – Mission Letter – Nicolas Schmit' (10 September 2019) 5 https://ec.europa.eu/commission/sites/beta-political/files/mission-letter-nicolas-schmit_en.pdf.

[68] K Ewing, 'Jeremy Corbyn and the Law of Democracy' (2017) 29 *King's Law Journal* 343.

tension between paragraphs (1) and (2) of Article 119, TFEU, on the one hand, and the third paragraph of Article 3, TEU on the other. The former commit EU and Member States' action in the economic policy sphere and in the governance of the euro currency, to the 'principle of an *open market* economy with free competition'. The latter set for the EU the overarching objective of working for the 'sustainable development of Europe based on ... a highly competitive and *social market* economy'. Ewing rightly reminds us that 'while US experience teaches that liberal democratic constitutions do not enable social democratic structures to be built, EU experience in contrast teaches that social democratic constitutions do not guarantee that such structures can be retained'.[69] It is not enough to proclaim that the EU should operate on the basis of a social market economy, when one of its crucial policies – the EMU – is underpinned by partisan imperatives such as 'stable prices, sound public finances and monetary conditions and a sustainable balance of payments'.[70] So how exactly does a 'social market economy' influence EU regulation and policy making, if at all?

An important indication of how the EU tries to reconcile the apparent contradiction between the 'open market' ambitions and the 'social market' aspirations of its project can arguably be found in the decision of the CJEU in C-201/15 – *AGET Iraklis*.[71] On the face of it, this decision was about the compatibility between the Greek Ministry of Labour power to veto collective redundancies – a vestigial prerogative that several European national public authorities enjoyed in the heyday of social democracy and until the 1980s – and the EU rules on free movement of services and establishment. But more profoundly, the decision was also about the ongoing bras-de-fer between the then left leaning, Syriza led, Greek Government and the IMF-ECB-EC 'Troika', the latter demanding a complete deregulation of the national collective redundancies regime, with EU Directive 98/59/EC in effect becoming (at best) a maximum harmonisation instrument.[72]

The opening lines of the scathing Opinion of the Advocate General left no doubt as to the approach that he was directing the Court towards: 'The European Union is based on a *free market economy, which implies that undertakings must have the freedom to conduct their business as they see fit*.' Unsurprisingly AG Wahl concluded that the power vested with the Greek Ministry of Labour was incompatible with 'Article 49 TFEU, interpreted in the light of Article 16 of the Charter of Fundamental Rights of the European Union'.[73]

The Court however approached the question from a different angle noting that

> as is apparent from Article 3(3), TEU, the European Union is not only to establish an internal market but is also to work for the sustainable development of Europe, which is based, in particular,

[69] Ibid, 359.

[70] TFEU 2007, Art 119(3).

[71] *Anonymi Geniki Etairia Tsimenton Iraklis (AGET Iraklis) v Ypourgos Ergasias, Koinonikis Asfalisis kai Koinonikis Allilengyis* ECLI:EU:C:2016:972 (*AGET Iraklis* Judgment). The following paragraphs draw heavily on the co-authored blog post N Countouris and A Koukiadaki, 'Greek Glass Half-Full: The CJEU And Europe's 'Highly Competitive Social Market' Economy' (Social Europe, 13 February 2017) www.socialeurope.eu/glass-half-full-cjeu-europes-highly-competitive-social-market-economy.

[72] An acknowledgement of this fact transpires from AG Wahl's Opinion, *Anonymi Geniki Etairia Tsimenton Iraklis (AGET Iraklis) v Ypourgos Ergasias, Koinonikis Asfalisis kai Koinonikis Allilengyis* ECLI:EU:C:2016:429 (*AGET Ikralis* Opinion), para 80.

[73] *AGET Ikralis* Opinion (n 72), para 82.

on a highly competitive social market economy aiming at full employment and social progress, and it is to promote, inter alia, social protection.[74]

In a very nuanced judgment the European judges inferred from 'Article 5 of Directive 98/59 that that directive is intended [...] to provide minimum protection with regard to informing and consulting workers in the event of collective redundancies and that the Member States remain free to adopt national measures that are more favourable to those workers'.[75] In other words, Greek legislation allowing a public authority the power to prevent collective redundancies was not incompatible in principle with Directive 98/59. The possibility of setting a higher national social standard is an essential aspect of the principle of accommodation in a social market economy, and this was a crucially important recognition.

Second, and equally important, the CJEU held that the mere fact that a Member State stipulates a requirement that any projected collective redundancies must be notified to a national authority, which has simultaneously the right to oppose these redundancies on grounds relating to the protection of workers and of employment, 'cannot be considered contrary to freedom of establishment as guaranteed by Article 49 TFEU or the freedom to conduct a business enshrined in Article 16 of the Charter' either.[76] Third, while the CJEU re-affirmed its *Alemo Herron* understanding of Article 16 of the Charter as establishing a fundamental freedom to conduct a business, it then went on to stress that 'the freedom to conduct a business may be subject to a broad range of interventions on the part of public authorities that may limit the exercise of economic activity in the public interest', another essential aspect of the principle of accommodation. Unlike in *Alemo*, where the CJEU took the view that Member States cannot take measures, which, while being more favourable to employees in transfers of undertaking, are liable to adversely affect the very essence of the freedom to conduct a business, the CJEU held in *Aget Iraklis* that the veto by public authorities in collective redundancies was solely designed to impose a framework on the ability of companies to proceed to collective redundancies.[77] Finally, the CJEU accepted the arguments of the Greek Government that the veto right of the public authorities could both be justified, as its objective was to protect workers (expressly referring to Article 30 of the Charter), and be proportionate. It went as far as suggesting that 'it is not apparent that measures of a less restrictive kind would ensure attainment of the objectives thereby pursued as effectively as the establishment of such a framework'.[78]

But there were also words of caution. The CJEU noted that the three criteria, which the Greek public authorities take into account for the purpose of deciding whether they oppose collective redundancies ('interests of the national economy', 'situation of the undertaking' and the 'conditions in the labour market') were not up to the job. The first one was considered to relate to an economic aim, which cannot constitute a public interest reason justifying a restriction on EU fundamental freedoms. As for the second two, while in principle these were found to be capable of relating to the public interest, the CJEU lamented the fact that the administrative authorities' discretion was unfettered by their

[74] *AGET Ikralis* Judgment (n 71), para 76.
[75] Ibid, para 32.
[76] Ibid, para 83.
[77] Ibid, para 88.
[78] Ibid, para 93.

overly-generic wording. It then went on to express its expectation that the criteria relied upon by the public authorities be detailed and specific enough so as to allow employers a certain degree of predictability in terms of their application by public authorities and to allow courts to review how public authorities exercise their discretion.[79]

The judgment was considered by some a surprising tie, even a step forward in the development of a social market economy,[80] and by others more of the same, if not a net loss.[81] What is clear is that without this nuanced judgment Greece would have not been able to retain any scrutiny role for a public body in the context of collective redundancies, which it ultimately managed to negotiate with its creditors and is currently embodied in the reformed, tripartite, Supreme Labour Council[82] whose key function was accommodated in Europe's labour and economic constitutions.

A second instance of accommodation emerges from the recent legislative reform of the original Posted Workers Directive, in particular through Directive (EU) 2018/957.[83] The original Posted Workers Directive 96/71 had become a totemic and divisive issue for Europe, particularly since its extremely controversial interpretation by the CJEU in cases such as *Laval* and *Rüffert*.[84] As argued in previously published work, these two decisions 'changed the nature of the PWD by transforming it into a de facto "maximum" or "exhaustive harmonisation" instrument, and by anchoring it to the centrifugal force pulling "free movement of services" (FMS) away from its original [Equal treatment Principle] and increasingly towards a [Market Access] with [Country of Origin Principle] rationale'.[85]

Sources close to the European institutions had immediately acknowledged that 'The Court's cases have exposed the fault lines that run between the single market and the social dimension at national level'.[86] The European labour movement had also strongly demanded reforms leading to 'equal treatment of local and migrant workers'.[87] And the European Parliament had advocated reforms dealing 'in particular with issues such as applicable working conditions, pay levels, the principle of equal treatment of workers in the context of free movement of services, respect for different labour models and the duration of posting'.[88] These were all prompts for the fundamental social principle of equality to

[79] Ibid, paras 95–104.

[80] M Markakis, 'Can Governments Control Mass Layoffs by Employers? Economic Freedoms vs Labour Rights in Case C-201/15 AGET Iraklis' (2017) 13 *European Constitutional Law Review* 724; N Countouris and A Koukiadaki, 'The glass half full: collective redundancies, public interest, and the (unfulfilled) potential of Europe's "highly competitive social market economy"' (2017) 153 *Giornale di Diritto del Lavoro e di Relazioni Industriali* 193.

[81] S Deakin, 'In Search of the Social Constitution' in F Dorssemont et al (eds) *The Charter of Fundamental Rights of the European Union and the Employment Relation* (Oxford, Hart Publishing, 2019) 53.

[82] Άρθρο 17 – Νόμος 4472/2017 – Έλεγχος ομαδικών απολύσεων.

[83] Directive (EU) 2018/957 of the European Parliament and of the Council of 28 June 2018 amending Directive 96/71/EC concerning the posting of workers in the framework of the provision of services.

[84] Case C-346/06 *Dirk Rüffert v Land Niedersachsen* ECLI:EU:C:2008:189.

[85] N Countouris and S Engblom, '"Protection or Protectionism?": A Legal Deconstruction of the Emerging False Dilemma in European Integration' (2015) 6 *European Labour Law Journal* 20, 37.

[86] Monti (n 1).

[87] European Trade Union Confederation, 'The Posting of Workers Directive: proposals for revision- Resolution adopted at the ETUC Executive Committee on 9–10 March 2010' www.europarl.europa.eu/document/activities/cont/201006/20100601ATT75367/20100601ATT75367EN.pdf.

[88] European Parliament resolution of 22 October 2008 on challenges to collective agreements in the EU (2008/2085(INI)). See also N Countouris and S Engblom, 'Civilising the European Posted Workers Directive' in M Freednaldn and J Prassl (eds), *Viking, Laval and Beyond* (Oxford, Hart Publishing, 2014) 279; E Voss et al, 'Posting Of Workers Directive – Current Situation And Challenges' (*European Parliament*, June 2016) www.europarl.europa.eu/RegData/etudes/STUD/2016/579001/IPOL_STU(2016)579001_EN.pdf.

contrast and, in fact, reverse the drift of the EU single market towards an open, free market, economy (de)regulatory model.

Eventually the Commission tabled a series of reforms proposals[89] aimed at strengthening the role of the equal treatment principle within the PWD, an objective that was mainly pursued by substantially expanding the concept of 'remuneration' beyond the narrow confines defined by the pre-existing concept of 'minimum rates of pay', contained in Article 3 of Directive 97/71.[90] To be clear, the new provisions introduced by Directive 2018/957 are everything but a panacea to the complex challenges arising from the posting of workers, but they undoubtedly constitute a serious attempt to offer an accommodation to the various concerns brought to the fore by *Laval* and its progeny.

It is worth highlighting that the CJEU is currently examining an action for annulment jointly brought by the Polish and Hungarian Governments against the new Directive, alleging 'that the principal objective of the contested provisions on the remuneration of posted workers is to restrict the freedom to provide services by increasing the burden on service providers, with a view to eliminating their competitive advantage resulting from lower pay rates applicable in their country of establishment'.[91] But the Directive also offered an opportunity to the European labour movement to restate its common and unified position in support of the 'paramount principle of equal pay for equal work at the same place', with the main Central and Eastern European trade union confederations openly asserting their members' support for the new reforms, and demystifying the mantra perpetrated by many that equality generates a rift that pits Eastern European workers against their Western European colleagues.[92] And, since the intervention of the Polish and Hungarian Governments (both sustained by two right wing, nationalist, parties – respectively the Law and Justice Party and Fidesz) it could be an opportunity for the Court of Justice to elaborate further on the concept of social market economy as a cure for the social and political dysfunctionalities generated by free market ideologues.

VIII. Conclusions – The Principle of Accommodation in a Democratic Europe

There is no denying that the last three decades have seen the parable of social-democratic values and policies in Europe and, perhaps more importantly for the argument developed in this chapter, in the European macroeconomic constitutional settlement. The EU has developed a macroeconomic constitution that has both narrowed down the range of policy

[89] Commission, 'Proposal for a Directive of the European Parliament and of the Council amending Directive 96/71/EC of The European Parliament and of the Council of 16 December 1996 concerning the posting of workers in the framework of the provision of services' COM (2016) 128 final; See R Zahn, 'Revision of the Posted Workers Directive: A Europeanisation Perspective' (2017) 19 *Cambridge Yearbook of European Legal Studies* 187, 187.

[90] Directive 96/71/EC of the European Parliament and of the Council of 16 December 1996 concerning the posting of workers in the framework of the provision of services.

[91] Case C-626/18, *Republic of Poland v European Parliament and Council of the European Union,* [2018] OJ L/173, 16.

[92] Joint statement of trade unions of the Visegrad Group on the current situation with Posted Workers Directive and the complaint of the Polish and Hungarian Governments to the Court of Justice of the EU on the revised directive (Prague, 12 October 2018).

action permissible under its strict monetarist parameters and sought to constrain the national constitutions of the EU Member States, often successfully. But it is also fair to say that, on occasion, the Member States that have sought to test the narrowing EU constitution have exceptionally been able to do so with a certain degree of success. Sections 6 and 7 above offer a number of successful instances of contestation of the free market paradigm. The narrowing constitution, under certain conditions that would have to be explored further in future research, may thus be able to accommodate particular policy expressions of social-democratic values. It may even be able to accommodate particular structural manifestations of these values, for instance some highly coordinated industrial relations regimes. It is suggested that one of the most pressing question for the EU, its institutions, and for those scholars still interested in the process and project of European integration, is to define more clearly this embryonic principle of accommodation and test its limits further. In a way, to expand further the constitutional envelope of the EU.

A crucial aspect to focus on will be the contribution that the idea of a 'social market economy' can make to the expansion of this constitutional envelope. Ewing and Bogg have correctly pointed out that 'a social market is … a weak form of social democracy within a capitalist paradigm: it is a commitment to a social market economy not a socialised economy of the kind that might have been understood by earlier pioneers of social democracy'.[93] There is a sense that, in their view, the current settlement may rule out political projects linked, for instance, to more robust ideas of democratic socialism (which some national constitutions after World War 2 might have been designed to accommodate). But they have also acknowledged that 'equally it is a commitment to a social market economy, not a free market economy, which sets the TEU and the EU apart from the free market and liberal democratic constitutions to be found notably in the United States'.[94]

Some will suggest that this process of reconciliation and accommodation is already largely occurring.[95] Some will take the view that this is a political and perhaps legal impossibility.[96] But the reality is that the conceptual and empirical testing of these propositions can only be pursued by a genuinely social democratic (or democratic and socialist) project emerging from the ashes of Austerity in a Democratic Europe. The ashes are there and 'The triumph of neo-liberalism is not complete; social democracy is not dead after all'.[97]

[93] A Bogg and KD Ewing, 'A Tale of Two Documents The Eclipse of the Social Democratic Constitution' in E Nanopoulos and F Vergis (eds), *The Crisis behind the Eurocrisis: The Eurocrisis as a Multi-Dimensional Systemic Crisis of the EU* (Cambridge, CUP, 2019) 326.

[94] Ibid.

[95] See O Gerstenberg, *Euroconstitutionalism and Its Discontents* (Oxford, OUP, 2019). See some of the chapters in F Vandenbroucke, C Barnard and G De Baere (eds), *A European Social Union after the Crisis* (Cambridge, CUP, 2017).

[96] C Lapavitsas, *The Left Case Against the EU* (Cambridge, Polity Press, 2019).

[97] Ewing, 'Jeremy Corbyn and the Law of Democracy' (n 68).

20

Equality and Community for Migrant Workers

JOO-CHEONG THAM*

I. Introduction

Many migrant workers are in a situation of *abusive dependence*. Their conditions of work are often marked by severe exploitation, serious breaches of rights and pervasive discrimination.[1] In the political debates of their receiving countries, they find themselves denigrated and feared.[2] Yet, there has been a sustained increase in labour migration globally.[3] Migrant workers continue to migrate in the hope that their journeys will result in better lives for themselves and their families and the receiving countries continue to rely upon their work, so much so that key industries in these countries would collapse if migrant labour were completely withdrawn.

Migrant workers are also caught in *hyper-moralised amoralism*. The temperature of debates concerning labour migration is often high with migrant workers seen as threats to national borders, national cohesion, living standards and the rule of law. At the same time, a powerful strand of opinion seeks to locate these workers in a realm where ethical considerations do not apply, where these workers are not moral subjects; but rather objects for the use of the receiving states.

How should we think about equality and community – two cardinal principles of any social democratic project – when it comes to migrant workers? Is there a place for these ideals in the context of abusive dependence and hyper-moralised amoralism? If so, how should we understand them?

With a focus on migrant workers in a regular situation within their receiving countries, this chapter explores these questions through three Conventions central to the international standards on migrant work: the two International Labour Organization ('ILO') Conventions

* A special thank you to Chris Kaias for his excellent research assistance. Thank you too to the following for their insightful comments on a draft chapter: Sayomi Ariyawansa; Shreya Atrey; Laurie Berg; Bassina Farbenblum; Tarun Khaitan; Marius Olivier; Julian Sempill; and the editors of this collection.

[1] See OHCHR, 'Report of the Special Rapporteur on the Human Rights of Migrants, François Crépeau: Labour Exploitation of Migrants' (3 April 2014) UN Doc A/HRC/26/35.

[2] International IDEA, *Global State of Democracy: Exploring Democracy's Resilience* (International IDEA 2017) 202.

[3] International Labour Organization ('ILO'), *Fair Migration: Setting an ILO Agenda* (Report of the Director-General, International Labour Conference, 103rd Session, 2014) Report I (B) [50]–[51].

on migrant labour and their Recommendations; and the International Convention on the Protection of the Rights of All Migrant Workers and Members of their Families.[4] It adopts the definition of migrant workers in a regular situation International Convention on the Protection of the Rights of All Migrant Workers and Members of their Families (migrant workers authorised to enter, to stay and to engage in a remunerated activity in the state of employment pursuant to the law of that state);[5] it does not deal with migrant workers in an irregular situation because of the additional legal and moral complexities stemming from their irregular status.

Whilst suffering from low levels of ratification, these Conventions are significant, firstly for their regulatory role, having been affirmed in the United Nations General Assembly's 2016 *New York Declaration for Refugees and Migrants* and its 2019 *Global Compact for Safe, Orderly and Regular Migration*, both of which promoted ratification of these instruments.[6] More broadly, they are significant for the normative principles they express – including those of equality and community.

The chapter argues that, despite their limitations, these international standards offer significant normative resources for these workers in terms of the principles of equal treatment and equal human rights. They, however, offer far less on the question of community; and the chapter argues that these standards should be augmented by an understanding of community based on social membership and an ethic of care.

The first part of the chapter addresses the question of equality of migrant workers in a regular situation within their receiving countries by, firstly, assessing – and rejecting – the key arguments against such equality (national sovereignty; democratic self-determination; lack of membership of their receiving countries; choice; and fairness). It then elaborates upon the principles of equal treatment, equal human rights and equal consideration of needs and interests as found in these international standards; and turns finally to the limitations of these principles.

The second part deals with community for migrant workers by highlighting how these international standards fail to fully recognise these workers as members or even potential members of the receiving countries. It then moves to reject the arguments that might justify such silence and ends by spelling out an alternative approach based on social membership and an ethic of care.

II. Equality for Migrant Workers

A. The Arguments Against Equality for Migrant Workers

Equality for migrant workers faces significant challenges, not just in practice but also in principle. The characterisation by the ILO of 'equal treatment and non-discrimination' for

[4] The international standards on migrant workers go beyond the Conventions that are the subject of this chapter. They further include human rights treaties such as the International Covenant on Civil and Political Rights and the International Covenant on Economic, Social and Cultural Rights; ILO Conventions that apply generally to workers, including migrant workers; as well as international trade agreements such as the General Agreement on Trade in Services.

[5] International Convention on the Protection of the Rights of All Migrant Workers and Members of their Families (adopted 18 December 1990, entered into force 1 July 2003) 2220 UNTS 3 (UN Convention) art 5(a).

[6] UNGA Res 71/1 (19 September 2016) UN Doc A/RES/71/1 [48]; UNGA Res 73/195 (11 January 2019) UN Doc A/RES/73/195 [22][a].

migrant workers as 'universal values' clearly does not command general acceptance.[7] There are five significant arguments against equality for migrant workers: national sovereignty; democratic self-determination; lack of membership of the receiving country; choice; and fairness.

i. National Sovereignty

The first argument is based on what the ILO considers as 'the sovereign right of all nations to determine their own migration policies'.[8] It contends that because migration is a matter of national sovereignty, it is therefore up to each nation to determine its policies in this area. If accepted, this argument is not only fatal to applying principles of equality to migrant workers but also to any other normative principles.

As Joseph Carens has, however, pointed out, the difficulty with this highly influential argument is that '(i)t confuses the question of who ought to have the authority to determine a policy with the question of whether a given policy is morally acceptable'.[9] This is a confusion stemming in part from the ambiguity of the term, 'sovereign right' with 'right' doubling in referring to both power and correctness – and this confusion conflates legal with moral authority.

The better view is that arguments as to national sovereignty point decisively to the 'where' of authority (nation-states) but still leave open the question whether 'how' such authority is exercised is morally acceptable. An analogy can be made with parliamentary sovereignty. The principle of parliamentary sovereignty identifies the institution which has law-making power (Parliament), but clearly does not shield this exercise of power from moral criticism. Indeed, a key insight of those who emphasise the workings of the political constitution, including Keith Ewing, is that the exercise of parliamentary sovereignty is subject to political norms;[10] what John Stuart Mill described as 'positive political morality'.[11]

Equally, national sovereignty over migration is compatible with principles governing the exercise of such sovereignty. These principles may be sourced from domestic self-understandings concerning migration, including understandings of equality and community as well as global principles; the latter being found in non-binding documents such as ILO Recommendations as well as those giving rise to 'hard' obligations at international law, such as the UN and ILO Conventions. The last, it should be pointed out, is not incompatible with national sovereignty; indeed, the assumption of obligations at international law through ratification of treaties is an exercise of such sovereignty.

ii. Democratic Self-determination

This argument contends that a vital aspect of democratic self-determination is control by democratic states over migration as part of a collective right to determine its community – democracies should be able to determine who is within their 'demos'.

[7] ILO, *Fair Migration: Setting an ILO Agenda* (Report of the Director-General, International Labour Conference, 103rd Session, 2014) Report I (B) [42].

[8] ILO, *ILO Multilateral Framework on Labour Migration: Non-binding Principles and Guidelines for a Rights-based Approach to Labour Migration* (ILO 2006) vi.

[9] J Carens, *The Ethics of Immigration* (New York, OUP, 2013) 6.

[10] KD Ewing, 'The Resilience of the Political Constitution' (2013) 14 *German Law Journal* 2111.

[11] JS Mill, 'Considerations on Representative Government' in JS Mill, *On Liberty and Other Essays* (New York, OUP, 1991) 270.

It is useful here to distinguish between questions relating to admission of migrants into receiving countries and those relating to the conditions of their stay. It is the latter which is the focus of this chapter, the specific concern being with migrant workers in a regular situation already within the territory of the receiving country – therefore subject to its laws. Robert Dahl has pointed out the absurdity from a *democratic* perspective of the argument that democracies should be free to determine their 'demos' in relation to those subject to its laws. It would allow nation-states to be considered 'democracies' even when a significant proportion of their resident population is excluded from the demos. As Dahl argues, 'if a demos can be a tiny group that exercises a brutal despotism over a vast subject population, then "democracy" is conceptually, morally, and empirically indistinguishable from autocracy'.[12] And even when those excluded constitute a small proportion of the population, the difficulties from a democratic perspective persist. As Mill said in his *Considerations on Representative Government*, '(i)t is an essential part of democracy that minorities should be adequately represented' – '(n)o real democracy, nothing but a *false show of democracy*, is possible without it'.[13]

iii. Membership, Choice and Fairness

The third argument against equality for migrant workers contends that migrants are not members of their receiving countries as they are not citizens of these countries; and, therefore, are not entitled to equality (with citizens of these countries). This argument, in fact, rests upon two parts: the first turns on who is considered a member of the receiving country (citizens) and the second on when a claim to equality can be properly made (only on the basis of citizenship). Both parts will be refuted later: it will be argued that many migrant workers should be considered members of their receiving countries, even when they are not citizens; and claims to equality can be made on grounds other than membership, including the status of migrant workers as workers and human beings.

The fourth argument against equality for migrant workers is based on choice. Migrant workers, it is said, have chosen to migrate and therefore to accept whatever laws apply in their host countries, including laws that treat them unequally; after all, migrant workers have agency including in developing their migration projects. The argument based on choice also often expresses itself in terms of perceptions that migrants are willing to perform jobs that nationals are unwilling to undertake, particularly so-called 'dirty, dangerous and demeaning' jobs.

There are, however, several fallacies lurking in the argument based on choice. First, it conflates considerations at the individual level with those relevant to the design of laws and, in doing so, elevates individual choice to an institutional principle when, as will be seen later with minimum labour standards, such choice is either irrelevant or of little significance.

Further, the argument seeks to convert what may be a relevant condition of justice for migrant workers (choice in migration) into a sufficient condition. Rather than concluding

[12] R Dahl, *Democracy and its Critics* (New Haven, Yale University Press, 1989) 122.

[13] Mill, 'Considerations on Representative Government' (n 11) 307 (emphasis added).

the inquiry, such choice should be weighed in the balance with other moral considerations, including those based on equality. And in such an exercise, it should always be remembered that migrant workers do not typically migrate in circumstances of their choosing, and the most emphatic of these unchosen circumstances is that of birth. This is what John Stuart Mill has characterised as '(t)he most powerful of all determining circumstances'[14] in what he considered the 'lottery of life'.[15]

Crucially for migrant workers, their birthplace (jus soli) and/or their birth parents (jus sanguinis) will have positive and negative consequences on their rights of citizenship: it will confer rights of citizenship to the country of their nationality but also result in a lack of citizenship rights to other countries. This differential enjoyment of citizenship rights profoundly impacts upon the decisions to migrate. It is this that gives the edge to the key drivers of migration (disparities in development, democracy and demography).[16]

The arguments considered so far broadly reject the principle of equality for migrant workers. The last is specifically directed to unequal treatment at work – differential treatment of migrant workers is fair, it is said, because they receive more by way of wages than they would in their countries of origin. As the Director-General of the ILO has observed 'where income differentials are so powerful a driver of migration, it may be seen as acceptable for migrants to be offered wages and conditions lower than those generally prevailing in destination countries simply because they are higher than those in countries of origin'.[17] This reasoning, of course, draws support from research showing that for many migrant workers they have a 'dual frame of reference' that assesses the wages and conditions they experience in the receiving country with reference to those in their country of origin.[18]

This argument of fairness, however, suffers from similar flaws as the argument based on choice. It seeks to convert a relevant consideration of justice for migrant workers (improvement in relative financial position) into a sufficient condition. And it tends to assume that the circumstances of migration – differential enjoyment of citizenship rights and global disparities – are fundamentally fair. The ILO Director-General is correct in stressing the need to 'dismiss the notion that by virtue of the major disadvantages which migrants may face in their countries of origin, it is acceptable for them to be subjected to lesser disadvantages and injustice in the countries to which they go to seek work'.[19]

The analysis so far has been a ground-clearing exercise – it has sought to reject arguments against applying the principle of equality to migrant workers. What it has not done is provide positive reasons for applying this principle. It is to these reasons, as expressed in the ILO and UN Conventions, that I now turn to.

[14] JS Mill, 'Chapters on Socialism' in JS Mill, *On Liberty: with The Subjection of Women; and Chapters on Socialism* (Cambridge, Cambridge University Press, 1989) ch 2, 231.

[15] Ibid, ch 1, 227.

[16] Global Commission on International Migration, *Migration in an Inter-connected World: New Directions for Action* (Global Commission on International Migration, 2005) 5–7.

[17] ILO, *Fair Migration: Setting an ILO Agenda* (n 7) [43].

[18] M Piore, *Birds of Passage: Migrant Labour and Industrial Societies* (Cambridge, Cambridge University Press, 1979).

[19] ILO, *Fair Migration: Setting an ILO Agenda* (n 7) [46].

B. The Principle of Equal Treatment

i. ILO Conventions and Recommendations on Migrant Workers

A key foundation for the ILO's 'rights-based approach grounded in universal values of equal treatment and non-discrimination'[20] are the ILO Conventions and Recommendations on migrant workers:

- Migration for Employment Convention (Revised), 1949 (No 97) (1949 ILO Convention);
- Migration for Employment Recommendation (Revised), 1949 (No 86);
- Migrant Workers (Supplementary Provisions) Convention, 1975 (No 143); and
- Migrant Workers Recommendation, 1975 (No 151).

The key article of the 1949 ILO Convention is Article 6(1)(a) which requires signatories 'to apply … to immigrants lawfully within its territory, treatment no less favourable than that which it applies to its own nationals' in relation to various matters including remuneration, hours of work, membership of trade unions and enjoyment of the benefits of collective bargaining and social security. The Recommendation to this Convention extends the principle of equal treatment by recommending that signatories apply this principle to admission of employment 'as far as possible'.[21] While the latter qualification allows for restrictions on such admission, the Recommendation provides that these restrictions should 'as far as possible cease to be applied to migrants who have regularly resided in the country for a period, the length of which should not, as a rule, exceed five years'.[22]

The principle of equal treatment is centre-stage within the 1975 ILO Convention which has as its sub-title: 'Convention concerning Migrations in Abusive Conditions and the Promotion of Equality of Opportunity and Treatment of Migrant Workers'. Article 10 of this Convention provides:

> Each Member for which the Convention is in force undertakes to declare and pursue a national policy designed to promote and to guarantee, by methods appropriate to national conditions and practice, equality of opportunity and treatment in respect of employment and occupation, of social security, of trade union and cultural rights and of individual and collective freedoms for persons who as migrant workers or as members of their families are lawfully within its territory.[23]

Two other provisions impose more specific obligations. Article 12(g) obliges each signatory 'by methods appropriate to national conditions and practice' to 'guarantee equality of treatment, with regard to working conditions, for all migrant workers who perform the same activity whatever might be the particular conditions of their employment'. Article 8(2) further provides that migrant workers in a regular situation 'shall enjoy equality of treatment with nationals in respect in particular of guarantees of security of employment, the provision of alternative employment, relief work and retraining'.

[20] Ibid [42].
[21] ILO Recommendation R086: Migration for Employment Recommendation (Revised) (1949), art 16(1).
[22] Ibid, art 16(2).
[23] Article 2 of the 1975 ILO Recommendation reaffirms and extends these principles to vocational training and social services: ILO Recommendation R151: Migrant Workers Recommendation (1975).

The Recommendation to the 1975 Convention goes beyond these areas to suggest that the principle of equal treatment be applied to vocational guidance and placement services, vocational training and broadly to 'conditions of life including housing and the benefits of social services and educational and health facilities'.[24]

What can be discerned from the principle of equal treatment in the ILO Conventions and Recommendations and their application principally to work-related areas is the underlying notion that *migrant workers have equal status as workers*. This notion helps us understand that the principle of equal treatment does not necessarily stipulate identical treatment. In fact, it might be better understood as a negative principle, a principle of non-discrimination – that migrant status is irrelevant to the treatment of migrant workers under the laws and policies of the receiving countries.

The equal status of migrant workers might be said to rest upon the rights of all workers, a rationale that is clearly suggested by the ILO's emphasis on a 'rights-based' approach.[25] This rationale has cogency in relation to some of the areas covered by the ILO Conventions and Recommendations, particularly freedom of association and membership of trade unions.[26]

Nevertheless, it only goes part of the way in explaining the equal status of migrant workers as workers, as the areas covered by these instruments go beyond what are conventionally considered fundamental rights of all workers; encompassing all working conditions and also incidental topics such as placement services and vocational training. Such scope suggests a broader rationale that arises from the purposes of labour regulation: migrant status is not only irrelevant to these purposes but differentiation based on such status will also undermine these goals.

This point can be brought out clearly in terms of the minimum labour standards. The overriding purpose of these standards is to lay down a floor of rights and entitlements for the performance of work – it makes no sense from this perspective to differentiate workers according to their migrant status. More than this, such differentiation will run counter to this purpose by providing employers an incentive to undermine these standards by employing cheaper labour. The internal logic of minimum labour standards – and regulation of work more broadly – supports the principle of equal treatment for migrant workers.

Crucial to note here is how the internal logic of minimum labour standards relates to individual choices by workers. The foundational assumption of these standards are that these choices are inadequate to provide for decent working conditions especially when it comes to workers competing at the lower end of the labour market. Their intent is to provide a base-line from which individual choices can be made.

ii. International Convention on the Protection of the Rights of All Migrant Workers and Members of their Families

It might be surprising that I have not foregrounded human rights as a rationale for the principle of equal treatment under the ILO Conventions and Recommendations. Whilst

[24] ILO Recommendation R151: Migrant Workers Recommendation (1975), art 2.

[25] ILO, *ILO Multilateral Framework on Labour Migration* (n 8); ILO, *International Labour Migration: A Rights-based Approach* (ILO 2010).

[26] See 1998 ILO Declaration on Fundamental Principles and Rights at Work.

human rights are not mentioned in the 1949 ILO Convention, they figure in the 1975 ILO Convention which in its first Article obliges signatories to 'respect the basic human rights of all migrant workers'.[27] The 1975 ILO Convention, however, treats the principle of human rights as distinct from the principle of equal treatment by situating these principles in different Parts of the Convention.[28]

An important aspect of the International Convention on the Protection of the Rights of All Migrant Workers and Members of their Families ('UN Convention') is that it brings these two principles together – under this Convention, equal treatment at work is an aspect of human rights. Included in Part III – entitled 'Human Rights of All Migrant Workers and Members of their Families' – are two provisions that reflect the principle of equal treatment at work. Article 25 stipulates that '(m)igrant workers shall enjoy treatment not less favourable than that which applies to nationals of the State of employment' in respect of remuneration and other conditions of work.[29] In a pointed rejection of choice being able to override minimum standards, Article 25 further provides that '(i)t shall not be lawful to derogate in private contracts of employment from the principle of equality of treatment'.[30] In addition, Article 27 states that '(w)ith respect to social security, migrant workers and members of their families shall enjoy in the State of employment the same treatment granted to nationals in so far as they fulfill the requirements provided'.

These articles and their placement signal a crucial shift in the understanding of equal treatment at international law. It implies that the principle of human rights of migrant workers requires equal treatment at work. Underlying this appears to be the notion that the equal status of migrant workers as workers follows from the equal status of migrant workers as human beings. Arguably, this connection is supplied by the right to 'just and favourable conditions of work' as recognised in the Universal Declaration of Human Rights ('UDHR') and the International Covenant on Economic, Social and Cultural Rights ('ICESCR').[31] After all, central to the notion of justice – including justice at work – is the maxim, 'treat like cases alike'.[32] This would suggest that migrant status is not a sufficient ground for differential treatment in terms of working conditions.

Like the equal treatment principle, the principle of equal human rights is not displaced by the choices migrant workers make in migrating. These choices can hardly be characterised as decisions to surrender their human rights; and even if so, migrant workers are still entitled to these *inalienable* rights. Neither does the relative improvement in the economic position of migrant workers override the principle of human rights – these rights constitute a floor upon which economic distribution takes place.

[27] ILO Convention C143: Migrant Workers (Supplementary Provisions) Convention (1975), art 1.

[28] Article 1 is in pt I (Migrations in Abusive Conditions) while pt II is devoted to 'Equality of Opportunity and Treatment'.

[29] UN Convention, art 25(1).

[30] Ibid, art 25(2).

[31] Universal Declaration of Human Rights (adopted 10 December 1948) UNGA Res 217 A(III), art 23(1) (UDHR); International Covenant on Economic, Social and Cultural Rights (adopted 16 December 1966, entered into force 3 January 1976), art 7 (ICESCR).

[32] This is often traced to Book 5 of Aristotle's Nicomachean Ethics. See Aristotle, *The Nichomachean Ethics of Aristotle* 6th edn (London, Trench, Tubner & Co, 1895).

C. The Principle of Equal Consideration of Needs and Interests?

Many provisions of the ILO and UN Conventions seek to address the distinctive needs and interests of migrant workers, principally in three areas: migratory processes; maintenance of ties with their countries of origin; and family reunification. With migratory processes, the 1949 ILO Convention obliges signatories to 'take all appropriate steps against misleading propaganda relating to emigration and immigration';[33] to provide 'an adequate and free service to assist migrants for employment, and in particular to provide them with accurate information';[34] 'to facilitate the departure, journey and reception of migrants for employment';[35] and to provide appropriate medical services at time of departure, during the journey and on arrival.[36] The 1949 ILO Convention also prohibits signatories from returning migrant workers admitted on a permanent basis and their family members 'because the migrant is unable to follow his occupation by reason of illness contracted or injury sustained subsequent to entry'[37] and requires them to allow the transfer of earnings and savings by migrant workers.[38]

The UN Convention has a part dedicated to '[p]romotion of sound, equitable, humane and lawful conditions in connection with international migration of workers and members of their families'.[39] It also has various provisions specifically dealing with the migratory processes of migrant workers in a regular situation. It provides that these workers are to be fully informed before their departure or at least at the time of their admission to the receiving countries of the conditions of their admission;[40] and similar to the 1949 ILO Convention, it provides for these workers with a right to transfer their earnings and savings from the receiving countries.[41] And for all migrant workers, the UN Convention lays down various rights relating to the protection and assistance of the consular or diplomatic authorities of their state of origin;[42] deprivation of liberty due to violation of immigration laws;[43] destruction of identity documents, work permits, documents authorising entry to or stay, residence or establishment in the receiving countries;[44] and expulsion.[45]

These international standards also seek to enable migrant workers to maintain ties with their countries of origin. The 1975 ILO Convention obliges signatories to 'take all steps to assist and encourage the efforts of migrant workers and their families to preserve their national and ethnic identity and their cultural ties with their country of origin, including the possibility for children to be given some knowledge of their mother tongue'.[46] The UN

[33] Migration for Employment Convention (Revised), 1949 (No 97), art 3 (1949 ILO Convention). The Convention also has Annexes dealing with recruitment, introduction and placement of migrant workers.

[34] 1949 ILO Convention, art 2.

[35] Ibid, art 4.

[36] Ibid art 5.

[37] Ibid, art 8(1). The Convention allows signatories to apply these restrictions 'after a reasonable period which shall in no case exceed five years from the date of admission of such migrants': art 8(2).

[38] Ibid, art 9.

[39] UN Convention, pt VI.

[40] Ibid, art 37.

[41] Ibid, art 27.

[42] Ibid, art 23.

[43] Ibid, art 17(3), 17(8).

[44] Ibid, art 21.

[45] Ibid, art 22.

[46] 1975 ILO Convention, art 12(f).

Convention stipulates in relation to migrant workers in a regular situation that 'States of employment shall make every effort to authorise migrant workers and members of the families to be temporarily absent without effect upon their authorization to stay or to work';[47] and that these migrants 'shall have the right to participate in public affairs of their State of origin and to vote and to be elected at elections of that State'.[48]

The third area, family reunification, is addressed by the 1975 ILO Convention and the UN Convention, albeit in less than forceful terms. The 1975 ILO Convention states that signatories '*may* take all necessary measures … to facilitate the reunification of the families of all migrant workers legally residing in its territory'.[49] The UN Convention obliges signatories in relation to migrant workers in a regular situation to 'take measures that *they deem appropriate* … to facilitate the reunification of migrant workers with their spouses or persons who have with the migrant worker a relationship that, according to applicable law, produces effects equivalent to marriage, as well as with their minor dependent unmarried children'.[50]

These provisions suggest a normative basis other than equal treatment and human rights. They do not seek parity with citizens of the receiving countries in terms of the application of the law. And whilst some of these provisions can be explained by human rights (eg the right to politically participate in state of origin; deprivation of liberty; and expulsion), many cannot be justified on this basis.

Let me suggest that these provisions are offshoots of another egalitarian principle – equal consideration of needs and interests of migrant workers, including their vulnerability as migrants. This principle can be grounded in the obligations of receiving countries as receiving countries: that is, once a country decides to receive migrants, it is under some obligation to meet the distinctive needs and interests of migrant workers. More contentiously, consideration of the needs and interests of migrant workers might be an aspect of a broader principle mandating equal consideration of the needs and interests of individuals or, at the very least, members of the community – a point to which I will return.

D. Some are Less Equal than Others

What is proclaimed in these instruments is also restricted. Some workers are less equal than others; some rights are less equal than others; and some work is also less equal than others.

i. Some Workers are Less Equal than Others

As Leah Vosko has correctly argued, the international standards on labour migration provide 'a multi-tiered framework for migrant workers' protection'.[51] Under the ILO and UN Conventions, in particular, there are formal exclusions informed by three distinct

[47] UN Convention, art 38.
[48] Ibid, art 41.
[49] 1975 ILO Convention, art 13(1) (emphasis added).
[50] UN Convention, art 44(2) (emphasis added).
[51] L Vosko, *Managing the Margins: Gender, Citizenship, and the International Regulation of Precarious Work* (New York, OUP, 2009) 82.

logics: a perceived lack of vulnerability; transience of stay in the host country; and exclusion due to the application of other regulatory regimes.

The first logic is reflected in the qualified protection afforded self-employed workers under the Conventions. Under the 1949 Convention, these workers, whilst coming within the scope of the principle of equal treatment under Article 6(1)(a), do not generally benefit from clauses of the 1949 ILO Convention and its Recommendation addressing the distinctive needs and interests of migrant workers as these provisions tend to apply only to 'migrants for employment', that is, persons who migrate from one country to another with a view of being employed otherwise than on their own account.[52] This qualified exclusion is presumably on the basis that self-employed workers do not need protection.

Under the 1975 ILO Convention, self-employed migrant workers have even less protection. Unlike the 1949 ILO Convention, the 1975 ILO Convention denies the principle of equal treatment to these workers as the principle under the latter Convention only applies to 'migrant workers' and their family members, and, as defined under the 1975 ILO Convention, 'migrant workers' do not include self-employed migrant workers.[53]

The second logic of exclusion (transience of stay) is reflected in the exclusions under the ILO Conventions of various groups of workers whose habitual place of residence is not the country of employment (frontier workers; short-term entry by artists and members of the liberal professions; and seamen).[54] Similarly, seafarers and workers on offshore installations who have not been admitted to take up residence and engage in a remunerated activity in the host country are completely outside the scope of the UN Convention.[55] Further, Part IV (Other Rights of Migrant Workers and Members of their Families who are Documented or in a Regular Situation) has qualified application to frontier workers; seasonal workers; itinerant workers; project-tied workers; and specified-employment workers.[56]

The third logic (exclusion based on the application of other regulatory regimes) is found in the 1975 ILO Convention. Excluded from its scope are 'persons coming specifically for purposes of training or education'.[57] Presumably, the justification for this exclusion is that the employment of international students should be governed by the regulation of international education rather than the regulation of migrant workers. This logic is pressed further by the UN Convention which does not apply to students and trainees; certain workers sent to the country of employment by states or international organisations; and refugees and stateless persons.[58]

Equality under the ILO and UN Conventions may also in practice be denied to some migrant workers due to what Judy Fudge has characterised as 'the paradox of the international human rights regime' for migrant workers.[59] On the one hand, this regime promises

[52] ILO Convention C097: Migration for Employment Convention (Revised) (1949), art 11(1); ILO Recommendation R086: Migration for Employment Recommendation (Revised) (1949), art 1(a).

[53] Migrant Workers (Supplementary Provisions) Convention (1975), art 11(1).

[54] ILO Convention C097: Migration for Employment Convention (Revised) (1949), art 11(2); ILO Recommendation R086: Migration for Employment Recommendation (Revised) (1949), art 3.

[55] UN Convention, art 3(f).

[56] Ibid, pt V.

[57] Migrant Workers (Supplementary Provisions) Convention (1975), art 11(1)(d).

[58] UN Convention, art 3.

[59] J Fudge, 'Precarious Migrant Status and Precarious Employment: The Paradox of International Rights for Migrant Workers' (2012) 34 *Comparative Labor Law and Policy Journal* 131.

equality to migrant workers; on the other, it leaves restrictions relating to their migrant status very much as a matter of state autonomy. Yet precariousness in migrant status[60] may result in a failure of de jure equality translating into de facto equality.

This is notably the case when state autonomy confers power upon employers to determine the migration status of the worker – where state sovereignty brings about employer sovereignty. Migrant workers dependent upon employer sponsorship for their ability to stay and work in the receiving countries fall into this category. They are not expressly excluded from the scope of the international standards but may nevertheless fail to be protected by them because of the dependence on their sponsoring employers. Such dependence can amount to the reality and perception that sponsoring employers have the de facto ability to remove these workers from the receiving countries. This, in turn, could be a vector for exploitative practices, including breaches of labour regulation, as well as a powerful inhibitor of complaints by migrant workers.

ii. Some Rights are Less Equal than Others: Freedom of Employment

Freedom of employment is clearly relevant to the principle of equal treatment as nationals of receiving countries would typically enjoy such a freedom. It is also pertinent to equal human rights, which is recognised by Article 23(1) of the UDHR ('free choice of employment') and Article 6 of the ICESCR ('the right of everyone to the opportunity to gain his living by work which he freely chooses or accepts'). It is, nevertheless, a freedom that receives lesser protection under the international standards.

This freedom is not mentioned in the 1949 ILO Convention. Rather, there is the entreaty in Article 16 of its Recommendation to the 1949 ILO Convention that migrant workers in a regular situation and their family member 'as far as possible be admitted to employment in the same conditions as nationals' and that any restrictions on such admission not exceed five years.

Like the 1949 ILO Convention, the 1975 ILO Convention provides freedom of employment lesser protection compared to other rights at work. In strong contrast to the earlier Convention though, the 1975 ILO Convention expressly acknowledges this freedom (while subjecting it to certain conditions). Article 14 of the 1975 Convention provides that:

> A Member may —
>
> (a) make the free choice of employment, while assuring migrant workers the right to geographical mobility, subject to the conditions that the migrant worker has resided lawfully in its territory for the purpose of employment for a prescribed period not exceeding two years or, if its laws or regulations provide for contracts for a fixed term of less than two years, that the worker has completed his first work contract;
>
> …
>
> (c) restrict access to limited categories of employment or functions where this is necessary in the interests of the State.

[60] L Goldring, C Berinstein and JK Bernhard, 'Institutionalizing Precarious Migratory Status in Canada' (2009) 13 *Citizenship Studies* 239; L Berg, *Migrant Rights at Work: Law's Precariousness at the Intersection of Immigration and Labour* (London, Routledge, 2016).

Article 14 of the 1975 ILO Convention clearly provides for stronger protection of freedom of employment than the 1949 ILO Convention. Indeed, it has been described as a 'remarkable achievement which, at least on its face, greatly decreases state control over the employment of migrant workers and contributes to the overall reduction of their exploitation'.[61]

The UN Convention, however, retreats from the position taken by the 1975 ILO Convention. Despite such freedom being recognised as a human right under the UDHR and the ICESCR, it does not find a home in Part III of the UN Convention (Human Rights of All Migrant Workers and Members of their Families). Rather, it is dealt with in Part IV (Other Rights of Migrant Workers and Members of their Families who are Documented or in a Regular Situation). The key clause dealing with freedom of employment of migrant workers in a regular/documented situation is Article 52:[62]

> 1. Migrant workers in the State of employment shall have the right freely to choose their remunerated activity, subject to the following restrictions or conditions.
> 2. For any migrant worker a State of employment may:
>   (a) Restrict access to limited categories of employment, functions, services or activities where this is necessary in the interests of this State and provided for by national legislation;
>   (b) Restrict free choice of remunerated activity in accordance with its legislation concerning recognition of occupational qualifications acquired outside its territory. However, States Parties concerned shall endeavour to provide for recognition of such qualifications.

Further (possible) restrictions on freedom of employment are placed on migrant workers whose permission to work is limited in time with state signatories allowed to require a period of residence not exceeding two years prior to granting this freedom; and, significantly, to limit such freedom in pursuance of a policy granting priority to their nationals.[63] It is this set of restrictions that result in the UN Convention affording freedom of employment lesser protection than the 1975 ILO Convention. Not surprisingly, one commentator has concluded that this Article 'significantly undermine[s] the progress made in this area by Article 14(a) of the ILO Convention No 143'.[64]

iii. Some Rights are Less Equal than Others: Political Rights

Equal human rights clearly implicate political freedoms (freedom of political expression; freedom of political association) or rights of political participation.[65] So, too, does the principle of equal treatment when it applies to liberal-democratic societies (where nationals enjoy these rights). Political rights might also be implicated due to a connection between these rights and exploitation of migrant workers, including discriminatory treatment. For instance, Michael Walzer has argued that temporary migrant workers 'are exploited

[61] R Cholewinski, *Migrant Workers in International Human Rights Law: Their Protection in Countries of Employment* (New York, OUP, 1997) 110.

[62] UN Convention, art 53 is the provision dealing with freedom of employment of the family members of migrant workers in a regular situation.

[63] UN Convention, art 52(3).

[64] Cholewinski (n 61) 163.

[65] See ICCPR, art 19 (freedom of expression), art 22 (freedom of association), art 25 (political participation).

or oppressed at least in part because they are disenfranchised, incapable of organizing effectively for self-defense'.[66]

The ILO Conventions and Recommendations, however, do not expressly address political rights. By comparison, the UN Convention recognises freedom of expression as a human right of all migrant workers.[67] There is also recognition of freedom of association, including the right to associate in trade unions, albeit in a rather puzzling form: the right to join and participate in associations is considered a human right of all migrant workers[68] but the right to form associations is reserved to those in a regular situation.[69]

Through Article 42, the UN Convention addresses the question of political representation of migrant workers in a regular situation. Its ambivalence is, however, apparent in the weakness of its provisions. The first only requires signatories to '*consider* the establishment of procedures or institutions through which account may be taken, both in States of origin and in States of employment, of special needs, aspirations and obligations of migrant workers and members of their families' and to '*envisage*, as appropriate, the possibility for migrant workers and members of their families to have their freely chosen representatives in those institutions'.[70] The third provision provides that '(m)igrant workers may enjoy political rights in the State of employment if that State, in the exercise of its sovereignty, grants them such rights'[71] – this can hardly be described as an obligation. The only obligation of substance in Article 42 is the requirement that signatories 'facilitate, in accordance with their national legislation, the consultation or participation of migrant workers and members of their families in decisions concerning the life and administration of local communities'.[72]

iv. *Some Work is Less Equal than Others*

Migrant work is often concentrated in particular sectors such as agriculture, construction, hospitality and domestic work. This concentration brings about a double disability for migrant workers: not only do most of these sectors suffer from poor working conditions but migrant workers also often perform low-skilled jobs at the bottom end of these industries.[73]

Such segmentation of labour markets poses challenges to the equal treatment principle. The ILO Director-General has commented that '(p)opular perceptions that "migrants are ready to do those jobs that nationals no longer want to do" … raise questions about equal treatment in segmented labour markets'.[74] These questions present themselves in two different scenarios. The first is when there are 'migrant' sectors with a predominance of migrant workers in precarious employment: what is the benchmark then for the principle of equal

[66] M Walzer, *Spheres of Justice: A Defense of Pluralism and Equality* (New York, Basic Books, 1983) 59.

[67] UN Convention, art 13(2).

[68] Ibid, art 26. Compare the position under the ILO Declaration on Fundamental Principles and Rights at Work and its Follow-up (adopted by the International Labour Conference at its Eighty-sixth Session, Geneva, 18 June 1998; Annex revised 15 June 2010). See also A Bogg and M Freedland, *Labour Law in the Age of Populism: Towards Sustainable Democratic Engagement* (MPIL Research Paper Series, No 2018–15) where they call for '(c)onstitutional protection of the fundamental rights of migrants at work': ibid, 21.

[69] Ibid, art 40.

[70] Ibid, art 42(1) (emphasis added).

[71] Ibid, art 42(3).

[72] Ibid, art 42(2).

[73] See ILO, *International Labour Migration: A Rights-based Approach* (n 25) 83–94.

[74] ILO, *Fair Migration* (n 7) [43].

treatment? The second is when the industry in which migrant workers are employed is characterised by precarious employment of both local and migrant workers. The problem here is not identifying a benchmark but the value of the equal treatment principle itself. An application of the principle would in these circumstances secure only equality of misery for migrant workers.[75]

v. Some Understandings of Equality are Less Equal than Others

G A Cohen has distinguished between three understandings of equality of opportunity and the obstacles they correspondingly seek to remove: bourgeois equality of opportunity which seeks to remove socially constructed status restrictions; left-liberal equality of opportunity which aims to remove these restrictions and obstacles arising from social circumstances; and socialist equality of opportunity which targets the obstacles to bourgeois and left-liberal equality of opportunity, as well as those resulting from inborn advantage.[76]

The main understandings of equality reflected in the ILO and UN Conventions – equal treatment and equal human rights – correspond to bourgeois equality of opportunity; they seek to remove migrant status as a relevant circumstance in terms of the application of laws (equal treatment) and the enjoyment of human rights (equal human rights).

These understandings, however, stand at a great distance from left-liberal equality of opportunity with the provisions based on the distinctive needs and interests of migrant workers providing only a faint gesture towards this egalitarian understanding. For one, left-liberal equality of opportunity would require a concerted effort to reduce the disparities so that migration is made out of choice rather than of necessity.[77]

The understandings of equality reflected in the Conventions are further still from socialist equality of opportunity. Take, for example, the privileged treatment of high-skilled migrant workers over low-skilled migrant workers.[78] This will be objectionable from the perspective of bourgeois equality of opportunity when the unfavourable treatment of low-skilled migrants involves departures from the principles of equal treatment and equal human rights. It will also be objectionable in terms of left-liberal equality of opportunity as the circumstances for acquiring skills are unequally distributed. But insofar as this distinction between high and low-skilled migrants is based on the innate strengths of these workers, neither of these understandings of equality will see that as problematic. Socialist equality of opportunity, however, considers inequality due to differences in innate strengths as an additional source of injustice because these differences are also unchosen.[79]

Context, of course, matters. And in the present context, the bourgeois understanding of equality reflected in the Conventions on labour migration is progressive – indeed, radical – in some domestic contexts and most clearly so if adopted at the global level. The principles of equal treatment and equal human rights stand firmly against the pervasive discrimination, racism and xenophobia experienced by migrant workers, now fuelled by the upsurge

[75] See Cholewinski (n 61) 107; Fudge (n 59) 130.

[76] GA Cohen, *Why Not Socialism?* (Princeton, Princeton University Press, 2009) 12–19.

[77] The first principle of action laid down by the Global Commission on International Migration is 'Migrating out of choice': Global Commission on International Migration, *Migration in an Inter-connected World: New Directions for Action* (Global Commission on International Migration 2005) 4.

[78] M Ruhs, *The Price of Rights: Regulating International Labor Migration* (Princeton, Princeton University Press, 2013) ch 5.

[79] Cohen (n 76) 17.

of nationalism. They also reject a neo-liberal approach that sees migrant workers as 'flexible' labour in the 'bargain basement' of globalisation.[80]

III. The Principle of Community

A. Outside Community? Migrant Workers and International Standards

The ILO and UN Conventions do not expressly acknowledge migrant workers as members or potential members of the community within the receiving countries. Indeed, there are contrary indications in terms of rights usually enjoyed by such members at least in liberal democratic societies: the restrictions the standards tolerate in relation to freedom of employment; and their failure to robustly provide for political rights.

Sitting alongside these contrary indicators are also intimations of migrant workers being members of the community in the receiving countries. Article 12(3)(e) of the 1975 ILO Convention is of particular significance in requiring signatories to 'formulate and apply a social policy appropriate to national conditions and practice which enables migrant workers and their families to *share in advantages* enjoyed by its nationals'.[81] Arguably, it is the status of migrant workers as members of the community in the receiving countries that explain their entitlement to share in advantages enjoyed by nationals.

Apart from this provision, however, the Conventions only gesture towards migrant workers being members of a community; not of their receiving countries, but in their countries of origin.[82] There are stronger hints with their Recommendations but they do not rise higher than recognising migrant workers and their family members as participants in communal life of the receiving countries.[83]

The UN Convention similarly acknowledges migrant workers and their family members who are in a regular situation as participants in the communal life of the receiving countries through Article 45. This provision obliges signatories to provide these migrants with equality of treatment with their nationals in relation to access to educational institutions and services; vocational guidance and training institutions and services; social and health services; and more broadly to cultural life.

B. Contra Community

At this point, some might find all this talk of 'community' for migrant workers to be strange. After all, it may be said: migrant workers are not members of the community in the receiving countries unless these countries have determined them to be so.

[80] ILO, *ILO Multilateral Framework on Labour Migration* (n 8) 83.

[81] Emphasis added.

[82] See art 12(f) of the 1975 ILO Convention and art 7(1)(c) of ILO Recommendation R151: Migrant Workers Recommendation (1975).

[83] See ILO Recommendation R086: Migration for Employment Recommendation (Revised) (1949), art 10(e), 11; ILO Recommendation R151: Migrant Workers Recommendation (1975), art 24(a)–(b).

This position may be held on the basis of national sovereignty in relation to migration; it might also rest upon the view that control of migration is a central aspect of democratic self-determination. But we have seen earlier, there are serious difficulties with both these arguments.

There is, however, one argument I have not contended with – the view that, unless naturalised as citizens, migrant workers are not members of the receiving countries. This argument rests upon a citizens-only understanding of political community, an understanding often assumed in contemporary debates,[84] and indeed, might gain support from Article 25 the International Covenant on Civil and Political Rights ('ICCPR') which provides 'every citizen' with certain rights of political participation, including the right to vote.[85]

Article 25 speaks to an important moral truth – citizenship is a compelling basis for inclusion into the political community. It, however, has much less force in characterising non-citizenship as a necessary basis for exclusion from the political community. The *inclusionary* and *exclusionary* effects of citizenship are not symmetrical. Notably, Article 25 guarantees particular political rights to citizens, but it does not deny these rights to non-citizens, some of whom may be granted political rights and some of whom may be entitled to these rights. As the UN Human Rights Committee has recognised in its General Comment on Article 25, permanent residents may compatibly with that provision be provided political rights.[86] Indeed, Article 21(3) of the UDHR points to an understanding of political community broader than ones based on citizenship. It provides that '(t)he will of *the people* shall be the basis of the authority of government'[87] – a statement that clearly implies that 'the people', not just citizens, are entitled to political right.

Another fundamental difficulty with restricting political community to citizens comes from the hollow thickness of the idea of citizenship. Its thickness is apparent when we ask the question: what should be the entitlements of citizens? The answer, most would say, is equality in relation to the rights of citizens (civil, political, social and economic). But when we ask, 'when is a person entitled to be a citizen', no answer readily yields from the idea of citizenship.

It is this hollowness that allows a citizens-only understanding of political community to fit hand-in-glove with the view that it is up to each nation-state to determine who are members of its community (either on the basis of national sovereignty or democratic self-determination). And when we ask from this perspective when is a person entitled to be a citizen, the answer is clear enough: when the nation-state determines this to be case.

C. Social Membership as a Basis of Membership

As an alternative, I would like to adopt the theory of social membership as proposed by Joseph Carens.[88] This theory seeks to provide answers to the questions: When does

[84] Carens, *The Ethics of Immigration* (n 9) 160.

[85] Emphasis added.

[86] Human Rights Committee, *General Comment 25(57), General Comments under article 40, paragraph 4, of the International Covenant on Civil and Political Rights, Adopted by the Committee at its 1510th meeting*, UN Doc CCPR/C/21/Rev.1/Add.7 (1996) [3].

[87] Emphasis added.

[88] For a similar account, see R Rubio-Martin, *Immigration as a Democratic Challenge: Citizenship and Inclusion in Germany and United States* (New York, Cambridge University Press, 2000) 21–25.

membership of society arise? And what rights are there to membership (including access to citizenship)?

The answers, according to this theory, rest upon the connections a person has to their place of residence, their sense of belonging to the society in which they live – 'the relationships, interests, and identities that connect people to the place where they live'.[89] And as proxies for these dense connections, the theory advances two criteria: residence and length of stay.[90]

The implications of this theory for migrant workers and their family members in regular situations are significant. First, migrants are considered members of the receiving countries once they have resided on an ongoing basis – it is ongoing residence, not the legal status of citizenship, that is the basis of membership.

Second, the theory advances a differentiated scheme of membership rights for residents rather than one of equal rights for citizens. Whilst differentiated, this scheme operates upon a strong presumption in favour of equality. It operates upon a high base-line of equality with all members (including temporary migrants and permanent migrants) entitled to most membership rights that should be enjoyed by citizens, including human rights, rights of workers, as well as access to social programs such as education and health care.[91] Distinguishing between residents and citizens is tolerated under this theory but only in relation to a small number of areas, including security of residence, access to public employment and redistributive rights.[92] And even then, adequate passage of time in terms of ongoing residence would give rise to a claim to full equality, either through the option of citizenship or a status equivalent to citizenship.[93]

It is worth emphasising that membership entails having a role in determining the rules of the community, having a say in the political process. The work of Michael Walzer is crucial on this point. As Walzer correctly argues, being subject to the state's authority, migrants 'must be given a say, and ultimately an equal say, in what the authority does'[94] and 'they must be possessed of those basic civil liberties whose exercise is so much preparation for voting and office holding'.[95] Underlying this argument is the principle of political justice that:

> the processes of self-determination through which a democratic state shapes its internal life, must be open, and equally open, to all those men and women who live within its territory, works in the local economy, and are subject to local law.[96]

Echoing the views of Dahl and Mill, Walzer notes that democratic citizens 'can't claim territorial jurisdiction and rule over the people with whom they share the territory' – '[i[t is a form of tyranny'.[97] And, importantly, this injustice does not disappear because of the 'point in time' choice migrant workers have made in migrating – democratic justice requires ongoing consent.[98]

[89] Carens, *The Ethics of Immigration* (n 9) 164.
[90] Ibid, 164–68.
[91] Ibid, 97–100, 115–24.
[92] Ibid, 101–08.
[93] Ibid, 103–04.
[94] Walzer (n 66) 61.
[95] Ibid, 60.
[96] Ibid.
[97] Ibid, 62.
[98] Ibid, 58.

It might be said that the theory of social membership has a remote chance of being reflected in international standards on labour migration. Perhaps; perhaps not. It is a theory that extends the present recognition under international standards of migrant workers as participants in the communal life of the receiving countries. Other international documents, in fact, go further than such recognition. The Declaration of the High-level Dialogue on International Migration and Development, a resolution unanimously adopted by the UN General Assembly, acknowledges 'the important role that migrants play as *partners* in the development of countries of origin, transit and *destination*'.[99] The ILO Multilateral Framework on Labour Migration has a dedicated chapter on 'Social Integration and Inclusion',[100] the governing principle of which is that 'Governments and social partners, in consultation, should promote social integration and inclusion, while respecting cultural diversity, preventing discrimination against migrant workers and taking measures to combat racism and xenophobia'.[101] Amongst the guidelines to give effect to this principle are:

> 14.6. working with the social partners and migrant worker associations to ensure better representation and participation in economic, social and political life;
>
> ...
>
> 14.13. allowing migrant workers to participate in political activities after a period of legal residence in the country, in accordance with national conditions.

Importantly, the UN General Assembly's *Global Compact for Safe, Orderly and Regular Migration* aims to '(e)mpower migrants and societies to realize full inclusion and social cohesion', laying down a commitment to 'foster inclusive and cohesive societies by empowering migrants to become *active members of society*'.[102]

Neither is stipulating an entitlement to citizenship after a period of residence fanciful. Indeed, the ILO Protection of Migrant Workers (Underdeveloped Countries) Recommendation, 1955 (No 100) states that:

> where such action is not contrary to the policy of the country concerned, the competent authority should consider affording to migrant workers who have been resident for a period of not less than five years in the country to which they have migrated all opportunities of acquiring citizenship of the country of immigration.[103]

This threshold of five years is one that has been suggested by Joseph Carens[104] and is shorter than threshold suggested by others.[105]

As to migrant workers in a regular situation having a voice in the political process as members of receiving countries, we have seen gestures towards this in the UN Convention. Guidelines 14.6 and 14.13 of the ILO Multilateral Framework on Labour Migration also underscore political representation of migrant workers. The intergovernmental organisation

[99] UNGA Res 68/4 (3 October 2013) A/RES/68/4 [9] (emphasis added).

[100] ILO, *ILO Multilateral Framework on Labour Migration* (n 8) ch VIII.

[101] Ibid, 27.

[102] UNGA Res 73/195 (11 January 2019) UN Doc A/RES/73/195, Objective 16, [32] (emphasis added).

[103] ILO Recommendation R100: Protection of Migrant Workers (Underdeveloped Countries) Recommendation 1955, art 51.

[104] Carens, *The Ethics of Immigration* (n 9) 104.

[105] Rubio-Martin (n 88) 23 (ten years); P Mares, *Not Quite Australian: How Temporary Migration is Changing the Nation* (Melbourne, Text, 2016) 294–97 (eight years).

International IDEA has also proposed important recommendations, including: making political processes more transparent and accountable to migrants; considering granting migrants voting rights; and inclusive party platforms that engage migrants.[106]

D. An Ethic of Care

I would like to move onto a less familiar topic that is nonetheless crucial in terms of community – an ethic of care for members of the community. As G A Cohen explains it, 'the requirement of community that is central … is that people care about, and, where necessary and possible, care for, one another, and, too, care that they care about one another'.[107] This understanding of community strongly overlaps with ideas of fraternity. It is also connected with notions of solidarity with the latter's emphasis on mutual support expressing what is necessary to 'care for' each other.[108]

Some might query this emphasis on community as understood in this way. From a social democratic perspective, it might be said that equality is what we should focus on. If so, George Orwell might give us cause for reflection, specifically his view that '(t)he real objective of Socialism is human brotherhood … a world in which human beings love one another instead of swindling and murdering one another'.[109]

Another concern might be that the principle of community is too vague to yield any meaningful principles for action, including for laws and government policies. I would like to suggest otherwise. Cohen, for instance, has identified two modes of caring under the principle of community. The first curbs inequalities that result in a lack of community between those who are fortunate and those less so, that is where inequalities are such that it threatens a 'common life'.[110] And the second is based on a communal form of reciprocity: 'the antimarket principle according to which I serve not because of what I can get in return by doing so but because you need or want my service, and you, for the same reason, serve me'.[111] The key motivation in this mode of caring is 'commitment to one's fellow human beings' and not markets, and cash reward.[112]

Consider, for example, the concentration of migrant workers in 'dirty, dangerous and demeaning' jobs through the first mode of caring spelled out by Cohen. Even if there were not any objections from the point of view of equality (bourgeois, left-liberal or socialist), we would still be disturbed from the point of view of community given how this results in an intolerable distance between migrant workers and non-migrants. This distance becomes even starker when we consider it from the perspective of the socialist principle of distribution, 'from each according to abilities, to each according to needs'.[113] Migrants performing

[106] International IDEA (n 2) 237.

[107] Cohen (n 76) 34–35.

[108] There is also affinity here with the significant feminist literature on the ethics of care, see R Mahon and F Robinson, *Feminist Ethics and Social Policy: Towards a New Global Political Economy of Care* (Vancouver, University of British Columbia Press, 2011).

[109] G Orwell, 'Can Socialists be Happy?' in G Orwell, *Essays* (London, Everyman, 2002) 508–09.

[110] Cohen (n 76) 35–38.

[111] Ibid, 39.

[112] Ibid.

[113] J Carens, 'An Interpretation and Defense of the Socialist Principle of Distribution' (2003) 20 *Social Philosophy and Policy* 145.

these 'dirty, dangerous and demeaning' jobs are expected to contribute more than nationals and yet receive less in terms of their needs. Such a distance undermines a democratic culture, which requires that members of the society can view themselves as fundamentally equal.[114]

Let me also elaborate upon Cohen's modes of caring by proposing three maxims that are particularly pertinent in terms of how receiving countries treat migrants as members of their community. First, *show that you care*. This would not only imply acknowledgment of migrants as members but also embrace practices of recognition, including embrace of the diversity brought about by migrants.[115] Equally, it would extend to a duty not to denigrate the identities of migrants as fellow members.[116] Strong elements of 'showing that you care' can be seen in the 2016 *New York Declaration for Refugees and Migrants*, unanimously adopted by the UN General Assembly, where it was declared that:

> We strongly condemn acts and manifestations of racism, racial discrimination, xenophobia and related intolerance against refugees and migrants, and the stereotypes often applied to them, including on the basis of religion or belief. Diversity enriches every society and contributes to social cohesion.[117]

Second, receiving states should *act in a caring way* in terms of their laws and policies. This would include according equality to migrants based on their status as human beings, workers and members of the community and seeing migrants in these terms – and not solely as units of labour to address labour market shortages or units of population to meet demographic pressures.

We see here the significance of Cohen's second mode of caring, where interdependence between migrants and other members of receiving countries is seen not through the lens of market exchange but through a sense of communal reciprocity. It should also be emphasised that the absence of voting rights does not mean the lack of an obligation to act in a caring way. Whilst not *electoral constituents*, migrants without voting rights are still *moral constituents*.[118]

Third, receiving states should *cultivate caring relationships*. This includes provision of adequate 'voice' for migrants in the political process. It also involves a degree of 'give and take' on the part of receiving states – what Carens has characterised as reasonable mutual adjustment.[119]

IV. Conclusion

The backlash against globalisation poses difficult challenges for social democracy.[120] Amongst them is the task of integrating migrant workers into the social democratic project. These workers are often the target of the backlash with nativist sentiments narrowly drawing

[114] Carens, *The Ethics of Immigration* (n 9) 116. These objections from the perspective of community also apply to excessively-paid 'expatriates' who through their wealth live in a 'world' different from nationals.

[115] Ibid, 83–85.

[116] Ibid, 76–80.

[117] UNGA Res 71/1 (19 September 2016) UN Doc A/RES/71/1 [14].

[118] A Gutmann and D Thompson, *Democracy and Disagreement* (Cambridge, Belknap Press of Harvard University Press, 1996) 144–45.

[119] Language and education are two areas important for such mutual adjustment: Carens, *The Ethics of Immigration* (n 9) 67–71.

[120] C Crouch, *The Globalization Backlash* (Cambridge, Polity, 2018).

the 'us', resulting in migrant workers invariably being 'them'.[121] The answer is neither to acquiesce in such views nor to vacate the field. The Left must talk about migration, emphatically and unreservedly with an ethic of care for migrant workers.[122]

In doing so, it is worth recalling that John Stuart Mill considered that socialism 'as affording in many cases the guiding principles of the improvements necessary, to give the present economic system of society its best chance'.[123] According to G A Cohen, the two key principles of socialism are equality and community.[124] In exploring these principles through the ILO and UN Conventions on labour migration, this chapter has hopefully contributed to developing ways to shift the position of migrant workers from abusive dependence to egalitarian interdependence.

[121] B Anderson, *Us and Them? The Dangerous Politics of Immigration Control* (Oxford, OUP, 2013).
[122] A Hassel, 'Why The Left Must Talk About Migration' (*Social Europe*, 29 October 2018) www.socialeurope.eu/why-the-left-must-talk-about-migration.
[123] Mill, 'Chapters on Socialism' (n 14) ch 3, 259.
[124] Cohen (n 76).

21

Democratic Socialism, Citizenship and Migration: The Progressive's Dilemma?

JUDY FUDGE*

I. Introduction

In his work both as a scholar and public intellectual, especially through his affiliation with the Institute of Employment Rights, Keith Ewing has always been an exponent of social democracy or, as he prefers, democratic socialism because this term puts the emphasis on democraticising the economy. Ewing sees democratic socialism as different from, and preferable to, liberal democracy because he believes that only democratic socialism can result in true self-government in the political, social and economic spheres and cultivate substantive equality for individuals.[1] This commitment informs his view of the goals of labour law, which are to promote democratic self-governance of work and greater economic equality.[2] For democratic socialists, citizenship has a distinctive social and economic content, and requires distinctive institutions, especially collective representation through autonomous organisations, to achieve it. The key political space for democratic socialists is the nation state, which is where citizens exercise popular sovereignty.

Globalisation, which is the process of greater economic integration across national boundaries, has been promoted and accompanied by a neo-liberal political discourse that prioritises markets over politics and emphasises market mechanisms and individual approaches to solving or handling economic and social problems.[3] Neo-liberal globalisation poses a profound threat to democratic socialism. It is 'in the first instance a theory of political economic practices that proposes that human well-being can best be advanced by liberating individual entrepreneurial freedoms and skills within an institutional framework characterised by strong property rights, free markets and free trade.'[4] Neo-liberal

* I would like to thank the editors for their very helpful suggestions, although all errors and infelicities are my own. I would also like to thank Keith Ewing for introducing me to comparative labour law; I was a student in a comparative labour law class he taught in 1981/82 when he was visiting at Osgoode Hall Law School, which inspired me to become a labour law researcher.

[1] KD Ewing, 'Jeremy Corbyn and the Law of Democracy' (2017) 28 *King's Law Journal* 343.

[2] KD Ewing, 'Democratic Socialism and Labour Law' (1995) 24 *Industrial Law Journal* 103.

[3] J Fudge, 'Constitutionalizing Labour Rights in Europe' in T Campbell, K Ewing and A Tompkins (eds), *The Legal Protection of Human Rights: Sceptical Essays* (Oxford, Oxford University Press, 2011) 244.

[4] D Harvey, *A Brief History of Neo- liberalism* (Oxford, Oxford University Press, 2005) 2.

restructuring at the national level is closely associated with supranational free trade agreements. These agreements, which include the Treaty on European Union, seek to insulate 'key aspects of the economy from the influence of politicians or the mass of citizens by imposing, internally and externally, binding constraints on the conduct of fiscal, monetary, trade and investment policy.'[5] Such agreements are designed to bind future governments (since they are very difficult to amend) and thus foreclose certain options, such as nationalisation of key economic or industrial sectors, that the populations of nation states may want to preserve or adopt in the future.

One impact of most trade agreements has been to put downward pressure on labour standards.[6] In the European context, Ewing has argued that the Court of Justice of the European Union's controversial decisions in *Laval* and *Viking* subordinated fundamental rights such as the right to strike and collective bargaining to the four freedoms in the Treaty on European Union, 'which related mainly to the rights of free enterprise to cross frontiers.'[7] For this reason he is very sceptical of supranational agreements that promote the free mobility of goods, services, capital and workers because he believes that privileging market freedoms undermines social democracy.

Globalisation, especially if accompanied by a web of free trade agreements, can pose an existential threat to democratic socialism by fettering democratic control over the economy. What I am interested in is where democratic socialists stand on the issue of migrant workers. When it comes to the treatment of migrant and citizen/national workers, Ewing is like most domestic socialists and calls for equal treatment. However the prior question, about who and how many to let in and keep out, is a much more difficult one. Labour migration poses a particular problem for democratic socialists, who are committed simultaneously to a cosmopolitan and inclusive approach to membership within the community, and to broad popular support for redistribution and a high commitment to social welfare.

The UK, along with many European countries, has seen popular unhappiness with the levels of migration increase, which has fuelled populist parties on the right, such as the UK Independent Party (UKIP), that have embraced an anti-immigration politics.[8] Since 2010, three quarters of Britons favour reducing migration, and migration, including the free of movement of workers in the EU, was a huge factor in explaining the outcomes of the 2016 referendum on membership in the EU, in which 51.9 per cent voted to leave.[9] The rise of anti-immigrant populist parties on the right has hurt social democratic parties 'almost as much as, and in some cases possibly more than, their rivals on the centre-right'.[10] Populist parties keep immigration on the agenda, a topic that rarely assists social democratic parties, and they appeal to working class voters who traditionally support social democratic parties.

[5] S Gill, 'Globalization, Market Civilization, and Disciplinary Neoliberalism' (1995) 24 *Millennium: Journal of International Studies* 399, 412.

[6] J Tham and KD Ewing, 'Labour Clauses in the TPP and TTIP: A Comparison without a Difference?' (2016) 17 *Melbourne Journal of International Law* 369.

[7] Ewing, 'Jeremy Corbyn and the Law of Democracy' (n 1) 357.

[8] I Krastev, *After Europe* (Philadelphia, University of Pennsylvania Press, 2017).

[9] C Woolfson, 'The Politics of Brexit: European Free Movement of Labour and Labour Standards' (2017) 45 *Themes on Migration and Ethnic Studies* 1.

[10] T Bale, 'Putting it Right? The Labour Party's Big Shift on Immigration Since 2010' (2014) 85 *The Political Quarterly* 296, 296.

This push from the right puts pressure on social democratic parties to reconsider, if not change, their policies on immigration.

Even more troubling for democratic socialists is what has come to be known as the 'progressive's dilemma', which is the tension between diversity and solidarity.[11] This challenge, instead of coming from the right and from parties committed to preserving cultural traditions, is 'also emerging from the left and centre-left, which increasingly fear that multiculturalism makes it more difficult to advance the agenda of economic redistribution.'[12] Do diversity and multiculturalism undermine support for redistributive policies in social democracies? Is this dilemma structural or conjunctural? If the latter, are there, 'factors that mediate between ethnic diversity and solidarity, tipping the balance between inclusive or corrosive relationships in particular contexts?'[13]

I want to consider these questions by looking at Ewing's account of social democracy and its constitutional supports. In particular, I want to unpick his ideas of popular sovereignty and the status of the nation state in order to understand his conception of social democratic citizenship. I then turn to consider whether contemporary globalisation poses particular problems for democratic socialism before outlining the progressive's dilemma. After providing a typology of immigration policies, I outline the Labour Governments' and Party's immigration policies between 1997 and 2017 to see how democratic socialist governments and parties have sought to resolve the tension between inclusion/equality and exclusion/solidarity. The enduring nature of this tension suggests that its roots may lie within the prevailing conception of citizenship as much as with its social democratic manifestations. After exploring the different dimensions of citizenship, I suggest that social democrats need to constitutionalise institutions that are designed to countervail against the exclusionary practices of political democracy.

II. Democratic Socialism

In two articles, separated by 22 years, Ewing explicitly considered the relationship between democratic socialism, the constitutional supports needed to establish and to sustain it, and labour law.[14] The first was published in 1995, before the election of the Labour Party in 1997, and the second in 2017, after Jeremy Corbyn became leader of the Labour Party, signalling the Party's return to democratic socialism after its betrayal by New Labour under Blair. In these articles, Ewing explains what he means by democratic socialism, how he distinguishes it from liberal democracy and what he considers to be its essential constitutional supports. His understanding of democratic socialism is very similar in the two articles, but what has changed is his confidence in the European Union as an institution that contributes to democratic socialism. Ewing's growing concern that the EU is a neo-liberal force also reflects the Labour Party's changed position on the EU, from one of New Labour's embrace, to the

[11] D Goodhart, 'Too Diverse?' (2004) February *Prospect* 30; N Pearce, 'Diversity versus Solidarity: A New Progressive Dilemma' (2004) 12 *Renewal: A Journal of Labour Politics* 79.

[12] K Banting, 'Is There Progressive's Dilemma In Canada: Immigration, Multiculturalism and the Welfare State' (2010) 43 *Canadian Journal of Political Science* 797.

[13] Ibid.

[14] Ewing, 'Democratic Socialism and Labour Law' (n 2).

Corbyn-led Labour Party's decision to abide by the referendum results in favour of the UK's withdrawal from the EU.[15]

Ewing distinguishes social democracy from liberal democracy. Unlike liberalism, which favours establishing institutions and norms to hold the state to account, democratic socialists see state power as necessary for democratising social and economic life. While democratic socialists are careful to protect the civil liberties of individuals, they want to ensure that the state has power to tame capital. Nor do they regard individuals as the only significant unit of moral worth, but, instead, see collectivities, such as unions, as critical actors and valuable in their own right.[16]

The constitutional vision of democratic socialism that Ewing fashions is built on three overarching principles: (i) the primary source of constitutional authority is the sovereignty of the people through elected representatives; (ii) the social democratic state should promote the social, economic, and cultural well-being of citizens; and (iii) the socio-economic goals must be implemented in a manner consistent with the civil and political rights of citizens.[17] These general constitutional principles are designed to harness the legal and administrative power of the state, and direct it at the realisation of social and economic equality of citizens. Although Ewing acknowledged that the UK's political Constitution does not embrace democratic socialism, he was confident that it could be accommodated. He observed that the UK's political Constitution 'was a means through which democratic socialist governments governed without serious impediment or restraint, with a wide range of recognisably democratic socialist initiatives being implemented by legislation between 1945 and 1951 in particular".[18] This legislation 'included the creation of the national health service and the public ownership of many of the important means of production, distribution and exchange.'[19]

In his 2017 article, Ewing reassessed whether the UK's political Constitution was fit for democratic socialism. He emphasised the extent to which 'social democracy is based on a different balance of values, on the role of different actors, and on the extension of liberal principles to different sites of struggle' than liberal democracy.[20] Social democracy is 'about securing and sustaining equality, and doing so by':

- embracing the state, concentrating on power rather than accountability;
- engaging social partners as well as parliamentarians in decision-making; and
- democratising the social and economic spheres in addition to the political sphere.[21]

The UK's political Constitution guarantees a key component of democratic socialism – universal suffrage, which ensures the political equality of all citizens. Parliament is the institution through which popular sovereignty is expressed and this is the reason why the doctrine of parliamentary supremacy is critical. However, the UK's political Constitution

[15] The Labour Party subsequently changed its position, and after the European Union Parliamentary elections in May 2019, it advocated a new referendum.
[16] Ibid.
[17] Ibid, 105.
[18] Ibid, 104.
[19] Ibid.
[20] Ewing, 'Jeremy Corbyn and the Law of Democracy' (n1) 344.
[21] Ibid.

does not go far enough to support social democracy because it fails to provide support for autonomous collectives such as trade unions to exercise rule-making power and it does not guarantee the equal status of civil, political, economic and social rights.

Autonomous unions have, according to Ewing, a distinctive role to playing securing social democracy in the UK. In his 1995 article, Ewing referred to TH Marshall's classic essay, Citizenship and Social Class, which not only explained the importance of social rights for full citizenship, but how these rights were dependent upon trade unions. Marshall claimed that in the UK trade unions created a 'secondary system of industrial citizenship supplementary to the system of political citizenship' which is necessary for social citizenship.[22] In his 2017 article Ewing stressed that trade unions should not only participate in economic planning, but that they should 'also be involved in autonomous rule-making activity of a legislative quality.'[23] Thus, he saw the key challenge for democratic socialist constitutionalism as recognising 'not only the legitimacy of collective power, but also the legitimacy of collective institutions as sources of constitutional, political and legal authority'.[24]

Ewing's enduring commitment to democratic socialism has resulted in his increased scepticism of the EU as an institution that can propagate social democracy. In his 1995 article, he remarked that the Labour Party's process of fundamental revision 'has seen a major mood-swing with regard to membership of the European Union, it being quite clear that Labour in government would be a more committed participant, and much more willing to shape and embrace the social agenda of Brussels'.[25] He expressed his hope that the EU would achieve its social democratic potential, which was expressed in its commitment to full employment in 'a highly competitive social market economy' and to combatting 'social exclusion and discrimination' as well as its embrace of social dialogue.[26] This hope was later dashed. Ewing diagnosed the problem as resulting from a deep contradiction embedded in the Treaty of the Functioning of the European Union, 'namely that the social democratic values, procedures and policies have been casually undermined by the steps taken under Title VIII of the TFEU (economic policy) to pursue a neoliberal economic policy which is at odds with the values, procedures and policies referred to above.'[27] The decisions of the Court of Justice, which placed economic freedoms above fundamental rights, and the European Union, which imposed austerity on debtor states in response to the Eurozone crisis, reinforced his view that the foundation of social democracy is the 'equal participation of citizens (with all that that implies) and their representative institutions in making and administering the rules by which they are governed.'[28]

Popular sovereignty achieved through universal suffrage and bolstered by the doctrine of parliamentary supremacy remains the core constitutional supports of Ewing's vision of democratic socialism. He is sceptical of justiciable bills of rights that empower the courts and

[22] Ewing, 'Democratic Socialism and Labour Law' (n 2).

[23] Ewing, 'Jeremy Corbyn and the Law of Democracy' (n 1) 353.

[24] Ibid, 361.

[25] Ewing, 'Democratic Socialism and Labour Law' (n 2) 103. However, the Labour Party's embrace of the EU, which was at that time expanding its social dimension, came at the same time as the Labour Party gave up on the article in its constitution that committed it 'to the social ownership of means of production, distribution and exchange'.

[26] Art 3 of TEU and TFEU, Ewing, 'Jeremy Corbyn and the Law of Democracy' (n 1) 348.

[27] Ibid.

[28] Ibid, 362.

judges who are not accountable to Parliament.[29] However, he is not adverse to autonomous institutions, like trade unions, whose source of authority is not through parliamentary procedures.[30]

III. Migration and the Challenge for Democratic Socialism

A. Anti-Migrant Politics

In the two decades after World War II, in Western Europe the key actors were industrial unions, social democratic parties, sovereign nation states and large manufacturing firms, which were motivated to support autonomous collective action and protective and redistributive labour standards by mass mobilisation that was expressed in the workplace and the ballot box. Tariff walls and embedded liberalism created protective enclaves in which a virtuous circle of mass production and mass consumption in advanced economies could be forged and democratic socialist governments and policies could take root.[31]

The conditions today are profoundly different. Democratic nation states have, because of the power, instability and interconnectedness of finance capital and the constraints imposed by free trade and international monetary agreements, much less room to manoeuvre than they did in the past. Many private sector trade unions in the advanced economies appear to be in terminal, albeit slow, decline, and mass political and workplace mobilisation against capital is in most democratic advanced capitalist states increasingly rare because it has been so ineffective.

But it is more than neo-liberal economic policies and trade agreements that have accompanied globalisation that pose a profound challenge to social democracy. Some commentators attribute the erosion and, sometimes, collapse of support for mainstream social democratic parties across Europe to 'a fragmentation of political identities and the emergence of new populist movements operating outside the channels of Parliamentary government.'[32] Some of these political groups embrace nationalistic conceptions of civic identity and do not accept the 'normative ideal of universal human rights, especially where "non-citizens" are concerned'.[33] Post democratic political apathy has combined with populism and nationalism to create toxic politics that is not conducive to creating a political coalition that can sustain democratic socialism.[34]

In the UK, Carey and Geddes describe immigration and European integration as 'powerful undertows in contemporary British politics that raise profound questions; not least for connections between politicians and "the people"'.[35] Free movement of workers is a core freedom upon which the EU is based. Since the early 2000s much of the migration

[29] Ibid, 355.
[30] Ibid, 362.
[31] J Fudge 'The Future of the Standard Employment Relationship: Labour law, New Institutional Economics and Old Power Resource Theory' (2017) 59 *Journal of Industrial Relations* 374.
[32] Krastev (n 8) 97.
[33] Ibid.
[34] C Crouch, *Post-democracy* (Cambridge, Polity, 2004).
[35] S Carey and A Geddes, 'Less Is More: Immigration and European Integration at the 2010 General Election' (2010) 63 *Parliamentary Affairs* 849.

to the UK has been from other members of the EU or the EEA, and immigration has been relatively high since then.[36] UKIP, claiming that political elites are out of touch with ordinary people, led the call to leave the EU, and it derives its support from people who are opposed to immigration.[37] Immigration raises questions about economics – who wins and who loses – from specific policies, but is also raises critical cultural questions of national identity and belonging.[38] Views about immigration are increasingly polarised in the UK.[39]

Faced with anti-immigration politics, Bale claims that social democratic parties have three ideal-typical strategies:

> The left-of-centre can try to hold its existing, relatively liberal-internationalist position by unashamedly making the case for tolerance of migration and multiculturalism. Or it can try to defuse the situation by trying to play down the issues championed by the radical right in favour of those issues (normally on the so-called "state-market" dimension) that favour the centre-left. Or else it can adopt the radical right's agenda and hope to close down the issue space on the other ("authoritarian–libertarian") dimension by arguing that migration must be limited and multiculturalism tempered by an increased emphasis on "integration"; that done, politics can, fingers crossed, get back to "normal".[40]

As we will see, the Labour Party has tried these different strategies at different times.

B. The Progressives' Dilemma

The public's increasing concern about immigration and the rise of UKIP has prompted political scientists to consider 'wider questions about society and community in contemporary Britain.'[41] While nationalism is often seen as the preserve of the right and populist parties, liberal nationalists also believe that an idea of the national or national identity is necessary for engendering the trust and norms of reciprocity needed to support redistribution for both a welfare state and liberal democracy to function.[42] These liberal nationalists advocate a form of civic nationalism that is not embedded in an ethnic idea of the people and that can bind together people otherwise divided by economic and ethnic differences.[43]

[36] B Duffy, 'Perceptions and Reality: Ten Things We Should Know About Attitudes to Immigration in the UK' (2014) 85 *The Political Quarterly* 259.

[37] A Geddes, 'The EU, UKIP and the Politics of Immigration in Britain' (2014) 85 *The Political Quarterly* 289, 292.

[38] M Skey, '"How Do You Think I Feel? It's My Country": Belonging, Entitlement and the Politics of Immigration' (2014) 85 *The Political Quarterly* 326.

[39] Duffy (n 36).

[40] Bale (n 10) 296.

[41] C Leddy-Owen, 'Liberal Nationalism, Imagined Immigration and the Progressive Dilemma' (2014) 85 *The Political Quarterly* 340, 340.

[42] Ibid, 340.

[43] Banting (n 12) 801, referring to B Barry, *Democracy and Power: Essays in Political Theory* (Oxford, Oxford University Press, 1991); D Miller, *On Nationality* (Oxford, Oxford University Press, 1995); D Miller, 'Multiculturalism and the Welfare State: Theoretical Reflections' in K Banting and W Kymlicka (eds), *Do Multiculturalism Policies Erode the Welfare State?* (Oxford, Oxford University Press, 2006); R Rorty, *Achieving Our Country: Leftist Thought in Twentieth-Century America* (Cambridge MA, Harvard University Press, 1998); Y Tamir, *Liberal Nationalism* (Princeton NJ, Princeton University Press, 1993).

Social democrats also appreciate the need to develop bonds of solidarity as a condition for a functioning welfare state, one which is designed to reduce class divisions. Reflecting on post-war Britain, Marshall regarded a sense of community, one that transcended racial or ethnic identities, as critical for the welfare state. He wrote that 'citizenship requires a bond of a different kind, a direct sense of community membership based on loyalty to a civilisation that is a common possession.'[44] This account of community as the glue for solidarity is very similar to a liberal nationalists conception of civic nationalism.

Leddy-Owen's explains that generally immigration does not pose problems for liberal nationalists except 'when the rate of immigration is so high' that resources and 'mechanisms of integration [such as schools and other state services] may be stretched beyond their capacity'.[45] When 'the absorptive capacities of the society in question' are stretched so that crucial mutual trust and 'shared sense of nationhood' then it becomes legitimate to reduce the immigration rate'.[46] Drawing on the threat that immigration can pose to liberal nationalism, in his 2013 book, *The British Dream: Successes and Failures of Post-war Immigration*, David Goodhart argued Britain has reached the point at which it was no longer able to integrate the high numbers of immigrants entering its territory. According to him, the high rate of immigration combined with multicultural policies and a commitment to diversity undermine the idea of a British nation. He claims that the left in Britain today faces the 'progressive's dilemma' in which they must choose where they stand in the trade-off between ethnic diversity and solidarity.[47] Thus, in order to preserve social democratic ideals about the welfare state he recommends that immigration should be restricted and integration policies should be emphasised.[48]

IV. Charting the Labour Party's Stance on Labour Migration

On the basis of his study of the UK's policies on labour migration under successive governments from different parties, Bernard Ryan has identified four ideal types, which are a combination of immigration controls for labour migrants and labour market regulation.[49] Treating them as different axes, he evaluates immigration controls on how restrictive they are to labour migrants and assesses labour market regulation in terms of how protective it is to workers. Egalitarianism is an ideal policy that combines open migration with a high degree of labour market regulation. It grants migrants the right to work and to equal

[44] TH Marshall, 'Citizenship and Social Class' in TH Marshall and T Bottomore (eds), *Citizenship and Social Class* (London, Pluto Press, 1950) 8.

[45] Leddy-Owen (n 41) 340 quoting Miller, *On Nationality* (n 43) 98.

[46] Ibid.

[47] D Goodhart, *The British Dream: Successes and Failures of Post-war Immigration* (London, Atlantic, 2014).

[48] A recent book published by a group of Labour MPs reflects this view, arguing that a cosmopolitan approach risks alienating the communitarians who make up the majority of social democracy's constituents. They urge Labour to develop a patriotic and communitarian approach to politics. S Kinnock and J Jervis (eds), *Spirit of Britain, Purpose of Labour: Building a whole nation politics to reunite our divided country* (London, Labour Future Limited, 2018).

[49] B Ryan, 'Labour Migration after Brexit: New Questions, New Answers? Migration after Brexit: The Challenge for Labour Standards' (London, Institute of Employment Rights, 15 March 2017).

treatment with citizen workers, who are entitled to a broad range of enforceable labour rights. Labour protectionism restricts migration at the same time that it provides a range of labour standards. It views migrant labour as increasing competition in the labour market, which runs contrary to commitment to provide labour rights to citizens workers in order to protect them from the market and competition. The common dimension of these different ideal types of labour migration policies is to protect the labour and living standards of national workers.

By contrast, 'light touch' labour regulation, otherwise known as low labour standards, is the shared element in both economic liberalism, which favours open migration, and popular nationalism, which restricts migration. Economic liberalism believes that the labour supplied by migration and flexible labour markets will benefit national workers in their role as consumers, whereas popular nationalism emphasises the costs of migration to national identity and social provision while targeting labour regulation at clear abuses.

Most social democrats adopt either an egalitarian or labour protectionist approach to labour migration and labour regulation since their goal is to protect the labour and living standards of citizen workers. As we will see, a range of factors, including the rise of right wing anti-immigration politics, influenced how the Labour Party balanced maintaining an inclusive and open labour migration policy with protecting the interests of citizen workers.

Since the late 1950s, the Conservative Party has presented itself as more representative of public opinion on the issue of immigration – 'opinion which is for the most part ambivalent and at times actively hostile' – than the Labour Party.[50] Consequently, since the 1960s Labour has sought to balance efforts to control the numbers of migrants entering the UK in order to work and to settle, and promoting equality for ethnic and racial minorities. Overt racism and anti-immigrant opinion led the incoming Labour Government, with Conservative support, to impose immigration restrictions, although it broke with the Conservative Party by enacting the Race Relations Act 1965, which outlawed public discrimination.[51] Labour regarded this dual approach of restricting immigration while promoting integration by combatting race discrimination as essential for maintaining 'good race relations.'[52] Essentially, Labour adopted a labour protectionist immigration policy.

The balancing act that had characterised Labour's stance on immigration since the 1960s broke down when New Labour was elected in 1997. Under Blair's leadership Labour's position was that immigration is good for the economy. At the same time, the Labour Government was tough on asylum seekers.[53] The government not only shifted to managed migration, establishing a Migration Advisory Committee composed of academics to examine the economic impact of immigration policy, it decided not to impose transitional controls on workers from the eight states which joined the EU in 2004. Managed migration, which emphasised skilled workers and filling sectoral labour shortages, boosted Labour's business friendly credentials and marked a decisive break with the Conservative policy of restricting immigration.[54]

[50] Bale (n 10) 297.
[51] S Spencer, *The Migration Debate* (Brighton, Policy Press, 2011) 25.
[52] B Ryan, *Labour Migration and Employment Rights* (London, The Institute for Employment Rights, 2005) 13.
[53] Carey and Geddes (n 35).
[54] A Balch, *Immigration and the State: Fear, Greed and Hospitality* (Basingstoke, Palgrave Macmillan, 2016) 161.

The Blair Government also introduced a raft of individual employment rights, including a new minimum wage and paid vacations, which workers could enforce by bringing claims to employment tribunals. But, it only tinkered around the edges of the UK's very restrictive trade union legislation. Despite building a floor of statutory labour rights, given the very deregulated labour market that it inherited from the Conservatives, New Labour could continue to boast that Britain has a very lightly regulated and flexible labour market.[55]

The repercussions of this policy of economic liberalism regarding immigration were not felt until the Labour Government entered its second and third terms, when the UK experienced an 'unprecedentedly intensive and utterly unplanned wave of immigration, particularly (though by no means exclusively) from Eastern and Central Europe'.[56] This large-scale migration led to anti-immigration frenzy in the media, and the Labour Government responded by imposing transitional restrictions for the citizens of Bulgaria and Romania in the 2007 enlargement of the EU and tightening immigration controls for third country nationals.[57] At the 2007 party conference, where he took over the leadership of the Party and government from Tony Blair, Gordon Brown proclaimed 'British jobs for British workers'.[58] Moreover, in the run up to the 2010 general election, Labour adopted a much more restrictive approach to labour migration policy, which consisted of a points-based system for higher-skilled migrants, a reliance on EU migration to plug labour market gaps in lower-skilled employment and a closed door to non-EU, lower-skilled migration.[59] The Conservatives took an even more restrictive stance to immigration, proposing an annual limit on the number of non-EU economic migrants admitted into the UK to live and work. They also pledged to apply transitional controls as a matter of course in the future for all new EU Member States.[60]

Concern about high rates of immigration increased public support for UKIP and drew support away from Labour. Immigration and the UK's economic problems combined to result in Labour loss of the general election of 2010.[61] The Coalition Government under David Cameron promised to reduce migration numbers from hundreds of thousands to tens of thousands. In 2012, Theresa May, who was appointed Home Secretary in 2010, announced her intention to create a hostile environment for illegal migration at the same time as her government dramatically restricted labour migration from outside of the EU. The Coalition Government adopted a popular nationalist approach to immigration policy.

By contrast, the Labour Party initially attempted to diffuse the anti-immigration sentiment by diverting attention to enforcing labour standards and the hardship created by the Coalition Government's austerity policies. Labour's leader Ed Miliband acknowledged that the Labour Government's decision not to impose transitional controls on new Member States in 2004 was a mistake. He claimed that what was needed was 'tougher labour standards to do more to protect working people from their wages and conditions being undermined' and to move the British economy away from low-skilled foreign labour. However, this concession

[55] P Davies and M Freedland, *Towards a Flexible Labour Market: Labour Legislation and Regulation since the 1990s* (Oxford, Oxford University Press, 2007).
[56] Bale (n 10) 297.
[57] Balch (n 54) 162.
[58] Bale (n 10) 300.
[59] Carey and Geddes (n 35).
[60] Balch (n 54) 164.
[61] Carey and Geddes (n 35).

did not quiet the growing concern within the Party that labour migration, including from the EU, should be limited as it is putting 'pressure on wages, welfare, housing and public services in this country. Above all', they continued, 'such a move would prove to voters that we are intent on regaining control of our own borders'.[62] Miliband seemed to assume that Labour could and would do nothing about free movement of labour for EU citizens. Just before the 2015 election, Labour adopted the Coalition's cap on skilled labour, fully returning to its traditional labour protectionist immigration policy.[63]

The outcome of the 2015 election hinged on which party could be seen as taking control over immigration.[64] When the Conservatives won by a small majority, Prime Minister David Cameron made good on his promise to hold a referendum over the UK's continued membership in the EU. In the run up to the vote, Cameron negotiated a deal with the EU on free movement that would restrict migrants access to certain kinds of benefits and allow the UK to impose a break on newly arriving EU labour migrants.[65] This concession to free movement did not stem anti-EU public opinion and in June 2016, 51.9 per cent of votes cast favoured leaving the EU. While immigrants and not labour policies were blamed for wage stagnation, it is clear that the objection to immigration was not solely economic; 'matters of identity were equally, if not more strongly, associated with the Leave vote – particularly feelings of national identity and sense of change over time.'[66]

Under Jeremy Corbyn's leadership the Labour Party initially pledged to abide by the results of the referendum and to leave the EU.[67] Theresa May, the Prime Minster after Cameron's resignation, vowed that Britain would leave the EU and she intensified the hostile environment for all, not just illegal immigrants. In the snap election called for 2017, both parties had to make their positions on labour migration, from within and outside the EU, clear. This proved to be a more difficult challenge for Labour than the Conservatives because of Labour's previous support for free movement and the EU. Corbyn's economic agenda, which included public procurement, public ownership and strategic investment would likely be incompatible, to varying degrees, with EU competition rules.[68]

In its 2017 election Manifesto, the Labour Party accepted the EU referendum results as requiring the end of freedom of movement for EU citizens in UK.[69] However, it promised to guarantee that all existing non-British EU nationals would have the right to remain after Brexit. Labour refused to 'scapegoat migrants' and 'blame them for economic failure', and instead held the Conservative and Coalition Government's austerity policies accountable.[70] In contrast to the Conservatives, it also refused to impose, numerical targets on the number of migrants admitted to work and to settle on the UK, in favour of 'fair rules and reasonable management' that 'will not discriminate between people of different

[62] Bale (n 10) 300.
[63] Ibid.
[64] Woolfson (n 9) 5.
[65] Ibid.
[66] Ibid. 6, quoting K Swales, 'Understanding the Leave vote' (*NatCen Social Research*, 2016) 2 https://whatukthinks.org/eu/wp-content/uploads/2016/12/NatCen_Brexplanations-report-FINAL-WEB2.pdf.
[67] It changed its position, and committed to holding a referendum, after it was trounced in the 2019 European Union elections.
[68] Woolfson (n 9) 2.
[69] Labour Party Manifesto, *For the Many, Not the Few* (*Labour Party*, 2017) 28.
[70] Ibid, 28.

races or creeds'.[71] Labour promised to replace the existing income thresholds for migrants with a requirement that migrants cannot access public funds. The new system would balance 'economic needs against controls and existing entitlements,' and decisive action would be taken to end the 'exploitation of migrant labour undercutting workers' pay and conditions'.[72] Labour undertook to step up labour enforcement generally and to guarantee and improve labour standards. Moreover, for what dislocation was caused by migration, local communities could appeal to an enhanced Migration Impact Fund. Under Corbyn the Labour Party has strengthened its commitment to a labour protectionist immigration policy, although the policy contains significant strains of egalitarianism.

As the Labour Party has shifted from Blair's Third Way – a form of very 'light' social democracy – to Corbyn's much more explicit democratic socialism, its immigration policy has shifted from economic liberalism through to labour protectionism with a humanitarian emphasis. This very significant shift of Labour's policy stance towards greater labour protections for all workers and towards humanitarian concerns for refugees suggests that it considers the threat that immigration poses to the UK to be solely economic. However, 'a substantial literature suggests that anti-immigration attitudes in Britain are far more influenced by ideas surrounding "symbolic" threats – to culture, values and identities – than by "rational" personal economic interests or actual levels of immigration'.[73] This symbolic threat is much harder for Labour, which has long been committed to multiculturalism and inclusion, than the Conservatives, who are content to see ethnic and national identity blur, to combat. Moreover, studies suggest that 'these symbolic threats relate to imagined immigration and unreliable secondary information' and thus cannot be counteracted by an easy appeal to the facts.[74] Declining social trust seems to be linked to perceptions of migration, especially as they have been framed in nationalist media and political discourse, than to actual negative experiences of immigration.[75] While the hierarchies of belonging in Britain are still to a large extent constructed on the basis of racial and ethnic difference, they are beginning to change. Ethnic minorities born and brought up in Britain, including Sikhs, Hindus and Muslims, support tighter migration controls, and minorities are more willing to identify themselves as British.[76] It appears that British identity is gradually shifting from being an ethnic to civic marker.[77]

V. Democratic Socialism and the Dimensions of Citizenship

Migration poses a particular challenge for democratic socialists because of their commitment to inclusiveness, solidarity and equality, and antipathy to ethnic and racial versions of national identity. What migration does is reveal the different dimensions of citizenship – the political principle of democracy, the juridical status of legal personhood,

[71] Ibid.
[72] Ibid.
[73] Leddy-Owens (n 41) 345.
[74] Ibid.
[75] Ibid, 346.
[76] Skey (n 38) 330.
[77] However, in light of calls for greater devolution and Scottish nationalism, 'English', which is a much more exclusionary category than British', may be gaining importance as an identity, Skey (n 38) 331.

and the social status of membership. Political theorist Jean Cohen explains that these dimensions 'can and do come into conflict, and that every historical synthesis entails a set of political choices and trade-offs that tend to be forgotten once a conception becomes hegemonic'.[78] The democratic conception of citizenship puts political equality and participation at its centre, but it is also particularising and exclusionary because it requires a defined demos, which entails distinguishing between members and non-members. The democratic dimension is narrower than the juridical dimension, which conceives of the citizen as the legal person who is free to act by law and expect the law's protection. This component is inherently universal, and, according to Cohen, 'it is on this basis that transnational or global citizenship is at least conceivable'.[79] However, the very universality of the juridical dimension of citizenship tends to depoliticise and undermine solidarity. It is in tension not only with the democratic dimension, it also fits uneasily with the membership dimension, which hinges on notions of identity, belonging and community. Cohen emphasises the '"elective" affinity between a strong democratic stress on citizenship as the self-rule of a sovereign demos (which presupposes membership) and a communitarian stress on belonging and identity'.[80]

Cohen argues that the three elements of the citizenship principle appeared to map congruently onto each other in the terrain of the constitutional, national, territorial and welfare state. In the period after World War II, with embedded liberalism, these three dimensions appeared to be compatible within the political space of the nation state. T H Marshall's conception of social citizenship exemplifies the democratic socialist conception of citizenship which is anchored in the nation state. Marshall foregrounded the universal nature of citizenship, while at the same time linking citizenship to the principle of equality in ways that promoted social integration and inclusion. The underlying tension between juridical and democratic dimensions was easy to ignore so long as the 'cultural identity of the demos [was] construed as a nation.' But, if, as Cohen suggests, attention shifts from Marshall's 'focus on the substantive rights of citizenship … to the formal dimension of membership' then citizenship becomes an instrument of social closure and exclusion because the nation state can exclude those who are not its members.[81] The background presumption of this paradigmatic conception is that citizenship involves membership in a sovereign, territorial nation-state within a system of states. Here Hannah Arendt's insight that 'the attribution of exclusive territoriality and inviolable sovereignty to each nation state over internal matters contributed to the willingness of states to deprive non-citizens of basic rights and to threaten the rights of national minorities, even if they were citizens' is crucial.[82] Cohen highlights the exclusionary side of citizenship, one that democratic socialists, who emphasise the political dimension, tend, unlike their conservative counterparts, to minimise.

The critical point of Cohen's argument is that the three dimensions of citizenship are in essential tension and cannot be resolved by the same institutions or within the national scale.[83] Because, unlike conservatives, social democrats are committed to inclusion, they

[78] Cohen, 'Changing Paradigms of Citizenship and the Exclusiveness of the Demos' (1999) 14 *International Sociology* 245-268, 248.
[79] Ibid, 249.
[80] Ibid, 250.
[81] Ibid, 253.
[82] Ibid, 253.
[83] Ibid, 265.

face a dilemma when dealing with migration. The principles of political citizenship – popular sovereignty – is not well suited for protecting non-citizens. Thus, democratic socialists need to consider the rights of non-citizens to reside, to work and to participate in social life in the UK when developing a constitutional framework. Ewing claims that it is only possible to achieve social citizenship by embracing the state, engaging social partners in decision-making and democratising the social and economic spheres.[84] These mechanisms need not be confined to citizens. Yet, the only institutions that Ewing identifies as critical to democratic socialism are the universal franchise, parliamentary sovereignty and autonomous trade unions. These institutions are critical for ensuring the political and membership dimensions of citizenship. But while membership in the demos must be limited in order to keep it active and vital, the presence of large numbers of non-citizens in most countries means that many people who are subject to the law had no say in authoring it. For this reason, migrants must be protected by international human rights that are enforced by institutions that are not subject to the will of the majority.[85] Human rights provide an important resource for deepening and disaggregating the juridical dimension of citizenship from the other two components.

Democratic socialist need to consider other mechanisms and institutions to ensure that the political and membership dimensions of citizenship do not become exclusionary of non-citizens. What kinds of autonomous and membership-based organisations can represent non-citizens? What kinds of institutions need to be embedded and constitutionally protected into order to enable non-citizen residents to participate in social dialogue? How do we democratise the social and political space? The right to vote in local government elections based on residence is a step in the direction of giving migrants democratic voice. Regardless of the precise institutional configuration, what is clear is that the components of citizenship need to be embedded in a variety of institutions – including parliaments and courts – if the rights of migrants are to be protected.

It is also important to take into account of how institutions may shape attitudes. Drawing on the work of political scientists who explain the feedback loops between policies, institutions and public opinion, Banting reminds us:

> policy regimes set a frame which helps shape attitudes, and expands or narrows the opportunities for political elites to mobilize the darker side that exists in any democratic citizenry. Phrased in another way, how much cultural glue a society needs depends not only on the extent and nature of diversity as such, but also on the ways in which public policies structure the distribution of benefits and burdens across a diverse population.[86]

Policy feedback includes the ways programs and institutions both 'distribute material and political resources across different groups and the larger interpretive implications about politics and the welfare state implicit in their structure and operation'.[87] Banting explains that policy regimes influence public preferences in three ways: generating negative feedback from the public and triggering direct changes in policy; altering the nature of information flows to the public by, for example, targeting particular groups of beneficiaries make

[84] Ibid.
[85] Ibid, 264.
[86] Banting (n 12) 814–5.
[87] Ibid, 802.

their dependency more visible; and policies, especially those celebrating cultural motifs and symbols, may influence the public's sense of national identity. This approach, instead of treating 'diversity as an independent variable that affects the welfare state', inverts 'the question to ask how the welfare state shapes diversity'.[88]

Thus, it is also crucial to consider whether and how the policies and institutions that give the British welfare state is distinctive shape influence the public's commitment to diversity and immigration. How welfare programs are structured – means-tested or universal, general revenue or contribution based – influences whether or not immigrants are seen as a drain on, or contribution to, the host society. Integration and cultural policies are also significant to whether or not immigrants are considered to be 'them' or 'us'.

VI. Conclusion

Migration poses a particular challenge for democratic socialists because democratic socialists are committed to inclusion *and* equality. The problem is that 'in an age of migration, democracy has begun to act as an institution of exclusion, not inclusion.'[89] Democratic socialists need to consider constitutionalising institutions that will help to minimise the tension between the different dimensions of citizenship. Because of their commitment to autonomous forms of collective power and democraticising economic, political and social life, social democrats have the greatest capacity to defeat authoritarian populism. If economic shocks like austerity and the financial meltdown are linked to the rise of authoritarian populism then social democratic policies are an important antidote to rising anti-immigrant sentiment.[90] The Labour Party's 2019 Election Manifesto decisive rejection of the strategy of the 'demonisation of migrant workers' and explicit commitment to 'a humane immigration system' and re-regulating the labour market rejects is a step in a progressive direction.[91] It is also possible that the progressive's dilemma is not 'the appropriate question to pose' and that the nation is not as liberal nationalists and democratic socialists presume 'the basic structure of society'.[92] Class structures or competition between rising and established elites may have a greater influence on solidarity than nationality. This is another reason why democratic socialism of the kind Ewing advocates is a necessary, if not sufficient, step for ending exclusionary, anti-immigrant populism.

[88] M Smith, 'Diversity and Canadian Political Development' (2009) 42 *Canadian Journal of Political Science* 831, 837.

[89] Krastev (n 9) 14.

[90] D Rodik, 'What's Driving Populism?' (*Social Europe*, 23 July 2019) www.socialeurope.eu/whats-driving-populism.

[91] Labour Party Manifesto, *It's Time for Real Change* (Labour Party, 2019) 70.

[92] Leddy-Owens (n 41) 346.

22

State Surveillance and Social Democracy: Lessons after the Investigatory Powers Act 2016

CIAN C MURPHY*

I. Introduction

This chapter uses the passage and content of the Investigatory Powers Act 2016 (IPA) to argue that social democrats are failing to address threats to civil liberties – to their detriment. For Ewing, in a social democratic state, constitutional authority derives from the sovereignty of the people and vests in elected representatives. Its goals are 'the promotion of the social, economic and cultural well-being of citizens' and those socialist reforms are to be done consistently with civil and political rights.[1] Thus, social democracy entails 'the extension of liberal principles to different sites of struggle'.[2] As a result there is a strong socio-economic focus and it is therefore unsurprising that many of the chapters in this book focus, for example, on labour law. However, to borrow a phrase from Ewing and Gearty, 'the struggle for civil liberties'[3] remains vital. This chapter argues that the failure by the Labour Party (and other social democrats) to get to grips with the IPA illustrates an ambivalence towards civil liberties. This ambivalence persists despite a history of state misuse of powers against social democrats, and despite (earlier) vocal opposition to the legislation by those who were party leaders while the Bill became law.

This chapter proceeds with the following parts. Part II presents a historical analysis as the foundation for the study. It intertwines two histories: the rise of state surveillance capacity, in particular surveillance of telecommunications, in the UK; and the legal protection of civil liberties and its relationship with surveillance law. Part III examines the origins and adoption of the IPA. It demonstrates how, despite significant political review, and civil society engagement, there was little prospect of extensive changes in Parliament because of the acquiescence of the Labour Party with the government's Bill. Part IV considers the

* Thanks to P Hirst for research assistance, and to the editors, and D Lock, for comments. I have endeavoured to state the law as of 1 October 2019.

[1] KD Ewing, 'Democratic Socialism and Labour Law' (1995) 24 *Industrial Law Journal* 103.

[2] KD Ewing, 'Jeremy Corbyn and the Law of Democracy' (2017) 28 *King's Law Journal* 343.

[3] KD Ewing and CA Gearty, *The Struggle for Civil Liberties: Political Freedom and the Rule of Law in Britain, 1914–1945* (Oxford, OUP, 2000).

fruit of this failure: weak protections for lawyers, journalists, and trade unionists. The final part highlights ongoing litigation and the potential future evolution of surveillance. The IPA demonstrates 'the re-assertion of the surveillance realist insistence that there is no alternative'.[4] This perception helps to perpetuate profound legal powers of surveillance. All of this is made possible, in part, by a failure to protect the civil liberties which underpin all progressive struggles.

II. State Surveillance, Civil Liberties & Social Democracy

Three decades ago Ewing and Gearty described the tension between democracy and state surveillance of communications: 'although it may be necessary to tolerate the practice, it should be conducted only in exceptional and highly controlled circumstances under which there is adequate scrutiny and review by institutions independent of the executive branch of government'.[5]

Social democrats, and those on the Left in general, have had good reason to be sceptical.[6] In the last century, those who identified as Communist or who were under suspicion of it, came under particular scrutiny. By 1952 the Security Service (MI5) had identified 90 per cent of the Communist Party of Great Britain's 35,000 members. As a *Guardian* headline put it, 'Being a Communist was all it took'.[7] Prior to World War II, 'civil liberties politics appeared to offer some obvious shared ground between socialist and liberal principles, potentially offering a unifying theme for adherents of such ideologies'.[8] However, as the century developed, a gap grew between those who were willing to pay the price of such associations and those who were not. Suspicion of the Communist Party of Great Britain (CPGB) influence over organisations such as the National Council of Civil Liberties (NCCL – now Liberty), the conflation in the minds of the Metropolitan Police of Communism and anti-fascism, and Cold War ideologies all contributed to a breakdown in the solidarity between civil libertarians and social democrats.[9]

At the same time the state's capacity for surveillance grew. Telecommunications surveillance is not the only form of state surveillance.[10] However, it merits particular scrutiny for several reasons. First, it is covert (and sometimes secret). Thus, the subject of a covert surveillance operation will not be aware of the fact. And, in the case of secret surveillance, the existence of a power to conduct such surveillance might not even be known. In *Klass*, one of the earliest judgments on surveillance, the European Court of Human Rights (ECtHR)

[4] L Dencik, 'Surveillance Realism and the Politics of Imagination: Is There No Alternative?' (2018) 1 *Krisis* 31, 40.

[5] KD Ewing and CA Gearty, *Freedom Under Thatcher: Civil Liberties in Modern Britain* (Oxford, OUP, 1990) 48.

[6] Ewing and Gearty, *The Struggle for Civil Liberties* (n 3) 48.

[7] M Kettle, 'Historians' work meant little to an MI5 obsessed with cold-war communists' *The Guardian* (London, 24 October 2014). See C Andrew, *The Defence of the Realm: The Authorised History of MI5* (London, Penguin, 2012) and Ewing and Gearty, *The Struggle for Civil Liberties* (n 3) 112–118.

[8] C Moores, 'From Civil Liberties to Human Rights? British Civil Liberties Activism and Universal Human Rights' (2012) 21 *Contemporary European History* 169, 171.

[9] Ibid, *passim*.

[10] See S Chesterman, *One Nation Under Surveillance: A New Social Contract to Defend Freedom Without Sacrificing Liberty* (New York, OUP, 2013) 131–156.

held that '[p]owers of secret surveillance of citizens, characterising as they do the police state, are tolerable under the Convention only in so far as strictly necessary for safeguarding the democratic institutions'.[11]

Second, covert surveillance often arises in the context of state regulation of political opposition. A recent database of another covert surveillance power – undercover policing – identifies targets including campaigns for animal rights and the environment, or a wide range of 'anti-' campaigns: apartheid, capitalism, nuclear power/weapons, racism, and war.[12]

Third, telecommunications surveillance is at the forefront of the development of the law. The history is one of state empowerment of intelligence agencies, litigation to vindicate civil liberties, and imperfect political responses to legalise identified rights violations.

The starting point for the contemporary legal framework is the reaction to the *Malone* judgment of the European Court of Human Rights (ECtHR). Mr James Malone was an antiques dealer under suspicion of crime. His telephones were tapped. In the national court, when Sir Robert Megarry VC could find no 'breach of the law' by the phone-tapping, he concluded that no authority in law was necessary. The European Court of Human Rights disagreed, and found a violation of Article 8 ECHR, on the grounds that the interference with privacy was not 'in accordance with law'.[13] The legislative response was the Interception of Communications Act 1985 – which provided the necessary authority.

In 1989, Patricia Hewitt and Harriet Harman of the NCCL were in pursuit of relief from the European Commission on Human Rights from surveillance without a basis in law. To address the matter, the government published a draft statute which became the Security Services Act 1989.[14] Five years later, the Intelligence Services Act 1994 gave statutory legal basis to the activities of the Secret Intelligence Service (MI6) and Government Communications Headquarters (CGHQ), and brought about certain arrangements for oversight.[15] The cases illustrate the tendency of UK governments to only address the issues of lawfulness and oversight when litigation makes it unavoidable.

In contrast to the earlier cases, *Kennedy* offers a counter-point, in which the UK legal framework was upheld.[16] The ECtHR had to consider the operation of the Investigatory Powers Tribunal which was established by the Regulation of Investigatory Powers Act 2000 to hear complaints against the intelligence services. After a complaint to the IPT about potential surveillance Mr Kennedy was told only that there was no determination in his favour. This meant he was either not under surveillance or, in the IPT's view, any surveillance was lawful. The ECtHR held that there was no violation of Article 8 ECHR when the law was read alongside the Code of Practice. There is a tension here with the values of accountability which the rule of law promotes. Although the interference with Article 8 had a basis in law (ie the statute and Code of Practice) it was not, for Mr Kennedy, clear whether or not he had been subject to surveillance.

[11] *Klass v Germany* (1978) 2 EHRR 214, para 42.

[12] R Evans, 'UK political groups spied on by undercover police – search the list' *The Guardian* (London, 13 February 2019).

[13] *Malone v United Kingdom* (1984) 7 EHRR 14.

[14] *Hewitt and Harman v United Kingdom* (1992) 14 EHRR 657.

[15] For a contemporaneous critique see: J Wadham, 'The Intelligence Services Act 1994' (1994) *MLR* 916.

[16] *Kennedy v United Kingdom* (2011) 52 EHRR 4.

It may be that *Kennedy* was correct and the IPT scheme established by RIPA is in compliance with the Convention. RIPA was, nevertheless, much-maligned even before the Snowden revelations. In the words of David Anderson QC it was 'incomprehensible to all but a tiny band of initiates'.[17] In the debate on his report, *A Question of Trust*, the Shadow Home Secretary Yvette Cooper MP admitted that the only way she could understand the law was 'with a wet towel wrapped around [her] head'.[18] This was the state of play as the IP Bill was about to be published.

What to make of this from the point of view of social democracy? Many powers are used in the absence of legal authority. This runs contrary to the idea of the constitutional authority of the people-in-Parliament under Ewing's conception of social democracy. Several of these powers have been upheld by the national judiciary before being found contrary to the UK's international legal obligations by a supranational judiciary. Furthermore, when the breaches were identified, the response of the legislature was, by and large, to alter the law not to protect civil liberties but to authorise the surveillance powers. In terms of the form of the law, the development of surveillance law offers little support for the claim that the legislature will offer better protection than the judiciary. In terms of the substantive content of such laws, legislation which provides powers that are open to political abuse ought to be of concern to those who have been subject to such abuses – such as social democrats.

The ECHR, of course, contains civil and political rights rather than social and economic ones. As Gearty, who is largely supportive of the ECHR and the HRA, notes: the post-war constitutional settlement in Europe allows social democracy only of 'a fairly timid sort'.[19] The HRA was brought about to fulfil the legacy of former Labour Party leader John Smith.[20] It afforded greater protection to civil rights and political freedoms in domestic law but had little impact on social and economic rights.[21] Indeed, social and economic rights have been in decline in UK and across Europe during the HRA's lifetime.[22] And the Party which legislated for the HRA became increasingly antipathetic towards it over the lifetime of the Blair Governments.[23]

Ewing has long been critical of both the ECHR and the EU Charter. The former, he argues, protects commercial speech and private property. The latter, even more contrarily to social democracy, includes the right to conduct business.[24] He is also sceptical of the judicial protection of rights as a vehicle for progressive politics. A social democratic model relies on Parliament to protect rights.[25] And he warns against 'the empowerment of lawyers as a class … self-appointed, self-regulating, and accountable to no-one outside their own community'.[26]

[17] D Anderson QC, *A Question of Trust: Report of the Investigatory Powers Review* (London, TSO, 2015), para 35.

[18] *Hansard*, 25 June 2015, vol 597, col 1086.

[19] CA Gearty, 'Neo-democracy: 'Useful Idiot' of neo-liberalism?' (2016) 56 *British Journal of Criminology* 1087, 1096.

[20] See F Klug, *Values for a Godless Age: The Story of the United Kingdom's New Bill of Rights* (London, Penguin, 2000).

[21] Ewing, 'Democratic Socialism and Labour Law' (n 1) 108–109.

[22] KD Ewing, 'The Death of Social Europe' (2015) 26(1) *King's Law Journal* 76.

[23] See KD Ewing, *Bonfire of the Liberties: New Labour, Human Rights, and the Rule of Law* (Oxford, OUP, 2010).

[24] Ewing, 'Jeremy Corbyn and the Law of Democracy' (n 2) 346, 357.

[25] Ewing, 'Democratic Socialism and Labour Law' (n 1) 110.

[26] Ewing, 'Jeremy Corbyn and the Law of Democracy' (n 2) 357.

Yet lawyers (and their clients) have been responsible for the development of constraints on the executive/legislature. The ECHR and EU Charter may have effect in the UK because of Acts of Parliament: the HRA and European Communities Act 1972 respectively. But it is the judiciary which has taken the opportunity the legislation gave them to resist legal and operational overreach by the legislature and executive.

The litigation set out both above and below centres on the right to privacy found in Article 8 ECHR. However, a range of other rights are also engaged by telecommunications surveillance. Article 10 ECHR, on freedom of expression, protects journalists. Article 11 ECHR on freedom of assembly offers protections for trade unions and other political groups. Article 14 ECHR sets out a prohibition on discrimination which may also be relevant.[27]

The EU Charter is engaged because national legislation which is 'within the scope of EU law' must be compatible with the Charter. This compatibility is overseen by the EU Court of Justice (CJEU).[28] The standards are, by and large, in concordance with the ECHR. Article 7 of the EU Charter is near-identical to Article 8 ECHR. Article 8 EU Charter adds to the general privacy protection with more explicit data protection rights. The CJEU's supervisory jurisdiction, used to significant effect in *Digital Rights Ireland*,[29] and then in *Watson*,[30] has put it at the forefront of the debate on surveillance. Those judgments are set out later.

The rationalisation of telecommunication surveillance powers results, at the very least, from a 'dialogue'[31] between the judiciary and the legislature/executive. Part III of this chapter examines the adoption of the IPA. The principal opposition to the Act came not from those advocates of social democracy but rather from 'civil libertarians' – in particular privacy activists. This ought to be of concern because, as Part IV demonstrates, the law has a detrimental impact on three professions which could play a role in achieving social democracy: lawyers, journalists, and trade unionists.

III. The Investigatory Powers Act 2016

The IPA has put the UK at the forefront of the development of lawful surveillance powers. It is in part a response to the revelations of Edward Snowden.[32] In 2013, Snowden revealed widespread digital surveillance by the US Government and its allies. These allies, in particular, were in the 'Five Eyes' states: Australia, Canada, New Zealand, the UK (and the US).[33] For parliamentarians, Snowden's revelations were an indication that their knowledge of state surveillance capacities and operations was limited. For the public, there was outrage at the extensive surveillance of their telecommunications. However, unsurprisingly, the UK and other governments did not welcome the publication by journalists of extensive

[27] P Bernal, 'Data gathering, surveillance and human rights: recasting the debate' (2016) 2 *Journal of Cyber Policy* 243, 244.

[28] See D Anderson and CC Murphy 'The Charter of Fundamental Rights' in A Biondi, P Eeckhout and S Ripley (eds) *EU Law after Lisbon* (Oxford, OUP, 2012).

[29] C-293/12 *Digital Rights Ireland* EU:C:2014:238.

[30] Joined Cases C-203/15 and C-685/15 *Tele2 Sverige* and *Watson v GCHQ*, EU:C:2016:970.

[31] See A Young, *Parliamentary Sovereignty and the Human Rights Act* (Oxford, Hart Publishing, 2008) 10–12.

[32] A Hintz and I Brown, 'Digital Citizenship and Surveillance| Enabling Digital Citizenship? The Reshaping of Surveillance Policy After Snowden' (2017) 11 *International Journal of Communication* 782, 792.

[33] See the symposium in 2020 *Common Law World Review* for a discussion.

classified materials. Prime Minister David Cameron warned of the potential for government to intervene: 'If [journalists] don't demonstrate some social responsibility it will be very difficult for government to stand back and not to act'.[34] Implicit, of course, in this threat was a denial that publication was in itself a fulfilment of the journalists' social responsibility.

The Snowden revelations are one half of the story. The fate of the Data Retention Directive is the other half. The 2014 judgment of the CJEU in *Digital Rights Ireland* held that the Directive was unlawful. The Directive had required the retention, and making available to law enforcement authorities, of telecommunications data across the EU. CJEU case-law continues to develop but in that first case the court set out the need for such powers to be restricted and subject to appropriate oversight.[35] To avoid any doubt over the legal basis for data retention and access in the UK, Parliament enacted the Data Retention and Investigatory Powers Act 2015 (DRIPA). This legislation gave the powers a new basis in national law. It too was the subject of a successful challenge to its lawfulness brought, initially, by two MPs: Tom Watson (Labour Party) and David Davis (Conservative Party).[36] By the time the case was resolved, DRIPA had been replaced by the IPA.

DRIPA anticipated its own demise. It included a requirement that the Independent Reviewer of Terrorism Legislation, David Anderson QC, conduct a review of 'the operation and regulation of investigatory powers'.[37] It included a sunset clause to repeal it on 31 December 2016.[38] Anderson's report was therefore always likely to significantly influence DRIPA's replacement. The report, *A Question of Trust*, runs to 373 pages (including annexes) and offers a comprehensive assessment of the legal, ethical, and technological questions which surround telecommunications surveillance. Two other reports were also influential. *Privacy and Security: A Modern and Transparent Legal Framework* was published by the Intelligence and Security Committee of Parliament.[39] The third, *A Democratic Licence to Operate*, was written by a panel appointed by the Royal United Services Institute.[40] In addition, several parliamentary committees (including the ISC) scrutinised and reported on the draft legislation.[41]

Not all the evidence which influenced the legislation has been published. Sir Nigel Sheinwald undertook confidential work for the Prime Minister in his role as the Special Envoy on Intelligence and Law Enforcement Data Sharing.[42] A two-page summary of his work was published. The recommendations focus on improving bilateral co-operation,

[34] 'Cameron Says May Act Against Press Over Spy Leaks' (*Reuters*, 28 October 2013).

[35] CC Murphy, *EU Counter-terrorism Law: Pre-emption and the Rule of Law* (Oxford, Hart, Expanded Paperback Edition 2015) 257–263.

[36] Upon his appointment as Secretary of State for Exiting the European Union, David Davis MP withdrew from the litigation. Open Rights Group and Privacy International were interveners.

[37] DRIPA 2015, s 7.

[38] DRIPA 2015, s 8(3).

[39] Intelligence and Security Committee of Parliament, *Privacy and Security: A Modern and Transparent Legal Framework* (HC 2015, 1075).

[40] RUSI, *A Democratic Licence to Operate* (London, RUSI, 2015).

[41] Anderson points to reports on the Bill by the ISC, Science and Technology Committee, Joint Bill Committee, a Public Bill Committee, Joint Committee on Human Rights, Constitution Committee, and Delegation and Regulatory Reform Committee. See D Anderson QC, 'The Investigatory Powers Act 2016 – an exercise in democracy' (*David Anderson QC*, 3 December 2016) www.daqc.co.uk/2016/12/03/the-investigatory-powers-act-2016-an-exercise-in-democracy/.

[42] Sir N Sheinwald, *Summary of the Work of the Prime Minister's Special Envoy on Intelligence and Law Enforcement Data Sharing – Sir Nigel Sheinwald* (London, The Cabinet Office, 2015).

Mutual Legal Assistance Treaties, and the development of an international legal framework. The Independent Reviewer conducted a review of the operational case for bulk data collection.[43] This use of the office of Independent Reviewer was possible because of his access to classified materials.[44] It was a successful strategy by the government, both because of the office's access to classified materials, and the high esteem in which Anderson was held across the political spectrum. This reliance on 'hybrid institutions' such as the Independent Reviewer (and perhaps the Special Envoy) indicates a limitation on Parliament's capacity to perform its function –which exists because of the necessary secrecy which national security demands.[45]

The role of global civil society in the regulation of communications is significant. They are 'increasingly part of multistakeholder processes that expand policy authority beyond governments'.[46] The most prominent example is that of the Internet Corporation for Assigned Names and Numbers (ICANN) in the regulation of domain names.[47] However, the role also involves 'normative interventions' – lobbying – governments on law and regulation. The prospect of influence on the content of legislation (rather than just its existence or not) has led to a shift in some civil society strategies – away from outright opposition and towards constructive collaboration.[48] However, these groups did not always get the 'traction' they sought. The civil society response to the Investigatory Powers Bill was strong and, to an extent, co-ordinated. Organisations including Liberty, Big Brother Watch, and Privacy International were part of a broader campaign entitled *Don't Spy On Us*. The campaign described itself as 'a coalition of the most influential organisations who defend privacy, free expression and digital rights in the UK and in Europe'.[49] The trade union movement appears to have left the lobbying to more specialist groups. TUC Congress in 2016 'congratulate[d]' the NUJ on the amendments it secured to the Bill.[50] Indeed, the NUJ remains active in resistance to the legislation – in particular via participation in strategic litigation.[51]

Anderson applauded the legislative process.[52] He wrote that the Act 'gets the big things right' and that it is a 'victory for democracy and the rule of law'.[53] To support this conclusion he cites the numerous parliamentary committee reports on the Bill, as well as the role of civil society, and public commentators.[54] This is persuasive, to an extent, and yet in a 2017 study Hintz and Brown found most of their interviewees agreed that 'a true public debate

[43] D Anderson, *Report of the Bulk Powers Review* (Cmd 9326, 2016).

[44] See in general D Anderson, 'Shades of Independent Review' in G Lennon, C King and C McCartney (eds), *Counter-terrorism, Constitutionalism, and Miscarriages of Justice: A Festschrift for Professor Clive Walker* (Oxford, Hart Publishing, 2019).

[45] PF Scott, 'Hybrid institutions in the national security constitution: the case of the Commissioners' (2019) 39 *Legal Studies* 1. On the Independent Reviewer's role see: D Anderson QC, 'The Independent Review of Terrorism Laws' (2014) *Public Law* 403.

[46] Hintz and Brown, 'Digital Citizenship and Surveillance| Enabling Digital Citizenship? The Reshaping of Surveillance Policy After Snowden' (n 32) 784.

[47] See: www.icann.org.

[48] Ibid, 794.

[49] See: www.dontspyonus.org.uk.

[50] TUC Congress 2016, *Preliminary Agenda*, 11–14 September 2016, 21.

[51] See below at IV.B.

[52] Anderson, 'The Investigatory Powers Act 2016 – an exercise in democracy' (n 41).

[53] Ibid.

[54] Ibid.

has not yet taken place'.[55] Bernal suggests the debate post-Snowden has been 'limited and miscast'.[56] He observes that, despite the volume of the conversation, there remains unhelpful disagreement on what constitutes surveillance, the distinction between 'metadata' and content data, and the impact of both covert and overt surveillance.[57] The breadth of the law, in terms of the agencies which are empowered by it, the powers which it contains, and the potential targets of those powers, is one limitation on the effectiveness of the parliamentary process. A challenge for those organisations was the sheer scope of the Bill. Given the limited time for the consideration of any Bill in Parliament, an omnibus Bill such as this, would be a serious challenge. It is for this reason that calls to also revise and re-codify other investigatory powers, such as those in the Police and Criminal Evidence Act 1984, as part of the process, were rightly resisted.

The legal and technological complexity of many of the Act's provisions adds to the challenge to adequately scrutinise it. The Act has been commended for being 'technology-neutral' – ie written in broad language to capture future technological developments as well as the services currently in use. However, some of the Act's engagement with technological matters confounds even technologists. The chief example is 'internet connection records'. For the Home Office, the requirement to retain ICRs is the only novel power for which the Act provides. However, there remains little clarity on what ICRs are and how they can be collected. Some technologists consider that they do not constitute an existent type or category of data – with the result that service providers will have to collect far more data than appears on the face of the Bill (see for instance various evidence put before Parliament).

Given the challenges for civil society engagement the responsibility for Parliament is even greater. The Constitution relies on the Opposition to hold the government to account. And yet the role of civil society contrasts sharply with that of the Labour Party. On 9 September 2015, a group of Labour Party MPs and trade unionists, including influential figures such as Tom Watson MP and Len McCluskey of UNITE, wrote to *The Guardian* to urge the next Labour leader to be ready to deal with the IP Bill, and to ensure there is no 'unnecessary trade-off between security and privacy'. They explicitly invoked 'the historical surveillance and subversion of the union movement'.[58] It is remarkable, then, that the official policy of the Labour Party was to welcome the Bill on first reading, abstain on second reading, and support it on third reading. The Leader of the Labour Party, Jeremy Corbyn, was absent for the Commons votes on the Bill.[59] The chief resistance in the House of Commons came from the Liberal Democrats, Scottish Nationalist Party, and Caroline Lucas of the Green Party.

The Labour Party's failure to oppose the Bill led to criticism from fellow parliamentarians and in the press.[60] Corbyn was not the only member of the Party to face direct criticism.

[55] Hintz and Brown, 'Digital Citizenship and Surveillance| Enabling Digital Citizenship? The Reshaping of Surveillance Policy After Snowden' (n 32) 796.

[56] P Bernal, 'Data gathering, surveillance and human rights: recasting the debate' (2016) 2 *Journal of Cyber Policy* 243, 244.

[57] Ibid, 248–250.

[58] 'Investigatory powers bill must be a priority for Labour's next leader' *The Guardian* (London, 9 September 2015).

[59] R Williams, 'How Tim Farron, Theresa May, and Jeremy Corbyn voted on mass surveillance' *iNews* (London, 31 May 2017).

[60] K Fiveash, 'Can We Please Stop Peddling the Myth that Labour Opposes Gov't Spying' (*Ars Technica*, 19 October 2016) https://arstechnica.com/tech-policy/2016/10/ipb-stop-peddling-myth-labour-opposed-surveillance/;

Shadow Home Secretary, Diane Abbott MP, as well as Shadow Attorney General, Baroness Shami Chakrabarti, were also singled out. The criticism referred to past unlawful surveillance of Abbott, and well as Chakrabarti's outspoken response to surveillance as director of Liberty. The reason for this silence, in the words of one commentator, 'remains a mystery'.[61] Andy Burnham MP did sponsor an amendment supportive of trade unions which the government accepted – but its value, as we will see, is limited.

The absence of Labour Party leadership of opposition to the Bill gives the lie to the promises of *The Digital Democracy Manifesto*, launched by Jeremy Corbyn in August 2016, during the Labour leadership election.[62] It also renders risible the claim in the party's 2017 election manifesto, *For the Many Not the Few*, that in relation to civil liberties and investigatory powers, '[the Party] will reintroduce effective judicial oversight over how and when they are used, when the circumstances demand that our collective security outweighs an individual freedom'.[63] Aside from the indecipherable grammar the statement rings hollow.

Indeed, at least since the 11 September 2001 attacks, surveillance, like counter-terrorism,[64] has been a 'bi-partisan' policy field. The two parties which have led every government since the end of World War II are largely aligned on the issue. Andy Burnham MP admitted as much when he acknowledged that 'in the past – *under Governments of both colours, it has to be said* – trade unions have indeed been monitored'.[65]

The Labour Party relied on amendments to the legislation to justify their support for it at third reading.[66] However, these amendments, as shown in Part IV below, fail to address several serious concerns with the legislation. Furthermore, governments have long known the lesson of the Incitement to Disaffection Bill of 1934, of which a contemporary commentator observed '[it] reminds one of the traditional horse-dealer … Place your demands sufficiently high, and you can graciously make numerous concessions and still get all you want'.[67]

IV. Some Implications for Social Democrats

The IPA is extensive and a comprehensive analysis is beyond the scope of this chapter.[68] It includes powers for the targeted and bulk interception of communications, requirements on telecommunications service providers to retain communications data (records

B Paddick, 'The Lib Dems oppose this snooper's charter. Why doesn't Labour?' *The Guardian* (London, 19 October 2016).

[61] P Bernal, 'How the UK passed the most invasive surveillance law in democratic history' (*The Conversation*, 23 November 2016) https://theconversation.com/how-the-uk-passed-the-most-invasive-surveillance-law-in-democratic-history-69247.

[62] J Corbyn, *The Digital Deomcracy Manifesto* (August 2016) https://d3n8a8pro7vhmx.cloudfront.net/corbynstays/pages/329/attachments/original/1472552058/Digital_Democracy.pdf?1472552058.

[63] The Labour Party, *For The Many, Not the Few: The Labour Party Manifesto 2017* (Labour Party, London, 2017) https://labour.org.uk/manifesto/ 77.

[64] L Morgan and F de Londras, 'Is There A 'Conservative' Counter-Terrorism?' (2018) 29 *King's Law Journal* 187.

[65] *Hansard* 6 June 2016 vol 611, col 955 (emphasis added).

[66] K Fiveash, 'Investigatory Powers Bill passes through Commons after Labour backs Tory spy law' (*Ars Technica*, 6 July 2016) https://arstechnica.com/tech-policy/2016/06/labour-backs-principle-of-investigatory-powers-bill/.

[67] *The New Statesman*, 14 July 1934.

[68] S McKay, *Blackstone's Guide to the Investigatory Powers Act 2016* (Oxford, OUP, 2017).

of telephone and internet use) for access by various governmental offices and agencies. It also includes powers for targeted and bulk 'equipment interference' (ie hacking). There is much in the Act which empowers state surveillance. The principal safeguards against such powers are now found in the Investigatory Powers Commissioner's Office (ICPO). Amongst the Act's innovations is the requirement that (most but not all) warrants to exercise powers under the Act must be approved first by the Home Secretary and then by a Judicial Commissioner.[69] Three aspects of the Act's impact on social democracy are examined, each of which were the subject of lobbying during the legislative process. These are the protections of legal professional privilege, journalistic material, and trade union data.[70] The legal profession is required, on ethical grounds, to be independent (see for example the Core Code of Conduct for barristers). Furthermore, for the press, and trade unions, to serve their societal functions, they must be independent of the state. The erosions of the special legal protections afforded to these institutions weakens their capacity to be agents of social democratic reform. And, as we shall see, the IP Act continues that erosion.

A. Legal Professional Privilege (LPP)

The legal profession is not necessarily an instrument of social democracy – as Ewing makes clear. However, the capacity of lawyers to protect their clients, in particular through legal privilege, can be of benefit to social democrats. That trade unionists, or journalists, for example, can access confidential legal advice is essential to their performance of their roles. And the existence of the Haldane Society of Socialist Lawyers is evidence that lawyers may organise in pursuit of social democracy.[71]

The justification for LPP doesn't focus on the legal professional but on the client. It is, as Lord Phillips put it, 'the fundamental requirement that a man should be able to speak freely and frankly to his lawyer'.[72] In *re McE (Northern Ireland)* the House of Lords had to consider whether it was lawful to target LPP communications for interception.[73] RIPA did not mention LPP but some protections for privilege were found in a Code of Practice. The Lords held that as RIPA did not prohibit the targeting of LPP communications then it was lawful to do so.

The IPA, at first, was set to follow this practice, because the draft Bill only required that a Code of Practice address 'legally privileged material'.[74] A joint briefing prepared by The Law Society and the General Counsel of the Bar, amongst others, identified several failings of the Bill. These included an absence of adequate protections for privilege in relation to communications data, when an individual outside the UK communicates with a lawyer inside the UK, and when warrants are modified. The briefing called for a statutory requirement to avoid the capture of privileged material as well an obligation to report annually on

[69] See in particular Pt 8, ch 1. For a critical consideration see Scott, 'Hybrid institutions in the national security constitution: the case of the Commissioners' (n 45).

[70] There is not space here to consider the question of confidentiality of MPs communications.

[71] See: www.haldane.org.

[72] Lord Phillips of Worth Matravers in re McE (Northern Ireland) [2009] UKHL 15, [2009] 1 AC 908 [10].

[73] Ibid.

[74] Secretary of State for the Home Department, *Draft Investigatory Powers Bill* (Cmd 9152, 2015) Sch 6, clause 4.

the number of privilege authorisations granted.[75] Not all of these recommendations were agreed but amendments in the House of Lords introduced some safeguards.[76]

These are found in section 27 of the IPA. A warrant application must state that its purpose(s) include the interception or examination of 'items subject to legal privilege'.[77] It can only be done in the interests of national security or to prevent death or serious injury.[78] The decision-maker on the warrant must have regard to the public interest in confidentiality of LPP material.[79] For the warrant to be lawful there must be 'exceptional and compelling circumstances'[80] which make it necessary and specific arrangements for its 'handling, retention, use, and destruction'.[81] The Act also makes explicit reference to the 'iniquity exception': the rule that legal privilege does not attach to communications which aim to further a criminal purpose.[82]

In comparison with RIPA, the IPA makes explicit that law enforcement authorities and intelligence agencies may target LPP material. It also makes the welcome shift of protections from the Code of Practice to the legislation itself. Nevertheless, the Act confirms that privilege is under strain by telecommunications surveillance, which may have a chilling effect on communications between clients and their lawyers. Chantal-Aimée Doerries QC, Chairman of the Bar Council, said: 'sadly what was passed in the end fell significantly short of what we would consider sufficient to protect this important and fundamental right, underpinning the rule of law'.[83] The matter is not only of national concern. The UK is a leader in global legal services. There is much international public interest work done by UK firms and chambers for overseas civil society groups. As Ben Jaffey QC writes: 'when my clients in national security cases ask me 'can I speak to you confidentially', my answer is still 'no'.'[84]

B. Journalistic Material

The protection of journalists finds legal expression in Article 10 ECHR. In *Goodwin v United Kingdom* the Court held that to force journalists to reveal their sources would have a chilling effect on the press' ability serve as a public watchdog.[85] In *Sanoma Uitgevers BV* the

[75] Bar Council of England and Wales, and Others, *Joint Briefing on Legal Privilege for House of Lords Second Reading of the Investigatory Powers Bill*, June 2016.

[76] For consideration of the Lords amendments see E King and D Lock, 'Investigatory Powers Bill: Key Changes Made by the Lords' (*UK Constitutional Law Blog*, 1 December 2016) https://ukconstitutionallaw.org/2016/12/01/eric-king-and-daniella-lock-investigatory-powers-bill-key-changes-made-by-the-lords/.

[77] IPA 2016, s 27(2).

[78] Ibid, s 27(6).

[79] Ibid, s 27(3).

[80] Ibid, s 27(4)(a).

[81] Ibid, s 27(4)(b).

[82] Ibid, s 27(11)–(12).

[83] The remark was made at the 10th Annual Rule of Law Lecture as quoted in J van der Luit-Drummond, 'UK's "world-leading" spy powers "a beacon for despots"' (*Solicitor's Journal*, 29 November 2016) www.solicitorsjournal.com/news/201611/uk%E2%80%99s-%E2%80%98world-leading%E2%80%99-spy-powers-%E2%80%98-beacon-despots%E2%80%99.

[84] B Jaffey QC, 'Legal Professional Privilege in jeopardy' in Big Brother Watch (ed), *The State of Surveillance in 2018* (London, Big Brother Watch, 2018).

[85] *Goodwin v United Kingdom* (1996) 22 *EHRR* 123. See further *Sanoma Uitgevers BV v The Netherlands* [2010] ECHR 1284.

Court developed its jurisprudence on safeguards. Principal amongst these is the 'guarantee of review by a judge or other independent and impartial decision making body'.[86] Such a review should take place *before* the journalist is compelled to reveal the source.

The IP Act likely fails to live up to these standards. The draft Bill did not protect journalists in relation to interception powers – but did provide that Judicial Commissioner approval was necessary for access to communications data when such access was for the purpose of identifying a journalist's source.[87] In response to the Bill's publication, the NUJ launched a 'Speak in Safety' campaign.[88] The Press Gazette shifted the focus of its campaign, 'Save Our Sources', from RIPA to the IP Bill.[89] Submissions to parliamentary committees were also made by Guardian News and Media, the Media Lawyers Association, News Media Association, Scottish PEN, as well as several individual journalists.[90] The NUJ sought 'automatic and mandatory prior notification [of requests for warrants]', 'an independent and judicial process', and 'mechanisms to challenge an application with the right of appeal'.[91] Few of the recommendations became part of the law.

The legislation as enacted makes several references to 'journalistic information' and 'confidential journalistic information'.[92] The protections are broadly analogous to those for LPP material. The safeguards therefore draw unfavourable comparisons with the Police and Criminal Evidence Act 1984 (PACE). Under PACE section 9 and schedule 1, journalists have the opportunity – prior to access – to challenge police access to journalistic materials.[93] The test for access to the material includes a requirement that there are reasonable grounds for belief that an indictable offence has been committed. These are much more stringent controls than appear in either RIPA or the IPA. The IPA's broad powers make it likely that journalists' communications can be swept up by bulk powers – for example of interception – with no means for the journalists to challenge the use of such powers in advance.

That better safeguards are necessary is clear. There is ample evidence of journalists' sources being at risk – even in democracies such as the UK.[94] Article 19 and English PEN, in their submission to the UK Universal Periodic Review, argue that bulk data collection contributes to a 'global chilling effect' on human rights organisations.[95] Even before the IPA, in October 2014, the Metropolitan Police used a power under RIPA to obtain journalist sources in relation to the 'plebs' scandal.[96] It's little wonder, then, that Reporters Without

[86] *Sanoma Uitgevers BV* (n 85) para 90.

[87] Secretary of State for the Home Department, *Draft Investigatory Powers Bill* (n 74) clause 61.

[88] See: 'Safeguarding journalists and their sources' (*National Union of Journalists*, 20 October 2014) www.nuj.org.uk/campaigns/safeguarding-journalists-and-their-sources/.

[89] See: 'Save our Sources' (Press Gazette) www.pressgazette.co.uk/subject/save-our-sources/.

[90] For evidence given to the Joint Committee on the Draft Investigatory Powers Bill see: www.parliament.uk/draft-investigatory-powers/.

[91] National Union of Journalists, Written Evidence to Draft Investigatory Powers Bill Committee, 21 December 2015 (IPB0078), para 18.

[92] See IPA 2016, ss 28, 264.

[93] PACE 1984, s 9 and sch 1.

[94] UNESCO, *2018 DG Report on the Safety of Journalists and the Danger of Impunity*, CI-18/COUNCIL-31/6 REV.2 https://en.unesco.org/themes/safety-journalists/dgreport.

[95] Article 19 and English PEN, 'Joint submission by ARTICLE 19 and English PEN to the Universal Periodic Review of the United Kingdom' (5 October 2016) www.englishpen.org/campaigns/upr-2016-submission/.

[96] The scandal involved an allegation that Andrew Mitchell MP, the government Chief Whip, had called police officers 'plebs' during an altercation with them.

Borders' 2019 World Press Freedom Index cites the IP Act as a 'menacing' threat to press freedom in the UK.[97]

C. Trade Union Data

Whatever might be said of lawyers and journalists, trade unions are central to social democracy.[98] Analyses of the role of unions in social democracy in the UK focus, for example, on the unions as sites of social democracy (ie in their own governance) and as promoters of social democracy through their influence over, and participation in, governance by the state.[99] Their political power, and the potential to disrupt both government and the economy, have led to trade unions being subject to (lawful and unlawful) surveillance throughout the past century.

The importance of trade union membership to the individual, and to collective society, has made the fact of such membership a 'special category' of personal data alongside 'religious or philosophical beliefs' and 'biometric data'.[100] As such it attracts particular protection in data protection law. The explicit mention of trade unions in the IP Act is limited to one (recurring) provision – an amendment accepted by the government in the House of Commons Report Stage. The provision states that, in relation to a range of different warrants (interception of communications, equipment interference, communications data, and bulk personal datasets), the fact that the information which would be obtained by the warrant relates to the activities of a trade union will not be sufficient to establish the necessity of the warrant.

As safeguards go this is rather flimsy. It does not prevent the capture of trade union data via (bulk) interception of communications, (bulk) equipment interference, retention and access to communications data or ICRs, or the issuance of technical capability notices. It merely notes that the necessity test for such activities is not met *solely* by the trade union character of the data. Given inferences by the intelligence services and police force of links between trade unions and subversive organisations, it doesn't take much linguistic dexterity to conceive of a reason for access that does not rest *solely* on the trade union character of the data but nevertheless captures such data. Furthermore, the amendment does not prevent, and the Act provides no particular protection against, the general capture of data on trade union membership or activities in the context of other searches.

If the protections for journalistic and LPP materials are weak then the protection for 'trade union material' is negligible. This suggests that the trade union movement's seeming decision to leave lobbying to the NUJ was mistaken. The NUJ had distinct and significant concerns, set out below, which they sought to address. Apart from the NUJ, no trade unions gave evidence to the Draft Investigation Powers Bill Committee in Parliament.[101] The Labour Campaign for Human Rights, a signatory to the 2015 letter to *The Guardian*,

[97] See: www.rsf.org/en/united-kingdom.

[98] Ewing, 'Democratic Socialism and Labour Law' (n 1) *passim*.

[99] Ewing, 'Democratic Socialism and Labour Law' (n 1) 118.

[100] GDPR 2018, Art 9.

[101] For the written and oral evidence see: www.parliament.uk/business/committees/committees-a-z/joint-select/draft-investigatory-powers-bill/publications/.

did give evidence, and drew attention to surveillance of unions throughout the last century. However, it did not call for any particular protections for trade unions.[102]

That trade unions might have been preoccupied with other legislation – the Trade Union Bill (now Act) 2016 – in the early stages of consideration of the IP Bill might provide some explanation but little excuse. It also doesn't explain why the Labour Party was, in general, so broadly receptive to a Bill that its Leader, Shadow Attorney General, and Shadow Home Secretary, had all spoken about in such bold terms. As one commentator puts it: Another asks: 'If social democrats are too frightened to stand up for what they believe in, then why bother voting for them?'[103]

V. (The Impossibility of) Conclusion

The Act was always likely to face legal challenge. Liberty's response was 'See You In Court'.[104] Before Liberty made it to court, however, Privacy International were successful in getting the IPT to refer several questions to the CJEU on bulk data collection.[105] During the legislative process which led to the IPA, the government admitted that since the late 1990s, GCHQ had been using section 94 of the Telecommunications Act 1984 as the legal basis for bulk data collection.[106] This was done on the basis of a very wide statutory power and by relying on a national security exemption to avoid laying the direction before Parliament. Privacy International challenge this practice. At the heart of the *Privacy International* reference is whether the principles which underpin the *Watson* judgment, which dealt largely with bulk data collection for the purposes of crime control, also apply in relation to national security.

Watson has already had an impact on the IP Act. In April 2018, in the first part of Liberty's challenge to the IP Act, the High Court held that, insofar as it relates to criminal justice, Part 4 of the Act was incompatible with EU law.[107] The decision implements in national law the reasoning of the *Watson* judgment. It holds that the issue of retention notices for crimes other than serious crimes, and access to retained data without prior review by a court or independent administrative body, are unlawful. Indeed, the government had conceded as much, and the principal dispute in the case was over the appropriate remedy. The Court gave until 1 November 2018 for the legislation to be amended. This was done by statutory instrument.[108]

[102] Labour Campaign for Human Rights, 'Written Evidence to Investigatory Powers Bill Public Bill Committee' (IPB 52), 6 April 2016 https://publications.parliament.uk/pa/cm201516/cmpublic/investigatorypowers/Memo/IPB52.htm.

[103] M Harris, 'Shami Chakrabarti and Jeremy Corbyn were the loudest critics of the Snooper's Charter – but now they're in power, they've gone quiet' *The Independent* (London, 11 October 2016).

[104] Liberty, '"See You In Court' – Liberty Responds to Passing of the Snoopers" Charter' (17 November 2015) www.libertyhumanrights.org.uk/news/press-releases-and-statements/see-you-court-liberty-responds-passing-snoopers-charter.

[105] The CJEU case is pending: *Privacy International v Secretary of State for Foreign and Commonwealth Affairs and Others* (Case C-623/17).

[106] O Bowcott and R Norton-Taylor, 'UK spy agencies have collected bulk personal data since 1990s, files show' *The Guardian* (London, 21 April 2016).

[107] *R (Liberty) v Secretary of State for the Home Department and Secretary of State for Foreign and Commonwealth Affairs* [2018] EWHC 975 (Admin), [2019] QB 481.

[108] Data Retention and Acquisition Regulations 2018.

In September 2018, in *Big Brother Watch v United Kingdom*, the ECtHR held that bulk interception of communications under RIPA was contrary to the Convention.[109] In particular bulk interception of communications was a violation of Article 8, the regime to obtain communications data was a violation of Article 8 on grounds of the principle of legality, and bulk interception and communications data regimes were in violation of Article 10 for failure to safeguard journalistic material. The Court rejected claims in relation to sharing intelligence with foreign governments and in relation to the right to a fair trial and prohibition on discrimination. The judgment, if affirmed by the Grand Chamber, has implications for the IPA – though the latter legislation does, of course, have new oversight provisions.

In the final days of writing this chapter the High Court refused Liberty's latest application for judicial review of the IP Act.[110] The challenge was to the powers to request warrants for bulk interception, bulk and thematic equipment interference, bulk personal datasets, and bulk acquisition of communications data. Liberty had sought a declaration under section 4 HRA that the powers were incompatible with the ECHR. The Court's refusal notes that in *Big Brother Watch* the ECtHR had held that bulk powers per se could be lawful and that the case was to be heard by the Grand Chamber.[111]

Litigation is not the only reason that conclusion is impossible. If the legislative process for the IP Act gave cause to hope for a culture shift then that optimism has already been put to the test. In October 2017 the Home Secretary, Amber Rudd, said that even though she didn't understand end-to-end encryption, she would take steps to 'combat it'.[112] Indeed, draft regulations leaked earlier that year made clear that the government considered it possible to require service providers to remove such encryption (or at least provide a 'backdoor' to allow it to be circumvented) using the power to issue a 'technical capability notice' under the IP Act.[113] This question remains a live one as the 'Crypto-War' once more comes to the forefront of debate.[114]

In 2018 the IPCO appointed Eric Kind its first Head of Investigations. However, his appointment was ultimately prevented by the Home Office on 'national security grounds'.[115] Kind was told that this was because of his 'previous work and associations'.[116] He had, in the past, been Deputy Director of Privacy International and co-ordinator of the DSOU campaign on the IP Bill. David Anderson QC wrote 'As one of Eric's referees and admirers, I share his disappointment in the outcome'.[117]

In May 2019 the Home Secretary, Sajid Javid, laid before Parliament a statement which identified certain 'compliance risks' in MI5's treatment of data after its acquisition

[109] *Big Brother Watch v United Kingdom*, App nos 58170/13, 62322/14 and 24960/15, judgment of 13 September 2018.

[110] *R (Liberty) v Secretary of State for the Home Department, Secretary of State for Foreign and Commonwealth Affairs* [2019] EWHC 2057 (Admin), [2019] 7 WLUK 488 ('*Liberty II*').

[111] Ibid [10].

[112] A Griffin, 'Amber Rudd admits she doesn't understand WhatsApp technology but intends to 'combat it' *The Independent* (London, 2 October 2017).

[113] C Baraniuk, 'Investigatory Powers: 'Real-time surveillance' in draft update' (*BBC News*, 5 May 2017) www.bbc.co.uk/news/technology-39817300. The power in question is in s 253, IPA 2016.

[114] See, eg, I Levy and C Robinson, 'Principles for a More Informed Exception Access Debate' (*Law Fare Blog*, 29 November 2018) www.lawfareblog.com/principles-more-informed-exceptional-access-debate.

[115] M Townsend, 'Home Office under fire for blocking new spy watchdog' *The Guardian* (London, 19 January 2019).

[116] Ibid.

[117] See: www.twitter.com/bricksilk.

by interception.[118] The statement notes the Investigatory Powers Commissioner's Office concluded that the risks were serious, required mitigation, and ought to have been disclosed at an earlier stage. The decision on Eric Kind, as well as the 'compliance' failures at MI5, suggest that significant problems remain with the culture within law enforcement and intelligence agencies.

The Shadow Home Secretary, Diane Abbott, said the MI5 disclosure 'highlights the failure of government legislation, which only facilitates more and more public bodies having access to and gathering information'.[119] However, like the Leader of the Opposition, she was absent for the key votes on the IP Act. Ewing argues 'social democracy is different from liberal democracy … [i]t is about a difference balance of values …'.[120] He may be right. But social democrats, in particular in Parliament, ought to remember that however hard the struggle for social democracy, it will be harder still without civil liberties. Failure to stand up for protections for lawyers, journalists, and trade unions only makes them weaker agents of social democratic change.

The necessity of (certain) surveillance powers, acknowledged by Ewing and Gearty decades ago, remains subject to deep contestation by civil libertarians and technologists. It is difficult to adequately interrogate that necessity because of the inevitable secrecy which surrounds such powers and their use. There is agreement in Parliament, at least amongst the two largest parties. More fundamental opposition has been left to smaller parties and to civil society. As a result, and contrary to Ewing's social democratic vision, it has taken judicial intervention to prompt Parliament to act. If social democrats do not do better when given such opportunities they run the risk of further misuses of the power – misuses that, in the past, have been to their own detriment.

[118] S Javid MP, 'Investigatory Powers Act 2016: Safeguards Relating to Retention and Disclosure of Material', HCWS1552, 9 May 2019 www.parliament.uk/business/publications/written-questions-answers-statements/written-statement/Commons/2019-05-09/HCWS1552/.

[119] O Bowcott, 'MI5 accused of 'extraordinary and persistent illegality' *The Guardian* (London, 11 June 2019).

[120] Ewing, 'Jeremy Corbyn and the Law of Democracy' (n 2) 343–344.

23

Just Transitions for Workers: When Climate Change Met Labour Justice

NAVRAJ SINGH GHALEIGH*

I. Introduction

This chapter commences a conversation between labour law and social democratic thought, and environmental and climate law. It does so tentatively given that these are bodies of law, practice, and scholarship which have traditionally had limited contact. Indeed, Part I of this chapter details a track record of suspicion between the two, ranging from indifference to outright hostility. It is argued however that this is an unproductive stance as there are shared interests and mutual gains to be had from a more engaged relationship. This is especially true when we consider the relationship between social democracy and climate change, and particularly the changes to labour markets, policy, and law which will be wrought by a meaningful response to climate challenge. It could equally be argued that the physical and social devastation which will follow from a non-meaningful response to the climate challenge will also radically reform labour markets, but that is outwith the scope of this chapter. Part II introduces the concepts of Just Transitions, and Just Transitions for Workers (JTW) as an aspect of the response to climate change. As a concept JTW draws on a larger literature of Just Transitions, but finds its narrower, labour law focus in instruments including the Paris Agreement (2015) and various International Labour Organisation instruments. The central idea of JTW is that the necessary transition to a low-carbon economy requires a radical reorganisation of the means of production and distribution and that this entails significant transitional challenges for workers, communities and industries. Although still nascent as a policy concept, JTW has already had some significant impact on national and sub-national planning for climate action. Part III identifies the legal landscapes in which JTW may find purchase. They range across different legal levels, from public international law to domestic, and take in a variety of legal tools. As such it maps the emerging regulatory frameworks of labour law pertinent to climate change, or of potential relevance to it, from bespoke ILO instruments such as the Silesia Declaration (2018) to broader discussion of active labour market policies and 'flexicurity'.

* Sincere thanks to David Cabrelli, and to Clare Tuohy for her research assistance. The comments of the editors were invaluable.

Particular contexts are focussed upon, with the political economy of the coal industry being one. This is of course a totemic sector in labour relations in the UK's past, and very much a present concern in EU Member States, as well as in emerging economies.

The overarching framing to these parts is the conviction that climate change, like robotics or globalisation, is a 'megatrend' which has the potential to change fundamentally the operation and character of labour markets, another 'precarity'.[1] As has been noted elsewhere:

> [The future] will be radically different from where we are now if we are going to solve climate change, and, if not, it is going to be radically different because of climate change.[2]

This neat formulation applies to labour markets no less than the car, or oil and gas industry and its plausibility becomes clear when the current science of climate change is considered. At the time of writing (summer 2019) the leading statement of climate science is to be found in the so-called '1.5 degree report' of the Intergovernmental Panel on Climate Change[3] – 'Global Warming of 1.5°C: An IPCC Special Report (2018)'.[4] The report, which is essentially a digest of the most authoritative peer reviewed climate science, makes a number of unequivocal findings: that global heating was likely to reach 1.5°C between 2030 and 2052 if it continued to increase at the current rate, with significantly higher levels of heating very likely;[5] that even if contained to between 1.5–2°C, the impacts of such warming include the loss of habitats such as coral reefs which are major contributors to planetary systems, will most likely be irreversible.[6] This is but one of the many climate-related risks to health, livelihoods, food security, water supply, human security, and economic growth which are projected to increase with global warming of 1.5°C and increase further with 2°C.[7] Closer to home, as hundreds of millions of people are exposed to climate-related risks and poverty, including in the Mediterranean and Central Europe[8] but especially in the tropics,[9] the prospect of migration in affected agricultural communities and associated conflict is real. New patterns of oppression and inequality will likely be engendered by unabated climate change, whilst existing ones will be exacerbated. It is no surprise that climate change will have varying effects in differing polities, with the poorer being less resilient than the richer. Identical sea level rises will affect the Netherlands and Bangladesh very differently. To the extent then that social democracy sets itself against the suffering and inequalities created by unchecked market forces, the consequences of and responses to climate change are social democratic concerns.

There is a risk though in such accounts of overly-deterministic or even climate-reductionist frames, of the dominant assumption perhaps inadvertent that scientific

[1] See generally, G Standing, *The Precariat: The New Dangerous Class* (London, Bloomsbury Academic, 2011).

[2] House of Commons, Environmental Audit Committee, 'UK Export Finance' (House of Lords 2019) 19th Report of Session 2017–19, HC 1804, Professor Kevin Anderson at para 97.

[3] On the IPCC, see generally, NS Ghaleigh, 'Science and Climate Change Law – The Role of the IPCC in International Decision-Making' in KR Gray, CP Carlarne and R Tarasofsky (eds), *The Oxford Handbook of International Climate Change Law* (Oxford, Oxford University Press, 2016).

[4] 'Global Warming of 1.5°C: An IPCC Special Report' (*IPCC*, 2018) www.ipcc.ch/sr15/.

[5] Ibid, 6.

[6] Ibid, Summary for Policy Makers, para B.4.2.

[7] Ibid, para B.5.

[8] Ibid, para B.5.1, B.5.3.

[9] Ibid, para 3.4.10.

prediction simply imposes its own logic on social relationships. Mike Hulme has written of the 'predictive authority' and 'hegemony' exercised by natural scientific modelling in which all futures are determined by climate and ultimately reduced to a function of it. This holds sway, he says 'over contingent, imaginative, and humanistic accounts of social life and visions of the future. It is a hegemony that lends disproportionate power in political and social discourse to model-based descriptions of putative future climates.'[10] This chapter is part of the effort on the part of the humanities and social sciences to build the organisational complexity and values of law and legal actors into those narratives. In particular, it offers social democratically informed avenues by which legal action can ameliorate climate impacts and play a positive role in climate action. Indeed, on the specific issue of just transitions for workers, the International Labour Organisation takes a positive view of the potential of a structured low carbon transition:

> Managed well, transitions to environmentally and socially sustainable economies can become a strong driver of job creation, job upgrading, social justice and poverty eradication. Greening all enterprises and jobs by introducing more energy and resource efficient practices, avoiding pollution and managing natural resources sustainably leads to innovation, enhances resilience and generates savings which drive new investment and employment.[11]

In this light, climate determinism is challenged by democracy.

Avoiding such climate impacts – the parade of horribles – requires an energy transition similar in nature to the shift from horse-drawn to steam and then electric power, albeit that the energy transition would be one of moving energy production and supply from fossil fuel to low-carbon alternatives, and across every conceivable sector. The shift from fossil fuels would have to be almost complete by 2050 in historically high-emitting nations, and by century's end globally, to avoid catastrophic global heating. One obvious consequence of such a transition would be the loss of employment to those working in the fossil fuel sector. In the UK alone c.300,000 jobs depend on this sector in 2019, a figure already depressed by historic destruction of the coal industry, oil market pressures, and the recognition of the climate challenge.[12] This is but one of the arenas in which the low carbon transition will be played out – from the end of peat harvesting in Ireland, to rapid coal phase outs in South Africa, the US, and China – meeting the challenge of climate change means almost unimaginable economic and social upheaval. (A sense of the vast costs involved can be gleaned from the recent compensation agreement struck between the Federal German Government, the coal industry and unions. Consisting of a phase out (by 2038) for coal-fired power plants in eastern Germany and the Rhineland, and the roster of regeneration and retraining projects, the plan will cost €40 billion.)[13] An aspect of this will be major changes to the nature of work. The *potential* tension between environmental and social democratic labour concerns is easily recognised then. Despite its various guises though, these tensions

[10] M Hulme, 'Reducing the Future to Climate: A Story of Climate Determinism and Reductionism' (2011) 26 *Osiris* 245, 255, 264.

[11] International Labour Organization, 'Guidelines for a Just Transition towards Environmentally Sustainable Economies and Societies for All' (2015) www.ilo.org/wcmsp5/groups/public/---ed_emp/---emp_ent/documents/publication/wcms_432859.pdf.

[12] House of Commons, Environmental Audit Committee (n 2) para 99.

[13] T Buck, 'Germany to Spending €40bn to soften blow from coal closures' *The Financial Times* (London, 22 May 2019).

are far from inevitable. That is especially the case when we consider the role of hierarchical and networked governance in the transition.[14] Much of the discourse of climate action has privileged the position of the market and its capacity to respond effectively. The market mechanisms of the Kyoto Protocol, and EU Emissions Trading Scheme are but two of the better known such examples.[15] A similar dereliction on the part of the state, and in particular the regulation of labour markets, cannot occur if labour justice is to be delivered in the low carbon transition.

II. An Uneasy Relationship – Social Democracy and Environmentalism

At a high level of abstraction, social democracy and environmentalism have generally existed in a state of tension, if not indifference. Social democracy is variously defined as a compromise between capitalism and socialism, or as a distinct body of thought which deploys collective action to extend freedom and equality from the political sphere into those of economy and society, thereby operating as a corrective to unchecked capitalism. For the purposes of public law Ewing, drawing on Kahn-Freund, has described this as the task of 'entrench[ing] social and economic rights within the constitutional structure of the nation [and] a process of constitutional integration in which social and economic rights are accorded *at least* equal status with civil and political rights.'[16] Specifically for the purpose of labour law, the social democratic constitutional order would 'promote a measure of democracy within the enterprise'[17] via mechanisms such as collective bargaining and its recognition, and workers' participation and representation.[18] These socio-economic objectives would preferably be incorporated politically with courts being marginalised whilst legislatures (at least in the Westminster model) pass laws and scrutinise the executive. So much is familiar. Many of the structures and debates in labour law can be understood within this frame. However, the concerns of the environment and climate have generated a fraction of this attention in the realm of social democratic legal and political thought. Rather, economic arrangements have dominated – whether ownership should be private or public, the market decentralised and 'free' or centralised with planned production. From such a perspective, the tension between social democracy and environmentalism arises when economic growth is cast as a solution to unemployment and precarity, and environmental protection as a brake on that same growth. Jacobs characterised that perspective (which he did not share himself) as follows:

> Environmental improvement costs money, and this inevitably raises prices; often for basic needs, such as water and food. In other cases higher prices are specifically the means by which

[14] See generally, GF Thompson, *Between Hierarchies and Markets: The Logic and Limits of Network Forms of Organization* (Oxford, Oxford University Press, 2003).

[15] NS Ghaleigh, 'Two Stories about E.U. Climate Change Law and Policy' (2013) 14 *Theoretical Inquiries in Law* 43.

[16] KD Ewing, 'Democratic Socialism and Labour Law' (1995) 24 *Industrial Law Journal* 103, 106, 108.

[17] Ibid, 112.

[18] Ibid, 115.

> environmentalists seek to reduce environmental consumption – the case of VAT on domestic fuel being a pertinent example. In both cases this is inequitable, not to say politically damaging, and cannot be countenanced by a government of the left.[19]

Although such macro-economic issues *could* readily be turned to cast light on environmental protection, they rarely are. Consider Polanyi's well-known definition of socialism as 'essentially, the tendency inherent in an industrial civilisation to transcend the self-regulating market by consciously subordinating it to a democratic society.'[20] Environmental degradation and particular instances thereof such as climate change are easily understood as failures of poorly-regulated markets, as Stern famously characterised climate change.[21] Moreover, to the extent that climate action is genuinely a 'public good', one which is non-rivaled and non-excludable, that no one can be effectively excluded from using, it is inevitable that the market will not supply it adequately.[22] As such, a Polanyian 'subordination' of the market to democratic control is well placed to supply the public good of climate action, in one of the two phases of what he identified as the 'double movement', with societies either disembedding markets from society or re-embedding markets into society (respectively in phases of liberalisation, or political interventionism),[23] or indeed the two occurring simultaneously at different levels.[24]

Despite the logical coherence between social democracy and environmentalism, it has often appeared that the former views the latter with disdain. The view is often that environmentalism is a bourgeois playground,[25] an affectation of tree huggers, an indulgence of those who lack a proper cause.[26] This is almost exactly the mirror image of the view from liberal environmentalism, especially the 'cool kids' of Davos who see the trade union movement as a lost cause, desperately clinging onto the handful of remaining mining jobs, seeking to protect their dwindling members rather than the wider public good. Both positions contain a good deal of deliberate misrepresentation, as well as truth. There is however scope to move beyond this discourse such that the two are better aligned. If the radical transformation of society and economy necessary to avoid catastrophic climate change is to occur, social democratic values will need to be engaged from the first if the goals of human dignity, equality and flourishing working lives are to be fulfilled. Even if social democracy has no patience with environmentalism,[27] environmentalism must make time for social

[19] M Jacobs, *Sustainability and Socialism* (London, Socialist Environment and Resources Association, 1995) 6.

[20] K Polanyi, *The Great Transformation: The Political and Economic Origins of Our Time* (Boston, Beacon Press 2014) 242.

[21] N Stern, *The Economics of Climate Change: The Stern Review* (Cambridge, Cambridge University Press, 2007). 'Climate change is the greatest market failure the world has ever seen, and it interacts with other market imperfections.'

[22] NS Ghaleigh, 'Economics and International Climate Change Law' in KR Gray, CP Carlarne and R Tarasofsky (eds), *The Oxford Handbook of International Climate Change Law* (Oxford, Oxford University Press, 2016) 79–80.

[23] See generally, C Joerges and J Falke (eds), *Karl Polanyi, Globalisation and the Potential of Law in Transnational Markets* (Oxford, Hart Publishing, 2011).

[24] JG Ruggie, 'International Regimes, Transactions and Change: Embedded Liberalism in the Postwar Economic Order' (1982) 36 *International Organization* 379, 393, 399.

[25] R Inglehart, 'Post-Materialism in an Environment of Insecurity' (1981) 75 *The American Political Science Review* 880, 895–7.

[26] T Farnhill, 'Environmental Policy-Making at the British Trades Union Congress 1967–2011' (2014) 25 *Capitalism Nature Socialism* 72, 72–7.

[27] A De-Shalit, 'Socialism and the Environment' in A De-Shalit (ed), *The Environment: Between Theory and Practice* (Oxford, Oxford University Press, 2000) 177–9.

democracy. Social democracy illuminates the global ecological crisis and provides pathways by which responses are inclusive and just. Rather than 'saving the planet' now and worrying about just distributions later, the approach of JTW identifies how the crises of social democracy and the environment are interconnected, and the solutions likewise.

The extent of sympathy between social democracy and environmentalism should not be understated, however. From both 'sides', there is something of a track record of engagement. The journalist Naomi Klein's characterisation of the climate problematic as 'capitalism vs the climate' is a case in point.[28] Her 2014 book *This Changes Everything* is, as its subtitle suggests, a focussed attempt at fully aligning the ambitions of both environmentalism and social democracy. Indeed, her claim is no less than an argument that social democracy is best for the environment in that it is more likely to protect the environment when the means of production are commonly held.[29] Most interestingly from the position of labour law, in a section entitled 'A Movement Digs Its Own Grave', Klein links US trade policy and the development of NAFTA, the role of organised labour and environmental NGOs ('ENGOs').[30] In the formative stages of the NAFTA negotiations, both groups were opposed to NAFTA, knowing that it would 'drive down labor and environmental standards.'[31] Although both interest groups shared a common goal – opposing NAFTA – their failure to fully coordinate their actions led to the ENGOs being peeled off from the mainstream NAFTA opposition, owing to the 'growing influence of corporate "partners" and donors.'[32] Although some ENGOs resisted – notably Greenpeace and Friends of the Earth – the Clinton administration was able to assuage public opinion in the knowledge that 'groups representing 80% of national [environmental] group membership have endorsed NAFTA.'[33] The failure to hold the line on NAFTA, Klein argues, led to a generation of agreements, including the WTO Agreement (1995) which have simultaneously undermined both environmental and labour standards.[34]

Klein's proposal is not autarky but an approach to trade which better accounts for environmental harm, and the 'localisation' of economies to combat offshoring. In one respect, Klein's narrative affirms the Polanyian observation that markets do not arise spontaneously but through the advocacy and actions of states, supported by the social groups with most to gain.[35] Pertinently for present purposes, their creation necessitates new modes of economic exchange which are destructive to traditional practices. Moreover, and building on the move against determinism above,

> markets are not autonomous, self-regulating institutions (as suggested by some readings of neo-classical economic theory and modern neoliberal political philosophy) that might be treated

[28] N Klein, *This Changes Everything: Capitalism vs. the Climate* (New York, Simon & Schuster, 2014).

[29] In this Klein follows political scientists of socialism such as De-Shalit. See generally, De-Shalit (n 27), and the citations therein.

[30] Klein (n 28) 73ff. Klein's narrative in turn draws heavily on M Dowie, *Losing Ground: American Environmentalism at the Close of the Twentieth Century* (Cambridge, Mass., MIT Press, 1995).

[31] Klein (n 28) 73. 'The connection between pollution and labor exploitation has been true since the earliest days of the Industrial Revolution.'

[32] Ibid.

[33] Ibid.

[34] Ibid, 74–5.

[35] Polanyi (n 20) 138.

> as separate from the societies in which they operate [but] are ultimately subordinate to law, politics, religion and other social relations.[36]

This degree of subordination of course varies over time, as recognised by Polanyi in his discussion of the 'dis-embeddedness' of the economy from society. What Klein identifies is a phase of powerful disembedding which begat yet more.

More detailed approaches in a similar vein to Klein's can be found in, for example, the writings of Michael Jacobs. In a substantial body of work[37] Jacobs outlines the deep linkage between environmentally sustainable growth and job creation. Just as the UK Climate Change Act (2008) creates a long-term goal[38] and stable institutions (principally the Climate Change Committee)[39] for guiding climate action to 2050, Jacobs proposes a Sustainable Economy Act supplemented by a Green Industrial Strategy. The Act would require government to set out plans and targets to meet a goal of sustainability, monitored by an independent 'Committee on Sustainability'.[40] It should be noted that the Climate Change Act has been criticised for setting ambitious aspirations and targets, but not necessarily providing for means by which they can be met. In large part these criticisms stem from an anxiety surrounding the vagueness of the language in section 1 of the Act.[41] What are the means by which the duty should be enforced? When is the duty triggered? In 2049, at which point it is too late, or at some point earlier when it is clear that the target cannot be met, when again it is too late?[42] Whilst these are valid points, it should be noted in the decade since its enactment, the UK has made some of the deepest emission reductions amongst any advanced economy, principally in the field of electricity generation decarbonisation. These are not facts to be lightly discarded. To the extent that there is criticism about meeting the newly coined 'net zero' by 2050 target, contained in the draft Climate Change Act 2008 (2050 Target Amendment) Order 2019 to amend the Climate Change Act 2008,[43] these revolve around uncertainty about meeting future carbon budgets (the periods when emissions are to be met, ie 2023–2027, 2028–2032).[44] Whilst valid, these criticisms fall into the 'counsel of perfection' category. When compared with the achievements of comparable jurisdictions, the Climate Change Act is arguably the most significant carbon reduction policy instrument

[36] J McGee and J Steffek, 'The Copenhagen Turn in Global Climate Governance and the Contentious History of Differentiation in International Law' (2016) 28 *Journal of Environmental Law* 37; F Block, 'Karl Polanyi and the Writing of "The Great Transformation"' (2003) 32 *Theory and Society* 275.

[37] M Jacobs and M Mazzucato, *Rethinking Capitalism: Economics and Policy for Sustainable and Inclusive Growth* (Chichester, Wiley-Blackwell, in association with The Political Quarterly, 2016); M Jacobs, *Greening the Millennium?: The New Politics of the Environment* (Oxford, Blackwell, 1997).

[38] Climate Change Act 2008, s 1, as amended.

[39] www.theccc.org.uk/.

[40] M Jacobs and Institute for Public Policy Research, *Prosperity and Justice: A Plan for the New Economy. The Final Report of the IPPR Commission on Economic Justice* (London, IPPR / Polity, 2018) 226 ff.

[41] 'It is the duty of the Secretary of State to ensure that the net UK carbon account for the year 2050 is at least 80% lower than the 1990 baseline.'

[42] M Stallworthy, 'Legislating against Climate Change: A UK Perspective on a Sisyphean Challenge' (2009) 72 *MLR* 412; CT Reid, 'A New Sort of Duty? The Significance of "Outcome" Duties in the Climate Change and Child Poverty Acts' [2012] *Public Law* 749.

[43] www.legislation.gov.uk/ukdsi/2019/9780111187654/pdfs/ukdsi_9780111187654_en.pdf.

[44] The first three carbon budgets were met by the UK, but in June 2018 in the CCC's Progress Report to Parliament called on the government to bring forward new fully funded policies to ensure the fourth and fifth carbon budget are met. Committee on Climate Change, 'Reducing UK emissions: 2018 Progress Report to Parliament' (June 2018) www.theccc.org.uk/publication/reducing-uk-emissions-2018-progress-report-to-parliament/.

in the world. More pertinently perhaps, criticisms of the CCA's mechanisms may stem from an uneasiness with its overtly political constitutionalist character. Rather than granting the court's the capacity to review governmental action in this sphere, instead the architecture of the Act relies instead on expertise and institutional independence (of the Climate Change Committee), persuasion (of the Committee on the Government), accountability (of Government to Parliament), and good faith (of the Government to nation by not diluting or repealing the Act). These are the same non-judicial mechanisms that Ewing advocated in his 1995 statement of democratic socialism. This discomfort of the environmental law community with the Climate Change Act may owe less to its effectiveness than their unfamiliarity with the arguments in that seminal paper.

Viewed in these terms, Jacobs' *Sustainable Economy Act*, modelled on the CCA, could be seen as a plausible response to familiar problems of plastic, air, and water pollution, not least with an expert Committee, like the CCC, providing guidance to government on how these targets could be feasibly achieved through technological and policy change, and reporting on the success or otherwise of policy in doing so.[45] Furthermore, workers and communities affected by the inevitable change would be supported through the transition, supplemented by new forms of economic constitutionalism and devolution, in harness with the trade union movement.[46] In this vein, a more fine-grained approach, specific to the labour-environment debate, is considered in Part III below. It is also important to note, if only *en passant*, that the 'tension' can be overstated as a matter of practical action. Jacobs' discussion of JTW for example relies almost exclusively on an ITUC sponsored and supported report for the OECD.[47] Similarly, as Farnhill painstakingly records, there is a long record of trade union environmental activism, albeit that it is a 'subordinate tradition' and concentrated in a small number of sectors, namely, transport, energy, manufacturing and local and central government.[48] As a matter of practice therefore at the level of the labour movement in the UK and to some extent internationally, the supposed opposition between labour and the environment is frequently a strawman.

III. Just Transitions: A Conspectus

Properly addressing major environmental challenges, and climate change in particular, entails massive economic and societal reorganisation. Whether there is the will to undertake this remains unclear – one suspects it is absent. Nonetheless, *if* the climate challenge is to be met, it will need comprehensively to address the concerns of workers and communities that are affected.

The 'Just Transitions' (JT) or 'sustainable transitions' literature is large and growing rapidly. At its core is the contention that environmental problems such as climate change are hugely complex – sometimes known as 'wicked problems'[49] or grand challenges – and

[45] Jacobs and Institute for Public Policy Research (n 40) 226.
[46] Ibid.
[47] Samantha Smith, 'Just Transition: A Report for the OECD' (*Just Transition Centre*, 2017) https://www.oecd.org/environment/cc/g20-climate/collapsecontents/Just-Transition-Centre-report-just-transition.pdf.
[48] Farnhill (n 26).
[49] HWJ Rittel and MM Webber, 'Dilemmas in a General Theory of Planning' (1973) 4 *Policy Sciences* 155.

can only be addressed by radical systems changes, not incremental tweaks.[50] As such, 'a central aim of transitions research is to conceptualise and explain how radical changes can occur in the way societal functions are fulfilled.'[51] Among the many aspects of transitions which the literature encompasses are their politics, governance, geography, and the role of industry. For present purposes, two further aspects are of particular importance, namely civil society, and social movements in transitions (principally trade unions), and the ethical aspects of transitions.

An obvious concern of just transitions is the risk of them being conceived as a set of purely technocratic questions and decisions, existing in a moral vacuum. As regards the ethical or normative aspects of just transitions, the literature to date, especially that addressing energy justice, has sought to identify exclusionary technologies before they fully develop so as to drive more socially just innovation, and also to develop normative criteria for making such assessments. The ambition is that by making JT a 'matter of priority at the landscape level [they] could exert pressure on the regime below, leading to the widespread reappraisal of our energy choices, and integration of moral criteria.'[52] This still leaves open the question of what the appropriate values of the just transition are, who gets to shape them, how, and by whom are they implemented. But in amongst all the other competing considerations, this is a literature that makes the case for the active consideration of values and actors in transitions.

With issues of values and their authorship in mind, a particularly interesting perspective on *Just Transitions for Workers* is provided by the Just Transition Centre and Samantha Smith.[53] Acknowledging that climate change means that the 'transformation we face is on a scale and within a time frame faster than any in human history [and that there] is a real potential for stranded workers and stranded communities,'[54] the report acknowledges the need for a structured approach in order to ensure a non-stranded, just transition: '[it] will not happen by itself. It requires plans and policies … Social dialogue is the key.'[55]

At the normative level, legal instruments are less well developed. The founding treaty of the so-called climate regime, the UN Framework Convention on Climate Change (1992)[56] makes no reference at all to transitions, labour rights, or even justice. Given the date of the instrument, a decade before the just transition debate had even begun, let alone flourish, this is understandable. Moreover, as a 'framework' treaty, which establishes the broad objectives of the regime in terms of mitigation, and its institutions, its limitedness is somewhat understandable. Although UNFCCC Article 3 states a number of principles – intergenerational equity, precaution, common but differentiated responsibility, sustainable development – none of which explicitly refer to just transitions, there is clearly scope for them to be used

[50] B Elzen, FW Geels and K Green, *System Innovation and the Transition to Sustainability: Theory, Evidence and Policy* (Cheltenham, Edward Elgar, 2004). See generally, M Grubb, JC Hourcade and K Neuhoff, *Planetary Economics: Energy, Climate Change and the Three Domains of Sustainable Development* (Abingdon, Routledge, 2014).

[51] J Köhler et al, 'An Agenda for Sustainability Transitions Research: State of the Art and Future Directions' 31 (2019) Environmental Innovation and Societal Transitions 1.

[52] K Jenkins, BK Sovacool and D McCauley, 'Humanizing Sociotechnical Transitions through Energy Justice: An Ethical Framework for Global Transformative Change' (2018) 117 *Energy Policy* 66, 67.

[53] Smith (n 47).

[54] Ibid, 1.

[55] Ibid, 1–2.

[56] UNTS 1771.

as interpretative tools which could both accommodate and advance just transitions, with intergenerational equity being the principle most amenable to such an approach.[57]

IV. Just Transitions for Workers: An Emerging Framework

A. Public International Law

i. Climate Regime

Although neither the UNFCCC nor its famous offspring, the Kyoto Protocol, make any explicit reference to JTW, it is in its latest iteration, the much-heralded Paris Agreement, that the climate regime has finally made a step in this direction. One would not know this from the secondary legal literature. As if to confirm the prejudices of those who view environmental law as a bourgeoise playground, the voluminous literature on the Paris Agreement has little to say about just transitions for workers – one searches the major textbooks in vain for a reference.[58]

The first substantive discussion of JTW in the climate regime came at the 2010 meeting of the UNFCCC at Cancun, the sixteenth 'Conference of the Parties' known as COP 16.[59] The Decision (1/CP.16) – a non-binding instrument – of that COP determined that 'just transition of the workforce [which] creates decent work and quality jobs' was a necessary feature of the 'paradigm shift towards building a low-carbon society'.[60] As Jenkins puts it, travelling on parallel lines to the 2015 ILO Guidelines:

> Just Transition agenda requires that we take into account the rights of the workforce, and throughout a period of unprecedented change, encourage the creation of decent work and quality jobs in sustainable economic sectors in accordance with nationally defined development priorities. It sets out that the burden of climate action should not be borne unequally by one set of workers or communities or by any one country. The result is an agenda that represents a once-in-a-lifetime opportunity to build a fairer world with diversified and resilient economies, and one that can address the positive and negative consequences of climate action.[61]

This ambitious agenda was given greater teeth by virtue of the Preamble to the Paris Agreement which takes: '*into account* the imperatives of a just transition of the workforce and the creation of decent work and quality jobs in accordance with nationally defined development

[57] C Redgwell, 'Principles and Emerging Norms in International Law: Intra- and Inter-Generational Equity' in KR Gray, CP Carlarne and R Tarasofsky (eds), *The Oxford Handbook of International Climate Change Law* (Oxford, Oxford University Press, 2016).

[58] D Bodansky, J Brunnée and L Rajamani, *International Climate Change Law* (Oxford, Oxford University Press, 2017); KR Gray, CP Carlarne and R Tarasofsky (eds), *The Oxford Handbook of International Climate Change Law* (Oxford, Oxford University Press, 2016); B Mayer, *The International Law on Climate Change* (Cambridge, Cambridge University Press, 2018).

[59] UNFCCC (2011) Report of the Conference of the Parties on its sixteenth session held in Cancun from 29 November to 10 December 2010: https://unfccc.int/resource/docs/2010/cop16/eng/07a01.pdf.

[60] Ibid, para I.10. See also, para III.E.

[61] KEH Jenkins, 'Implementing Just Transition After COP24' [2019] Climate Strategies Policy Briefing.

priorities.'[62] Preambular language does not of course amount to a binding commitment in Public International Law, even if the instrument in question is a binding treaty.[63] Preambles serve the specific function not of creating legal obligations but in establishing the context in which an instrument was agreed, and may operate as an interpretative aid. As such, the identification of just transitions and the nature of work as a contextual factor in the overall agreement amounts to an incorporation of the parties' motivations in the concluding of the treaty. As Mbengue puts it, 'Preambles are *indicia* of the intention of the parties to a treaty.'[64] The interpretative potential of this recital is aided by its relative precision. As noted by the Appellate Body in US-Shrimp,[65]

> While Article XX [of the GATT] was not modified in the Uruguay Round, the preamble attached to the WTO Agreement shows that the signatories to that Agreement were, in 1994, fully aware of the importance and legitimacy of environmental protection as a goal of national and international policy. The preamble of the WTO Agreement – which informs not only the GATT 1994, but also the other covered agreements – explicitly acknowledges "the objective of sustainable development" … From the perspective embodied in the preamble of the WTO Agreement, we note that the generic term "natural resources" in Article XX (g) is not "static" in its content or reference but is rather "by definition, evolutionary" … As this preambular language reflects the intentions of negotiators of the WTO Agreement, we believe it must add colour, texture and shading to our interpretation of the agreements annexed to the WTO Agreement, in this case, the GATT 1994.

In short, the greater the precision, the greater the chance that a recital can guide interpretation. In this case, the reference to 'just transition of the workforce', and the references to decency and quality of work – both ILO concepts – goes beyond a more generic reference to just transitions, which as noted above, can have a very broad range of meanings and implications.[66] 'Just transitions' are not merely noted, but described as an 'imperative'. Moreover, there is an emphasis on the 'creation of decent work and quality jobs'. Following the approach in *US-Shrimp*, this is language which adds colour and texture in the mode of that case and could therefore contribute to establishing the meaning of treaty provisions and clarifying their purpose.

Supplementary to the Paris Agreement itself, the Conference of the Parties at Paris also agreed to adopt a work programme comprising the 'Just transition of the workforce, and the creation of decent work and quality jobs.'[67] This mandate, combined with the outputs of that work programme,[68] and the supportive text in the Paris Agreement itself, provided the legal cue for what became the Silesia Declaration.

[62] Paris Agreement, FCCC/CP/2015/L.9/Rev.1, (2015). Preambular recital 10.

[63] A Aust, *Modern Treaty Law and Practice*, 3rd edn (Cambridge, Cambridge University Press, 2013).

[64] MM Mbengue, 'Preamble' in *Max Planck Encyclopedia of Public International Law* (Oxford, Oxford University Press, 2006).

[65] United States – Import Prohibition of Certain Shrimp and Shrimp Products, India and ors v United States, Report of the Appellate Body, WT/DS58/AB/R, Report No AB-1998-4, Doc No 98-3899, ITL 012 (WTO 1998), DSR 1998:VII, 2755, (1999) 38 ILM 118, 12 October 1998, World Trade Organization [WTO]. Paras 129–130, 153.

[66] Köhler et al (n 51).

[67] UNFCCC (2015) Report of the Conference of the Parties on its 21st session, held in Paris from 30 November to 13 December 2015: https://unfccc.int/sites/default/files/resource/docs/2015/cop21/eng/10a02.pdf.

[68] United Nations Framework Convention on Climate Change, 'Just Transition of the Workforce, and the Creation of Decent Work and Quality Jobs' (2017) https://unfccc.int/sites/default/files/resource/Just%20transition.pdf.

ii. International Labour Organisation and the Silesia Declaration

Despite the recent attentions of the climate regime, it cannot be gainsaid that the body of international climate and environmental law treats the just transition challenge relatively thinly. The recital discussed in the section above amounts to its primary standard, and a rather lonely and underdeveloped one at that, albeit one that was welcomed by the Director-General of the ILO.[69] The rather more substantial role of the International Labour Organisation in this space is to be noted.[70] In 2015 it published its 'Guidelines for a just transition towards environmentally sustainable economies and societies for all.'[71] Initiated by the 102nd Session (2013) of the International Labour Conference and its conclusions concerning sustainable development, decent work and green jobs, the Guidelines amount to a soft law, non-binding policy framework for a just transition. In broad terms the Guidelines are prescriptions to guide the transition to environmentally sustainable economies and societies, including planning, investment, and implementation of a transition to environmentally and socially sustainable jobs, sectors and economies and measures to address inequality and poverty, as well as striving to create decent, fair and high value work, which does not negatively affect the current workforce.[72] The influence of the Guidelines is noteworthy, not least in the work of the UNFCCC itself whose Technical Paper on the topic relies extensively, explicitly and implicitly, on it.[73]

A significant elaboration of the Guidelines is found in the Silesia Declaration (2018). The context of this declaration is perhaps no less important than its substance. Poland was to be the host of the 24th Conference of the Parties of the UNFCCC. This was a controversial choice given the recidivist tendencies of the Polish state and Government in respect of human rights, the rule of law,[74] as well as EU climate policy. The coal industry looms large in the Polish consciousness and culture. As well as a significant employer (though not as large as is often assumed[75]), coal provides up to 90 per cent of Polish electricity, and is commonly perceived to provide energy security and autonomy, especially given the alternative of reliance on Russian gas. Accordingly, in a European Union which must decarbonise to practically zero by 2050 according to most climate models, the fate of the Silesian coal workers and communities is a pressing one.

Given this context, it was particularly welcome that the Polish Presidency of COP 24 (2018) took the initiative on agreeing the 'Solidarity and Just Transition Silesia Declaration', which was adopted by governments at COP24.[76] The ILO played a significant role in the

[69] ILO, 'ILO welcomes new climate change agreement committing nations to a just transition and the creation of decent work' (15 December 2015) www.ilo.org/global/topics/green-jobs/news/WCMS_436322/lang--en/index.htm.

[70] See generally, ILO, 'Climate change and jobs: Why does climate change matter for employment?' www.ilo.org/global/topics/green-jobs/areas-of-work/climate-change/lang--en/index.htm.

[71] ILO, 'Guidelines for a just transition towards environmentally sustainable economies and societies for all' (n 11).

[72] Ibid, Pt IV.

[73] United Nations Framework Convention on Climate Change (n 68) See especially B04-08.

[74] W Sadurski, *Poland's Constitutional Breakdown* (Oxford, Oxford University Press, 2019).

[75] N Berrah and X Wang, 'Poland Energy Transition: The Path to Sustainability in the Electricity and Heating Sector' (*World Bank*, 2018) http://documents.worldbank.org/curated/en/983941544623112019/pdf/132871-WP-PETallvweb.pdf.

[76] 'Solidarity and Just Transition Silesia Declaration' (2018) https://cop24.gov.pl/fileadmin/user_upload/Solidarity_and_Just_Transition_Silesia_Declaration_2_.pdf.

development of the Declaration, listed as it is as a core organisation in the implementation of the Declaration.[77] The core of the Declaration is the agreement, by Heads of States and governments, that 'just transition of the workforce and the creation of decent work and quality jobs are crucial to ensure an effective and inclusive transition to low greenhouse gas emission and climate resilient development, and to enhance the public support for achieving the-long term goals of the Paris Agreement.'[78] The need for wide-ranging support to deliver the low carbon transition is acknowledged,[79] as well as its gender implications.[80] Particularly important, procedurally, is the acknowledgement of the need for 'participatory and representative process of social dialogue involving all social partners to promote high employment rates, adequate social protection, labour standards and wellbeing of workers and their communities.'[81] By agreeing to the Silesia Declaration, countries are demonstrating their intention to seriously engage with the impact of climate change and climate change policies on workers and surrounding communities.

The Silesia Declaration is now a part of the larger policy[82] and international organisation debate over how to achieve coal closures in a manner consistent with JTW.[83] It is of course the case that ILO Recommendations and Declarations under discussion do not have binding force under international law, although they do also entail certain general obligations for the Member States, including reporting obligations. They also aim to provide guidance in the drafting of national legislation and policy, to which we now turn.

B. Domestic Law

The precise means by which labour law might engage with the JTW concept has yet to be fleshed out in either the policy or scholarly literature. What follows is an attempt to test the capacity of known legal and institutional tools to deliver JTW. Are they suitable models for delivering the low carbon transition, and with it, justice for workers?

i. Social Dialogue and Collective Bargaining

The language of social dialogue is woven through the fabric of the JT literature. Although some recent and important 'state of the debate' papers do not discuss the concept, much less collective action and trade union action,[84] it has a larger presence in ILO instruments and the cognate literature. At its most basic, social dialogue depends on respect for fundamental principles and rights at work, such as freedom of association and protection of the

[77] Ibid, para 7.
[78] Ibid, para 1.
[79] Ibid, paras 4, 6(iii).
[80] Ibid, para 2.
[81] Ibid, para 5.
[82] Oliver Sartor, 'Implementing Coal Transitions: Insights from Case Studies of Major Coal-Consuming Economies' (*IDDRI*, 2018) https://coaltransitions.files.wordpress.com/2018/09/coal_synthesis_final.pdf.
[83] World Bank, 'Managing Coal Closure: Achieving a Just Transition For All' (2018) http://documents.worldbank.org/curated/en/484541544643269894/pdf/130659-REVISED-PUBLIC-Managing-Coal-Mine-Closure-Achieving-a-Just-Transition-for-All-November-2018-final.pdf.
[84] Köhler et al (n 51).

right to organise, as enshrined in ILO Convention nos 87 and 98,[85] as well as ILO Convention no 144 which provides guidelines on consultative procedures and structures, and the tripartite participation of governments, workers and employers.[86]

In Smith's definition, social dialogue and tripartism include formal processes of negotiation, consultation and information exchange, as well as economic and social policies and agreements. It can either be a bilateral process (between unions and employers), or a trilateral one (including governments).[87] This draws upon the ILO's own recognition that,

> sustainable development is only possible with the active engagement of the world of work. Governments, employers and workers are not passive bystanders, but rather agents of change, who are able to develop new ways of working that safeguard the environment for present and future generations, eradicate poverty and promote social justice by fostering sustainable enterprises and creating decent work for all.[88]

These processes in turn rely upon the existence and enforcement of freedom of association and the effective recognition of the right to collective bargaining. In a series of case studies, Smith and the UNFCCC go on to parse effectively the differing nature of social dialogue depending on scale and level, the role of governments and investors, tools such as shareholders resolutions, and the necessity of retraining and reskilling.[89] Included in these are online tools for identifying 'green collective agreements' which include clauses related to climate change, dealing with training and education, workplace environmental committees, commuting, green procurement, energy conservation, workforce adjustment and social responsibility.[90] Across sectors as diverse as public services, steel and mining, railways, oil and gas, energy and others, over 200 climate transition clauses have been compiled drawn from numerous jurisdictions.

Inevitably the character of social dialogue varies across jurisdictions. The UNFCCC notes, somewhat predictably, that social dialogue in Sweden and Germany differs in its degree of coordination between levels of government from Greece. Whereas the former maintains a system of social dialogue which is highly coordinated, in the latter the bargaining structures were recast as a consequence of austerity-imposed policy changes.

> Those countries that maintained or reinforced social dialogue structures [were able to] better cope with the socioeconomic impacts of the economic crisis [whereas] where such structures were not well established, led to social unrest and further economic downturn. Similar consequences may be seen in the near and medium future in relation to climate change policies.[91]

Two of Ewing's five categories of trade unions functions – being a workplace representative function, and a regulatory function – are pertinent herein, relating as they do to trade

[85] Freedom of Association and Protection of the Right to Organise Convention (1948), and Right to Organise and Collective Bargaining Convention (1949).

[86] Tripartite Consultation (International Labour Standards) Convention (1976).

[87] Smith (n 47) 1–2.

[88] ILO, 'Guidelines for a Just Transition towards Environmentally Sustainable Economies and Societies for All' (n 12) 4.

[89] United Nations Framework Convention on Climate Change (n 68) para 154ff.

[90] Green Agreements Library at www.zotero.org/green_agreements/items.

[91] United Nations Framework Convention on Climate Change (n 68) para 156. For a wider discussion of tripartite structures of the ILO, see A Trebilcock, 'The International Labour Organization' in MJ Bowman and D Kritsiotis (eds), *Conceptual and Contextual Perspectives on the Modern Law of Treaties* (Cambridge, Cambridge University Press, 2018).

unions' collective representation of employees in the workplace, and through regulatory legislation which trade unions play a part in securing.[92] As noted above, in his 1995 piece Ewing characterises collective bargaining as a 'means of delivering a standard of social and economic security',[93] delivering full citizenship, and reliant upon the 'State providing a developing framework of protection not only to form a basis from which bargaining may take place, but also to drive the bargaining agenda as new frontiers are opened in the fertile landscape of citizenship.'[94] Drawing on this categorisation however, Ford and Novitz illuminate the challenges of collective bargaining, with consequences for the prospects of JTW.[95] Amongst various factors, declining member rolls, an increasingly heterogeneous workplace, the gig economy, and a hostile legal framework all contribute to an ever more vulnerable system of union-led collective bargaining in the UK. Both the representative and regulatory functions are under a sustained assault from legislation and macro-economic developments, although not without pushback. Whilst radical instability may well be the name of the game (in Ford and Novitz's terminology), the sheer volume of 'green collective agreements', in numerous important sectors and jurisdictions, with clauses related to climate change, cannot be gainsaid. At the very least they represent a new front worthy of further research.

ii. Flexicurity: From Job- to Employment-Security

The model of flexicurity revolves around the notion that flexibility and security in the labour market are not contradictory, and in many situations can be mutually supportive.[96] Flexicurity challenges the traditional model of labour law which prizes permanent full-time employment, employment relationships regulated by labour law with a contract of employment, and the presence of a single entity employer accountable for the obligations placed upon the employers.[97] First developed in the context of globalisation debates, ongoing restructuring and the move towards a knowledge-based economy, from the perspective of some, including the European Commission, European labour markets needed to be more inclusive and responsive to innovation and change.[98] Likewise, the UK Department of Trade and Industry (DTI) argued that 'equipping people to manage and take advantage of change rather than to seek and protect specific sectors or jobs is the best way to manage the uncertainties and opportunities of globalisation.'[99] First coined in the Netherlands, the notion of flexicurity sought to modify employment protection for employees working on

[92] KD Ewing, 'The Function of Trade Unions' (2005) 34 *Industrial Law Journal* 1, 3–4.

[93] Ewing, 'Democratic Socialism and Labour Law' (n 16) 115.

[94] Ibid, 116.

[95] See chapter in this volume.

[96] H Jørgensen and PK Madsen, 'Flexicurity and Beyond – Reflections on the Nature and Future of a Political Celebrity' in H Jørgensen and PK Madsen (eds), *Flexicurity and beyond: finding a new agenda for the European social model* (Copenhagen, DJØF Pub, 2007).

[97] European Commission, 'Modernising Labour Law to Meet the Challenges of the 21st Century' (European Commission 2006) COM(2006) 708 final http://ec.europa.eu/employment_social/labour_law/green_paper_en.htm.

[98] Ibid.

[99] House of Lords, European Union Committee, 'Modernising European Union Labour Law: Has the UK Anything to Gain?' (House of Lords 2007) 22nd Report of Session 2006–07, HL 120 www.publications.parliament.uk/pa/ld200607/ldselect/ldeucom/120/120.pdf.

standard contracts and to improve it for temporary workers, whilst simultaneously driving a shift from job security and towards employment security.[100]

Flexibility can take different forms of flexibility, but the focus herein is on 'functional' flexibility – the ease with which workers can be redeployed to new tasks or are able to adapt to change. For present purposes changes would be those arising from the transition to the low carbon economy, but in other contexts could be driven by innovation and improvements in technology.[101] They key tool by which flexicurity purports to be delivered are known collectively as 'Active Labour Market Policies' (ALMPS). ALMPS seek to facilitate the matching process between the supply and demand for labour so that a given number of jobseekers will be associated with fewer vacancies. They manage this by maintaining the level of effective labour supply by keeping the long term unemployed and other groups of outsiders tight to the labour force. Further, they seek to affect the demand for labour, therefore increasing the number of available jobs, as well as boosting the productivity of the labour force, through the direct effect of the ALMPs on programme participants and also through general productivity increases associated with externalities.[102]

Of those states which have experimented with flexicurity, Denmark is the poster child, routinely described as the most successful EU Member State in achieving flexible labour markets combined with a high level of social security for the unemployed and short transition periods between jobs.[103] Flexicurity has found favour in Denmark because it exhibits a higher rate of employment and a lower rate of unemployment than the UK's economy, but without the accompanying degree of income inequality and poverty.[104] The main elements of the Danish labour market have been described as a 'Golden Triangle', consisting of:

1. Flexible workforce, highly mobile work force.
2. Strong income support system.
3. Active labour market and educations policies[105] – with rights and obligations for the unemployed.

High employee turnover and easy structural adjustments can be attributed to the existence of generous income support systems for the unemployed and the positive attitudes by the workers to active labour market measures. Activation and vocational training and further education have been strong elements in reforms of labour market policy and are backed up by stringent controls on job seekers.[106]

The success of the Danish system undoubtedly relies on the high level of social trust in the system, the atmosphere of cooperation and the acceptance of the responsibility to be adaptive to change. Public organised and financed education and activation helps workers to acquire more skills and ability needed for re-entering the labour force.[107]

[100] Jørgensen and Madsen (n 96).

[101] Ibid.

[102] V Escudero, 'Are Active Labour Market Policies Effective in Activating and Integrating Low-Skilled Individuals? An International Comparison' (2018) 7 *IZA Journal of Labor Policy* 4.

[103] European Commission, 'Modernising Labour Law to the Meet the Challenges of the 21st Century' (European Commission 2007) COM(2007) 627 final http://ec.europa.eu/employment_social/labour_law/green_paper_en.htm.

[104] House of Lords, European Union Committee (n 99) ch 4 'Flexibility and Employment Security'.

[105] Jørgensen and Madsen (n 96).

[106] Ibid.

[107] Ibid.

The unemployment benefits and training provision places a higher burden of taxation upon the higher earning members of Danish society. This therefore allows for relatively high expenditure on social security and active labour market policy as a proportion of GDP – 4.5 per cent of GDP rather than 1 per cent in the UK.[108]

The Danish experience is characterised by a high degree of trade union involvement and relatively little state engagement. Danish tripartite agreements amongst employers, workers and the state are supported by an intricate system that allows for an active response from the state which supports the activation of workers. Government is not engaged in elaborating deliberative flexicurity policies.[109] The system protects the primacy of employers and the unions in the process. Developments in social dialogue at national, industry and enterprise level, geared towards introducing new forms of internal flexibility have also demonstrated how workplace rules can be adapted to changing economic realities. The evolving relationship between law and collective agreements is reflected in the ways in which such agreements cover new issues – restructuring, competitiveness, access to training – and apply to new categories of workers. Collective agreements no longer merely play an auxiliary role in complementing working conditions already defined by law, and serve as important tools adjusting legal principles to specific economic situations and to the particular circumstances of specific sectors.[110]

The European Commission has added to the debate with its own vision of flexicurity, based on five elements.[111]

1. The availability of contractual arrangements, providing adequate flexibility for both workers and employers to shape the relationship according to their needs.
2. Active labour market policies to support transitions between jobs as well as from unemployment and inactivity to jobs.
3. Credible life-long learning systems to enable workers to remain employable throughout their career.
4. Social Security systems to ensure that all workers are adequately supported during absences form the labour market and to facilitate labour market mobility and transition.
5. Active involvement of social partners, partnerships and consensus.[112]

These elements point towards a vision of labour market in which flexibility for employments is provided by frequent transitions of workers between jobs and between labour market states; and where security for workers follows from support in fostering employability, active labour market policies aimed at making transitions run smoothly, social security support during periods without employment.[113] Individuals derive security from employability – lifelong learning is the key to this kind of security; the constant upgrading of skills

[108] House of Lords, European Union Committee (n 99) ch 4 'Flexibility and Employment Security'.

[109] Jørgensen and Madsen (n 96).

[110] European Commission, 'Green Paper Modernising labour law to meet the challenges of the 21st century', COM (2006) 708 final, 22 November 2006.

[111] Annex to the Communication from the Commission to the Spring European Council, 'Time to Move up a Gear', CEC 2006a 31–40.

[112] M Keune and M Jepsen, 'Not Balanced and Hardly New: The European Commission's Quest for Flexicurity' in H Jørgensen and PK Madsen (eds), *Flexicurity and beyond: finding a new agenda for the European social model* (Copenhagen, DJØF Pub, 2007).

[113] Ibid.

would improve chances of finding a job and reduce the chances of becoming unemployed.[114] The Commission's flexicurity concept calls for higher flexibility through increased use of flexible contracts and the limiting of job protection and increased security through life-long learning which is supposed to improve employability.[115] In this mode, flexicurity is seen as a way to preserve the European Social Model while maintaining and improving the competitiveness of the European Union. It is argued that in the context of globalisation and technical change, which places great demands on business to adapt continuously, high levels of employment security will not depend only on protection of workers' specific jobs but mainly on the means for workers to stay on the job market, manage smooth transitions between jobs and make progress in their career.[116] Further, it is in line with calls by the European Council to mobilise all appropriate national and community resources to promote a skilled, trained and adaptable workforce and labour market responses to the challenges stemming from the combined impact of globalisation and of the ageing European societies.[117]

Examples of ALMPs – to foster labour market participation and reduce unemployment through the reduction of the disincentive effect of benefit entitlements[118] – do exist outwith Denmark. The European Coal and Steel Community adopted a strategy of active labour market policy based on the adaptation of workers to economic change. The idea was that workers ought not to have to bear the consequence of economic change which technical progress makes inevitable. Enterprises which are being transformed can be given temporary assistance to avoid the need to lay off employees and if they close down, wholly or partly, assistance can be given directly to the workers to enable them to search for work elsewhere or to retain other jobs.[119] That said, there are obvious challenges to implementing flexicurity elsewhere.

At the level of national law, it is the case that labour and social security laws in most EU Member States were designed to provide protection for dependent employees in particular jobs. They may not therefore be sufficient to assist workers in making transitions from one status to another.[120] The opportunities to enter, remain and make progress in the labour market vary considerably with both employment protection legislation and the legal contractual framework at national level having a strong impact on job status transitions.[121] There is a degree of scepticism concerning the transferability of the Danish experience.[122] Denmark's success in achieving flexibility is based on high expenditure on social security supported by high taxation, a model which would present budgetary and political challenges for other Member States where expenditure is lower. Moreover, the success of the Nordic model is premised on high trade union membership, and as noted above high levels of collective bargaining coverage, which is far from universal. Only in jurisdictions with

[114] Ibid.
[115] Ibid.
[116] European Commission, 'Modernising Labour Law to Meet the Challenges of the 21st Century' (2006) www.europarl.europa.eu/meetdocs/2004_2009/documents/com/com_com(2006)0708_/com_com(2006)0708_en.pdf.
[117] Ibid.
[118] Keune and Jepsen (n 112).
[119] European Commission, 'Modernising Labour Law to the Meet the Challenges of the 21st Century' (n 116).
[120] Ibid.
[121] Ibid.
[122] House of Lords, European Union Committee (n 99) ch 4 'Flexibility and Employment Security'.

high standards of protection for the fundamental rights of association, collective bargaining and collective action could the Danish model be plausible. Labour law which supports trade unions could achieve better results in the form of flexible labour markets, with trade unions managing active labour market policies, including short transition periods between jobs.

In a larger (European Union) frame, this is a debate that can be located within the terms of a debate about the (im)balance in the European polity between the 'market' and the 'social', and the increasing social deficit which has exacerbated in the decade since the global financial crisis and austerity policies. Often termed as the European Social Union, a key policy here is the European Pillar of Social Rights (2017) which enumerates 20 principles and rights in respect of labour market access, working conditions, and social protection to address problems of social dumping and fragmentation.[123] In one sense it is a social policy sibling to European monetary union, a means by which flexible labour markets agendas are meshed with those for investment in labour market opportunities and the development of 'enabling' policies, such as to generate a real-life system of flexicurity.[124]

Yet for all its promising principles – rights to life-long learning, job search and retraining, as well as adaptable employment and social dialogue – the European Social Pillar will be judged by its implementation which is, as yet pending. Moreover, from a JTW perspective, this is a policy menu which on its face is as likely to sunder JTW as support it. For example, it is notable that Principle 8 ('Social dialogue and involvement of workers') makes great play of 'social partners' (an undefined term), yet contorts itself in minimising the role of trade unions. The closest that the text comes to providing a traditionally understood role for unions in collective bargaining comes in paragraph two of Principle 8. This states that 'Workers or their representatives have the right to be *informed and consulted* in good time on matters relevant to them, in particular on the transfer, restructuring and merger of undertakings and on collective redundancies.'[125] This rather passive role is to be contrasted with paragraph one of Principle 8 which affirms that

> social partners shall be consulted on the design and implementation of economic, employment and social policies according to national practices … encouraged to negotiate and conclude collective agreements … agreements concluded between the social partners shall be implemented at the level of the Union and its Member States.

The contrast in language is noteworthy, nor do the principles make reference to environmental change, or its implications. That said, 'transitions' in the labour market are referenced, albeit at a high level of abstraction.[126] In sum, the importance and impact of the Pillar remain difficult to ascertain. Much depends on its implementation and which actors are most successful in turning its open-textured language to their ends.

It should also be noted that ALMP exist in many other parts of the world including the US, Canada, India, and China, with varying degrees of intensity, commitment, and effectiveness. In the US for example, although programmes include employment services,

[123] See generally, European Commission, 'European Pillar of Social Rights' https://ec.europa.eu/commission/priorities/deeper-and-fairer-economic-and-monetary-union/european-pillar-social-rights_en.

[124] F Vandenbrouke, The European Pillar of Social Rights: From Promise to Delivery (*EU Visions*, December 2018) www.euvisions.eu/europea-social-union-public-forum-debate-vandenbroucke/.

[125] Emphasis added.

[126] Principles 1, 4, and 5.

job search assistance, job training schemes and employment subsidies, the level of investment in active labour market policies by the US is low by both international and historical standards.[127] Member countries of the Organisation for Economic Operation and Development (OECD) spent, on average, 0.5 per cent of GDP on active labour market policies in 2004 spending by the US was just 0.1 per cent. The level of public investments in active labour market policies in the US has also fallen over time. Relative to the overall economy, the US now spends less than half of what it did on such programs 30 years ago. Limited, and shrinking, investments in active labour market policies raise important questions about how best to connect workers with strong employment opportunities, ensure they have the skills to succeed in these roles, and support the overall efficiency of the US labour market. Despite multiple initiatives to revitalise the process – Presidential Memorandum on Job-Driven Training for Workers, 2014; Workforce Innovation and Opportunity Act 2014; Middle Class Tax Relief and Job Creation Act of 2012; the Partnerships of Opportunity and Workforce and Economic Revitalisation (POWER) initiative; Trade Adjusted Assistance (TAA) 2015 – the persistence of poor performance indicates the challenges at hand.[128]

The Canadian experience appears to be more promising. Prompted by the prospect of mass de-industrialisation – Canada's manufacturing sector lost over 600,000 jobs in the two decades to 2015 – and the loss of lifelong careers, Canada enacted the Employment Insurance Act 1996 which implemented a series of changes in the structure and eligibility rules of the unemployment benefit system and put more emphasis on active labour market policies and introduce a new, more coherent organisation of them. For example, in 2012–13, $2.1 billion was spent on Employment Benefits and Support Measures, which accounted for 12 per cent of total employment insurance spending for the year and just over 1 per cent of the total governments expenditures, assisting 662,260 clients. Bramwell's is a less optimistic analysis, noting how Canada has devolved responsibility for planning, implementing and administrating active labour market policies from national to regional levels over the past two decades.[129] ALMP performance has been generally patchy and lacklustre in Canada over the past 20 years leading observers to express serious doubts about Canada's ability to come up with a coherent and comprehensive national skills development strategy.[130]

In a broader ILO study of six Asian jurisdictions, Vandenberg provides a rich narrative of experiences and practices in a diverse and very fast moving region.[131] Among the

[127] 'The Active Labour Market Policies: Theory and Evidence for What Works' (*Council of Economic Advisers Issue Brief*, December 2016) https://obamawhitehouse.archives.gov/sites/default/files/page/files/20161220_active_labor_market_policies_issue_brief_cea.pdf.

[128] LS Jacobson, R LaLonde and D Sullivan, 'Is Retraining Displaced Workers a Good Investment?' (2005) 29 *Economic Perspectives* 47; PT Decker and CV Thornton, 'The Long-Term Effects of Transitional Employment Services' (1995) 58 *Social Security Bulletin* 71.

[129] A Bramwell, 'Training Policy for the 21st Century: Decentralization and Workforce Development Programs for Unemployed Working-Age Adults in Canada' (*Mowat Centre for Policy Innovation*, 2011) https://tspace.library.utoronto.ca/bitstream/1807/80100/2/Bramwell_2011_Training_policy_21st.pdf.

[130] See also M Gunderson, 'Active labour market adjustment Policies: what we know and don't know', Report prepared for the Ontario Role of Government Panel. Canada. Parliament. House of Commons. Standing Committee on Human Resources, Skills and Social Development, (2015), Renewal of the Labour Market Development Agreements, 9th Report, 41st Parliament, Second Session www.parl.gc.ca/HousePublications/Publication.aspx?DocId=6839662&Language= E&Mode=1&Parl=41&Ses=2&File=15.

[131] P Vandenberg, 'Is Asia Adopting Flexicurity? A Survey of Employment Policies in Six Countries' (*IMI – International Management Institute*, 2008) 4 www.ilo.org/empelm/pubs/WCMS_113927/lang--en/index.htm.

findings are that China and South Korea have made the transition to broader systems of labour market security over the past decade by reducing restrictions on retrenchment while introducing unemployment insurance and active measures; that where informal and rural economies are large (China, India and Sri Lanka), governments have used public works, self-employment programmes and skills training to support labour market outcomes; policies in Sri Lanka and India provide employment security, not labour market security, where government approval is required to retrench workers in larger firms and income support in the event of lay off is reorganised at the enterprise level in the form of severance and gratuity payments. There are additional problems of compliance and enforcement of the law meaning that protection may be strong de jure but weak de facto. These findings merely scratch the surface of Vandenberg's work. The important point is that ALMP are broadly deployed in both India (ie Skills Development Initiatives, Centres of Excellence, Expansion of Educational Institutions), and also in China and South Korea. Although space precludes a proper investigation, there is clearly scope for a discussion of the role of social dialogue and the development of industrial policy and general labour market policy. In particular, is there a relationship between polities with practices of social partnership and employment creation of 'green' jobs and emerging industries?

iii. Commissions

Finally, it is worth briefly surveying a novel institutional development which may, in time, become important. This is the emerging number of 'Just Transition Commissions'. Without delving too deeply into the comparison, readers will have already noted that the just transitions literature and movement shares features with that of 'transitional justice', now an established feature of public international and human rights law, if not a self-standing legal sub-discipline of its own.[132] Despite the differences – transitional justice is principally concerned with shifts from repressive regimes, and is highly integrated into NGO networks and UN processes[133] – both approaches are interdisciplinary approaches to major societal changes with shared institutional features. One of the best known of these in transitional justice settings is the truth commission or commission of inquiry, which may also have restorative justice mechanisms.[134]

The practice of JTW have followed this 'commission-approach', a number of which have recently been established – in Scotland in 2019[135] and Canada in 2018.[136] Naturally these Commissions differ in their mandate, legal basis, scope, outputs and ambition. The Scottish Commission makes direct reference to, and aims to apply the ILO Guiding Principles. It aims to advise the Scottish Government on the economy-wide path to net-zero, and will make its recommendations in two years. The NGO community has been quick to note

[132] See generally, C Bell, *On the Law of Peace: Peace Agreements and the Lex Pacificatoria* (Oxford, Oxford University Press, 2008).

[133] See generally, C Bell, 'Transitional Justice, Interdisciplinarity and the State of the "Field" or "Non-Field"' (2009) 3 *International Journal of Transitional Justice* 5.

[134] For one of very many accounts, see P Hayner, 'Fifteen Truth Commissions–1974 to 1994: A Comparative Study' (1994) 16 *Human Rights Quarterly* 597.

[135] Just Transition Commission, www.gov.scot/groups/just-transition-commission/.

[136] Task Force: Just Transition for Canadian Coal Power Workers and Communities, www.canada.ca/en/environment-climate-change/services/climate-change/task-force-just-transition.html.

that the Scottish Government had established the Commission whilst simultaneously pursuing a policy and promoting increased extraction of fossil fuels.[137] Similarly, the UK Government's policy framework that it has established in response to job losses in the North Sea (Maximising Economy Policy)[138] is more concerned with financial support to the oil and gas industry rather than protecting workers' jobs. It is noteworthy that in 2016, Friends of the Earth and the Scottish Trade Union Council established the Just Transition partnership between Trade Unions and environmentalists which has an agenda which could coordinate with that of the Commission with these challenges, again undermining the alleged 'tension' between the two communities and facilitating unions to have a voice on climate change, and ENGOs on economic and industrial issues.

The Canadian Commission makes no direct reference to the ILO, unlike the Scottish Commission and is narrower in its scope with a focus on 'Canadian Coal Power Workers and Communities'. The *Just Transition Task Force* produced a report to help shape Canada's phase-out of traditional coal-fired electricity. Parallel initiatives have included the announcement in January 2019 of Prime Minister Trudeau $25.6 million in funding for Canada's first geothermal power facility, an area that will be impacted heavily by Canada's coal phase out, which will create 1,000 jobs during construction, provide the provincial power grid with clean, renewable energy and create new business opportunities for local communities. As part of the 2018 Budget, Canada announced $35 million in funding to support skills development and economic diversification for workers and communities in the affected coal regions.

In Spain a different, more flexible, approach has been adopted whereby trade unions, the government, and other social partners have brokered a €250 million package to invest in mining communities as the country's coalmines are shut down by 2027. The funding supports clean energy initiatives in mining regions, early retirement for miners, retraining for green jobs, and environmental restoration.[139]

V. Conclusion

Effective climate action poses an almost existential challenge to existing systems of economy and society, and law. If this is true, what I term as *just transitions for workers* amount to an emergent example of what, a quarter of a century ago, Ewing described as a new frontier opening in the fertile landscape of citizenship.[140] It will be a thread of this volume that Keith's work has a rare ability to transcend its time and context. As demonstrated by this chapter, it has the capacity to cast light on new landscapes and timescapes. This contribution has sought to make a number of straightforward points. First, that there is no necessary inconsistency between social democratic and environmental thought and practice.

[137] M Crighton, 'Is the Scottish Government working towards a Just Transition?' (*Friends of the Earth Scotland*, 2019) https://foe.scot/scottish-government-working-just-transition/.

[138] Parliament, 'The Future of the Oil and Gas Industry' https://publications.parliament.uk/pa/cm201719/cmselect/cmscotaf/996/99606.htm.

[139] 'Spain guarantees a just transition for miners' (*Syndicat European Trade Union*, 2018) www.etuc.org/en/spain-guarantees-just-transition-miners.

[140] Ewing, 'Democratic Socialism and Labour Law' (n 16).

Second, that a process of mutual engagement would be to the benefit of both communities, bridging what are increasingly strawman disagreements. As Rosemberg notes, 'job losses are not an automatic consequence of climate policies, but the consequence of a lack of investment, social policies and anticipation.'[141] Third, there is great scope for the two bodies of thought and practice to engage on the specific, emergent issue of just transitions for workers in the context of the low carbon transition. There is great promise in bringing together initiatives from the deep and recent past of labour market policy such as collective bargaining, social dialogue, ALMPs, and participation in the transition from across civil society. The detail of those policies and processes of engagement require detailed working out. This is not, as yet, a well explored area although legal research is now emerging.[142] With that in mind, there are reasons for optimism. The number of collective agreements with 'green' clauses is significant and rising. They encompass all major industrial sectors and several important jurisdictions. The trade union movement, both national and transnational, is engaged in the climate debate and has a well articulated vision for its own role in that debate. Although flexicurity is a concept with its origins in the richest of western European states, practically all of the planet's largest emitters have some considerable experience with Active Labour Market Policies. The world's top ten emitters are, in order: China, US, India, Russia, Japan, Germany, Iran, Saudi Arabia, South Korea, Canada. Collectively these ten countries account for 66 per cent of global emissions with the other circa 190 nations of the world being responsible for the other 34 per cent. As such, these are precisely the jurisdictions that need to decarbonise most urgently, subject to the requirements of differentiation. The confluence of major emitters, and experience of ALMP is a narrow basis for optimism that they can and will adopt policies of decarbonisation that will simultaneously deliver just outcomes for affected workers and communities. Although slim, it is tangible and in the context of climate debates, where optimism is in short supply, that makes it important.

[141] A Rosemberg, 'Building a Just Transition: The Linkages between Climate Change and Employment' (2010) 2 *International Journal of Labour* 125.

[142] See the EU-funded 'Agreement' project on collective bargaining and labour relations, and DJ Doorey, 'Just Transitions Law: Putting Labour Law to Work on Climate Change' (2017) 30 *Journal of Environmental Law and Practice* 201.

PART VI

Afterword

24

Interview of Professor Keith Ewing by Lord Hendy QC on 13 September 2018

HENDY: Can we start by talking about your education?

EWING: Well I started off at a local school, near where we lived in Cowdenbeath in Fife which was where the family was from. We moved when I was six to just south of Edinburgh and I went to the local high school, Penicuik High School. It was 1966, the first year of fully comprehensive education. I think I was the second person in the school to go on to do law. The person before me, I remember him quite well, he was a good bit older than me but I think I was the second. So, that was an unusual thing.

HENDY: Did you get good results at school?

EWING: Quite good. I mean, I wasn't brilliant to be honest but two A's and two B's at Higher level, which was good enough.

HENDY: Were you political at school?

EWING: So, I did have fairly well developed political views by then. Actually, one of the papers I did (the equivalent of A-levels, in Scotland they were called Highers) was economics. And one of the questions in the exam I still remember was about trade union organisation and structure. And I remember – this is true – I remember writing an essay in the exam about the importance of industry-wide collective bargaining. And that would be in the early 1970s.

HENDY: Wow! And where did that come from?

EWING: No idea.

HENDY: But where did your appreciation of the significance of this come from?

EWING: I don't know, I guess it was just because I had a very acute interest in history, economics and politics. Even at that stage. I read a lot of politics when I was young – from about 16 onwards, I remember going to a bookshop and buying the *Communist Manifesto*, buying some of Connolly's early writings. In those days you could buy – Progress Publishers used to sell independent stuff – pamphlets around the revolution, the state ---

HENDY: Yes, for pennies.

EWING: Yes, basically sixpence or something. And there was a shop in Edinburgh, in Causewayside called James Thin and they used to sell all this stuff, so I used it to buy that. And I think I've still got that stuff I bought then I used to take it home and bind it with plastic covers so it would be protected and then underline everything. But anyway – I had a fairly well-developed sense of politics.

HENDY: And where did that sort of attention to detail, of underlining text, where did that come from?

EWING: I think it was something just to help to understand. An aid. I always looked at books, really, as tools really. So a book was something to be used. Also to be respected. Well, not so much the book to be respected, but the ideas in the book to be respected.

HENDY: Yes.

EWING: You've got to get the most out of it. And to get the most out of it, you've got to engage with it in a very thorough way. And underlining just helped me to remember.

HENDY: Extraordinary. I only ask because, you know, I've never written in a book – ever.

EWING: You've not written in a book? Yes, I can understand that, it's sacrilegious.

HENDY: I just feel I would defile it if I even put a pencil mark on it.

EWING: Yeah, I know, I do actually. Well, I have felt like that and I've thought, look you've got to get past this.

HENDY: Yes.

EWING: Because these are your tools.

HENDY: Yes.

EWING: And this is where you do your work. So a carpenter wouldn't decide, well I'm not going to get the hammer or whatever, the plane out of the box because it gets dirty. I've got to use it.

HENDY: Yes. I understand. That's a very sensible attitude.

EWING: I use it until it becomes worn. Its less of an issue as you get older, things become less difficult to follow, you develop skills to read quickly.

HENDY: At that age, I did read some texts but actually I was just reading 100s of novels.

EWING: Right.

HENDY: Just you know, all of existentialist novels ---

EWING: Right.

HENDY: --- and trying to plough my way through the English classics ---

EWING: Yes.

HENDY: --- and American literature and Russian literature and so on.

EWING: Well, I've never – that would be a, what would you say? A failing on my part that I didn't do that. And I suppose, most of my reading has been quite instrumental, in a sense.

HENDY: The failing was more on my part for not reading more politics.

EWING: I never sort of, read for pleasure in that sense. And even today when I'm reading a novel, I'm trying to see: what are the deep politics of this novel?

HENDY: What message is it conveying?

EWING: Yes, well probably a message never intended by the author. But political ideas interest me, I suppose, intrigue me. Just politics generally, the politics of any situation interest me.

HENDY: Yes.

EWING: Trying to understand what's going on. So, that would be true of a meeting, a crowd, a match, a book, an experience on the train, or whatever. So I think everything's about politics and power and how it's played out and expressed.

HENDY: Yes. And the idea that there's an explanation for everything – what is ostensibly said to be the cause of something, even by the actor herself, is normally completely different to the true explanation?

EWING: Exactly, yes. So it's about interpretation then too.

HENDY: Yes. And so, to what do you attribute that quest for the hidden meaning, then?

EWING: I don't know.

HENDY: Was that just something that was in you? No particular mentors of the day?

EWING: At that stage, I can't think of anybody that had sort of, fired me up, at that stage. Not really, just something that in many ways, I felt I had come to, stumbled across, myself. So, I don't know quite how I got there. At the time I was also playing football and going to the football and ---

HENDY: Well, I was going to ask about that. Football was presumably a big part of your life at that time?

EWING: Oh yes, a big part of my life. It's partly where I learned my politics. And actually, maybe it was one of the guys I used to go to games with. He was a bit older and he was an active trade unionist, in what became one of the print unions. So we used to go to Hibs' away games on the train or on the bus, and you know home games nearby. So we used to go to a lot of football as well, and we talked – but I don't know where this interest in politics really came from – but once you get hooked, it's – it's there.

HENDY: Were there particular books that sort of, opened your eyes to it? I mean, for me, reading the *Communist Manifesto* – that just opened my eyes.

EWING: Yes, indeed. I remember buying that and I've still got the first copy I bought, all marked up. I remember in that Penguin edition the introduction was by the historian AJP Taylor who I liked at the time. Actually, I think the *Manifesto* was influential.

HENDY: Yes.

EWING: After I did my Highers I was encouraged by my father. Actually, both my mother and father have been a big influence in my life. So was my maternal grandfather. He worked in a pit in Cowdenbeath. All his forbears had been coalminers. He lived to 100 and died in 2008. As a young man he took part in the General Strike and in the lockout in 1926. I remember talking to him about it. After he left the pits, I think he had a dispute with a manager and just walked off a job and signed on at the army recruiting place and joined up.

HENDY: Yes.

EWING: He was in, I think, it was both Royal Scots and Black Watch. During the war he was left behind at Dunkirk and eventually made his way home, to be sent back to defend Gibraltar, before being captured at Cassino in 1944, where he was wounded in the face and patched up by an Australian army surgeon. He came home after the War, and had various jobs.

HENDY: Yes.

EWING: Actually, the great thing about his life, I often felt, was that he was somebody who started life in 1908 in what would be seen today as really poor circumstances. But from 1945 onwards, he saw his life improve after the Attlee government. So he had social housing, a National Health Service, nationalised industries. And a pension and a job. He was rarely unemployed in the post-war years. His generation had the benefit of experiencing real improvements.

HENDY: Yes.

EWING: Real improvements that were sustained and sustainable. And that was, you know, something that couldn't be said, I think, as easily about subsequent generations, but his generation was a unique generation. But, of course, from 1979 onwards, the community in which he lived, his family lived, was just torn apart by the Thatcher changes.

HENDY: Absolutely.

EWING: His life experience had a big impact on me, which showed the benign power of the state and how the state can really help people. On, you know, on every front in terms of jobs, housing, education and health.

HENDY: And vice-versa: the role the state has played in diminishing those things since 1979?

EWING: Exactly. These were conscious decisions, of course, that were taken from '79 onwards. How did we get onto that? Ah yes, encouraged by my father to do A-levels which was unusual in Scotland at the time. I did British history and British Constitution, of all things. That sort of, reinforced my political interest and that took me into some of this other stuff as well. So, my dad had done British Constitution A-level at night school a couple of years before, and he'd the books so he gave them to me and I did the A-level. I didn't do very well by the way, in the A-level but I did the exam and I didn't have any tuition either, so again, I had to learn it just by reading on my own. So anyway, I did the exam and got a pass. But it took me into this other field.

HENDY: Yes.

EWING: It stimulated an interest in political ideas and then took me to all these sources. In the house, we had Engels, *The Condition of the Working Class in England* and I read that. And that took me to the *Communist Manifesto* and other works. I remember buying

C Wright Mills' compilation of Marxist authors. It's where I first came across Karl Kautsky, Bernstein and Rosa Luxemburg, completely out of my depth of course, at that stage.

HENDY: Yes. And what about law? Why did you settle on law? How did that come about?

EWING: Well actually, I wanted to be a union lawyer, I wanted to work for the NUM as it then was. So I signed up for law and I thought, well if I become a lawyer, that will be a good thing to do but if I don't, it'll be a good degree to have. I didn't really know much at that stage, I was only 17 when I went to university and 16 when I applied.

HENDY: Why was that? Why so young?

EWING: Well, I was moved up a year at school when we moved from Fife to Midlothian. It was a matter of pride that Fife schools were the best in the country at the time.

HENDY: Right.

EWING: So I was a year younger than my peer group.

HENDY: Wow.

EWING: So I went to university when I was 17. I wanted to work for the union.

HENDY: Did you know people in the NUM? Had you met people?

EWING: I must have done, yes. Actually, there were people – the town in which I lived, the guy next door where we first lived was the safety officer at the pit and people my dad worked beside, through the Labour party, were all trade union members.

HENDY: Yes.

EWING: I was a member of the Labour party when I was at school, I gave my first speech at a Labour party branch meeting when I was about 15. It was on the reunification of Ireland.

HENDY: Right, wow.

EWING: And it was agreed to send a letter of solidarity about Irish reunification to Gerry Fitt MP, at the beginning of the Troubles. Must have been 1970. At the constituency they sent the letter to Gerry Pitt MP, who I think was a Birmingham MP! We think it was a deliberate act of sabotage by an Orange group which was then running the Midlothian party. Sectarianism was a fact of Labour Party life in those days.

HENDY: Nice.

EWING: Anyway, so that – how did we get onto that? That was, how did I get into law? So basically, I was moving in Labour circles. I didn't know at the time, the unions didn't employ lawyers directly because I wanted to be an in-house lawyer.

HENDY: Yes.

EWING: I wrote to the NUM and they wrote back and said, 'Well, our lawyers are so and so.' So I went to see so and so (and others as well), and the first question I remember being asked at one of these interviews was, 'What school did you go to?' And that was it. I had not gone to the right school! So the NUM, sensibly I guess, used a commercial law firm to do their work, mainly personal injury work I suppose.

HENDY: Wow.

EWING: Edinburgh was a pretty closed community. Certainly, for people from my background. And there'd be no question of going to the bar, I mean that would just not be an issue at that time.

HENDY: No, no. But this application was after you'd done the law degree?

EWING: It maybe in my second year, I was thinking about what to do next. So I wrote to a number of firms asking if I could come and speak to them.

HENDY: So, during your law degree?

EWING: Yes. I went to law school in 1972. So I was an undergraduate '72 till '76, it was a four-year degree.

HENDY: Were there influential figures for you in the legal world? Lecturers, or legal writers?

EWING: Yes, there were people in the law school who I found inspiring. I was more interested in the public law, labour law side. So I was very impressed for lots of reasons with Tony Bradley, who taught me constitutional and administrative law. I couldn't wait to study labour law which was in the third year. And I did labour law with Breen Creighton.

HENDY: Oh Breen, of course.

EWING: He was a really good teacher and a good mentor. I think I was very lucky to be supported and encouraged by both Tony Bradley and Breen Creighton. There was also Eric Clive, who did family law, who was for me a very influential role model. A very dedicated academic, very open minded and he was just everything you would want to see in a law professor.

HENDY: Yes.

EWING: So there were a number of people that, in a sense, by their presence gave you a confidence which you need at that age, in that kind of environment. And I needed confidence and inspiration and, in a sense, encouragement. Everybody needs that. So I would say, thinking about it, these would be the three legal people that influenced me then. There are people that were not as generous, but you know, that's always the case.

HENDY: Yes. I don't think I got to the bottom of why you wanted to be a union *lawyer*? I mean, you could have been a union officer or representative or --- ?

EWING: Yes, that's a good point. I mean, I couldn't probably articulate now why I wanted to do that. My career expectations when I was at school were much different, that was certainly not the type of job I had initially been thinking about. But I did quite well in my O-grades as they were called in Scotland so I thought, well I could probably give it a go.

HENDY: Yes.

EWING: So, it was a question of using what skills you had to a productive end and that, for me, would have been a productive end. It could have been something else, I guess, but I had no experience of being a union research officer of the kind that you have now, or a journalist, I didn't know anybody who did that.

HENDY: No. Or you could have studied politics or history?

EWING: Could have studied – I did study history actually, in my first year at university. Because I thought I might not like law, so I'll do history. In Edinburgh, in your first year doing law, you could elect to study a non-law subject. So I did British history, just to make sure that I wasn't doing the wrong thing by doing law.

HENDY: Oh.

EWING: And I realised very quickly that I actually see law as an extension of politics and I guess I saw that from the beginning. And for me, law is simply the currency, the language of politics. It's what happens – it's the outcome of the political process. It's what happens when politics has finished.

HENDY: Yes.

EWING: You end up with a statute. And so, whatever lawyers may think to the contrary, the law is simply the product of a political process.

HENDY: Sure.

EWING: And indeed, the legal process itself is a political process. But a political process of a different kind. I'm not saying that I saw that at the time but maybe instinctively, that was part of my understanding.

HENDY: Yes.

EWING: And maybe, I also had ambitions, political ambitions, I think I probably wanted to be an MP at one time, but I quickly lost that ambition.

HENDY: Yes. Can we come back to how you see law and what the function of it is. What about your politics while you were at university?

EWING: I was politically engaged with progressive causes, and had briefly left the Labour Party for something more politically satisfying. We were married by this time, and I recall going off to meetings, often when Gail was working. Meetings were often held in the university, conveniently, so actually it was a great place. I remember, this would be around the time of Portugal and the revolutionary developments there.

HENDY: 1974?

EWING: Yes, this is the early to mid-70s. And they were great meetings, bringing together this remarkable mix of people from both the university and the local community. I remember meeting an old guy with memories of the Spanish Civil War and the like. I mean, it was a fantastic melting pot of progressive ideas. And it was a great equaliser or leveller actually, reminding me now of a great passage in *Homage to Catalonia* where Orwell writes about experiencing a foretaste of socialism.

HENDY: Yes. And you were reading widely as well, outside law?

EWING: The politics reinforced the reading, the reading reinforced the politics. I read Lenin – and Connolly was up there, I read a lot of Connolly's stuff. I was quite inspired by his life story, humble origins in Edinburgh. His attempts to reconcile nationalism and socialism with the burden of religion that he bore. Another influential figure was John Maclean, who was a Scottish revolutionary figure from Glasgow. Quite an inspirational character, I think. But you know, he was then celebrated in Russia after the Russian revolution. He fell out with Lenin on tactics, but he was a very impressive man.

HENDY: Who were your great intellectual heroes at that time?

EWING: Well, I would say Connolly, Maclean and Lenin. I think Lenin's piece on the state and revolution was magisterial. And a great critique of liberal constitutional law. The tradition is continued by others but it is a fantastic read.

HENDY: Yes, yes.

EWING: Marx on *The Civil War in France* contains some fantastic stuff. I had bought Marx's Selected Works, of course. There's a page there on the constitution of the Paris Commune, which is what a constitution should look like. And it still bears reading – so I still go back to that for inspiration. It's just one page.

HENDY: So, after Edinburgh University when you had got your degree, where next?

EWING: I went to Cambridge, Trinity Hall in 1976. Again, both Breen Creighton and Tony Bradley were very powerful influences in me going there to do a PhD. There I met Patrick Elias and that great group of people that Bob Hepple and Paul O'Higgins had assembled. Brian Bercusson was still there – he was a bit older than me. I was just a young student. Gillian Morris was there at the time. We were really the back end of that group. Bob Hepple had gone to Kent, so Paul O'Higgins was left on his own. Patrick Elias had stepped up and was my supervisor. And he was a very generous character and a great academic, He was very open minded. He asked awkward questions and he just had that clinical academic mind. He was fearless as well, so he would ask unpopular questions. I didn't agree with everything he said, but I really respected him, just for showing me how academics should conduct themselves.

HENDY: Yes.

EWING: Actually, he suggested the subject of my thesis. He said, 'Look here are five titles, topics, why don't you go away and think about them?' One of them was on trade union political activities, he said, 'I was thinking about doing it myself, but if you want to do it, why don't you take it?' And I thought, well this has all been done, but actually it hadn't.

HENDY: I see.

EWING: I did part of the PhD and I went back to Edinburgh in 1978 to teach, but I had a year left on the PhD and I finished it while I was teaching in Edinburgh.

HENDY: Yes.

EWING: It was great to get immersed in the detail. For example, there is a case that is often underestimated, the *Osborne* judgment.[1] It's important for two reasons. One is because the

[1] *Osborne v Amal. Soc. of Rly. Servants* [1910] AC 87.

House of Lords and the Court of Appeal below, sought to control trade union political voice, as you know.

HENDY: Yes.

EWING: But also, there's a remarkable judgment by Lord Shaw,[2] which doesn't get the attention it deserves, in which he creates a kind of liberal theory of the constitution which is designed to put a blanket over imminent universal suffrage by basically protecting members of Parliament from the pressures of their constituents.

HENDY: Right.

EWING: And creating the model of a representative democracy, not a democracy in which the people are sovereign. So, Parliament will listen to the people but Parliament will not necessarily represent the views of the people.

HENDY: Yes, yes.

EWING: And so, it was an extraordinary judgment and it was used to constrain democratic expectations and aspirations, and to constrain the democratic role of trade unions in the constitution. He refers to people like Locke and Burke and other liberal thinkers and writers. But it was really the concept of a constitution as a restraint on popular power.

HENDY: Yeah.

EWING: That judgment is worth having a look at.

HENDY: The other judges were completely dishonest in stating the law, weren't they?

EWING: Yes.

HENDY: The conclusion that Parliament in the Acts of 1871 and 1876[3] intended to exclude the possibility of trade union political activity was just a dishonest fiction.

EWING: Yes, well exactly. Earlier decisions got it right in that case. I mean, they made it clear what Parliament had intended in 1876.

HENDY: Isn't *Osborne* the case that the Lord Chancellor – I had the name—

EWING: Earl of Halsbury, wasn't it?

HENDY: Yes. Halsbury changed the date of the hearing to dates in late July, because he knew that the more liberal members of the Judicial Committee of the House of Lords would be attending a conference in New York and wouldn't be able to get back for it.

EWING: It was heard in 1909 and decided in the December, but reported in 1910, so it might have been.

[2] At 106–116. He held that it was unlawful for parliamentary candidates to be financially supported by the union on condition that they adhered to the policies of the recently created Labour Party as being contrary to 'sound public policy'. He went further and held (at 114) that payment of MPs to abide by party policy was 'an unconstitutional and unwarrantable interference with the rights of the constituencies of the United Kingdom'.

[3] Trade Union Act 1871 and Trade Union (Amendment) Act 1876.

HENDY: Trade union capacity to have a political voice is something that has sort of echoed down the years for you, hasn't it? You've done a lot of writing on it.

EWING: My first book, actually from the PhD thesis, was *Trade Unions, the Labour Party and the Law*. It was published, at the time of the third Tory anti-union Act, the Trade Union Act 1984. It was unbelievably fortuitous because Part 3 of the 1984 Act was on the political funds and the introduction of the political fund ballots. So, this book, just by pure chance, got a lot of coverage, and was widely reviewed in newspapers, law reviews, and so on. It was also picked up by the Labour front bench, who were then, of course, in opposition. And the two front bench speakers at the time, were Brown and Blair.

HENDY: Yes.

EWING: And they were also on the Standing Committee on the bill. John Smith was the leader and he read out bits of the book in Parliament and Brown used it in a parliamentary debate. I had written a piece in *Modern Law Review* about company political donations which Brown also referred to in other debates at the time. So I got a lot of coverage, just by the accident of timing. There's nothing like that to give you a bit of encouragement!

HENDY: I can imagine.

EWING: I did another book called *The Funding of Political Parties* in 1988. It was designed to defend the trade union link but attack the Tories and their funding arrangements. It was an argument for more equitable funding legislation.

HENDY: Yes.

EWING: And that as well, for some reason, got a lot of publicity and it got reviewed in the middle pages of the FT and covered on radio. It was just amazing. Anyway, it was quite a topical issue at the time, so I did quite well out of these two books. It was on the basis of the 1988 book that I was asked by the Labour party to draft their evidence to the Neill Committee on the funding of political parties 10 years later. The book boiled down actually was the basis of that evidence. And that evidence then influenced, basically, the recommendations of the Neill Committee for radical reform. And those recommendations became the Political Parties Elections and Referendums Act of 2000.

HENDY: Wow!

EWING: So academics can have an impact, but you've just got to be constantly pushing away and have a bit of luck as well. But you've got to engage with the political process in order to get these ideas implemented.

HENDY: Would you say that all your writing has a political purpose to it?

EWING: All of it, yes. I mean, absolutely all of it. All writing is political, whether or not people are prepared to acknowledge it or not.

HENDY: Whether it's intended or not, but in your case it is intended?

EWING: Exactly. Otherwise you're wasting your time. You should write for a purpose and the purpose is to change. Because you've identified a problem, you want to resolve the problem, you want a change.

HENDY: Yes.

EWING: Now, I'm not saying as a simple academic that I can change things, but you can contribute to a climate which helps. So you're just one extra paddle in the water which helps to carry the debate. You're providing ammunition for those on the front line in the debate.

HENDY: I don't mean to invite a critique of colleagues, but that's perhaps not a widely shared view?

EWING: Well, it goes back to the question of what is the purpose of an academic. And I think you can see it as a job, or you can see it as a vocation. And if you see it as a vocation, I think you have certain responsibilities. And I think the responsibility of the academic was quite well expressed by Edward Said in his Reith Lectures in 1993. In a sense, you're there to represent certain points of view. You don't have a mandate, but in a sense, you have a voice. And you're there to express that voice. I think a part of that responsibility is to ensure that that voice is heard. It's also to critique other views, to hold to account. As an academic you have a great privilege, which I think not enough of us make fullest use of. You might say the privilege is that you are paid by the State to be a critic of the State. It's an extraordinary privilege.

HENDY: Yes.

EWING: And that is your responsibility. So if you come into this job, you have a responsibility to perform that role. You're not there to sleepwalk into retirement. You have a function. And the function in my view, is quite clear. It's not to serve your own personal interests, not to serve the interests of any corporation or any governments, you're there as a critic. The harder the criticism, the more difficult making it will be, but I think that is your function.

HENDY: I mean, you could see that in another way, couldn't you? I mean, the way I see my role is not that I'm paid to give voice to the concerns of the people with whom I sympathise, but more that the status my job gives me a platform to do so. And I would feel that impulsion whatever I did in life.

EWING: Right.

HENDY: Although I am quite clear that in other jobs, I wouldn't have that status, I wouldn't have the soapbox to stand on that the status of being a barrister provides me with.

EWING: Right. But you have an opportunity.

HENDY: I have an opportunity.

EWING: I have an opportunity.

HENDY: But the duty to speak out emanates from me and is not a responsibility deriving from my job.

EWING: Right. But for me I think I have an opportunity but I also have a responsibility to the profession which I have entered. And I see the function of the academic as being a critical one. And that role can be performed in whatever field of law you occupy. I think it's probably easier for lawyers to do this – we've got the opportunity but also have the responsibility.

HENDY: Absolutely.

EWING: Because we're engaging with, as I said before, politics. And the meat on the table is called justice. So we engage with politics in at least two ways. One is the substance of the law, its meaning, but also the legal process itself is deeply political.

HENDY: Yes.

EWING: It's political, it's about choice, arguments ---

HENDY: That's indisputable, yes.

EWING: Well, a lot of people would dispute it. A lot of people would consider the science and rationality and the majesty of the law to be apolitical. I think I see my job as to debunk that and to say, actually that's not what law is. The sooner we appreciate that, the sooner we understand what's going on.

HENDY: Yes, sure. One of the things I know that you and I both enjoy is the opportunity to reveal the hypocrisy of the rules of the law to demonstrate the fact that they are often not actually applied.

EWING: Yes, an example of that hypocrisy – which I feel quite deeply about – would be the willingness of governments to sign up to international legal obligations and insist that other countries comply with them while themselves refusing to do so. I mean, since 1989, we've both, in different ways – I mean, you more directly than me – been insisting that British governments of both parties (three parties in government by now) must comply with their obligations under international labour standards. Yet none of them complied. Yet all of them have signed, subsequently, commitments in free trade agreements or OECD guidelines or elsewhere to comply with obligations that they're manifestly in breach of.

HENDY: And have no intention of ever complying with ---

EWING: And we're about enter into free trade agreements, with multiple other countries in which we will solemnly declare our commitment to the ILO principles, freedom of association and so on. In the meantime, you see legislation is still in the ark as it was in the 1990s.

HENDY: This is the stuff of hypocrisy of the rule of law, isn't it?

EWING: Yes, and the hypocrisy of the Strasbourg court which you and I have written about. How can it be that under article 11, you bring a complaint from any of the other 40-odd countries and you're very likely to succeed in an article 11 claim. Bring five cases from the UK and you're almost certain to lose all five.

HENDY: I know.

EWING: And actually, none of them is convincing. I've been looking again at some of these cases, for a new edition of our textbook on labour law and you have to say that the reasoning is pretty ropey. So, I see the hypocrisy at every level.

HENDY: Yes.

EWING: And it's our job to expose that. Whether anybody wants to hear it is another question, but our job is to provide the tools for the analysis.

HENDY: Absolutely, absolutely. Another example is the Brexiteer argument for parliamentary sovereignty which has ever since, been scoffed at by the Brexiteers.

EWING: Exactly, that's another example of hypocrisy.

HENDY: So, just going back to your central thesis, you have a responsibility as an academic to try and change things, which you might say is really a manifestation of the epitaph on Marx's grave.[4] You say that that is an obligation which is incumbent on you as an academic throughout academic life.

EWING: Yes.

HENDY: Well, now we have an opportunity, with a potential change of government, of actually doing more than critiquing from the side-lines but actually participating in that. How do you view that possibility?

EWING: Well, I wouldn't see me as a direct participant in government. But I think what you're trying to do is to produce material, arguments, analyses of a progressive nature that you would hope that a progressive government would be able to adopt and endorse. But I think there comes a point when, in a sense, having provided the material, your role is also to withdraw from the process. In a sense, that's when your job then changes so you then become in a sense, a guardian, a critic of the implementation and operation of any of these procedures. Now, that is a position that we haven't really been in. My working life has been one of decline of the organised labour movement from the heady days of the the 1970s, and we were really disappointed by the failings of the Blair and Brown governments. The closest I got to involvement in the process of government was defending the trade union political link to the Labour Party, I spent a lot of time doing that.

HENDY: Go on.

EWING: Well after the Neill Committee recommendations, which accepted the trade union/Labour Party link, defending the link has been a constant challenge. There have been attempts from the Right to undermine it. One way by which they've tried to do this was by introducing caps on donations to political parties – five or ten thousand pounds from each source. That would completely cut out trade union funding and completely transform the nature of the relationship with the Labour Party. The Political Parties, Elections and Referendums Act 2000, which respects the structure of the Labour Party, did the job of protecting the link. So I was able to influence the outcome of the legislation. But the political process doesn't stop. It continues and those who are hostile to the outcome are continually biting away, trying to change it.

HENDY: For example?

EWING: I remember we had an attack from the IPPR in 2002. In 2006 there was an attack from within Downing Street following a scandal involving donations and loans by rich individuals to the Labour Party. In 2011, there was the Committee on Standards in Public Life. Then you get to the Miliband-inspired Collins Review in 2014. So, effectively, what your role there is, is to defend what it is that you had been able to influence and able to establish. So, I would say, an academic role in a progressive government would be to defend progressive ideas, to defend the framework you helped to establish, from constant challenge.

[4] 'The philosophers have only interpreted the world, in various ways. The point, however, is to change it.' Karl Marx, *Eleven Theses on Feuerbach.*

HENDY: Yes.

EWING: I spent a lot of time working with trade unions and trade union leaders in TULO,[5] dealing with each of these attacks. We held them off in 2002, we held them off in 2006, we held them off in 2011, but we lost under Miliband and Collins and I think that was an absolute disaster to the structure of the party, to the heritage of the party. I was so, so disappointed by that.

HENDY: Although, ironically, it was what helped Jeremy Corbyn get into power.

EWING: I know. It was. Exactly. That has been incredible. But we're taking a long-term view of it.

HENDY: Yes, of course, understood.

EWING: Because it then became very easy for the Tories to come in with the Trade Union Act, 2016, 'OK, you've individualised what has been a collective relationship. We'll take it a step further and do it by law, we'll require union members to opt in to the political levy.'

HENDY: It was obvious too, wasn't it?

EWING: It was so, so stupid. They just walked into that, frankly.

HENDY: Yes.

EWING: But anyway, I would say, if we had a progressive government in the future which were to adopt some of the stuff that you and I have been working on together with many other academic. legal and trade union colleagues, I would say that would be principally the role of the academic to protect and defend.

HENDY: I absolutely agree with that. And of course, it is not only governments which change; the present Labour leadership may change and then you may be engaged in an internal defence.

EWING: Yes.

HENDY: But at the present stage, it's not merely putting forward ideas that the progressives and trade unions can adopt, it's actually proselytising those.

EWING: Yes, yes.

HENDY: Which is an unusual activity for an academic.

EWING: Well, I learned this from John Foster, former general secretary of the NUJ who taught me so much: there's no point in having an idea, putting it out there once and saying, 'Well, that's it.' You've actually got to go and reach as many people as possible with that idea.

HENDY: Sure. But it also calls on slightly different skills, doesn't it? I mean, the academic who writes ---

EWING: A learned paper.

[5] The Trade Union Labour Party Liaison Organisation.

HENDY: --- a learned paper, which is completely impenetrable to anybody who's not of that faculty or discipline or sub-specialty will convince no-one outside that specialism.

EWING: No.

HENDY: But you personally have the knack both of speaking and writing in an academic fashion or to students who are familiar with the terms and the concepts but not perhaps the ideas, and of putting the ideas across to trade union and lay audiences who are familiar neither with the terms nor the concepts.

EWING: Well, since I was 21 (in 1976) I've always done trade union education classes. The first class I did was for the National Union of Tailors and Garment Workers. Full week's course, four sessions a day in Glasgow. I used to go through every day to Glasgow from Edinburgh to give this course. So that was a great, great learning experience for me. I'm not sure they learned much, but I learned an awful lot about how to express myself. Then, I used to run a course, with Brian Bercusson, from 1983 four times a year for about ten years, to a NALGO education centre up in Scotland. We used to teach the branch officers and stewards. Locked in for a week in a small hotel in Largs on the Ayrshire coast. It was a fantastic course. We used to do that and then I used to go and do a course at Northern College near Barnsley. ASTMS had a college down in Bishops Stortford, and I also taught there. So I've always had that string to my bow. And one-off talks to trades councils, trade union branches, committees, conferences and so on. Whenever I ever get asked, I always say yes if I can, because it's a great opportunity.

HENDY: Yes.

EWING: What an academic needs is an audience, right? Because you've got ideas that you want to project and get across. You and I have spoken many, many times together on the same platform in the past. We've gone round and we've spoken to people and you get these really great responses which are sometimes very challenging. And they do challenge what you think and what you've said, but you've got to think through these problems.

HENDY: Yes, yes.

EWING: You need an audience to present your views to, an audience to persuade, but you also need an audience to challenge and to strengthen your views.

HENDY: I find what happens is that they open up another dimension to the argument that is either supportive or destructive but you've got to work your way round that.

EWING: Something you hadn't thought about.

HENDY: Yes absolutely. Listen, we've run out of time. We should resume on another occasion. I'd like to ask you about theories of labour law. Also, how you see the interaction of public law and labour law and the importance of equality, sovereignty of the people, and parliamentary sovereignty. And then the theory of law itself.

EWING: Right.

HENDY: Well, we'll do that next time.

INDEX

Lightning Source UK Ltd.
Milton Keynes UK
UKHW051624070720
366138UK00008B/413

9 781509 916573